Dynamics of Identification and Conflict

Dynamics of Identification and Conflict

Anthropological Encounters

Edited by Markus Virgil Hoehne, Echi Christina Gabbert
and John R. Eidson

berghahn
NEW YORK • OXFORD
www.berghahnbooks.com

First published in 2023 by
Berghahn Books
www.berghahnbooks.com

© 2023, 2025 Markus Virgil Hoehne, Echi Christina Gabbert and John R. Eidson
First paperback edition published in 2025

All rights reserved. Except for the quotation of short passages
for the purposes of criticism and review, no part of this book
may be reproduced in any form or by any means, electronic or
mechanical, including photocopying, recording, or any information
storage and retrieval system now known or to be invented,
without written permission of the publisher.

Library of Congress Cataloging-in-Publication Data

Names: Hoehne, Markus Virgil, editor. | Gabbert, Echi Christina, editor. | Eidson, John R., editor.
Title: Dynamics of Identification and Conflict: Anthropological Encounters / edited by Markus Virgil Hoehne, Echi Christina Gabbert, and John R. Eidson.
Description: New York: Berghahn Books, 2023. | Includes bibliographical references and index.
Identifiers: LCCN 2022027939 (print) | LCCN 2022027940 (ebook) | ISBN 9781800736757 (hardback) | ISBN 9781800736764 (ebook)
Subjects: LCSH: Group identity—Case studies. | Ethnicity—Case studies. | Ethnic conflict—Case studies. | Pastoral systems—Case studies. | Migration, Internal—Case studies. | Emigration and immigration—Social aspects—Case studies.
Classification: LCC HM753 .D96 2023 (print) | LCC HM753 (ebook) | DDC 305—dc23/eng/20220719
LC record available at https://lccn.loc.gov/2022027939
LC ebook record available at https://lccn.loc.gov/2022027940

British Library Cataloguing in Publication Data

A catalogue record for this book is available from the British Library

ISBN 978-1-80073-675-7 hardback
ISBN 978-1-83695-049-3 paperback
ISBN 978-1-83695-162-9 epub
ISBN 978-1-80073-676-4 web pdf

https://doi.org/10.3167/ 9781800736757

Contents

List of Illustrations   viii

Acknowledgements   ix

Introduction. Approaching the Dynamics of Identification and
Conflict through the Anthropology of Günther Schlee   1
   John R. Eidson, Echi Christina Gabbert and Markus Virgil Hoehne

Part I. Pastoralists and Others: Identity, Territoriality, History and Politics

Chapter 1. What Do (Pastoralist) Women Want? Warfare, Cowardice
and Sexuality in Northern Kenya   27
   Bilinda Straight

Chapter 2. Negotiating Complexity in East Africa: Landscape,
Territoriality and Identity among Maa Speakers, North to South   49
   John G. Galaty

Chapter 3. Where Do They Belong and What Belongs to Them?
Acceptance of 'Sedentarizing' Fulɓe and Rejection of Arab Returnees
in Blue Nile State and Sennar State, Sudan   63
   Elhadi Ibrahim Osman and Al-Amin Abu-Manga

Chapter 4. Ethnicity, Identity and Citizenship of Recent Migrant Groups
in Ghana   85
   Steve Tonah

Chapter 5. Studying Conflict and Ethnicity through Performative
and Audio-Visual Research Methods: Examples from Cameroon   105
   Michaela Pelican

Part II. Conflict and Identification, Interests and Integration

Chapter 6. The Topography of Terrorism: Between Local Conflicts and Global Jihad   135
Sophie Roche

Chapter 7. Politics of Belonging and the Litmus Test of Retaliation   154
Bertram Turner

Chapter 8. Heroes and Identities: Relativism, Myth and Reality   174
Aleksandar Bošković

Chapter 9. 'Košta akwa': What an Italian Pidgin Poem from Tigray Says about Self-Image, Resistance and Conflict   186
Wolbert G.C. Smidt

Chapter 10. Integration Through Conflict: The Proliferation of Mutually Constituted Sacred Narratives in the Process of State (Re-)Formation in Ethiopia   196
Dereje Feyissa

Chapter 11. 'A Dimpled Spider, Fat and White': US Exceptionalism and the Accumulation of Terror   216
Stephen P. Reyna

Part III. Migration and Exclusion, Displacement and Emplacement

Chapter 12. From Bases of Identifications to Acts of Exclusion? Günther Schlee's Contributions to the Max Planck Research Initiative on Migration   239
Marie-Claire Foblets and Zeynep Yanasmayan

Chapter 13. Dilemmas of Identification: The Trader's Dilemma among Khorezmians in Tashkent   255
Rano Turaeva

Chapter 14. Is Migrating a Rational Decision? Motives and Procedures of Qazaq Repatriation   272
Peter Finke

Chapter 15. Transnational Communities and Shifting Moral Values: Migrants between the Netherlands and the Moluccas   291
Keebet von Benda-Beckmann

Chapter 16. Multiscalar Social Relations of Dispossession and Emplacement   308
Nina Glick Schiller

Epilogue. Emancipatory Cosmopolitanism or Global Neighbourhood?   335
    John R. Eidson, Echi Christina Gabbert and Markus Virgil Hoehne

Afterword. Charisma: Ethnographers and Their Host Societies   347
    Ivo Strecker

Interview with Günther Schlee, Halle (Saale), 10 December 2018   357
    Markus Virgil Hoehne

To Günther Schlee, with Thanks …   377
    Abdullahi A. Shongolo

Published Works by Günther Schlee (Selection)   381
    Compiled by Viktoria Giehler-Zeng

Index   395

Illustrations

Figures

5.1–5.5. Farmer-grazier conflict, role-play of the Ballotiral staff, Nkambe, 29 January 2001. — 114

5.6–5.10. *Sippoygo* (selling milk), role-play of the Mbororo women's group of Chako, 8 April 2001. — 119

5.11–5.12. Misaje Film Festival, 27 October 2001. — 122

Maps

3.1. Blue Nile administrative map OCHA. Source: OCHA/ReliefWeb. — 65

3.2. Sennar administrative map OCHA. Source: OCHA/ReliefWeb. — 68

Tables

10.1. Ethiopia's religious demography. Source: 1994 and 2007 national censuses of Ethiopia, Central Statistics Authority. — 198

14.1. Demographic changes in Hovd-*sum*. Source: Statistical Office of Hovd-*sum*. — 278

Acknowledgements

As one saying in German goes, 'Was lange währt, wird endlich gut' – things that take a long time turn out well. We hope that the contributing authors, the many others who have supported us, our readers and, of course, Günther Schlee find this to be a fitting epigram for this book. Those at the Max Planck Institute for Social Anthropology in Halle (Saale), Germany, whom we wish to thank include Marie-Claire Foblets and Ursula Rao for generously authorizing human and financial resources to facilitate the production of this volume; Bettina Mann for being a benevolent advisor along the way; Brian Donahoe for editorial assistance; and Conny Schnepel and Viktoria Giehler-Zeng for doing everything that is necessary to get a manuscript ready to submit to the publisher. As we raced to the finish line, Viktoria worked behind the scene, formatting, ensuring stylistic consistency, checking references and even taking on the task of compiling a list of the published works of Günther Schlee. We also thank the Max Planck Society for subsidizing the publication of this volume. Our sincere thanks go to Elisabeth Schlee, Günther's sister, who, during an important phase of our work on this book, encouraged us to keep at it. At Berghahn Books, Marion Berghahn, Anthony Mason, Tom Bonnington and Elizabeth Martinez provided professional guidance in a friendly way. It has been a pleasure to work with them. Our thanks go as well to the anonymous reviewers, who gave us some good advice. Finally, we want to thank the members of our families for their understanding and for giving us the extra time we needed to find solutions to all the puzzles that arise when one brings a volume of this size and scope to light.

INTRODUCTION

Approaching the Dynamics of Identification and Conflict through the Anthropology of Günther Schlee

JOHN R. EIDSON, ECHI CHRISTINA GABBERT
AND MARKUS VIRGIL HOEHNE

In a programmatic article, published shortly after he took up his post as one of the founding directors of the Max Planck Institute for Social Anthropology, Günther Schlee referred to a situation that arose fairly often during his fieldwork among the Rendille and their neighbours in northern Kenya and southern Ethiopia:

> When a herdsman meets a stranger at a watering-hole – the typical trigger-situation for violent conflicts – ... the existence of cross-cutting ties opens up the following possibilities ... He can either emphasize their difference ('We belong to different tribes, go away before our young men come!'), or he can refer to a shared identity ('Though we belong to different tribes, we belong to the same clan', or 'You belong to my wife's clan'). (Schlee 2004: 144)[1]

This illustration, which touches on a range of themes, including social structure, social networks, territoriality, resources, history, conflict, identification, agency and choice, provides a fitting point of departure for introducing Schlee's empirical and theoretical contributions to anthropology and the social sciences, generally. Once the type of situation depicted in this quotation is contextualized, unpacked, generalized and prepared for recontextualization, it may also serve as a framework for introducing the themes of the various contributions to this volume.

Schlee began his fieldwork in the mid-1970s among the Rendille on the Kenyan side of the border between northern Kenya and southern Ethiopia – in 'the hot, dry lowland from Lake Turkana in the west to the Juba River in the east and beyond', which, for the last several centuries has been 'populated by pastoral nomads and hunter-gatherers', who often also practise shifting cultivation

(Schlee 1994: 31). In the late nineteenth century, Emperor Menelik pursued the southward expansion of the Ethiopian empire, sending troops into this region, which, '[a]ccording to Abyssian ideology', was 'wild and dangerous, infested with disease, and inhabited by savages' (Donham 2002: 20). As the historian Bahru Zewde (1991: 93) writes, '[s]outh-western Ethiopia became a hunting-ground for humans as well as animals', as the Ethiopians imposed their rule in the territory, massacring and enslaving local inhabitants in the process (Almagor 2002; Donham 2002; Gabbert 2012). The British colonialists, in reaction to this expansion, moved to establish their northern Kenyan territories as a buffer zone against Ethiopia's imperial ambitions (Schlee 1994: 44), while building 'hardly any roads or schools or hospitals' there and even denying entry to missionaries, lest they 'instil new desires in the local population' (Schlee 1994: 45). Under these conditions, northern Kenya and southern Ethiopia remained relatively isolated peripheries characterized, culturally, by 'heterogeneity in a very confined space' (Schlee 2008: 11). The region is home to multiple ethnic groups of varying sizes, including the Boran Oromo, Somali, Gabra, Garre, Sakuye, Rendille and Arbore (Hor), some of whom had resided in the region for quite some time, while others, including some Somali groups, had arrived from the northern Horn only in the second half of the nineteenth century (Fekadu Adugna 2009; Schlee 2010c).

Clearly, the various ethnic groups in northern Kenya and southern Ethiopia are not timeless features of the ethnographic landscape; rather, they are manifestations of historical processes of migration, separation and incorporation, operating in accord with principles of social fission and fusion that Schlee, among others, has sought to unravel. What he observed during fieldwork were dynamic relations among the various groups that modulated between alliance and enmity, ritual exchange and raiding, and between expansion, dispossession, dispersal and regrouping. Such social and political fluctuation was, evidently, the general rule, at least before ethnicity became more rigidly territorialized under the corresponding colonial and postcolonial administrations (Schlee 2010c).

The relationship of the ethnic groups in northern Kenya and southern Ethiopia to the territory they occupy and to each other may be understood in terms of several variables, including a common pastoralist livelihood, the history of the migration to this peripheral region, conflicts and agreements over the use of resources, the establishment of cooperative relations and coalitions that have been periodically revamped, and the actions of representatives of Ethiopian, British and Kenyan administrations. During his fieldwork, Schlee found that, despite current divisions among ethnic groups, traces of past connections were kept alive through an 'inter-ethnic network of clan identities' (Schlee 1994: 3). That is, many ethnic groups included clans that were also represented in the other groups, so that, for example, 'some of the clans found among the Gabra were believed to be the same as certain Rendille, Sakuye or Garre clans' (Schlee 2010b: 218). Therefore, clan members had the option of activating ties based on descent and alliance within their own ethnic group or of referring to shared narratives of common origins across ethnic boundaries.

Schlee (1997) refers to links between ethnic groups through common clan membership as cross-cutting ties, which, taken together, form an alternative network spanning local divisions among groups, the members of which are often in conflict over scarce resources – pasture, water and cattle.[2] Max Gluckman (1965: 13, 20–21) stressed the importance of divided loyalties for cohesion and for 'peace in the feud' in societies without centralized rule. With reference to E.E. Evans-Pritchard's (1940) description of Nuer society, Gluckman (1965: 12) argued that the co-residence of Nuer from different patrilineal descent groups in villages used mainly during the rainy season diminished the probability that conflicts between descent groups would escalate into violence – since their members depended on each other as neighbours in the villages. What is more, the rule of exogamy and relationships established through marriage forced a man not only to be loyal to his agnates but also to maintain good relations with his in-laws. While emphasizing the significance of cross-cutting ties, Schlee cautions against taking too sanguine a view of their effects, noting that they serve less to prevent violent conflict than to provide some sort of social support in its wake (Schlee 2008: 50–52).[3]

With the arrival of agents of the British and Ethiopian empires in northern Kenya and southern Ethiopia, respectively, another dimension of social complexity and normativity was superimposed on the multifaceted relations among local people: the policies of colonial and, later, postcolonial administrations, the representatives of which, typically, have viewed pastoralists and their way of life as 'primitive' or 'underdeveloped'. While Ethiopian forces sought ivory and slaves (Almagor 2002; Bahru 1991; Donham 2002; Turton 2002), the British, though largely uninterested in this apparently unproductive land, wanted to quell what they saw as 'incessant conflicts over pasture and water' (Schlee 1994: 45). On the basis, first, of their assumptions about the nature of tribal organization and, second, of their misunderstandings of the pastoralist adaptation to regional ecological conditions, colonial administrators attempted to impose rigid ethnic categories on the inhabitants and to promote the territorialization of ethnicity and pastoralism, irrespective of the mobility that is required to cope with 'the uneven and unpredictable spatial distribution of the rains' (Schlee 1994: 45). These policies only aggravated the economic and ecological problems, which the British wrongly attributed to soil erosion due to overgrazing (Schlee 1994: 45). The postcolonial Kenyan governments, beholden to dominant ethnic groups in the agricultural south of the country, have adopted measures similar to those of the British – measures which have deepened distinctions among ethnic groups and intensified their competition for resources (Schlee 2010c; see also Galaty in this volume). For their part, successive Ethiopian governments have used the label 'backward' as a kind of political magic formula to dispossess pastoralists and drive them from their territories (Schlee 2021; Gabbert et al. 2021).

The basis for understanding pastoralists in social, political and ecological context and for reflecting, more generally, on the complex dynamics of conflict and identification is, of course, intensive and long-term fieldwork – to which Schlee, his collaborators and his students are committed. Schlee's general approach to anthropological research can be described as a form of 'critical empiricism' that finds expression in two closely interrelated orientations: a commitment to ethnographic research in the spirit of 'epistemological realism' (Schlee 2010b: 215) and engagement with people in the field – socially, personally and politically. Schlee has expressed confidence that, through fieldwork, facts can be established adequately enough for the purposes of anthropological scholarship, even if these facts must be regarded as provisional and subject to revisions in light of further evidence (Schlee 2010b: 221–25). By combining classical participant observation, linguistic analysis, genealogical research and oral history, Schlee has laid the foundation for his social and political analysis and for his theoretical reflection, both of which have led him to challenge widely held misconceptions, for example, about pastoralism, conflict, identity, migration and social integration – the themes featured in this volume.

In Schlee's view, working to establish the facts of people's lives is an obligation not only to scholarship but also to the people themselves – in whose interests he has often spoken out (e.g. Schlee 2013, 2021). Accepting the responsibility to get to know and to represent people's way of life as best one can by conducting fieldwork conscientiously and creatively is a prerequisite for grounding one's understanding and also for speaking truth to power.

Over the years, Schlee has returned repeatedly to field sites in northern Kenya and in other regions of northeast Africa, including Sudan, establishing many close personal ties. Characteristically, his relationships with the people in these places have always been 'coeval' (Fabian 1983). For example, drawing on people's knowledge of their own history, among the Rendille and others, Schlee has gone to great lengths to acknowledge the contribution of his interlocutors, whom he has always viewed as research partners. This attitude, which, according to one reviewer, lends Schlee's work 'a dialogical postmodern scent' (Galaty 1992: 220), is evident in his decision to cite these partners by name whenever this is possible without endangering them:

> What would give me the right to treat my conversation partners among the pastoral nomads of northern Kenya differently from colleagues in Germany? The fact that ... they have never undergone any formal education in the Western sense? To me all that mattered little in comparison to their right to individual acknowledgment. (Schlee 2010b: 219–20)

As Director of the Max-Planck-Institute for Social Anthropology, Schlee has collaborated with a number of colleagues with whom his interests overlap. He has also trained a new generation of anthropologists (including many from the

'Global South'), funded long-term fieldwork and encouraged the use of innovative ethnographic methods; and he has supported and worked together with research partners in northeastern Africa. In many ways, this volume bears witness to this collaboration, training and support.

Part I. Pastoralists and Others: Identity, Territoriality, History and Politics

The chapters in the first section of this volume concern, on the one hand, the flexibility of identification and re-identification among pastoralists and, on the other hand, conflicts between pastoralists and sedentary people such as agriculturalists, urbanites, state authorities and development agents – conflicts which are based in part on the latter's misinterpretations of and discrimination against the former. Bilinda Straight challenges pejoratively tinged interpretations of gender identities among the Samburu of northern Kenya, paying particular attention to relations between young women and young men and to the oft reported role of the women in inciting violent behaviour among the men. With reference to his long personal history of research on pastoralist Maa-speakers of southwestern Kenya and northeastern Tanzania, commonly referred to as Maasai, John Galaty provides insight into the history of population movements, the permutations of social formations and the development of 'protocols' for the allocation of resources among groupings that are often in intense competition. As elsewhere, however, the social and geographical flexibility of herding communities has been hindered by the demarcation of Maasailand by state authorities, which took the form of the administrative crafting of sectional boundaries during the colonial period and which today continues with the so-called Group Ranches of the postcolonial state.

State policies vis-à-vis pastoralists take an even more drastic turn in the chapter by Elhadi Ibrahim Osman and Al-Amin Abu-Manga, which traces the widely varying fate of two different pastoralist groups of the Blue Nile area whose patterns of transhumance were foiled by civil war, the imposition of an international border between Sudan and the new state of South Sudan, and the expansion of mechanized farming. Finally, members of the two groups were forced to settle in different regional states of Sudan under conditions that were favourable, in one case, and highly unfavourable, in the other.

With the chapter by Steve Tonah, we shift to Ghana in West Africa, where the state is controlled, once again, by those with social origins among agriculturalists, and where basic rights are denied to members of mobile populations, including pastoralists and traders. Michaela Pelican employs innovative ethnographic methods to explore relations among pastoralists, agriculturalists and traders in the Grasslands of northern Cameroon, where she documents and analyses theatrical performances and local video productions that dramatize such relations.

The authors of the chapters in this first part of the volume focus either on relations among pastoralists or on pastoralists in relation to agriculturalists, traders, and representatives of state and development agencies. They intend not only to depict social, political and economic dilemmas, while exploring their implications, but also to correct misperceptions of pastoralists and their way of life. Schlee and his colleagues, including contributors to this volume, have analysed pastoralism as a kind of double adaptation: first, to harsh environmental conditions and, second, to the presence of others with whom resources are perforce shared (e.g. Catley et al. 2013; Schlee 2013).

Schlee, among others, has repeatedly refuted social-evolutionist clichés which hold that nomadic pastoralism represents an early stage of human development by referring to ethno-archaeological and socio-geographical evidence of shifts between agricultural and pastoralist adaptations throughout history (Schlee 1991: 137; Schlee 2012a; Scholz and Schlee 2015). Pastoralism did not precede agriculture, it co-exists with it; and it has evolved together with it under varying ecological conditions. Today, pastoral nomadism is 'a rather sophisticated, economically successful and sustainable way of life' in drylands (Scholz and Schlee 2015: 838), where herders may now use mobile phones to coordinate the movements of herds, to plan attacks in remote areas in the context of feuds, to negotiate and make peace, and to be able to react flexibly to changing climatic challenges (Krätli 2006; Schlee 2012a: 3; Hoehne 2022: 155–57).

Herding in semi-arid regions under unpredictable climatic conditions requires good range management, which is achieved through an intimate knowledge of the environment, through mobility and also through adaptation to the prevailing social and political conditions. Well organized livestock distribution, ownership variation, multiple property rights and strategic livestock exchange provide social security networks through ties of friendship and kinship, which buffer risks in challenging environments and foster bonds of solidarity and cooperation within and across ethnic and clan boundaries (Schlee 1989; see also Khazanov and Schlee 2012; Schlee 2012b). As Schlee's friend Ginno Ballo, a herder from Arbore in southern Ethiopia, states: 'Cattle open as many ways between people as they have hair on their hide' (Ginno Ballo personal communication with Gabbert, August 2011). Clearly, however, these 'many ways between people' may serve as the basis for the formation of groups, alliances and coalitions not only with but also against others – a point to which we return below.

On the basis of his ethnography, Schlee has helped to lead the way in developing a grounded critique of state-driven and developmental discourse that is directed against pastoralists (Gabbert 2021). In many African settings, as Schlee describes in detail for the Sudan, the state favours farmers and urban dwellers, 'from whom a larger proportion of the ruling class has been recruited' (Schlee 2015: 134). This helps to explain the harmful policies that Elhadi and Schlee (2014) saw in the Blue Nile region, where nomads were taxed multiple times and had to pay to use pastures on fenced but uncultivated land to feed their animals. Here, state policies actually increased inequality, disorder and conflict potential through land registration and taxation (Schlee 2013: 13). The same is true elsewhere: nomads from Kenya compare government chiefs who collect money from pastoralists to lions, who 'wait at the water holes and prey on the animals that come to drink' (Schlee 2013: 13).

Even more extremely, authorities cause pastoralists to be removed from their land, often violently, because of so-called 'development' interventions such as the implementation of large-scale agricultural projects in southern Ethiopia, Tanzania and Kenya (Gabbert et al. 2021). In-depth studies show, however, that land taken from pastoralists often provides less revenue than it did before 'development' occurred (Atkeyelsh 2019; Behnke and Kerven 2013; Gabbert 2021).

If, however, land is under-used after it has been taken from pastoralists, what is its benefit even for elites? Schlee considers a number of possible answers to this question, ranging from corruption, i.e. the identification of elites not with the whole national community but with their own narrow interests (Schlee 2013), to class warfare in the name of 'development' (Schlee 2021). The class warfare in question takes the form of the war of 'progressive' forces, including, especially, national elites, against the 'backward' sectors of the population, for example, the agro-pastoralist communities of southern Ethiopia:

> If your group is classified as backward, then your ethnicity is not associated with any entitlement to resources and does not have a voice in politics. So this distinction might mark a new class division that runs across the entire country. Ethiopia is divided into those who know the direction of progress and therefore know where the directions 'forward' and 'backward' point and those who are said not to know. (Schlee 2021: 67)

In this context, it does not matter if the land was used more productively or less destructively before being 'developed'. What matters is which class membership or ideological orientation defines the rules and goals of what is 'better'. To 're-lieve' people of their 'backward' existence benefits those who claim to know the right direction, insofar as they get credit for this noble achievement.

Of course, this brief review of Schlee's critique of the policies of East African states that are harmful to pastoralist only scratches the surface of a complex set of issues, which, however, Schlee, his colleagues and his students continue to explore in greater depth (Abbink et al. 2014; Gabbert et al. 2021). Recently, ethnographic and historical insights have led some of them to ask if the nation-state may be considered to be the wrong model for politics in the Horn of Africa (Markakis et al. 2021).

In situations of resource conflict between farmers and pastoralists, 'development' agents, more often than not, support official goals of the state that are detrimental to pastoralist economies and ecologies. They fail to recognize that pastoralists already contribute to developing agendas of long-term national sustainability and to finding solutions for global challenges in times of ecological crisis.

Clearly, there are a number of dedicated NGO staff members who have devoted themselves to understanding the value of pastoral livelihoods. Often, however, those involved in development aid have project assignments that do not exceed a few years. Consequently, they have limited possibilities to learn about the many time-tested practices of pastoralists that are based on flexibility, mobility and continuous innovation. A low yield cow that does not give large amounts of milk might be sorted out quickly by quantitative enhancement measures, ignoring the fact that families in drylands prefer animals that lactate steadily over the year and survive with limited inputs (Schlee 1988; Schlee und Salentin 1995: 102). Such drylands might look like a disaster to a sedentary person who seeks stable planning patterns; but a pastoralist with a mobility map in mind sees which measures are necessary for maintaining good environmental conditions, e.g. letting the dry pasture rest until the rains come (Schlee 1991: 134). Land titling and fencing only makes sense to those who do not understand the concept of free movement of people and livestock on open lands, where rainfall is unpredictable and water sources are impermanent. Based on short-term and spatially static observations, development interventions such as privatization and concentration of land ownership are often counterproductive to long-term land-use challenges (Schlee 1991). Therefore, weighing the historically grounded evaluation of the costs of misconceived development against the benefits of the subsistence economies of pastoralists (Schlee 1984, 1989: 44; 1991; Schlee and Shongolo 2012), Schlee concludes that 'anti-pastoralism policies are outdated' and that, 'in most of the world's dry belt, mountainous areas and tundra, reliable food production depends on mobile livestock-keeping' (Schlee 2013: 6; see also Schlee 2012a: 11; Istomin and Habeck 2016; Istomin et al. 2017).

Rather than pursing this topic further, however, we shift gears, thematically, turning to the next part of this volume, which shows how Schlee's empirical research may serve, and has served, as a point of departure for developing a theory of conflict and identification in human societies generally.

Part II. Conflict and Identification, Interests and Integration

For Schlee, field research – on the political ecology of pastoralists of northern Kenya (e.g. Schlee 2010c) and the Blue Nile region of Sudan (Elhadi and Schlee 2014) and on the peace process in Somalia (Schlee 2006, 2008: 107–48) – has resulted not only in contributions to the specialist literature on pastoralism on the Horn of Africa but also in the formulation of a general theory of conflict, identity, interests and integration. While, in Schlee's scheme of things, these four concepts are intimately intertwined, it is 'identity' that seems to have aroused the most controversy among anthropologists, social scientists and historians.

In the vast literature on 'identity', there is scant acknowledgment that the term is used rather indiscriminately in a number of different senses. Historical semantic investigation shows that the English-language term 'identity' – along with its cognates in French, German and no doubt other languages as well – has long been used in the fundamental sense of the 'sameness' of two or more things: the identity of x and y or of x_1 and x_2 (Eidson 2019; see also Dubiel 1976; Fraas 1996; Wagner 1999: 63). On this fundament, the idea of individual identity emerged in the early modern period; but the two senses invoked most commonly in the human sciences, which might be glossed, respectively, 'collective identity' and 'social-psychological identity', became widely established, beginning in the mid-twentieth century (Gleason 1983; Mackenzie 1978; Weigert 1983; see also Eidson 2019).[4] In the literature of the various human sciences, 'identity' began to appear more often in the 1950s and 1960s; and, by 1980, the frequency of the use of this term had increased dramatically, as competing concepts, such as 'character', which had served a comparable function in setting apart and distinguishing one collectivity from another, were largely abandoned (Eidson 2019; Riesman 2020: lx).

As is well known, the ascent of 'identity' to conceptual or at least terminological dominance has been accompanied by a critical reaction, especially because the use of this term may entail the reification of groups in ways that can be, and have been, exploited for political purposes, many of them reprehensible (e.g. Handler 1994; Brubaker and Cooper 2000; Malešević 2002; Judt 2010). However, in early ethnological and social anthropological texts, the term 'identity' was used to express the fact that tribal segments often set themselves off and distinguish themselves from other segments of the same order (e.g. Marett 1920: 190; Mooney 1902: 385; Schoolcraft 1845: 28–29). Subsequently, Fortes (1940: 251–53), Gluckman (1940: 40, 49) and Nadel (1950: 346–48), among others, showed that the concept of 'identity' is thoroughly compatible with approaches emphasizing the flexibility inherent in processes of identification and in relations of amity or enmity.

More recently, some of the fiercest critics of the concept of 'identity' have seemed to concede that it is sometimes useful. At the turn of the millennium, Rogers Brubaker, with Frederick Cooper, published a widely cited article excoriating common usage of 'identity', suggesting, practically, that it be stricken from the social scientific lexicon (Brubaker and Cooper 2000). Subsequently, however, Brubaker published a book in which 'identity' serves as a central concept – indeed, it appears in plural form in the title – and which contains no critical reflection on the use of the term (Brubaker 2016). Given the near ubiquity and the apparent indispensability of the term 'identity', the solution to any difficulties surrounding its use is not to purge it but to define and employ it in analysis appropriately.

For Schlee, the identity of a collectivity, or of its members in their relations to that collectivity, is based on the actors' activation of one or more available categories of likeness, distinction and solidarity (e.g. Schlee 2004; Eidson et al. 2017). It is something that may vary, within the limits of plausibility, depending on the circumstances, the social situation, the motivations and the intellectual agility of different actors – a point to which we return below. For now, perhaps the most important issue to clarify in a discussion of Schlee's understanding of identity and processes of identification is his rejection of the distinction between resource-based conflicts and identity-based conflicts.

> 'Identity' and 'resources' are not qualifiers of different kinds of conflict but different aspects of all conflicts . . . The . . . study of 'identification' aims at answering questions starting with 'who'; while the resource issue addresses the question 'about what'. Who-questions (e.g. who sides with whom against whom, along which lines of identification, religious, ethnic or whatever) need to be asked in the analysis of any conflict, and the same is true for the question 'about what' (e.g. water, oil, jobs, political representation, etc.). (Schlee 2018a: 11)

Since, in conflict situations, the question 'about what' always involves resources of some sort, whether natural, economic or political, and since the determination of the resources in question varies with each particular case, Schlee focuses in his general conflict theory on 'who-questions', that is, on the bases of identification. Thereby, he distinguishes three relevant aspects: (1) 'social structures and their cognitive representations'; (2) 'the politics of inclusion and exclusion'; and (3) 'the economics of group size' (Schlee 2004: 137). Articulating these aspects of the larger problem and their interrelations also serves to provide the rationale for Schlee's own way of synthesizing such apparently diverse approaches as structural functionalism, cognitive anthropology, sociolinguistics, rational choice theory, ecological anthropology, action anthropology and theories of agency and the self.

With the phrase 'social structures and their cognitive representations', Schlee is referring especially to the following aspects of identification processes: dimensions of identification, i.e. frames of reference for purposes of identification (e.g. nationality, ethnicity, clan, lineage, gender, religion, 'race', etc.); and categories of identification within such frames (e.g. Rendille or Samburu within the frame 'ethnicity', or Rengumo or Matarbá within the frame of Rendille 'clans' and so on). These social structural and cognitive aspects also include various combinatory principles governing the perceived compatibility or incompatibility of different categories, the relations of nesting among them and their susceptibility to prototypical interpretations, i.e. the degree to which they allow for distinctions between central and marginal members (Eidson et al. 2017).

Identities are set in motion in the second phase of Schlee's analysis, when actors engage in the 'politics of inclusion and exclusion' by choosing, consciously or unconsciously, between alternative forms of identification in particular situations and under particular circumstances. Schlee (2004: 136) argues that, very often, there is 'room for identity work – that is, room for people reasoning about their identities and changing them'. Given the cases on which he has focused – for example, competition among Somali warlords in raising forces (Schlee 1995: 283–86) – Schlee has often emphasized the role of the 'virtuoso' of identification processes, whom he defines as 'someone who successfully navigates different identities, responding to threats, expectations, and opportunities, while always remaining himself' (Eidson et al. 2017: 355). Whether or not actors are virtuosi of identification, and whether they are engaging in power politics or simply navigating the variegated situations of everyday life – from, say, family life to extra-familial forms of sociability – they necessarily make choices, with or without reflecting on these choices, among categories of identification that include some other actors as their fellows, while excluding others.

Finally, with his emphasis on the 'economics of group size', Schlee explores the qualitative and especially the quantitative consequences of inclusion and exclusion via choices among categories of identification – consequences that may have far reaching effects in situations of conflict. Some options in identification may result in larger, more heterogeneous collections of group members and some in smaller, more homogeneous ones; and, for some strategically minded actors, having many comrades or associates may be advantageous when sharing the costs of collective action, while having fewer may be preferable when sharing the benefits that result from that action.

Schlee is intrigued by the possibility of manipulating identification and re-identification in order to minimize costs and maximize benefits – from the point of view of a particular actor or of a small set of closely allied actors. But he also notes that the possibilities open to the virtuoso of identification may be limited by 'social structure and the conventional logic of identification' (Schlee 2008: 58). Thus, the clan organization in Somalia provides warlords 'with the tools and the material of military recruitment', but it also 'limits their freedom of choice in recruiting whom they want', for example, by preventing them from discriminating, during recruitment, among more or less suitable members of any given clan. For, when manipulating the terms of identification, the warlords in question 'need to behave plausibly and follow socially accepted patterns' (Schlee 2008: 58). By taking into account both the narrow interests of individual actors and the social obligations in which they are entangled, Schlee merges, in his conception of agency in processes of identification, the rationally calculating, gain-maximizing *Homo oeconomicus* with the role-fulfilling and norm-abiding *Homo sociologicus* (Schlee 2008: 53, 58; cf. Elwert 1997, 2002).

Of course, Schlee's conception applies not only to the local logic of self-identification or mutual identification, e.g. in the Somali setting during the escalation of civil war, 1991–1993. It may also help to illuminate the mobilization of categories globally, for example, when the USA and its allies declare war on 'terror' and define certain individuals as 'terrorists'; or, conversely, when Al Qaeda and ISIS invoke the category 'mujahideen' to attract followers from around the globe (see Roche and Reyna in this volume). Therefore, external delineations of identities, following their own normative and ideological logic, need to be taken into account when analysing local dynamics of identification.[5]

Although inspired by empirical research in particular locations and directed, initially, toward solving particular problems, Schlee's scheme for the analysis of identification processes is universal in scope, providing a matrix for analysing a wide range of problems in various settings – as is clear in the case of the contributions to the second part of this volume. Sophie Roche applies Schlee's ideas on group size to what are basically regional conflicts between the Tajik government and the political opposition in a peripheral area, showing how some representatives of oppositional forces, deprived of access to political channels domestically, align themselves with jihad on an international scale, thus giving the central government the opportunity to seek allies among international players in the 'war against terrorism'. Reflecting generally on identification processes in cases of transgression and retaliation, Bertram Turner, with reference to Schlee's work in East Africa and his own in Morocco, shows how diverse injured parties may discover or rediscover the identificatory bases of their solidarity – although he also emphasizes 'the fragility of large sizes and great numbers' in groups formed in this way, a point for which Roche's case study might serve as an example.

Aleksandar Bošković continues with the theme of group size by focusing on potential contradictions between the commitment to a particular national identity – Serbian, in this case – and to universal human rights, which are, arguably, an expression of 'the collective identity' that is 'most difficult to mobilize', namely, 'our common humanity' (Schlee et al. 2018: 230). Contradictions between ways of identifying that are particular or universal in scope emerge with force when the concept of human rights is broadened to include cultural rights – a potentially dangerous development, according to Bošković, insofar as the right to exist as a nation might seem to imply the right to defend the integrity of the nation in the face of 'enemies'.

At very different scales, Wolbert G.C. Smidt, Dereje Feyissa and Stephen P. Reyna focus on narratives of identity, conflict and integration as expressions of dominance, resistance or counter-hegemony. In the oral tradition of the Tigray of northern Ethiopia, Smidt has discovered a poem that was composed in the 1940s in a kind of Italian pidgin. In the poem, the Italians lament being driven from the good land that they have occupied by a Tigrayan bandit; but, on closer inspection, Smidt discovers a narrative formula for resistance to usurpation, which, in Tigrayan oral tradition, has been applied to conflicts in various contexts and at different scales. Dereje shows how the claim of representatives of Orthodox Christianity to provide the sacred narrative underpinning Ethiopian national identity is being challenged by Muslims advocating a counter-narrative that offers an alternative basis for national identity. Thus, in their efforts to distinguish themselves from one another by offering mutually exclusive bases for identification, 'enemies become alike' (Schlee 2008: 11). In seeking to illuminate the causes of contemporary conflict on a global scale, Reyna characterizes two forms of ostensibly deviant behaviour in the Global South – cargo cults and terrorism – as reflections, respectively, of the ideology and the military force of the imperial powers of the Global North, particularly the United States. Participants in so-called cargo cults anticipate the arrival of abundant riches from the land of the imperialists, because the imperialists have first identified themselves as suppliers of these riches; similarly, those branded as terrorists respond in kind to the violence perpetrated against the populations of the former colonies.

Part III. Migration and Exclusion, Displacement and Emplacement

In our presentation of the contributions to this volume, we set migration apart as a special topic to which Schlee's approach to processes of conflict and identification may be applied fruitfully. While migration has always numbered among Schlee's topics, he had for many years restricted his attention to population movements within East Africa or from West Africa to East Africa (Dereje and Schlee 2009). Then, during his time as director at the Max Planck Institute for Social Anthropology, Schlee started to engage in diasporic and transnational issues, investigating, together with Nina Glick Schiller and others, pathways for the integration of migrant groups in Germany (Glick Schiller et al. 2004). As part of the larger EU-funded project 'Diasporas for Peace', coordinated by colleagues at the University of Jyväskylä (2008–2011), with Markus V. Hoehne, Dereje and Schlee involved at the Max Planck Institute for Social Anthropology in Halle, Schlee and Isir Schlee examined the transnational engagement of Somalis in Germany, especially that of the second generation of Somali migrants who were losing interest in social ties to and affairs in war-torn Somalia (Schlee and Schlee 2010).

Schlee took up the topic of migration from the Global South to the Global North in 2017 when he joined the Max Planck Initiative 'The Challenges of Migration, Integration and Exclusion' (known by the German acronym WiMi), which is the subject of the contribution by Marie-Claire Foblets and Zeynep Yanasmayan. Conceived in the wake of 'the memorable summer of 2015', when the German government, largely in response to the Syrian crisis, decided to admit a record number of immigrants, this initiative combined the expertise of six Max Planck institutes and included Foblets, Yanasmayan and Schlee in the planning commission. Not wanting to replicate the work of earlier or of parallel projects on the topic of immigration, which have focused overwhelmingly on 'pathways to successful integration of immigrants', the members of the commission chose to emphasize 'processes and mechanisms of exclusion' in migration. In accord with Schlee's thinking, 'exclusion' was conceived not as the opposite of integration but as an inevitable, if highly variable, aspect of it. Inspired by that conception, Hoehne and Tabea Scharrer (2021), who were part of the WiMi initiative, have emphasized that, among Somalis in Germany, certain practices that are often thought to be (self-)exclusionary, such as establishing ethnic associations, can become a basis for linking with the non-Somali majority society in Germany, while seemingly inclusionary practices, such as leaving behind basic Islamic provisions of clothing for women in public, might effectively lead to more exclusion (within the Somali diaspora, but sometimes also within the larger society). As Foblets and Yanasmayan show in this volume, social anthropological projects within the WiMi initiative, which address migration within Africa (often a precondition of migration from Africa to Europe) and the experience of migrants in Halle (Saale), Germany, challenge the common assumptions that the integration of migrants depends necessarily on their 'sameness' with the receiving society and that the receiving society necessarily displays social and cultural homogeneity or 'sameness' with itself (see also Schlee and Horstmann 2018).

In her chapter, Rano Turaeva focuses on internal migration in Uzbekistan, specifically on the dilemmas confronting migrants from the western province of Khorzem to the distant capital, Tashkent. In Tashkent, Khorezmian migrants are torn between ethnic solidarity, on which they are dependent, both economically and legally, and their narrower interests as individuals or as household heads, which cannot be ignored if they and their families are to survive. Turaeva thus provides a classic example of the need to shift strategically between wider and narrower forms of identification, depending on the elusive answer to the questions 'Who?', 'With whom?' and 'For whom?'.

Peter Finke and Keebet von Benda-Beckmann offer contrasting case studies, both of which concern transnational relations among members of a single ethnic group or nation who, in the course of history, were separated geographically and then reunited, decades later, only to discover the degree to which they had, in the interim, grown apart. In Finke's case, which features the concept of 'bounded rationality' in an analysis of decisions regarding migration, political restrictions on the movement of pastoralists were suddenly lifted when the Soviet Union dissolved and the new Qazaq (or Kazakh) state invited Qazaqs living in Mongolia and elsewhere to 'return home'. In Benda-Beckmann's case, Moluccans who had migrated to the Netherlands in the 1940s, when the Dutch colony in island Southeast Asia became the new nation of Indonesia, attempted, decades later, to re-establish ties with compatriots with whom they had little in common in a 'homeland' that was no longer their home.

This final section closes with the contribution by Nina Glick Schiller, who, while acknowledging the ubiquity of migration, along with the resulting transnational relations, also sees it as something of a red herring. Rather than focusing on the exclusion of migrants in receiving societies and, thus, emphasizing the binary of 'native' and 'stranger', Glick Schiller directs our attention to the displacement of people, including migrants and non-migrants alike, through capital accumulation worldwide. All victims of displacement, whether from the city centre to the low-rent district, or from one corner of the world to another, seek emplacement through activation of 'multiscalar' social relations within 'hierarchies of networks of power'. The search for emplacement may lead to 'fundamentalist ethnonationalism', often coupled with religious beliefs; but it can also take the form of engagement in political movements for social and economic justice. Understanding these processes requires, Glick Schiller suggests, following Schlee's lead in linking the actor's perspective with the system perspective.

Processes of Identification across Scales of Social Integration

> [W]hen the different individual rationalities behind individual identification and bonding have been explained, what comes next? An obvious question concerns the connections between processes understood at the level of particular actors and the behavior of large aggregates of people, in other words the micro/macro problem. This remains among the most intractable of social science conundrums. (Schlee 2008: 17)

Schlee addresses what he calls the micro/macro problem by working, simultaneously, with the concepts of 'identification' and 'integration' – concepts he associates with theories of action, in the first case, and with system theory, in the second. Compared with 'identity', 'integration' – though occupying, along with a number of equivalent expressions, a central position in the vocabulary of the social sciences – has not, in recent years, received the same degree of critical scrutiny, with some exceptions (e.g. Schinkel 2018; Wimmer and Glick Schiller 2003). It is, however, no less deserving of re-examination, since, like 'identity', it is used extensively not only as a 'category of analysis' but also as a 'category of practice' (Brubaker and Cooper 2000: 4), especially in public discourse regarding immigration (Hoehne and Scharrer 2021: 2). Schlee clarifies his understanding of 'integration' by noting that he uses it 'not in the sense of politicians or social workers who want to achieve something and for whom the idea is laden with a positive value, but in the sense of system theory' (Schlee 2018a: 31, note 2). By way of example, he adds that '[i]f we understand our enemies to the extent that we can engage in meaningful hostile relationships with them, we are part of the same social system' (Schlee 2008: 11).

What are the implications of a theory of action, based on the idea that identities are (within limits) mutable, for a theory of systems, based on the idea that integration entails both the linking and separating of participants in larger aggregates (cf. Brubaker and Cooper 2000: 23)? While offering no simple answer to this question, Schlee does find his own path through the corresponding difficulties by exploring social relations across different scales of social integration, such as those one might call tribal, national or ethnic, imperial and universal. Glick Schiller, in this volume, insists that human subjects occupy and engage in networks that are 'unbounded' and 'multiscalar' insofar as the search for integration or 'emplacement' does not proceed systematically through a hierarchy of bounded territorial units, from local to national to global, but branches out simultaneously, if selectively, in all directions at once. This precision of Schlee's position might serve as a fitting point of departure for highlighting the varying approaches to problems of integration in this volume.

Straight, Galaty and Smidt start with local or tribal relations, which they follow outward or inward in various ways. Straight shows how gender relations among young Samburu women and men vary in sync with intertribal relations in subtle ways. In Galaty's chapter, we find an example of pastoral groupings with 'self-chosen names' but with no 'fixed outside border', so that the demarcation 'between the "we" and "the others" shifts depending on the point of view of the observer' (Schlee 2008: 7). 'Here, ethnicity frequently only emerged as a result of colonial administration, when districts were divided according to the tribes allegedly settled there' (Schlee 2008: 7). Smidt shows how people in the part of Tigray where he has done fieldwork apply a kind of narrative schema that opposes an in-group to an out-group, establishing a demarcation that can be expanded, contracted or shifted this way or that, depending on the circumstances and the intentions of the narrator and the understanding of his or her audience.

Agents of colonial administrations operate at a grander scale, according to a mode of integration that entails 'the levelling of ethnic differences among members of the ruling elite . . . and . . . the maintenance and even formalization and instrumentalization of ethnic difference between ruler and the ruled and within the ruled populations' (Schlee 2018b: 191; see also Dabhoiwala 2021). Members of the ruling elite often identify with a homogeneous national or international community, while the subjected peoples are divided into ethnic groups that are perceived to be homogeneous within but heterogeneous vis-à-vis one another. Upon gaining independence from colonial rule, the former colonies were faced with the apparent necessity of becoming a nation, bridging ethnic diversity or other differences, be they sectarian, regional or cultural. In different ways, the chapters by Elhadi and Abu-Manga, Tonah, Pelican, Dereje, Foblets and Yanasmayan, Turaeva, Finke and Benda-Beckmann all deal with manifestations of such postcolonial dilemmas.

In the contributions by Roche, Bošković, Reyna and Glick Schiller, integration at a universal scale clashes either with various forms of ethnonationalism or with alternative visions of universality. In the chapter by Roche, the former member of the Tajik presidential guard who vanished mysteriously, only to reappear in a video from Syria in which he announced his impending return to

Tajikistan in the name of jihad, opts to identify with – or, in Glick Schiller's terms, to seek emplacement in – what he understands to be a just and universally valid movement against corrupt political regimes, including that of his own country of origin. Bošković, in contrast, reports on Serbians who choose a particular form of national integration over integration in a larger community of nations that are united, supposedly, in the name of international law and human rights. For Reyna, the claim, particularly, of the United States to be ushering in a new era of peace and prosperity on a global scale is, in truth, an imperial quest for domination, which provokes resistance in the form of 'terrorism'. His analysis challenges us to ask which side, in this struggle, really represents generally valid human values. Finally, Glick Schiller shows how the dispossessed and displaced people of two cities in the USA and in Germany, respectively, seek emplacement through the activation of what she calls 'multiscalar social relations ... within various hierarchies of networks of power'.

In the ways just cited, this volume takes the herdsman at the watering-hole, whom we met in the quotation at the beginning of this introduction, through a whole series of transformations. It ends with the conviction that all herdsmen and women – indeed, all people everywhere – should be included within the circle of those whose experiences and whose opinions matter, so that they do not end up among the dispossessed and displaced, as too many already have.

John R. Eidson is a social anthropologist with a PhD from Cornell University and with interests in modern Germany, social theory, historical semantics and the history of anthropology. He has taught at the University of Maryland, the University of New Hampshire, the University of Leipzig and the Martin Luther University of Halle-Wittenberg. He is editor of *Das anthropologische Projekt* (Leipziger Universitätsverlag, 2008) and editorial board member of the *Integration and Conflict Studies* series published by Berghahn Books. After eighteen years as a senior research fellow at the Max Planck Institute for Social Anthropology, he retired in 2020 and continues now with his research as an independent scholar.

Echi Christina Gabbert is an anthropologist and a lecturer at the Institute for Social and Cultural Anthropology at Göttingen University, Germany. Her research foci are agro-pastoralism, music and oral history, political ecology and peace and conflict studies. Her long-term fieldwork in Ethiopia resulted in the award-winning PhD thesis 'Deciding Peace'. She has extended the 'Cultural Neighbourhood Approach' to 'Global Neighbourhood' scenarios, where global investment schemes meet smallholders' livelihoods, and she is coordinating the Lands of the Future Initiative, an interdisciplinary project about pastoral livelihoods in the twenty-first century. She is also co-editor of the volume *Lands of the Future: Anthropological Perspectives on Pastoralism, Land Use and Tropes of Modernity in Eastern Africa* (Berghahn, 2021).

Markus Virgil Hoehne is lecturer at the Institute of Social Anthropology at the University of Leipzig. He received his PhD from the Martin-Luther University Halle-Wittenberg and worked for ten years at the Max Planck Institute for Social Anthropology in Halle (Saale). His long-term research interests are Somali affairs and the anthropology of conflict; his most recent project deals with forensic anthropology in cultural context, based on research in Somaliland and Peru. He authored *Between Somaliland and Puntland: Marginalization, Militarization and Conflicting Political Visions* (Rift Valley Institute, 2015) and is co-editor of *Borders and Borderlands as Resources in the Horn of Africa* (James Currey, 2010) and *The State and the Paradox of Customary Law in Africa* (Routledge, 2018).

Notes

1. For reflection on why, in such cases, a herder might decide one way or another, see Gabbert (2012: 105) and Schlee (2010a: 10).

2. More recently, Gabbert and Thubauville (2010) have referred to communities that traverse ethnic boundaries with the concept of a 'cultural neighbourhood', to which we return in our epilogue.

3. Hoehne (2016: 1389) has emphasized that cross-cutting ties during the civil war in northern Somalia (1988–1991) helped to keep lines of communication open between the enemy groups. 'Given the intensity of civil war', however, 'the power of these ties to curtail conflict was limited'. Earlier, Helander (1996: 198) took inspiration from Schlee's original findings, when he emphasized that 'Rahanweyn clans' living in southwest Somalia 'do contain large numbers of members from other Somali clan-families'; and, in the context of domestic migration, relatives help each other to become adopted into the Rahanweyn grouping. The personal networks which transgress clan boundaries reminded Helander of what Schlee had found among the Rendille, Gabbra, Sakuye and some Somalis in northern Kenya. Helander has concluded 'that the existence of such cross-clan kinship links serves to mitigate inter-clan warfare' (ibid.).

4. By 'collective identity' we mean the notion that a collectivity may have an identity that is in some ways analogous to that of the individual person; and by 'social-psychological identity' we mean 'the identity which an individual can find through a collectivity' (Mackenzie 1978: 39; see also Eidson 2019).

5. This has been illustrated by Schlee (2008: 167), who, while serving in 2002 and 2003 as an expert at the peace conference for Somalia that took place in Kenya, was able to observe how some of the Somali participants, in the wake of the 9/11 attacks, tried to outdo each other in depicting themselves as 'moderates' and their opponents as 'terrorists'.

References

Abbink, Jon, Kelly Askew, Dereje Feyissa Dori, Elliot Fratkin, Echi Christina Gabbert, John G. Galaty, Shauna LaTosky, Jean Lydall, Hussein A. Mahmoud, John Markakis, Günther Schlee, Ivo Strecker and David Turton. 2014. 'Lands of the Future: Transforming Pastoral Lands and Livelihoods in Eastern Africa', *Max Planck Institute for Social Anthropology Working Papers* No. 154. Retrieved from https://www.eth.mpg.de/pubs/wps/pdf/mpi-eth-working-paper-0154.

Almagor, Uri. 2002 [1986]. 'Institutionalizing a Fringe Periphery: Dassanetch-Amhara Relations', in Donald L. Donham and Wendy James (eds), *The Southern Marches of Imperial Ethiopia*. Oxford: James Currey, pp. 96–115.

Atkeyelsh G.M. Persson. 2019. *Foreign Direct Investment in Large-Scale Agriculture in Africa: Economic, Social and Environmental Sustainability in Ethiopia*. London and New York: Routledge.

Bahru Zewde. 1991. *A History of Modern Ethiopia 1855–1974*. Addis Ababa: Addis Ababa University Press.

Behnke, Roy and Carol Kerven. 2013. 'Counting the Costs: Replacing Pastoralism with Irrigated Agriculture in the Awash Valley', in Andy Catley, Jeremy Lind and Ian Scoones (eds), *Pastoralism and Development in Africa: Dynamic Change at the Margins*. Abingdon and New York: Routledge, pp. 57–70.

Brubaker, Rogers 2016. *Trans: Gender and Race in an Age of Unsettled Identities*. Princeton, NJ: Princeton University Press.

Brubaker, Rogers and Frederick Cooper. 2000. 'Beyond "Identity"', *Theory and Society* 29(1): 1–47.

Catley, Andy, Jeremy Lind and Ian Scoones (eds). 2013. *Pastoralism and Development in Africa: Dynamic Change at the Margins*. Abingdon and New York: Routledge.

Dabhoiwala, Fara. 2021. '"Imperial Delusions". Review of *Time's Monster: How History Makes History* by P. Satia, *Neither Settler nor Native: The Making and Unmaking of Permanent Minorities* by Mahmood Mamdani and *Worldmaking after Empire: The Rise and Fall of Self-Determination* by Adom Getachew', *The New York Review of Books*, 1 July 2021, Volume LXVIII(11): 59–62.

Dereje Feyissa and Günther Schlee. 2009. 'Mbororo (Fulɓe) Migrations from Sudan into Ethiopia', in Elisabeth E. Watson and Günther Schlee (eds), *Changing Identifications and Alliances in North East Africa. Volume II: Sudan, Uganda and the Ethiopia-Sudan Borderlands*. New York and Oxford: Berghahn, pp. 157–78.

Donham, Donald. 2002 [1986]. 'Old Abyssinia and the New Ethiopian Empire: Themes in Social History', in Donald L. Donham and Wendy James (eds), *The Southern Marches of Imperial Ethiopia*. Oxford: James Currey, pp. 3–48.

Dubiel, Helmut. 1976. 'Identität, Ich-Identität', in Joachim Ritter and Karlfried Gründer (eds), *Historisches Wörterbuch der Philosophie, Volume 4*. Darmstadt: Wissenschaftliche Buchgesellschaft, pp. 148–51.

Eidson, John R. 2019. 'The Concept of Identity in the Ethnology and Social Anthropology of the Nineteenth and Early Twentieth Centuries – A Preliminary Report', *Max Planck Institute for Social Anthropology Working Papers* No. 196. Retrieved from https://www.eth.mpg.de/pubs/wps/pdf/mpi-eth-working-paper-0196.

Eidson, John R., Dereje Feyissa, Veronika Fuest, Markus Virgil Hoehne, Boris Nieswand, Günther Schlee and Olaf Zenker. 2017. 'From Identification to Framing and Alignment: A New Approach to the Comparative Analysis of Collective Identities', *Current Anthropology* 58(3): 340–59.

Elhadi Ibrahim Osman and Günther Schlee. 2014. 'Hausa and Fulbe on the Blue Nile: Land Conflicts between Farmers and Herders', in Jörg Gertel, Richard Rottenburg and Sandra Calkins (eds), *Disrupting Territories: Land, Commodification and Conflict in Sudan*. Woodbridge: James Currey, pp. 206–25.

Elwert, Georg. 1997. 'Gewaltmärkte: Beobachtungen zur Zweckrationalität der Gewalt', in Trutz von Trotha (ed.), *Soziologie der Gewalt: Kölner Zeitschrift für Soziologie und Sozialpsychologie*, Sonderheft 37: 86–101.

———. 2002. 'Switching Identity Discourses: Primordial Emotions and the Social Construction of We-Groups', in Günther Schlee (ed.), *Imagined Differences: Hatred and the Construction of Identity*. Hamburg: LIT Verlag, pp. 33–54.

Evans-Pritchard, Edward E. 1940. *The Nuer: A Description of the Modes of Livelihood and Political Institutions of a Nilotic People*. Oxford: Clarendon Press.

Fabian, Johannes. 1983. *Time and the Other: How Anthropology Makes its Object*. New York: Columbia University Press.

Fekadu Adugna. 2009. *Negotiating Identity: Politics of Identification among the Borana, Gabra and Garri around the Oromo-Somali Boundary in Southern Ethiopia*. Halle (Saale): Martin-Luther-Universität Halle-Wittenberg, Dissertation.

Fortes, Meyer. 1940. 'The Political System of the Tallensi of the Northern Territories of the Gold Coast', in Meyer Fortes and Edward E. Evans-Pritchard (eds), *African Political Systems*. London: Oxford University Press, pp. 239–71.

Fraas, Claudia. 1996. *Gebrauchswandel und Bedeutungsvarianz in Textnetzen: Die Konzepte IDENTITÄT und DEUTSCHE im Diskurs zur deutschen Einheit*. Tübingen: Gunter Narr Verlag.

Gabbert, Christina. 2012. *Deciding Peace: Knowledge about War and Peace among the Arbore of Southern Ethiopia*. Halle (Saale): Martin-Luther-Universität Halle-Wittenberg, Dissertation.

Gabbert, Echi Christina. 2021. 'Futuremaking with Pastoralists', in Echi Christina Gabbert, Fana Gebresenbet, John Galaty and Günther Schlee (eds), *Lands of the Future: Anthropological Perspectives on Pastoralism, Land Deals and Tropes Of Modernity in Eastern Africa*. New York and Oxford: Berghahn, pp. 1–38.

Gabbert, Echi Christina, Fana Gebresenbet, John G. Galaty and Günther Schlee (eds). 2021. *Lands of the Future: Anthropological Perspectives on Pastoralism, Land Deals and Tropes of Modernity in Eastern Africa*. New York and Oxford: Berghahn.

Gabbert, Echi Christina and Sophia Thubauville (eds). 2010. *To Live with Others: Essays on Cultural Neighborhood in Southern Ethiopia*. Cologne: Rüdiger Köppe Verlag.

Galaty, John G. 1992. 'Review of *Identities on the Move: Clanship and Pastoralism in Northern Kenya* by Guenther Schlee', *Man* 27(1): 219–20.

Gleason, Philip. 1983. 'Identifying Identity: A Semantic History', *Journal of American History* 69(4): 910–31.

Glick Schiller, Nina, Boris Nieswand, Günther Schlee, Tsypylma Darieva, Lale Yalçın-Heckmann and Lazlo Fosztó. 2004. 'Pathways of Migrant Incorporation in Germany', *Transit* 1(1). http://dx.doi.org/10.5070/T711009697.

Gluckman, Max. 1940. 'The Kingdom of the Zulu of South Africa', in Meyer Fortes and Edward E. Evans-Pritchard (eds), *African Political Systems*. London: Oxford University Press, pp. 25–55.

———. 1965 [1956]. *Custom and Conflict in Africa*. Oxford: Basil Blackwell.

Handler, Richard. 1994. 'Is "Identity" a Useful Cross-cultural Concept?', in John R. Gills (ed.), *Commemorations: The Politics of National Identity*. Princeton, NJ: Princeton University Press, pp. 27–40.

Helander, Bernhard. 1996. 'Rahanweyn Sociability: A Model for other Somalis?', in Richard J. Hayward and Ioan M. Lewis (eds), *Voice and Power: The Culture of Language in Northeast Africa*. London: Routledge, pp. 195–204.

Hoehne, Markus Virgil. 2016. 'The Rupture of Territoriality and the Diminishing Relevance of Cross-Cutting Ties in Somalia after 1990', *Development and Change* 47(6): 1379–1411.

———. 2022. 'Beyond "African Political Systems"? The Relevance of Patrilineal Descent in Moments of Crisis in Northern Somalia', in Aleksandar Bošković and Günther Schlee (eds), *African Political Systems Revisited: Changing Perspectives on Statehood and Power*. New York and Oxford: Berghahn, pp.139–62.

Hoehne, Markus Virgil and Tabea Scharrer. 2021. 'Balancing Inclusion and Exclusion among Somali Migrants in Germany', *International Migration* 2021: 1–15. https://doi.org/10.1111/imig.12856.

Istomin, Kyrill V. and Joachim Otto Habeck. 2016. 'Permafrost and Indigenous Land Use in the Northern Urals: Komi and Nenets Reindeer Husbandry', *Polar Science* 10(3): 278–87.

Istomin, Kyrill V., Alexandr A. Popov and Hye-Jin Kim. 2017. 'Snowmobile Revolution, Market Restoration, and Ecological Sustainability of Reindeer Herding: Changing Patterns of Micro- vs. Macromobility among Komi Reindeer Herders of Bol'shezemel'skaia Tundra', *Region* 6(2): 225–50.

Judt, Tony. 2010. 'Edge People', *The New York Review of Books*, 25 March 2010, Volume LVII(5).
Khazanov, Anatoly M. and Günther Schlee. 2012. 'Introduction', in Anatoly M. Khazanov and Günther Schlee (eds), *Who Owns the Stock? Collective and Multiple Property Rights in Animals*. New York and Oxford: Berghahn, pp. 1–23.
Krätli, Saverio. 2006. 'Cultural Roots of Poverty? Education and Pastoral Livelihood in Turkana and Karamoja', in Caroline Dyer (ed.), *The Education of Nomadic Peoples: Current Issues, Future Prospects*. New York and Oxford: Berghahn, pp. 120–40.
Mackenzie, William J.M. 1978. *Political Identity*. New York: St. Martin's Press.
Malešević, Siniša. 2002. *Making Sense of Collectivity: Ethnicity, Nationalism and Globalisation*. London: Pluto Press.
Marett, Robert Ranulph. 1920. *Psychology and Folklore*. London: Methuen & Co. Ltd.
Markakis, John, Günther Schlee and John R. Young. 2021. *The Nation State: A Wrong Model for the Horn of Africa*. Open Access Edition 14. Berlin: MaxPlanck-Gesellschaft zur Förderung der Wissenschaften. DOI: 10.34663/9783945561577-00.
Mooney, James. 1902. *Myths of the Cherokee*. Extract from the nineteenth annual report of the Bureau of American Ethnology. Washington: Government Printing Office.
Nadel, Siegfried F. 1950. 'Dual Descent in the Nuba Hills', in Alfred Reginald Radcliffe-Brown and Daryll Forde (eds), *African Systems of Kinship and Marriage*. London: Oxford University Press, pp. 333–59.
Riesman, David. 2020 [1961]. 'Preface to the 1961 Edition', in David Riesman, with Nathan Glazer and Reuel Denney, with an Introduction by Richard Sennett, *The Lonely Crowd: A Study of the Changing American Character*. Abridged and revised edn. New Haven and London: Yale University Press, pp. xxix–lx.
Schinkel, Willem. 2018. 'Against "Immigrant Integration": For an End to Neocolonial Knowledge Production', *Comparative Migration Studies* 6(1): 1–17.
Schlee, Günther. 1984. 'Nomaden und Staat: das Beispiel Nordkenia', *Sociologus* 34(2): 140–61.
———. 1988. 'Camel Management Strategies and Attitudes towards Camels in the Horn', in Jeffrey C. Stone (ed.), *The Exploitation of Animals in Africa: Proceedings of a Colloquium at the University of Aberdeen, March 1987*. Aberdeen: Aberdeen University African Studies Group, pp. 143–54.
———. 1989. 'The Orientation of Progress: Conflicting Aims and Strategies of Pastoral Nomads and Development Agents in East Africa – A Problem Survey', in Elisabeth Linnebuhr (ed.), *Transition and Continuity of Identity in East Africa and Beyond: In Memoriam David Miller*. Bayreuth: Breitinger, pp. 397–450.
———. 1991. 'Erfahrungen nordkenianischer Wanderhirten mit dem kolonialen und postkolonialen Staat', in Fred Scholz (ed.), *Nomaden, mobile Tierhaltung: Zur gegenwärtigen Lage von Nomaden und zu den Problemen und Chancen mobiler Tierhaltung*. Berlin: Das Arabische Buch, pp. 131–56.
———. 1994 [1989]. *Identities on the Move: Clanship and Pastoralism in Northern Kenya*. Nairobi: Gideon S. Were Press.
———. 1995. 'Regelmäßigkeiten im Chaos: Elemente einer Erklärung von Allianzen und Frontverläufen in Somalia', *Africa Spectrum* 30(3): 274–92.
———. 1997. 'Cross-Cutting Ties and Interethnic Conflict: The Example of Gabbra Oromo and Rendille', in Katsuyoshi Fukui, Eisei Kurimoto and Masayoshi Shigeta (eds), *Ethiopia in Broader Perspective: Papers of the XIIIth International Conference on Ethiopian Studies*. Kyoto: Shokado Book Sellers, pp. 577–96.
———. 2004. 'Taking Sides and Constructing Identities: Reflections on Conflict Theory', *Journal of the Royal Anthropological Institute* 10(1): 135–56.
———. 2006. 'The Somali Peace Process and the Search for a Legal Order', in Hans-Jörg Albrecht, Jan-Michael Simon, Hassan Rezaei, Holger-Christoph Rohne and Ernesto Kiza (eds), *Conflicts and Conflict Resolution in Middle Eastern Societies – Between Tradition and Modernity*. Berlin: Duncker & Humblot, pp. 117–67.

———. 2008. *How Enemies Are Made: Towards a Theory of Ethnic and Religious Conflicts*. Integration and Conflict Studies 1. Oxford and New York: Berghahn.

———. 2010a. 'Choice and Identity', in *Max Planck Institute for Social Anthropology. Report 2008–2009, Volume 1*. Halle (Saale): Max Planck Institute for Social Anthropology, pp. 9–28.

———. 2010b. 'Epilogue: How Do Paradigm Shifts Work in Anthropology? On the Relationship of Theory and Experience', in Olaf Zenker and Karsten Kumoll (eds), *Beyond Writing Culture: Current Intersections of Epistemologies and Representational Practices*. New York and Oxford: Berghahn, pp. 211–27.

———. 2010c. 'Territorialising Ethnicity: The Political Ecology of Pastoralism in Northern Kenya and Southern Ethiopia', *Max Planck Institute for Social Anthropology Working Papers* No. 121. Retrieved from https://www.eth.mpg.de/pubs/wps/pdf/mpi-eth-working-paper-0121.

———. 2012a. 'Introduction', in Günther Schlee and Abdullahi A. Shongolo, *Pastoralism and Politics in Northern Kenya and Southern Ethiopia*. Woodbridge, Suffolk and Rochester, NY: James Currey, pp. 1–34.

———. 2012b. 'Multiple Rights in Animals: An East African Overview', in Anatoly M. Khazanov and Günther Schlee (eds), *Who Owns the Stock? Collective and Multiple Forms of Property in Animals*. New York and Oxford: Berghahn, pp. 247–94.

———. 2013. 'Why States Still Destroy Pastoralism and How They Can Learn That in Their Own Interest They Should Not', *Nomadic Peoples* 17(2): 6–19.

———. 2015. 'Competing Forms of Land Use and Incompatible Identifications of Who is to Benefit from Policies in the South of the North: Pastoralists, Agro-Industry and Farmers in the Blue Nile Region', in Sandra Calkins, Enrico Ille and Richard Rottenburg (eds), *Emerging Orders in the Sudans*. Bamenda: Langaa Research & Publishing CIG, pp. 121–37.

———. 2018a. 'Introduction: Difference and Sameness as Modes of Integration', in Günther Schlee and Alexander Horstmann (eds), *Difference and Sameness as Modes of Integration: Anthropological Perspectives on Ethnicity and Religion*. New York and Oxford: Berghahn, pp. 1–32.

———. 2018b. 'Ruling over Ethnic and Religious Differences: A Comparative Essay on Empires', in Günther Schlee and Alexander Horstmann (eds), *Difference and Sameness as Modes of Integration: Anthropological Perspectives on Ethnicity and Religion*. New York and Oxford: Berghahn, pp. 191–224.

———. 2021. 'Unequal Citizenship and One-Sided Communication: Anthropological Perspectives on Collective Identification in the Context of Large-Scale Land Transfers in Ethiopia', in Echi Christina Gabbert, Fana Gebresenbet, John G. Galaty and Günther Schlee (eds), *Lands of the Future: Anthropological Perspectives on Pastoralism, Land Deals and Tropes of Modernity in Eastern Africa*. New York and Oxford: Berghahn, pp. 59–77.

Schlee, Günther and Alexander Horstmann (eds). 2018. *Difference and Sameness as Modes of Integration: Anthropological Perspectives on Ethnicity and Religion*. New York and Oxford: Berghahn.

Schlee, Günther, Alexander Horstmann and John Eidson. 2018. 'Epilogue', in Günther Schlee and Alexander Horstmann (eds), *Difference and Sameness as Modes of Integration: Anthropological Perspectives on Ethnicity and Religion*. New York and Oxford: Berghahn, pp. 225–30.

Schlee, Günther and Kurt Salentin. 1995. 'Ernährungssicherung in Nomadengebieten Nordkenias: Ergebnisse einer Lehrforschung', *Zeitschrift für Ethnologie* 120(1): 89–109.

Schlee, Günther and Isir Schlee. 2010. 'Limits to Political Engagement: The Case of the Somali Diaspora', *Max Planck Institute for Social Anthropology Working Papers* No. 125. Retrieved from https://www.eth.mpg.de/pubs/wps/pdf/mpi-eth-working-paper-0125.

Schlee, Günther and Abdullahi A. Shongolo. 2012. *Pastoralism and Politics in Northern Kenya and Southern Ethiopia*. Woodbridge, Suffolk and Rochester, NY: James Currey.

Scholz, Fred and Günther Schlee. 2015. 'Nomads and Nomadism in History', in James D. Wright (ed.), *International Encyclopedia of the Social and Behavioral Sciences* 16. 2nd edn. Amsterdam: Elsevier, pp. 838–43. DOI: 10.1016/B978-0-08-097086-8.62018-4.

Schoolcraft, Henry Rowe. 1845. *Oneóta, or Characteristics of the Red Race of America*. New York: Wiley & Putnam.
Turton, David. 2002 [1986]. 'A Problem of Domination at the Periphery: The Kwegu and the Mursi', in Donald L. Donham and Wendy James (eds), *The Southern Marches of Imperial Ethiopia*. Oxford: James Currey, pp. 148–71.
Wagner, Peter. 1999. 'Fest-Stellungen: Beobachtungen zur sozialwissenschaftlichen Diskussion über Identität', in Aleida Assmann and Heidrun Friese (eds), *Identitäten*. Frankfurt a.M.: Suhrkamp, pp. 44–72.
Weigert, Andrew J. 1983. 'Identity: Its Emergence within Sociological Psychology', *Symbolic Interaction* 6(2): 183–206.
Wimmer, Andreas and Nina Glick Schiller. 2003. 'Methodological Nationalism, the Social Sciences, and the Study of Migration: An Essay in Historical Epistemology', *International Migration Review* 37(3): 576–610.

PART I

PASTORALISTS AND OTHERS
Identity, Territoriality, History and Politics

CHAPTER 1

What Do (Pastoralist) Women Want?
Warfare, Cowardice and Sexuality in Northern Kenya

Bilinda Straight

Introduction

Günther Schlee has published an extensive theoretical and ethnographic corpus supported by fine-grained empirical data on questions that include the techniques by which individuals create, understand and communicate their identities within and between communities, including in the context of war (e.g. Schlee 2003, 2004, 2007, 2008; see also Donahoe et al. 2009; Eidson et al. 2017). Schlee's work on conflict has been a natural and fruitful progression from his classic monograph, *Identities on the Move* (1989), which advanced anthropological thought with respect to the relationships through which pastoralists in northern Kenya create identities that crosscut 'ethnicity'.

In Schlee's view, resources constrain identity-forming criteria of inclusion and exclusion even as the system is reproduced by individuals manoeuvring within the system's own logic (Schlee 2009). Schlee references Giddens (1976, 1979); also relevant is Bourdieu's (1977) structures of the habitus by which individuals are at once hypnotized by their own cultural-historical programming and yet capable of contributing to change through improvisational increments. Most likely because of this tension between constraint and freedom, Schlee does not offer a final comment on the causes of conflicts even though he supports a materialist view of pursuit of advantages over limited resources as well as the sociological explanation of pursuit of power – which he notes provides the conduit to greater control over resources. Nevertheless, he leaves motivation ultimately open-ended.

In this homage to Schlee's considerable contribution to anthropology, I examine pastoralist Samburu women's roles and choices in relation to warfare. Women's interests and decision-making freedom are constrained by elements of a Samburu cultural logic by which women are life givers, not life takers, and thus must not engage in combat, and depend on male relatives for access to life-sustaining livestock. My focus is on how women's culturally shaped interests pertaining to warfare support Schlee's corpus with respect to the situationally advantageous framing and reframing of collective identities in situations of conflict (including, here, generational and gender conflicts). At the same time, it is worth highlighting the fact that women's interests can both subvert and reproduce normative (masculine) collective identities. With that in mind, the chapter also critically reframes women's agency through an issue well celebrated in anthropological scholarship on warfare – the potential relationship between men's conduct in war and their success in obtaining wives and lovers within their communities. Thus, I also discuss the sexuality of pastoralist young men insofar as they are the subjects – or not – of women's desires.

Warfare and Gender in Small-Scale Societies

Cross-culturally and historically, women are represented in scholarly and popular discourses as occupying five potentially simultaneous roles in warfare: peacemaker (brokering agreements or protesting), target (victim of violence including sexual violence, traumatized witness, captive, sexual acquisition), combatant (soldier-combatant or participant-perpetrator), supporter (providing domestic and sexual labour, economic and/or ritual support) and inciter (through praise, shame and encouragement) (e.g. Cameron 2016; Das 2007; Gabbert 2012; Hutchinson and Pendle 2015; Lynn 2008; Mamdani 2001; Martin 2007; Sugiyama 2014). Of these, scholarly and popular discussions of the peacemaker role often reflect problematic gendered assumptions about women as 'natural' peacemakers. Although contemporary trends in the military industrial complex are changing the scale of women's participation as soldier-combatants, this role has typically been the rarest, particularly in small-scale societies. Thus, anthropological scholarship tends to examine the 'doing' of warfare as an aspect of masculinity. Partly for this reason and partly based on socially constructed biases, women can be invisible in scholarship and popular media depicting warfare, whereas men in warfare cannot help but be highly visible. Nevertheless, warfare pervades societies, and whether humans evolved, or historically developed, the capacity for collective violence, women have played a role.

Francesca Merlan has examined women's varied roles in Papua New Guinea warfare from the theoretical perspective of agency, which is congenial to Günther Schlee's work as well as the purposes of this contribution (see also Gabbert

2012 for women's active role in warfare and peacemaking in southern Ethiopia). Merlan's approach to agency is by way of a reinterpretation of Mahmood's (2001) theorizing of women's Islamic pietistic practices that considers (New Guinean) women's 'involvement and intervention in social action – in what are strongly constrained as well as changing circumstances' (Merlan 2016: 394). Merlan recounts two periods of warfare in which women played prominent roles: in one, resolving a conflict; in the other, as economic and weapons support, as assistants in plundering enemy supplies, and in a few cases, as combatants (dressed as men).

Women's roles in these two episodes of warfare described by Merlan are consistent with portrayals elsewhere. In an edited volume devoted to women's varied and important roles in twentieth-century wars in Eastern Europe, Rachamimov (2006) describes high-ranking women referred to as 'nurses' and yet making key economic and personnel decisions directly affecting the soldiers in the camps in which they served. In his survey of the roles of non-combatant women camp followers of the European early modern period, Lynn (2008) describes women as participants who were crucial to the warfare enterprise. Even as non-combatants, early modern European women engaged in injurious practices towards enemy villages, and additionally, they managed the pillaging economy that was a central aspect of these wars.

Two points emerge from these examinations of women's active, though non-combatant, participation in warfare. First, women's 'support' role bears more scrutiny than the typical connotation of that adjective. 'Support' evokes a dichotomous gendered assumption of women performing necessary but uninteresting work while men perform the valued and interesting labour. In scholarship as in popular media, it is 'politically correct' to describe warfare as 'tragic' and 'lamentable', but few would deny its 'sexy' and 'intriguing' representational social capital. Here, women camp followers may get a passing nod, but the main attention will be on the combatants. Nevertheless, writers such as Rachamimov and Lynn demonstrate through carefully supported historical sources that there are flourishing economies encompassing soldiers, with their own cultural grammars and politics of inclusion and exclusion. Second, and related to the first point, in spite of an assumption that women's interests are the same as those of combatants they 'support', this is an empirical question with potentially complicated answers.

Samburu: Warfare, Gender and Sexuality

Warfare and *Lmurran*

Samburu are livestock herders who raise goats, sheep, cattle and, in some families, camels in north-central Kenya's semi-arid lands. Over the past several decades, Samburu have practised an increasingly diversified economy, augmenting subsistence pastoralism with cash-based livestock trade, petty hawking, and wage employment ranging from positions in teaching and government to jobs as 'watchmen' and itinerant unskilled labour, both locally in Samburu and in urban centres as far away as Nairobi, Nakuru and Mombasa. Annual mean rainfall is too low for agriculture in most parts of Samburu County, but in highland areas that can support it, Samburu augment livestock herding with both subsistence and cash-based farming. In spite of a diversified economy, livestock herding remains a central aspect of Samburu collective identity, and even the wealthiest educated elite maintain herds, often purchasing imported dairy goats and cattle with high milk yields in addition to indigenous breeds.

With respect to representations in the media and scholarship, Samburu are among the East African pastoralist groups who are well known for their participation in coalitional lethal violence specifically framed as 'cattle raiding', which has transformed over time in the context of periodic extreme drought, colonialism, the independent Kenyan state, wage labour and formal education (e.g. Abbink 1993; Anderson and Bollig 2016; Blystad 2005; Bollig 1990; Heald 2000; Hodgson 2001; Holtzman 2017; Knighton 2003; Lamphear 1992; McCabe 2004; Rigby 1985; Schlee 2003; Straight et al. 2016). The proliferation of small arms, competition for political representation, and highly organized theft resulting in the movement of large numbers of livestock have also contributed to transforming warfare between Samburu and their neighbours such as Pokot, Turkana and Borana (e.g. Bollig and Oesterle 2008; Straight 2009a; Greiner 2012, 2013). Education has provided an alternative for many young men, truncating without eliminating the livestock role for boys who attend school.

The Samburu age set system prescribes seven to fourteen years (ideally) of membership in a cohort of young men who are expected to care for the community and its livestock. All young Samburu men (even those attending school) are initiated into a cohort through an extended rite with circumcision at its centre. Although raiding has historically been an important component of the construction of Samburu young men's masculine identity, their role is more than martial, and referring to them as 'warriors' bears scrutiny. These young men are referred to in the Samburu vernacular as *lmurran* (*lmurrani*, sing.), a word unrelated to violence, but which refers instead to the rite of circumcision (see Marmone 2017). Thus, Marmone's chosen translation of 'young circumcised' would be a better gloss to reflect the broad role of these young men, which includes defending the community and livestock not only against enemies but also against wild predators, such as lions, hyenas and leopards. Their task of long-distance herding of livestock in semi-arid environments is hazardous even in the absence of enemy combatants.

Youth and Sexual Freedom

Until approximately eight years of age, Samburu boys' and girls' labour obligations are largely undifferentiated, although they are already emulating their older counterparts in a number of ways. Small boys and girls both assist with penning goat and sheep kids, bringing kindling into the house, and undertaking various errands. Both are also called upon to perform food processing tasks, although boys perform these in the context of either caring for ailing grandparents or serving older boys and *lmurran* at livestock camps. While girls engage in food processing tasks associated with home, uninitiated girls may also prepare food for *lmurran*. Thus, uninitiated girls and boys occupy a symbolic zone between home and bush, while *lmurran* belong entirely to the bush, a fact that becomes clarified in the case of death (Straight 2007).

Besides labour obligations near home, boys and girls serve their communities by engaging in the most physically demanding and hazardous labour. Although *lmurran* undertake the most dangerous – and violent – role, boys and many girls (the latter in the lowlands especially) nevertheless engage in potentially dangerous herding tasks that take them far from home on a daily basis. They climb into bushy and forested areas with small stock, sometimes accompany camels, and climb trees to cut animal fodder. Boys are sent to cattle camps to assist *lmurran*, and if a family's male labour supply is lacking, girls may also be sent to cattle camps, typically in the company of *lmurran* whom their families trust.

The labour demands placed upon older girls, boys and *lmurran* accord them a degree of unsupervised freedom that has a symbolic dimension. Girls transition to sexual freedom gradually, while for boys the rite of passage into *lmurran*-hood is a prerequisite to sexual activity (Spencer 1965; see also Marmone 2017). In families following traditional clothing and adornment practices, parents increase the quantity of their daughters' neck beads as they grow, and young girls imitate older girls in dancing and singing. Similarly, boys watch *lmurran* very carefully, attempt to sing like them, and are eager to wear beaded ornaments like them. The importance of beaded ornaments to *lmurran* identity is evidenced by the fact that older boys who wear too many ornaments can be beaten by *lmurran* for transgressing the border between boy and initiated *lmurran*.

Both fathers and mothers play a role in encouraging the behaviour that will aid their sons in the transition to *lmurran*-hood; by the time of initiation, parents and other relatives and community members have done a great deal to shape young men's masculinity as eventual protectors of the community. Once young men have become glamorous, sexy *lmurran* in the eyes of Samburu girls, lowland (and some highland) *lmurran* are indeed visually stunning with their long braids covered in red ochre and elaborate beadwork lovingly constructed by mothers and girlfriends. Samburu *lmurran* are even internationally iconic, representing Kenya on posters, postcards, billboards, travel brochures and coffee-table books for Kenyan domestic as well as European and US audiences. Young girls, like *lmurran*, are colourfully and beautifully adorned whether daily or for ceremonies and other dance occasions, and as with *lmurran*, families encourage their daughters to become excellent singers and to enjoy their time as somewhat carefree young girls. There is no expectation of virginity – traditionally, Samburu have permitted *lmurran* and uninitiated girls to engage in sexual activities so long as girls do not become pregnant. There is no denying that adornment, songs and sexual behaviours and expressions are entangled cultural expressions, much like high school dances and prom nights in the United States.

Travellers have remarked upon *lmurran* and girls' intertwining adornment and sexual freedom, beginning with Count Teleki's 1888 expedition into northern Kenya (Höhnel 1894) and achieving notoriety in the 1930s in tandem with the unsolved death of a British ranch hand named Theodore Powys (Holtzman and Straight 2004; Straight 2020 and 2005a).[1] In the aftermath of the Powys case, the colonial government dramatically curtailed the martial role of *lmurran* and went so far as to ban specific song styles and some of the beads that girls wore. The ambivalence of older generations and Europeans towards Samburu young people's sexuality and adornment has continued into the twenty-first century. Over the past decade, a number of organizations and movements have been founded aimed at abolishing 'beading', the practice in which *lmurran* forge monogamous unions with girls by giving them large quantities of beads. Documentaries such as *Silent Sacrifice* and *Beads of Bondage*, and organizations such as the Samburu Women Trust and Samburu Girls Foundation, take the position that the monogamous unions between *lmurran* and adolescent girls are responsible for female genital surgeries, rape, abortion and forced marriage.[2] In doing so, these groups run the risk of what is akin to blaming rape on fancy dresses worn to high school dances and conflating consensual unions with forced ones. With respect to clitoridectomy, the controversy surrounding this practice is undeniable, although it is preparatory to Samburu marriages (which are typically arranged) and not at all to unmarried relationships (which are typically consensual). Likewise, in the absence of contraception and safe, legal abortions, any Samburu abortion is risky.

To be clear, I do not support forced marriage, forced abortion, forced surgery or rape in any cultural context. Moreover, as will be apparent in what follows, age and gender inequalities in Samburu often place girls and women in untenable situations. At the same time, I would not suggest that adornment, singing, dancing and consensual unions between young people should be banned and held responsible for rape and forced bodily practices. Samburu adolescent and young adult women celebrate their own adornment and sexuality, particularly in their choices of *lmurran* partners. Yet external representations (popular and scholarly) of young women's identities persist in focusing on a victimized sexuality or a sexuality as the target, the bounty.[3] How do teen girls and young women actually choose their lovers? Is it based on martial prowess, singing reputation or something else? What is at stake for women in contexts of warfare?

Warfare and Milk for Mothers

You descend to narrow paths, my Sweety Light-Black, my father's mouth,
You turn the stones, my Light-Black; you create narrow paths, my Sweety Light-Black . . .
You entered the bush before the wild animals, my Sweety Light-Black,
Short One of my father, we also call you Trouble Maker,
We have also called you Trouble Maker, my Sweety Light-Black, because
Short One of my father, you put warriors in danger.
(Women's Milking Song, lowlands, 2005)[4]

In 2003–2006 I conducted 76 (49 women, 27 men) intensive, tape-recorded interviews about warfare and migration. The women's ages ranged from young women who were dancing with then-active *lmurran* (Lmooli cohort, 1990–2006) to octogenarians who had danced with Lkileku (1923–1936), while the men's ages ranged from Lmooli cohort to Lmekuri cohort (1936–1948). Of the 49 interviews with women, 36 (19 Samburu lowlands, 17 Samburu highlands) included structured, quantifiable questions concerning warfare, cowardice, bravery and sexuality. I conducted the men's interviews with Samburu men as research assistants, the women's interviews with Samburu women as research assistants, and conducted some interviews myself (in Samburu or, rarely, Kiswahili).

Themes included women's direct experience of warfare, disposition of livestock acquired or lost in raids, perspectives on women's role in warfare, which categories of women (if any) encourage *lmurran* to engage in offensive raiding, and finally, women's opinions about bravery and cowardice. Since Samburu women do not serve as combatants but experience warfare if under attack, I do not discuss here women's direct experiences of raiding (as that belongs to a discussion about warfare and trauma). Rather, consistent with this chapter's focus on women's interests and agency in warfare in a small-scale society, I examine two overlapping aspects of the interviews: (1) women's perspectives on warfare and *lmurran*'s conduct in it as these pertain to women's culturally shaped roles and interests; and (2) women's sexuality and desires in relation to the question of cowardice and bravery.

Samburu Women and Warfare

Given the interactive combination of living in semi-arid and arid lands, climate change, uneven economic development, the machinations of local and national political campaigns, and the gender and age inequalities of Samburu social structure, it is perhaps not surprising that coalitional lethal violence – 'cattle raiding' – persists even if internal justifications and understandings are dynamic.[5] In spite of warfare's historical transformations, every Samburu generation finds common ground in discussing collectively sanctioned and transgressive forms of intercommunity violence that are irreducibly entangled in sexuality. At its most concise, *lmurran* defend their communities against attacks by enemy groups and attack other groups in turn, and these attacks have persisted up through the time of this publication. Historical reasons for attacks include the need to replenish livestock after the decimation of herds following disease and drought, although of course the human and livestock losses sustained in the violence undermine recovery. Violence has its own logic, becoming its own cultural expression (Whitehead 2004). In that regard, there is an unresolvable contradiction: indigenous explanations for violence may support or be consistent with evolutionary, materialist and historical explanations for violence. That does not make any of the justifications correct or enduringly necessary.

It is in the daily lived experience of a livestock economy that features chronic intercommunity violence that women's own interests and constraints can be understood. Paul Spencer (1965) offered an accurate and insightful assessment of Samburu age and gender inequalities and the structural differences circumscribing girls' versus women's personal and sexual liberties. Unmarried girls choose their lovers among *lmurran*, while families arrange marriages in which husbands exert control over wives (on Maasai, see Llewelyn-Davies 1981; Talle 1988). If a *lmurrani* 'beads' a girl, monogamy is expected on both sides and a girl will remove the beads in the case of an unfaithful boyfriend.[6] Historically, the consequences of infidelity within unmarried unions – particularly if *lmurran* were discovered having affairs with married women – have been disastrous. A girl's curse reportedly led to a hero being defeated in battle in one celebrated nineteenth-century case, and in a case from Lkileku generation (1920s–1930s), a *lmurrani* allegedly disappeared: 'He went and got lost up to now; we don't know where he went to die. [Up to now?] Up to now. His beaded girlfriend accused him of befriending [married] women' (F24-2004).

Spencer's (1965) monograph made the generational tensions between Samburu men widely known to future scholars, yet generational tensions between women also bear scrutiny. Older women condemn unmarried girls' perceived role in 'inciting' *lmurran* to warfare (Straight 2009b), while in the domain of sexuality, unmarried girls can be so enraged over *lmurran* liaisons with married women as to curse their lovers to death. Unmarried girls and married wives both refer to affairs between married women and *lmurran* in the idiom of theft but in vastly different emotional registers. There is ample irony and collective ambivalence for both women and men. Whether active raiders have more affairs with married women than non-raiders is questionable. Nevertheless, from the perspective of married elders (who remember their own youth nostalgically) protecting cattle, raiding, and affairs with married women all belong to *lmurran* identity. Thus, *lmurran* raiding must be held to moderation for reasons of sexual control as well as peace, even as husbands vary in vigilance against adulterous wives.

Meanwhile, women's relationships with *lmurran* and the activity of warfare change across the life course. Or, stated differently, *lmurran* raiding is never simply about livestock but rather about bringing cattle to women – first to their girlfriends in the bush and ultimately to their mothers at home. While married elders sit together in the cool of a shade tree sharing songs and stories of their own and earlier generations' raiding behaviour (Straight 2005b), the primary players in warfare are *lmurran* and the women they love – women who simultaneously want, do not want and consistently fear the reality of warfare.

With respect to girls' role in warfare, unmarried girls sing songs of praise and shaming aimed at inciting *lmurran* to raid. This does not mean that girls' songs are causal in warfare, and thus, condemnation of girls' perceived incitement occurs alongside the ubiquitous assertion that no one 'sends' *lmurran* because no one controls them. In a few well-known cases in which Samburu were attacked with many fatalities and thousands of livestock taken, such as the Somali attacks on Samburu during the Lkishili period (1961–1976), the community as a whole did expect *lmurran* to respond, and in some cases even married elders who were physically able joined the fight (see Holtzman 2017 on the Samburu-Somali violence). Aside from such cases, married elders attempt to limit *lmurran* raiding behaviour but with limited success. One Samburu octogenarian woman told this story:

> When *lmurran* want to go for a raid they don't want to hear the words of elders, not at all. You know, there was one *lmurrani* whose father said, 'My son, give me your ear', by which he meant, 'Listen to me, my son'. Then the *lmurrani* cut off his ear, handed it to him, and said, 'Here, now you have it'. And then he went to the raid without that ear. [Laughter.] And he didn't get killed because he had given his father his ear. [Continued laughter.] (F44-2005)

Nevertheless, even as *lmurran* actions cannot be attributed to unmarried girls in any simple sense, the relationships between *lmurran* and girls are central to the poetics of warfare. The space of *lmurran*-girlfriend interactions is the bush, where praise and shaming songs, warfare and its aftermath all occur. If brave, the songs might go like this:

> Le— pushed through the gunfire
> he pushed through the gunfire because he can face it
> to push raiders from behind
> push the raiders from behind [to embolden them]
> (Lterito generation song – 1893–1912)

In the same song, girls are encouraged/wooed to take *lmurran* boyfriends because 'beauty can diminish but the cattle will never finish'. And the sexual play might be sung like the following:

> My black girl of Le—
> My black girl of Le—
> My black black girl of Le—
> Greetings, my black girl of Le—
> She opens the glass
> she opens the glass
> on the bed
> on the bed
> on the bed
> on the bed
> What will you do to me
> heart of my life
> King of the dance ground?
> (Lkishili generation song 1961–1976)

If praise is the way in which girls reward their lovers (and *lmurran* reward themselves – in these songs sung by one gender or both together), shame is the way in which they punish *lmurran* for not performing their martial role. During the Lmekuri generation (1936–1948), the British colonial government banned spears as well as girls' beads. Lmekuri girls sang their opinions about their boyfriends' behaviour:

> May you be stricken by worms
> bitten by a monkey
> because the last time our cattle had real *lmurran*
> was during Lkileku of [place name].

Lmekuri carried sharpened sticks instead of spears and did not raid, but many of their generation did see combat eventually as it turned out – in the Burma campaign of the Second World War. European-imported goods were eventually incorporated into songs:

> My boyfriend's eyes are like light bulbs
> lighting up the house

Wars fought in distant places, however, were not similarly incorporated; rather, Lmekuri girls had to content themselves with the shape of their boyfriends' bodies and their mutual love of cows.

After a raid, if it has been successful and without fatalities, *lmurran* return singing. If they have killed, the bush is the space of cleansing; regardless of killing, the bush is both liminal and transformative, the place where girls, but not married women, may eat slaughtered meat with *lmurran*, and the place where girls are treated to the sight of newly acquired animals. Since most girls belong to the same clan as their lovers, this is also a space where the identities of sisters and lovers are conflated:

> I won't say a girl is my sister
> I won't say a girl is my sister
> So as not to miss one to touch
> (sung at Ntotoi stone game, 2002)

Livestock are not given to girlfriends but they are given to sisters, who are biological sisters of some *lmurran*, lovers of others, and clan sisters of all *lmurran* fighting together:

> When her brother goes to the raids he will bring cows and the girl's mother's house will have plenty of milk. So that girl has plenty of milk to give to the *lmurrani* and to her fellow girls, like the song, 'I'm delighted and happy because the young *lmurrani* of my mother has succeeded in his duty' [bringing cows to milk]. (F44-2005)

Girls meet the stolen cattle first, praising and blessing *lmurran*:

> Our bulls who take long to herd
> I will just run and get into my sisters' intestines
> (get a blessing from my sisters; song sung at Ntotoi game, 2002)

Sisters' blessings can also have a material dimension since sisters – and once sisters marry, sisters' husbands – contribute cows with which to buy guns, and goats to buy ammunition.

After passing through the bushy space of raiding, meat camp, song ground and meeting point with sisters and lovers, successful *lmurran* bring the livestock home, not to their fathers, but to their mothers. The most closely aligned interests in a Samburu polygynous home are between mothers and their *lmurran* sons. Initiation into *lmurran*-hood includes the practice of *lminong*, whereby *lmurran* are no longer permitted to eat food prepared or seen by initiated and married women, including their own mothers. However, *lmurran* continue to be strongly bonded to their mothers in a relationship reinforced through milk. Mothers cannot cook for their sons, but women's livestock are apportioned through their sons, and *lmurran* drink milk and sleep in the homes of their mothers and the mothers of other *lmurran*. Raided livestock then become the source of milk for women, their younger children and the *lmurran* who are the source of the livestock in the first place:

> L— has led the *lmurran*
> Those who have killed the ones dying of diarrhoea [euphemism for fright]
> And my mother doesn't stay hungry
> My mother doesn't go around begging for food
> (Lkishili song)

> We have raided a large herd
> because we thought no one would notice
> during the rainy season my beloved

> Give milk to my mother
> We have raided a large herd, my beloved
> We thought no one would notice
> during the rainy season, my beloved
> Give milk to my mother
> (Lmooli song)

This role of bringing milk cows to their mothers is perhaps the greatest source of poignant ambivalence. Every woman I interviewed asserted that mothers do not want their sons to go to war, fearing they might be killed.

> She keeps on thinking about him, thinking, this child of mine who has gone, isn't he going to get killed? And she can't believe he can return [safely] until she sees him. (F25-2004)

> The mother of *lmurran* gets scared and just prays for him and fastens her stomach [braces herself]. (F26-2004)

Nevertheless, the lure of warfare is strong when all goes well; if a group of *lmurran* returns safely, bringing livestock, mothers of those who remained behind feel bad.

> The mother of 'I-cannot-go' will be angry. Those women [mothers of *lmurran* who raided] will be milking the cows from the raid and the mother of 'I-cannot-go' will be angry. (F25-2004)

Between the sexual freedom of girlhood and the power of being a mother to *lmurran*, a woman's young reproductive years are a time of relative powerlessness. There are two paths to constrained liberation for these women: taking lovers of their own choosing, and running away – becoming *kitala*, an institutionalized practice that permits women days, weeks and sometimes years away from controlling and/or abusive husbands.

> I stand at the middle slopes and I look for one thing only
> I look for a white cloth [*lmurran* fashion at that time]
> Coming around the bottom of that hill
> Ho, my husband, don't beat me in the evening
> Let me milk cattle for you
> Because if you say I can't milk them, I will go
> I will go straight to the place you don't like
> I will go to the home of *lmurran* / where there is equality
> (Lkishili song)

Married women are continually subjected to the possibility of interpersonal violence and lost access to food through their husbands' actions (as in the song, not being permitted to milk). Infidelity surfaces in songs, stories and everyday conversation as a fact so embedded in the social fabric that all of the Samburu I have asked informally over the past several decades (over sixty individuals, men and women) estimate that 80–97 per cent of married individuals have extramarital affairs. Since marriage is viewed as a social contract, not a companionate one, many men ignore their wives' affairs so long as they are discreet – even boasting that once weaned, lovers' children increase the husband's labour pool. Others, though, are enraged by jealousy. In the case of one woman, who bore many scars from her husband's abuse, rage prevailed and she spent many years of her marriage *kitala*.

> You know what sent me? He [husband] wakes me hitting my house with rocks. Other Samburu told me to run away to avoid being killed and so that sent me. [Did he hit you?] Yes, he hit me. And he threw stones at my house, tu tu tu tu! So I went to our [natal] home. You know the kind of problems a Samburu husband can subject you to? You may even be denied food from your own livestock . . . He can even make you starve, you don't eat food . . . Whenever I got pregnant I ran away [accused of infidelity, to which she confessed] . . . You see at my [natal] home, there weren't problems because my family is rich and I was given cattle, I was given goats, so I had no problems. (F50-2002)

Family histories are replete with the stories of sons conceived in extramarital affairs or by uninitiated girls managing to survive these circumstances and found successful lineages. In one nineteenth-century story, a husband (of a daughter of a Laikipiak man adopted by Samburu) tries to force his wife to kill the infant she has conceived with her lover:

> A man can see a woman he wants and a woman can see a man she wants. And so, these two (adulterers) mated and had a boy. After the boy was born, the husband said, 'I don't want this child', and he ordered his wife to kill the boy but she refused. She told him to kill the child himself but everyone was afraid to kill small babies back then. Even the married men were afraid to kill them and the women were afraid to kill them. So, the woman took the child to her mother. (M8-2003)

After more discussions and debate, the grandmother raised the child and he founded a lineage, while the husband continued to live a successful life – a happy ending for all. In another story though, the outcome was less favourable for the cheated-on husband. The man was of Lmarikon generation (1880–1893), the son of a renowned Lkipiku (1837–1851) *lmurrani*. Lkipiku was a period of drought, famine and smallpox, and the Lkipiku father escaped to Baringo and later returned, celebrated for his fierceness. Although his Lmarikon son was also a well-known *lmurrani*, his bravery did not survive married life. Soon after the wedding, his wife

> went back to her former *lmurrani* boyfriend while she was still just a bride, staying with the family of that *lmurrani* who had beaded her. Thus, it was Le— (her lover) who sired the elder brother (her first child). When she was brought back (to her husband) he escaped to K— (place name), escaping this beautiful girl who disliked him because he had an ugly face and was very black. He escaped to the plains. Boy,

this madness can take men and get them lost. It will kill them. That foolishness kills men! He got sick and died there. (M9-2003)

Samburu social structure mutually reproduces age and gender inequality in a system in which married men enjoy power over women and younger men, leading *lmurran* (chronological adults) to rebel against the authority of elder men, while girls try to protect their claims to sexual exclusivity with *lmurran* against the transgressions of young married women barely older than themselves. Even as married elders hold (and wield) social and political authority, the fact that a young cohort of *lmurran* take the largest share of risk in protecting – and stealing – livestock means that *lmurran* are the sexual targets of girls and women, and the objects of affection of their mothers, with cow love uniting them all.

Sexuality and Desire for Cowards and Heroes

According to a prominent anthropological paradigm, there is a direct, linear relationship between men's combat behaviour in small-scale societies and their success with sexual liaisons. In its evolutionary theoretical form, this means equating warfare and reproductive success – women in the 'target' role of warfare. Sexual violence and abduction are relevant here, with potentially far-reaching consequences (Cameron 2016). Captivity features prominently in Samburu stories, but these are stories with happy endings, in which new lineages were founded and heroes prevailed, often through women's empowering actions. For example, in one story, Kamba *lmurran* succeeded in getting away with both cattle and Samburu girls. The Samburu *lmurran* followed their enemies' tracks and pursued them quietly as it started to rain. Realizing that their boyfriends and brothers had come, the captive girls invited their captors to dance – deliberately creating a distraction and disarming their captors at the same time because, before dancing, the Kamba untied their bows and quivered their arrows. The Kamba sang,

> Samburu *lmurran* are like their mothers' light-coloured shit
> Kamba *lmurran* are like the eyes of lions.

One of the Samburu *lmurran* had stoppered the war bell on his leg, saying he would let it ring only as they faced their enemies to release the girls. As the Kamba continued their song, this *lmurrani* jumped into their midst and speared the song leader.

> Haai! Haai! They [Kamba] tried to shoot him with arrows. Pupu! The Kamba were finished. There were very few survivors. That was the last time the Kamba tried to raid the Samburu [during Lterito 1893–1912]. (M9-2003)

Empowerment can depend then on the perspective of the narrator. In this story (narrated to my research assistant and me in 2003 by a Lkileku [1923–1936] man), Samburu girls developed their own strategy, and the success of their boyfriends is credited partly to them. In Samburu stories generally, women often play an active role, and their choices of lovers are celebrated or lamented but never condemned.

In 1988, Napoleon Chagnon published his highly controversial paper providing demographic evidence to argue that Yanomami who had killed had more wives and children than those who had not killed. In doing so, he narratively framed his anecdotal evidence that cowards' wives received sexual attention from other men as if women lacked agency. In a recent, less controversial paper on Nyangatom pastoralists in East Africa, Glowacki and Wrangham (2014) support the reproductive success argument with data that accords more wives and children to elders peer-identified as 'prolific' stealth raiders in their youth. Limitations of this paper have been noted (Zefferman, Baldini and Mathew 2015). While the authors claim that sexual affairs are more or less non-existent, hearing from women respondents would be helpful to further support their claims concerning paternity. Stephen Beckerman et al. (2009) provide contrasting data of lower reproductive success for aggressive Waorani warriors based on interviews with both men and women and complete raiding histories of 95 warriors.

In my structured set of 36 interviews with Samburu women, in answer to the question of whether *lmurran* known as 'cowards' have girlfriends (unmarried girls and also married women lovers), 29 asserted that they do, 4 asserted that they do not (3 from highlands, 1 from lowlands), and 3 (all from highlands) were equivocal. Women were typically first asked whether *lmurran* who are not praised (for their raiding activity) could remain without girlfriends, and then were asked directly whether cowards could attract girlfriends, lovers and wives. The term Samburu typically use for 'coward' is *guret*, which means fearful, although sometimes the more pejorative word *laron* (*laroi*, sing. – stingy) is used. If using *laron*, the speaker is emphasizing an overall demeanour of not acting on behalf of others, whereas those who are fearful may act in other ways that benefit the group.

Women's detailed answers to the questions were often spirited and humorous, particularly on the question of sexuality, which Samburu women enjoy discussing, and at other times quite serious, as when we discussed the warfare involvement of sons and brothers (see Straight 2009b). In explaining why girls and women might choose cowards, women often discussed the importance of looks, personality and that hard-to-define attraction which those in the United States refer to when they say, 'the heart wants what it wants'. One woman in her twenties from the lowlands said, 'It is just the *nkosheke* [stomach/kindness] of the person that matters' (F38-2004). A woman in her forties from the highlands said,

> There may even be a *lmurrani* with a good *ltau* [heart/personality] and then he also has a good tongue [singing voice] for girls and then the girls just love that *lmurrani* even if he doesn't go on raids. (F25-2004)

One woman in her thirties from the lowlands went further as to whether cowards could attract girlfriends:

> Cowards can even get more girlfriends than brave warriors if handsome . . . It's not required that a person is brave. (F28-2004)

Some women were sexually playful or explicit. One woman, using the term *laroi* for a coward, said,

> He can get the best bride [as a lover, not referring to his wife], a hot one. (F37, young lowland woman, 2004)

A woman in her fifties from the lowlands spoke of having *lmurran* lovers when she was a young married woman:

> They just tell each other so when he comes to look for her, they get each other anywhere, even in the river, they do it there. He just grinds you there and leaves [laughter].

Of cowards, she said pragmatically,

> Samburu want cowards because the brave one usually dies first. (F29-2004)

A younger woman (in her thirties, from the highlands), whom I know fairly well, launched into sexual playfulness in this way:

> Me: *Are there those [warriors] who are not praised who stay without [girls]?*
>
> Answer: How can they stay without? They just have, every person gets because they borrow that 'thing' if it's that 'thing' one wants. [laughter] Isn't that thing being borrowed? Even you now, can't someone borrow your 'thing'? [laughter] If you like his face, if you like his face and you understand each other.
>
> Me: *What if he's a coward?*
>
> Answer: Even if he's a coward, it's okay. It's whatever your heart likes. (F46-2005)

A woman from the lowlands in her thirties who likewise spoke of the importance of sexual attraction additionally made clear that young women were able to choose lovers, so long as they were not 'beaded' by a *lmurrani* (as it marks exclusivity):

> A girl is just in charge of herself. A girl without beads just drives herself. She goes to anyone her body wants . . . (F35-2004)

While they might love 'cowards' if they were handsome, kind-hearted or because the two were simply mutually attracted, women also said they liked 'heroes' (*lain'goni*, bulls) and strong men (*ltun'gani ogol*). Here, some women spoke directly of the relationship between a man's personality and the offspring he sires:

> I don't know why these 'cowards' [*gureti*] get girlfriends but girls say they do. [What about heroes?] Heroes get because women want to perpetuate their genes [*mpekoi*, from Kiswahili *mbegu*, seeds]. (F24-2004)

Another woman, drawing a comparison between personality and the qualities of the child, condemned 'cowards' (using first *laroi* and then *guret*), but then she went on to describe a desirable 'strong man' in ways that complicated the simple dichotomy between hero and coward:

> Bilinda, if you have a child with a *laroi* like this one, even the child will be *guret* [We laugh – she is referring to one or both of our husbands]. Even his child will just be *guret* because his father is *guret* ... When it is said that a great man, a strong man has sired a child, the child is liked by everyone because it is known that the child will be strong and work hard. A great person knows that he can do great things and not kill anyone. [Even if he goes on raids frequently?] Yes, even if he raids frequently, he knows how to bring himself back alive. (F45-2005)

In sum, in explaining why *lmurran* attract girlfriends and lovers even if they are cowards, women offered a range of statements that focused on looks, personality (*ltau*), kindness (*nkosheke*), sexual attraction and even their qualities for producing admirable children. Women also evaluated bravery and cowardice in relation to their excellence in performing their expected role, looking after the cattle and defending one's own herd. As one woman said, when stating that Samburu do not like *lmurran* going on offensive raids, the right time to die is defending one's own animals in one's own place (F39, woman in her fifties from the highlands, 2005). Another woman summarized a common sentiment connecting a *lmurrani*'s willingness to do what is most essential to his role and loving him independently of raiding:

> There is no one who doesn't love a *lmurrani* who is just looking after his cows. It's just a matter of getting a *lmurrani* first so if he happens to go on raids, he's already yours. (F25-2004)

Conclusion

In reality, in the absence of warfare, as during the Lmekuri period, *lmurran* nevertheless perform crucial duties in the context of the extreme challenges posed by Kenya's semi-arid lands. As Neil Whitehead (2004: 9) eloquently states: 'Violent actions, no less than any other kind of behavioral expression, are deeply infused with cultural meaning and are the moment for individual agency within historically embedded patterns of behavior'.

Raiding is not necessary, but by its logic, Samburu women exert their interests materially and symbolically in ways that differ relationally and change across the life course, and which often represent successful, non-violent forms of conflict and protest. Schlee's thinking provides a useful theoretical framework for understanding the positioning and repositioning of Samburu women's interests even as those interests bear examining by their own optic. *Lmurran* ensure that the cattle remain safe and get the sweetest pasture, so that their mothers, sisters (and lovers) have enough milk. Those sisters and mothers, in turn, provide the material and symbolic edifice of the *lmurran* social world of livestock theft and protection. Moreover, mothers and married sisters embody the bridges between lineages, clans and ethnic groups that afford *lmurran* a material advantage when needed. As one motherless *lmurran* informed me concerning his challenges raising the livestock capital for marriage:

> If my mother were still alive, she would go into her father's and brothers' herds and take animals for me by force!

While perhaps exaggerated, this young man's statement highlights the structural aspects that reinforce love between *lmurran* and mothers, *lmurran* and sisters, and simultaneously create generational conflict between mothers who might prefer to broker peace where their own sons' lives are at stake, and daughters perceived (accurately or not) to 'send' *lmurran* into war.

Lmurran's relationships with unmarried girlfriends and the young wives of married elders likewise point to yet another conflict: between the interests of unmarried girls to whom *lmurran* 'belong' and the young married wives who 'steal' *lmurran* for their reproductive and playful potential. In this sense, *lmurran* are the licit sexual capital of one group of women (unmarried, uninitiated girls) and the illicit reproductive capital for married women who thereby achieve sexual freedom while also potentially (and deliberately) conceiving children with qualities they (as mothers) value. If Samburu men manage key aspects of the political world and the needs of livestock, women consciously and strategically manage the world of human reproduction in ways that shape kin relationships and undermine the very real (too often violent) control that married elders exert over their physical and sexual labour.

Samburu women share with men the challenges of chronic low-intensity violence, food insecurity and limited access to education and health services, but these issues are compounded for women by more limited rights over themselves as persons. In their relationships with *lmurran*, girls and women sing, dance, make love and war as the primary symbolic actors of Samburu society. They create spaces of freedom through performative cultural expressions and through relationships of their own choosing. It is to be hoped that Samburu women will continue to expand their current strategies and create new paths to gender equality.

Acknowledgements

I thank the Samburu communities who have permitted and supported this research, and the Kenyan Ministry of Education for permission to conduct research on which this contribution is based. Funding was provided by National Science Foundation Grant #0413431 (Jon Holtzman, co-PI), National Science Foundation Grant #1430860, and Western Michigan University. Any opinions, findings, and conclusions or recommendations expressed in this material are those of the author and do not necessarily reflect the views of the National Science Foundation. I would also like to thank the editors of this volume for their helpful comments in making this a better contribution.

Bilinda Straight is Professor of Anthropology and Gender & Women's Studies at Western Michigan University. Earlier in her career, she published on the anthropology of experience, gender, aesthetics and material culture. Since 2008, she has focused on the nature of emotion and human experience through the impact of cultural and moral norms on pastoralists in the midst of northern Kenya's extreme environment and chronic, low-intensity warfare. Most recently, her National Science Foundation funded projects have examined the intersection between humans and world suggested by epigenetics, utilizing an ethnographic and multi-disciplinary approach.

Notes

1. See the authors cited for more detailed scholarly consideration of this complicated case. In sum, a British ranch hand from a celebrated British literary family died in mysterious circumstances. His death was first attributed to an accident (possibly his pony shied and threw him), and his remains were subsequently scavenged by wild predators. However, colonial British settlers later blamed it on Samburu *lmurran* – conveniently in the midst of a land dispute as the same settlers attempted to move Samburu off of Leroghi Plateau. Samburu were acquitted and the settlers likewise failed to acquire Leroghi, but Samburu were nevertheless punished through livestock confiscation, brutality at the hands of Kenyan soldiers, and social engineering that included banning beads and cultural expressions that British colonial officers associated with Samburu *lmurran* violence.

2. This association coincides with a discourse of 'harmful cultural practices' perpetuated by Christian missionaries but also consistent with British colonial discourses (see note 1).

3. This expectation of girls' and women's victimhood extends beyond sexuality, as discussed in Gabbert (2014). Gabbert provides rich stories exemplifying Arbore women's agency, and, with respect to girls specifically (see ibid.: 198), prompts a discussion of Arbore girls' ability to be more disobedient and outspoken than boys.

4. This song was sung by a woman milking her cows, referencing the fact that cows' needs for pasture and water lead to warfare between Samburu and their neighbours. *Lmurran* also sing to cows when milking them in cattle camps – Samburu sing to their cows in order to relax the latter during milking, and in general, songs sung to cows represent a cultural expression marking intimate human-animal interactions.

5. I am separating the fact of persisting interethnic violence from its forms and justifications. Violence may endure while its logic transforms, and in contrast, one hopes it is possible for violence to end. In 2008, when Pokot abruptly initiated attacks on Samburu highland farms, many Samburu inhabitants of those lands were taken completely by surprise. The majority had educated their boys through secondary school, and thus their young men had been initiated as *lmurran* as a cultural identity but had never engaged in any raiding behaviour. They viewed themselves as *lmurran* and as Samburu but did not view these identities as requiring violence – animal husbandry (and a love of cows), yes, but violence, no. As the Pokot attacks continued, Samburu from lowland areas arrived to assist highland Samburu, and some highland Samburu (often reluctantly) learned to use firearms.

6. See Schlee (2014 [1979]: 108) for similar practices among the Rendille.

References

Abbink, Jon. 1993. 'Ethnic Conflict in the "Tribal Zone": The Dizi and Suri in Southern Ethiopia', *Journal of Modern African Studies* 31(4): 675–82.

Anderson, David M. and Michael Bollig. 2016. 'Resilience and Collapse: Histories, Ecologies, Conflicts and Identities in the Baringo-Bogoria Basin, Kenya', *Journal of East African Studies* 10(1): 1–20.

Beckerman, Stephen, Pamela I. Erickson, James Yost, Jhanira Regalado, Lilia Jaramillo, Corey Sparks, Moises Iromenga and Kathryn Long. 2009. 'Life Histories, Blood Revenge, and Reproductive Success among the Waorani of Ecuador', *Proceedings of the National Academy of Sciences of the United States of America* (PNAS) 106(20): 8134–39.

Blystad, Astrid. 2005. 'Fertile Mortal Links: Reconsidering Barabaig Violence', in V. Broch-Due (ed.), *Violence and Belonging: The Quest for Identity in Post-Colonial Africa*. London: Routledge, pp. 112–30.

Bollig, Michael. 1990. 'Ethnic Conflicts in North-West Kenya: Pokot-Turkana Raiding, 1969–1984', *Zeitschrift fur Ethnologie* 155: 73–90.

Bollig, Michael and Matthias Oesterle. 2008. '"We Turned our Enemies into Baboons": Warfare, Ritual and Pastoral Identity among the Pokot of Northern Kenya', in Aparna Rao, Michael Bollig and Monika Boeck (eds), *The Practice of War: Production, Reproduction and Communication of Armed Violence*. Oxford and New York: Berghahn, pp. 23–51.

Bourdieu, Pierre. 1977. *Outline of a Theory of Practice*. Cambridge: Cambridge University Press.

Cameron, Catherine M. 2016. *Captives: How Stolen People Changed the World*. Lincoln: University of Nebraska Press.

Chagnon, Napoleon. 1988. "Life Histories, Blood Revenge, and Warfare in a Tribal Population." *Science* 239 (4843): 985–92.

Das, Veena. 2007. *Life and Words: Violence and the Descent into the Ordinary*. Berkeley: University of California Press.

Donahoe, Brian, John R. Eidson, Dereje Feyissa, Veronika Fuest, Markus Virgil Hoehne, Boris Nieswand, Günther Schlee and Olaf Zenker. 2009. 'The Formation and Mobilization of Collective Identities in Situations of Conflict and Integration', *Max Planck Institute for Social Anthropology Working Paper* No. 116. Retrieved from http://www.eth.mpg.de/pubs/wps/pdf/mpi-eth-working-paper-0116.

Eidson, John R., Dereje Feyissa, Veronika Fuest, Markus Virgil Hoehne, Boris Nieswand, Günther Schlee and Olaf Zenker. 2017. 'From Identification to Framing and Alignment: A New Approach to the Comparative Analysis of Collective Identities', *Current Anthropology* 58(3): 340–59.

Gabbert, Echi Christina. 2012. 'Deciding Peace: Knowledge about War and Peace among the Arbore of Southern Ethiopia', Ph.D. dissertation. Halle (Saale): Martin Luther University Halle-Wittenberg.

———. 2014. 'Powerful Mothers, Radical Daughters: Tales about and Cases of Women's Agency among the Arbore of Southern Ethiopia', *Paideuma* 60: 187–204.
Giddens, Anthony. 1976. *New Rules of Sociological Method: A Positive Critique of Interpretative Sociologies*. New York: Basic Books.
———. 1979. *Central Problems in Social Theory*. London: Macmillan Press.
Glowacki, Luke and Richard Wrangham. 2014. 'Warfare and Reproductive Success in a Tribal Population', *Proceedings of the National Academy of Sciences (PNAS)* 112(2): 348–53.
Greiner, Clemens. 2012. 'Unexpected Consequences: Wildlife Conservation and Territorial Conflict in Northern Kenya', *Human Ecology* 40: 415–25.
———. 2013. 'Guns, Land, and Votes: Cattle Rustling and the Politics of Boundary (Re)Making in Northern Kenya', *African Affairs* 112(447): 216–37.
Heald, Suzette. 2000. 'Tolerating the Intolerable: Cattle Raiding among the Kuria of Kenya', in Göran Aijmer and Jon Abbink (eds), *Meanings of Violence*. Oxford: Berg, pp. 101–21.
Hodgson, Dorothy L. 2001. *Once Intrepid Warriors: Gender, Ethnicity, and the Cultural Politics of Maasai Development*. Bloomington: Indiana University Press.
Höhnel, Ludwig von. 1894. *Discovery of Lakes Rudolf and Stefanie, Volumes I and II*, trans. N. Bell. London: Longmans, Green.
Holtzman, Jon. 2017. *Killing Your Neighbors: Friendship and Violence in Northern Kenya and Beyond*. Berkeley: University of California Press.
Holtzman, Jon and Bilinda Straight. 2004. 'Echoes of the Vultures: Multivalent Memories of a Colonial "Murder" in Samburu District, Northern Kenya', paper presented at the 2004 Ethnohistory Meetings in Chicago, October.
Hutchinson, Susan E. and Naomi R. Pendle. 2015. 'Violence, Legitimacy, and Prophecy: Nuer Struggles with Uncertainty in South Sudan', *American Ethnologist* 42(3): 415–30.
Knighton, Ben. 2003. 'The State as Raider among the Karamojong: "Where There Are No Guns, They Use the Threat of Guns"', *Africa* 73(3): 427–55.
Lamphear, John. 1992. *The Scattering Time: Turkana Responses to Colonial Rule*. Oxford: Oxford University Press.
Llewelyn-Davies, Melissa. 1981. 'Women, Warriors and Patriarchs', in Sherry B. Ortner and Harriet Whitehead (eds), *Sexual Meanings: The Cultural Construction of Gender and Sexuality*. Cambridge: Cambridge University Press, pp. 330–58.
Lynn, John A. II. 2008. *Women, Armies, and Warfare in Early Modern Europe*. Cambridge: Cambridge University Press.
Mahmood, Saba. 2001. 'Feminist Theory, Embodiment, and the Docile Agent: Some Reflections on the Egyptian Islamic Revival', *Cultural Anthropology* 16: 202–36.
Mamdani, Mahmood. 2001. *When Victims Become Killers: Colonialism, Nativism, and the Genocide in Rwanda*. Princeton, NJ: Princeton University Press.
Marmone, Giordano. 2017. 'Danser et chanter un système d'âge: Anthropologie musicale des Samburu (Kenya)', MA thesis. Paris: Université Paris Nanterre.
Martin, Elaine. 2007. 'Is War Gendered? Issues in Representing Women and the Second World War', in Aparna Rao, Michael Bollig and Monika Boeck (eds), *The Practice of War: Production, Reproduction and Communication of Armed Violence*. Oxford and New York: Berghahn, pp. 161–73.
Merlan, Francesca. 2016. 'Women, Warfare, and the Life of Agency: Papua New Guinea and Beyond', *Journal of the Royal Anthropological Institute* 22: 392–411.
McCabe, Terrence J. 2004. *Cattle Bring Us to Our Enemies: Turkana Ecology, Politics, and Raiding in a Disequilibrium System*. Ann Arbor, MI: University of Michigan Press.
Rachamimov, Alon. 2006. '"Female Generals" and "Siberian Angels": Aristocratic Nurses and the Austro-Hungarian POW Relief', in Nancy M. Wingfield and Maria Bucur (eds), *Gender and War in Twentieth-Century Eastern Europe*. Bloomington: Indiana University Press, pp. 23–46.
Rigby, Peter. 1985. *Persistent Pastoralists: Nomadic Societies in Transition*. London: Zed Books.

Schlee, Günther. 1989. *Identities on the Move: Clanship and Pastoralism in Northern Kenya*. London and New York: Routledge.
———. 2003. 'Redrawing the Map of the Horn: The Politics of Difference', *Africa* 73(3): 343–68.
———. 2004. 'Taking Sides and Constructing Identities: Reflections on Conflict Theory', *Journal of the Royal Anthropological Institute* 10(1): 135–56.
———. 2007. 'Brothers of the Boran Once Again: On the Fading Popularity of Certain Somali Identities in Northern Kenya', *Journal of Eastern African Studies* 1(3): 417–35.
———. 2008. *How Enemies Are Made: Towards a Theory of Ethnic and Religious Conflicts*. Integration and Conflict Studies 1. Oxford and New York: Berghahn.
———. 2009. 'Introduction', in Günther Schlee and Elisabeth E. Watson (eds), *Changing Identifications and Alliances in North-East Africa, Volume I: Ethiopia and Kenya*. Oxford and New York: Berghahn, pp. 1–13.
———. 2014 [1979]. 'The Social and Belief System of the Rendille, Camel Nomads of Northern Kenya', English version (German Original: Berlin, 1979), *Max Planck Institute for Social Anthropology, Department 'Integration and Conflict' Field Notes and Research Projects* VII. Retrieved from http://www.eth.mpg.de/pubs/series_fieldnotes/vol0007.html.
Spencer, Paul. 1965. *The Samburu: A Study of Gerontocracy in a Nomadic Tribe*. Berkeley: University of California Press.
Straight, Bilinda. 2005a. 'Cutting Time: Beads, Sex, and Songs in the Making of Samburu Memory', in Wendy James and David Mills (eds), *The Qualities of Time: Temporal Dimensions of Social Form and Human Experience*. ASA Monograph Series. New York: Routledge, pp. 267–83.
———. 2005b. 'In the Belly of History: Memory, Forgetting, and the Hazards of Reproduction among Samburu in Northern Kenya', *Africa* 75(1): 83–104.
———. 2007. *Miracles and Extraordinary Experience in Northern Kenya*. Philadelphia: University of Pennsylvania Press.
———. 2009a. 'Making Sense of Violence in the "Badlands" of Kenya', in Michael L. Harkin and Neil L. Whitehead (eds), Special Issue, 'Ethnographies of Violence', *Anthropology and Humanism* 34(1): 21–30.
———. 2009b. 'The Sense of War Songs', in Parvis Ghassem-Fachandi (ed.), *Encountering Violence in the Field*. New York: Berg, pp. 71–78.
———. 2020. 'Land Conflict, Murder, and the Rise of "Timeless Culture" and Girl Blaming (Samburu, Kenya)', *Ateliers d'anthropologie: Laboratoire d'ethnologie et de sociologie comparative* 47(2020, Special Issue). Retrieved from http://journals.openedition.org/ateliers/12553.
Straight, Bilinda, Paul J. Lane, Charles Hilton and Musa Letua. 2016. '"Dust People": Samburu Perspectives on Disaster, Identity, and Landscape', *Journal of Eastern African Studies* 10(1): 168–88.
Sugiyama, Michelle S. 2014. 'Fitness Costs of Warfare for Women', *Human Nature* 25: 476–95.
Talle, Aud. 1988. *Women at a Loss: Changes in Maasai Pastoralism and Their Effects on Gender Relations*. Stockholm: University of Stockholm, Department of Social Anthropology.
Whitehead, Neil L. 2004. 'Introduction: Cultures, Conflicts, and the Poetics of Violent Practice', in Neil L. Whitehead (ed.), *Violence*. Santa Fe and Oxford: School of Advanced Research and James Currey.
Zefferman, Matthew R., Ryan Baldini and Sarah Mathew. 2015. 'Solving the Puzzle of Human Warfare Requires an Explanation of Battle Raids and Cultural Institutions', *Proceedings of the National Academy of Sciences of the United States of America* (PNAS) 112(2): E2557.

CHAPTER 2

NEGOTIATING COMPLEXITY IN EAST AFRICA
Landscape, Territoriality and Identity among Maa Speakers, North to South

JOHN G. GALATY

Introduction

Due to the works of Günther Schlee (1985, 1989, 2008), Richard Waller (1985a, 1985b, 1993) and others, we now have a nuanced understanding of the emergence of ethnic entities in East Africa out of the interactions between a confluence of families and clan groups moving across territories. What emerged were socially complex communities tied together through cultural and linguistic codes that provided symbolic ingredients through which people experienced 'recognition' of their mutual affinities and differences. The imposition of internal colonial boundaries often affected constituent groups that saw districts crafted around them in which they were to live, resulting in the severance or weakening of ties with their neighbours as boundaries were enforced and trans-border movements criminalized (Dereje and Hoehne 2010; Galaty 2016a). Two strong arguments seem today indefensible, namely that ethnicity travelled unaffected through the colonial experience to postcolonial realities, or that ethnicity in general and in its particular manifestations was a colonial artefact, with groups being products of colonial interventions in structures of administration and territoriality. The interplay of history and anthropology, illustrated by Schlee's work on Cushitic speakers in northern Kenya and Waller's among the Maasai, is what moves us beyond primordialist and instrumentalist views to grasp how social and cultural orders both engage with and assimilate regional influences while maintaining both the realities and ideologies of continuity. In this chapter,[1] I will focus on the interplay between a generalized Maasai sense of identity (or 'ethnicity') and the actions of particular Maasai territorial sections (Iloshon), as the latter emerged and were distinguished from one another, as well as on the integrative interactions between Maasai and neighbours, which often created interstitial though sometimes ephemeral bilingual groups. In what ways did sections exercise territorial governance over what would today be recognized as a 'commons',[2] and over time how did they reconfigure themselves and experience reintegration after being shattered? And, by means of assimilation and reintegration, did they indeed change, and if so, was it in order to remain the same?

Ethnicity and Territorial Politics in the Maasai Expansion

Today the distinction between Maasai territorial polities and Maa culture and language seems quite clear, given that mutually intelligible dialects of Maa are spoken by diverse social groups from northern Kenya (Samburu, Chamus, Ariaal, Elmolo, Laikipiak) through southern Kenya (the 'Maasai' as such, most prominently Purko and Kaputiei sections), northern Tanzania (i.e. Kisongo, Arusha), and from eastern and south-central Tanzania to northern Zambia (Parakuiyo). In recent years, 'Maasai' has become a universal ethnonym for almost all Maa speakers, given their mutual interest in identifying themselves with a single ethnic body, comparable to the composite notion of 'The Kalenjin', which could provide them with a modicum of political power in the postcolonial epoch to counter-balance their relative weakness vis-à-vis other major national groups that number in millions.

But, prior to about 150 years ago, it appears that the encompassing ethnonym for Maa speakers was 'Iloikop', a term still associated with Samburu (who call themselves 'Lokop'), possibly associated etymologically with 'Laik-ip-iak', and used in early explorer and administrative accounts to describe such groups as the Iloogolala that have now through historical shape-shifting become Il-parakuiyo (Baraguyu or Parakuiyo). In the earliest records in which the 'Maasai' nomenclature is used (Krapf 1860; Wakefield 1870), we are also told that they, together with the 'Kwavi' or 'Kuapi', called themselves Il-oikop (Jennings 2005). These several groups shared a single language and sets of institutions and social practices, so despite being distinct polities were culturally very similar. Despite their cultural affinities, the history of the seventeeth, eighteenth and nineteenth centuries in Kenya and Tanzania was in large part driven by the expansion of Maa speakers, not just at the expense of other groups, such as the South Kalenjin Il-Tatwa (now known as Tatoga and Barabaig), but also through conflicts between Maa-speaking groups, which led to the dissolution of some, the absorption of others, the structural fissioning of some and the re-amalgamation of others. Vossen's (1988) and Sommer and Vossen's (1993) work on Maa dialects makes clear the grand linguistic and historical distinction that exists between North Maa and South Maa, which divides Samburu and Chamus from the rest of the Maa speakers, who again are divided into the Kenyan South Maa and the Tanzanian South Maa, the former including the majority of Maa-speaking sections from Kenya that we know today, the latter the Arusha, Kisongo and Parakuiyo who inhabit Tanzania.[3] Based on the assumption that the Kore of Lamu represent nineteenth-century Laikipiak refugees, a Central Maa group has been hypothesized, spatially and linguistically interstitial to the North and South Maa (Heine and Vossen 1979). But more complex historical associations also exist, such as between the Samburu and Parakuiyo, that give some linguistic justification to Jacobs' (1968) hypothesis of an association between Iloikop from north and south (Sommer and Vossen 1993: 32–35).[4]

Turton's (1991) seminal notion that pastoral groups, such as the Mursi of the Omo Valley in Ethiopia, were outcomes of the expansionary process ('A journey made them') may provide insight into how Maa-speaking societies evolved as they expanded. A contrasting and more orthodox view would be that it is groups themselves that expand. Keeping this distinction in mind, we can consider several moments of Maasai expansion, the first when 'early' Maa (with related Ongamo), who may have represented 'old pastoralists' with more diversified economies, expanded southward 1000 to 1500 years ago (Ehret 1971; 2002: 276–77). The 'Later Maasai', practising a more specialized form of pastoralism, would have represented another wave of southward expansion, which undoubtedly brought a social body known as Iloikop into the northern Rift Valley, possibly centred on the Baringo Basin and the plateau northwest of Mount Kenya, or further south into the Nakuru basin (Galaty 1993: 66–67; Ehret 2002: 394, 445). From here, several groupings emerged, presumably by peripheral movements to the plateau lands of the Rift Valley. Firstly, the North Maa 'Kore' (Samburu) moved northward, then the Central Maa Laikipiak moved eastward, then the 'Kwabuk' Uasin Gishu, Siria and Ilosegelai moved westward, and finally the Iloogolala moved southward. We can presume that a group of Iloikop, who would later adopt an innovative ethnonym, 'Maasai', occupied the Baringo-Nakuru lake basin. It was undoubtedly the processes of movement of these Later Maa speakers outward from an ethnic core that saw their emergence as separate groups, with certain distinctive dialectics and institutions (Sommer and Vossen 1993: 35). Of course, each of these groupings came into intimate contact with non-Maa speakers, and the resulting friction contributed to the cultural amalgam that their respective expansions stimulated.

Sommer and Vossen's (1993) observation that the Iloogolala lived in proximity to the Loitai for several hundred years suggests a progressive movement southward of those who would come to call themselves 'Maasai', at the same time that their neighbours continued to call them by versions of earlier names associated with Maa speakers, whether Iloikop or derivatives like 'Kuapi', 'Kapi' or

'Kuavi'. The first explorer, mission and colonial records reflect a period when the Iloikop wars were already retrospective events for Maasai, who had experienced long-term strife mixed with paroxysms of violence as central Maasai confronted peripheral Maasai sections, competing with one another, partly for livestock and grazing, and partly in 'deadly jousts' between age-set battalions, sometimes acting out rivalries between Iloibonok, their respective ritual leaders (Galaty 1991). Were Maasai Iloshon the agents of conflict and expansion or outcomes of it? First, the Loita mounted the western escarpment, scattered the Iloogolala and drove the Siria back to the Mara River. Second, the 'Osilalei' (lowland lily) Maasai, who would later be called Kaputiei, Loodokilani and Matapato, moved up the eastern escarpment and southward, dislodging the Iloogolala and occupying the current domain of Kajiado, still called 'Kaputie' by Maasai. The movement of the Maasai from the Nakuru-Naivasha basin eastward brought them into conflict with a congeries of groups associated with the Iloogolala, on the Loita highlands, the eastern escarpment, and then on the Kaputie plains, which stretched from Oldoinyo Sapuk to Kilimanjaro (where a group called Enkang Lema, probably an element of the Iloogolala, lived). The Maasai expansion into territories of Iloogolala quite likely resulted in their fissioning, with regional groupings emerging, including the Matapato as such in the vicinity of Oldoinyo Orok (Namanga), the Loodokilani straddling the eastern escarpment to the Magadi basin, and the Kaputiei onto the plains of the same name. The three sections recognized their continuing unity well into the twentieth century by their joint celebration of age-set ceremonies, under the leadership of the Kaputiei, until jealousy over the monopoly held by the Kaputiei over the ritual office of the Olotuno led the other two sections' age-sets to separate their celebrations from the Kaputiei, later followed by the split of the Matapato from the Loodokilani. In this way, territorial realities in what we must presume was the emergence of distinct Iloshon out of an expanding group of southern Maasai were over time reflected in the ritual split of age-sets into localized groups. The Iloogolala regrouped to the northeast of Mount Kilimanjaro and to the southeast along the Pangani River and throughout Kiteto, where they lived in proximity to the Kisongo. Over time, tension between the two led to the Iloogolala (also called 'Kwavi' or 'Parakuiyo') being pushed out or assimilated by the Kisongo (Galaty 1993).

Bernsten (1979) observed that the Kisongo as such represented such a diverse set of Maasai groups that their unity, as such, was forged by their common recognition of the authority of the Oloiboni who derived from the Enkidong family of Sikirari (some members of which moved to western Kilimanjaro and Monduli, and then Namanga, Loitokitok and, finally, Ngong). The Kisongo had to fight for their territory, against Parakuiyo or Kwavi and also against the southern Nilotic-speaking Barabaig and Tatoga, who now occupy the western highlands of northern Tanzania. Like the Osilalei Maasai of Kaputiei, it would appear that the Kisongo as such did not expand, but the expansion of the southern Maasai resulted in the emergence of groups that began to see themselves as Kisongo due to their shared age-set affiliations and ritual leadership.

In the north, the Uasin Gishu came into conflict with Laikipiak, who defeated them. Then the Purko successfully fought with the related Ilosekelai, dispersing and absorbing them, and, together with the Laikipiak, defeated and dispersed the Uasin Gishu, absorbing many but leaving refugees who revitalized themselves under colonial rule. The Laikipiak then came into conflict with the Purko and the 'Tarakwai' (highland cedar) alliance they led (which included Damat, Keekonyokie and Ildalalekutuk). The Laikipiak came to dominate the Nakuru basin, but were later decisively defeated by this Purko cluster, which absorbed many Laikipiak and pushed others northward. There, they initially prevailed over the Rendille and Samburu, until the latter rose up, defeating them in a decisive encounter near Laisamis, since known as 'the place of stinking' (Sobania 1993). In this way, the Purko, swelled by families and adoptees from the wars of the north, came to dominate the region from the Naivasha-Nakuru base northward through the Laikipia Plateau. We must recall Waller's observation that when a Maasai group was defeated and its livestock taken, it had little recourse except to follow its own livestock into the kraals of the victors; in this way, the Purko cluster accepted in turn Iloogolala, Ilosekelai, Uasin Gishu, and Laikipia families, marrying their daughters or adopting their children, leading to a more complex clan and sub-clan structure and family names associated with those groups. I received an account in Keekonyokie of the assimilation of Iloogolala families, who were indignant when the prevailing Maasai began to change the place names of the locale, as if to erase the former's historical memory, to which they clung despite their social integration.

Clanship, Culture and Sectional Cluster Identities

It is impossible to say with certainty whether particular Maasai Iloshon existed as such prior to conflicts associated with occurrences of expansion on various Maasai fronts. In the mid-nineteenth century, Krapf (1860) wrote of the 'Eloikob' and the 'Masai', but did not mention particular Maasai or Iloikop sections. Nor does Ehret (2002), in his sweeping review of African history, refer to territorial sections, but rather 'The Maasai', who are depicted as distinctive actors in East Africa over the last fifteen hundred years. But if we consider the history of present-day sectional clusters, which share distinctive dialectical features and ritual practices, it is not unlikely that Maasai began as a territorial section of the Iloikop from which the divisions of Kwapuk, Iloogolala, Lokop (Samburu) and Laikipiak hived off (all representing distinct sections or sectional clusters). Bernsten described Maasai sections as 'clan clusters', though Maasai often describe their system of clanship more simply, in terms of five original clans emanating from different wives of a founder. But in fact, the system of Maasai clanship reveals great diversity, in the structure and depth of segmentation of clans and in the array of clan and sub-clan names, which may well represent evidence for the early associations between or later interactions among different sections, similar to interclan relations described by Schlee (1985, 1989) for northern Kenya.

For instance, the Ilukumai clan is strongly represented among Keekonyokie (from the Tarakwai cluster), while Ilaiser is the most prominent clan among the Osilalei sections (e.g. Kaputiei, Loodokilani and Matapato), within which, when it occurs at all, Ilukumai only represents a sub-clan. Outside of the original Maasai sections, Ilukumai is quite prominent as a territorialized clan or 'phratry' among Samburu, but is also found in good numbers among Arusha and Parakuiyo. Thus clanship provides another source of evidence of the deeper connection between the far northern and far southern Iloikop sections that Vossen and Jacobs noted. Ilaiser, which was said to have adopted the Enkidong family, is strongly represented in southern sections, but much less so among northern sections, which suggests that this major clan group was part of the Maasai southward migration. Systematically examining clan affinities between sections represents a challenging study of its own, which would parallel the careful work already done by Vossen and Ehret to trace semantic and syntactic relations between sectional dialects. But clearly Iloshon have represented historical vacuum cleaners as they swept up families after conflict or in the aftermath of migratory movements. In this way, the locales and sections in which particular clans and sub-clans are now found represent a reverberation of past dynamics of integration and trajectories of movement.

As some Maasai clashed with other Maa speakers and moved outwards in various directions, they would have experienced political fission, initially between clusters, and then progressively as distinct Iloshon within each cluster. But each would have maintained especially close social and ritual ties with members of the same sectional cluster even as they experienced greater and greater autonomy borne out of their establishing new areas of grazing and social life. While clearly centrifugal cultural and political forces were at work, what is most interesting is how connectivity was maintained between communities living at increasing distances from one another. Awareness of social affinity between distant groups was maintained in three ways: through ideologies of historical attachment between different clan groups, such as Schlee (1985, 1989) described; by means of continuing sociability that occurred at times and places of overlap; and through structural linkages between members of the same age-set distributed across different neighborhoods and even political sections, which brought them together informally and formally as coevals. This occurred through celebrations of inaugural and promotional age-set rituals, which also highlighted their shared cultural competencies (e.g. in language, dance and song, dress, and apparel) and which signaled and acted out their degrees of social intimacy.

So, even as each congeries of sections absorbed other Maa and non-Maa communities and in so doing experienced transformations in language and culture across generations, they would have seen themselves not as the sort of disjunctive personages that some theories of ethnic complexity would suggest, but as singular communities with clear identities.[5] The remarkable aspect of human identities is that individuals and collectivities invariably manifest situational complexity, characterized by social and linguistic 'shifting' according to context, while resisting loss of a centre of gravity for their emergent selves. So even today the Tarakwai cluster made up of Purko, Keekonyokie and Damat (and to a lesser extent Dalalekutuk, otherwise known as Kangere, and Uasin Gishu) maintain their social affinities (not without conflicts, which have arisen in the context of land allocations), as do members of the Osilalei cluster made up of Kaputiei, Iloodokilani and Matapato (and more distantly the Kisongo). It is not by chance that in the postcolonial period, when only approximate sectional boundaries sketched out during the later colonial period were being pressed into service when Group Ranch boundaries were demarcated, eruptions of violence occurred not between sections of the same clusters but between those of different clusters (Galaty 1994). These experiences of friction and outbreaks of conflict occurred between sections derived from different cluster affinities who had been pressed together after the second Maasai Move in 1914–1915 (Hughes 2006). At that time, Purko and Damat moved up the Mau and onto the Loita plains up to the Mara region, displacing Loitai and Siria, and, in lesser numbers, along with the Dalalekutuk, into the Kaputiei region from Kajiado to Bisil, pushing the Matapato southward and pressing the Loodokilani both from the east and the west (near Mosiro), all sites of continuing unrest (Hughes 2006).

Linguistic Complexity

There is something quite self-consciously persistent about Maa speakers' sense of identity, seen from the culture of daily interactions and speech, to the collective presentations of selves to one another in daily life and special ceremonial events, to the stylized performances enacted in touristic or media interactions. Yet each Olosho (singular of Iloshon, territorial sections) has also assimilated diverse cultural influences stemming from encounters, intermarriages and ethnic assimilation with neighbours, which appear in historical marks on the language and on customary life. Maa speakers have been called 'Cushitized Nilotes' due to the profound cultural and linguistic effects on those Eastern Nilotic speakers who moved away from their Lotuko compatriots in Southern Sudan into a cultural sphere of Eastern Cushitic speakers somewhere in the vicinity of Lake Turkana, probably a thousand years ago (Heine et al. 1979). As Ehret (1971, 2002) has so insightfully revealed, borrowings of both vocabulary and grammar reveal a history of contacts that inflect the languages of today. Kwabuk Maasai intermingled with Abaluyia, Luo and Kisii, Laikipiak and Samburu with Rendille and Borana, various segments of Maasai with Kikuyu from the north (Nyeri), south (Kiambu) and east (Murang'a), with Sonjo, Meru and Chagga in northern Tanzania, and Parakuiyo with numerous Bantu-speaking farmers of central and eastern Tanzania.

Waller (1985b) used the metaphor of Maasai and Kikuyu 'blurring together' in the forests above Kijabe to describe the sort of intimate interactions, in cohabitation, inter-marriage, joint age activities and bilingualism, that founded new bicultural communities of people equally comfortable in both societies. The Ariaal were described by Spencer (1973) and then Fratkin (1991) in terms of their bilingual Rendille-Samburu admixture, borne out of camel-keeping Rendille taking up cattle-keeping like Samburu and at the same time Samburu wives, spawning a generation of culturally ambidextrous children. Between Archer's Post and Isiolo live Turkana migrants, known as Ilgira, or 'the silent ones' (Hjort 1981), some brought in by colonial officials to build the road, who have melded with Samburu of the region to create another bilingual community, one linked to a similar Turkana/Samburu community around Baragoi. Jacobs (1968) identified the Ilkurrman as bilingual Sonjo-Maasai, who emerged when Sonjo farmers migrated northward along the Nguruman Escarpment below the Loita Hills to found irrigation colonies that used waters flowing from the highlands, and married sisters and daughters to Loodokilani Maasai, again creating a bilingual community. And Waller (1993) described how Kikuyu intermarried with Maasai along the Mau from Nairragie-Enkare to Ntulele during the early colonial period, at one stage respecting the need to accommodate themselves to the Maasai language and culture, at a later stage, strengthened by numbers, withdrawing from this sort of accommodation to become Kikuyu agricultural colonies within and but not of the Maasai community.

These and many other cases challenge simple notions of identity because plurality is ingrained in the knowledge and practices of each individual and in the patterns of social life in these interstitial communities. But complex identities are neither confused nor indistinct; bilinguals perform 'code switching', their shifting according to context between the languages they command demonstrating that languages do not blur together but are used deliberately and strategically, even if with magical facility. The sort of coordinated competences manifested by the Ariaal (Rendille and Samburu), Ilgira (Turkana, Samburu and often Borana), and Ilkurrman (Maasai and Sonjo) is what we see today among the several generations of schooled Maasai who in their exchanges may shift between Maa, English, Swahili and Sheng in the same sentence, not confusing but using the several languages they share. Such cosmopolitan identities, which are gaining stability in contemporary Kenyan or Tanzanian Maasai societies, may represent profiles for the future. Some bilingual communities may in fact be what Jacobs described for the Nguruman area, a 'halfway house' for Sonjo becoming Maasai.

But a study today might find that Pagasi was now peopled by Maasai for whom their Sonjo linguistic ancestry was a memory associated with grandparents. In the same way, I found that numerous Ariaal defined their identities as follows: What is your ethnicity or tribal group? Rendille. Are you an Ariaal? Yes I am. What language do you speak? Samburu. How can you then claim to be a Rendille? Because my father and his father were Rendille. How did you learn Samburu? From my mother. One Ariaal, bilingual in Rendille/Samburu, maintained that he was refusing to speak Samburu in an effort to revive the Rendille language in the Ariaal community. The Elmolo, a very small fishing community on the eastern shores of Lake Turkana, have almost completely lost their ancestral Eastern Cushitic language in favour of Samburu, although many are now learning Turkana, given the large Turkana community now living in the vicinity of Loyengelani. In short, for some, bilingualism may be a short-lived phenomenon, of only one or a few generations' duration, a sign of a one-way cultural assimilation rather than of a dynamic multi-lingual community. For many small communities, Maa and Samburu represent dominant and absorptive languages, the attraction of which follows from those regional communities' strong economic and social profiles over the last century. On the other hand, faced with nationalist and urban cultures, Maasai and other rural-based languages may give way in those urban families whose children favour Swahili and English as means of communicating with an ethnically plural community.

Iloshon Territoriality Today and 'The Commons'

The previous sections of this chapter describe the process by which Maasai moved into the regions they now occupy and in their expansion and penetration of these regions 'became' the sections they now are. I am suggesting that during a 'formative' expansion those occupying certain areas assumed the qualities of an Olosho (see below) while movements during the colonial period also involved displacement of Iloshon that already existed, which moved into other areas that were already occupied: Purko to Laikipia and then to the Loita plains; Uasin Gishu to Oldama Ravine and then to the Trans-Mara; Dalalekutuk from Laikipia and nearby Meru to central Kajiado; and smaller numbers of Purko and Damat to central Kajiado.

How did Iloshon relate to territory in the places to which they gravitated after their historical expansion (Galaty 2013)? Areas controlled by members of particular sections invariably included both wet season and dry season grazing, and both permanent and seasonal water sources, to which herders from other sections could request and, through negotiation, gain access. Some pastoralists and their herds intermingled in regions of wet season gazing, otherwise inaccessible due to lack of standing water, or converged on dry season pastures in swamps and lowland pastures near permanent water sources. The territoriality enacted along what might be seen as 'borders', where age-set warrior villages (*imanyat* or 'manyatta') gravitated, thus involving intermixture of sections and ongoing negotiations. This does not mean that friction and overt conflict did not occur, since 'frontiers' were often where gradual expansion occurred, cattle raiding took place, and age-set struggles and 'deadly jousts' occurred; what is important to recognize is that it was where the sections involved had a history of cooperation borne out of sharing sectional cluster identities that friction was perceived as between coevals.

The key institution through which decisions were made and action coordinated was the local age-group, which represented a seven-year cohort (each two 'hands' later structurally amalgamated into a fourteen to fifteen year age class), led by a spokesman (Olaiguenani) and his team. Coordination would then occur between such age groups and classes, between alignments of alternate age-sets, and through coordination between successive age-sets. The localized contingents of age-sets, which would join together to form section-wide age groups to carry out major ceremonies or for concerted action, were the anchors of sectional politics, helping to decide on the opening of dry season reserved pastures, coordinating watering regimes, and providing both for sectional defence and for coordination across allied sections. In times of drought, frontiers softened and movements of livestock herds across conventional borders, arranged through negotiations, occurred.

During the colonial period, the Maasai Moves involved the demarcation of a region that as a whole constituted what the colonial administration called 'Masailand' (Hughes 2006). Just as Samburu District demarcated areas allocated to the Samburu, in contradistinction from the Rendille and many Ariaal (as well as Gabra and Borana) who primarily inhabited Marsabit District, and instilled a sense of fixity into a much more fluid sense of territory, so Maasailand sealed off Maasai from flows of people and livestock that had long kept them closely tied to their neighbours (Waller 1993; Bernsten 1976). Waller has told the story of how Kikuyu and Maasai alike conspired to undermine colonial attempts to preserve Maasailand for the Maasai alone. Progressively, administrators tried to identify sectional boundaries, which were resisted by the stronger and more aggressive sections (i.e. Purko) while being welcomed by the smaller and more dominated sections (i.e. Damat), so finally such boundaries were less identified than imposed (Galaty 2009). I have already mentioned the conflicts that arose out of the administrative crafting of sectional boundaries during the colonial period when the demarcation originally occurred, and during the postcolonial period when Group Ranch boundaries were crafted to accord with sectional boundaries: between the Matapato and Kaputiei (in different areas) and the Kisongo-Loitokitok, between the Lodokilani and Keekonyokie and the Purko near Mosiro, between the Purko and the Loita near Naikara and Narosura, and, near the Mara triangle, with Uasin Gishu.

Maasai tend to state that they manage pastures as commons, with any herder having the right to take livestock to graze anywhere in Maasailand and to move their homes where they wish. Recent work has described conditions under which common pool resources have been successfully managed by collectivities (Ostrom 1990). The basic 'design principles' suggested by Ostrom created an idealized portrait of common property: defined boundaries, defined membership, rules arrived at by resource users, self-monitoring with graduated sanctions, etc. Maasai Iloshon have always had fuzzy geographical and social boundaries; its members are generally known, although creative ambiguities may be based on heritage, residence, and age-set affiliations, as movements and shifting social ties occur, and may change over time. Governance relies on informal councils of local age-sets, through which deliberations occur that make allocating and using resources an ideally orderly process, despite involving what has been described as opportunistic and highly reactive movements of herders to benefit from grazing opportunities, often in competition with one another. Protocols define the use of common watering points, with anxious herds managed by tough herders counterpoised while waiting their turn, or disorderly, with pastoralists fighting to push ahead of the line. Group Ranches created in the 1970s have generally taken over responsibility for territorial governance, though under numerous conditions herders can move between Group Ranches within the same Olosho, not however without negotiation. For instance, the swamp areas of the lower southern Ewaso Ng'iro, though lying in Shompole Group Ranch, have usually been used in common by the herders of neighbouring Olkiramatian Group Ranch, who, as neighbourhoods of Loodokilani, have long constituted a single amalgamated age-group with them. Yet as communities anticipate sub-division of commonly held lands, Group Ranch borders have begun to ossify, leading to exclusions and refusals of reciprocity. In the severe drought of 2007–2009, herders from both sections, and those farther north in Keekonyokie, crossed the border from Kenya into Tanzania and sought out pastures in the Simanjiro area south of Arusha. Informants on both sides confirm that negotiations were held, but that Simanjiro Maasai recognized the legitimacy of Maasai from Loodokilani and Keekonyokie (and perhaps elsewhere) seeking out pastures from their brethren in times of severe stress, and they agreed. Tanzanian government officials, on the other hand, were not amused, and on the principle of sovereignty have sought to bar such episodes of ethnic solidarity from recurring in the future.

What is demonstrated is the following: social entities that manage rangeland resources in common are not undifferentiated, but represent a multi-layered structure, with 'commonality' sometimes refused and sometimes recognized, depending on context and social identities. The governance of rangeland resources does not operate like a well-oiled machine but as a disputatious and complex process, where commonality represents a claim to be asserted rather than a right to be recognized. This chapter has sought to present the complex process whereby a congeries of Maasai Iloshon emerged through migration and conflict, with emblematic cultural forms representing ways of both displaying and asserting affinities on the basis of which the society both cohered and fragmented. Notions of common property have some utility as we seek to understand how sectional communities manage themselves and interact more widely across sectional boundaries, and, today, across Group Ranch, district, county and national borders. How these social dynamics evolve in the face of the subdivision of Group Ranch lands in Kenya or the future enforcement of village and Wildlife Management Areas (WMAs) in Tanzania, with the possibility of increasingly strict systems of land use zoning that might constrain grazing rights, remains to be seen, as Maasai territoriality enters another phase in their complex history (Galaty 2016b).

John G. Galaty is Professor of Anthropology at McGill University, with a research focus on pastoralism, tenure and conservation in Eastern Africa. He is the founding Director of the Centre for Society, Technology and Development and has served as Chair of Anthropology, Interim Dean of Arts, Associate Dean of Arts and of the Faculty of Graduate Studies, and President of the McGill Association of University Teachers. He was President of the Canadian Association of African Studies, Secretary of the Commission on Nomadic Peoples (IUAES), and member of the Editorial Board of *Nomadic Peoples* and the Scientific Advisory Board for the Max Planck Institute for Social Anthropology.

Notes

1. An earlier version of this chapter was presented in a Panel on 'Becoming Maasai; Becoming Maasailand: papers in honour of Richard Waller' at the African Studies Association Meeting held in San Diego in 2015, under the title 'Range Land-Scapes and -Claims: How "Common" was/is Maasai territoriality?' Research in Kenya has been supported by the Social Sciences and Humanities Research Council of Canada (SSHRC), the International Development Research Centre (IDRC), the Canadian Centre for Innovation (CFI) and McGill University, and carried out through affiliation with the Ethnography Unit of the National Museums of Kenya, Mainyoito Pastoralist Integrated Development Organisation (MPIDO), and the African Conservation Centre (ACC), through the Pastoral Property and Poverty project (PPPP) and the partnership project on the Institutional Canopy of Conservation (I-CAN). I acknowledge and appreciate the assistance over time of Joseph Ole Simel, Amos Ole Kaitei, Justus Lesiamon and Daniel Lemoile in Kenya, and Julia Bailey, Stephen Moiko and Anne-Elise Keen at McGill, and institutional support provided by the Max Planck Institute for Social Anthropology in Halle/Saale, the Centre for Society, Technology and Development (STANDD) and the Department of Anthropology at McGill University.

2. I should note that the proposition that pastoral territorialities, at least in West Africa, represent 'open' (access) rather than common property regimes has been discussed recently, the key issue being whether pastoralists forgo exclusion in the interest of wider access to pastures (Moritz 2016).

3. In Sommer and Vossen's (1993: 32) account, North Maa dialects include Samburu and Chamus, Kenyan South Maa the Loitokitok, Dalalekutuk, Damat, Kaputiei, Keekonyokie, Matapato, Loita, Loodokilani, Purko, Sikirari (of Ngong and Loitokitok), Siria and Uasin Gishu, Tanzania

South Maa the Arusha, Kisongo and Parakuiyo. This account does not include the Laitayok, Salei and Serengit of northern Tanzania, the Moitanik of Kenya, nor the Ariaal and Elmolo of northern Kenya.

4. Jacobs' historical theory was overgeneralized as representing an enduring enmity between agricultural Loikop and pure pastoral Maasai, evidence for which was based on colonial reports on settled refugees of internecine wars of Maasai and peripheral sections over the nineteenth century, which Bernsten's (1976; 1980) work puts into historical perspective.

5. One is reminded here of the theoretical associations some have proposed between hybridity and splintered selves, critiqued by Friedman (1997) for confusing cultural complexity and actual social life. Against conceptions of history as formed out of timeless continuities, it is important to realize that social and cultural forms are all hybrid, but that people nonetheless usually constitute themselves as whole selves.

References

Bernsten, John. 1976. 'The Maasai and Their Neighbors: Variables of Interaction', *African Economic History* 2: 1–11.

———. 1979. 'Maasai Age-Sets and Prophetic Leadership, 1850–1912', *Africa* 49: 134–46.

———. 1980. 'The Enemy is Us: Eponymy in the Historiography of the Maasai', *History in Africa* 7: 1–21.

Dereje Feyissa and Markus Virgil Hoehne. 2010. 'State Borders and Borderlands as Resources: An Analytical Framework', in Dereje Feyissa and Markus V. Hoehne (eds), *Borders and Borderlands as Resources in the Horn of Africa*. Woodbridge: James Currey, pp. 1–25.

Ehret, Christoph. 1971. *Southern Nilotic History*. Evanston, IL: Northwestern University Press.

———. 2002. *The Civilizations of Africa: A History to 1800*. Oxford: James Currey.

Fratkin, Elliot. 1991. *Surviving Drought and Development: Ariaal Pastoralists of Northern Kenya*. Boulder, CO: Westview Press.

Friedman, Jonathan. 1997. 'Simplifying Complexity: Assimilating the Global in a Small Paradise', in Karen F. Olwig and Kirsten Hastrup (eds), *Siting Culture: The Shifting Anthropological Object*. New York: Routledge, pp. 268–91.

Galaty, John G. 1991. 'Pastoral Orbits and Deadly Jousts: Factors in the Maasai Expansion', in John G. Galaty and Pierre Bonte (eds), *Herders, Warriors and Traders: Pastoralists in Africa*. Boulder, CO, San Francisco and Oxford: Westview Press, pp. 171–98.

———. 1993. 'Maasai Expansion and the New East African Pastoralism', in Thomas Spear and Richard Waller (eds), *Being Maasai: Ethnicity & Identity in East Africa*. Oxford: James Currey, pp. 61–86.

———. 1994. 'Rangeland Tenure and African Pastoralism', in Elliot Fratkin, Kathleen A. Galvin and Eric A. Roth (eds), *African Pastoralist Systems: An Integrated Approach*. Boulder, CO and London: Lynne Rienner, pp. 185–204.

———. 2009. *Walling in or Walling Out? Demarcating Maasai Sectional Boundaries in Kenya*. Workshop on 'Ethnicisation of Politics and Governance in the Borderlands and the State in the Horn of Africa', Max Planck Institute for Social Anthropology and Egerton University, Kenya, 7–8 July.

———. 2013. 'The Indigenization of Pastoral Modernity: Territoriality, Mobility, and Poverty in Dryland Africa', in Michael Bollig, Michael Schnegg and Hans-Peter Wotzka (eds), *Pastoralism in Africa: Past, Present and Future*. New York and Oxford: Berghahn, pp. 473–510.

———. 2016a. 'Boundary-Making and Pastoral Conflict along the Kenyan-Ethiopian Borderlands', *African Studies Review* 59(1): 97–122.

———. 2016b. 'Reasserting the Commons: Pastoral Contestations of Private and State Lands in East Africa', *International Journal of the Common* 10(2): 709–27.

Heine, Bernd, Franz Rottland and Rainer Vossen. 1979. 'Proto-Baz: Some Aspects of Early Nilotic-Cushitic Contacts', *SUGIA, Sprache und Geschichte in Afrika* 1: 75–91.

Heine, Bernd and Rainer Vossen. 1979. 'The Kore of Lamu: A Contribution to Maa Dialectology', *Afrika und Übersee* 62: 272–88.

Hjort, Ander. 1981. 'Ethnic Transformation, Dependency and Change: The Ilgira Samburu of Northern Kenya', in John G. Galaty and Philip Carl Salzman (eds), *Change and Development in Nomadic and Pastoral Societies*. Leiden: Brill, pp. 50–67.

Hughes, Lotte. 2006. *Moving the Maasai: A Colonial Misadventure*. Basingstoke: Springer Palgrave.

Jacobs, Alan. 1968. *The Irrigation Agricultural Maasai of Pagasi: A Case Study of Maasai–Sonjo Acculturation*. Makerere Institute of Social Research/Social Science Research Conference Papers.

Jennings, Christan Charles. 2005. *Scatterlings of East Africa: Revisions of Parakuyo Identity and History, c.1830–1926*. Austin: The University of Texas at Austin, PhD Dissertation.

Krapf, Johann L. 1860. *Travels, Researches and Missionary Labours during Eighteen Years Residence in Eastern Africa*. Boston: Ticknor and Fields; London: Trübner and Co.

Moritz, Mark. 2016. 'Open Property Regimes', *International Journal of the Commons* 10(2): 688–708.

Ostrom, Elinor. 1990. *Governing the Commons: The Evolution of Institutions for Collective Action*. Cambridge: Cambridge University Press.

Schlee, Günther. 1985. 'Interethnic Clan Identities among Cushitic–Speaking Pastoralists', *Africa* 555: 17–38.

———. 1989. *Identities on the Move*. Manchester: Manchester University Press.

———. 2008. *How Enemies are Made: Towards a Theory of Ethnic and Religious Conflict*. Integration and Conflict Studies 1. New York and Oxford: Berghahn.

Sobania, N. 1993. 'Defeat and Dispersal: The Laikipiak and Their Neighbours at the End of the Nineteenth Century', in Thomas Spear and Richard Waller (eds), *Being Maasai: Ethnicity & Identity in East Africa*. Oxford: James Currey, pp. 105–19.

Sommer, Gabriele and Rainer Vossen. 1993. 'Dialects, Sectiolects, or Simply Lects? The Maa Languages in Time Perspective', in Thomas Spear and Richard Waller (eds), *Being Maasai: Ethnicity & Identity in East Africa*. London: James Currey, pp. 25–37.

Spencer, Paul. 1973. *Nomads in Alliance*. London: Oxford University Press.

Turton, David. 1991. 'Movement, Warfare and Ethnicity in the Lower Omo Valley', in John G. Galaty and Pierre Bonte (eds), *Herders, Warriors and Traders: Pastoralists in Africa*. Boulder, CO, San Francisco and Oxford: Westview Press, pp. 145–69.

Vossen, Rainer. 1988. *Towards a Comparative Study of the Maa Dialects of Kenya and Tanzania*. Hamburg: Buske.

Wakefield, T. 1870. 'Routes of Native Caravans from the Coast to the Interior of East Africa', *Journal of the Royal Geographical Society* 40: 303–38.

Waller, Richard 1985a. 'Ecology, Migration, and Expansion in East Africa', *African Affairs* 84: 347–70.

———. 1985b. 'Economic and Social Relations in the Central Rift Valley: The Maa-Speakers and Their Neighbours in the Nineteenth Century', in Behwell A. Ogot (ed.), *Kenya in the Nineteenth Century*. Nairobi: Bookwise, pp. 83–151.

———. 1993. 'Acceptees & Aliens: Kikuyu Settlement in Maasailand', in Thomas Spear and Richard Waller (eds), *Being Maasai: Ethnicity & Identity in East Africa*. London: James Currey, pp. 226–57.

CHAPTER 3

WHERE DO THEY BELONG AND WHAT BELONGS TO THEM?
Acceptance of 'Sedentarizing' Fulɓe and Rejection of Arab Returnees in Blue Nile State and Sennar State, Sudan

ELHADI IBRAHIM OSMAN AND AL-AMIN ABU-MANGA

Introduction

The establishment of South Sudan as an independent nation in 2011 has had far-reaching repercussions on the pastoral groups in the Blue Nile Area who, for decades, have been using the rich pasture of Southern Sudan as their main dry-season grazing area. Many of them have been forced to return to settle in Blue Nile State and Sennar State in the Republic of Sudan and have been known as 'the returnees'. In Blue Nile State, where the pastoral Fulɓe, also known as Fulani and Mbororo, form the majority of the returnees, the state has welcomed them and provided settlements and services to them. However, in Sennar State, where the Rufaʿa al-Hoi form the majority of the returnees, the state has not welcomed them and has failed to provide settlements and adequate services to a significant portion of them. In other words, while the returnees have been accepted and smoothly accommodated in Blue Nile State, they have been rejected in Sennar State. This chapter endeavours to explain the factors behind the different situations facing the different groups in these two states.

Apart from secondary data, the information used in this chapter is a product of several fieldwork trips conducted by a group of researchers[1] from November 2012 to April 2018. These trips were part of a research project by Max Planck Institute for Social Anthropology titled 'Pastoralism in Interaction with Other Forms of Land Use in the Blue Nile Area, Sudan'. Several interviews were conducted with ordinary people among the pastoralists, the leaders of the pastoralist groups, mechanized farmers, representatives of the local agricultural authority, and the range and fodder manager.

In this chapter, the researchers encountered some difficulties in attempting to bring together in a single study different groups with different cultural heritages and different pastoral strategies whose experiences are notably varied in their relations to the state and the wider society. This complexity invites a perspective with an appreciation of broader socio-economic causes and the connection of these causes to other factors. These factors include, but are not limited to, demographic growth, agricultural encroachment, incorporation of pastoralists into the market economy, general insecurity arising from civil war and conflict, faulty national and international policies, as well as factors arising from physical and environment changes (Manger and Ahmed 2000). Most, but not all, of these factors are relevant to the case discussed in this chapter.

The term 'Mbororo' – unless precisely given as 'Mbororo proper' – stands for all the pastoral Fulɓe in Southern Blue Nile, irrespective of the self-ascribed names of their different segments. This term also stands for and is used interchangeably with 'pastoral Fulani'.

The organization of this chapter is as follows: after this short introduction we will provide an overview of the Fulɓe and Rufaʿa al-Hoi pastoralists and their interaction with the state and society within the context of the Blue Nile Area (BNA).[2] The main body of the chapter deals with the acceptance of the 'sedentarization' of Fulɓe in Blue Nile State and the rejection of the Rufaʿa al-Hoi returnees in Sennar State. Finally, the chapter closes with concluding remarks.

The Pastoral Fulɓe and Rufaʿa al-Hoi in the Blue Nile Area

Background

The Blue Nile is a densely populated migrant-receiving area in the southeastern corner of the Sudan. It has rich natural endowments that have attracted migrants from different parts of the country, consequently leading to a rapidly growing population. Since the beginning of the twentieth century, the Blue Nile Area has witnessed increasing competition over land use among different stakeholders. Traditional small-scale agriculture and nomadism have been the dominant modes of living. The Rufaʿa al-Hoi, the Ingessana and the pastoral Fulɓe are the major pastoral groups in the Blue Nile Area. Other groups include the Kenana and the White Nile Baggara.[3] These nomadic groups spend the dry season in the southern part of the region and move to the north in the rainy season.

But in recent decades, the area has undergone many transformations such as environmental degradation, the huge expansion of mechanized farming, the civil war and the decline of security (Ahmed 2001). The combined effect of these

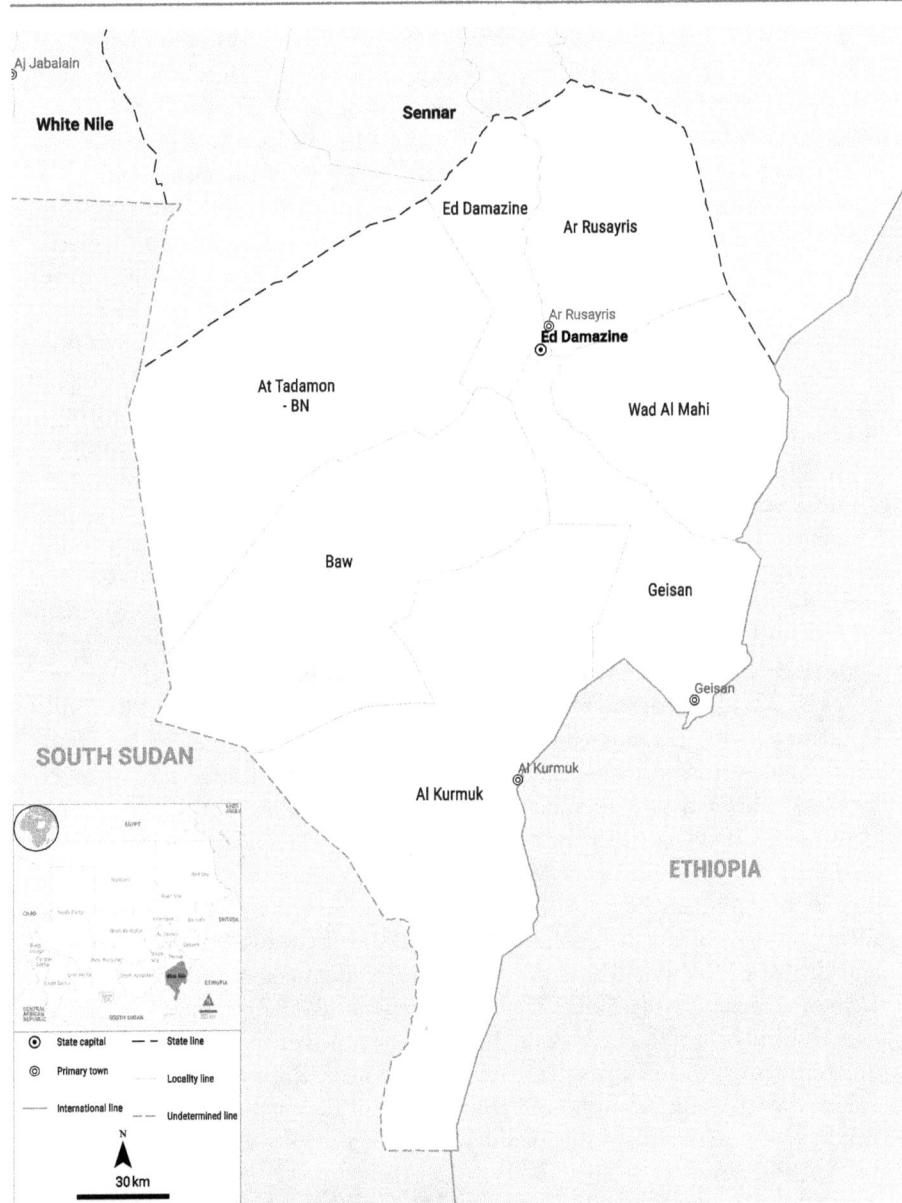

Map 3.1. Blue Nile administrative map OCHA. Source: OCHA/ReliefWeb.

factors has been the reduction of pasture, constrained pastoral mobility, increased competition between farmers and herders and among the herders themselves, the privatization and commoditization of pastoral resources, and changes in gender roles. To adapt themselves to these transformations, pastoralists have resorted to changing the direction of their seasonal migration, stock diversification, interbreeding, militarization and sedentarization (Osman 2013; Ahmed 2009).

Before the expansion of mechanized farming, the area south of Damazin was regarded by the pastoralists as a winter grazing area, where animals could graze inside the forests, depending entirely on the fallen flowers and leaves of trees (*baram* and *ʿuleef*) (Schlee 2012). The Blue Nile Area witnessed a dramatic expansion of mechanized farming in the 1970s; almost all the land used by the nomads on both sides of the river was distributed to companies and individuals, mostly from outside the region, to promote rain-fed mechanized farming schemes. The pastoralists were left with no choice but to push further south through the lands of local ethnic groups. Sporadic clashes used to occur between the nomads and the small farmers in these lands, but were usually settled peacefully. With the increasing expansion of mechanized farming, however, the pastoralists were obliged to move further south, crossing deep into the Upper Nile Province in South Sudan and the Ethiopian territories. At the beginning of the twenty-first century, these areas became the only places where the pastoralists spent the dry season.

The Funj region[4] has suffered from political instability and insecurity for most of its modern history. Since 1987, several local groups have expressed their grievances by gravitating to the SPLM,[5] with many joining its war against Khartoum (Human Security Baseline Assessment 2012). Civil war and the decline of security have disrupted human and animal mobility and hindered any prospect for sustainable agricultural production. Competition among pastoral groups has intensified. Complementary and symbiotic relations between farmers and herders in the region, which had contributed to peaceful coexistence in the past, gave way to military raids, looting of herds and crops, and other forms of violence, including the holding of hostages (Ahmed 2001). By the same token, Osman and Schlee (2014) noted that the different ethnic groups in the area south of Damazin, including the Fulɓe, Hausa and others, like farmers and herders all over the arid belt of the Old World, had managed to avoid competition by using different resources and by exchanging their products. But avoidance of conflict failed when those different ethnic groups claimed the same resources. In other words, peace can be most easily maintained among peoples who do not compete for the same resources (Schlee 1989).

The groups whose animal routes extended up to Kurmuk, Yaabuus, Grinti and Jaamuus before the war now are restricted to the northern part of the region (Schlee 2012). Concern for security has become the single biggest factor that shapes the livelihoods of the pastoralists. Pastoralists have changed their system of grazing, becoming cautious in their movements. They have armed themselves, trained in the use of sophisticated weaponry and fought on behalf of the government. The civil war in what is now South Sudan intensified with the advent of the Islamic regime in 1989 and began to expand further north into Southern Kordofan (Nuba Mountains) and Southern Blue Nile. The government (i.e. the national army), finding itself incapable of confronting the rebels by itself, decided to organize two forms of supporting military forces: the Popular Defence Forces (PDF) and tribal militias. The recruits for the former were derived from young adherents of the ruling Islamic Movement, whereas recruits for the latter were mainly from the pastoral groups, who have been obliged to penetrate through the war zones in their seasonal migrations. Of course, the main objective of the militia fighters has been to defend themselves and their wealth, but at the same time they have been expected to fight on the side of the government, hand in hand with the national army.⁶

The Rufaᶜa al-Hoi

The Rufaᶜa al-Hoi constitute one of the early groups that established itself in the northern part of the Blue Nile Area as their wet-season grazing area. They once extended their northward wet-season migration up to Maᶜtuug in the Gezira (Schlee 2012), but the introduction of irrigated farming in the Gezira and Al-Manaagil and the sugar schemes in west Sennar and Kenana restricted their movement to the area south of the Sennar-Kosti railway line (Ahmed 1973). As a result, they began to spend the wet season northeast of Ad-Daali and Al-Mazmuum in the area of Jabal Moya and Sagadi, and some of them spent the dry season south of Abu-Hujar, forming what has come to be known as the northern *baadiya*.⁷ Part of the group crosses to the eastern bank of the Blue Nile and reaches Khoor Al-ᶜAgaliyyiin. Other group members spend the dry season south of Damazin up to Yaabuus, forming what has come to be known as the southern *baadiya* (Ahmed 1974: 25).

The Rufaᶜa al-Hoi have been negatively affected by the huge expansion of mechanized farming in the 1970s and 1980s, which reduced the area available for the pastoralists. They lost the small plots they used to cultivate to supplement their diet and also lost their gum gardens as a source of additional income. Coupled with the severe drought of the 1980s, these various issues forced 70–80 per cent of the northern *baadiya* to settle in Singa and the small towns south of it. Likewise, 10–15 per cent of the southern *baadiya* established their new villages in places such as Mazmuum in Sennar State and in Guli, Buut and Wad Dabook in Blue Nile State.

With settlement, a transformed form of pastoralism has come into existence in which pastoralists diversify their economic activities: they practise farming, petty trade and wage labour, and they enjoy social services (water, education and

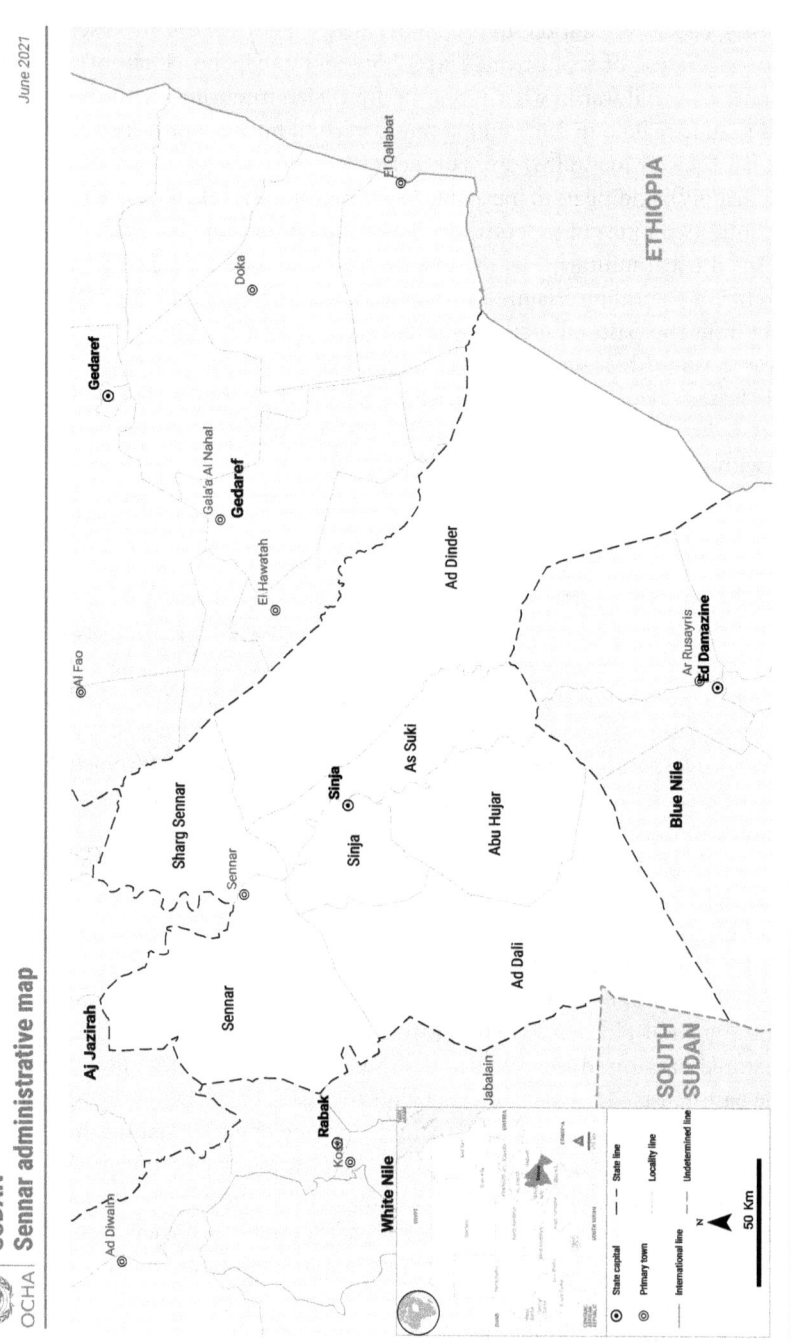

Map 3.2. Sennar administrative map OCHA. Source: OCHA/ReliefWeb.

health) with an aim to invest in the advancement of future generations, while the young men continue to move with the herds (Ahmed 2009).

The pressure caused by a combination of factors, mechanized farming expansion prominent among them, forced a considerable number of Rufaʿa al-Hoi pastoralists to desert their 'homeland' in the old Abu-Hujar Rural Council and to establish themselves as citizens in the Southern Blue Nile and Upper Nile regions. They came to be known as ʿArab As-Saʿiid.[8] Since the early 1980s onwards, they have been integrating socially and economically into the host communities and have acquired the languages spoken by some of the indigenous groups such as the Ingessana, Burun and Maban. After their settlement, as they remember it, they led easy and prosperous lives, utilizing the rich natural endowments of the south to combine animal husbandry with farming,[9] hunting and the collecting of wild fruits and honey.

The Rufaʿa al-Hoi were subjected to attacks and robbery during the time of the civil war (1985–2005) but nevertheless they remained there. They trained themselves in the use of sophisticated firearms and proper war tactics. Some of those who were trained followed the herds while others stayed at nearby camps to be ready in case of emergency. With this defensive strategy, the southern *baadiya* pastoralists insisted on going as far south as possible, despite the dangers they were destined to face. However, they divided their loyalty between the northern opposition and the ruling National Congress Party (NCP); they became identified as being on the side of the government (Salih et al. 2001). They fought many battles against the Sudan Peoples Liberation Army (SPLA) and the tribal militias and registered many 'martyrs' (*shuhadaa*),[10] resulting in a considerable portion of female-headed households. After the signing of the Comprehensive Peace Agreement (CPA) in 2005, the Popular Defence Forces (PDF) were disarmed and the pastoralists were subsequently helpless in the face of the indigenous groups' militias, recruited from the local tribes of the Southern Blue Nile and attached to the SPLA. Ironically, at this point, the pastoralists complained of suffering from the 'culture of peace' (Schlee 2012). The situation was aggravated after the secession of South Sudan, as a result of which the Popular Defence Forces were restricted to the area of Buut and the nomads could no longer carry their arms south of it.

The Pastoral Fulɓe

The pastoral Fulɓe are relative newcomers to the Blue Nile Area. It is likely that the migration of the pastoral Fulɓe to Sudan began in 1930 and intensified during the 1940s, coming from present-day Nigeria, Niger Republic and Cameroon.[11] It is unlikely, however, that their migration was in search of pasture;[12] it could be attributed to the new system of tax collection established by the colonial government in West Africa (Stenning 1957). Being ill at ease with the huge number of animals arriving and uncertain about the kind of diseases these animals might be carrying, the local people did not welcome the pastoral Fulani immigrants, nor did the British (colonial) administration or subsequent national governments. The coming of the pastoral Fulɓe in the Blue Nile Area disturbed the local authority and the host community, adding to the pressure over land and to the competition among the various pastoral groups (Ahmed 1973). Being proper cattle people, the Mbororo were always winners when competing against other non-Fulani pastoralists over resources in the area; so, pasture envy led the leaders of the Rufaꜥa al-Hoi to demand the authorities in the Blue Nile Province to expel the immigrants from the area, but the attempt to expel them failed.

The vanguard of the pastoral Fulani appears to have reached the Blue Nile in 1930. On their arrival in the (former) Blue Nile Province, they were attached to the Sultan of Maiurno (Maiwurno), the closest paramount – and perhaps spiritual – chief to them. They were labelled as '*baadiyat Maayirno*' (Maiurno nomadic group) with the understanding that they fell within the jurisdiction of the Sultan and paid their taxes through him.

The reference spots of the pastoral Fulani in Southern Blue Nile[13] spread to both western and eastern sides of the Blue Nile, with Damazin and Rosseiris as their central markets, respectively. Until the early 1970s, those living on the eastern side used to roam within the Sudanese territories north to the reserved area of Dinder National Park (locally known as the *haziira*) and southeast to the Ethiopian border. Likewise, those living on the western side of the river roamed within the former Blue Nile Province north up to the Sennar area and southwest to the edges of the province. Until that time, very few of them used to cross into Ethiopia or the Southern Sudan provinces because there was enough vacant land for their animals to graze (as well as the animals of the other non-Fulani nomads). An informant confirms that their transhumance process used to run smoothly.[14]

In 1983–1984, a number of the local tribes in the southwestern parts of Southern Blue Nile (mainly, Uduk, Burun and Jumjum) rebelled under the leadership of Malik Aggar and followed him to join the SPLM/SPLA under the late John Garang (Human Security Baseline Assessment 2012). With this development, both the dry-season grazing areas and the passages to it became insecure. As noted by Dereje and Schlee (2009), the Fulani cattle and wealth became exposed to raids by the local militias, which caused the Mbororo to join the Popular Defence Forces, ally with the armed forces and receive training in the use of firearms.

In 1990, a charismatic personality from the Woila section of the pastoral Fulani called Salih Haruun, well known as Salih Bank, came from Kordofan accompanied by some lieutenants with the idea of establishing a Fulani militia. In the same year they were granted permission by the central government to form this militia, which came to be known as '*Katiiba Maa Yanuum*'[15] (Osman 2013: 228). Within a short time, this militia became prominent in the area and well trained in the use of sophisticated weaponry.

The fighting between the Fulɓe militia and the rebels continued for many years, during which the pastoral Fulani witnessed good times as well as bad, as is the case in any guerrilla war. But among the hardest of all was the killing of their leader (Salih Bank), together with his first two lieutenants, in one of their incursions in 2004. Another equally difficult time was what is known in Arabic as the *Darbat al-Girinti* (Engl.: Girinti Strike)[16] in Upper Nile State in Southern Sudan on 28 April 2002. All of their camps at Girinti, counting more than forty, together with other groups of Rufaᶜa and the White Nile Baggara, were 'struck' at the same time, resulting into heavy losses and casualties. Almost all of their animals were either killed or looted or dispersed into the bush to die of thirst. The *Darbat al-Girinti* remains, for the Fulɓe, the most tragic event in the history of the civil war in Southern Blue Nile. But it is worth noting that regardless of what happened to them in Girinti, they never stopped migrating to it; they just changed their pastoral strategy, as will be explained later.

In November 2005, the Comprehensive Peace Agreement was signed by the government and the SPLM to end the war. Afterwards, the area witnessed six years of nominal peace: 'nominal' because the agreement stipulated that the SPLA retain its arms, while the northern militias should be disarmed. Not surprisingly, raids on Fulɓe, Rufaᶜa and other groups' cattle by uncontrolled local militia groups continued, and this time with the Fulɓe unable to defend themselves and their wealth. Thus, all our informants confirmed their preference for the time of war over the time of peace.

In November 2011, a referendum in South Sudan resulted in its secession. Immediately afterwards, war broke out once again in Southern Blue Nile (and South Kordofan, i.e. the Nuba Mountains), aggravating the situation of the still unarmed pastoral Fulɓe as well as other groups.

Another landmark in the history of the war in Southern Blue Nile is what is known as *Darbat ad-Damaazin* (Damazin Strike), when skirmishes between a contingent of Sudan Armed Forces (SAF) and a convoy of the SPLM–North[17] Joint Integrated Unit (JIU) at the southern gate of Blue Nile State's capital city, Damazin, on 1 September 2011 quickly ignited a large-scale confrontation between the national army and paramilitary groups, on one side, and the SPLM–North under the leadership of Malik Aggar, on the other. Upon their failure to occupy Damazin, the SPLM–North army withdrew to the bush, harshly attacking not only the nomads but also those settled in villages, thus creating an overwhelming atmosphere of chaos.

Acceptance of the Fulɓe and Rejection of the Rufaᶜa al-Hoi Returnees

From the above, it is clear that the pastoral Fulɓe and the Rufaᶜa al-Hoi were not left equally able to absorb or respond to the shock of the South Sudan separation. Apart from different pastoral strategies and different social and cultural backgrounds, they were positioned at different distances from the political circles in their respective states.[18]

Acceptance of the Fulɓe in Blue Nile State

In the early 2000s, the central government of Sudan called upon the states that included nomadic groups to design and implement policies for settling the nomads. Blue Nile State – being endowed with a huge amount of animal wealth, being a war zone with a large number of nomads suffering from insecurity in the newly established state of South Sudan, where they used to spend the dry season, and being in a position to provide the necessary land for the settlement – was the first to respond to that call. Some groups of the Rufaᶜa al-Hoi and Kenana were the first nomads to be settled in Blue Nile State within the framework of this structured arrangement, but on the condition that they affiliate themselves officially to Blue Nile State and not to Sennar State, where their historical roots lay.

Many individual households among the nomadic Fulɓe had experienced sedentary life temporarily in the past in certain circumstances, and many households had settled after the infamous attack on Girinti in 2002 (Osman 2013: 94–96). But their organized sedentarization started about ten years later. They established their settlements along the outskirts of Damazin and north up to Goni Village (ca. 5 km) on the western side of the river. Around the same time, others settled to the south and east of Rosseiris on the eastern side of the river in places such as Ab-Zoor, Badoos, Gaddaala and ᶜAzaaza. Almost all of those who settled on the western side established their villages on farming lands owned and cultivated by the Borno (Kanuri) living in villages such as Yarwa, Jarmaari, Shin-Tashrab, Abu-Ramaad and Goni; these Borno released their farms voluntarily to the Fulɓe, who were their relatives in Islam and with whom they shared ancestral homes (West Africa). Al-Firdaus II (ca. 5 km north of Damazin) is one of the villages that benefitted from this Borno hospitality; its Omda[19] confirms:

> they [the Borno people of Abu-Ramaad] themselves brought us to this place and showed us the limits: 'Take from here to here [i.e. there]; don't enter into so-and-so place'. The person who brought us here is a Borno, because he said that the place is his farm.[20]

The Mbororo of Azaaza village on the eastern side of the river (Rosseiris Locality), however, were not accorded a similarly warm reception by the Abu-Janna Rufaᶜa al-Hoi and Riisiyya Arabs with whom they wanted to become neighbours; on the contrary, those Arabs stood firmly against the Fulɓe settling there on the grounds that the land (or part of it) belonged to them. But then the state government intervened and supported the Fulɓe with equal strength; the locality commissioner, who belonged to the SPLM at the time,[21] told them: 'Build [your houses] even on the [trucks'] road and let the trucks find another road. Build in the face of anybody'.[22]

Thus, three main bodies contributed to the smooth and successful settling of the nomadic Fulɓe in Blue Nile State: the (Borno) citizens, the state government and a non-governmental organization, namely, the Pastoralists Union.

As we have seen above, the Borno released their lands voluntarily to their Fulɓe brothers. The state government, on the other hand, with the project of nomad settlement as one of its priorities, gave its utmost attention to this question. It instructed the land office to establish plans for all the vacant land in and around Damazin for this project. Thus, five residential plans (villages) were completed by 2016,[23] and its residents now enjoy most of the basic services, especially water stations and schools;[24] only medical services have yet to be provided. One such village is the above-mentioned al-Firdaus II of the Uda Fulɓe sub-tribe. It was established in February 2013 about 5 km north of Damazin. When we visited it for the second time in February 2016 (the first visit was in June 2013), we found that it had already been planned as a Class IV Residence[25] and officially entered in the locality's register; plots were distributed and all the households received their papers (certificates) of plot possession/ownership. A mosque was constructed from permanent material (cement and baked bricks), and now the people are working towards the construction of a second mosque. There was a complete mixed basic school (years one through eight), and a big water tank (tower) besides four water pumps, with a plan to set pipelines (water supply network) and connect electricity. As such, the village qualifies for promotion to a Class III Residence; the people have already started the process to that effect.[26]

The main factor behind this fast development is the Fulɓe's financial ability to bear the cost of many basic – and non-basic – services or, at least, to contribute to them. The nomadic Fulɓe are indeed the wealthiest segment of the population in Blue Nile State; their wealth amounts to about 8 million head of cattle and 3 million head of sheep. One sub-tribe (probably the Mbororo) alone bought forty-eight tractors with their trailers, which they load with consumer goods to sell at nomad camps far south towards the border with South Sudan.[27]

The Pastoralists Union represents the right hand of the state government with regard to the project of settling nomads. It so happened that its chairperson for two tenures (eight years) was a Fulani and himself a former nomad. The union did its best to ensure that the settling process progressed satisfactorily. It coordinated between the settling citizens and the state government, in addition to intervening to facilitate the implementation of services in the new settlements, especially education and water supplies. Moreover, it used to advise the NGOs on the kind of services needed and where. It is worth noting that many international NGOs used to have offices in Damazin (the Southern Blue Nile being a war zone), including, among others, UNICEF, Red Cross and ECOM.[28] Each of them offered specific services.

In settling down, however, the nomadic Fulɓe have not abandoned cattle rearing; they decided to differentiate the work between herds and households; young men and hired shepherds take cattle to distant grazing areas, leaving the households behind. Contact between herders and households is maintained via mobile phones.

Rejection of the Rufaᶜa al-Hoi in Sennar State

During the years of escalating warfare, ᶜArab As-Saᶜiid – i.e. the Rufaᶜa al-Hoi groups who had earlier settled in what became South Sudan – moved their households northwards to the border area in places such as Gooz Faame near Renk. After the secession of South Sudan, they became foreigners in the space in which they had lived for decades and successfully pursued their livelihoods. The newly established state brought an army from the inner South and stationed it in the Gooz Faame border zone. Some of these soldiers harassed the Arabs, entering their houses and confiscating their belongings. The Arabs, who could no longer carry arms after the secession of South Sudan, were anxious about their families' 'honour';[29] that is – in their own words – they would not 'tolerate seeing drunken soldiers wandering in the vicinity of their settlements'. So, they moved further north to the Buut district in Tadamun Locality. Most of them fled overnight without carrying their belongings and thus lost almost everything they had. Some of them only managed to take kitchen utensils and light luggage. They halted for a while on the border side of Sudan, hoping that Khartoum would do something to make their return to the south possible. When they realized that no serious efforts had taken place in that direction, they continued their northward movement, returning to their 'homeland' in Sennar State. It should be mentioned that this northward movement was encouraged and facilitated by the leaders of the pastoralist groups in Sennar State, who may have seen in it an opportunity to press local and national authorities to allocate (or reallocate) land to them.

But the coming of these groups disturbed Sennar State authorities as well as the farmers. In fact, the state was not prepared and lacked the financial ability to accommodate such a huge number of returnees. To deal with the crisis, it encouraged the settlement of these returnees in Mazmuum town and in At-Tarru (west of Mazmuum) so that they could make use of the available services in these places, and then promised to provide them with more services later.

The returnees were allotted demarcated plots on the outskirts of Mazmuum town in places that came to be known as the Al-ᶜIzza and Al-Mujaahidiin quarters. This land belonged to small farmers who have yet to be compensated. Some services were provided to these groups by the government and the NGOs (the Red Crescent/Cross organization and Unity Support Fund) such as water, medical centres, schools and public pit latrines. But with regard to water, as of 2016, the network had not reached the Al-ᶜIzza quarter and people were left to fetch water by donkey cart, whereas a low-quality network was extended to the Al-Mujaahidiin quarter but still failed to supply the inhabitants with enough water. In general, these settlements lack necessary services, and more importantly the settled people lack the land badly needed for farming and grazing.

Two major groups resisted the state government's instructions to settle in Mazmuum and At-Tarru, namely, the Wad ᶜIweeda group of Sheikh Saᶜiid and the ᶜArakiyyiin group of Sheikh Ibrahim Al Masri.

After the secession of South Sudan and the decline of security with respect to the southerners, the group of Awlad ᶜIweeda of Sheikh Saᶜiid, which consists of about a thousand households, sent a pickup truck to scout the Rufaᶜa al-Hoi *dar* (tribal land). The scouts led them to Kookri in As-Sahba near the booster station of the Wad an Nayyal–Mazmuum water pipeline, better known as the *balif* (valve). Kookri was regarded as being suitable for settlement because of its sandy soil, the availability of water and the existence of a tree belt. They hired trucks to transport households to the area. Meanwhile Sheikh Ibrahim Al Masri of the ᶜArakiyyiin headed a group of 3,500–4,000 households migrating from Upper Nile to Sennar State. They decided to go to the At-Tiruus livestock resting area, which is located along the stock route linking At-Tiruus to Ahmar ᶜEen west of Mazmuum.

After the settlement of the returnees in As-Sahba (precisely, Kookri), Al-Rakha Agricultural Company complained to the state government and demanded the expulsion of these groups from the area, describing their presence as a threat to their agricultural business. At first, the state authority tried to use force to expel the groups that had settled in Kookri and At-Tiruus without even suggesting alternative locations. A group of soldiers armed with heavy artillery was deployed to the area. The Wali (governor) went to Kookri himself and ordered the people to evacuate the area. The same was said to the groups of the ᶜArakiyyiin in At-Tiruus just seven days after the welcoming visit by the commissioner of the locality. The response of the two groups, who had been fighting on the side of the government during the civil war, was to resist the instructions of the state governor and to further advocate that they should return to their 'homeland',[30] which they left due to the pressure exerted by mechanized farming, and they insisted that they would stay where they were, showing their readiness to fight to the death towards that end.

Faced with the pastoralists' resistance, the state authorities suggested alternative locations such as Mazmuum town, At-Tarru and other places near Garabiin, and promised to provide them with services if they settled there instead. The pastoralists refused all of the suggested locations on the grounds that none of the areas were amenable to the kind of life they lead. The government, in an attempt to force the pastoralists to evacuate the land they occupied and go to the suggested locations, resorted to withholding services from these returnees and encouraged or bribed some potential or rival leaders to split from their groups to settle on the outskirts of Mazmuum, where they promised to provide them with services. This strategy has, to some extent, proved successful – in 2012, a group split and moved to the outskirts of Mazmuum in what has come to be known as Hay Al-Izza (al-Izza Quarter). Two years later, another group split and moved also to the outskirts of Mazmuum and settled in the Al-Mujaahidiin Quarter.

The farmers who opposed the settlement of the pastoralists in Sennar State used different tactics against the returnees. In addition to demanding that the state authorities expel the pastoralists from the mechanized farming area, they resisted a resolution by the state governor to reduce their land holdings for the sake of the returnees. Moreover, they began to cultivate any available space so as to establish a continuous farming zone that would prove inaccessible to herders.

Another aggressive tactic used by farmers against the pastoralists was to hand over or rent contested land to the armed forces. This happened in At-Tiruus, where there are four mechanized schemes within the grazing domain inside the livestock corridor that extends from At-Tiruus to Ahmar ᶜEen (115 km). When the work on the demarcation of the stock route started, the pastoralists warned the farmers not to cultivate these areas. The farmers stopped cultivation, but two of them handed over or rented their areas to the army stationed in Mazmuum district. This conduct brought the pastoralists into direct interaction with the armed forces; the former complained of excessive fines and cruelty in the case of crop damage or for simply trespassing on the crop area. According to the pastoralists, the army had been given a green light by the state government as a means to press them to evacuate the area. Similarly, in Kookri, some soldiers cultivated land plots that were claimed by the pastoralists. The pastoralists contacted the military command in Singa, the state capital, and managed to stop the soldiers from cultivating their land.

The state government formed a committee to handle the question of the returning pastoralists, but many of the returnees did not accept it and described it as being weak and ineffective. Another committee was formed at the national level and made recommendations such as the reduction of farming land and the provision of services to the returnees, and proposed a land use plan that considered the rights of all stakeholders. In 2011, after the intervention of the national government, the governor of Sennar State, whom the returnees accused of siding with the farmers, resolved to reduce farming land by deducting 10 per cent from the mechanized schemes in the state to provide space for pasture, stock routes and reforestation, but after three years had passed – as of November 2014 – no tangible progress was achieved in this regard.

The national committee for the settlement of the returnees proposed a budget in the amount of SDG 5 billion. The budget was approved, but as of 2016 the money had not been released. Various delegations of the returnees went to Khartoum to investigate. One of these delegations noted that they had met the *Nazir*[31] of the tribe there and he told them that he had asked the central government to delay the fund release in order to avoid disputes that were likely to ensue between the different leaders of the tribe.

Eventually, the government provided scant services[32] to a portion of the returnees but failed to support their livelihood. The main issue of concern to the pastoralists – land – remained unsolved. So, in 2016, the *Nazir* of the Rufaᶜa al-Hoi group warned that if the government failed to provide land to the pastoralists by the coming of the rainy season, they would not allow any farmer to cultivate his farm. In response to the *Nazir*'s warning, the state governor called upon the Central Reserve Force (CRF), a police force that specialized in protection and violence control, and based them at the Al-Rakha Agricultural Company. Early in 2016, some of the pastoralists' leaders complained about the cruelty and harassment used by the CRF in As-Sahba. On 23 October, one of the patrols of the CRF came across a group of returnees in Kookri gathering to harvest a sesame plot in a land contested with the farmers and ordered them to stop the work. Upon the pastoralists' insistence on harvesting their crop and their violent response, the policemen used force, shooting and killing one of the pastoralists. The pastoralists withdrew, and after mobilizing the support of their kinsmen from Buut and Mazmuum, launched a counter-attack on the police camp. They killed some of the police and burned the camp to the ground after the police had withdrawn.

It is obvious that both state authorities and the farmers did not welcome the pastoral groups and exerted strong pressure to evacuate them from the area, employing various tactics, including use of force, withholding services, playing upon internal differences, handing over contested land to the army, and establishing an agricultural continuum to block the passage of stock.

Explaining the Different Experiences

In what follows, we will investigate possible factors and reasons behind the stark differences in the two situations. The entire southern part of Blue Nile State has been – and still is – a war zone and has suffered from repercussions of this, as the state shares a long border with South Sudan. Moreover, almost all of the ethnic groups living in the southern part of this state (Uduk, Ingessana, Burun, Surkum, Jumjum and so on) rebelled and carried arms and joined the SPLA under the leadership of Malik Aggar. The war ended with the CPA, which facilitated the entrance of a number of international NGOs into the war-affected areas (here, the Blue Nile State) for peace-keeping and peace-building, including re-habilitating the war victims.

The effects of war on Blue Nile State may have been why its state government responded seriously to the national government's call regarding the settlement of nomads. The efforts exerted by the state government in the matter of such settlement, assisted by the international NGOs, which covered a considerable portion of the cost, was one of the main reasons that the nomadic Fulɓe were able to settle without difficulties. These circumstances did not apply to Sennar State, to the disadvantage of the Rufaᶜa Arab returnees from South Sudan. Sennar State was not part of the war zone, sharing only a very short border with South Sudan, and, apart from some groups of the Rufaᶜa al-Hoi, none of its ethnic groups near that border entered into the war. Despite the involvement of the Rufaᶜa al-Hoi in the civil war, they were not regarded as part of the war-affected groups simply because Sennar State was not regarded as one of the war-affected states. They thus received less attention from the state government and far fewer services from international NGOs than the Fulɓe received in Blue Nile State.

Another point is that, although all the vacant land in both of the two states has been occupied by mechanized farming schemes, the citizens in the Borno villages north of Damazin in Blue Nile State were nevertheless ready to release their farms to their 'relatives', the nomadic Fulɓe, as mentioned earlier; besides, the citizens of two settled Fulani villages (Abu-Hashim and Sereu) also agreed to incorporate them in additional quarters along the outskirts of their villages. Thus, the nomadic Fulɓe had the advantage of seeking settlement, or being settled, among people with whom they share ethnicity and/or home origin (i.e. West Africa).

This brings to mind Schlee's (1989) examination of interethnic clan relationships between a number of Cushitic-speaking groups of northern Kenya and southern Ethiopia: the Rendille, Gabbra, Sakuye and Garre. He found that their linguistic, religious and other cultural differences are quite distinct, but nevertheless their cross-ethnic ties form a dense web and traverse ethnic boundaries.

Likewise, the Borno, being committed Muslims, tried to observe the Islamic injunction to offer assistance to brother Muslims. This is especially true in a state such as Blue Nile that includes a large number of different ethnic groups (some of which are not Muslim) and that is not free of ethnic tensions; in such a situation, a certain degree of solidarity between related groups can be decisive.

This is not the case in Sennar State. While it is true that the people who objected to the Rufaᶜa Arabs' settling in their neighbourhood are also Arabs, they do not belong to the Rufaᶜa al-Hoi tribe and thus may not have a strong feeling of obligation towards them to the extent of sacrificing their farms for them. Additionally, there is no ethnic and religious diversity in this state that necessitates interethnic solidarity.

An alternative explanation could be that competition over pasture is an issue of concern to the mechanized farmers in Sennar State; many of them also own large herds of sheep and cattle and are not in a position to welcome more herds, so they resisted the returning Rufaᶜa al-Hoi, who represented competition over shrinking pastoral resources. This is not the case for the Borno farmers in Blue Nile State.

While in seeking sedentarization, the bar for the pastoral Fulɓe is set relatively low – basically a matter of the provision of adequate land and access to adequate social services – the Rufaʿa al-Hoi have a high bar to clear in that they repeatedly emphasize that they are returning to their 'homeland', from which they were pushed out due to mechanized farming schemes. Not only do they intend to return to their 'homeland', but their leaders have made overt demands that the land taken from them by the state-backed mechanized farmers be reallocated equally to the various stakeholders.

The difference in attitudes of the two state governments with respect to the settlement of nomads has also played a role in causing the different situations. We mentioned earlier that the national government's call regarding the settlement of nomads has received varying degrees of response by the two states. For reasons discussed above, Blue Nile State gave much attention to its nomads under the care of the (state) Directorate of Range and Fodder, as the nomads in this state constitute an important element of the population in terms of their size. Many long corridors have been opened, with water spots and resting areas; pasture seeds have been broadcast along some corridors; and projects to improve animal breeding are being implemented. The state also began to implement the national government's resolution regarding a 20 per cent deduction of land allocated to mechanized farming schemes, partially for the purpose of making provision for the nomads (and partially for reforestation).

Sennar State is lagging far behind in its treatment of the nomads when compared with Blue Nile State. In Sennar State, apart from opening (incompletely) a few corridors, nothing else tangible has been achieved – or even initiated – to help the nomads. While in Blue Nile State the state government and its successive governors have been always keen to see that the nomads' problems, especially concerning their settlement, are smoothly resolved, in Sennar State the government itself and its former governor are part of the problem, as we have seen earlier. The Rufaʿa al-Hoi leaders complained that in the 2008 census, the governor refused to send teams to include the Rufaʿa al-Hoi living in South Sudan on the grounds that he was only concerned with the people living within the boundaries of the state.

Another difference between the nomadic Fulɓe in Blue Nile State and the Rufaʿa Arabs returning to settle in Sennar State relates to the degree of connection with their respective states. The Rufaʿa Arabs had been nearly permanent residents of Southern Sudan for a long time and had established themselves as citizens in Southern Sudan while it was part of the unified Sudan. After the secession of South Sudan, the insecure situation left them little choice but to return to their original home in Sennar State. In contrast, the transhumance system of the nomadic Fulɓe led them to migrate annually to South Sudan only for the dry season, and in the wet season they returned to Blue Nile State, which meant that, unlike the Rufaʿa Arabs, they remained tightly linked with the state and its citizens, and their leaders maintained connections in Blue Nile State political and administrative circles. Furthermore, their annual taxes – paid regularly –

provided the state treasury with billions of pounds, in light of their considerable wealth. All of this contributed to them being deserving of the facilities they received from the state government, including providing for their settlement. On the other hand, despite the Rufaᶜa al-Hoi's support of the National Congress Party (NCP) and their alliances with the Sudan Armed Forces during the civil war, and despite the fact that prominent figures among them assumed high positions in the government,[33] their relations with the state authority and in party circles are not stable, which could be partly attributed to their historical link with the Umma (opposition) Party, which remains strong.

As we have seen earlier, the rapid development of the nomadic Fulɓe's settlements, particularly when compared to the exclusion of the Rufaᶜa Arabs who have sought similar settlements, is also due to the fact that the former are wealthy, whereas some of the latter were not even able to secure the cost of their transportation from South Sudan to Sennar State. Viewed from another angle, the wealth of the Fulɓe can be an incentive – rather than a source of envy – to the host community, which can benefit from the Fulɓe's purchasing power and their contribution to the provision of social services. The Rufaᶜa al-Hoi Arabs, conversely, do not enjoy a similar advantage.

Another important point is that most of the land in Sennar State falls within the domain of the proposed Kenana Irrigated Scheme, whereas only a small area in Blue Nile State falls within the domain of that scheme. The irrigated scheme is expected to increase the value of land in the area, and therefore people in Sennar State are fighting for a foothold in the area so as to qualify for the compensation that is expected to be dispensed at the project's inception.

Conclusion

What we have described in this chapter is a stimulating case related to the challenging question of land use in a politically unstable country. However, not only Sennar State but all of the other states in the Sudan that include farmers and herders may be able to learn from the experience of Blue Nile State.

The Rufaᶜa Arabs, on the one hand, are obliged to cope with the reality of being settled, against their will, in locations in the southwest of the state, far away from the seat of their Native Administration and the state capital (Singa). They have been provided with insufficient services, especially with respect to water. The lack of stability of their new life is reflected in the intermittent skirmishes between them and the farmers, whom they claim are favoured by the state government. However, with such limited options, their new situation appears to have become an unavoidable reality and they are expected to have no choice but to adapt themselves to it.

The nomadic Fulɓe in Blue Nile State, on the other hand, having been allowed to settle in the vicinity of the state capital (Damazin), have already commenced a second phase – planning their villages, installing water pumps and tanks, building schools and mosques and so on. Some of them have entered into the trade business. Now, they are intent on connecting electricity and acquiring farmland. In most of the villages we visited in 2014, the people confirmed that they had settled permanently without any intention to return to bush life. Yet, at our last visit to the field (2016) we asked a group of informants a critical question: 'Suppose the civil war in both Sudan and South Sudan ended and South Sudan became secure, is it possible that you would go back to your former system of transhumance?' They smiled and kept silent for a while and then one of them responded: 'Don't trust a nomadic Fulani'. They all laughed, meaning that, if this happened, they might do so.

Elhadi Ibrahim Osman received his PhD in Social Anthropology from the University of Khartoum in 2008 for his research on the pastoral Fulɓe. He is an Assistant Professor at the Faculty of Agriculture, University of Sinnar, Sudan. He has conducted several consultancies on pastoralists' integration into irrigation projects in central and eastern Sudan (2009–2012) and in support for reconstruction in Darfur (2017–2019). Currently he is a member of the project 'Assisting Regional Universities of Sudan (ARUS)' within which he published his article 'Pastoral Women in Town: The Case of the Migrant Fulbe in Sinja, Sudan' (CMI, Bergen, 2020).

Al-Amin Abu-Manga is head of the department of Sudanese and African Languages, University of Khartoum, where he has worked since 1987. He completed his PhD in African Languages and Literature at the University of Marburg/Lahn (Germany) in 1986. He has authored thirteen books and booklets and forty-seven book chapters and journal articles. He cooperated closely with the Max-Planck Institute for Social Anthropology in Halle (Saale) in projects headed by Günther Schlee. He is the author of *Fulfulde in the Sudan: Process of Adaptation to Arabic* (Berlin, 1986) and *Hausa in the Sudan: Process of Adaptation to Arabic* (Cologne, 1999).

Notes

1. Al-Amin Abu-Manga, Elhadi Ibrahim, Günther Schlee and others.
2. The Blue Nile Area, also known as the Funj region and once called the Blue Nile Province, lies in the southeastern part of Sudan between latitudes 9° and 14° north and longitude 32° and 36° and now includes Sennar State and Blue Nile State (Sennar State n.d; Sennar State 1997; Blue Nile State 1995: 10). Generally speaking, Blue Nile State with its current boundaries (see Figure 3.1: Blue

Nile State map) is an administrative-geographical unit created relatively recently under the present regime; the Blue Nile Area excludes the extreme northern and extreme southern parts of the state; Southern Blue Nile extends roughly from Damazin south to the border with the Republic of South Sudan.

3. 'Baggara' from Ar. *bagar* = cattle. Cattle keepers from the White Nile through Kordofan up to Darfur are known as 'Baggara'; that is, cattle people, as opposed to 'Abbala' = camel people.

4. A nomenclature relating to the Native Administration system that was used in the early literature; it corresponds roughly to 'Blue Nile Area'. See also note 2.

5. Sudan Peoples Liberation Movement, under the banner of which operated the South Sudan rebels, led by the late John Garang.

6. Omda/Usman al-Arabi, age 53, born in Tulus (S. Dafur) and grew up in Blue Nile Area, interviewed in Damazin on 16 June 2013.

7. Semantically, 'rural land'; but as a term, *baadiya* refers to the nomads and their animals (the households and herds).

8. Ar. = the Arabs of the south; i.e. south of their home area, but not necessarily South Sudan.

9. That is, the young men take herds to distant grazing areas while household members practise farming.

10. In the present Islamic regime's slant on the civil war between the (Northern) government and the South Sudan rebels, whoever was killed fighting for the government's cause was considered a martyr (*shahiid*) who sacrificed his life for the nation and for Islam.

11. An informant (Abdu ᶜUmar [Darwe], age 44, interviewed in Sereu on 19 June 1998) claimed that his grandfathers started along with Attahiru/Mai-Wurno's *hijra* (migration of religious nature in Islam) (1903) and stayed behind in Borno, but pastoral Fulani were not mentioned in any source or reference on this *hijra*.

12. Because even now in many areas of Nigeria and Cameroon, pasture is as abundant as it is in Sudan, if not more so.

13. By 'reference spots' we mean the places from where the nomads depart to go on dry season migrations, and to which they return in the rainy season. The term refers to the camps (or villages) where they leave the families and the old people when they move with the animals.

14. Bello Abdu Waziri (Dimo), age 51, born in Damazin area, interviewed in Damazin on 15 June 2013.

15. Literally, 'Batallion Never Sleeps', i.e. it fights day and night without pause.

16. 'Strike' = Ar. *ḍarba*, which means 'attack', but the event in question is popularly known among the pastoral Fulani in the area as *ḍarbat al-Girinti* = the Girinti Strike. Girinti, located some 40 km north of Nasir in South Sudan, is where a large number of the pastoral Fulani and Arabs spend the dry season.

17. After the secession of South Sudan, the rebels belonging to areas within the territories of the old Sudan – namely, Southern Blue Nile and the Nuba Mountains – were allowed to keep their arms until their issues were resolved through what the CPA termed the 'Popular Consultancy' (*al-mashuura sh-shaᶜbiyya*). These rebels decided to maintain the name of the movement under which they were fighting, i.e. Sudan Peoples' Liberation Movement (SPLM), but added 'North' to it.

18. They had both been allies of the ruling party, and some of them had shifted their loyalty and supported the SPLM/SPLM-N and/or the Northern Sudanese Opposition, but the Fulɓe remained more identified with the ruling party than did the Rufaᶜa al-Hoi.

19. 'Omda' is a tribal section leader; he occupies the intermediate level of the native administration hierarchy, senior to village *sheikhs* and junior to the *nazir*.

20. Omda/ Usman Abbakar, age 57, al-Mujlad (Darfur), interviewed at al-Fidraus II, 18 June 2013.

21. That was during the period of the 'National Government' after the signing of the CPA, in accordance with which the SPLM–North participated with the NCP in forming the government.

Accordingly, the *walis* (governors) of Blue Nile State were to hold office by rotation (NCP-SPLM-NCP). The above event took place during the tenure of the SPLM. We had the impression that the support of the Fulɓe by the then commissioner could be understood, at least in part, in the context of 'Arabs versus non-Arabs'.

22. Sudaani Muhammad ᶜUmar Buuba, age 44, ᶜAzaaza, interviewed on 18 June 2013.

23. Interview with Mustafa Daoud Yousif (land senior officer of the Blue Nile State), age 57, interviewed in Rosseiris, 13 June 2016.

24. Ibid.

25. In Sudan, residential quarters are categorized into classes, Class I being the highest and Class IV the lowest. The first three classes are registered at the Land Office at the state level and allocated with paper possession documents, whereas Class IV quarters are registered only at the locality level without paper possession documents (subject to promotion to Class III).

26. See note 25 above.

27. Oral information (by phone) from Muhammad Ahmad Tunfafe (chairperson of the Fulani Amara in Blue Nile State), age 62, born in Sereu, consulted on 5 May 2018.

28. ECOM is an American organization that implements the development projects which are funded through American aid; it has an office in Damazin and Khartoum.

29. In Arab tribal culture, females are regarded as 'honour' (Ar. *sharaf*) and must be protected against strangers; failure to do so signifies a loss of dignity.

30. The Rufaᶜa al-Hoi consider the plains where semi-mechanized schemes have expanded, as well as some of the lands on the bank of the river, as their *dar* (homeland) (Ahmed 2009).

31. An office within the Native Administration system; the system is headed by the *Nazir*, who has a number of *omdas* under him, and each *omda* has a number of *shaikhs* under him.

32. Main water service has not reached all places, and the entire town suffered from water shortages from March to September 2016, depending instead on *hafiir* water (a dug water reservoir).

33. The present *Nazir* was appointed as an advisor to the state governor for nomad affairs and he is now a member of the Federal Legislative Council.

References

Ahmed, Abdel Ghaffar M. 1973. 'The Nomadic Competition in the Funj Area', *Sudan Notes and Records* 54: 43–56.

———. 1974. *Shaykhs and Followers: Political Struggle in the Rufaᶜa al-Hoi Naazirate in the Sudan.* Khartoum: Khartoum University Press.

———. 2001. 'Livelihood and Resource Competition, Sudan', in M.A. Mohamed Salih, Ton Dietz and Abdel Ghaffar Mohamed Ahmed (eds), *African Pastoralism: Conflict, Institutions and Government.* London: Pluto Press, pp. 172–93.

———. 2009. 'Transforming Pastoralism: A Case Study of the Rufaᶜa al-Hoi Ethnic Group in the Blue Nile State, Sudan', *Sudan Working Paper.* Bergen: Christian Michelsen Institute.

Blue Nile State (BNS). 1995. *Ministry of Agriculture and Animal Wealth, the Investment Map, Part 1.*

Dereje Feyissa and Günther Schlee. 2009. 'Mbororo (Fulɓe) Migration from Sudan into Ethiopia', in Günther Schlee and Elizabeth E. Watson (eds), *Changing Identifications and Alliances in North-East Africa, Volume II: Sudan, Uganda and the Ethiopia-Sudan Borderlands.* New York and Oxford: Berghahn, pp. 157–78.

Human Security Baseline Assessment (HSBA). 2012. 'The Conflict in Blue Nile', *Small Arms Survey.* Geneva: Graduate Institute of International and Development Studies.

Manger, Leif and Abdel Ghaffar M. Ahmed. 2000. *Pastoralists and Environment: Experiences from the Greater Horn of Africa.* Addis Ababa: Organization for Social Science Research in Eastern and Southern Africa (OSSREA).

Osman, Elhadi Ibrahim. 2013. *The Pastoral Fulɓe in the Sudan Funj Region: A Study of the Interaction between State and Society*. Bergen: Christian Michelsen Institute.

Osman, Elhadi Ibrahim and Günther Schlee. 2014. 'Hausa and Fulɓe on the Blue Nile: Land Conflict Between Farmers and Herders', in Jörg Gertel, Richard Rottenburg and Sandra Calkins (eds), *Disrupting Territories: Land, Commodification and Conflict*. Woodbridge: James Currey.

Salih, Mohamed Abdelrahim, Tom Dietz and Abdel Ghaffar Mohamed Ahmed. 2001. *African Pastoralism: Conflict, Institutions and Government*. London and Sterling, VA: Pluto Press in association with OSSREA.

Schlee, Günther. 1989. *Identities on the Move: Clanship and Pastoralism in Northern Kenya*. Manchester: Manchester University Press.

———. 2012. 'Pastoralism in Interaction with Other Forms of Land Use in the Blue Nile Area of Sudan: Project Outline and Field Notes, 2009–10', *Max Planck Institute for Social Anthropology, Department 'Integration and Conflict' Field Notes and Research Projects* I. Retrieved from http://www.eth.mpg.de/pubs/series_fieldnotes/vol0001.html.

Sennar State. 1997. *Annual Report, Sinjah*. Ministry of Agriculture.

Sennar State. n.d. *The Investment Map Project: The Agricultural Sector, Phase 1, Sinjah*. Ministry of Agriculture and Animal Wealth.

Stenning, Derrick J. 1957. 'Transhumance, Migratory Drift, Migration', *Journal of Anthropological Institute* LXXXVII (1).

CHAPTER 4

ETHNICITY, IDENTITY AND CITIZENSHIP OF RECENT MIGRANT GROUPS IN GHANA

Steve Tonah

Introduction

In Ghana, just as in other multi-ethnic West African countries, several forms of group or collective identity tend to exist side by side and are used by the various segments of the population depending on the particular situation or location.[1] Some of the most common markers of group identity include language, clan or kin group, religion, occupation, race or colour, region of origin or nationality. The specific form of identity or 'we group' that is emphasized will vary depending on the occasion. At a certain time the group may emphasize their belonging by way of a narrower criterion such as lineage or hometown association, and at another time it may rely on a broader criterion such as ethnic group, religion, region of origin or race (cf. Schlee 2009). Besides belonging to several groups, each with its unique identity, the primary form of group identity may also change over time (cf. Amoah-Boampong and Duah 2014). Indeed, Schlee (1994: 1) draws attention to the fact that 'social identities are subject to constant redefinition by their bearers and others. Groups can change their composition, or their status, or their name, or their affiliation, or even all these features' (see also Schlee 2003).

Furthermore, while some 'we group' identities may be less emotive (such as membership in a professional association), others may be very emotive, such as the religious, ethnic and nationality group to which one belongs. Across West Africa the group identity that elicits the strongest emotions and sense of bonding is the ethnic group. Although other forms of identity are also relevant and may be stressed occasionally, ethnic identification remains the most prevalent and enduring, particularly in the competition for power and resources in multi-ethnic nation states. Additionally, the drawing of administrative boundaries along ethnic lines and the amalgamation of hitherto clan-based groups into larger units based on a common language and cultural affinity resulted in the 'ethnicization' of many societies across West Africa during the colonial period (Tonah 2007; Lentz and Nugent 2000; Bening 2010).

This chapter examines the relationship between ethnicity, identity and citizenship in Ghana, with particular reference to three non-autochthone immigrant groups: the Fulani, the Lebanese and the Hausa. It elaborates on how members of each group see themselves as well as how they are perceived by the autochthone groups, including widely held stereotypes and prejudices. It also analyses the different forms of identity found within each of the three migrant groups. Furthermore, the chapter establishes a link between their identity as recent migrants or late-comers and how that has shaped their experiences of Ghanaian citizenship. Tracing the roots of citizenship from the colonial period to recent times, the chapter elaborates on attempts by successive postcolonial governments and segments of the population to limit Ghanaian citizenship to the autochthone ethnic groups.

Research Methods

The approach to this chapter is largely historical and ethnographic, and focuses primarily on three case studies: the Fulani, the Hausa and the Lebanese. The author relies mainly on his extensive fieldwork among the Fulani and Hausa in Ghana and Burkina Faso that spans nearly two decades (Tonah 2000, 2005, 2015). A detailed ethnographic study of the Fulani was carried out in West Mamprusi in 2005 and 2006 (see Tonah 2006). This was supplemented by several months of interviews and focus group discussions on identity and citizenship among the Fulani and the Hausa in Northern Ghana and Accra between 2014 and 2016. Additional information on the history and identity of the Hausa in Ghana was obtained from secondary sources and the internet. The section on the Lebanese in Ghana relied extensively on the works of Akyeampong (2006a, 2006b) and Ohene Marfo (2012). Besides these primary and secondary sources, the chapter also relied on several newspaper articles and discussion fora in the Ghanaian media and internet sources.

Autochthones and Recent Migrants

Ghana, with a population of 29,460,000 in 2018, has upwards of ninety-three ethnic groups (Ametewee 2007). The dominant ethnic groups (in terms of numbers) include the Asante (14.8 per cent of the population), Fante (9.9 per cent),

Brong (4.6 per cent), Dagomba (4.3 per cent), Dagaaba (3.7 per cent), Ga (3.4 per cent) and the Konkomba (2.7 per cent) (GSS 2002, 2012). Conspicuously absent from the extensive list of ethnic groups in Ghana are the Hausa, Yoruba, Fulani, Lebanese, Kotokoli and others although they are found in sufficiently large numbers in Ghana. Thus the Ghana Statistical Service (GSS 2002) makes a distinction between first-comers or autochthone groups and others that are categorized as late-comers or immigrant groups. This is in spite of the fact that some of these immigrant groups have been living in the country since at least the eighteenth century. This division of residents into first-comers/autochthones and late-comers/allochthones is, of course, not unique to Ghana but a widespread phenomenon throughout Africa (see Geschiere 2009; Lentz 2013; Pelican 2015). State institutions commonly argue that autochthone groups have been territorialized since the fifteenth century while later migrant groups do not have any territory they can call their 'Traditional Area'.

Schlee (2011) has also drawn attention to how the state and sedentary groups act under the assumption that 'bounded surface areas are inhabited by particular ethnic groups' and how the elite in Kenya and other northeast African countries have been the main drivers of the process of territorial subdivision among ethnic groups. In Ghana and neighbouring West African countries the belief in the idea that autochthone ethnic groups have fixed territories and boundaries is widespread and serves as the basis for denying allochthone groups the full benefits of citizenship. These issues as they affect the Fulani, the Hausa and the Lebanese will be expatiated in this chapter.

Colonial Rule and the Roots of Ghanaian Citizenship

One major impact of colonial rule in the then Gold Coast (now Ghana) is that it transformed the relationship between autochthones and later migrant groups in the country. Following the imposition of formal colonial rule in 1896, both autochthones and late-comers became subjects of British rule. However, it was the late-comers who benefitted most from the new order as they were freed from many of their obligations to the traditional leadership. Besides, late-comer groups were given some recognition under colonial rule because they were prepared to do the back-breaking and demanding jobs that the natives were not prepared to do (Anebo et al. 2010). The colonial government consequently encouraged migration to the Gold Coast, resulting in the rapid growth of the migrant population. By 1960, migrants constituted about 12 per cent of Ghana's population of 6.7 million, and groups such as the Hausa, Fulani, Yoruba, Zerma, Kotokoli, Syrians and the Lebanese constituted the bulk of the farm labourers and controlled the vibrant trading sector as well as the trade in gold, diamond and other minerals (Addo 1974).

The colonial administration created new categories of residents, and by implication, identity based on the British Nationality and Status of Aliens Act of 1914. This act divided the residents of the Gold Coast into three main groups: 'natives', 'subjects' and 'migrants'.[2] Both subjects and natives enjoyed the same rights and privileges, while migrants were considered immigrants or 'aliens' who were subject to expulsion from the colony if considered a threat to public order. Furthermore, the British Nationality Act of 1948 conferred citizenship on all British subjects who had not acquired the citizenship of another country.[3] However, the act did not affect the status of migrants from the French colonies as they continued to be regarded as French subjects (Kobo 2010). Generally, most migrants took advantage of the protection of residency and the privileges offered them by the colonial government. At the provincial level, migrants also frequently served as a buffer between the colonial administrators and the natives. This made them somewhat unpopular amongst the autochthone population.

Independence and the Emergence of New Citizenship and 'Alien' Identity

The attainment of independence in 1957 brought considerable changes to the social, economic and legal status of immigrants in Ghana. While complaints about the increasing immigrant population remained muted during the colonial period, they became overt after independence. Many amongst the autochthone population were resentful of the relatively privileged status that migrants enjoyed under colonial rule. There were widespread complaints that migrants dominated the retail, wholesale and other sectors of the economy (Peil 1974). However, despite the mutual suspicion that characterized the relationship between autochthones and immigrants, the latter felt at home in Ghana. Many immigrants, particularly those of the second and subsequent generations, were granted citizenship during the colonial period and were expected to retain their citizenship after independence. They were further assured by the Ghana Nationality Act (Act 1) of May 1957, under which an individual was considered a citizen of Ghana if one of his/her parents or grandparents was born in Ghana.

Although their dominant economic role made migrants increasingly unpopular amongst the autochthone population, it was the exercise of their rights as citizens by participating actively in politics that made them incur the wrath of the ruling government, the political elite and the autochthone population. The acrimonious and violent nature of party political activities in the immediate post-independence era soon affected the immigrant community. Despite a court ruling that affirmed the status of some prominent immigrants who supported the opposition National Liberation Movement as Ghanaians, the Nkrumah government (1957–1966) declared them as 'aliens', quickly passed the Deportation

Act of 1957 and expelled them to neighbouring countries (Kobo 2010). Those affected were mainly of Hausa, Mossi, Gao, Fulani and Yoruba extraction, but the Lebanese and Syrian merchants were also affected (Schildkrout 1978; *West Africa*, 14 December 1957). According to Kobo (2010: 75), 'with this selective deportation [of immigrants], Nkrumah initiated the construction of the "alien" identity in post-colonial Ghana, which was to be expressed in both popular and formal discourses'. The deportations created fear and panic amongst the immigrant population. It clearly indicated a shift in government policy with respect to immigrants. While under colonial rule all persons born in Ghana were regarded as citizens of the country, the Ghana Nationality Act of May 1957 limited citizenship to 'a person born in Ghana before 1957 with at least one of his/her parents or grandparents being born in Ghana'. In practice, citizenship became reserved to members of the autochthone ethnic groups in Ghana. Thus, within a year after independence, immigrant groups in Ghana were suddenly transformed from 'subjects' and 'migrants' to 'aliens' who were to be excluded from the privileges of citizenship (cf. Sudarkasa 1979).

After the demise of the Convention Peoples Party (CPP) government in 1966, successive governments continued with the policy of disregarding the citizenship rights of immigrant groups, and the 'alien' identity foisted on immigrants became commonly used in the media and daily vocabulary of residents. Migrants were blamed for the worsening economic situation in the 1960s and 1970s, and there were calls for the autochthone population 'to capture the commanding heights of the economy' by breaking the migrants' domination of the distributive trade (Peil 1971). The practice of discriminating in favour of autochthones and limiting the rights of immigrants intensified. In 1968, a law compelling non-autochthones to obtain residence permits before either accepting employment or participating in commercial activities was promulgated. In 1969 citizenship was limited to persons married to autochthone Ghanaians and children from such a relationship, thereby depriving many migrants and their descendants of their Ghanaian citizenship. In November 1969 the Aliens Compliance Order, under which non-Ghanaians were required to acquire a residence permit or leave the country within two weeks, was passed (Shack and Skinner 1979). More than a million migrants left Ghana following threats on their lives and the confiscation of their properties (Adomako-Sarfoh 1974; Peil 1971, 1974), reducing the migrant population considerably. In 1979, the Armed Forces Revolutionary Council (AFRC) government blamed migrant businesses for the economic decline and for engaging in dubious and corrupt practices. In response, the government nationalized some businesses belonging to individuals of Lebanese and Indian origin, revoked their Ghanaian citizenship and deported them (Akyeampong 2006a, 2006b).

Since the return to civilian rule in 1992, Ghana's economic fortunes have improved and the migrant population that was decimated following the Aliens Compliance Order of 1969 has again risen to about 5 per cent of the total population. Most migrants are from the West African subregion, but there are significant numbers of Indian, Lebanese and Chinese nationals, some of whom are second-, third- or fourth-generation migrants in the country. Although the 1992 Constitution and the Citizenship Act of 2002 (Act 591) limit citizenship to persons born in or outside Ghana with a parent or grandparent being a citizen of Ghana, Ghanaian citizenship can also be acquired through registration, adoption and marriage, while Ghanaians abroad can now apply for dual citizenship. Generally, migrants are welcome, particularly if they are investing in the country, but resentment against those in the retail trade and the small-scale mining business remains high. While the civic and socio-economic rights of migrant groups have been largely granted, there have been attempts to limit their political rights, including the right to vote in elections, compete for political office and hold public office. Indeed, the participation of migrants in the political process in Ghana remains a contentious issue (see Akyeampong 2006a; Amoah 2009).

In the next section we examine the experiences and perspectives of Fulani, Hausa and Lebanese immigrants in Ghana with regard to ethnicity, identity and citizenship as well as the perspectives of the autochthone groups and the state on these three immigrant communities. We also expatiate on attempts by individuals and the migrant groups to claim their rights as citizens of Ghana as well as the reaction of the majority autochthone population to these claims.

The Fulani in Ghana: Cooperation, Estrangement and Exclusion

Fulani migration to Ghana dates back to the late nineteenth century when they moved in small numbers to the north of the area that eventually became part of the Gold Coast (later, Ghana). These movements occurred mainly during the dry season and were part of their seasonal transhumance across the West African savanna in search of water sources and pasture for their livestock. As the rainy season approached, the Fulani moved their livestock back to the northern savanna and the Sahelian countries (Tonah 2005, 2006). It was not until the early twentieth century that the first Fulani herders settled permanently in the savanna areas of the Gold Coast. Later, the Fulani population in the area increased following the decision of the colonial government to employ Fulani herders to manage the newly established cattle farms and stimulate cross-border trade in livestock (Tonah 2006). In the 1920s and 1930s some of these Fulani herders relocated south to the Accra Plains while others moved to the Middle Volta Basin and the savanna-forest transitional zone during the 1960s and 1970s. Currently, the Fulani population in Ghana is estimated between 200,000 and 300,000, with only about half of them working in the pastoral sector as herders, livestock owners, traders and middlemen, butchers and so on. The rest have settled in towns and taken up work as traders, drivers, clerks, security personnel, religious leaders and other skilled professions such as teachers, journalists and social workers (cf. Hill 1970). The pastoral Fulani are largely sedentary agro-pastoralists who combine livestock herding with the cultivation of food crops (mainly maize and vegetables). While two to three generations of Fulani have lived in the north of the country, there are also those who have settled in Ghana only since the last decade. Some groups of Fulani herders from the subregion migrate seasonally to Ghana while others have remained nomadic herders, moving their stock across borders in West Africa in search of water and pasture (Tonah 2005).

Relations between the pastoral Fulani and the autochthone population are mixed. In some parts of the country the Fulani have developed cordial and reciprocal economic relations with their neighbours, but in others this relationship is characterized by mutual suspicion, animosity and violent conflicts. Cattle owners, traders, butchers, chiefs and landowners tend to have more cordial relations with the Fulani, whereas farmers, youth groups, government officials and urban residents loathe their presence in Ghana. The Fulani are frequently accused of engaging in cattle rustling, destruction of food crops, pollution of water bodies, environmental degradation, and in recent times, armed robbery and rape (*Ghanaian Times*, 6 February 2011; *Daily Graphic*, 23 February 2011). In response to recurring conflicts between the pastoral Fulani and farmers, the Ghanaian government expelled some Fulani herdsmen from the country in 1988, 1994 and 1998 (Tonah 2002, 2003).

Conflicting Perspectives on Fulani Identity and Citizenship

Fulani identity, just as with all ethnic groups, is a complex and varying phenomenon and can be classified in very broad terms to include all those who speak their language (Fulfulde) and share in significant aspects of their culture, particularly their concept of *pulaaku*, which involves the qualities appropriated by the group, their value system and social norms. *Pulaaku* represents the characteristics that guide the Fulani (or Fulɓe; singular: Pullo) in their intercourse with their neighbours, including the whole range of rights and duties peculiar to the Pullo (cf. Tonah 2005: 132–34; Stenning 1994; Riesman 1977). When asked to expatiate on the concept of *pulaaku*, most Fulani make reference to character traits befitting and actions unbefitting of a Pullo. The positive traits include honesty, patience, trustworthiness and deference or shyness, while the negative actions include stealing, drinking alcohol, eating unwholesome foods (for example, pork) and flirting with other people's wives. There is thus a sense of identification and belonging with all persons who share in the Fulani culture and tradition, although they are quick to acknowledge that most of them no longer follow 'the true Fulani way of behaving'. In Ghana being a Fulani has also become synonymous with being a Muslim, keeping cattle or having a sentimental attachment to cattle (cf. Oppong 2002).

There are, of course, numerous subgroups of the Fulani, each with its peculiar identity. We have already mentioned the pastoral and the non-pastoral Fulani. Even amongst the pastoral Fulani, there are the Ghanaian-born and the non-Ghanaian Fulani as well as the sedentary, the transhumant and the nomadic Fulani. There are also differences among the different generations of Fulani residents in Ghana, just as there are differences with respect to the countries of origin of the Fulani. The Fulani who trace their ancestry to Burkina Faso (the majority) do not always closely associate themselves with those from Niger, Mali and Nigeria. While there are national associations that fight for the interests of all ethnic Fulani residents in Ghana, there are several conditions under which an individual Fulani may choose to identify more closely with local associations (narrower identities) with specific interests (cf. Donahoe et al. 2009; Schlee 2009). The reasons for this, among others, include their integration into the autochthone community, the close relationship with other stakeholders (such as cattle traders and butchers) in the livestock industry, lack of knowledge about the neighbouring Sahelian countries, preoccupation with their local situation/environment, and differences in cultural practices amongst the various Fulani groups.

The autochthone population in Ghana has varied perspectives on Fulani identity and citizenship. The Ghanaian state, the media and large sections of the urban population are very opposed to Fulani pastoralists' presence in Ghana and frequently blame the pastoralists for the increasing farmer-herder clashes, insecurity, stock rustling, pollution of water bodies, destruction of the environment, and more recently, for highway robbery and rape. There are also widespread stereotypes about the Fulani being 'illiterate, backward, aggressive aliens and foreigners' (cf. Bukari and Schareika 2015). The media, government officials and the general public frequently call for the abolition of nomadic pastoralism and the expulsion of herdsmen from Ghana (Tonah 2007, 2016). Generally, urban residents are unable to make a distinction between the Fulani and persons from other immigrant groups such as the Hausa, Djerma, Kotokoli and Gao. Most Fulani immigrants in the towns reside in the *Zongo* communities where they are often presumed to be 'Northerners' or of Hausa origin (cf. Oppong 2002).[4] The urban Fulani are also politically active and participate in the electoral processes and compete for political leadership positions.

In the rural communities where the pastoral Fulani have resided for decades, they are commonly regarded as 'strangers' who have settled amongst the autochthone population and, besides engaging in economic exchanges, have adopted the indigenous language, dress and diet, as well as the cultural and religious practices, of the autochthones.[5] Here, second and subsequent generations of Fulani, although they may still remain 'strangers', are accepted as citizens of Ghana and benefit from services provided by the state including education and training, health insurance, agricultural subsidies and other services. In the rural areas, the autochthone population frequently makes a distinction between 'our Fulani' –

the sedentary Fulani who were born in the community – and 'other Fulani' – the nomadic pastoral Fulani with whom they have no contact.

The Fulani acknowledge the fact that they are, in comparison with the autochthone population, more recent migrants to Ghana. They are, however, quick to point out that because they never settled permanently at one location and therefore are not 'territorialized' in Ghana they are often considered to be 'strangers' and 'aliens' by many Ghanaians. While acknowledging the fact that most Fulani people in Ghana originated from the Sahelian region, second and subsequent generations of Fulani consider themselves to be Ghanaians. Most of them indicated that they were born in Ghana and have integrated quite well into the host community wherever they settled. They speak the local language fluently, are conversant with the local culture and have adopted some local practices. They also mix well with the autochthone population, assist their neighbours with farm duties and herd cattle belonging to local residents. Furthermore, because they consider themselves Ghanaians, they participate in local and national elections. In contrast, recent Fulani migrants consider themselves as being of dual nationality since they have a citizens' identity card from a neighbouring West African country (mainly Burkina Faso or Niger) and that of Ghana. Although this is technically an illegal practice, they argued that it facilitated their smooth and trouble-free movements when attending marriages, births, funerals and other social ceremonies of relations living across the borders. Besides, they believe that they cannot completely give up their foreign identity cards because of the insecurity that characterizes their stay in Ghana as a result of the frequent expulsion of Fulani pastoralists from the country. They have close kin relations both in Ghana and across the borders and prefer to move between Ghana and the neighbouring countries.

Hausa Immigrants – Between Exclusion and Integration

The earliest contacts between Hausa traders and the inhabitants of the Middle Volta Basin can be traced as far back as the fifteenth century. These Hausa people were engaged in long-distance trade, moving between their home areas in Northern Nigeria and the savanna kingdoms (Yatenga, Wagadugu, Gurma, Tenkodugu, Dagbon, Nanun) in the Middle Volta Basin where they exchanged goods such as leather wares, textile products, metal locks, horse equipment and other articles for slaves, gold, kola nuts, elephant tusks and other products (Davis 1997). Hausa migrations and trading across the West African savanna led to the establishment of trade routes with rest stops and markets along the routes. Upon successfully establishing themselves in the savanna areas, they moved further south into the forest region (Gonja, Bono and the Ashanti Kingdoms) to develop trade and proselytize among the population. According to Kobo (2010) the disturbances that ensued following the invasion of Hausaland by Fulani jihadists led by Uthman Dan Fodio and the subsequent establishment of the Sokoto caliphate prompted the migration of more Hausa traders to the West African savanna region. Thus, by the eighteenth century, Hausa diaspora settlements had emerged in the savanna and forest regions of Ghana where they established trading and religious centres and worked as Islamic clerics, Koranic schoolteachers, and Malams among the ruling clans in Mamprugu, Dagbon, Gonja and Ashanti (Davis 1997).

In the savanna areas, the Hausa migrants intermarried with the autochthone population, successfully converting sections of the local population and the ruling class to the Islamic faith (Wilks 1965, 1989; Ferguson 1972). However, in the forest region, the Hausa migrants lived in their own Muslim quarters (*Zongo*), quite separate from the autochthone Guan and Akan groups. Wherever they settled, Hausa migrants had considerable influence as powerful Islamic clerics who provided charms, amulets and other protective wares for the warriors and leadership of the host population (Owusu Ansah 1991). Besides trading and establishing Koranic schools, Hausa migrants were also recruited by their hosts in the forest region to work in the mines, cocoa and food crop farms. Within a short period, the Hausa language and their religion (Islam) defined the migrant quarters, and they soon took up most of the religious and secular leadership positions within the migrant community (Kobo 2010).

By the time of formal colonial rule in 1896, Hausa communities had been well established in the Gold Coast. The British colonial government recruited many Hausa residents into the colonial police force (that is, the Gold Coast Constabulary), and many of them assisted the British in their campaigns during the First and Second World Wars as part of the West African Frontier Force.[6] The British considered the Hausa as having migrated from British West African territory, and therefore the British Nationality and Status of Alien Act of 1914 accorded Hausa immigrants and other Nigerians in the Gold Coast colony the same rights, privileges and responsibilities as the 'native' or autochthone population.

However, following independence in 1957 the citizenship status of the Hausa and other non-autochthone groups was altered frequently and has remained contested ever since. The Ghana Nationality Act of May 1957 granted *de jure* Ghanaian citizenship to second and subsequent generations of Hausa immigrants in Ghana 'if one of his/her parents or grandparents were born in Ghana'. However, *de facto*, many autochthones believed and acted as if citizenship was a preserve of the autochthone population and therefore regarded the Hausa as non-nationals or 'aliens' from Nigeria.[7] These populist views were confirmed by national legislation and government policies, particularly with the establishment and enforcement of the Deportation Act of 1957, the Aliens Act of 1963 and the Aliens Compliance Order of November 1969. These legislations were used to deport leaders of immigrant groups, including some prominent Hausa in 1963 and 1969 (Peil 1974; Schildkrout 1978; Sudarkasa 1979).

Since around the early twentieth century, almost every major urban settlement in Ghana has a suburb (*Zongo*) inhabited mainly by the Hausa and other northern Ghanaian and savanna Muslims. In these surburbs, which are under the leadership of a Hausa traditional leader (*Sariki Zongo*), the Hausa language is the lingua franca, Islam is the dominant religion, and social and cultural activities are predominantly Muslim-influenced (cf. Amoah-Boampong and Duah 2014). These suburbs are typically densely populated and bustling with economic activities. With the creation of their own suburbs in virtually every urban settlement, the Hausa people in Ghana became the promoters and defenders of the Islamic way of life and the creation of what has become the '*Zongo* identity'. Unlike other immigrant groups, they also succeeded in territorializing their presence in the country and creating a semi-autonomous space where they live according to their Islamic and traditional Hausa customs and practices without much interference from the autochthone population and the state (cf. Pellow 1991).

The Hausa in Ghana work mainly in the security services and as merchants, traders, livestock/cattle owners and traders, butchers, and in the informal sectors of the urban economy. They provide spiritual and psychological services and run their own Koranic schools where English and Arabic as well as the Islamic religion are taught. For a long time the Hausa and other Muslims shunned the formal educational system in the country (Schildkrout 1978; Pellow 2002). The consequences of this are the high illiteracy rate, lack of skills, training and education, and low representation of the Hausa, and Muslims in general, in government and state institutions. Most *Zongo* today are unplanned, overpopulated and impoverished settlements with poor sanitation, an absence of social infrastructure and a high proportion of low-income earners. The widely held stereotypes about the Hausa and indeed all *Zongo* residents is that they are either 'hardworking, devout and spiritually powerful persons' or 'illiterates, lack understanding and are prone to violence'; particularly with respect to the latter view, *Zongo* communities are negatively perceived to be hotbeds of social vices and criminal activities including armed robbery, black marketeering, fraud and internet scams among others.

Besides the broad '*Zongo* identity', which is multi-ethnic but dominated by the Hausa language and Islamic religion and culture, there are several shades of uniquely Hausa identity within the *Zongo* settlement. There is the community of Hausa residents who accept the authority of their traditional chief and the religious leadership of the Imam. They strive to maintain the Hausa culture and tradition as related to them by their forefathers by organizing traditional festivals and Muslim religious celebrations. During these festival celebrations the diversity of traditional social life in the *Zongo* communities is often on display with ethnic groups such as the Mossi, Fulani, Gao, Dagomba, Frafra and other northern groups joining the Hausa in cultural displays and route marches amidst drumming and dancing.

From the 1950s to the 1980s there was also the division of the Hausa community: those born in the Gold Coast/Ghana, commonly called the '*yankasa*', and recent Hausa migrants from the subregion (that is, strangers – *baaki*) as well as those born abroad (*tabouse*) (see Kobo 2010). These divisions resulted primarily from attempts by the state to promote indigenes or members of the autochthone groups to take up the businesses, commercial activities and institutions headed by recent Muslim migrants or non-Ghanaian Hausa. There were also attempts by other groups to challenge the authority of the Hausa Imam to lead the Islamic community, but these divisions appear to have subsided following the acceptance of the foremost role of the Hausa in Islamic affairs in Ghana.

While the Hausa and other *Zongo* residents are socially and economically quite well integrated into Ghanaian society, there are still suspicions amongst segments of the autochthone population and state institutions with respect to their citizenship status and political rights. The Hausa are still not listed and accepted as an ethnic group in Ghana and are sometimes refused the acquisition of citizenship documents such as national passports and identity cards. Some state institutions such as the Ghana Statistical Service and the Ghana Immigration Service also frequently challenge the citizenship of the Hausa in Ghana (see *The Chronicle*, 27 March 2012).

The Lebanese in Ghana: A Diaspora with Changing Fortunes and an Uncertain Future

There are colonies of Lebanese diaspora in all West African countries, including Ghana, and Lebanese migration and experiences are interesting because of their non-African origin and their identity as a visible minority in a subregion dominated by 'black' people. According to Akyeampong (2006b) Lebanese emigration to coastal West Africa commenced in the 1860s with the arrival of a Lebanese migrant by sea in Dakar. This was followed by a wave of Lebanese migration to neighbouring francophone West African countries. By the early twentieth century, small numbers of Lebanese migrants had settled in the Ivory Coast, Ghana and Nigeria (Bierwirth 1999). The first Lebanese to settle in Ghana were William Ibrahim Chedid and Elias el-Khoury, who arrived there (then the Gold Coast colony) in 1884. They were Maronite Christians. They were soon followed by other migrants from their home area in Lebanon in what has been described as a chain migration involving friends, family members and relatives from the same town or locality in Lebanon. For example, most of the Lebanese in Accra migrated from Tripoli in northern Lebanon (Ohene Marfo 2012). A few years after arriving in Ghana, most of the migrants gradually brought over their wives, children and relatives, while the unmarried men soon went back to Lebanon to get their brides to join them in Ghana. From a few individuals who trickled into the country in search of greener pastures, the population of Lebanese in Ghana grew to 570 by 1931, reaching its peak of 12,000 by 1969. The number of Lebanese in Ghana has since declined considerably following Ghana's expulsion of foreigners after the promulgation of the Aliens Compliance Order in 1969.

The bulk of the Lebanese migrants in Ghana worked as merchants, filling the role of middlemen between British companies and the local Ghanaian population. These Lebanese merchants served as wholesalers and retailers for the large multinational companies and distributed household, consumer and agricultural goods to the local inhabitants. They eventually established trading posts in the hinterland areas where the British did not venture, thereby incorporating those areas into the European cash economy. Subsequent generations of Lebanese migrants in Ghana soon relied on their knowledge of Ghanaian society and culture to branch into different sectors of the Ghanaian economy including automobile, manufacturing, entertainment, communication, hospitality, sports and construction works, among others (Ohene Marfo 2012).

With respect to citizenship, the Lebanese in Ghana and other British colonies in West Africa fell into two categories, 'aliens' and 'subjects'. The first category consisted of those who maintained their Lebanese citizenship as well as those who had acquired the citizenship of other countries. The second were those who chose to become British subjects. All second-generation Lebanese were British-protected persons and from 1949 were given the option of being 'Citizens of the United Kingdom and the Colonies'.

With respect to their ethnic identity, it is certainly a fact that this has varied considerably over the years. The first Lebanese migrants came to West Africa at a time when their country (Lebanon) was classified together with Syria, Jordan and Palestine/Israel as one territory under the Ottoman Empire. The collapse of the Ottoman Empire in 1922 resulted in the emergence of the different independent countries that we know today and hence a budding Lebanese identity (Akyeampong 2006b). This explains why the autochthone population did not initially make a distinction between the Lebanese and the Syrians and people from the Arabian Peninsula in general. They were all considered Arabs or Syrians, although the fact that the first migrants were Christians made it difficult for locals to classify them. An independent Lebanese identity only emerged over time. The Lebanese national identity also became prominent in the national psyche following the creation of a national association, a clubhouse and sports centre, a cultural centre, schools and through numerous philanthropic activities that included the provision of scholarships, renovation of hospital wards and engagement in civic and voluntary duties. Lebanese-owned companies also regularly supported community activities as part of their corporate social responsibility.

Their national identity was by no means their only identity, or even the most important, to the individual Lebanese. Religious identity played a significant role. While the Maronite Christians were more prominent in the capital towns, the numbers of Shiite Muslims from southern Lebanon expanded. It can be concluded that the religious and sectarian divisions found in the Lebanese homeland ultimately found their way into Ghana, although unlike at home, this was not a source of friction or conflict.

Both Akyeampong (2006b) and Ohene Marfo (2012) have drawn attention to the fact that Lebanese emigration to Ghana has a localized pattern, as related families migrated from a particular locale in Lebanon. Furthermore, marriages amongst the Lebanese are largely endogamous; that is, they mostly marry within their ethnic group. In the past, male migrants went to their home region in Lebanon to take their brides, but more recently, with the growth of the Lebanese community, marriages amongst Ghanaian-born Lebanese are increasingly common. These factors explain the strong identification of the Lebanese with their kin network and their region of origin in Lebanon.

Furthermore, many Ghanaian-born Lebanese feel very much at home in Ghana. Besides Arabic, they speak one or two local languages as well as English, and understand the Ghanaian culture and attitudes well. They typically attend schools in Ghana and Lebanon and have links in both countries to relatives and business partners. Many of them have taken over businesses established by their parents while others have moved into other sectors of the economy. Just as are many Ghanaian elite, they are transnationals with links in Ghana and abroad. The fragile nature of the Ghanaian economy and the poor social infrastructure compel them to maintain links abroad. They have, of course, also not forgotten the bitter experiences of the 1960s, 1970s and 1980s in Ghana when the properties of prominent and wealthy Lebanese were expropriated and the people themselves expelled from the country.

Like all late-comer immigrant groups in Ghana, the Lebanese have been victims of prejudice and stereotyping by the autochthone groups. Because the Lebanese have been predominantly engaged in trading and manufacturing, they have often incurred the wrath of the local population. The Lebanese have at different times been made scapegoats due to a malfunctioning and deteriorating economy by successive Ghanaian governments. Their relative wealth and their thriving businesses are often the source of anger and envy amongst large sections of the autochthone population. They are frequently accused of engaging in corrupt and shady business practices, siphoning foreign exchange out of the country and being racist (Ohene Marfo 2012).

After independence in 1957, the Lebanese, particularly the second and third generations, were encouraged to switch their allegiance to the new nation by acquiring Ghanaian citizenship. Many did, fearing that the wave of racial antagonism and economic nationalism would endanger their businesses and other investments in the country. The fears of the Lebanese community at independence soon became a reality as the nationalist leaders enacted laws to reduce Lebanese participation in the economy, particularly the trading sector. Generally, the Lebanese have had a chequered experience with successive Ghanaian governments since independence. Their businesses have at different times been seized by governments and vandalized by the populace, while individual Lebanese have been de-naturalized and deported out of the country. Fearing victimization by successive governments and backlash from the elite, generations of Lebanese have largely opted to stay out of Ghanaian politics and governance. Since the return to civilian rule in 1992, the Lebanese community has gradually expanded and made significant contributions to the development of industry, education, trade, sports, music, entertainment and the information technology sectors. Second and subsequent generations of Lebanese feel at home in Ghana but their integration into Ghanaian society remains tenuous.

General Conclusions

This chapter examined the changing notions and experiences of ethnic identity among three non-autochthone immigrant groups in Ghana. It showed that, besides their broad categorization as an ethnic group based primarily on their language, religion and culture, each of these immigrant groups has other forms of lower-level identities with which they are more closely associated. The chapter also supports the notion that ethnic identity is not immutable.

Ghana is a multi-ethnic, multi-cultural and multi-religious society. In contrast with ethnic group identities that are quite well established, a national identity can be regarded as still under construction. The social order is largely based on ethnic diversity, and the national goal is to achieve 'Unity in Diversity'. To be integrated into Ghanaian society, recent immigrant groups are not required to be the same or different from the autochthone groups or even the urban elite.[8] However, ethnic identities and differences become accentuated when late-comer migrant groups such as the Fulani, the Hausa and the Lebanese who have specialized in the lucrative trading and livestock sectors become far wealthier than most autochthone groups. This generates hatred and envy on the part of the autochthone groups, and any existing ethnic differences with these migrant groups can become an obstacle to the latter's integration into Ghanaian society (see Schlee 2018).

Furthermore, the chapter has shown the rigidity of traditional notions of nationality that are largely based on membership in an autochthone ethnic group (first-comers) that is territorialized in Ghana, while 'late-comers' or more recent immigrant groups who cannot claim a settlement or area as their ancestral home within Ghana's territory are regarded as 'strangers' and sometimes 'aliens'. This is in spite of the fact that the colonial government already introduced a concept of citizenship that recognized immigrant groups from anglophone West African countries as Ghanaian citizens with the same rights and responsibilities as the autochthone groups. After independence, however, successive Ghanaian constitutions and laws have defined citizenship mainly in terms of membership in an ethnic group autochthonous to Ghana. The status of non-autochthone immigrant groups such as the Fulani, Hausa, Yoruba, Lebanese, Kotokoli, Zerma and so on, with respect to their social and political integration, remains ambiguous.

Successive postcolonial governments fostered the perception that immigrant groups controlled and dominated the key sectors of the economy and were to blame for the economic and social woes experienced during the post-independence era. As a result, businesses belonging to immigrants were repeatedly attacked and the owners expelled from the country. Although since the Fourth Republic (January 1992), the spectre of being labelled as 'aliens' and forcibly expelled from the country has receded, the general perception among autochthones that citizenship should be limited to members of their groups persists. Late-comer groups may be given Ghanaian citizenship, but should not become involved in local politics and governance issues. Politics, it is believed, should remain the preserve of the autochthones.[9]

Currently, the 1992 Constitution of Ghana and the Citizenship Act of 2002 do not distinguish adequately among the various categories of migrants. Thus, second and subsequent generations of immigrants are treated just like those who have settled in the country in the last decade: they are all expected to prove that they were born in Ghana and one of their parents or grandparents was also born in Ghana or that they were born outside Ghana but one of their parents was born in Ghana. Alternatively, they may obtain citizenship through adoption, marriage or naturalization. Furthermore, the decision to grant dual citizenship to Ghanaians abroad was made with respect to members of the autochthone population residing and working abroad. The situation of immigrant groups from the West African subregion and beyond residing in Ghana who are actually in the same situation as Ghanaians abroad was not considered. Subsequently, the dual citizenship law did little to resolve the ambiguous situation of non-autochthone groups in Ghana. Perhaps the issue of Ghanaian citizenship can be best regulated at the subregional level, that is, within the framework of the Economic Community of West African States (ECOWAS), whereby all long-term residents (including those from the subregion) are given dual citizenship with full rights and responsibilities in every ECOWAS country.

Steve Tonah is Professor of Sociology at the University of Ghana, Legon. He holds a BA in Economics and Sociology (University of Cape Coast) and an MPhil and PhD in Development Sociology (University of Bielefeld, Germany). He worked as a Project Coordinator for the Christian Council of Ghana (1993–1998) before joining the University of Ghana in 1999. Tonah has collaborated with several development organizations and research institutions in Africa and Europe. His areas of specialization include migration, chieftaincy, Fulani pastoralism and ethnicity. He is a fellow of the Ghana Academy of Arts and Sciences and the Alexander von Humboldt Foundation, Germany.

Notes

I am most grateful to Echi Christina Gabbert for her very helpful comments on an earlier version of this chapter and for providing relevant materials used in its revision.

1. Donahoe et al. (2009: 1) define collective identities as 'representations containing normative appeals to potential respondents and providing them with the means of understanding themselves, or being understood, as members of a larger category or assemblage of persons'.

2. 'Natives' referred to all members of the autochthone population, while 'subjects' consisted of immigrants from other English colonies such as Nigeria, Gambia and Sierra Leone, as well as from East Africa and India. Migrants, on the other hand, were residents from the neighbouring French Territories who came to seek work in the country.

3. This law appeared to have been selectively applied. After independence in 1957 migrants and residents who did not enjoy Ghanaian citizenship and wanted to take advantage of the law to obtain British citizenship were denied this right. This was particularly the case with Lebanese migrants (personal communication of Sylvia Marfo, September 2011).

4. The *Zongo* was originally a 'stranger's' quarter or an area in a settlement where Muslim traders and migrants from the savanna region (Hausa, Mossi, Kotokoli, Kanjarga and so on) resided (Schildkrout 1978; Amoah-Boampong and Duah 2014). In urban Ghana, *Zongo* settlements have been dominated by the Hausa people and their language was the lingua franca. *Zongo* settlements in Ghana have increasingly become more multi-ethnic and multi-religious with people from diverse cultures and nationalities residing there.

5. Among many ethnic groups in Ghana a 'stranger' simply refers to a migrant, that is, someone who belongs to another ethnic group and has not (yet) been integrated into the indigenous group. Among the Mamprusi, for example, a stranger may become an indigene after a long period of residency in the area and upon acquiring the local culture (personal communication, Dr Abdulai Abubakari, 12 November 2016 at Tamale).

6. Personal communication, Prof. Bawa Awumbila, 15 March 2018, at University of Ghana, Legon.

7. In the 1960s and 1970s, most Ghanaians considered anyone who lived in the *Zongo*, dressed like a Muslim in their long robe (*Jalabia*) and spoke Hausa to be an alien.

8. Schlee and Horstmann (2018) in their recent book *Differences and Sameness as Modes of Integration* discuss extensively the question of when and how social and political integration into a host society depends on sameness or requires difference or a combination of both.

9. See Akyeampong (2006a: 47). Bierwirth (1999: 93) states with respect to the Lebanese in neighbouring Côte d'Ivoire that there is also 'an implicit color bar to political participation' by the Lebanese. See also Geschiere (2009).

References

Addo, O.N. 1974. 'Foreign African Workers in Ghana', *International Labour Review* 109: 47–68.
Adomako-Sarfoh, J. 1974. 'The Effects of the Expulsion of Migrant Workers on Ghana's Economy with Particular Reference to the Cocoa Industry', in Samir Amin and Daryll Forde (eds), *Modern Migrations in West Africa*. Oxford: Oxford University Press, pp. 138–55.

Akyeampong, Emmanuel K. 2006a. 'Race, Political Identity and Citizenship in Ghana: The Example of the Lebanese', *Inaugural Lecture, Ghana Academy of Arts and Science*. Accra, 12 April 2006.

———. 2006b. 'Race, Identity and Citizenship in Black Africa: The Case of the Lebanese in Ghana', *Africa* 76: 297–323.

Ametewee, Viktor K. 2007. 'Ethnicity and Ethnic Relations in Ghana', in Steve Tonah (ed.), *Ethnicity, Conflicts and Consensus in Ghana*. Accra: Woeli, pp. 25–41.

Amoah, Michael. 2009. 'The Most Difficult Decision Yet: Ghana's 2008 Presidential Elections', *African Journal of Political Science and International Relations* 3(4): 174–81.

Amoah-Boampong, Cyrelene and Manna Duah. 2014. 'The Invention of Belonging among Rural Migrants in Asante', in Nana Y.B. Sarpong and J. Otto Pohl (eds), *Replenishing History: New Directions to Historical Research in the 21st Century in Ghana*. Banbury: Ayebia Clark, pp. 90–107.

Anebo, Felix, Yaw Benneh, John Agyei, Takyiwaa Manuh and Yao Gebe. 2010. 'Legal and Institutional Dimensions of Migration in Ghana', *Technical Paper* No. 4. Centre for Migration Studies. Legon: University of Ghana.

Bening, Bagulo R. 2010. *Ghana Administrative Areas and Boundaries*. Accra: Ghana University Press.

Bierwirth, Chris H. 1999. 'The Lebanese Communities of Côte d'Ivoire', *African Affairs* 98(390): 79–99.

Bukari, Kaderi Noagah and Nikolaus Schareika. 2015. 'Stereotypes, Prejudices and Exclusion of Fulani Pastoralists in Ghana', *Research, Policy and Practice* 5: 20–32.

Davis, David C. 1997. 'Renaissance, Reformation and Revolution: Islam in Eighteenth Century Mamprugu', *Journal of Muslim Minority Affairs* 17(1): 43–63.

Donahoe, Brian, John R. Eidson, Dereje Feyissa, Veronika Fuest, Markus Virgil Hoehne, Boris Nieswand, Günther Schlee and Olaf Zenker (eds). 2009. 'The Formation and Mobilization of Collective Identities in Situations of Conflict and Integration', *Max Planck Institute for Social Anthropology Working Paper* No. 116. Retrieved from http://www.eth.mpg.de/pubs/wps/pdf/mpi-eth-working-paper-0116.

Ferguson, Phyllis. 1972. 'Islamization in Dagbon: A Study of the Alfanema of Yendi', PhD dissertation. Newnham College, University of Cambridge.

Geschiere, Peter. 2009. *The Perils of Belonging: Autochthony, Citizenship and Exclusion in Africa and Europe*. Chicago: University of Illinois Press.

Ghana Statistical Service (GSS). 2002. *2000 Population and Housing Census – Summary Report of Final Results*. Accra: GSS.

———. 2012. *2010 Population and Housing Census – Summary Results of Final Report*. Accra: Statistical Service.

Hill, Polly. 1970. 'The Occupations of Migrants in Ghana', *Anthropological Papers* No. 42. Museum of Anthropology. Ann Arbor: University of Michigan.

Kobo, Ousman. 2010. '"We Are Citizens Too": The Politics of Citizenship in Independent Ghana', *Journal of Modern African Studies* 48(1): 67–94.

Lentz, Carola. 2013. *Land, Mobility and Belonging in West Africa*. Bloomington: Indiana University Press.

Lentz, Carola and Paul Nugent. 2000. *Ethnicity in Ghana: The Limits of Invention*. London: Macmillan.

Ohene Marfo, Sylvia. 2012. 'Immigrant Businesses in Ghana: A Study of the Lebanese in Accra', MPhil thesis. Legon: University of Ghana, Department of Sociology.

Oppong, Yaa P.A. 2002. *Moving Through and Passing On: Fulani Mobility, Survival, and Identity in Ghana*. London: Transaction.

Owusu Ansah, David. 1991. *Islamic Talismanic Tradition in Nineteenth-Century Asante*. Lewiston, NY: Edwin Mellen Press.

Peil, Margaret. 1971. 'The Expulsion of West African Aliens', *Journal of Modern African Studies* 9(2): 205–29.

———. 1974. 'Ghana's Aliens', *International Migration Review* 8(3): 367–81.
Pelican, Michaela. 2015. 'Ethnicity as a Political Resource: Indigenous Rights Movements in Africa', in UoC Forum Ethnicity as a Political Resource (ed.), *Ethnicity as a Political Resource: Conceptualizations across Disciplines, Regions, and Periods*. Bielefeld: Transcript, pp. 135–49.
Pellow, Deborah. 1991. 'The Power of Space in the Evolution of an Accra Zongo', *Ethnohistory* 38(4): 414–50.
———. 2002. *Landlords and Lodgers: Socio-Spatial Organization in an Accra Community*. Chicago: University of Chicago Press.
Riesman, Paul. 1977. *Freedom in Fulani Social Life: An Introspective Ethnography*. Chicago: University of Chicago Press.
Schildkrout, Enid. 1978. *People of the Zongo: Transformation of Ethnic Identity in Ghana*. Cambridge: Cambridge University Press.
Schlee, Günther. 1994. *Identities on the Move: Clanship and Pastoralism in Northern Kenya*. Nairobi: Gideon S. Were Press.
———. 2003. 'North-East Africa as a Region for the Study of Changing Identifications and Alliances', in *Max Planck Institute for Social Anthropology Report 2002–2003*: 163–70.
———. 2009. 'Introduction', in Günther Schlee and Elisabeth E. Watson (eds), *Changing Identifications and Alliances in North East Africa, Volume 1: Ethiopia and Kenya*. New York and Oxford: Berghahn, pp. 1–13.
———. 2011. 'Territorializing Ethnicity: The Imposition of a Model of Statehood on Pastoralists in Northern Kenya and Southern Ethiopia', *Ethnic and Racial Studies* 36(5): 857–74.
———. 2018. 'Introduction: Difference and Sameness as Modes of Integration', in Günther Schlee and Alexander Horstmann (eds), *Difference and Sameness as Modes of Integration: Anthropological Perspectives on Ethnicity and Religion*. New York and Oxford: Berghahn, pp. 1–32.
Schlee, Günther and Alexander Horstmann (eds). 2018. *Differences and Sameness as Modes of Integration: Anthropological Perspectives on Ethnicity and Religion*. New York and Oxford: Berghahn.
Shack, William A. and Elliot P. Skinner (eds). 1979. *Strangers in African Societies*. Berkeley: University of California Press.
Stenning, Derrick J. 1994. *Savannah Nomads: A Study of the Woodabe Pastoral Fulani of Western Bornu Province Northern Region, Nigeria*. Münster: LIT.
Sudarkasa, Niara. 1979. 'From Stranger to Alien: The Sociopolitical History of the Nigerian Yoruba in Ghana, 1900–1970', in William A. Shack and Elliot P. Skinner (eds), *Strangers in African Societies*. Berkeley: University of California Press, pp. 141–68.
Tonah, Steve. 2000. 'State Policies, Local Prejudices and Cattle Rustling along the Ghana-Burkina Faso Border', *Africa* 70(4): 551–67.
———. 2002. 'The Politics of Exclusion: The Expulsion of Fulani from Ghana 1999/2000', *Max Planck Institute for Social Anthropology Working Paper* No. 44. Retrieved from http://www.eth.mpg.de/pubs/wps/pdf/mpi-eth-working-paper-0044.
———. 2003. 'Conflicts and Consensus between Migrant Fulani Herdsmen and Mamprusi Farmers in Northern Ghana', in Franz Kröger and Barbara Meier (eds), *Ghana's North*. Frankfurt: Peter Lang, pp. 79–100.
———. 2005. *Fulani in Ghana: Migration History, Integration and Resistance*. Accra: Yamens Press.
———. 2006. 'The Challenge of Fulani Pastoralism in Ghana', *Legon Journal of International Affairs* 3(1): 75–94.
——— (ed.). 2007. *Ethnicity, Conflicts and Consensus in Ghana*. Accra: Woeli.
———. 2015. 'The Relationship between Farmers and Fulani Herdsmen in Ghana', in Dan-Bright S. Dzorgbo and Steve Tonah (eds), *Sociology and Development Issues in Ghana*. Accra: Woeli, pp. 222–42.
———. 2016. 'Conflict and Fulani Migration in Northern Ghana', *paper presented at a Conference for the Project 'Society and Change in Northern Ghana'*, Leiden, Netherlands, 9–10 December 2016.

Wilks, Ivor. 1965. 'A Note on the Early Spread of Islam in Dagomba', *Transactions of the Historical Society of Ghana, Volume* 8: 87–97.

———. 1989. *Wa and the Wala: Islam and Polity in North Western Ghana*. Cambridge: Cambridge University Press.

CHAPTER 5

STUDYING CONFLICT AND ETHNICITY THROUGH PERFORMATIVE AND AUDIO-VISUAL RESEARCH METHODS
Examples from Cameroon

MICHAELA PELICAN

Introduction

The Max Planck Institute (MPI) for Social Anthropology in Halle (Saale), Germany, has provided a particularly conducive environment for methodological experimentation and innovation. Günther Schlee has encouraged many of us to explore alternative approaches, both during fieldwork and with regard to publication formats. While a researcher at MPI between 2000 and 2006, I greatly benefitted from institutional support as well as from inspiring discussions with colleagues, many of whom used innovative approaches in their previous and ongoing research. Andreas Dafinger, for example, made use of aerial photographs of Bisa compounds to analyse the correlation of social and spatial organizational patterns in Burkina Faso (Dafinger 2004). Tilo Grätz organized a fairy tale festival with a local nongovernmental organization and a radio station in Benin that sparked his later interest in contemporary African mediascapes (Grätz 1997, 2014). John Ziker used elaborate network analysis to explore food-sharing practices among Dolgan hunter-gatherers in northern Siberia (Ziker and Schnegg 2005). Patrick Heady integrated qualitative and quantitative approaches in his studies on kinship and social security in Europe. He and his team developed a computerized Kinship Network Questionnaire (KNQ), enabling them to combine interpretive and mathematical analyses and to develop a sound database for historical and cross-national comparison (Heady 2014; see also Grandits 2010; Heady and Schweitzer 2010; Heady and Kohli 2010).

Besides supporting the exploration of different research methods, Schlee also encouraged us to think of alternative publication formats beyond the genre of academic articles and books. Setting an example, he published two field diaries (based on selected trips to Sudan and Ethiopia) on the Max Planck Institute website, with the aim to share his primary data with interested scholars and students (Schlee 2008, 2013).[1] The diaries have also proven instructive for educational purposes, such as in my class on research methodology and field diaries. More recently, Schlee initiated the open-access series *Field Notes and Research Projects* as a complement to authors' peer-reviewed publications.[2] As stated in the editor's preface, the series devotes ample space to visual and primary data and aims at enhancing the authors' public outreach. Several MPI researchers have published in this series; for example, to reflect on their research process (e.g. Jiménez-Tovar 2016) or to experiment with alternative publication formats (e.g. Köhler 2017). Some of us also made use of the MPI's institutional support to publish audiovisual outputs from our research (e.g. Beyer and Knee 2007; Pelican and Orland 2002; Rudolf 2010, 2011).

In this chapter, I will focus on the insights gained through the use of role-playing and video documentation as interactive tools in studying conflict and ethnicity in northwest Cameroon (see also Pelican 2015). More generally, the chapter contributes to a discussion of quasi-experimental methods in anthropology, a term I owe to Tilo Grätz (2010). The term refers to innovative, collaborative or participatory methods that are applied in conjunction with standard anthropological methods and with an aim to generate additional insight into specific research questions. Such methods may include the use of role-playing and video documentation, as explored in this chapter, as well as photo or film diaries, radio broadcasts, public film screenings, video or storytelling workshops and press conferences, among many others. Authors often mention their use of quasi-experimental methods only peripherally or as a complement to established anthropological methods. I argue, however, that these methods deserve more attention as they significantly contribute to extending and refining anthropologists' methodological toolkit.

The material presented in this chapter is drawn from fieldwork in Cameroon conducted between 2000 and 2002. Here, I focus on a specific aspect of my research, namely local actors' various uses of role-playing as a medium of entertainment, communication and social critique vis-à-vis state agents, NGO workers and researchers, as well as among themselves. The practice of role-playing was introduced to the region in the 1990s in the context of development initiatives and was soon adopted by local communities. It relied upon on the expertise of Cameroonian playwrights as well as local familiarity with theatre and dance performances in school.[3] In my fieldwork, I employed a variety of anthropological methods, including approaches from visual and performance anthropology. Over the course of fourteen months I witnessed, and participated to a degree, in fifteen role-plays performed by members of local women's groups, youth groups, a regional nongovernmental organization and an informal drama group of which I was a founding member. These role-plays covered an array of topics, ranging from marital issues to interethnic tension, the benefits of Islamic education, the opposition of 'traditional' beliefs and Western education, and the nature of anthropological research. The topics were developed in collaboration with members of theatre groups. While some of the role-plays were simply intended for entertainment, many touched on topics relevant to my research and often entailed an educational component. Integrating the role-plays into my ethnographic writing and analysis, however, proved somewhat challenging, as I will discuss in this chapter.

Besides role-playing, I also used photography and video to document everyday life and cultural events (Pelican and Orland 2002). Moreover, some of the plays were videotaped, edited and later screened for local audiences. This was part of a public event in my field site of Misaje, which I co-organized with a team of local collaborators (Pelican and Ngeh 2006). During the Misaje Film Festival we presented a cross-section of our audio-visual material with an aim to render comprehensible the objectives of my research. This approach proved rather successful and engendered basic understanding and widespread support among the local population in my field site. Some of the audio-visual documents also proved useful for public presentations back in Germany, as well as for classroom teaching on research methodology and topics related to my fieldwork.

For the purposes of this chapter, I have selected two role-plays: one performed by the nongovernmental organization Ballotiral that deals with strained relations between farmers and herders; the second enacted by a group of Mbororo women who reflected on their experiences of selling milk products. Both address the subject of conflict and ethnicity, which resonates with several contributions in this edited volume. As I will show, the role-plays provide insights into how local actors deal with cultural difference and make use of play and satire to challenge cultural norms. At the same time, they address various topics beyond my thematic scope, which illustrates the challenge of effectively integrating qualitative-explorative data into scholarly analysis and ethnographic writing.

Quasi-Experimental Methods in Visual and Performance Anthropology

As the above examples illustrate, anthropologists have been innovative in using quasi-experimental methods to address a wide array of topics. In most cases, these methods have been elaborated in the context of visual and performance anthropology.[4] Within the subdiscipline of visual anthropology, Sarah Pink and Marcus

Banks have been particularly instructive in discussing and developing diverse uses of (audio-)visual methods in ethnographic research (Banks 2007; Banks and Zeitlyn 2015; Pink 2013, 2015). With regard to studying performance, researchers have drawn inspiration from the classical works of Victor Turner (1974, 1982, 1988), Johannes Fabian (1990) and Dwight Conquergood (1982, 2006) who have emphasized the relevance of cultural performance as a venue to express and negotiate vital social issues.

In both subfields, reflections on the politics of anthropological research, the positionality of researchers and the relevance of collaborative and participatory methods have been illuminating (e.g. Lassiter 2005; Madison 2005; Zoettl 2012). Chalfen (2011) distinguishes between collaborative and participatory research with regard to how research subjects are involved in the process of generating data. Taking the example of video productions, a collaborative approach emphasizes the exchange and joint contributions of researcher and research subjects in producing the video. Conversely, a participatory approach foregrounds the active role of the research subjects who construct their own videos and texts with minimal intervention by the researcher. Accordingly, 'a central aim of the participatory visual media process is to create pictorial narratives that convey what respondents want to communicate in the manner they wish to communicate' (Chalfen 2011: 188). A clear-cut distinction between collaborative and participatory methods, however, is not always possible, as they frequently overlap and may be used interdependently in the same research project. The boundaries between visual and performance anthropology are fluid, as collaborative and participatory video productions often involve an element of performance.

As a pioneer of collaborative and performative video production, we may consider Jean Rouch and his approach of 'shared anthropology' in the 1950s. Together with his longtime African collaborators, Rouch produced a number of – for his time – highly innovative documentaries and docu-fictions to illustrate the lives and dreams of Africans in motion (Henley 2010; Rouch 1974).[5] Current examples include, among others, the works of Peter Anton Zoettl and Francesco Bondanini, both of whom integrated participatory video workshops in their research on identity in northeastern Brazil (Zoettl 2012) and on African migrants' narratives in the Camp for the Temporary Stay of Migrants (CETI by its Spanish acronym) in Melilla (Bondanini 2017).

The genre of performance anthropology also overlaps with the anthropology of popular culture and theatre studies. For my approach to role-playing, I draw on the Manchester School, whose proponents have interpreted cultural performance 'as a methodological metaphor for exploring issues of conflict and contradiction in wider society' (Parkin 1996: xix). While most of them focused on ritual, it was Victor Turner (1974, 1982, 1988) who connected drama to theatre by introducing the metaphor of the social drama, and by subsequently including theatrical performances in his analysis. As he pointed out, 'performance is often a critique, direct or veiled, of the social life it grows out of' (Turner 1988: 22); it centres on conflict and social change, and may in itself be an active agent of change.

A second source of inspiration is Johannes Fabian's (1990) study *Power and Performance: Ethnographic Explorations through Proverbial Wisdom and Theatre in Shaba, Zaire*, where he analyses the development and performance of a drama that centred around the proverb 'Le pouvoir se mange entier/Power is eaten whole'. In his introduction, Fabian (1990: 12) uses the iceberg as a metaphor: whereas the actual performance represents only what is visible above water, its greater submerged bulk comprises a plethora of experiences, ideas, discussions, repetitions and rehearsals. Secondly, he (1990: 17–20) reminds us that cultural performances are not just fantasy and entertainment, but critically reflect on actual political and economic conditions as well as global power inequalities.

A different take on performance in anthropological research has been proposed by Soyini Madison. Taking inspiration from Conquergood's plea to rethink ethnography in terms of cultural politics (Conquergood 1982, 2006), Madison opted for performance as a medium to convey the findings of her research and contribute to public discussions (Madison 2005, 2006, 2010). Based on her fieldwork on traditional religion, modernity and human rights debates in Ghana, she scripted a play entitled *Is It a Human Being or a Girl?*, which she staged in collaboration with colleagues and students of the University of Ghana in Legon. Besides critically engaging with the subject of civic rights, the play was also aimed at questioning her positionality as a researcher. Madison (2006: 397) argues that the enactment of 'the living performances of everyday remembrances, imaginings and deeply felt encounters of ethnographic fieldwork is a radical act of translation'. It creates a symbolic reality that, by enacting a people's reality as well as enacting its representation, speaks to the inseparability of fiction and nonfiction.

The subject of theatre has also been central to the work of Karin Barber (1997a, 2000), who linked her study of the Yoruba travelling theatre to the wider field of popular culture. Barber asks us to situate popular expressions of culture and art – such as theatre, music, paintings, cinema and fiction – in time and space, and when doing so, to pay careful attention to the historical and cultural contexts in which these expressions emerge as well as their continuous modification in relation to social and economic change. Furthermore, she draws attention to the audience as a constitutive element of a performance's production and reception (Barber 1997b), an element also relevant with regard to the methodological use of role-playing in fieldwork.

This leads me to another strand of research on theatre, namely Theatre for Development, also known as the popular theatre approach (Eyoh 1991; Mlama 1991), people theatre (Doho 2006) or culture-drama (Kirby and Shu 2005, 2010).[6] Theatre for Development is a participatory tool applied in international development work that gained prominence in the 1980s and 1990s (Breitinger 1994; Mda 1993). It is based on the works of two Brazilian educationalists and theatre practitioners, Paulo Freire and Augusto Boal. While Freire (1970) argued for a liberated education, supporting the act of cognition rather than the simple transmission of information, Boal (1979) applied his colleague's approach to theatre. He developed a participatory form of theatre that involves both actors and audience in the process of play-making and performance. Theatre for Development may take different forms in different parts of the world, as it is supposed to take into account the particularities of the local settings and social groups involved.[7]

The literature on Theatre for Development focuses largely on the capacity of performance to facilitate community engagement and social communication; i.e. drama is interpreted as an agent of social change (e.g. Boon and Plastow 2004; Mda 1993; Mlama 1991). Besides engaging with the plays' subjects, many researchers pay close attention to the workshop-like structure associated with Theatre for Development as well as the fluid interchange of actors and audience. Jon Kirby and Gong Shu (2005, 2010) apply culture-drama, as they call it, to the post-conflict situation in Ghana. Drawing on their experience as workshop facilitators and researchers, they advocate culture-drama as an effective tool in promoting intercultural understanding and peace building. Culture-drama for them is based on the idea that actors exchange roles and thus get a chance to embody the other parties' experiences; that is, they feel how it is to be in the others' social position (for example, of power or subjugation). This change in perspective, they argue, is particularly fruitful for research and conflict resolution, as it generates grounds for mutual understanding.

While most studies of popular theatre analyse performances with regard to their content, the process of their making and the role of the audience, they also share in common a methodological involvement. Most researchers have not only studied but participated in public culture performances, be it as an actor, spectator, facilitator or 'catalyst' (e.g. Barber 2000; Madison 2010; Mda 1993). Similarly, in my work with role-playing in Cameroon, I have been involved in various roles, and it was both enjoyable and enlightening to take part in developing storylines and to play the 'white woman's' part. Yet in the two role-plays selected for this chapter, my involvement centred on observing and video-recording the event.

Role-Playing and Theatre for Development in Northwest Cameroon

Cameroon is one of the numerous African countries where Theatre for Development has become a popular tool in the work of international development agencies. This is also reflected in the number of studies on Theatre for Development in different parts of Cameroon (Doho 2006; Samba 2005; Takem 2005). In the anglophone part of the country – where my research site was located – the Cameroonian playwright and professor of African literature Bole Butake was a prominent promoter (Butake 1991, 2001). In collaboration with the Swiss development agency Helvetas, he facilitated several workshops and produced a number of manuals in co-authorship with other researcher-practitioners.[8] A few of the plays have been televised and broadcasted by the Cameroonian national television station.[9]

At my research site Theatre for Development was used by Ballotiral, a partnership programme of three nongovernmental organizations (MBOSCUDA, SIRDEP and Village AiD), run by Cameroonian personnel and largely British-funded. Ballotiral's aim was to address the situation of the Mbororo minority in northwest Cameroon (Duni et al. 2009; Hickey 2002, 2011; Pelican 2008a; Salihu and Hickey 2005). After the programme ended in 2003, Ballotiral's activities were continued by MBOSCUDA (Mbororo Social and Cultural Development Association) and extended to other parts of the North West Region. Ballotiral made use of Theatre for Development in two ways. Firstly, the Ballotiral staff performed role-plays at public occasions to communicate crucial issues to the administration and the wider public. Secondly, they integrated it in their work with Mbororo women's groups, encouraging them to articulate their problems in improvised role-plays. While Ballotiral stands in an established tradition of Theatre for Development in this region, the introduction of role-playing to Muslim population groups in the late 1990s was a novelty (Samba 2005).

To the Mbororo – a Muslim, agro-pastoral group belonging to the Fulɓe ethnic category – role-playing was a new means of communication. In Mbororo society, social relations are guided by Islamic norms as well as *pulaaku*, the 'Fulɓe code of conduct', which entails a strong emphasis on modesty, reserve and self-control (Riesman 1977; Virtanen 2003). As a consequence, members of different gender and age groups generally do not interact freely in public, and dissent is seldom openly expressed. Ballotiral thus considered role-playing as a means for Mbororo women to overcome the constraints of *pulaaku* in their interactions both within the women's group and with their male counterparts. As it turned out, Mbororo women willingly adopted role-playing as a way of playfully addressing vital issues in their lives. However, it was hardly possible to overcome the gender segregation, and the most acceptable way for Mbororo men to watch their women's role-plays was via video recordings (cf. Samba 2005).

In the course of my fieldwork I was able to participate in social drama training workshops organized by Ballotiral, and to observe two role-plays performed by the organization's staff at public meetings – both focusing on the subject of farmer-herder conflict. I also witnessed several role-plays initiated by participants during women's group meetings that addressed aspects of their daily lives, such as economic activities, education or health issues. For the purpose of this chapter, I have selected two role-plays that exemplify the different applications of Theatre for Development at the research site and that relate to the subjects of conflict and ethnicity, central to this volume.

Researching Conflict and Ethnicity through Role-Playing

The area under study is the anglophone North West Region, which together with the francophone West Region forms a geographical and cultural unit, also known as the Cameroon Grassfields. The largest and longest established population group is the Grassfielders, or *Garafi* in local parlance (in Cameroon Pidgin English), who account for approximately 85 per cent of the North West Region's inhabitants. They belong to linguistically distinct communities but share common features of economic and socio-political organization (Chilver and Kaberry 1967; Nkwi and Warnier 1982). For the purpose of my study that focuses on the coexistence of culturally and religiously different population groups, I have regarded them as a single ethnic category (Pelican 2015). Grassfielders are largely subsistence farmers and are organized in centralized chiefdoms and confederations; most are Christians and/or adherents of African local religions. They consider themselves 'natives' and 'guardians of the land', and claim political supremacy over population groups that joined them later, such as the Mbororo and Hausa. The latter are Muslim minorities who arrived in the Grassfields in the late nineteenth and early twentieth centuries (Awasom 1984; Boutrais 1995/96). The Mbororo belong to the ethnic category of Fulɓe and are primarily cattle pastoralists. They account for about 15 per cent of the population and, due to their wealth in animals, occupy a vital role in the region's economy. The Hausa is a heterogeneous group that comprises all Muslim village dwellers. They engage in trade and service jobs, and are in close relationship with the Mbororo, with whom they share cultural and religious similarities. At less than one per cent of the population, they are a tiny minority, found in most urban and rural centres.

The coexistence of Grassfielders, Mbororo and Hausa is at the same time peaceful and conflicted. While their economic specialization in farming, cattle rearing and trade respectively is perceived as complementary, farmers and herders' coexistence is not without problems (Chilver 1989; Dafinger and Pelican 2006; Harshbarger 1995). Conflicts over crop damage and land allocation have been reported since the colonial period and have occasionally resulted in violent outbursts. While the colonial and postcolonial administration responded with changing measures, no viable solution could be achieved (Njeuma and Awasom 1990). At the time of my research, the issue of farmer-herder conflict was addressed by nongovernmental organizations, such as Ballotiral, that used Theatre for Development to engender new solutions.

The subject of farmer-herder conflict has also been central to my research, but has presented challenges from a methodological standpoint. First-hand observation of actual incidents was hardly feasible, and it was only in 2009 – years after the completion of my study – that I was invited to witness a case from its inception to its trial. I thus based my analysis on administrative documents as well as conversations with individuals and parties who had been involved in farmer-herder disputes. When Ballotiral came up with a role-play on farmer-herder conflict, it offered the opportunity to study the subject from different angles. Firstly, it allowed me to observe the interactive dimension and the dynamics of conflict that are difficult to reconstruct from interviews. Secondly, the Ballotiral role-play utilized and palpably illustrated the popular discourses and ethnic stereotypes commonly associated with farmer-herder conflicts.

Role-Play on Farmer-Herder Conflict, Performed by the Ballotiral Staff

In January 2001, Ballotiral convened a one-day seminar entitled *Farmer-Grazier Conflict: Awareness and Transformation* to which representatives of the administration and the different population groups were invited.[10] The motive for this initiative was not a recent incident, but a general attempt to improve interethnic relations by alerting farmers, herders and civil servants as to their rights and duties. For the purpose of this seminar, the Ballotiral staff devised a three-act role-play in which they portrayed a farmer-herder dispute in its most simplistic form, pitting Mbororo herders against Grassfields farmers and state officials.

While the role-play could be analysed with regard to various aspects, I here concentrate on the cultural logics and ethnic stereotypes deployed by the actors.[11] Ethnic stereotypes against Fulɓe pastoralists have also been the subject of an article by Kaderi Bukari and Nikolaus Schareika (2015) with regard to Ghana. Drawing on social and cognitive categorization theory, they argue that negative attitudes towards Fulɓe pastoralists have become an important part of national and local community policies and overshadow farmer-herder relations. Their main research methods include focus group discussions and the analysis of print and online media. Unlike the above role-play, their data is somewhat partial, as it only reveals ethnic stereotypes and exclusionary practices against Fulɓe pastoralists, while ignoring ideas about the character of local farmers and state representatives. I argue that while ethnic and cultural difference is conveyed in everyday life, it is in the fictitious context of an educative role-play that it is expressed most pointedly. The stereotypes elucidated in this role-play include the hysterical Grassfields woman farmer, the aggressive Mbororo herdsman, the opportunistic Grassfields chief, the conceited Mbororo leader, the well-intentioned but ineffectual headmaster and the corrupt state counsel. Furthermore, the role-play reflects the different stages entailed in farmer-herder disputes, namely negotiations on the interpersonal level, on the group level and on the level involving government officials.

The first act deals with the stereotype of the excessive emotionality and tendency to overreact among Grassfields women. Women farmers are generally reputed to exaggerate and dramatize damage done to their farms. This assessment suggests underlying gender issues within Grassfields society (Chilver 1989; Ottiger 1996). A second stereotype refers to the allegedly aggressive behaviour

The first act portrays the complaint of a Grassfields woman whose crops have been destroyed by trespassing cattle. We see the woman farmer arriving at the Grassfields chief's palace in tears, claiming that cattle have destroyed her entire farm and that she has been attacked by the Mbororo herdsman. The news of the incident reaches the local headmaster, who attempts to reconcile the two parties.

The second act portrays the attempted resolution of the conflict by the two parties' representatives, the Grassfields chief (*fon*) and the Mbororo leader (*ardo*), mediated by the headmaster. The *fon* claims that his people came first and hence are the landlords of this place. Mbororo herders arrived only later; but now they want to occupy the land so that nothing will be left for the farmers and their future generations. The *ardo*, on the other hand, argues that his family has stayed in the area for many decades. They have always tried to be on good terms with the Grassfields chief, providing him with gifts. He cunningly asks the headmaster, 'Would you bring your bicycle to the petrol station?', implying 'Would you pay for crop damage if you had no benefit from it?' Dissatisfied with the headmaster's mediation, the *ardo* seeks redress from a higher institution.

The third act portrays the Mbororo leader negotiating legal action with the state counsel (state lawyer). The latter promises to send the farmer to jail, but warns the *ardo* of potential consequences if he does not reward him for his services. The *ardo* is taken aback at first, but regains his self-confidence in view of his wealth in cattle. He leaves the scene with the words: 'I have you all in my pocket!'

Figures 5.1–5.5. Farmer-grazier conflict, role-play of the Ballotiral staff, Nkambe, 29 January 2001 (original approximately 20 minutes). Video footage/photos: Michaela Pelican.[12]

of Mbororo herdsmen who are regularly blamed for unjustly attacking Grassfields farmers. However, the Mbororo reputation for resorting to violence refers predominantly to youths whose unruliness is also regretted by their elders (cf. Boutrais 2002).

In the second act, the matter is brought to the next higher authority, namely the community leaders. The case has thus become a political matter, in which not only personal but group interests are at stake. The staged confrontation between the Grassfields chief (*fon*) and the Mbororo leader (*ardo*) is exemplary of the formulaic charges commonly exchanged between representatives of the two parties. The *fon* claims political and economic ascendancy on the grounds of his group's anteriority and his ancestral links with the land. Conversely, Mbororo leaders are generally viewed as arrogant and flaunting their economic and political influence. In the Ballotiral role-play the *ardo* is portrayed as shifty and sly. He responds to the *fon*'s claims not by querying the Grassfielders' claims to anteriority, but by emphasizing the Mbororo's lengthy presence and their significant economic contribution to the chiefdom's development. The *ardo* is also portrayed as speaking only rudimentary Pidgin English, the lingua franca in anglophone Cameroon. Grassfields informants and administrators often interpret the Mbororo's lack of mastering Pidgin English as a sign of their contempt for Western education and as an impediment to progress. The headmaster, finally, represents members of an educated, liberal elite who attempt to bring the two community leaders together in order to facilitate viable solutions. This is the role administrators and nongovernmental organizations such as Ballotiral seek to fill. Yet in the perspective of many civil servants and NGO workers, the rural population – in its seeming backwardness and unwillingness to collaborate – frustrates all attempts towards conflict resolution and progress.

In the last act of the Ballotiral play, we observe a third dimension of negotiating farmer-herder relations in the appeal to external institutions, namely state officials, here represented by the state counsel. It is a popular conviction that Mbororo herders prefer bribing civil servants over compensating farmers. Conversely, it is assumed that state officials' backing is conditional on their generous remuneration. They are thus widely suspected of corruption and extortion, and held responsible for exacerbating farmer-herder conflicts. The role-play ends with the Mbororo leader's triumphant words 'I have you all in my pocket!' Yet everyone in the audience is aware of the decline of Mbororo wealth and the *ardo*'s self-delusion, which benefits third parties like government officials, while the occurrence of farmer-herder conflicts is perpetuated.

Ballotiral's objective was to entertain and, more importantly, to educate its audience by confronting it with its own stereotypes and predicaments in order to generate reflection and discussion about possible solutions to the farmer-herder problem. Ballotiral only partially succeeded in its endeavour. On the one hand, spectators responded to the play with laughter and affirmation, and several speakers acknowledged their own contribution to the perpetuation of farmer-herder disputes. On the other hand, participants tended to reiterate stereotypical allegations, giving little room for reconciliation. The resultant discussion of possible solutions remained on a hypothetical level and ended in administrative resolutions with limited practical implications.

According to Kirby and Shu (2005, 2010) peace building is not just a matter of discussion and negotiation but requires that both sides undergo some kind of 'cultural conversion' (Kirby and Shu 2010: 150). They see culture-drama as an effective tool to experience each other's ways of thinking and acting, and posit role reversal as the crucial technique to achieve full understanding of divergent cultural pathways. In the Ballotiral role-play, such a role reversal did not take place. Thus, despite their ambitions, by reproducing rather than reversing popular stereotypes and discourses of farmer-herder dispute, Ballotiral may have contributed to their reinforcement.

In the meantime, there has been a shift in NGO approaches away from stressing ethnic and cultural differences and towards emphasizing mutual benefits and shared interests. This is also reflected in one of the latest programmes of MBOSCUDA, which was funded by the British Big Lottery Fund and realized in collaboration with the British NGO Village Aid. The programme *In Search of Common Ground* has promoted alliance farming between farmers and herders as well as the creation of dialogue platforms as a desirable alternative to involving state institutions in the resolution of farmer-herder conflicts (Asong, Anchang and Shu 2015; Nchinda et al. 2016).[13] This new approach has laid the grounds for the amicable coexistence of the farmers and herders involved in the programme. Since 2016, however, Cameroon's Anglophone North West and South West Regions have been home to an ongoing violent conflict over the regions' political status (Pommerolle and Heungoup 2017; Bang and Balgah 2022). Sadly, the conflict has overshadowed the relationship between farmers and herders (Pelican et al. 2022), and has rejuvenated many of the ethnic stereotypes and historically developed cognitive and social categorizations enacted in the above role-play.

In the following, I turn to a second role-play I video-recorded during my research in the early 2000s. Again, the theme is conflict and ethnicity, but with a focus on female perspectives. Unlike the Ballotiral performance, I played a more (inter-)active role in this instance, as the performance was triggered by my presence.

Challenging Cultural Norms through Satire

While the negotiation of farmer-herder conflict is a male-dominated domain, the relations of Mbororo women with their Grassfields and Hausa neighbours were equally part of my research. In general, their encounters seemed rather friendly and largely related to social events (Pelican 2012). In informal conversations, however, and more palpably in two role-plays performed by Mbororo women's groups, one subject arose as a contentious issue: the practice of milk sales.

The sale of milk products has long been a vital source of income for Mbororo women. Yet with their settlement in the Grassfields and in conjunction with the gradual adoption of Islamic gender ideals, many families abandoned this practice in favour of agro-pastoralism. Others continued to sell milk products, but found themselves subjected to the deprecations of fellow, often better-off Mbororo. The practice of milk sales thus became a marker of backwardness, poverty and lack of Islamic virtue. While I was aware of these dynamics as a result of my earlier research on the socio-economic position of Mbororo women in the Grassfields (Pelican 1999, 2004), it is the role-plays that made me understand the gravity of this stigma and its impact on interethnic relations.

Mbororo women's engagement with Theatre for Development is rather new and a result of Ballotiral's initiative. At the same time, however, they draw on established genres of cultural performance in Mbororo society, such as song, dance and storytelling.[14] Mbororo women call their role-playing *fijirde* in Fulfulde, meaning play, amusement, fun. Similar to singing, dancing and storytelling, it is, for them, primarily a form of entertainment. Most plays are addressed to themselves and occasionally to visitors or the Ballotiral staff. They are not elaborate masterpieces but improvised sketches of possible real-life situations, with which performers and audience are generally familiar.

For the purpose of this chapter, I have chosen a rather short and improvised role-play, the performance of which took me by surprise. The play brings to the fore two issues: Mbororo women's predicaments over selling milk products, and their capacity to make use of play and satire to challenge cultural norms.

Role-Play on Milk Sales, Performed by a Mbororo Women's Group

In April 2001, I visited a Mbororo women's group whose president I had known for a long time and was a close friend of mine. I had just come back from Burkina Faso, bringing decorated calabashes as presents. Eight women had assembled, among them five elderly women who were well acquainted with each other and three younger women. One of the elderly women initiated a role-play by picking up a decorated calabash. Soon the guiding theme emerged: *sippoygo*, which means 'selling milk' in Fulfulde. Without further discussion of the storyline, the women embarked on the role-play, drawing on their experiences and imagination.

Although I did not ask the women to perform a role-play for me, my presence and the gifts from Burkina Faso were the decisive trigger. Several of the women knew me quite well and were familiar with my research interests and my appreciation for role-playing. The topic of milk sales had come up in earlier conversations, and was likely prompted by the gifted calabashes that often serve as containers for Mbororo cow milk. Moreover, the play was performed in the cosy setting of my Mbororo friend's house, a private space reserved for women and children, as male and female spheres are largely separated in Mbororo society (see also Pelican 1999). This setting enabled them to address the subject of Mbororo reputation and female rivalries in a humorous, even mocking manner that would have been culturally inappropriate in the presence of men. The use of my video camera gave the women an additional impulse to 'perform', even more than without the camera. They knew from earlier occasions that we could later watch the video footage on my small camera screen. This provided them with the opportunity to concentrate on acting their roles, while enjoying the performance and jokes afterwards.

Both Fabian (1990) and Barber (2000) highlight the wealth in symbolism and meaning of popular theatre in Africa. This also applies to the role-play that, despite its rough and improvisational character, entails a number of current themes, such as Mbororo exploitation, their nascent claims to civil rights, as well as their ethos of self-control and restraint (*pulaaku*). As the play is addressed to an audience familiar with Mbororo culture and society, it draws on a shared cultural transcript to convey its message and irony. Much of the action portrayed is neither realistic nor culturally acceptable, and turns the play into a satire that ridicules established cultural norms.

The role-play starts with a common situation: a Mbororo woman selling milk to a Hausa or Grassfields customer. The argument that Mbororo milk is diluted with water and not very fresh is a popular conviction and often used as a bargaining strategy. The scene then evolves into a more unusual situation with Madujo's calabash being stolen – an act, repeated in the third scene, which is rather unlikely but here serves as a plot device. Madujo's warning to take the thief to court draws on Ballotiral's paralegal programme, instructing Mbororo women and men on their civil rights, and brings it to a putative practical level.

In scene two Madujo introduces herself as a visitor from Senegal. The Fulɓe of West Africa here are seen as more 'traditional' than the Mbororo in northwest Cameroon who have settled and diversified their economic activities (cf. Pelican 1999). The Mbororo from Senegal are portrayed as being pure pastoralists who exclusively live on animal products, including the sales of milk. Madujo's dancing and her blessings represent assumed pre-Islamic practices, which the Mbororo in northwest Cameroon have abandoned. Her licking the calabash spoon is a sign of her lack of *pulaaku* (sense of shame) and her uncultured life. The image of Madujo thus represents the opposite of how Mbororo women see themselves. At the same time, it reflects the Mbororo past and their cultural heritage. The character Madujo is a parody of both the ideal herdswoman and the popular stereotype of the Mbororo as backwards, uneducated and nomadic cattle pastoralists.

Scene one: Madujo (Fulfulde for 'old woman') heads off to sell milk. She is called by a customer who wants to taste her milk and asks if it has been diluted with water. Madujo gets annoyed at the customer's attempt to beat the price, but finally agrees to sell her some milk. A second customer distracts Madujo's attention and her calabash is stolen. She holds the interrupter responsible and threatens to take the case to court. She finally regains her possessions, but the milk is gone.

Scene two: Madujo introduces herself as a Fulɓe woman from Senegal. A local woman wants to give her seeds of maize and vegetables to plant, but Madujo declines. She points out that she lives only on milk and does not eat maize. Also, her family has cattle but no chickens. She shows her decorated calabash spoon and boasts that she sold a cow to buy it. She then scrapes the milk remains off her calabash and licks her spoon, a behaviour the others find disgraceful. Moreover, she begins to dance publicly and to utter superstitious blessings.

Scene three: Madujo again leaves to sell milk. She meets customers but cannot understand their language (Pidgin English). She is robbed. While the thieves make fun of her, a friend comes to her aid. The friend wants to attack the thieves, but is held back. In the meantime, Madujo has grabbed a stick and threatens the thieves. They return Madujo's possessions. Her friend is so upset that she breaks into tears, and is eventually consoled by her neighbour. The performers and audience are highly amused and the play ends in laughter.

Figures 5.6–5.10. Sippoygo (selling milk), role-play of the Mbororo women's group of Chako, 8 April 2001 (original approximately 20 minutes). Video footage/photos: Michaela Pelican.[15]

In the third scene the participants return to the issue of milk sales and Mbororo women's assumed mistreatment. Madujo's property is again stolen, but this time a different solution is suggested: Madujo and her friend become violent and attack the thieves with a stick. While I have never witnessed Mbororo women being aggressive in public, the suggestion is not implausible, as it is said that both Mbororo men and women are well accustomed to using a herding staff, be it as a walking stick, a herding tool or a weapon of defence. In the end, Madujo's friend is overwhelmed by her emotions and bursts into tears. The audience responds with laughter to this scene, as bursting into tears is unthinkable behaviour for an elderly woman in Mbororo society, where emotions and pain are generally concealed, even in the face of birth and death. This, to me, is the most intriguing moment of the play, as it renders palpable the imaginative capacity of its performers as well as their readiness to make fun of themselves and their culture, and to challenge cultural norms.

The Mbororo women's role-play reflected on processes of social change, namely their contemporary reality as a settled, Islamized, agro-pastoral people (as opposed to their nomadic past) and their growing political self-confidence as promoted by NGO programmes. A central feature of the performance was its playful, humorous quality. Unlike the Ballotiral role-play on farmer-herder conflict, this performance was not aimed at being educational but entertaining. Moreover, it was of a more hypothetical character, as the women experimented with common elements drawn from their experience, sometimes exaggerating, sometimes inverting them. The women's role-play beautifully illustrates what Madison (2006) calls symbolic reality: it represents both Mbororo women's experience of social change as well as their humorous reflections on it. Their role-play thus clearly speaks to the inseparability of fiction and non-fiction, a quality that also applies to my writing about it.

Video Recording Role-Plays

In the two role-plays chosen for this chapter, my role was not one of actor or facilitator but of spectator and camerawoman. It would be wrong, however, to believe that my presence and action (video recording) had no impact on the actors' performance or choice of subject. It did, but in context-specific ways. Moreover, by occupying the role of camerawoman, I became a collaborator and participant, thus rendering the performance an interactive and collaborative project.

The Ballotiral role-play *Farmer-Grazier Conflict* took place six months into my fieldwork, when I had established a good working relationship with the Ballotiral staff and was frequently invited to join their activities in the neighbouring town of Nkambe. In this case, my role was limited to camerawoman, as I did not participate in the scripting or the rehearsals of the role-play but only joined them the day before the workshop. The role-play was based on a script developed and performed at earlier occasions by members of MBOSCUDA, some of whom had been integrated into the Ballotiral programme. While it was part of the NGO's performative repertoire, it had never been videotaped. My proposal to record the role-play was welcomed by the Ballotiral staff. The video documentation was intended for my own research but was also shared with the Ballotiral staff, so they could use it for their own purposes. My role as camerawoman placed me in an active relationship with the performers and workshop organizers, and gave me the opportunity to observe not only the performance but also the audience.

Unlike the Ballotiral role-play performed in a public context, the role-play *Sippoygo* arose in the intimate space of a Mbororo woman's house. By addressing their performance to me and my research interests, the women assumed a participatory approach, as defined by Chalfen (2011); i.e. they constructed their own storyline and conveyed what they wanted to communicate to me in the manner they wished. As my video camera was at hand, I seized the opportunity to record the play with the women's approval. The camera not only stimulated their performance, but also helped to elicit further information. Immediately after the performance, we jointly watched the recording on the small camera screen. Excited to see themselves performing, the women discussed the fictitious characters and commented on the stereotypes and symbolisms involved. This elicitation process was crucial to arrive at the role-play's interpretation presented in this chapter.

The equipment I used during my research was relatively basic and editing facilities were limited.[16] The recordings were on mini-DVs, which we copied to VHS tapes to be screened on old-fashioned television sets. This was also the technical set-up available for the Misaje Film Festival, which I co-organized with my research collaborators and a Ballotiral colleague. The event included public screenings of a cross-section of my audio-visual material, which were followed by feedback sessions. The event drew a large audience – not least because of using film as the medium of dissemination. It generated new data on the subject of conflict and ethnicity and contributed to popularizing my research (Pelican and Ngeh 2006).

Throughout my research, audio-visual devices (photo and video camera) played an important role in recording and eliciting information. They were part and parcel of my research tools, sometimes operated by myself, sometimes by my collaborators. Yet visual recording devices were not new to this environment but formed part of the 'local visual culture' (cf. Pink 2013), more so for the photo camera than the video camera, but the latter also gained ground during the period of my research and in the subsequent years.

The presence of the video camera to document cultural events and role-plays gave these performances a new or additional quality. The actors were definitely well aware of and at times amazed, even excited, at the idea of being recorded. This was clearly expressed during the Misaje Film Festival, when participants spoke on camera about their responses to being filmed, seeing themselves and

Figures 5.11–5.12. Misaje Film Festival, 27 October 2001. Photos: Michaela Pelican (2001).

others on screen. While they were used to watching Hollywood/Bollywood blockbusters in the town's privately run video hall (a simple room equipped with a television, video deck and benches), the experience of being an actor in a documentary or role-play and the potential of the film to be globally disseminated opened up a wholly new perspective (Pelican and Ngeh 2006).

While local demand for the video recordings of the cultural events and role-plays existed, there were no functional facilities for their conservation and distribution. The VHS tapes I left with trusted individuals and the Ballotiral staff quickly deteriorated due to local climatic and technical conditions. Upon my return to Germany, I opted for electronically editing and storing the audio-visual data, part of which is accessible online.[17] It is important to note, however, that the audio-visual material is not self-explanatory, as it was primarily collected for research purposes. To local audiences and the anthropologist familiar with the cultural and linguistic context, the edited video documents may well make sense. But to non-specialists, the visual data cannot speak for themselves and need to be embedded in textual analyses, as exemplified in this chapter.

Integrating Audio-Visual and Performative Data in Ethnographic Writing

In the following, I wish to highlight the benefits of using role-playing and video documentation in anthropological research, but also to discuss some of the challenges we face in integrating audio-visual data and their analysis in our ethnographic writing.

The methods I understand to be quasi-experimental often include collaborative and participatory elements, which I believe is one of their particular strengths. Providing the opportunity to our collaborators to express their views and experiences in different ways, to bring to the fore the subjects they consider relevant, and to actively intervene in our research, may produce surprising and illuminating insights. Moreover, it renders the research a shared enterprise from which both sides – the researcher and the researched – may derive pleasure and knowledge.

A particular advantage of using role-play in the research of conflict and ethnicity lies in the nature of drama and performance. Drama as a theatrical form uses the expression of conflict as a way of communicating its content. It demands condensing the complexity of everyday life and elaborating on characters and storylines. Furthermore, a staged performance allows for mockery, criticism and the candid expression of conflicting views and practices, as it has no immediate effects on actual social relations. Some of the ways in which these qualities of drama may be fruitfully exploited have been illustrated in the above examples.

Video recording role-plays and cultural events adds an additional, media dimension to the staging of cultural conflict. As my analysis has shown, the production of still and moving images goes hand in hand with participants' awareness that production for public media starts already at this early point. This insight leads us to critically question the idea of observational methods of visual anthropology, as propounded for example by Meyer and Schareika (2009) in their article on neoclassical fieldwork and the microscopic analysis of social events (cf. Heiss and Pelican 2009). I believe that anthropologists working with audio-visual methods should be aware of the methods' collaborative and participatory qualities and test their usefulness in regard to specific research themes and contexts.

The difficulties related to quasi-experimental methods often do not arise in the process of research, but when faced with the question of how to incorporate their content and findings in our analysis and writing. These difficulties are of a formal and conceptual nature. Firstly, anthropology is a discipline of words. Only a few anthropology departments and publishers encourage non-textual – for example, audio-visual or performative – forms of representation. In this regard, Günther Schlee and the Max Planck Institute for Social Anthropology in Halle have been exemplary in promoting alternative publication formats. Secondly, the technicalities of professionally archiving video files, and of combining textual and audio-visual data by means of accompanying websites or hypermedia, are a major challenge to many of us. Here, recent investments in the development of sustainable data archiving systems by research institutions, universities and funding agencies may, in the long run, help to resolve the problem.

More demanding than the formal difficulties, however, is the conceptual challenge of how to analyse and present a performance in view of a specific research question. Several authors have centred their analyses on selected performances, developing the themes therein. Fabian's *Power and Performance* (1990), for example, engages with a single play to explore the subject of chiefly power as well as the process of translating a proverb into a play. Similarly, *The Generation of Plays* by Barber (2000), while focusing on the work of a travelling theatre company, delves into a plethora of themes, including gender, language, politics and tradition, as well as rapid social and economic change. These authors highlight the wealth of symbolism and the multilayered meanings entailed in performance. However, when approaching audio-visual and performance data with a defined research topic in mind, different challenges emerge. The skill then lies in reducing complexity, eluding loose ends, carving out sequences of interest and rendering them comprehensible to an audience unfamiliar with the performance's underlying cultural transcript. The above case studies illustrate this process.

Conclusion

Being a researcher at the Max Planck Institute for Social Anthropology in Halle provided me, and many others, with the intellectual freedom and institutional support to experiment with different conceptual approaches, research methods, ethnographic genres and publication formats.

My experiences of working with performative and audio-visual methods have also shaped my later work. For example, in researching transnational relations of Cameroonian migrants in Gabon and the United Arab Emirates, I used video-letters to study migrants' communication with relatives back home and the quality of their relationship (Pelican 2008b, 2014; Pelican and MacKinnon 2009). In my recent research on African migration to China, I have worked with the Chinese documentary photographer Li Dong to study how African migrants have been represented in the Chinese public and how they respond to these representations (Pelican 2014; Pelican and Li 2017). My interest in audio-visual methods has also trickled down to my classroom teaching, resulting, for example, in the production of a podcast series as part of the practical research seminar 'Research, Action and Art'.[18] Importantly, I have learned to cherish publication formats off the beaten path. They allow for integrating different forms of reflection, such as academic, personal and photographic accounts (e.g. Pelican and Steinberger 2017), and help us reach out to audiences beyond academia.

While quasi-experimental methods and alternative publication formats may come with their own challenges, I believe that they significantly contribute to extending and refining the anthropologists' methodological toolkit.

Michaela Pelican is Professor of Social and Cultural Anthropology at the University of Cologne, principal investigator of the Global South Studies Centre Cologne and speaker of the international research unit 'The Production and Reproduction of Social Inequalities: Global Contexts and Concepts of Labour Exploitation'. She has conducted extensive fieldwork in Cameroon, the United Arab Emirates and China. She has published widely on South-South migration, entrepreneurship, forced migration, intersectionality, ethnicity, the indigenous rights movement, farmer-herder conflict, friendship and witchcraft. She has used audio-visual methods in much of her research, and has produced documentary shorts and photo exhibitions.

Notes

1. The first diary is a compilation of field notes on the topic of Fulɓe pastoralist migration from Sudan into Ethiopia, extracted from Schlee's original field diaries of research trips between 1996 and 2002. The second is the Ethiopian diary that contains thematically mixed field notes from three research trips, undertaken in 2001 and 2002.

2. Günther Schlee, ed., *Field Notes and Research Projects (Series)*, Max Planck Institute for Social Anthropology, Department 'Integration and Conflict'. Retrieved 18 June 2018 from http://www.eth.mpg.de/3346002/series_fieldnotes.

3. Information about the history of role-playing and theatre for development in the North West Region will be provided later in this chapter.

4. Anthropologists working on performance have used different terms to denote their field of studies, including anthropology of performance (Turner 1988), performance ethnography (Conquergood 1982, 2006; Madison 2005) and anthropology of popular culture (Barber 1997a; Fabian 1998). In this chapter, I will use the term performance anthropology to encompass these closely related strands.

5. For example, *Jaguar* (1957), *Moi, un Noir* (1958), *Petit à petit* (1970), *Cocorico monsieur Poulet* (1974).

6. For an overview of different genres of popular theatre in Africa, see Kerr (1995).

7. Compilations of Theatre for Development in different parts of Africa are provided, for example, by Banham et al. (1999); Byam (1999); Eyoh (1991).

8. These include manuals on empowering women through theatre; theatre, democracy and human rights; land use management; children's theatre for environmental education (retrieved 8 August 2012 from http://cameroonperformance.blogspot.de/2012/01/).

9. Among the plays that have been televised is a set of role-plays on participatory governance entitled *Gomen na We: People Talking . . . People Doing*, which was realized in 2004 and distributed on VCD.

10. The seminar included a number of instructional speeches by administrators and resource persons, a short role-play by the Ballotiral drama group, general discussions and the formulation of resolutions. More than 60 per cent of the 103 workshop participants were officials representing government services and nongovernmental organizations, roughly 25 per cent were representatives of the Mbororo community, and 15 per cent represented local Grassfields communities.

11. A more comprehensive analysis of the role-play is found in Pelican (2006: 227–41).

12. A succinctly edited version (2:46 minutes) of the role-play is accessible at http://www.michaela-pelican.com/research_media.php#theatre4development.

13. As Schlee (2004) has argued with regard to Fulɓe in different parts of Africa, carving out complementary ecological niches has been an effective strategy to create a peaceful environment despite potentially antagonistic relations between farmers and herders. While some Mbororo herders in Sudan have resorted to extreme forms of cattle nomadism to avoid competition over pastures with Arabs (Dereje and Schlee 2009), sedentary Fulɓe in West Africa have developed systems of shared land use by farmers and herders, similar to the alliance farming promoted by MBOSCUDA (see also Dafinger and Pelican 2006; Diallo, Guichard and Schlee 2000).

14. Within Mbororo society, the singing and dancing of adult women is limited to specific occasions, such as marriage and child naming ceremonies, and is addressed to an exclusively female audience. Storytelling is a leisure activity during a typical evening, and is performed in the family-nexus, from which adult men are normally excluded.

15. A succinctly edited version (4:27 minutes) of the role-play is accessible at http://www.michaela-pelican.com/research_media.php#theatre4development.

16. Village-wide electrification has only recently been established in Misaje. At the time of my research (2000–2002) we had to rely on generators to work with audio-visual equipment. The actual editing of the footage was done back in Germany during a return visit in 2001 and after completion of the fieldwork.

17. Part of the audio-visual data is accessible at http://www.michaela-pelican.com/research_media.php#theatre4development.

18. The podcast series is available on the website of the Department of Cultural and Social Anthropology of the University of Cologne: http://ethnologie.phil-fak.uni-koeln.de/content.php?kid=99.

References

Asong, Valentin, Juliana A. Anchang and Martin Shu. 2015. *Conflicts over Land and Pasture in North West Cameroon: Listening to the Voices of Farmers and Grazers*. Pan African Institute for Development in West Africa (PAID-WA).
Awasom, Nicodemus. 1984. 'The Hausa and Fulani in the Bamenda Grasslands 1903–1960', Ph. dissertation. Yaoundé: University of Yaoundé.
Bang, Henry N. and Roland A. Balgah. 2022. 'The Ramification of Cameroon's Anglophone Crisis: Conceptual Analysis of a Looming "Complex Disaster Emergency"', *Journal of International Humanitarian Action* 7(6). https://doi.org/10.1186/s41018-022-00114-1.
Banham, Martin, James Gibbs and Femi Osofian (eds). 1999. *African Theatre in Development*. Oxford: James Currey.
Banks, Marcus. 2007. *Using Visual Data in Qualitative Research*. London: SAGE.
Banks, Marcus and David Zeitlyn. 2015. *Visual Methods in Social Research*, 2nd edn. London: Sage.
Barber, Karin (ed.). 1997a. *Readings in African Popular Culture*. Bloomington: Indiana University Press.
———. 1997b. 'Preliminary Notes on Audiences in Africa', *Africa* 67(3): 347–62.
———. 2000. *The Generation of Plays: Yoruba Popular Life in Theatre*. Bloomington: Indiana University Press.
Boal, Augusto. 1979. *Theatre of the Oppressed*. New York: Urizen.
Bondanini, Francesco B. 2017. 'Migration on the Borders of Europe: The Case of Melilla', in Michaela Pelican and Sophie Steinberger (eds), 'Melilla: Perspectives on a Border Town', *Kölner Arbeitspapiere zur Ethnologie* 6. Cologne: University of Cologne, Department of Social and Cultural Anthropology, pp. 71–79.
Boon, Richard and Jane Plastow (eds). 2004. *Theatre and Empowerment: Community Drama on the World Stage*. Cambridge: Cambridge University Press.
Boutrais, Jean. 1995/96. *Hautes terres d'élevage au Cameroun*. Paris: ORSTOM.
———. 2002. 'Nderkaaku: La folle jeunesse chez les Foulbés de l'Adamaoua', *Journal des Africanistes* 72(1): 165–81.
Breitinger, Eckhard (ed.). 1994. *Theatre for Development – Théâtre au service du développement*. Rossdorf: TZ-Verlagsgesellschaft.
Bukari, Kaderi Noagah and Nikolaus Schareika. 2015. 'Stereotypes, Prejudices and Exclusion of Fulani Pastoralists in Ghana', *Pastoralism Research, Policy and Practice* 5(20): 1–12.
Butake, Bole. 1991. 'Conscientizing the Urban Masses', in Hansel N. Eyoh (ed.), *Beyond the Theatre*. Bonn: German Foundation for International Development (DSE) and Education, Science and Documentation Centre (ZED), pp. 8–23.
———. 2001. 'Children's Theatre for Environmental Education: Helvetas Cameroon Trainers Manual'. Unpublished manuscript..
Byam, Dale L. 1999. *Community in Motion: Theatre for Development in Africa*. Westport, CT and London: Bergin and Garvey.
Chalfen, Richard. 2011. 'Differentiating Practices of Participatory Visual Media Production', in Eric Margolis and Luc Pauwels (eds), *SAGE Handbook of Visual Research Methods*. London: SAGE, pp. 186–200.
Chilver, E.M. 1989. 'Women Cultivators, Cows and Cash-Crops: Phyllis Kaberry's Women of the Grassfields Revisited', in Peter Geschiere and Piet Konings (eds), *Proceedings/Contributions of a Conference on the Historical Economy of Cameroon: Historical Perspectives, 1–4 June 1988*. Leiden: Centre of African Studies, pp. 383–421.
Chilver, E. and Phyllis Kaberry. 1967. *Traditional Bamenda: The Pre-Colonial History and Ethnography of the Bamenda Grassfields*. Buea, Cameroon: Government Printer.

Conquergood, Dwight. 1982. 'Communication as Performance: Dramaturgical Dimensions of Everyday Life', in John I. Sisco (ed.), *The Jensen Lectures: Contemporary Communication Studies*. Tampa: University of South Florida Press, pp. 24–43.

———. 2006. 'Rethinking Ethnography: Towards a Critical Cultural Politics', in Soyini D. Madison and Judith Hamera (eds), *The SAGE Handbook of Performance Studies*. Thousand Oaks, CA: SAGE, pp. 351–49.

Dafinger, Andreas. 2004. *Anthropologie des Raums: Soziale und räumliche Ordnung im Süden Burkina Fasos*. Cologne: Köppe.

Dafinger, Andreas and Michaela Pelican. 2006. 'Sharing or Dividing the Land? Land Rights and Herder-Farmer Relations in a Comparative Perspective', *Canadian Journal of African Studies* 40(1): 127–51.

Dereje Feyissa and Günther Schlee. 2009. 'Mbororo (Fulbe) Migrations from Sudan into Ethiopia', in Günther Schlee and Elisabeth E. Watson (eds), *Changing Identifications and Alliances in North-East Africa, Volume II: Sudan, Uganda and the Ethiopia-Sudan Borderlands*. New York and Oxford: Berghahn, pp. 157–78.

Diallo, Youssouf, Martine Guichard and Günther Schlee. 2000. 'Quelques aspects comparatifs', in Youssouf Diallo and Günther Schlee (eds), *L'ethnicité peule dans des contextes nouveaux*. Paris: Karthala, pp. 235–55.

Doho, Gilbert. 2006. *People Theatre and Grassroots Empowerment in Cameroon*, trans. M. Lathers. Trenton, NJ: Africa World Press.

Duni, Jeidoh, Robert Fon, Sam Hickey and Nuhu Salihu. 2009. 'Exploring a Political Approach to Rights-based Development in North-West Cameroon: From Rights and Marginality to Citizenship and Justice', *Global Development Institute Working Paper Series 10409*. Manchester: GDI, University of Manchester.

Eyoh, Hansel N. (ed.). 1991. *Beyond the Theatre: Interviews Conducted by Hansel Ndumbe Eyoh with Bole Butake, Stephen Chifunyise, Kemani Gecau, Andrew Horn, Daniel Labonne, Sophia Lokko, Penina Mlama, Dickson Mwansa, Ngugi wa Mirii, Nugi wa Thiongo, and Articles by Tar Ahura, Bole Butake and Guarav Desai*. Bonn: German Foundation for International Development (DSE) and Education, Science and Documentation Centre (ZED).

Fabian, Johannes. 1990. *Power and Performance: Ethnographic Explorations through Proverbial Wisdom and Theatre in Shaba, Zaire*. Madison: University of Wisconsin Press.

———. 1998. *Moments of Freedom: Anthropology and Popular Culture*. Charlottesville, VA: University of Virginia Press.

Freire, Paulo. 1970. *Pedagogy of the Oppressed*. New York: Herder and Herder.

Grandits, Hannes (ed.). 2010. *Family, Kinship and State in Contemporary Europe, Volume 1: The Century of Welfare: Eight Countries*. Frankfurt and New York: Campus.

Grätz, Tilo. 1997. *Contes de Gouandé*. Manuel de lecture en Biali. Campagne de Post-Alphabétisation, avec le soutien de Tagali Yambouali; Saré Dacosa Sahgui; Bampo Théophile; Sambieni Moussa; Sambieni Séraphin. Tanguiéta.

———. 2010. 'Soziokulturelle Experimente in der ethnologischen Feldforschung', Presentation at the Conference *Soziologische vs. ethnologische Ethnographie: Zur Belastbarkeit und Perspektive einer Unterscheidung*, 22 May 2010. Berlin: Humboldt University, Institute of European Ethnology.

———. 2014. *Technologische Dramen: Radiokulturen und Medienwandel in Benin (Westafrika)*. Bielefeld: Transcript.

Harshbarger, Camilla. 1995. *Farmer-Herder Conflict and State Legitimacy in Cameroon*. Gainesville: University of Florida.

Heady, Patrick. 2014. 'Thinking Scientifically about Kinship: Towards an Axiomatic Formulation of Ethnographic Insights', *Max Planck Institute for Social Anthropology Working Paper* No. 158. Retrieved from http://www.eth.mpg.de/pubs/wps/pdf/mpi-eth-working-paper-0158.

Heady, Patrick and Martin. Kohli (eds). 2010. *Family, Kinship and State in Contemporary Europe, Volume 3: Perspectives on Theory and Policy*. Frankfurt and New York: Campus.
Heady, Patrick and Peter Schweitzer (eds). 2010. *Family, Kinship and State in Contemporary Europe, Volume 2: The View from Below: Nineteen Localities*. Frankfurt and New York: Campus.
Heiss, Jan Patrick and Michaela Pelican. 2009. 'Kommentar', *Zeitschrift für Ethnologie* 134: 114–17.
Henley, Paul. 2010. *The Adventure of the Real: Jean Rouch and the Craft of Ethnographic Cinema*. Chicago: University of Chicago Press.
Hickey, Sam. 2002. 'Transnational NGDOs and Participatory Forms of Rights-Based Development: Converging with the Local Politics of Citizenship in Cameroon', *Journal of International Development* 14(6): 841–57.
———. 2011. '"Hometown Associations" as Social Movements for Citizenship: A Case Study from Northwest Cameroon', *Africa Today* 57(4): 29–47.
Jiménez-Tovar, Soledad. 2016. 'The Anthropologist as a Mushroom: Notes from a PhD Research Project in Central Asia', *Max Planck Institute for Social Anthropology, Department 'Integration and Conflict' Field Notes and Research Projects* XIV. Retrieved from http://www.eth.mpg.de/pubs/series_fieldnotes/vol0014.html.
Kerr, David. 1995. *African Popular Theatre: From Pre-Colonial Times to the Present Day*. London: James Currey.
Kirby, Jon and Gong Shu. 2005. 'Culture-Drama: A New Enactment Genre for Peacebuilding', in David Millar et al. (eds), *African Knowledges and Sciences: Understanding and Supporting the Ways of Knowing in Sub-Saharan Africa*. Leusden: Compas, pp. 149–61.
———. 2010. 'Re-Reconciling Culture-Based Conflicts with "Culture-Drama"', in Eva Leveton (ed.), *Healing Collective Trauma Using Sociodrama and Drama Therapy*. New York: Springer, pp. 207–33.
Köhler, Florian 2017. 'The Sedentarization of Dwelling: Continuity and Change in the Habitat of Fulɓe Woɗaaɓe Pastoralists and Urban Migrants in Niger. Text and Photo Essays', *Max Planck Institute for Social Anthropology, Department 'Integration and Conflict' Field Notes and Research Projects* XV. Retrieved from http://www.eth.mpg.de/pubs/series_fieldnotes/vol0015.html.
Lassiter, Luke E. 2005. 'Collaborative Ethnography and Public Anthropology', *Current Anthropology* 46(1): 83–106.
Madison, Soyini. 2005. *Critical Ethnography: Methods, Ethics, and Performance*. Thousand Oaks, CA: SAGE.
———. 2006. 'Staging Fieldwork/Performing Human Rights', in Madison Soyini and Judith Hamera (eds), *The SAGE Handbook of Performance Studies*. Thousand Oaks, CA: SAGE, pp. 397–418.
———. 2010. *Acts of Activism: Human Rights as Radical Performance*. Cambridge: Cambridge University Press.
Mda, Zakes. 1993. *When People Play People: Development Communication through Theatre*. Johannesburg: Witwatersrand University Press.
Meyer, Chris and Nikolaus Schareika. 2009. 'Neoklassische Feldforschung: Die mikroskopische Untersuchung sozialer Ereignisse als ethnographische Methode', *Zeitschrift für Ethnologie* 134(1): 79–102.
Mlama, Penina. 1991. *Culture and Development: The Popular Theatre Approach in Africa*. Uppsala: Nordiska Afrikainstitutet.
Nchinda, Valentine, Tata Ijang, Marcellus Che, Shidiki Abubakar and Chi Napoleon. 2016. *In Search of Common Ground: The Farmer Grazer Conflict in the North West Region of Cameroon – Midterm Evaluation Report*. Bamenda: MBOSCUDA.
Njeuma, Martin and Nicodemus Awasom. 1990. 'The Fulani and the Political Economy of the Bamenda Grasslands, 1940–1960', *Paideuma* 36: 217–33.
Nkwi, Paul N. and Jean-Pierre Warnier. 1982. *Elements for a History of the Western Grassfields*. Yaoundé: University of Yaoundé Press.

Ottiger, Nadja. 1996. *Die Ökonomie der Geschlechter: Kooperation und Konflikte bei den Mmen im Kameruner Grasland*. Zurich: Argonaut Verlag.
Parkin, David. 1996. 'Introduction: The Power of the Bizarre', in David Parkin, Lionel Caplan and Humprey Fisher (eds), *The Politics of Cultural Performance*. London: Berghahn, pp. xv–xl.
Pelican, Michaela. 1999. *Die Arbeit der Mbororo-Frauen früher und heute: Eine Studie zum Wandel der sozio-ökonomischen Situation semi-nomadischer Fulbe-Frauen in Nordwest Kamerun*. Bayreuth: Universitätsbibliothek Bayreuth.
———. 2004. 'Im Schatten der Schlachtviehmärkte: Milchwirtschaft der Mbororo in Nordwestkamerun', in Günther Schlee (ed.), *Ethnizität und Markt: Zur ethnischen Struktur von Viehmärkten in Westafrika*. Cologne: Köppe, pp. 131–58.
———. 2006. *Getting along in the Grassfields: Interethnic Relations and Identity Politics in Northwest Cameroon*. Halle (Saale): Universitäts- und Landesbibliothek Sachsen-Anhalt.
———. 2008a. 'Mbororo Claims to Regional Citizenship and Minority Status in Northwest Cameroon', *Africa* 78(4): 540–60.
———. 2012. 'Friendship among Pastoral Fulbe in Northwest Cameroon', *African Study Monographs* 33(3): 165–88.
——— (ed.). 2014. 'Baohan Street: An African Community in Guangzhou – Documentary Photographs by Li Dong', *Kölner Arbeitspapiere zur Ethnologie* 4. Cologne: University of Cologne, Department of Social and Cultural Anthropology. Retrieved 18 June 2018 from http://kups.ub.uni-koeln.de/5782/.
———. 2015. *Masks and Staffs: Identity Politics in the Cameroon Grassfields*. Oxford and New York: Berghahn.
Pelican, Michaela and Li Dong. 2017. 'Photo Essay: Baohan Street: An African Community in Guangzhou', in Dorothy L. Hodgson and Judith Byfield (eds), *Global Africa*. Oakland: University of California Press, pp. 193–201.
Pelican, Michaela and Billy MacKinnon. 2009. *Face to Face: Synopsis and Characters*. Retrieved 18 June 2018 from http://www.michaela-pelican.com/research_media.php#face2face.
Pelican, Michaela and Jonathan Ngeh. 2006. 'Misaje Film Festival 26–28th October 2001', in Michaela Pelican, *Getting Along in the Grassfields: Interethnic Relations and Identity Politics in Northwest Cameroon*, Appendix A. Halle (Saale): Universitäts- und Landesbibliothek Sachsen-Anhalt, pp. 486–522.
Pelican, Michaela, Kim Schumann, Sina Plücken and David Drew. 2022. 'Mbororo under Attack: Extreme Speech and Violence in the Anglophone Conflict in Cameroon'. *ABI Working Paper* No. 21. Freiburg: Arnold Bergstraesser Institute. https://www.arnold-bergstraesser.de/projekte/cameroon-legacies-of-violence-and-prospects-for-peace-new-impulses-from-research.
Pelican, Michaela and Sophie Steinberger (eds). 2017. 'Melilla: Perspectives on a Border Town', *Kölner Arbeitspapiere zur Ethnologie* 6. Cologne: University of Cologne, Department of Social and Cultural Anthropology. Retrieved from https://kups.ub.uni-koeln.de/7700/.
Pink, Sarah. 2013. *Doing Visual Ethnography*, 3rd edn. London: SAGE.
———. 2015. *Doing Sensory Ethnography*, 2nd edn. London: SAGE.
Pommerolle, Marie-Emmanuelle and Hans de Marie Heungoup. 2017. 'The "Anglophone crisis": A Tale of the Cameroonian Postcolony', *African Affairs* 116(464): 526–38.
Riesman, Paul. 1977. *Freedom in Fulani Social Life*. Chicago: University of Chicago Press.
Rouch, Jean. 1974. 'The Camera and Man', *Studies in the Anthropology of Visual Communication* 1(1): 37–44.
Salihu, Nuhu and Sam Hickey. 2005. 'Paralegal Extension in North-West Cameroon', *Participatory Learning and Action* 52: 12–18.
Samba, Ngufor E. 2005. 'Women in Theatre for Development in Cameroon: Participation, Contributions and Limitations', *Bayreuth African Studies* 74.

Schlee, Günther. 2004. 'Einleitung', in Günther Schlee (ed.), *Ethnizität und Markt: Zur ethnischen Struktur von Viehmärkten in Westafrika*. Cologne: Köppe, pp. 1–10.

———. 2008. *Ethiopian Diary 2001–2002 / Tagebuch Äthiopien 2001–2002*. Retrieved 2 June 2018 from http://www.eth.mpg.de/subsites/schlee_tagebuch/index.html.

———. 2013. *Fulbe Pastoralists in Eastern Sudan and Western Ethiopia: A Documentation*. Retrieved 2 June 2018 from http://web.eth.mpg.de/subsites/schlee_diary_02/index.html.

Takem, John T. 2005. 'Theatre and Environmental Education in Cameroon', *Bayreuth African Studies* 76.

Turner, Victor. 1974. *Dramas, Fields and Metaphors: Symbolic Action in Human Society*. Ithaca, NY: Cornell University Press.

———. 1982. *From Ritual to Theatre: The Human Seriousness of Play*. New York: Performing Arts Journal.

———. 1988: *The Anthropology of Performance*. New York: Performing Arts Journal.

Virtanen, Tea. 2003. 'Performance and Performativity in Pastoral Fulbe Culture', PhD dissertation. Helsinki: Helsinki University.

Ziker, John and Michael Schnegg. 2005. 'Food Sharing at Meals: Kinship, Reciprocity, and Clustering in the Taimyr Autonomous Okrug, Northern Russia', *Human Nature* 16(2): 178–210.

Zoettl, Peter A. 2012. '"Participatory Video" as a Means of Reflection and Self-Reflection about the Image and Identity of Re-Emerging Indigenous Groups in North-Eastern Brazil', *Anthropology in Action* 19(2): 17–26.

Visual Documents

Beyer, Judith and Roman Knee. 2007. *The Wall. Ethnographic Documentary. Talas Province, Kyrgyzstan*, video recording. Retrieved 2 June 2018 from https://youtu.be/f_dZSIRQzTk.

Gomen na We: People Talking . . . People Doing: A Film on Participatory and Transparent Local Governance, 2004. Kwasen Gwangwa'a, Helvetas and CRTV, 2004.

Pelican, Michaela. 2001a. *Farmer-Herder Conflict*, Role-Play of the Ballotiral Staff. Nkambe, video recording, hdl:10681/00-0000-0000-0000-0025-C. Retrieved 2 June 2018, http://www.michaela-pelican.com/films/conflict_roleplay.mp4.

———. 2001b. *Sippoygo (Selling Milk)*, Role-Play of the Mbororo Women's Group of Chako, video recording, hdl:10681/00-0000-0000-0000-0023-9. Retrieved 2 June 2018 from http://www.michaela-pelican.com/films/milksale_roleplay.mp4.

———. 2008b. *Face to Face: Cameroon – Gabon – Dubai – Geneva*, documentary short. Retrieved 18 June 2018 from http://www.michaela-pelican.com/research_media.php#face2face_film.

Pelican, Michaela and Judith Orland. 2002. *Getting along in the Grassfields: Aspects of Village Life in Misaje (North West Cameroon)*, documentary film, 38 min., English subtitles, hdl:10681/00-0000-0000-0000-002A-0. Retrieved 18 June 2018 from http://www.michaela-pelican.com/research_media.php#more.

Rudolf, Markus. 2010. *Coopération au Développement dans un conflit oublié = Entwicklungszusammenarbeit in einem vergessenen Konflikt*, DVD. Max Planck Institute for Social Anthropology, Department 'Integration and Conflict'.

———. 2011. *'We Are Tired of Running Away'– Voices in a Forgotten Conflict ('Wir sind es leid wegzulaufen' – Stimmen in einem vergessenen Konflikt*, DVD. Max Planck Institute for Social Anthropology, Department 'Integration and Conflict'.

PART II
Conflict and Identification, Interests and Integration

CHAPTER 6

THE TOPOGRAPHY OF TERRORISM
Between Local Conflicts and Global Jihad

SOPHIE ROCHE

Introduction

Gulmurod Halimov (Gulmurod Khalimov) left his apartment on 23 April 2015 and promised to be back in three days.[1] Yet he did not return; instead, he and ten other persons disappeared for the next few weeks. It was not until 28 May 2015 that he announced in a video message directly from Syria that he would return to Tajikistan in the name of the jihad. Halimov, born in 1975, had belonged to the presidential guard during the civil war of 1992–1997. Over the years he had moved up through the ranks and been given command of OMON (the special forces unit) within the Ministry of the Interior. He had eight children and, according to Ozodi (Radio Free Europe), had become a practising Muslim in 2001 and devoted himself to studying the history of Islam. The Ozodi report further detailed: 'The US State Department declared that from 2003 to 2014 Gulmurod Halimov, commander of the Ministry of Internal Affairs OMON special forces of Tajikistan, had participated five times in innovative counterterrorism exercises' (ozodi.com).

The Halimov episode is particularly interesting for two reasons. First, here was someone who, having been trained in counterterrorism, became a terrorist himself, which raises the question: what exactly is terrorism? Second, the discussion surrounding Halimov's radicalization has focused on his religious interests and conduct rather than conditions in Tajikistan in the post-Soviet era or the presence of international actors in Central Asia. Such focus implies that religion is the gateway to terrorism and that terrorism in turn is the link to global events.

Following the current debates in political geography and social anthropology on scale and group size, I will examine two examples: the 2010 military intervention in the Rasht mountainous region in Tajikistan; and Halimov's defection to 'terrorism' in 2015. One important event in the recent history of Tajikistan is the conflict in 2010–2011 that broke out in the Rasht Valley. Even before it became clear as to what was taking place on the ground, the government had quickly labelled the actors as 'terrorists' and thus turned the area into an active battleground in the 'War on Terror'. Although the conflict did not gain international attention, it was very consequential for Tajikistan. For one, the country became an active site with respect to the 'topography of terrorism', thereby justifying vast international military and political support for a questionable regime. And second, it gave online jihad activists an opening to include Tajikistan in the 'Crescent of Jihad'. In this chapter, I am interested in the way in which different levels shape how conflicts are contextualized. In other words, the study of terrorist conflicts emerges as a problem of differing scales. The analysis is based on fieldwork in Tajikistan since 2002 and in Russia and Turkey since 2010 as well as extensive online research at the time of and after the conflict (Roche 2019).

In this chapter, I approach the question of terrorism as a problem between different geopolitical scales. I draw on Günther Schlee's (1989, 2006, 2008, 2013) idea of scale and group size that he had examined in the context of conflict studies and later of migration. Whereas Hechter (1988: 37) applies group size to cost-sharing, Schlee employs the concept of group size to study the dynamics of identification among conflict parties. Actors regulate group sizes through criteria of inclusion and exclusion and are constantly working to produce the biggest possible advantage for their members. Scale, however, is concerned with the levels where groups are formed, where they operate, and where they are defined. Groups obviously cannot define their boundaries entirely, as external conditions and the recognition of their own criteria play vital roles (emic-etic group definition).

Geographers proposed to look at politics through the study of 'scales' – that is, at different (administrative and political) levels of society. The map of terrorist threats has been produced on the basis of the 'political map' that was drawn by the global North. I propose to change that type of categorization and instead use a topographic, more layered perspective on terrorism. On a topographic map, features become increasingly uniform as one zooms farther out (e.g. mountain ranges, plains and oceans start to appear unicolour). As one steadily zooms in, however, the subtleties of the different nuances become increasingly distinguishable. A similar varying of scale also brings about a changed perspective on the interrelations between involved actors and levels. Moving between different levels also means changing group sizes. Local actors might thus become global actors, if their actions are deemed to reach across certain scales and if they are considered to be part of a global network or group.

Whereas the military conflict yielded geographical sites as reference points, Halimov's example shows that it is not only territorialization that can be used to characterize a terror group. Halimov was categorized as a representative of potential terrorists in Tajikistan, and the country then received large sums from Europe and the United States to fight this 'group', whose existence was never proven. The problem lay both in group size and in scale, which is by no means specific to Tajikistan. Similarly, alleging that the terrorists in Syria belonged to a single group allowed for individuals in Tajikistan to identify as members of that group. Depending on the scale, the group size can be referenced as regional, national or international. The characterization of the international 'Islamic State terror group', for instance, made it possible to subsume all other groups under its umbrella. The scales were blurred in order to establish regional and international ties.

The topography of terrorism produced particular reflexes that developed in many diverse places in very similar ways. Jihad and the term terrorism have become opposed notions of the same phenomenon, an emic and etic notion of violent militant Muslims, not only in Tajikistan, even though these terms are neither synonymous nor semantically linked. Nevertheless, terrorism and jihad are two forces that shape the topography of terrorism in the current political context. Both terms are used for situations and events that may be interpreted on different levels (namely local, national and global). Different sides use different terms to ascribe danger, and while the terminology affords little insight into the course or cause of a conflict, it reveals much about the scale of analysis and the group size of the involved parties.

Defining Terrorism by Scale

Terrorism is primarily a political construct to describe events and situations that seem more closely tied to socio-political contexts than to geographic areas (Feldman and Ruffle 2008; Herman and O'Sullivan 1990; Eckert 2005; 2008; Schlee 2016; Schmid 2004; Weinberg et al. 2004). In explaining terrorism, researchers usually centre on sociological factors and political realities. Researchers put much effort into studying the successes and failures of terrorism research (e.g. Silke 2004) and into disclosing what interest governments have in terrorism research (Herman and O'Sullivan 1990). Further, scholars try to find a consensus of terms (Weinberg et al. 2004) and to identify the role of ideologies in terrorism (e.g. religion) (Feldman and Ruffle 2008). One approach used in social anthropology focuses on terrorism from the perspective of the political consequences of counterterrorism policies (e.g. Eckert 2005, 2008; Goerzig 2010). Terrorist actors themselves have rarely been studied, as the direct examination of such research subjects remains fraught with danger (Elwert 2001; Goerzig 2010; Schlee 2016). In addition, terror has often been described as a political context in, for example,

South American countries, where it shaped the daily conditions of people's lives (Sheper-Hughes 1993).

Over the last decades, the term has increasingly been tied to geography, leading to the development of a 'topography of terrorism', which marks certain areas as terrorist or potentially affected by terrorism. The choice of these areas is neither random nor necessarily coinciding with actual events. The areas are rather marked as potentially terrorist on different scales of a time-space axis, and often they are peripheral areas – both in the colonial sense and concerning the urban-rural dichotomy. Tajikistan belonged to the outer periphery of the Soviet Union and was also conceptualized as such. During the entire Soviet era, the country remained economically dependent on Moscow and also embodied the threat of Islamic opposition as well as Islamic 'backwardness'. In the words of social anthropologist Muhiddin Faizulloev, this led to a sort of 'laboratory situation' (Roche and Faizulloev 2014: 28). Zooming in closer, in Tajikistan itself the Rasht Valley in particular was considered an exemplar of 'backward areas' to which was ascribed the potential for danger. To date, the area's reputation has not been repaired.

The current terrorism debate is based less on facts and more on differing scales of interpretation that are transferred from political geography to physical and social geographies. And yet, the topography of terrorism is not merely an arbitrary map of the present day; instead, areas that have already been marked are contextualized and then interpreted accordingly, while truly new additions to this topography are quite rare. Historic references can play as decisive a role as geographic features. In the case of Tajikistan, the ascription of danger goes back to the relation between Moscow as the centre and Tajikistan as the periphery. Upon the country's independence in 1991, that same ascription was adopted by the West without question. However, such relational dynamics have thus far mostly been discussed in the context of postcolonial and post-socialist approaches (e.g. Chari and Verdery 2009; Hann 2002; Heathershaw 2009).

If the description of terrorism is expanded to include the level of colonial relations and the perspective of 'scales', new approaches can be accessed. Kevin Cox (1998) argues that the interdependence of different 'scales' is of particular interest. He identifies the nation state as the main actor, controlling the administration and division of geographic space and thus creating dependencies. He examines five examples that – as Marston (2000) critiques – are all concerned with 'capitalist problems'. Cox studies contexts such as land allocation, the labour market, housing policies, class divisions and so on, and views scale in terms of networks that create dependencies. He finds that the local level of the community is the most important potential space for action; however, actors often pass over it to engage directly at the national level.

To Cox's approach I then add Schlee's concept of group size – highlighting not only networks and political interests but also focusing on which actors engage at which respective levels. The lone actor Halimov was branded as a representative of all former opposition members who had been admitted into the military and political ranks after the peace treaty of 1997. Anyone having had any kind of connection to Halimov could (after 2015) be accused of being a terrorist, which led to the arrests of hundreds of members and politicians of the Islamic Renaissance Party of Tajikistan and to the banning of the party as a 'terrorist party'. Although many dozens of Tajiks had joined the Islamic State before Halimov, he was the person with enough significance to reach across different scales and connect them. Cox calls it 'jumping scale' when a superordinate scale is directly accessed. Similarly, Schlee (2013) describes the activities of migrants in cities and points out that their group size has great impact on which demands they may make at which levels. Local actors can thus become national or even international actors and, in Halimov's case, such a shift between scales was made possible by his defection to Syria and a group photograph with Tajiks there. The photo implied that Halimov led a large group of Tajiks.

Schlee emphasizes that group size can be steered in conflicts to match the group size to the expected goal. Group size does not always correspond to the actual number of members (it can be favourable for a group to appear bigger and more dangerous than it really is). Rather, a group carefully gauges at which level it can command respect. As a lone actor, Halimov was of little interest to the press and politicians. He only became a feared terrorist in Syria. Scales can be used to purport group sizes and to affect a group's ability to attract members. In the context of the conflict in the Rasht Valley in 2010–2011, the government naturally assumed the entire population of the area to be supporters of the rebels. The comprehensive military operation in 2010 illustrates that the government considered it a war – applying the national scale – and not merely a small band of rebels, whereas a small group causing trouble in the area could easily have been arrested by the police, containing the situation at the local scale.

Dennis Judd (1998) criticizes Cox's approach of 'jumping scales' by arguing that it is not at all a given that levels can be jumped because some political systems do not have a regional scale. The state directly engages local institutions and thus denies political groups the chance to engage at the regional level and to draw in supporters at that level. Markus Hoehne (2014) showcased one example in his analysis of a conflict in northern Somalia. He describes how the Warsangeli area on the border between two autonomous regional administrations, Somaliland and Puntland, had become a haven for Islamist fighters since 2006. The Warsangeli live in the mountainous hinterland, where no infrastructure exists, and the regional governments considered the population to be second-class citizens and potential troublemakers. When valuable ores were found in the area, the government of Puntland utilized military action to exploit these resources without consulting the local population. Armed locals resisted the government, but soon Islamist fighters from South Somalia – through connections of a local preacher – joined the marginalized Warsangeli in support against the Puntland military. Puntland actually cooperated with the provisional government of South Somalia (backed by external actors, such as Ethiopia, the United States and the European Union, among others) that was the main adversary of the Islamists. Consequently, the conflict was elevated to a higher level, even connecting it to the global War on Terror, with the United States flying several drone and missile strikes against terror suspects in the area from 2010 to 2018. At the same time, most Warsangeli have viewed it and still view it as a dispute over local resources and over the fair allocation of participation and power in Puntland.

The conflict in Tajikistan in 2010 developed in a similar way. The government granted coal mining concessions without any regard for realities on the ground, where the locals were already mining these resources. In Tajikistan, regional divisions are not instruments of a decentralized administration but rather a tool to maintain the dependency of all regions on the governing family. The quasi-royal family established itself as the ruling power by advancing this political development and bound almost all regions directly to itself over the past twenty years through political positions and personal ties (Roche 2010, 2017: 38). The established family and its allies eliminated all actors who had been critical of them and at the same time refused any national or regional political claims. This left local political or oppositional movements with few opportunities to acquire any space or to jump from the village to the regional or national level. As a result, protest groups increasingly tried to engage directly at the global level – an option that Cox did not consider but that is highlighted by Michael P. Smith (1998). In the Tajik conflict, the dispute over access to resources in the Rasht Valley was not categorized as a political democratic conflict but instead was interpreted as a global terrorist threat to the nation state. In other words, the government presented itself as the underdog in a fight against global terrorism. The goal was to obtain military support from abroad even when, in reality, the violent actors from the Rasht Valley were poorly equipped, small in number and very loosely interlinked. And in the winter, the conditions for a guerrilla war were already extremely adverse.[2] In effect, the government wilfully distorted the group size and the scale in order to obtain international support, which it utilized to eliminate as many political dissidents as possible. Halimov defected to IS five years after the conflict and thus was used as belated proof for the global relevance of the local actors. He was the first piece of tangible 'evidence' of the link between the different levels.

Terrorism Is 'Politics in Becoming'

The terms 'Wahhabism' and later 'extremism' had been used in the Soviet Union since the 1970s and were then relied upon in the 1980s to distinguish between a non-political and a politicized Islam. The former was deemed to be compatible with the system and labelled 'official Islam' while the latter was deemed 'illegal Islam', 'unofficial Islam', and so on (Malashenko 2006).

These categories were not an accurate representation of actual religious networks, groups and activities, but were instead utilized to condemn actors to whom these categories were ascribed when necessary. The actors themselves engaged at different levels and from different positions, but they were usually well connected through networks. However, the categorizations were not only employed politically; they were also adopted by the population. In his research on Uzbekistan, Johan Rasanayagam (2011: 130–31) convincingly showed that '[t]he law explicitly places the state in the position of arbiter, deciding what religious expression is permissible; guaranteeing the observance of what it considers good, tolerant practice; and excluding "fanaticism" and "extremism" (article 5)'. In this context, extremism, Wahhabism and later terrorism are categories of exclusion used by the state, but these same categories are also adopted by communities and used to label actors who do not conform to the moral expectations of the community. Further, they are used against scores of actors, including Muslims, Christians and any person acting contrary to the norms or expectations of the community or the state.

In Central Asia, the organization of the political space was to a considerable extent influenced by physical-geographical features, essentially blurring the lines between political and geographic characteristics. Tajikistan as a whole represents the potentially dangerous periphery to Russia since the Soviet period and until today. Zooming into the country, however, the regions show a differentiated topography including both political and physical geography. For example, the people in the northern parts of Tajikistan (the Ferghana Valley) were reputed to be better educated than other Tajiks and therefore were preferred for important political positions during the Soviet period.[3] Other regions, such as the Rasht Valley, were categorized as dangerous, both in the socio-political context as well as due to 'landslides' and the 'inaccessibility' of the mountains, so that the physical geography contributed to the 'dangerous' label in this case.[4] The geographic information underscores the threat of an actor to national security. 'The ones from the mountains' were labelled as 'backward' and 'unpredictable'.[5]

After 1991, the newly independent Central Asian states continued to use the terms Wahhabism, extremism and so on in similar fashion before the events of 9/11 reshaped the global terminologies. These terms allowed governments and their subordinate institutions to draw the lines between Islam and dangerous extremism and radicalism according to their own needs. This was primarily used to isolate political actors and to define political spaces.

Since 2001, the term 'terrorism' has blurred the categories even further in Tajikistan, as it has in many other countries where terrorism is tied to Islam. Jack Draper (quoted in Baker 2006: 107) states that terrorism means 'to reify the act as a commodity of pure negativity, a commodity which can then be inscribed with whatever moral or political connotations the translator deems expedient'. Veena Das (2001), Julia Eckert (2005, 2008) and M.Y. Omelicheva (2007, 2011) have described similar developments in Central Asia, where the use of the term terrorism led to arbitrary government practices. In Central Asia, as in many other regions, 'terrorism' expanded the terminology but did not really change the political landscape. The term is primarily used as a measure to 'jump scales' so that a local conflict can be interpreted as a global threat to the nation state. It also functions to influence group size. Depending on the scale, the group can be characterized as overwhelmingly big or quite small – the same is true for the self-presentation of terrorist groups. Schlee described repeatedly how mechanisms of inclusion and exclusion are used to regulate group size. For a time, there had been rumours that an international terrorist group of more than four thousand fighters had formed in Tajikistan. Both the supposed number and the claim of internationality were demonstrably false, but were utilized by both sides to suggest a group size that could elevate a local conflict to relevance on a global scale.

In Tajikistan, the contexts of Islam and political activism are decisive for the use of the terms extremism, radicalism, Wahhabism and terrorism. At the same time, even international organizations that fulfil important advisory functions in Central Asia use the term terrorism just as ambiguously. It is simply wrong to understand terrorism as an objective reality, especially since there is no clear, universally accepted legal definition.[6] 'There exists no general (historical) theory of terrorism: there is no comprehensive explanation or set of principles accounting for the origin, development, and – possibly – end of this political phenomenon. . . . According to the mainstream of experts, *the* issue obstructing the path toward a general theory of terrorism is the notorious lack of agreement as to what terrorism is' (Verhoeven 2009: 4). To phrase it differently, Claudia Verhoeven (2009: 7) introduces the idea that 'terrorism is politics in becoming'. She examined the political assassination attempt on the Russian tsar by Karakozov in 1866, for which the term terrorism was used for the first time to describe an assassination attempt, and not terror by the state as in '*la grande terreur*' of 1794. Verhoeven concludes that terrorism is the beginning of a new kind of politics in the face of a willingness to employ violent actions. Karakozov utilized violence as an individual political expression. 'When the tension between this knowledge of the coming community and the prohibition to participate in its construction becomes unbearable, the body may break out of its bind through action known as terrorism' (Verhoeven 2009: 7) The novelty in this context is that it is not a mass movement but instead a small group with radical political ideas. The term terrorism implies unpredictable, politically motivated violence perpetrated by a small group or individual actors. Terrorism can thus be viewed as the counterpart to state terror, which is the systematic oppression of alternative political views and the use of unpredictable and systematic violence against the population.

Again and again, the fear of terrorism leads to faulty assessments of scale and danger and thus continuously eliminates spaces for non-violent political confrontation. Conflict research has shown that acts of terrorism may result in heightened control over the society by the government and thus never bring about the freedoms that the acts were committed to achieve. The employed scale then also suggests a group size that is often hard to grasp. An act of violence committed by a Muslim activist is astonishingly hoisted to the global level immediately, as if all other considerations of scale were completely irrelevant. In turn, this immediate elevation endows such an act of terrorism (especially since 9/11/2001) with great allure, as the individual actors gain a disproportionate amount of notoriety, which would not be possible if they faced an ordinary trial or if they engaged in peaceful political confrontations. The marking of a person or of a conflict as 'terrorist' immediately elevates the event or person to the global level and thereby frequently triggers a military response. Against this backdrop, other conflicts, e.g. those taking place without the use of physical violence in the streets or in a courtroom, no longer are viewed worth much consideration; they are downscaled.

Nevertheless, the term terrorism cannot simply be discarded as a 'diffuse category'; rather, it represents one of the most important global political concepts today. It connects different levels that can be considered scales. In the following, I want to use the term to zoom in to specific events and look at the interdependency of different scales.

The Conflict on Different Scales

On 19 September 2010 a truck carrying soldiers on their way to a remote area in the Rasht Valley was attacked by armed men. All twenty-three soldiers were killed.[7] In response, the government dispatched its army to the area to crush the 'terrorists'. Only a few weeks earlier, there had been a successful prison break during which a group of 'terrorists' managed to escape from one of the best guarded prisons in the country. It was assumed that they had been able to make their way to Rasht because one of the group members had originated from the area that had long since been considered 'problematic'. The military engagements that ensued over the course of eight months were only sporadically reported by official state television, while many rumours circulated among the population. Some believed that four thousand foreign terrorists had gathered in the mountains around Rasht and that the hospitals in the capital Dushanbe were overflowing with wounded soldiers. The narrative of the War on Terror drowned out other interpretations, such as the conflict being caused by a dispute over a coal mine, where the local population had originally been mining coal before it was sold to foreign investors. It was to secure the visit of the president to this coal mine that the truck carrying soldiers had gone on that day in September. Another interpretation was that of an organized political uprising and yet another that it was the aftermath of an attempted attack on the president. While it may be futile to try to find 'the truth' among these manifold versions, it seems clear that the coal mine played a significant role. During my fieldwork prior to the conflict, I gained first-hand knowledge of residents rejoicing that they no longer had to cut firewood and instead had access to affordable coal at locally set prices.

The government elevated the conflict from the level of a local act of violence and conflict over a constant lack of fuel in a region with long and harsh winters to the level of a globally situated act of terror. Thus, geographic characteristics – the Rasht Valley as a mountainous, dangerous area and the assumption of it being a haven for political refugees and terrorists – were linked to the political threat and thereby the government zoomed out from a local to a global scale. A few months later, state television presented the re-establishment of 'peace' as the result of the national government taking control over the regional political establishment. Neither at the regional nor national level were any means of negotiation available.

On the one hand, using the term terrorism served as the continuation of the 'discourse of danger'[8] from the Soviet era; on the other, the term had become a geographic ascription of danger. To these ends, political, physical-geographic and social spaces are interlinked across local and global levels. At the local level, terrorism is understood as a political attack that enables actors to try to break through from the regional to the national level. At the regional level, local actors sometimes hold, or rather held, considerable power before the government pressed the regions into near complete dependence. As a result, Islamic activists were left without negotiation spaces and were essentially forced to take the recourse to the global level.

As I learned one year after the event, the attack on the truck and the ensuing military engagements originated from the village where I had conducted fieldwork since 2002. I had never before seen 'terrorists' there, although the question remains whether 'terrorists' have discernible identifying features. At the time of the conflict, I could only guess what had happened based on the official media and the few bits of information I had picked up from taxi drivers. The phone lines had been cut, and neither foreigners nor non-residents, not even journalists, were allowed in the area. I could only complete the picture one year later, when I returned to the village.

The Ascription of Danger

The Rasht district lies to the east of the capital Dushanbe in the Qarategin Valley. In the nineteenth century, the area belonged to the Emirate of Bukhara but was more than a week's march on foot or ride on horseback from the capital of Bukhara. When the Bolsheviks invaded the area, the residents organized their resistance against the well-armed revolutionaries through local farmers remembered in local history as both heroes and bandits (*basmachi*) equipped with hoes and sickles. There were massacres on both sides. During the Soviet era, ethnographers classified the region as a 'stronghold of traditions', an area that withstood Soviet modern developments and exemplified the 'backwardness' of traditional life (Kisljakov and Pisarčik 1972, 1976).

For more than a century, Rasht has been associated with backwardness, danger, extreme religiosity and traditionalism. Starting with the *basmachi*, the ascription of danger continued and was again perpetuated by Buškov and Mikul'skij (1995, 1996) when they named the area a 'stronghold of the opposition' in their initial reports on the civil war in the early 1990s. The region seems destined to play the role of the opposition in many conflicts in Tajikistan. To date, the government ascribes general dangerousness to the region. When I prepared for my fieldwork in Rasht in the years 2002, 2003 and again in 2006, I could not find a single person in the capital who would be willing to work for me as a field assistant in this 'dangerous area'. Urban residents imagined the people of Rasht as extremist, traditionalist and armed-to-the-teeth fighters. Those of my assistants who finally dared to go for financial reasons were astounded to discover the population to be incredibly hospitable and peaceable. So there is not only the colonial ascription to the space, but even inside Tajikistan the ascription of political danger is reproduced through the geographic space.

As the ascription of dangerousness is embedded in the construction of a historical continuity, every conflict in this region is immediately viewed as a political threat. The use of the term 'terrorism' for the conflict of 2010/11 can be understood as an ascription that qualified the relation between the political centres in Moscow and Dushanbe and the mountainous Rasht region.

After the attack on the military transport in 2010, the historical ascriptions of dangerousness were revived within hours of the incident. It was presented as a given that the attackers were terrorists who threatened the government. Using this ascription, the government restricted the area – no journalists or non-residents allowed – and dispatched an outsized military response, including international support, in order to immediately quash the 'terrorist threat'. The terminology had changed from *basmachi* and traditionalists or 'opposition stronghold' to a haven for terrorists, but the reaction and ascription of dangerousness have remained the same since the last century.

The conflict also comprised another dimension with far-reaching consequences: the *mujahedeen* from the Caucasus welcomed the Tajik *mujahedeen* into the fold of the international jihad. This was not the result of the actors' 'terrorist' methods – if their actions followed any strategy at all – but was instead purely based on the ascription of Islamic extremism and the use of the term terrorism by the Tajik state and its anti-terror partners. An online group called Ansarullo also posted a number of texts on the conflict that jihadi groups then leaned on to affiliate with the Tajik fighters. The jihadi website Kavkazcentre.ru saw the texts[9] as evidence that the conflict in Rasht was part of the 'Crescent of Jihad' stretching from the Caucasus to Afghanistan – this established a geography of jihad next to the topography of terrorism.

Further social anthropological analysis of the conflict could draw on much more detail that for reasons of space I have addressed elsewhere (Roche 2019). For the present discussion it suffices to establish that a topography can define entire regions physically, socially and politically. Such a generalized ascription of dangerousness is based on the experience of specific political relations and historically selective remembrance rather than on a sound analysis of specific conflicts. In the course of the recent conflict, individual conflict actors were considered to be representative of national and even international (terrorist) groups. The ascription made it possible to establish links across scales.

Zooming into the Ethnographic Field

In the summer of 2011, I returned to a village in the Rasht Valley I had visited for fieldwork years earlier. There were hardly any men of working age left – they had moved to Russia in order to avoid the arbitrary arrests that had ensued after the conflict and frightened many families in the area. In previous years it had been my custom to first visit the homes of families who had lost a relative since my last visit. I did so again on this occasion and went with my host mother on the first Thursday after my arrival to say a *fotiha* prayer with the families. Those who had died included the elderly, migrants and also fighters involved in the military conflict of the previous year. The families of the fighters were afraid to grieve openly and the bodies of their relatives had not been returned to them. The official justification was the prevention of a mortuary cult to 'idolize' the dead fighters. It had been explained to the families that these measures corresponded to the case of Osama bin Laden, whose body had been buried at sea to prevent a martyr cult. There is no tradition of a mortuary cult in this area and thus the repeated reference to the US War on Terror made little sense to the grieving families. The decision not to return the bodies was not made by local politicians, but came down from the highest level of the state and bestowed global relevancy on the local conflict. The state thereby ignored the regional political tensions. Three young men from the village had died. All of them had previously fought in the civil war but had since lost much of their influence in the village. The families I visited grieved for young fathers, brothers and sons, not for terrorists or heroes.

What had happened? Different versions about the reason for the state military action circulated in the village. The attack on the truck just outside the village in 2010 was seen as only one episode of the conflict and not the main cause, as it had been portrayed in the media. Some believed the coal deposits to be the reason for the conflict. Others invoked the civil war and the remaining *mujahedeen*. And yet others blamed the state for provoking the conflict itself against a peaceful population in order to quash demands for political freedom and social justice. None of these explanations were meant to represent the truth but rather to identify the scale of reference. At the global and state levels it was unmistakeably clear: terrorists had attacked soldiers. At the local level, however, the ascriptions became blurred and the actions of the national military and international security forces were incomprehensible to the residents. Relations to the state were renegotiated on the basis of the manifold possible interpretations of the conflict, and eventually the 'terrorist' version was widely accepted by the international media and political partners of Tajikistan as the least complex, most ideologically clear, and most encompassing interpretation.

In addition to the political and resource conflict, the village had been the stage for a mullah who had spent many years in Afghanistan and established himself in the village in 2009. He taught children a jihadist version of Islam and trained them to use weapons, as it later turned out. The government knew about these developments but never arrested this person, to the chagrin of many villagers who expected the police to take care of their safety.

Young men and even children were arrested and questioned for months after the end of the conflict. Collective accusations were standard operating procedure: brothers working in Moscow were accused of supporting terrorism and were arrested upon their return. Fathers were accused of coordination and cousins of collaboration. While the media emphasized the image of foreign intruders, of international terrorists, the state laid the blame on the local population and on the political Islamic activists from Rasht. The state mapped the country with collective ascriptions and accusations and then claimed to be the sole guarantor of peace, at both regional and national levels.

The power struggle in Rasht, however, was no novelty. The state had repeatedly attempted to undermine the 1997 peace treaty, which guaranteed 30 per cent of political posts to the opposition, and tried to criminalize and marginalize oppositional actors. In return, individual militant actors during the civil war had tried to gain control over Rasht, forced their Islamic views on the population and wanted to establish an 'Islamic system' and social justice according to their rules.

The residents never considered the fighters from the village terrorists, with the exception of the 'foreign mullah'. In their view, only others could be terrorists – those who 'had lost the connection to their family and their home'. Terrorists are the others who act without social reference; they are a global threat. Since the military intervention of 2010/11, the term has come to be used for any and all acts of violence, whether in mafia films, media reports or even everyday conversations. 'Terrorism' is used to describe the violent act of a person who feels no personal connection to the place of the attack. At the same time, the government increasingly uses the term for any politically motivated opposition activities. The term thereby becomes a shortcut to link different scales on the basis of mimicry rather than facts.

The state utilizes the topography of terrorism to gain complete control over all regions without political negotiation. The arbitrary use of terrorism at the global level enables the Tajik state to usurp all political levels and regions. Rather than conducting appropriate politically and socially critical analyses across scales, analogies are drawn based on different geographic and political scales. From afar, Tajikistan has its place in the topography of terrorism. Zooming in to the level of the country, however, reveals complex crosslinks among events, terminology and politically driven military reactions that are not necessarily a response to a real threat but rather representations of national or local interests.

The Tajik nation state has utilized the local conflict to obtain international support and at the same time marked the country, and particularly the Rasht region, in the topography of international terrorism. This will undoubtedly guide the interpretation of future conflicts in the region. In order to understand how different levels are connected and affect one another, the approach of scales from the field of human geography has been helpful. Cox emphasizes that the nation state plays a pivotal role in situating local conflicts in the context of existing conflict zones. In the case of Tajikistan, the state connects local and global scales but itself considers only the national level to be legitimate, denying other levels the agency to negotiate. Thus, the independent Tajikistan of today still offers no political spaces for local political activists to negotiate or protest peacefully.

This helps to explain why Halimov's disappearance and defection to the Islamic State in Syria, on the one hand, inspired many young men to follow him and, on the other, threw the Tajik security apparatus into a panic. In his role as a partner in the fight against terrorism, Halimov had to go along with the government's anti-Islamic policies. His turn to and active practice of Islam later made Halimov suspect. The media coverage emphasized the timing of his conversion to Islam as if it were identical with him becoming a 'terrorist'. According to social media posts, Halimov had been ordered by the counterterrorism group to produce a propaganda film wherein young Muslim, headscarf-wearing women were supposed to say that they actually work as prostitutes. That had reportedly been the last straw, leading to his decision to defect. Halimov's individual action is examined less as a political act and more through the prism of his religious development. The latter could be fit easily into the linking of different scales by simply assuming group sizes. An individual who is a devout Muslim and acts politically may potentially become a threat because he acts in the name of and as a representative of a locally, nationally or globally active group. Following Smith's (1998) argument, Halimov became active at the global level when there were no spaces for action at the local or national political level. Through the term 'terrorism', scales can be jumped and actors can link different levels. Halimov's choice of Syria and not Europe or any other destination shows that he knew the topography of terrorism well and could read it with opposite signs, notably, terrorism became jihad. In a world marked by radical topographies, it is actually easier to turn from one radical ideology to another than to normality or responsible political discussions.[10]

Conclusion

Günther Schlee examined group formation processes, emphasizing the importance of group affiliation in conflict situations. He analysed the Who, When and Why of joining a particular group or being affiliated with it. Schlee proposed three basic criteria for the analysis of identification: the social structure, the politics of inclusion and exclusion, and the economy of group sizes. I focused mainly on the last two criteria and combined them with the concept of scales taken from human geography. Using as an example the term terrorism, I have shown how different political scales produce imagined rather than real group sizes. Terrorism operates along the lines of clear-cut oppositions: either one is a terrorist or part of a terrorist group, or one is against terrorists and terrorist groups. In this way, a political actor like Halimov can utilize strategic travel and his knowledge of the topography of terrorism to become the representative of a (large) jihad group – the group's actual size remains unknown and yet it is combatted by a large international military force. Inclusion is achieved here by jumping scales, which, at the same time, also brings new actors onto the scene. This kind of scaling is utilized by the state in order to eliminate political activists and also by the activists themselves, who jump scales as their only option to voice their resentment of arbitrary state practices.

The term terrorism has come to be used geographically. When a group or an individual is condemned as 'terrorist', the underlying conflict is thereby elevated from the local or even individual level to the global level and is reinterpreted as a threat to the nation state. Geography looks at space and time as a matter of scale, which can be transferred to the term terrorism and yield new insights. This is possible because each specific level is associated with a certain capacity to act and to link to a group or movement. Terrorism politics at the global level directly impact interpretations and methods of combat at the local level. As the conflict in Rasht exemplified, the initial catalyst on the ground can be a handful of local activists who should have been arrested by the police (there had been requests by residents to have the 'foreign mullah' arrested). Only when global-scale terrorism is invoked can local actors appear as part of a large (terrorist) group and thus represent a plausible threat to the nation state. In both examples cited in this chapter the state plays a major role in linking various geopolitical scales through its own interpretation, thereby denying local actors any space for political negotiation at the district or national level.

In this chapter, I focused on two particular cases in order to systematically demonstrate the scaling processes, with one example zooming in and the other zooming out. Examining persons or conflicts on a certain scale also 'paints' them in a certain light. Once a region is marked as a potential 'terrorist area' it is inscribed into the topography of terrorism. This topography is then again reproduced online with terminology that often bears little resemblance to the actual events on the ground but rather follows along the lines of existing discourses. Initially, the state plays the central role in drawing this topography of terrorism, but it increasingly loses influence over the process as actors utilize the topography both locally and globally in order to circumvent the state.

Political analysis at only one level ignores the topography behind the concept, fails to critically zoom into the geographic and political areas, and fails to correlate the national level with other levels. When viewed from the perspective of scales, it becomes clear that counterterrorism policies can produce more violence than they prevent: first, because spaces of political negotiation are eliminated at intermediary levels; second, because such policies can establish a route or narrative of scaling that jihadi groups can now follow in reverse (this was exemplified by Halimov who found that his engagement in Syria with jihadi groups and with an Islamic military vocabulary was the only possibility to articulate grief and challenge the political structure in Tajikistan); and third, because the size of terrorist groups is not estimated according to numbers but according to the potential of a group to develop across levels.

Sophie Roche works on conflicts and environmental disasters in Central Asia, Iran and Germany. She specializes in the social and political history and ethnography of Central Asia. She received her PhD from the Martin Luther University of Halle-Wittenberg and her habilitation degree at the Ruprecht Karls University of Heidelberg. She currently heads the asylum documentation and research centre at the Higher Administrative Court of Baden-Württemberg. She has authored two monographs, several edited volumes and more than forty articles and book chapters.

Notes

This chapter builds on the ethnographic material that was used in a previous study published as *Domesticating Youth* (Berghahn, 2014).

1. I want to thank Daniel Münster for his constructive advice on the theoretical approach as well as Felicitas Fischer von Weikersthal and Markus Hoehne for their insightful comments.

2. According to residents in the area, one fighter had been walking around for several weeks deprived of sleep and food. When he came to the village to surrender, he collapsed from exhaustion.

3. The northern part of Tajikistan had, since the seventeenth century, belonged to Russian-controlled Turkestan, whereas the south had been part of the Emirate of Bukhara and enjoyed relative autonomy well into the twentieth century.

4. In 1947, the village Hoit was buried under a mudslide. This disaster was used as a pretence for the resettling of all villages in the area, either to the plains in the south and north or at least from the inaccessible mountains to more accessible thoroughfares.

5. Recent events reaffirm the topographic view of terrorism, when General Abduhalimov Nazarzoda and his group, all accused of terrorism, had retreated back to the area under his command. The topographic information is always mentioned in media reports: 'The Interior Minister and the Committee for the National Security of Tajikistan report on 16 September [2015] that General Abduhalimov Nazarzoda of the Romit Valley has been eliminated by Special Forces. . . . It is reported that the military search operation was accomplished after one-and-a-half days, when the terrorists were pinned near the city of Gusgev, in the Romit Canyon, 130km from Dushanbe at an altitude of 3700m' (translated from the original Russian, ozodi.org, 2015).

6. One OSCE document states, for example: 'There is no settled definition of terrorism in international law, despite many attempts to achieve one by intergovernmental organizations, governments, and academics. One International Court of Justice judge has observed, "terrorism is a term without any legal significance. It is merely a convenient way of alluding to activities, whether of States or individuals, widely disapproved of and in which either the methods used are unlawful, or the targets protected, or both" (Marks and Clapham 2005: 345). However, as such, much is at stake in the definition of terrorism. To call an act terrorism is to assert not just that it possesses certain characteristics, but that it is wrong. To define an act as a terrorist act also has significant consequences with regard to co-operation between states, such as intelligence sharing, mutual legal assistance, asset freezing and confiscation and extradition' (Cooper 2007: 21).

7. An overview of the conflict from the perspective of the International Crisis Group can be found at Crisisgroup.org (16 April 2011): 'Tajikistan: The Changing Insurgent Threats – International Crisis Group'. The book *The Faceless Terrorist* (Roche 2019) provides an in-depth analysis of the conflict, the online discussions and the ethnographic contexts.

8. On the 'discourse of danger': 'By "Western discourse of danger on Central Asia" we mean how Western policy, popular and even academic accounts identify Central Asia as obscure, ethnically and politically fractious, essentially Oriental and – for this reason – dangerous' (Heathershaw and Megoran 2011).

9. Tadzhikistan: Modzhachedy Tadzhikistana vystupili s obraščeniem v svjazi s Šachadoj amira Mullo Abdullo, in Kavkazcenter.com, 21 April 2011.

10. In 2015, rumours emerged that Halimov was actually a secret agent of the Tajik state. Although this idea seems quite fantastical, it demonstrates how quickly actors and events can be transformed and adapted through rumours.

References

Baker, Mona. 2006. *Translation and Conflict: A Narrative Account*. London: Routledge.
Buškov, V.I. and D.V. Mikul'skij. 1995. *Tadzhikskaja revolutsija i grazhdanskaja voyni (1989–1994 gg.)* [The Tajik Revolution and the Civil War (the Years 1989–1994)]. Moscow.
———. 1996. *Anatomija grazhdanskoj voyni v Tadzhikistane (etno-social'nie processi i političeskaja bor'ba 1992–1995)* [Anatomy of the Civil war in Tajikistan (Ethno-Social Processes and Political Struggle 1992–1995)]. Moscow.
Chari, Sharad and Katherine Verdery. 2009. 'Thinking Between the Posts: Postcolonialism, Postsocialism, and Ethnography after the Cold War', *Comparative Studies in Society and History* 51(1): 6–34.
Cooper, Jonathan. 2007. *Countering Terrorism, Protecting Human Rights: A Manual*. Warsaw: ODIHR. Retrieved 2013 from http://www.osce.org/odihr/29103?download=true.
Cox, Kevin R. 1998. 'Spaces of Dependence, Spaces of Engagement and the Politics of Scale, or Looking for Local Politics', *Political Geography* 17(1): 1–23.

Crisis Group. 2011. 'Tajikistan: The Changing Insurgent Threats – International Crisis Group', 16 April. Retrieved from Crisisgroup.org, http://www.crisisgroup.org/en/regions/asia/central-asia/tajikistan/205-tajikistan-the-changing-insurgent-threats.aspx.
Das, Veena (ed.). 2001. *Remaking a World*. Berkeley: University of California Press.
Eckert, Julia. 2005. 'The Politics of Security', *Max Planck Institute for Social Anthropology Working Paper* No. 76. Retrieved from http://www.eth.mpg.de/pubs/wps/pdf/mpi-eth-working-paper-0076.
———. 2008. 'Laws for Enemies: Introduction', in Julia Eckert (ed.), *The Social Life of Anti-Terrorism Laws: The War on Terror and the Classifications of the 'Dangerous Other'*. Bielefeld: transcript, pp. 7–31.
Elwert, Georg. 2001. 'Terroristen: Rational und lernfähig' [Terrorists: Rational and Fast Learning], *Der Überblick* 3: 5.
Feldman, Naomi E. and Bradley J. Ruffle. 2008. 'Religious Terrorism: A Cross-Country Analysis', working paper, *Economics of National Security*: 1–32.
Goerzig, Carolin. 2010. 'The Boomerang Effect of the War on Terror', *Historia Actual Online (HAOL)* 22: 163–71.
Hann, Chris (ed.). 2002. *Postsozialismus: Transformationsprozesse in Europa und Asien aus ethnologischer Perspektive*. Frankfurt and New York: Campus.
Heathershaw, John. 2009. *Post-Conflict Tajikistan: The Politics of Peacebuilding and the Emergence of Legitimate Order*. London: Routledge.
Heathershaw, John and Nick Megoran. 2011. 'Contesting Danger: A New Agenda for Policy and Scholarship on Central Asia', *International Affairs* 87(3): 589–612.
Hechter, Michael. 1988. *Principles of Group Solidarity*. Berkeley: University of California Press.
Herman, Edward A. and Gerry O'Sullivan. 1990. *The Terrorism Industry: The Experts and Institutions That Shape Our View on Terror*. New York: Pantheon.
Hoehne, Markus Virgil. 2014. 'Resource Conflict and Militant Islamism in the Golis Mountains in Northern Somalia (2006–2013)', *Review of African Political Economy* 41(141): 358–73.
Judd, Dennis R. 1998. 'The Case of the Missing Scales: A Commentary on Cox', *Political Geography* 17(1): 29–34.
Kisljakov, N.A. and A.K. Pisarčik. 1972. *Tadzhiki Karategina i Darvaza* [The Tajiks of Karategin und Darvaz], Volume I. Dushanbe.
———. 1976. *Tadzhiki Karategina i Darvaza* [The Tajiks of Karategin und Darvaz], Volume II. Dushanbe.
Malashenko, Alexei V. 2006. 'Islam, The Way We See It', *Russia in Global Affairs*, 12 October. Retrieved from http://eng.globalaffairs.ru/print/number/n_7325#.
Marks, Susan and Andrew Clapham. 2005. *International Human Rights Lexicon*. Oxford: Oxford University Press.
Marston, Sallie A. 2000. 'Social Construction of Scale', *Progress in Human Geography* 24(2): 219–42.
Omelicheva, Mariya Y. 2007. 'Counterterrorism and Human Rights: Explaining Differences in the Scope and Brutality of States' Responses to Terrorism', PhD dissertation. ETD Collection for Purdue University. Retrieved from https://www.researchgate.net/publication/27235307_Counterterrorism_and_human_rights_Explaining_differences_in_the_scope_and_brutality_of_states'_responses_to_terrorism
———. 2011. *Counterterrorism Policies in Central Asia*. London: Routledge.
Rasanayagam, Johann. 2011. *Islam in Post-Soviet Uzbekistan: The Morality of Experience*. Cambridge: Cambridge University Press.
Roche, Sophie. 2010. 'Friendship Relations in Tajikistan: An Ethnographic Account', *Ab Imperio* 3: 273–98.
———. 2017. 'The Family in Central Asia: New Research Perspectives', in Sophie Roche (ed.), *The Family in Central Asia: New Perspectives*. Berlin: Klaus Schwarz, pp. 7–38.
———. 2019. *The Faceless Terrorist: A Study of Critical Events in Tajikistan*. Heidelberg: Springer.

Roche, Sophie and Muhiddin Faizulloev. 2014. 'The Faithful Assistant: Muhiddin Faizulloev's Life and Work in the Light of Russian Ethnography', *Working Paper of FMSH*. Retrieved from http://www.fmsh.fr/en/c/6540.

Schlee, Günther. 1989. *Identities on the Move: Clanship and Pastoralism in Northern Kenya*. Manchester: Manchester University Press.

———. 2006. *Wie Feindbilder entstehen: Eine Theorie religiöser und ethnischer Konflikt*. Munich: C.H. Beck.

———. 2008. *How Enemies Are Made: Towards a Theory of Ethnic and Religious Conflicts*. Integration and Conflict Studies 1. Oxford and New York: Berghahn.

———. 2013. 'Collective Identification in Cities: Reflections on City Scale and Group Size', presentation at the Plenary Session of the Tenth Congress of Russian Ethnographers and Anthropologists, 'Modern Cities and Social and Cultural Modernization of Russia', Moscow, 2 July.

———. 2016. 'Wie Terroristen gemacht werden' [How Terrorists are Made], Max-Planck-Gesellschaft. Retrieved 12 January 2016 from https://www.mpg.de/9853139/terrorismus-ursachen.

Schmid, Alex P. 2004. 'Frameworks for Conceptualising Terrorism', *Terrorism and Political Violence* 16(2): 197–221.

Sheper-Hughes, Nancy. 1993. *Death without Weeping: The Violence of Everyday Life in Brazil*. Berkeley: University of California Press.

Silke, Andrew (ed.) 2004. *Research on Terrorism: Trends, Achievements and Failures*. London: Frank Cass.

Smith, M.P. 1998. 'Looking for the Global Spaces in Local Politics', *Political Geography* 17(1): 35–40.

Tadzhikistan 2005. 'General'naja prokuratura: Nazarzoda dejstvoval po ukazaniju Kabiri' [Attorney General's Office: Nazarzoda Acted on Behalf of Kabiri], 17 September. Retrieved from *Ozodi.org*, http://rus.ozodi.org/content/article/27253239.html.

———. 2011. 'Modzhachedy Tadzhikistana vystupili s obraščeniem v svjazi s Šachadoj amira Mullo Abdullo' [The Mujaheds of Tajikistan Made a Statement in Relation to the Shahada of Amir Mullo Abdullo], 21 April. Retrieved from *Kavkazcenter.com*, http://www.kavkazcenter.com/russ/content/2011/04/21/80912.shtml.

———. 2015. 'Ziddi Gulmurod Halimov parvandai 'muzdurī' boz šud' [A Case Against Gulmurod Halimov as Mercenary was Opened], 31 May. Retrieved from *Ozodi.com*, http://www.ozodi.org/content/interpol-head-of-tajik-omon/27045651.html.

Verhoeven, Claudia. 2009. *The Odd Man Karakozov: Imperial Russia, Modernity, and the Birth of Terrorism*. Ithaca, NY: Cornell University Press.

Weinberg, Leonard, Ami Pedahzur and Sivan Hirsch-Hoefler. 2004. 'The Challenges of Conceptualizing Terrorism', *Terrorism and Political Violence* 16(4): 777–94.

CHAPTER 7

Politics of Belonging and the Litmus Test of Retaliation

Bertram Turner

Introduction

In his writings on retaliation Günther Schlee emphasizes the close correlation between identifiable and internally solidary coalitions of actors based on descent and the competitive striving for power and domination among such formations within society (Schlee 1996, 2002: 260, 2017, 2022; Schlee and Turner 2008: 63–65). Schlee refers here to societies in East Africa whose political self-understanding is conventionally characterized as segmentary and in which central political authority and vertical alignment are minor formative principles. In his examples clan-based retaliation groups (revenge-seeking, compensation-paying or compensation-receiving groups), in accordance with the Islamic notion of *diya* groups, represent such cohesive units. While the principle of retaliation is acknowledged as a universal social phenomenon or total social fact, such forms of socio-political organization are considered as the *locus classicus* of an archetype or primeval form of retaliation.

Taking Schlee's argument as the point of departure, I assert in this chapter that the conjunction between the logics of retaliation and the politics of belonging takes effect, on the one hand, based on the composition and stability of retaliation groups and, on the other, according to how the distribution of power among such groupings is negotiated. Retaliatory action may serve as a litmus test, making evident to what extent politics of belonging to a cohesive reference unit and the arithmetic of power differentials between such coalitions correlate. I further argue that, as regards retaliatory units, not only the claim to domination but also the incessant exchange of checks and balances inform the production of cohesion and of inclusion and exclusion. Moments of retaliation provide an opportunity to update kin relations and alliances and to harmonize kin-based claims with a cohesion that is based on solidarity and control of power. Retaliatory logic thus entails more than law and kinship as modes of calculation. It highlights the uncertainty of proof making that would allow for the allocation of responsibility based on 'true facts' and constitutes a challenge to the sustainability of markers of identification in situations that demand the translation of such ties of belonging and shared frames of identification into solidary action with a view to the future.

There is widespread consensus in the literature that descent and retaliatory solidarity form a set whereby it is often assumed that retaliatory solidarity emanates from kinship relations. Thus the belonging to a retaliation network appears in various situations of crisis or conflict as a litmus test that proves the individual's rooting in kinship relations. However, there is ample indication that it also may work the other way around, namely that acting in solidarity and taking sides are translated into kinship relations whereby the latter proves to be a flexible frame that allows for quite a number of ways to construct a collective identity. Such modes of inferring the one from the other indicate that 'frames of reference for the purpose of identification' (Eidson et al. 2017: 341, 355–56) that are translatable into each other are mutually constitutive. The 'likeness' (Eidson et al. 2017: 341) shared by members of retaliatory networks is the solidarity in their dealing with acts of social transgression for which either one or several members of their unit are responsible or of which they compose the injured party. The legitimacy of such cohesive communities is quite often expressed in the terms and language of kin but may also associate people who share interests based on other criteria such as professional cooperation, trade relations or territorial proximity.[1]

Then what does retaliatory solidarity as a frame allow us to learn about identity dynamics within and across communities? Considering that retaliation groups compose a larger unit of socio-political organization as a community of law in which retaliatory logics inform the ways disputes are dealt with, more questions follow. To what extent and in what way does 'size matter' and how does the accumulation of power within solidary revenge parties translate into models of political organization and eventually politics of belonging? Does striving for the greater number of members provide a means that allows fostering solidary bonds within the groups? Or do identity markers such as kin and retaliatory solidarity begin to lose their cohesive force when a certain number of adherents is exceeded? Dynamics of change draw into play what Eidson et al. (2017) call co-determinants of identification.

In a first step I briefly sketch out the concept of retaliation and its embeddedness in larger institutional assemblages. I then present two examples, an ethnographic vignette and a reference to a source of authority, on the basis of which Günther Schlee has elaborated upon his understanding of group-based arithmetics of power differentials and retaliation. In a next step I argue that the law of the powerful does not produce social stability. On the contrary, the accumulation of power may unleash a plethora of counterbalancing strategies. Such dynamics identified in situations of retaliation are then addressed in terms of processes of identity formation and the generation of social cohesion as they are theorized extensively in a wide range of publications produced by Günther Schlee and co-authors (e.g. Schlee 2004, 2006; 2008; Eidson et al. 2017). Politics of belonging are discussed with reference to empirical examples. The chapter draws on data from African and MENA (Middle Eastern and North African) societies, especially Morocco, and revisits the classic debate on the correlation between segmentarity and retaliation. In the conclusion the correlation between calculation and identity, between 'size matters' and its cohesive force, is seen in light of institutional arrangements and individual agency.

Retaliation

After two volumes on retaliation co-edited with Günther Schlee (2008, 2017), I provide here only a brief account of some main principal aspects of retaliation, which should be sufficient to develop the line of argumentation for this chapter.

One may define retaliation as a human disposition to reactively balance conflict or other types of situations perceived as unjust. The basic principle of retaliation, however, is more than simply an automatic reaction to an offence, especially if violence is involved. It refers broadly to the full range of reactions to circumstances that are perceived to be deviant or socially transgressive. Such a constellation presupposes two opposed, nominally equal parties. Understood in this sense, retaliation occurs at all levels of socio-political organization, from individual face-to-face interaction to nation states and transnational organizations.

As an expression of the principle of reciprocity, retaliatory logics may inform the whole gamut of conflict resolution procedures, from avoidance to consensual settlement to compensation to violent reprisal and escalation. The question is, how can the great variety of retaliatory reactions be explained? The most fundamental common denominator seems to be the equalizing and balancing quality that is inherent in the principle of reciprocity. Retaliatory reaction thus exhibits two properties: on the one hand, it entails a preventive principle, as the threat of retaliation can prevent someone from committing an inappropriate act directed against another; on the other, it implies the right to react in a way that allows an offended party to rebalance a perceived injustice. A perpetrator should not enjoy any advantage from such action. If the prevention mechanism fails and an initial violent act takes place, then reactive violence is acknowledged as legitimate; otherwise, the implicit threat of retaliation would lose its deterrent function. However, the legitimate right to violent retaliation does not necessarily lead to its immediate execution; it can be substituted by compensation. This also proves to be true in situations where there is not only a right to a violent reaction, but an actual duty to react violently. Even in such cases there are usually a number of exit options available. These allow the involved parties to avoid a sustained violent relationship without waiving their claims to retaliation. All this is subject to negotiation. Retaliation is thus about decisions between violent or compensatory reactions to an initial act that disrupts the balance.

The moments of transition, where avoidance turns into compensation-oriented and then confrontational reactions and vice versa, are the vital juncture in this field of action. This is where it becomes evident under which social conditions the principle of retaliation will entail what consequences (Turner 2017a: 10–11). This is also exactly the interface where the embeddedness of relations in a wider institutional assemblage comes into play. Retaliation turns out to provide the basic principle for an effective conflict settlement that is performed in an institutional assemblage that combines protection with mediation and post-conflict settlement as components of the formal social reintegration of the parties involved in the conflict. Institutional arrangements of retaliatory claims between parties may thus be connected to an institutionalized grant of protection, asylum or exile informed by rules of hospitality, which in turn may carry over to established forms of negotiations (Turner 2005). Compensation itself can then be subject to such negotiations that, under favourable conditions, may take on the form of a mediation process.

Looking beyond the specifics of concrete cases, such decisions appear to be significantly informed by the quality of the social relations between the parties involved. It is already the exercise of a transgressive act that leads to the formation of two opposed parties, the perpetrator party and the injured party. In the process the action to be retaliated against is classified in terms of severity and also in terms of its social scope. Interestingly, there is a striking silence in the literature on how exactly this mobilization takes place, which is the prerequisite for any further action and apparently has an impact on the way the two opposed parties interact and how the course of events proceeds. Schlee (2017: 220) considers the sheer power of numerical superiority the decisive factor that materializes in solidary action: 'It is clear that numbers matter a great deal in this power game'.

Power Sensitivity and the Enforcement of Claims in Retaliatory Relationships

In this section I assess, with reference to two vignettes, how the size of retaliatory networks and the power of numbers and calculation relate to each other. The first example highlights the basic assumption that 'size matters' in retaliation. It also reflects the integration of the law of retaliation in local normative registers – and to what extent or under what circumstances such rules are applied.

In his vignette Schlee (Schlee and Turner 2008: 63–65 [translation mine]) refers to a strong group that is the one representing the perpetrator of an act of brutal rape.

> In 1990, I witnessed negotiations for blood compensation in northern Kenya. The two parties were the Degodia and the Sakuye. The Degodia are a Somali clan that is associated with the Hawiyye clan family by way of a uterine link. They are a large group of well-armed nomadic pastoralists. The formerly also nomadic Sakuye are Islamized Oromo speakers. In the 1960s, they stood with the Somali in the fruitless attempt to force the integration of the region into Somalia (Shifta Uprising). Both their own numbers and those of their herds were depleted by Kenyan government forces. The survivors tried to engage in agriculture in the less arid foothills of the Ethiopian plateau, gathered honey, poached leopards as long as there was still a market for the furs, and slowly grew their herds again. In comparison with the Degodia the Sakuye are demographically and economically weak and without military clout.
>
> A young Degodia had raped a Sakuye girl, who had tended her herd far away from the settlement. She was disfigured by stab wounds and had almost lost her voice. The Sakuye demanded five camels as compensation (*diya*), and the Degodia agreed that this amount was appropriate to the damage. However, they also countered: 'If you now demand the full *diya*, what will you do in the opposite case, if for example one of your young men killed one of ours? Would you be able to pay one hundred camels? Surely not! You would ask us to be brotherly and to waive the *diya* and instead accept a gift of reconciliation, as it is done within a clan. So now it is your turn to be brotherly!' In the end, the Sakuye accepted only one single camel as compensation. They were forced into this brotherliness – one that had little to do with freedom or equality.

In his analysis Schlee remarks:

> Large groups demanding compensation have the option to take an offer (without having to accept curtailments as the Sakuye had to) or to exert revenge. Weaker opponents would not dare to strike back. Not to resolve disputes but to keep them simmering might be useful, especially when the goal is to keep one's neighbours at a distance. All water holes in the area are then accessible and open the way to new grazing grounds. A big *diya* paying group is thus similar to the common slogans of insurance companies, that of the 'strong community'. The propensity to violence of such numerically big solidarity groups, which can have several thousand members, is deemed extremely high, even in cases of being responsible for a homicide. This is so even though the contribution of the individual to the total compensation sum is quite small. It seems tolerable to split the price of one hundred camels among several thousand group members. But that is not the point. Such an equation does not seem to correspond with Somali logic on the offsetting of violence with material compensation. A group that is large enough to spread the burden of compensation among so many members that it is not a burden to any individual, might also be large enough to refuse [to pay] compensation. It could rely on its potential to in-

timidate the opponent and thus discourages acts of revenge or to prevail in case violence does erupt.

Three things are remarkable here. There is power, there is law and there is the bending of the law by the powerful. The line of argumentation of the powerful perpetrator reveals the interplay between the register of rules and the situation of its application. In what way agency is informed by rules turns out to depend on various criteria. However, when rules are not applied, why are they invoked? As will be shown, they provide a guideline for the settlement of a concrete configuration.

One would be mistaken to conclude, however, that such strategic action results automatically out of the retaliatory power arithmetic between stronger and weaker but nominally equal groupings. I argue that decisions in situations of retaliation may take into consideration a wide range of contingencies that reflect the many ways through which an ideological concept may inform agency and practice. Accordingly, the significance of retaliatory action of segmentary units within given social formations goes far beyond the confirmation of internal social cohesion. I later address a few of those contingencies.

I often heard similar arguments about unequal size when I discussed violent conflicts in Morocco. Once, a peasant said to me when we debated his conflict with another villager about his claim to exercise his usufruct rights in a plot in the forest: 'What can I do? My son is in primary school. The other guy has five adult sons and one of them is even a butcher!'[2] One should add here that the claim to usufruct rights also depends on the ability of the claimant to defend those rights when challenged. Yet I will discuss later how size or number relates to additional criteria and why assumptions about 'stability in number' have to be taken into consideration. So the description of the power-accumulating Degodia clan keeping the weak Sakuye in a state of permanent insecurity lays bare an important instant in always dynamic societal configurations at large but at the same time it represents a snapshot in time.

Another aspect of the calculability of deviance becomes apparent and challenges the greater number of the strong party, a challenge that the strong party feels obliged to argue away. Two modes of calculation are set in opposition: the number of members making up the group size against prices to be paid according to fixed tariffs for injuries. In various normative orders claims to legitimate violent response and compensatory claims are clearly determined, and sophisticated catalogues of prices for bodily harm or homicide exist, as in the case of regulations that refer to Islamic normativity (e.g. Tyan 1965; Peters 2005: 50–53). The amount of the tariff translates social criteria such as status or rank into material compensation in the form of a 'currency', here 'camels'. Moreover, *diya* is also perpetrator related and presupposes forgiveness, factors in individual responsibility and intent. As Schlee shows, those tariffs, although 'sacred law', apply mainly on paper and inform concrete negotiations rather than determine them. In addition, powerful *diya* groups that are strong in members have the option to strategically decide whether they prefer compensation or violent retaliation. The criteria that inform strategic decision making may include considerations about the maintenance of power in the future and the question of how to weaken the opposed party – economically by high compensation or in terms of group size. However, as will be addressed below, other considerations of future making may also play a role.

Such a decision sometimes seems not even to take into consideration the position of the powerful group in a conflict – whether it is in the position of the aggrieved party or in the position of the offending party. Signalling a principally permanent propensity to violence, for instance, may at any rate work to the group's advantage.

The vignette also suggests that a propensity to violence is high if retaliatory costs are spread over a large number of members of a solidarity group. Now, the argument may also go the other way round than presented in Schlee's account. The propensity to split into smaller units may be as high as the propensity to violence because of the frequency with which costs may be inflicted on each member. Schlee's argument that large groups could have the capacity to bend the rules in their favour may of course devalue the calculation. However, such large groups may display a remarkably weak internal social cohesion as conflicts may occur within the formation on a regular basis. Of course, it is not only aspects of retaliation that may have an effect of internal solidarity; various other reasons may challenge the internal solidarity, especially those that arise out of the spatial and social proximity with one another. The moment described, when retaliatory parties facing each other are about to emerge, is exactly the litmus test: it is 'the situation' in which relationalities are laid bare; when under conditions of retaliation ties of belonging either translate into solidary action or lose their cohesive force. It may work out once again, but with a view to the future it may send a clear signal and mobilize others against the strong group. Moreover, there is another fuzzy aspect that reveals itself and may combine with the litmus test of identity: the trespassing of a threshold. If the stronger group overplays its hand, the many weaker parties may feel motivated to keep the powerful at a distance as far as is possible.

The second example highlights the basic assumption that 'counting matters' in retaliation and that the basic principle of retaliation – the balance between challenge and response – may appear subordinated to the law of the powerful. It is a classic quotation with a high authoritative power, and Schlee insisted that we had to deal with it in our introduction to the edited volume on retaliation in 2008. In the context where we discuss the various scientific approaches to the concept of retaliation and the sources from which they draw, we refer to the inherently inconsistent statements in the Old Testament. One such statement refers to Lamech:

Lamech, a descendant of Cain, boasted before his wives: 'Adah and Zillah, Hear my voice; ye wives of Lamech, hearken unto my speech: for I have slain a man to my wounding, and a young man to my hurt. If Cain shall be avenged sevenfold, truly Lamech seventy sevenfold'. (Gen. 4: 23–24)

With his claim to seventy-sevenfold revenge, which translates in numerical symbolism to 'absolute' revenge, Lamech may be referring to his capacity to mobilize a huge group, an abundant progeny obliged to take revenge. However, I argue it is less likely that the matter of power is addressed in the sense of a party's ability to take seventy-sevenfold revenge; rather, it is the basic problem of balanced reciprocity in socially stratified societies that worries Lamech. Here another fundamental principle of the concept of retaliation is addressed: the adequacy, proportionality or appropriateness of retaliatory action. The relationship in question becomes the appropriateness of the retaliatory reaction in relation to the social position of a hypothetical victim (Turner 2017a: 12, 16). It makes sense to see this appropriateness in relation to the social proximity between the parties involved. But what does this mean? Retaliation is proportional to what? Should retaliation be proportional to the social position of the victim, or of the perpetrator, or proportional to the damages suffered or to the unjustly acquired advantage? There is empirical evidence for each of the possibilities. What is important here, first, is that proportionality is basic to retaliation and, second, that it clashes with a logic of calculation that would allow the bending of the rules to the advantage of the strongest party. An isolated analysis, however, does not take us far enough. A closer look reveals that retaliation is part of a larger institutional arrangement.

Retaliatory Groups and the Power of Numbers

With respect to retaliation it should be clear at this point that collective identity provides the basis of, or materializes in, cooperation. The process of activating identity, of identification, 'designates the ways in which actors engage with the categories on which collective identities are based' (Eidson et al. 2017: 341). Taking action happens in relation to others. The 'category of identification' is shared solidarity in retaliatory relations. The cognitive ideology appears to be the shared blood of consanguine relatives, the affinity by consanguinity or alternatives to it. Herewith a categorical distinction is made with respect to alliances, in which each alliance partner may keep its identity while acting together on a contractual basis. So why then is the attraction of the great number empirically not as clearly evident as calculation exercises may suggest?

Retaliation parties are mutually exclusive identifications. One is either a giver or a receiver, and cannot be both. As a community of accrued gains, the distribution of compensation is traded against a previous contribution to an owed compensation. Therefore, no retaliation is possible within the minimal kin unit, the nuclear family. In the latter case, perpetrator and injured party are the same. This is basic to the logic of retaliation but true only to a certain extent. For one can nevertheless be in the same party, because the logic of segmentation may position the same actors who are facing each other as retaliatory opponents at one level of segmentation in one and the same solidarity group at a higher level of segmentation. Moreover, as Schlee (2017: 232, n20) himself points out, there is by far no automatism in this simple model as it 'does not extend necessarily to higher levels of segmentation', referring in his example to Somali clans and their recruitment of followers.

Thus, only the concrete act of transgression of one or more identifiable individual(s) that both mobilizes and transcends the retaliation network to which these individuals belong determines the positions of the other network members towards one another as they are either joining the emerging perpetrator or the victim party at another level of segmentation. The concrete solidarity group only forms in case of need and this according to criteria of kinship proximity. Although usually an identifiable kin-determined network is considered as the retaliation group, it is the concrete case scenario that determines how people get involved and are divided into opposing parties.

Moreover, there is evidence that the balancing between segments via fission and fusion resonates in a corresponding normative order. The assumption of a strong correlation between segmentary lineage systems and retaliation in the literature, however, seems to have blocked the view on context. The principle of retaliation as a concretization of the basic principle of reciprocity in situations of conflict does not exist independently. It appears instead to be integrated in a widely ramified and multi-layered model of order connecting political, normative, religious and economic features of human coexistence (Turner 2005). Without going into specifics here, the bargaining power of the greater number is embedded in an institutional assemblage that may dramatically restrict its effectiveness. Negotiations between the parties may take place while the weaker party finds itself in a situation of institutionalized protection, be it asylum or exile, during which the threat of the great number is neutralized and the negotiations concretize in the form of mediation among equals (Turner 2017a, b). Thus the litmus test of belonging always concerns individuals in relation to the mentioned conditions. From there, fragility and uncertainty emerge, because the number of possible constellations is indefinite.

Internal power differentials and hierarchies may take effect in the way that all members of a network position themselves against another network. However, power does not seem to be the major attraction or cohesive force in its relationality to the number of members. The large number may be at the base of the network's power, whereas the very same number may already challenge this power in that individual bonds within a large network are often less intense than in smaller ones. A network's power is something more than the sum of its individual members' ability to put up a fight. Moreover, apart from physical power and threat, the network's internal total amount of resources and/or its equal or unequal distribution may contribute to the fragility mentioned.

Hence, what should be added to the overall picture is the fragility of the large size and the great number. Also, in the case of the Degodia, it appears less likely that in cases when recourse to violence is on the agenda, the several thousand adherents can be mobilized and ready for action. This litmus test was not required in the example from Schlee. But once it is required, quite a number of different possibilities may materialize; nothing is sure. Moreover, the number of potential targets of retaliation in very strong solidarity formations is comparatively large, such that the protection of these persons constitutes a challenge even for a potent solidarity unit. In public opinion, so to speak, an imbalance of power is quite often looked at through the lens of appropriateness. As my interlocutors assured me regarding the Moroccan context, no one would agree, for instance, to join an alliance that mobilizes, say, five hundred people to proceed against three brothers.

In fact, as Schlee and I have suggested, the criterion of kinship does not seem unchallengeable as the basic condition for the social cohesion that is associated with the collective management of retaliatory claims. Instead, situations of retaliation may reveal divergent interests within a retaliation group and evoke or motivate the constant reinterpretation of social relations. The exercise of retaliatory solidarity may even result in kin relations.

Social Structure, Retaliation and Appropriate Response: Measurement and the Calculation of Proportionality

In order to analyse the entanglements of size, number and power, and the normative force of basic principles of reciprocity in situations of conflict, we are brought back to the question of how such groups are formed. The point of departure is the model of segmentary organization in combination with its orientation along unilineal, agnatic units. In this model genealogies serve as flexible instruments for defining social groups. A tribal unit consists of lineages that form a more or less autonomous socio-political identity pool. The lineages are integrated into a genealogy that determines the relationship between them as well as between individuals. In that way, reciprocal rights and duties are well defined. Several lineages descend from the same ancestor and can be subdivided into family units. In contrast to solidarity groups, lineages are considered to be relatively stable units. Each generation of ancestors constitutes a bond and a target breakpoint that leads to the fission of segments and forms a new level. All segments on one organizational level belong to the same rank, but affiliated or assimilated segments may constitute exceptions to this rule. According to the same criteria of social proximity, these social units, exclusive and complementary on one level, form a common unit on the next higher level of organization, which again faces a corresponding segment. From the actors' perspective these segments approximately form concentric circles. 'Medium social distance', then, exists between the respective units of reference on every level of segmentary organization. Segments are associated with different forms of cooperation between their members according to the respective level.

There is no standard terminology even for small ethnographic settings. A distinction is usually made among tribes, clans, sub-clans, lineages and sub-lineages. There remains an unresolvable dispute over the question of what constitutes a violation of these flexible rules and what may be considered a hint for the existence of contradictory sets of rules. Furthermore, segmentary order is associated with specific patterns of residence and a particular organization in space (Evans-Pritchard 1976 [1940]; Baştuğ 1998).

In practice, retaliation in segmentary order does not automatically translate into the emergence of stable power groups. Instead, processes of constant fusion and fission are expressed in terms of retaliation and solidarity whereby the principles of segmentation follow an ideal of complementary oppositions within society in the absence of central political institutions.

A standard quote cited by evolutionists is ascribed to John Burdan S. Haldane.[3] He looked at retaliation in his debate on cooperation and altruism from the perspective of simple genetic principles and inheritance patterns, an argument that in the form of socio-biological explanatory schemes continues to attract attention in the ongoing debate in social sciences on responsibility and solidarity. In his synthetic theory of evolution Haldane (1990 [1932]) portrays evolutionism as a natural mathematical calculation:

> 'I would be willing to risk my life for two brothers or eight cousins'.
> This quip is based upon the observation that brothers share an average of one-half of their genetic material, whereas first cousins share an average of one-eighth. Therefore, saving two brothers or four cousins would result in the same genetic contribution to the next generation as that represented by one's own genome. This quip was later cited by one of the founders of what is now known as the theory of kin selection.[4]

Apart from the fact that the quote is misleading and was not meant to be taken literally, because gene pools in hereditary transmission are always different, empirical data reveal that simple socio-biological arithmetic cannot lead us to an understanding of humans' strategic dealing with universal human conditions such as retaliation. Seemingly in the same vein, the Arabic proverb states a tenacious formula of the segmentary principle – in a variety of concrete versions – that is repeated across the entire Middle Eastern and North African region:

Me against my brother. My brother and me against our patrilineal cousins. All of us together against the rest of our clan, our clan against the rest of the tribe, and our tribe against the rest of the world.

Descent provides the language in which cooperation is addressed while descent ascriptions may appear as an outcome and not as the precondition of social cohesion. And cooperating groups always have better chances in competition irrespective of descent relation.

Politics of Belonging

The ways in which ideology and practice interact are reflected in the setup of reference units. At least according to the rules, the belonging to a kin-based retaliation network is not chosen; it is a given as it reflects social structure. However, one can choose to change kin affiliation and adopt another one. I will explore this issue by referring to another preferred topic of Günther Schlee. In his writings on identification, inclusion and exclusion, Schlee (2004) first asks the seemingly simple question, 'who against whom?' He then shows that while the institutional frameworks identifying opposed parties may show remarkable stability, the actors themselves may change loyalty, may form alliances and also belong to kin groups according to criteria detached from that framework. So the first issue of size and subsequent calculation is regarded under the conditions of the second, which emphasizes the incentives for group formation. Again, it is the framework, the institution and the clan structure that persist while actors are always moving and separating from and integrating in various alliances, networks and formations and combining such belonging as necessary.

Schlee (2017: 220) quotes Lewis 1999 [1961] as the authority for strategically dealing with numerical inferiority in the endless process of fission and fusion within segmentary societies.

> It is clear that numbers matter a great deal in this power game. As early as 1961, Lewis (1999 [1961]) pointed out that branches of a clan with slower demographic growth form alliances and combine into diya-paying groups with smaller lineage groups of other clans, in breach of the logic of the segmentary lineage system, which would posit that forms and degrees of mutual assistance reflect genealogical proximity.

This rather sounds like creative dealing with inferiority and resonates with the Degodia example above. Also, retaliation groups exhibit cross-cutting ties within a narrower frame (Schlee 1997). The difference that the team of authors around Schlee emphasizes between 'commitment' and 'strategy' informs such situational formation processes (Eidson et al. 2017: 347–48).

Related to the statement that size matters is obviously the fact that both sides in a conflict should be aware of who is included in, and who is excluded from, the opposed parties, all the more because the strategic flexibility of actors demands constant updates of the state of affairs. The critical phase in this respect during which the two parties are about to come into being is called in Arabic *fort [fawrat] ad-damm*, or 'the boiling of the blood', a limited period following an act of social transgression during which the opposed parties are constituted through complex processes of inclusion and exclusion, claimed and ascribed identification, but also by the normative power of facticity such as distance, economic circumstances and much more. There is, not surprisingly, variation regarding the patterns of behaviour associated with this forming phase. While various ethnographies from the MENA region suggest that during this rather short and clearly determined period of time the emerging retaliation group is expected to do nothing but seek a violent confrontation since the duty to perform violently prevails over everything else, the literature also suggests that this emotional state is perceived as a period during which early attempts to set up negotiations are deemed to fail but violence does not seem necessarily mandatory (e.g. Gabbert 2012: 176).

All such processes of group formation are informed by notions of social proximity and distance, which eventually open the door to a choice of possible options concerning how to deal with the concrete event. Since the composition of such parties is subject to constant fluctuation, this comes out as the decisive question.

To give an example close to my own work and also connected with the foundational myth of the International Max Planck Research School (REMEP) in which Günther Schlee and I cooperated for so many years and in which such topics have been central to the research agenda, I have chosen an ethnographic vignette from Morocco. In Ernest Gellner's *The Saints of the Atlas* (1969), he analyses the segmentary order of Tashlhit-speaking people, the so-called *khamsa khmas*, the fragmentation into the five fifths of the *Ait 'Atta*, a tribal confederation in southeastern Morocco. Integral to the model is the clear definition of revenge parties. Gellner asked a question that produced surprise and laughter among his *Ait 'Atta* interlocutors. He wanted to know if in a case where he was only the eleventh confederate (member of an oath group, *tagallit*, or revenge party)[5] of a perpetrator or target of retaliation, he could calmly stay at home despite impending retaliation, while the ten closest agnates, which formed the actual solidarity group, would have to go into exile or seek asylum.[6] He was told not to be so sure that, firstly, all members of the opposing party had the same opinion on this and, secondly, that his own group did not expect some contribution to their compensatory activities. After all, there were several persons who could be counted as fifth or tenth confederate, depending on the case. Another decisive restriction to the model of complementary oppositions becomes visible here: one cannot assume that all those affected by a conflict are equally familiar with structures of solidarity, alliances and coalitions and align their actions accordingly (Turner 2008).

Moreover, claiming kin solidarity may inform the taking of sides, a decision that actors can reach in various ways. The solidarity of members of a retaliation party may fade away in cases where the perpetrator among them and with whom they are called to solidarize turns out to be a notorious troublemaker. Recidivists or individuals who have exercised violence beyond the reasonable – that is, beyond appropriate and proportionate standards – may face problems in mobilizing their solidarity group. Members of his party may agree to pay compensation for his acts once or twice, but there will come a time when the problem seems to require internal regulation. Societal peace may require that the group itself stops the perpetrator in order to avoid perpetuating retaliatory relationships with other groups; he may be excluded if the opposed parties accept this procedure as a solution. It may also be that members dissatisfied with the regulation secede from the group. Thus a concrete case of mobilization may even bring about the end or dissolution of a solidary retaliation group.

Another aspect is illuminated by Otterbein's (1994) study on the connection between patrilinearity and postnuptial residence. Even if adherence to a revenge group is defined, this does not necessarily conclude in the capacity to mobilize. Otterbein regards commitment to solidarity as a result of the social and territorial proximity of actors. In accordance with patrilineal descent and patri- or virilocality, fraternal interest groups are seen as easy to mobilize and thus the configuration can lead to a high readiness to use violence. In a case of conflict, powerful solidarity collectives of consanguineous males are readily available as violent actors. In uxorilocally organized alliances, in contrast, solidary actors of violence live far apart from each other. In a case of uxorilocal postnuptial residence in patrilineal organized societies, male members of retaliation parties live in spatial distance from one another. Therefore, social cohesion is less pronounced while solidarity with the matrilateral kin is accentuated. Otterbein extrapolates from the low enthusiasm to take sides to a high propensity for a nonviolent settlement of the conflict.

This model proved to be rather mechanical. Upon closer examination it turned out that in actual conflict, members of fraternal interest groups also may belong to networks in the wider general public and intervene equally as matrilateral and affinal relatives. Apart from this, the model ignores the specifically high potential for conflict within patrilineal and patrilocal settings. Internal tension, for instance, between brothers falls outside of retaliatory logic, may weaken solidary cohesion and may lead to coalitions with external alliance partners. Such potential for conflict may include rank disputes, domestic stress, generational conflicts because of education and change, inheritance disputes and competition for women. In everyday life, accordingly, individuals may maintain close relationships across such retaliation networks within a community of law so that solidarity is more or less pronounced until it is put to the test in the critical moment when the principle of retaliation takes effect. Such a situation may arise, either when solidarity is rewarded in that compensation fees are distributed among members or, more critically, when all members are called upon to contribute to the compensation that their own group has to pay to an opposed solidarity group. Then, internal tensions may emerge around disagreements about the correlation between individual accountability and collective charge and much more. Thus, the concrete conflict at hand may shape the way in which internal solidarity is played out.

The degree of group homogeneity also plays a role. 'Blood solidarity' as a marker of identity may be ideologically emphasized, but it represents but one among various registers that hold actors together who may have not as much in common regarding other markers such as wealth, reputation, age set or grade.

Another classic ethnography may be adduced here to shed light on the entanglements between belonging, the formation of retaliation parties and their sustainability. Conventionally, Emrys Peters (1967) is relied upon for this analysis, in his case by reference to Aulad 'Ali Bedouins of the Cyrenaica. He showed to what extent the convictions about how retaliation groups should be formed and how such parties were composed diverged in practice. In the moment when a conflict emerged, the patrilineal relatives who actually should have joined the parties were nomadizing with their herds far away, and thus it was the matrilateral relatives and friends who joined ranks and intervened. This shows that while the institutional arrangements are taken as stable, the individuals and even the groups involved are not. The opposed parties may absorb members of other communities of interest such as pasture associations, or land owners united as field abutters, or other trans-segmentary groups. In sub-Saharan Africa, for example, age groups play a crucial role as solidarity groups with respect to certain types of offence. Interestingly, it may be exactly those units that display the highest probability to retaliate violently and to express their sentiments of belonging most intransigently, exceeding the limits of calculated appropriateness (see Gabbert 2012: 118, 128, 175–80). Moreover, when analysing case studies, quite often a gap can be identified between the number of those active in a conflict and the number of those in whose names activities are carried out.

I now return to a Moroccan case in order to investigate another possible configuration. It is a narrative about a confrontation among Haoura Arabic-speaking people in the Souss in southwest Morocco, the focus area of my research. The events took place in the early twentieth century and continue to be recounted in the present day. To summarize, it was a typical violent incident that may occur between holders of overlapping use rights – that is, between mobile herders and peasants. In this example, it was indeed two lineage segments that were the conflicting parties. Yet the social relationship between them was so close that their external relations did not differ. Under such circumstances one party is expected to join another alliance group (Montagne 1930). Thus, it becomes evident that it is not only descent groups that are involved in conflict management. Alliance building as an organizational principle secures solidarity ties that stand in contrast to the segmentary and territorial identity cluster and is often compared with transregional political parties in modern times. In the Moroccan context these principles are crucial. Nevertheless, processes of reconfiguration may also take place on the respective segmentary level. Genealogies may be continually reinterpreted; incorporations of hitherto only affiliated foreign segments, which were formerly refused, may be accepted; fissions at a low level may be provoked because of alliances established between one segment and an opponent group. To a degree, potential future alliances also have to be considered in present strategies. It may appear opportune to moderate violence against the allies of the actual opponent in order not to jeopardize the option of a future partnership. It is not only the power relations that are taken into consideration but also possible marriage alliances, the establishment of trade relations and much more.[7]

Thus, in negotiating who will enter the arena of violence and against whom, or who is ready to offer, or is entitled to receive, compensatory payments, the consequences have to be considered quite pragmatically. Bargaining power translates into the exercise of coercive violence if neglected by the weaker party. The one who has to perform the violence on behalf of the powerful party may position himself in a delicate relationship with both parties, e.g. in terms of solidarity within age sets, or hunting or herding parties. Bargaining power does not implicate a standard solution. There is quite a distance to be travelled from bargaining power to the achievement of the preferred result. Creativity and uncertainty line the path. The member of the strong and powerful clan opposing a weaker one may soon find himself in a situation in which he faces, together with a small number of solidary allies, a superior number of opponents with whom he may solidarize in different circumstances. Such interplay may have an effect on the sustainability of internal cohesion and power and also on decisions to be made in view of their possible future effects. This includes the possible reactions of the wider public that constitutes the larger category of socio-political organization. According to Eidson et al. (2017: 347), relations of power and authority are among the circumstances according to which situations are handled that involve identification and 'are witnessed by multiple others'.

The strategic decision to invest in a pool of compensation and thus to demonstrate cohesive solidarity may pay off in the future. All of a sudden the targeted weak solidary group of an offender finds itself surrounded by friends and distant relatives. Also, factual circumstances, prehistory and anamnesis of an offence may have an impact on those social dynamics whose outcomes are expressed in terms of kin solidarity, identity and social cohesion.

Here there comes into play what Schlee (2004) calls 'taking sides' because a conflict that is addressed as an affair between two parties is embedded in a social environment and other actors may join one of the parties for a variety of reasons. A major motivation for nominal outsiders to engage in a conflict may be to balance an accumulation of power on one side because this could lead to domination or hegemony within the society at large. Such checks to the social order may thus be met with strategic balancing. Moreover, weaker allies of the powerful, realizing that their protector behaves in alliance in a hegemonic way, tend to quit. The conflictive situation itself may provide new opportunities to unite, and even opposed parties may be set in social relations to each other by the conflict itself on the way towards its settlement. There is a great variety of social tools for the establishment or maintenance of social relations after violence, such as the arrangement of marriages and the replacement of victims by substitutes among many others. It is far from being the exception in Middle Eastern and North African societies, for instance, that compensation arrangements are never really fully executed in the course of time. Even after very detailed negotiations in which tariffs are applied to a concrete case of injury, even after all of the calculation exercises, the agreement that has been reached may not be fully executed. The insistence on the full settlement of the account would be interpreted as an interruption of bilateral social relations established through a compensation agreement after an act of violence.

Thus if we apply Schlee (on identification and taking sides) to Schlee (on bargaining power and size matters), we realize that power is just one factor and that the simple power of calculation is actually based on a number of unknown qualifications. The other frames beyond retaliatory solidarity come to the fore, such as spatial proximity, inequalities within the network and so on. Under what conditions actors chose to activate what combination of categories of identification eventually remains an empirical question (Eidson et al. 2017: 356).

Context-specific identities and belonging, sometimes associated with more power overlap, sometimes with less, exist simultaneously. Thus, the bargaining power resulting from the great number of co-bargainers towards the less strong party presupposes a certain temporality of the necessary cohesion. Hence, the argument that size matters in power play and allows for bending the rules may apply to the immediate situation of conflict but may have detrimental consequences in the long run. It may, however, collide with other concomitant circumstances.

The empirical question then is to what extent an individual may rely on a multiplicity of his identities in a situation of retaliation or associated compensation negotiations in which other frames of identification barely count. There may be, for instance, the intervention of central political authorities, state institutions or religious leaders to offer frames of identification that devalue the retaliatory one or split loyalties along different lines.

Group affiliation is not automatically achieved by individual decisions to share a frame of identification with others. There must be recognition of the claim by the others sustaining that frame. As the Gellner example reveals, one cannot even be sure about one's own belonging. Sometimes ascribed identities by far override the ones that are individually adopted. Thus, the moment when a retaliation party is formed is the litmus test that shows to what extent expected ties of belonging materialize or not. Retaliation is a frame for identification insofar as it urges actors to make clear their attitude towards a number of shared or not shared frames that in one way or the other overlap or intertwine with the reactive logic of retaliation.

Conclusion

The examples provided herein have shown that the arithmetic of power may not automatically lead to a stable social organization. The rhetoric of retaliation provides for a whole range of social dynamics, allowing for sophisticated manoeuvring and alliance building. Ideology laid down in legal registers and catalogues of fines and treatments on the one hand, and practice on the other, feature complex mutual entanglements. Narratives on retaliation, competition and conflict reflect such ambiguities. It is the litmus test itself that lays bare the politics of belonging. When in situations of conflict politics of belonging find expression in a variety of strategies, it seems to be less an operation of measurement that counts; instead, sentiments of solidarity may evolve out of a variety of motivations, among them a sense for compensatory justice beyond any formal criteria of calculation.

The appreciation for the great number and size thus finds itself embedded in the complex processes of identity formation and the production of social cohesion so convincingly described in the literature mentioned. Summarizing Günther Schlee's view one may state that the striving for power is an empirical fact that emanates clearly in situations of retaliation, while strategies for its accumulation and maintenance may trigger counterbalancing processes of identification and solidarizing. Even if institutional arrangements safeguarding hegemony and dominance stand the test of time, their personnel changes over time according to the above-mentioned dynamics.

Bertram Turner is an anthropologist and senior researcher in the department Law & Anthropology at the Max Planck Institute for Social Anthropology in Halle, Germany. He has conducted extended field research in the Middle East and North Africa, EU countries and Canada and has held university teaching positions in Munich, Leipzig and Halle. He is a member of the executive body of the Commission on Legal Pluralism and an associate editor of *The Journal of Legal Pluralism*. He has published widely on the anthropology of law and legal pluralism, religion, conflict, morality, development, governance, science and technology, and resource extraction.

Notes

1. Moreover, in some communities kin-based legitimacy may be overruled by other cohesive forms of social organization such as those based on age and generation. See, for example, Gabbert (2012).
2. Data from 2005 fieldwork in southwest Morocco.
3. For further details about the narrative and its expansion and use, see https://quoteinvestigator.com/2016/05/05/brothers/#note-13671-1.
4. 28 August 1975, 'New Scientist, Survival through Suicide' by John Maynard Smith (book review of Edward O. Wilson's *Sociobiology: The New Synthesis*), quote on p. 496, col. 2, New Science Publications, London; now published by Reed Business Information, UK (http://evolutionlist.blogspot.de/2009/03/modern-evolutionary-synthesis.html).
5. The ten closest agnates functioned not only as a solidarity unit in a case of retaliation, but especially as a minimal group of co-jurors who took a collective oath on the true content of a statement and the reputation of a candidate. Cf., e.g. Hart (1981: 158–66), Turner (2017c).
6. In other words, each individual has his own reservoir comprising a certain number of ascending and descending generations out of which the solidarity group constitutes itself. Cf. also Baştuğ (1998: 106f).
7. For a more detailed analysis, see Turner 2008.

References

Baştuğ, Sharon. 1998. 'The Segmentary Lineage System: A Reappraisal', in Joseph Ginat and Anatoly M. Khazanov (eds), *Changing Nomads in a Changing World*. Brighton: Sussex Academic Press, pp. 94–123.
Eidson, John R., Dereje Feyissa, Veronika Fuest, Markus Virgil Hoehne, Boris Nieswand, Günther Schlee and Olaf Zenker. 2017. 'From Identification to Framing and Alignment: A New Approach to the Comparative Analysis of Collective Identities', *Current Anthropology* 58(3): 340–59.
Evans-Pritchard, E.E. 1976 [1940]. *The Nuer: A Description of the Modes of Livelihood and Political Institutions of a Nilotic People*. New York and Oxford: Oxford University Press.
Gabbert, Echi Christina. 2012. 'Deciding Peace: Knowledge about War and Peace among the Arbore of Southern Ethiopia', PhD dissertation. Halle (Saale): Martin Luther University Halle-Wittenberg.
Gellner, Ernest. 1969. *Saints of the Atlas*. London: Weidenfeld and Nicolson.
Haldane, John B.S. 1990 [1932]. *The Causes of Evolution*. Princeton, NJ: Princeton University Press.
Hart, David M. 1981. *Dadda 'Atta and His Forty Grandsons: The Socio-Political Organisation of the Ait Atta of Southern Morocco*. Wisbech: MENAS Press.
Lewis, Ioan M. 1999 [1961]. *A Pastoral Democracy: A Study of Pastoralism and Politics among Northern Somali of the Horn of Africa*. Oxford: James Currey.
Montagne, Robert. 1930. *Les berbères et le Makhzen dans le sud du Maroc: Essai sur la transformation politique des Berbères sédentaires (groupe Chleuh)*. Paris: Félix Alcan.
Otterbein, Keith F. 1994. *Feuding and Warfare*. Amsterdam: Gordon and Breach.
Peters, Emrys L. 1967. 'Some Structural Aspects of the Feud among the Camel-Herding Bedouin of Cyrenaica', *Africa* 37(2): 261–82.
Peters, Rudolph. 2005. *Crime and Punishment in Islamic Law: Theory and Practice from the Sixteenth to the Twenty-first Century*. Cambridge: Cambridge University Press.
Schlee, Günther. 1996. 'Regelmäßigkeiten im Chaos: Die Suche nach wiederkehrenden Mustern in der jüngeren Geschichte Somalias', in Günther Schlee and Karin Werner (eds), *Inklusion und Exklusion*. Cologne: Köppe, pp. 133–59.

———. 1997. 'Cross-Cutting Ties and Interethnic Conflict: The Example of Gabbra, Oromo and Rendille', in Katsuyoshi Fukui, Eisei Kurimoto and Masayoshi Shigeta (eds), *Ethiopia in Broader Perspective, Volume II*. Kyoto: Shokado Booksellers, pp. 577–96.

———. 2002. 'Regularity in Chaos: The Politics of Difference in the Recent History of Somalia', in Günther Schlee (ed.), *Imagined Differences: Hatred and the Construction of Identity*. Münster: LIT, pp. 251–80.

———. 2004. 'Taking Sides and Constructing Identities: Reflections on Conflict Theory', *Journal of the Royal Anthropological Institute* 10(1): 135–56.

———. 2006. *Wie Feindbilder entstehen: Eine Theorie religiöser und ethnischer Konflikte*: Munich: C.H. Beck.

———. 2008. *How Enemies Are Made: Towards a Theory of Ethnic and Religious Conflicts*. Integration and Conflict Studies 1. New York and Oxford: Berghahn.

———. 2017. 'Customary Law and the Joys of Statelessness: Somali Realities Beyond Libertarian Fantasies', in Bertram Turner and Günther Schlee (eds), *On Retaliation: Towards an Interdisciplinary Understanding of a Basic Human Condition*. New York and Oxford: Berghahn, pp. 208–35.

———. 2022. 'Retaliation, Mediation and Punishment in Ankole: Revisiting the Chapter by Oberg', in Günther Schlee and Aleksandar Bošković (eds), *African Political Systems Revisited*. New York and Oxford: Berghahn, pp. 122–38.

Schlee, Günther and Bertram Turner. 2008. 'Rache, Wiedergutmachung und Strafe: Ein Überblick', in Günther Schlee and Bertram Turner (eds), *Vergeltung: Eine interdisziplinäre Betrachtung der Rechtfertigung und Regulation von Gewalt*. Frankfurt: Campus, pp. 49–67.

Turner, Bertram. 2005. *Asyl und Konflikt: Von der Antike bis heute*. Berlin: Reimer.

———. 2008. 'Recht auf Vergeltung? Soziale Konfigurationen und die prägende Kraft der Gewaltoption', in Günther Schlee and Bertram Turner (eds), *Vergeltung: Eine interdisziplinäre Betrachtung der Rechtfertigung und Regulation von Gewalt*. Frankfurt: Campus, pp. 69–103.

———. 2017a. 'Introduction on Retaliation: Conceptual Plurality, Transdisciplinary Research, Rifts, Blurrings and Translations', in Bertram Turner and Günther Schlee (eds), *On Retaliation: Towards an Interdisciplinary Understanding of a Basic Human Condition*. New York and Oxford: Berghahn, pp. 1–25.

———. 2017b. 'Conclusion: Retaliation in Specific Spheres of Effectiveness', in Bertram Turner and Günther Schlee (eds), *On Retaliation: Towards an Interdisciplinary Understanding of a Basic Human Condition*. New York and Oxford: Berghahn, pp. 283–305.

———. 2017c. 'Translating Evidentiary Practices and Technologies of Truth Finding: Oath Taking as Witness Testimony in Plural Legal Configurations in Morocco', in Yazid Ben Hounet and Deborah Puccio-Den (eds), *Truth, Intentionality and Evidence: Anthropological Approaches to Crime*. Abingdon: Routledge, pp. 112–29.

Tyan, E. 1965. 'Art: "Diya"', in *The Encyclopaedia of Islam*, new edition, Volume 2. Leiden: E.J. Brill, pp. 340b–343a.

CHAPTER 8

HEROES AND IDENTITIES
Relativism, Myth and Reality

ALEKSANDAR BOŠKOVIĆ

Introduction

In this chapter, I look at the blurring boundaries between the universalism of human rights, on one hand, and the construction and perception of local identities, on the other. I take as my example reactions in Serbia following the apprehension of General Ratko Mladić in late May 2011. These reactions show a striking inability, on the part of many Serbs, to come to terms with the country's recent past, while at the same time demonstrating anthropology's uneasiness in dealing with consequences of relativism. It is also worth pointing out that debates about relativism among anthropologists followed what has been referred to as a 'storm', within the discipline, 'of intense self-questioning in the late 1980s' (Clifford 1999: 643).

One of the most original contemporary philosophers, John Gray, recently summed up some of the problems with the concept of human rights: 'Human rights have two large virtues – they empower us against governments, and anyone can claim them. If we have rights we needn't approach power on our knees, as supplicants begging for favours. We can demand that our freedoms be respected. And it doesn't matter who governs us. Human rights can be invoked wherever they exist' (Gray 2013). At the same time, invoking them in the contemporary world can provoke all kinds of unwanted reactions – accusations of essentialism, objectification and the like. That is why Gray, following up on E.M. Forster's famous essay of 1938, proposed that we give them only 'two cheers'. However, human rights are a product of Western liberal philosophy (Gray traces the concept from the seventeenth-century philosopher John Locke), and their claim to universality has been vigorously contested throughout the last century. It is still contested today (Eriksen 2017).

Of relevance to anthropology is the long history of debates between proponents of universalism and those who favoured relativism – beginning with the arguments between the French writer and philosopher François-Marie Arouet (1694–1778), better known as Voltaire, and the German poet and philosopher Johann Gottfried Herder (1744–1803). While Herder believed that each nation (and people) had a specific 'spirit' (*Volksgeist*) that must be understood if one is to understand their culture, Voltaire argued that there are no particular peoples nor nations – there exists only a universal humanity. Herder's response was that, in Voltaire's ideal universal humanity, everybody speaks French (Eriksen and Nielsen 2013: 16; Bošković 2014: 32). The echo of these debates can be seen in the mid-twentieth century, when the executive board of the American Anthropological Association (1947) expressed serious concerns about the draft version of what would, in December 1948, be adopted as the United Nations Universal Declaration of Human Rights (UDHR) (American Anthropological Association 1947; Goodale 2006: 1; Eriksen 2017: 1143).

The declaration has been deemed problematic, in some respects, since its adoption. In the vote to adopt the UDHR, the socialist countries belonging to the UN (including Yugoslavia) abstained, citing the failure of the proposed text to mention 'economic rights'. As a matter of fact, the main reason why Yugoslavia abstained was that it did not want to further complicate its relations with the USSR at the time (Šeks 1989: 352). However, in the decades that followed, the concept gradually became more and more relevant, especially for the industrialized, developed countries, where the idea of human rights was perceived in terms of its liberal background – as a way of enabling individual people to be free to achieve the best for themselves and their families. On the other hand, as human rights 'can be invoked wherever they exist', they have also been instrumentalized as a way to claim a special status and to justify specific needs. Over the years, the whole concept has evolved:

> Socialist and welfare state concepts and nations added a 'second generation' of *socioeconomic and cultural rights* including rights to employment and fair working conditions; rights to a standard of living that ensures health and well-being; rights to social security, education, and participation in the cultural life of the community; and special rights of women and children. . . .
>
> Third World nations, especially in Africa, added a 'third generation' of *solidarity* or *development rights* to peace, a more equitable socioeconomic order, and a sustainable environment. At the same time, many rejected the universalism of the Western human rights notions as ethnocentric and insisted that the rights of individuals could not be separated from their collective context. Indigenous peoples are now in the process of adding a 'fourth generation' of *indigenous rights*, which will protect their rights to political self-determination and control over socioeconomic development. (Messer 1993: 222–23; references omitted, italics in original)

Throughout the conflicts of the 1990s, warring sides in the former Yugoslavia, offering their own perspective on human rights, pointed frequently to their inalienable right to protect their own culture and their way of life. Maintaining their specific ethnic identity was the prerequisite for their physical survival as nations. This, they claimed, could only be achieved if they were allowed to live separately from their neighbours. How this separation would be accomplished, and at what cost to their neighbours, was not really discussed. In fact, the cost was inestimably high: 'The wars and destruction that ravaged parts of former Yugoslavia (and especially Bosnia and Herzegovina) during the 1990s also meant the destruction of moral values that were traditionally believed to exist in South European cultures' (Bošković 2012: 128).[1]

Ethnicity, Nationalism and Myth

In the last fifty years, issues such as ethnicity have come increasingly into focus in anthropological research (Schlee 2008: 5; Eriksen 2010: 4), beginning with Barth's (1969) insistence on the fact that ethnic groups are constructed. The idea that identities are constructions (i.e. that they are artificial) was something that decisively influenced approaches to the study of ethnicity and related issues. In his detailed overview of theories of ethnicity and nationalism, Eriksen points to the role that self-identification plays in many contemporary expressions of nationalism. Self-identification is, in turn, related to the choices that people (as actors in the social arena) make, depending on the circumstances and on the outcomes that they desire. Sometimes actor's choices in identification and self-identification are related to 'cost-benefit' calculations (Schlee 2008: 27; Bošković and Ignjatović 2012: 291–93). When it comes to the relationship between ethnicity and identity, Günther Schlee has drawn attention to the fact that conflict may be motivated by difference between enemies but often requires a degree of 'sameness', if enemies are to engage with one another in any meaningful way. In this sense, 'enemies become alike' (Schlee 2008: 11; see also Schlee and Horstmann 2018).

The concept of identity in general (especially in the aspects where it touches upon – and diverges from – identification) was explored in detail in a recent article by John R. Eidson et al. (2017). However, there is still something to be said about the ease with which identification can turn into animosity, and here there is probably room to consider what Erik H. Erikson (who is mentioned, but not regarded as important, in Eidson et al. 2017) referred to as development of 'a healthy personality' (Chapter 2 in Erikson 1959). In the case of the former Yugoslavia and the wars that broke out in the 1990s, hostilities based on ethnic feelings were skilfully exploited by the ruling elites. For example, Serbian politicians frequently pointed out that they were just trying to protect 'their people', the Serbs, who remained in other parts of former Yugoslavia. It would be helpful to view these developments in light of Erikson's psychoanalytically influenced works, as well as with reference to what another psychoanalyst, Christopher Bollas, later called 'the fascist state of mind':

> I turn my attention to that state of mind which is the warrant for the extermination of human beings. I term it the Fascist state of mind, knowing that in some respects this is historiographically incorrect, as Fascism was a particular movement in human history with highly unique features to it, but I justify this license by playing on the double meaning of the word 'state'. There was a fascist state. The coming into being of that state and its political theory can tell us quite a lot about another state: the state of mind that authorized a Fascist theory. (Bollas 1994: 196)

In his study of nationalism, Bruce Kapferer begins from what Ernst Cassirer (1923: 11) called a move from form to function. Historically, nationalism was criticized by many social scientists as 'pre-modern' or destructive, and it was assumed that it would gradually dissipate, or retreat, when confronted with forces of modernization (Gellner 1983; Hobsbawm 1983). Kapferer demurs:

> How nationalist discourse develops as a humanly destructive force is an empirical matter and demands an interrogation of nationalist arguments and how they became vital in political and social dynamics giving rise to the force and shape of their violence. . . . The perspectives of Gellner (1983) and Hobsbawm (1983), who exemplify such positions [objectivist and rationalist – A.B.], dismiss nationalist arguments as mere figments of the imagination or constructions and distortions of reality. Theirs are important contributions, however, they risk an overdetermination in a European and North American historical experience. Furthermore, they do not confront thoroughly enough either nationalist arguments or the discursive structures of their appeal. (Kapferer 2012: xiv)

Kapferer's book is more than another approach to ethnicity and violence – it 'describes nationalism as an ontology; that is a doctrine about the essence of reality' (Eriksen 2010: 129). In nationalist discourse, war, birth and death are all used as powerful symbols, but they gradually transcend the symbolic and enter into nationalist 'reality'. In his understanding of the interplay between symbols and everyday life, and in his attention to the religious aspects of nationalism, Kapferer displays an appreciation for Benedict Anderson's (1983) insistence on the importance of understanding nationalist constructions. However, while he conceives of his book *Legends of People, Myths of State* 'as an extension of Anderson's kind of approach', he goes beyond it, insofar as his 'objective was to concentrate more on the diverse styles of nationalist imaginations than did Anderson, who in my view remained committed to a linear and too homogenized conception, one still honed within a Western historical perspective' (Kapferer 2012: xxii). I see Kapferer's argument as crucial in understanding how Serbs internalized their views of themselves and others in a way that led to the wars of the 1990s.

The relationship between myth and history is at the core of Kapferer's arguments. Both of these are different forms of discourse. In his article 'The Narrative Function', Paul Ricœur distinguished between two general types of narratives, historical and fictional. These two types can be analysed in terms of their common structure, as structuralists have done; or they can be analysed in terms of their historicity – a 'fundamental feature of our individual and social existence' that they share (Ricœur 1981: 274).

The very distinction between 'history' and 'fiction' is in itself fictional in many ways. Histories are written by humans and, as such, are works of fiction. Ricœur points to the role of the myth as mimesis (following the argument from Aristotle's *Poetics*), but this is a creative imitation (1981: 292–93), not a mere reflection of some 'objective' reality. Through this process of creative imitation, the world of narratives (Ricœur's 'world of fiction') brings us 'to the heart of the real world of action' (Ricœur 1981: 296). It seems, then, that 'fiction, by opening us to the unreal, leads us to what is essential in reality' (Ricœur 1981: 296). This can explain how people accept mythical stories that are served to them as facts – presented to them as a shared history that is supposed to help them establish a 'proper' sense of national identity. Communities are symbolically established and solidarities strengthened through fictions that open up worlds that scholars could interpret as unreal. For the specific actors, they are perfectly real.

Myths are important for people's sense of identity, as they offer a 'safe haven', a place where individuals can feel that their sense of belonging to a group (whether it is an ethnic group or a nation) could be in their best interest. Myths also form an important part of national ideologies, and one of the main achievements of Kapferer's study was to show how different national ideologies (in his case, Sinhalese and Australian) can be structured along very similar lines.

Nationalist ideology provides important symbolic markers that allow members of the society to focus their anxieties and experience a sense of unity (Billig 1995; Eriksen 2010; Jenkins 1994). It also helps members of a society to form what is sometimes called the 'ethnonational bond' (Connor 1993) and to achieve 'ethnonational mobilization' (Iveković 2000). This 'bond' serves, in turn, to create a feeling of belonging to a shared community. Despite the fact that stories based on fiction are used in the process of achieving unity, the experience is real, and so are its consequences – and thus it is very important to comprehend the mechanisms that shape public opinion when it comes to particular cases (Kapferer 2012: 90–93).

Getting to the General

In his discussion of the relation of myth to political violence, Kapferer (2012: 40–48) argues that there is a tendency among scholars to assume that myth and 'reality' can be easily distinguished. His analysis shows the opposite to be true. Myths establish a specific kind of 'historicity', the main actors in which are mythic figures. They can be gods or goddesses, but also local heroes or even members of the community, to whom the community attributes certain powers. These figures are mythical because a certain community feels that they represent their most fundamental hopes and goals (Rank 1914).

General Ratko Mladić, Bosnian Serb army commander between 1992 and 1996, was felt by many to epitomize some of the most important Serb cultural traits – bravery, cunning and the will to defend 'his' people. Celebrated by Serbs and feared by his enemies, he seemed to embody the Serb unwillingness to be dominated by foreign powers that forms an important part of local epic and folklore tradition.

But the image of Mladić as a proud national warrior had much darker associations, too: as one of the commanders responsible for the 'ethnic cleansing' that took place in Bosnia and Herzegovina between 1992 and 1995, as a ruthless man whose soldiers had already killed civilians in Croatia in 1991, and as someone accused of organizing the worst massacre on European soil since the Second World War.[2]

On 26 May 2011, Mladić was arrested in a small town in the northern Serbian province of Vojvodina. The capture of this archetypal villain of the modern era was deemed such an important event by the Serbian government that the country's president at the time, Boris Tadić, announced it himself at a televised press conference. Because Mladić was accused of masterminding the genocidal massacre that took place in the eastern Bosnian town of Srebrenica in July 1995 (among other things), the International Criminal Tribunal for the former Yugoslavia (ICTY) in The Hague had held a warrant for his arrest since that year, and sizable rewards were on offer from both the US and Serbian governments for anyone helping to bring him to justice.

But Mladić, who went into hiding in mid-2001 (having hitherto lived openly in Serbia's capital, Belgrade), had up until this point proved elusive, although in years before his arrest various European Union figures had made it clear to the authorities in Belgrade that the path of European integration, to which the Serbian government had committed itself, could only be successful after Mladić's arrest and subsequent extradition to The Hague.

In the days that followed the arrest of Mladić, the reactions of the Serbian public were mixed. Ultra-nationalist politicians, predictably, condemned the arrest, accusing government officials of 'treason'. Only one political party, the opposition Liberal Democrats, congratulated the government. Several dozens of – mostly young – extremists rioted in the centre of Belgrade and in the northern city of Novi Sad, and members of the Serb Radical Party organized a protest in front of the National Assembly on the Sunday following the arrest. The protest was poorly attended, despite oft-cited opinion polls showing a majority of the Serb public in support of Mladić, considering him a 'hero' and 'defender of Serbs'.

There were renewed attempts in the Serbian media to portray the general as a 'brilliant' military strategist, although it is clear from his track record that his victories during the war were achieved only when his troops had a huge advantage in terms of numbers and firepower. When the forces were roughly even, he did not fare very well.³

According to Jelena Grujić, a journalist who reported on the war in Bosnia and Herzegovina, Mladić won fame beyond Bosnian Serbs only after being indicted by the ICTY in 1995. As the tribunal was viewed by large parts of the Serbian population as unjust and 'anti-Serb', even a 'threat to the safety of Serbs' (Artz 2006: 231–32), anyone indicted by it almost instantly won national renown. Perceptions of injustice and the phenomenon of 'hereditary victimhood' (Bauman 1998) are not, of course, limited to the Serbs. Just a few months before Mladić's apprehension, many Croatians and almost all the political parties in Croatia condemned, with a vehemence approaching hysteria, the ICTY sentencing of two Croatian army generals for war crimes. However, in Serbia, the sense of grievance was intensified by the feelings of frustration and loss following defeat in the wars that erupted after the break-up of Yugoslavia. Despite the official state propaganda that claimed that 'Serbia never participated in any wars', the economic and social destruction that resulted from the armed conflicts of the 1990s was (and still is) very tangible. As Serbs tended to identify disproportionally with Yugoslavia, the 'loss' of the homeland of the southern Slavs was extremely traumatic for them.

Coping with the Loss

This widespread feeling of loss and disillusion, arising from a sense of humiliation, gave rise in Serbia to a prevailingly relativist understanding of the wars: as all sides committed crimes during 1990s, many argued, all sides were guilty in equal measure.⁴ The attempt to present all sides as responsible in equal measure for the war atrocities was especially strong among Serbia's elite (as evident from the essays collected in Popov 2000). This partisan position is framed in the Serbian media (as well as in the scholarly literature) in relativist terms and citing relativist references (for the list of examples up to 2007, see Bošković 2007). For many ordinary Serbs, as all sides committed crimes, it is wrong to single out Serbian crimes. Many of them reject even the well-documented events (such as the genocide in Srebrenica in July 1995 – which figures also in the verdict of the International Court of Justice), claiming that they are part of the smear campaign created to spread lies about Serbs and Serbia. At the same time, they are also quick to point to the colonial legacy of Western powers, to US-led military strikes in the Middle East, etc., as proof of the double standard of their accusers. This relativist position also consistently emerges from surveys of Serbian public opinion regarding the ICTY (Strategic Marketing Research 2009).

As in some African countries, where parts of the population have resented the prosecution by the international courts of their erstwhile leaders and have argued that the funds spent on the prosecution would have been better used to aid the country's economy and feed its poor (Akoth 2014), many Serbs view prosecuting war criminals as a waste of time and money, speaking disparagingly of 'human rights' as an unnecessary 'import' from the West. Human rights organizations are perceived as 'enemies of the state', financed and supported by 'the West' in order to further undermine Serbian national identity. But, while we might conclude, with Wilson, that in Serbia, 'a culture of human rights [has been] constructed upon the quicksand of a culture of impunity' (Wilson 2003: 369), it is true, nevertheless, that a human rights culture, inflected by relativism, has taken hold there, finding expression, in the wake of the move to democracy in 2001, in a new insistence on freedom of speech and expression.

Interestingly, this new emphasis on the freedom of speech and expression has meant that the authorities do not object to publications glorifying Bosnian Serb leaders, or to many other extreme publications, including those denying the Holocaust and promoting hatred towards non-Serbs and other minorities (both ethnic minorities, such as Roma, and other kinds, such as sexual minorities). Most likely, any attempt to ban such publications would have been considered an infringement of basic human rights (Bošković 2006).

Following the arrest of Mladić, Serb media were full of expressions of concern about his human rights – how did he look, was he ill, was he fit to stand trial, should he be allowed to visit the grave of his daughter? Although some news outlets reported reactions from Bosnia and Herzegovina, especially from the mothers of the Srebrenica victims, and from Croatia, the issue of how Mladić himself was feeling was what filled the front pages. Thus, all outlets reported that, on being brought before the presiding judge of the Special Court in Belgrade, the general had requested fresh strawberries. He had also requested a visit from the Serbian Minister of Health and the Speaker of the National Assembly. All these requests were granted. Unfortunately for the media, neither the minister nor the speaker wanted to say what they talked about with Mladić, describing the visits as 'private'.

Curiously enough, Serb media showed little or no interest in what Mladić was actually accused of. The topics of war crimes and genocide remain almost invisible in Serbia, and it is widely believed that any politician who dared to speak openly about them would be condemned to oblivion. In the week of the general's arrest, the editor of Belgrade's leading weekly magazine, *NIN*, expressed himself on the issue as follows:

> How is it that we are still unaware of the extent of the crime in Srebrenica, the causes of war? How is it that, as a society and a nation, we have not yet questioned our own responsibility for everything that happened to ourselves and what we did

to others? Numbed by the necrophilic mythology, where we see only the injustice committed against us, hung over from the smell of [the] blood of tens of thousands of [those] killed during the wars we were in, Mladić's arrest did not make us realize the basic fact – that in the time we live in, national, state and social issues do not relate to blood and soil, but to the corpus of civilizational values. (Spaić 2011: 3; translated by the author)

There have been several opportunities for Serbia to begin the process of coming to terms with the past. The first came in 2001, shortly after the change of government, when a documentary about the Srebrenica genocide was broadcast on national television (see note 4). The film provoked almost universal condemnation of the crime. Four years later, in June 2005, video footage was aired, showing members of the Serbian 'Scorpions' unit executing six Bosnian Muslims in July 1995.[5] The brutality of this crime shocked both the international and the Serbian public. But this state of shock did not last very long. At each point, whenever something like this would happen, some other event, such as an acquittal in The Hague of someone accused of crimes against Serbs, would turn the spotlight back on the perceived injustices and unfairness of the 'international community', making the road towards coming to terms with the past an even longer and more winding one.

Myths to Die For

Myths, histories and stories of struggle and salvation all come together in this extraordinary narrative. How is it possible to transform the idea that cultures (and peoples) should be studied in their own terms, in their own cultural idiom, into one that favours the exclusion of others, even to the point of physically destroying them? At the same time, what can these shifts tell us about the (re)constructions of identities? Can one conclude that the specific actors (ethnic groups or their leaders) are actually behaving quite rationally – given that they have received (and continue to receive) overwhelming popular support for their policies? In the words of one of the most popular scholars of myth in the last century, myths were something that people 'live by'. However, in the Serbian version, they seem more like something to 'die for'.

Anthropology provides important tools for understanding these events. In a historical context of long duration, anthropological studies of specific social interactions and their consequences can help to achieve an understanding of apparently ambivalent or even complicated shifts. For example, given Serbia's struggles with modernity, and the fact that the majority of Serbs always looked with suspicion on anything that they viewed as 'imported from the West' (Bošković 2017), it appears as if the ruling elite, of the late 1990s and early 2000s, had 'read' the prevailing popular sentiments and offered the people a hero. Then, when the political context changed with the government's decision to start negotiations with EU countries and to open the country for trade and foreign investment, the hero became expendable. Improving relations with neighbouring countries, which goes together with the increase in trade and communication, also became much more important.

Given all this, the arrest, extradition and eventual sentencing of one of the most wanted men of the past twenty-five years is still only a first step towards reconciliation – though, in view of Mladić's overall mythical status in Serbia, a highly significant one. Shifts in feelings of victimhood and perceived injustice will take more time, as will any moderation in the prevailing ethos of moral relativism. Given anthropologists' interest in all things 'relative', Serbia will remain an important field site for observing, testing and interpreting the limits of relativism.

Aleksandar Bošković is Senior Research Scientist at the Institute of Archaeology in Belgrade (Serbia) and Professor of social anthropology at the UFRN, Natal (Brazil). He has taught at the Universities of Ljubljana (Slovenia), Brasília (Brazil), Donja Gorica (Montenegro), Belgrade (Serbia) and St Andrews (Scotland, UK), at Rhodes University in Grahamstown (South Africa) and at the University of the Witwatersrand (Johannesburg, South Africa). He is the author of *William Robertson Smith* (New York and Oxford, 2021), *Mesoamerican Religions and Archaeology* (Oxford, 2017), editor of *Other People's Anthropologies* (New York, 2008) and co-editor of *African Political Systems Revisited: Changing Perspectives on Statehood and Power* (New York, 2022; with Günther Schlee).

Notes

This chapter draws in part from Bošković (2011). I am very grateful to Dr Gustaaf Houtman and the anonymous reviewers for their comments on that earlier sketch, which I have also taken into account in this chapter. Special thanks to John Eidson, who went into details that made me revisit some of the sources (and consult a few more). All the potential errors and omissions are my own.

1. This set of values was in anthropological literature sometimes referred to as the 'honour/shame' code (Peristiany 1966).
2. On 22 November 2017, Mladić was sentenced by the International Criminal Tribunal for the former Yugoslavia (ICTY) to life in prison for genocide and crimes against humanity. The summary of the verdict (abridged version for the media) is available at http://www.icty.org/x/cases/mladic/tjug/en/171122-summary-en.pdf.
3. See Anastasijević (2011), who describes military conflicts around Bihać in 1995, in which Bosnian Serb army units were defeated.
4. *Srebrenica: A Cry from the Grave*, 13/WNET production. When this documentary was broadcast in 2001, it was condemned by the opposition in the Serbian National Assembly, not because of the film's content but because it was shown on 'national television' (as opposed to being shown on one of the private TV channels). Among the most vocal opponents of the broadcasting of this film was Aleksandar Vučić, who became head of the country's ruling party in 2012 and president of Serbia in 2017.

5. The Scorpions and similar army and police units are often labelled as 'paramilitary', even though they were equipped and financed by the Serbian government. All of the top Bosnian Serb military commanders, including General Mladić, received their salaries from Belgrade. Mladić formally retired from active military service in 2002, and the decree confirming his retirement was signed by the then president of the Federal Republic of Yugoslavia, Vojislav Koštunica.

References

Akoth, Steve O. 2014. 'Human Rights Critique in Post-Colonial Africa: Practices among Luo in Western Kenya', *Anthropology of Southern Africa* 37(1–2): 94–106.
American Anthropological Association. 1947. 'Statement on Human Rights', *American Anthropologist* 49(4): 539–43.
Anastasijević, Dejan. 2011. 'Kako se Ratko Mladić odao genocidu' [How Ratko Mladić Gave in to Genocide], *Vreme* 1065, 31 May. Retrieved from http://www.vreme.com/cms/view.php?id=993392.
Anderson, Benedict. 1983. *Imagined Communities: Reflections on the Origin and Spread of Nationalism*. London: Verso.
Artz, Donna E. 2006. 'The Local Perception of International Criminal Tribunals in the Former Yugoslavia and Sierra Leone', *Annals of the American Academy of Political and Social Science* 603: 226–39.
Barth, Fredrik. 1969. 'Introduction', in F. Barth (ed.), *Ethnic Groups and Boundaries: The Social Organisation of Culture Difference*. Bergen: Universitets Forlaget, pp. 9–37.
Bauman, Zygmunt. 1998. 'The Holocaust's Life as a Ghost', *Tikkun* 13(4): 33–38.
Billig, Michael. 1995. *Banal Nationalism*. Newbury Park and London: Sage.
Bollas, Christopher. 1994. *Being a Character: Psychoanalysis and Self Experience*. New York: Hill and Wang.
Bošković, Aleksandar. 2006. 'Balkan Ghosts Revisited: Racism, Serbian Style', *Anthropos* 101(2): 559–64.
———. 2007. 'Nacionalizam kao sudbina: Nekoliko stavova srpskih intelektualaca o raspadu Jugoslavije' [Nationalism as Destiny: Some Attitudes of Serbian Intellectuals about the Dissolution of Yugoslavia], in M. Rašević and Z. Mršević (eds), *Pomeramo granice [We Are Moving the Borders]*. Belgrade: Institute of Social Sciences, pp. 67–80.
———. 2011. 'Ratko Mladić: Relativism, Myth, and Reality', *Anthropology Today* 27(4): 1–3.
———. 2012. 'The Question of Morality: "The Starry Heavens above Me" and Everyday Life in the Balkans', *Forum Bosnae* 55: 128–32.
———. 2014. *Antropološke perspektive* [Anthropological Perspectives]. Belgrade: Institute of Social Sciences.
———. 2017. 'Serbia and the Surplus of History: Being Small, Large, and Small Again', in Ulf Hannerz and Andre Gingrich (eds), *Small Countries: Structures and Sensibilities*. Philadelphia: University of Pennsylvania Press, pp. 195–209.
Bošković, Aleksandar and Suzana Ignjatović. 2012. 'Understanding Ethnic Conflicts through Rational Choice: A Review Article', *Ethnos* 77(2): 289–94.
Cassirer, Ernst. 1923. *Philosophie der symbolischen Formen. Erster Teil: Die Sprache*. Berlin: Bruno Cassirer Verlag..
Clifford, James. 1999. 'Review of *After Writing Culture: Epistemology and Praxis in Contemporary Anthropology*, edited by Allison James, Jenny Hockey, and Andrew Dawson', *American Anthropologist* 101(3): 643–45.
Connor, Walker. 1993. 'Beyond Reason: The Nature of the Ethnonational Bond', *Ethnic and Racial Studies* 16(3): 373–89.

Eidson, John R., Dereje Feyissa, Veronika Fuest, Markus Virgil Hoehne, Boris Nieswand, Günther Schlee and Olaf Zenker. 2017. 'From Identification to Framing and Alignment: A New Approach to the Comparative Analysis of Collective Identities', *Current Anthropology* 58(3): 340–59.

Erikson, Erik H. 1959. *Identity and the Life Cycle: Selected Papers*. New York: W.W. Norton.

Eriksen, Thomas Hylland. 2010. *Ethnicity and Nationalism: Anthropological Perspectives*, 3rd revised edn. London: Pluto Press.

———. 2017. 'Global Citizenship and the Challenge from Cultural Relativism', *Етноантропoлошки проблеми, н. с. год. 12 св. 4 (Issues in Ethnology and Anthropology* 12(4)): 1141–51.

Eriksen, Thomas Hylland and Finn Sivert Nielsen. 2013. *A History of Anthropology*, 2nd edn. London: Pluto Press.

Forster, E.M. 1938. 'Two Cheers for Democracy', *The Nation*, 16 July.

Gellner, Ernest. 1983. *Nations and Nationalism: New Perspectives on the Past*. Oxford: Blackwell.

Goodale, Mark. 2006. 'Introduction to "Anthropology and Human Rights in a New Key"', *American Anthropologist* 108(1): 1–8.

Gray, John N. 2013. 'A Point of View: Two Cheers for Human Rights', BBC, 27 December. Retrieved from http://www.bbc.com/news/magazine-25505393.

Hobsbawm, Eric. 1983. 'Introduction: Inventing Traditions', in Eric Hobsbawm and Terence Ranger (eds), *The Invention of Tradition*. Cambridge: Cambridge University Press, pp. 1–14.

Iveković, Ivan. 2000. *Ethnic and Regional Conflicts in Yugoslavia and Transcaucasia: A Political Economy of Contemporary Ethnonational Mobilization*. Ravenna: Longo Editore.

Jenkins, Richard. 1994. 'Rethinking Ethnicity: Identity, Categorization and Power', *Ethnic and Racial Studies* 17(2): 197–223.

Kapferer, Bruce. 2012. *Legends of People, Myths of State: Violence, Intolerance, and Political Culture in Sri Lanka and Australia*, new and revised edn. New York and Oxford: Berghahn.

Messer, Ellen. 1993. 'Anthropology and Human Rights', *Annual Review of Anthropology* 22: 221–49.

Peristiany, John G. 1966. *Honour and Shame: The Values of Mediterranean Society*. Chicago: University of Chicago Press.

Popov, Nebojša (ed.). 2000. *The Road to War in Serbia: Trauma and Catharsis*. Budapest: CEU Press.

Rank, Otto. 1914. *The Myth of the Birth of the Hero: A Psychological Interpretation of Mythology*, trans. F. Robbins and Smith E. Jelliffe. New York: Journal of Nervous and Mental Disease Publishing.

Ricœur, Paul. 1981 [1979]. 'The Narrative Function', in Paul Ricœur, *Hermeneutics and the Human Sciences*, edited and trans. by John B. Thompson. Cambridge and Paris: Cambridge University Press and Maison des Sciences de l'Homme, pp. 274–96.

Schlee, Günther. 2008. *How Enemies Are Made: Towards a Theory of Ethnic and Religious Conflicts*. Integration and Conflict Studies 1. New York and Oxford: Berghahn.

Schlee, Günther and Alexander Horstmann (eds). 2018. *Difference and Sameness as Modes of Integration: Anthropological Perspective on Ethnicity and Religion*. New York and Oxford: Berghahn.

Šeks, Vladimir. 1989. 'Jugoslavija i međunarodni pravni dokumenti o pravima čovjeka' [Yugoslavia and International Legal Documents on Human Rights], *Revija za sociologiju* 20(3/4): 351–62.

Spaić, Nebojša. 2011. 'Buđenje iz košmara' [Waking Up from a Nightmare], *NIN* 3153, 2 June.

Strategic Marketing Research. 2009. 'Stavovi prema ratnim zločinima, Haškom tribunalu i domaćem pravosuđu za ratne zločine' [Public Opinion and Attitudes Toward the ICTY in The Hague], April. Retrieved from http://bgcentar.org.rs.

Wilson, Richard A. 2003. 'Anthropological Studies of National Reconciliation Processes', *Anthropological Theory* 3(3): 367–87.

CHAPTER 9

'KOŠTA AKWA'

What an Italian Pidgin Poem from Tigray Says about Self-Image, Resistance and Conflict

WOLBERT G.C. SMIDT

The subject of this chapter is a short poem that was recorded in Färäs May in the Adwa area of central Tigray in 2010.[1] This so-called 'Italian' poem, which was orally transmitted, was once popular in Färäs May. An elder who had witnessed the Italian occupation of Ethiopia from 1935 to 1941 could still remember it. Its language was said to be Italian. According to the information provided by the elder, the poem was composed by young Ethiopians during the occupation in order to make fun of the Italian occupying forces and to praise a 'šəfta' ('bandit' or, in this context, member of the 'resistance' against Italian occupation) who made life for the Italians in the Färäs May area difficult. It therefore belongs to the well-known category of poems or songs praising heroes and heroic deeds.

I dedicate this brief study to Günther Schlee in memory of his recent visits to Tigray and of our many fruitful conversations – conversations about the Ethiopian regions and their diversity of claims and counter-claims, about the creation of identities and about the creative ways, in Ethiopia, of expressing and organizing conflict. With this dedication, I wish especially to honour his interest in the social context of language or, as in this case, the social and cultural-political context. In addition, this chapter is meant to appeal to his interest in oral literature,[2] even if certainly from an unexpected angle. I should add that I am deeply grateful for our cooperation within the film series 'Guardians of Productive Landscapes' at the Max Planck Institute for Social Anthropology. With this text I contribute one more performative element to our cooperation.

The Poem - Text and Translation

The documented text in Geez script is the following:

ኮሽታ ኣኳ ኮሽታ ኣኳ ባበይነ
ሰደረ ደርሚነ ቦነ
ኣስተሲራ ገብረህይወት ሩባረ
ሮቶ ደሚነ ድሞ ደማነ

The transliteration of the original text follows, using the *Encyclopaedia Aethiopica* (EAE) system of transliteration, with a word-to-word comparison with Italian and a translation (with a tentative explanation in brackets, based on the information provided by the elder).

košta akwa košta akwa babäynä
questa acqua questa acqua - va bene
this water, this water is good
(= this area is rich in water resources)

sädärä därminä bonä
sedere dormono (dormire) buono
sitting, sleeping, [that is all] good
(= the area is good to live in)

astäsira gäbrähəywät rubarä
a sta sera Ghebrehiwot[3] rubare
this evening Gäbrähəywät stealing[4]
(= Gäbrähəywät comes tonight as a thief/šəfta)

roto däminä dəmo dämanä
rotto domani dopodomani
broken tomorrow, after tomorrow
(= attacking / killing continuously, so that the Italians have to give up that place)

The Language of the Poem

What can we say about the claim that the language of the poem is 'Italian'? The spelling of words largely follows the patterns of Tigrinya phonology and, in some cases, is modelled after existing Tigrinya words or expressions. Examples for this are the following:

sädärä (ሰደረ) – past tense (masc., sing.) of *məsdar*, 'to do steps', cp. *sədri* 'step'
dəmo (ድሞ) – 'and' / 'and then'

roto (ሮቶ) – water container on top of a house (loanword in modern Tigrinya) / modern derived meaning: 'fat man'
däminä . . . dämanä (ደማን . . . ደማን): this combination of words strongly resembles *dämäna dammänä/dämminu* – 'clouds become thick (and dark) [hope for rain]'.

These similarities play a role in the creation of connotations linked with this orally presented poem (the written version is recent, as this is in principle an entirely oral piece of local poetry). Despite the fact that those reciting it and listening to it understood it to be composed in a foreign language, phonetic similarities to Tigrinya allow some vague associations with meanings in Tigrinya, especially when consonants are the same and only vowels differ, which is a basis for the creation of meaning in the root-centred Semitic languages. On this more below!

The poem, however, is really entirely composed of Italian or rather 'Italianizing' words, put together in a quite ungrammatical way. Its syntactic pattern follows, to some degree, local principles of oral poetic performances. These are often based on a simplified pattern of composition involving a focus only on the most important words, which are often repeated in a rhythmic pattern. An example for this is the first line, which can be translated as 'This water, this water is good'. Even if, locally, this poem is said to have been composed in 'Italian', this is neither Italian in the proper sense nor simply a faulty representation of Italian. The combination of Ethiopian phonetics with a simplified syntactic logic, following Ethiopian patterns of poem performance, composed in a harmonious and rhythmic way, producing a clear meaning, suggests, rather, that the text represents an early but somehow stabilized stage of a pidginized language. The poem shows a sovereign use of language, which appropriates the original language creatively, establishing its own new patterns of production of sense and meaning. It can therefore be regarded as a rare example of an early stage of language development, when elements of a foreign language are combined with those of a substratum (in this case Tigrinya), following a simplified grammar and pronunciation but also introducing new principles. I suggest, therefore, that this text is one of the few examples of the sort of early Italian pidgin that had started to develop in Ethiopia during the Italian occupation (possibly influenced by the specific use of Italian by locals in adjacent Eritrea).[5]

Typical for a pidgin (or a nascent pidgin as in this case) is the re-interpretation of words: a word with an originally more narrow meaning is transported into another context and given a wider meaning. For example, the expression *va bene* is used here for 'it is good'. The word *rotto* (from *rompere*, 'broken') is understood, according to the explanation of the elder, to mean 'to kill'. Another example is the simplified use of verbs, mostly in infinitive form (*sedere, rubare*), or in a mix between the infinitive and a conjugated form (*dormire/dormono*).[6] Very typical for a pidgin is also the phonetic transformation, e.g. from *va bene* to *babäynä* (v > b), or from *questa* to *košta* (ue > o).[7]

Evidently, one cannot yet speak of a fully developed pidgin, first, because the text is too short to offer conclusions and, second, because the use of Italian by locals (for example in conversations with their Italian employers or military commanders) had just started in that period. In addition, after the rather rapid downfall of *Africa Orientale Italiana* (Italian East-Africa), encompassing the Italian colonies of Eritrea and Somalia, together with Ethiopia and its dependencies, which were divided into new sub-entities or provinces, there was no further need for such a language. Therefore, we possess only a very few examples of this sort of Italian pidgin. Still, there are a considerable number of examples of Italian influences on Ethiopian and Eritrean languages, which were the result of this language contact. Today's Tigrinya is full of Italianisms and loanwords of Italian origin.[8]

Content and Composition: A Performative Poem

It is interesting that this 'Italian' poem was composed by Ethiopians and meant for Ethiopian ears, despite being composed in a foreign, or in a pidginized language. So, the Italian language – which younger Ethiopians had already begun to learn, if only at the level of some basic vocabulary, during the Italian occupation from 1936 to 1941 – was used in this case not for communication with the Italians, but for the amusement of an Ethiopian audience. The Italian words serve to mimic the speech of Italians amongst themselves. Certainly, then, the Ethiopians who listened to the poem anticipated that 'the Italians' would hear it and become angry, feeling that it undermined their authority. This is a key dramatic effect of this poetic piece. In this sense, the use of Italian had a pronounced performative function, based on its effect on the imagination of the audience.

At the same time, some words are identical or almost identical with Tigrinya, which allows those listeners who may not have a sufficient command of the corresponding Italian vocabulary to play with his or her imagination and infer some meaning. For example, *sädärä* means something like 'he made steps (forward)' – fitting well the general theme of the poem telling the story of the Italians stepping into the land. This quality of non-intended, fantasized meanings augments the performative aspects of the poem.

A further element which strengthens its performative quality is its narrative structure. The poem first achieves a positive climax, which is then followed by a quick, negative turn of events. The poem is virtually a short narrative of historical events. In a first phase, when the Italians arrive in Färäs May and construct their houses, they are imagined to have said something like the following to each other: 'Great, this area has good water and is beautiful – let us stay here. We will have a good life here!' But then a disturbance arises, and the Italians are said to exclaim in fear: 'Oh, this evening the bandit Gäbrähəywät is coming. He is killing and dispersing us – so we have to leave this nice place!' Thus, even if very short, the poem is an example of a narrative of the downfall of an illegitimate occupant, and a narrative of resistance. The invaders identify the place as good, but then it becomes terrible for them, due to local resistance. The message is clear: this good place does not belong to the Italians! As it is not theirs, they have to leave. Thus, justice is re-established. It is an example of evolved literary irony that the story of their failure is told in their own language, literally 'quoting' them. This inner tension increases the persuasive power of the poem.

In addition, the poem refers to a concrete local personality, Gäbrähəywät, a šəfta (roughly 'lawless person/bandit'), respectively a member of the resistance who was active in the Färäs May area in the late 1930s or early 1940s. Therefore, the poem also has the secondary function of praising a 'hero', honouring the capacity of this heroic personality to make life miserable for the occupying forces and even to drive them out. At the time of the composition of the poem, this may not have yet been reality, but the Ethiopian resistance did contribute to the quick failure of the Italian colonial plans. In some areas this resistance was systematically organized, and it was sometimes carried out in the traditional manner of šəfta resistance, i.e. by lawless groups attacking soldiers, military and administrative posts, the infrastructure, and so on. This makes the poem interesting from a comparative point of view as well. It belongs (if only secondarily) to the large category of hero poems and songs so widespread in the oral literature of northeastern Africa. Like the songs of heroes in other cultures of the region, there is a short narrative linked with a hero's name – as is the case in some *geerarsa* songs of the Oromo, some of which refer, in a similarly brief way, to the deeds of a hero in battle or in fights.[9]

A further inner tension is created by the contrast between the meaning of the Ge'ez name of this member of the resistance and the description of his activities in the poem. He is 'killing', but his name means 'Servant of Life'. His name is the only purely non-Italian element of the poem and thus deserves attention. It is a Ge'ez name, very typical for Tigray and for the Christian Orthodox naming tradition of the Ethiopian highlands. The audience of this poem would understand this contrast without difficulty, but would not perceive any contradiction. In fact, this is another typical feature of Ethiopian poems: working with sublayers of meanings and creating contrasts through double meanings. While the poem refers to a concrete personality, the meaning of the name creates a sublayer. The 'Servant of Life' kills – which cannot, however, be perceived as a hidden criticism of this 'bandit', who breaks the laws of life. On the contrary, this contrast fits perfectly a pattern of Ethiopian praise poems in which heroes and military leaders are often associated with heavenly laws, with powers and sacredness. They are compared, for example, to the Archangel Michael or Saint George, who killed devilish monsters, a snake and a dragon, respectively. The archangel and the saint are thus killers of evil, and they are both very popular in the traditions of Ethiopian highlanders, including praise poems. This militant aspect of Christian tradition allows the association of killing with the idea of a holy action. Thus, the contrast between the hero killing and the meaning of the hero's name would be read as one more variation of the established narrative of sacred struggles against evil. The poem contains, then, an underlaying reference to the idea of an (eternal?) sacred struggle of Christians against evil, justifying war as part of a long history of resistance against the devil and his emissaries.

The Context: Constructing a Self-Image of Resistance

The poem represents a purified version of events. It is based on the interpretative pattern of the (bad) invader versus the (good) resistance fighter, an important element in Tigrayan traditional narratives on war and conflict which corresponds to the Tigrayan image of themselves as patriots who resist against any and all foreign rule. Thus, this poem is one of many examples of a general political-cultural narration of heroic deeds in the face of illegitimate 'others' – be they the Italians of the 1930s (as in this case), or the Shewan soldiers under Menilek II, who took power in Ethiopia in 1889 (a central narrative in Tigrayan traditions), or the Egyptians of the Ethiopian-Egyptian wars under atse Yohannis IV – another important topos in oral poems in the Tigrayan tradition.[10]

To dramatize this narrative of the hero versus the invader, the poem utilizes another pattern not yet mentioned: the good and beautiful land that is desired by these 'others' and, in response, their destruction by 'us', by members of the we-group, who are the defenders. This pattern provides a historical explanation for the question why 'others' – the Italians, in this case – wish to take the land: it is a 'good land', rich in resources. If one inhabits a good land, others want to take it; therefore, one must always be ready to defend one's land and to destroy the invaders! This is a narrative which strongly marks Tigrayan political discourse and political identity-construction until this day. Invaders will be repelled – and must be repelled. The Tigrayan of this poem, Gäbrähəywät, represents an ideal image of a Tigrayan defending his people's land aggressively and effectively.

The last line of the poem is of interest here. As pointed out above, even if the language is meant to be Italian, due to the phonetic realization of the Italian words, there are sometimes strong similarities to local vocabulary. Because Ethiopian poetry tradition is marked by play with double meanings, audiences possess a developed sensitivity for any possible double meaning – even those which may not have been intended originally, but which emerge during performances and which are reproduced in subsequent recitations of such poems by members of the audience. In fact, double meanings are always an interactive process, not just something that is hidden between the lines by the original author. Connotations are produced in the process of performance and performances! Just one example: the line '*däminä dəmo dämanä*' – translated above from the 'Italian' as 'tomorrow, after tomorrow' – greatly resembles the Tigrinya words for cloud and 'clouds become thick'. Together with the Tigrinya word 'dəmo' (which means, according to the context, something like 'and' or 'and then'), the entire wording makes perfect sense: the Italian phrase is built on the Tigrinya phrase 'dämäna dəmo dammänä', with just a minor change of the vowels involved.[11] This can be translated as 'and then the cloud became [dark and] thick' – in the sense of heavy weather making for an uncomfortable situation for Italians, but bringing good rain for Ethiopians.

To be clear, this would not be understood as a real translation of that last line, but due to the similarity of the Italian words to specific Tigrinya vocabulary, such connotations can and will pop up during performances of this poem. And supposing that the audience would have a general idea of the meaning of the Italianizing word *roto*, one can easily think of something like 'the threatening clouds become thicker and darker'. That is, in effect, what happened to the Italians when they lost their decisive battles in early 1941 and, subsequently, had to leave. This may suggest that the poem dates approximately from the period of increased resistance against Italian rule, from around the months and weeks of their demise. In short, the poem gives expression to the self-image of heroic resistance against evil, that is, to a dichotomic view of the world and of the self. It refers to an established local definition of conflict: that there is one side that breaks the rules, one side that is evil or misguided. There is usually a good and a bad side in conflict, which is caused by the illegitimate desire of the 'other' for something that is not his.

Of course, if we look at the details, history tells us a different story. Especially at the beginning of the Italian invasion (1935 to 1936), reactions of local leaders and local groups were mixed. While the Ethiopian state organized a high-level of military resistance, there were numerous defections. In some regions, such as Wallaggaa (or Wollega), people did not always participate in the state's defence against the invasion, and leaders in these regions even used the occasion to declare their secession from Ethiopia – which they saw as an occupying force, as their declarations made clear. In Tigray, especially, large portions of the rural population of Rayya, who, traditionally, valued their autonomy highly, supported the Italian army, rather than the Ethiopian soldiers of Emperor Haylä Səllase (Haile Sellassie), who were, in fact, identified as the 'occupants from Shewa', not as the patriotic defenders of the nation. The most prominent Tigrayan leader to cross over to the Italians was *ras* Haylä Səllase Gugsa, governor of eastern Tigray. His defection to the Italian side is usually seen in historiography as an act of betrayal, a crime against the nation. If one looks more closely, however, at the political context, one can see that the supposed traitor had, in fact, entered into the local logic of resistance against Shewan domination, which was seen as illegitimate by the defenders of Tigrayan autonomy. From this perspective, cooperation with the Italians was a legitimate strategy.

Without insisting that Tigrayan resistance to Shewan domination fully explains such cases of cooperation or collaboration with the quasi-colonial occupants, I suggest that there can be (and often is) a local logic behind such acts that is usually overlooked by government-centric historiography. One can even observe, in oral accounts recorded during field research on local history in Tigrayan regions, that rural people often remember their encounter with the Italian occupants positively. Clearly, the simple economic fact that the Italians paid regular salaries exerted a strong influence on local perceptions, which contrast with official narratives. The observation to be underlined here is that the resistance against Italian occupation was not general and all-encompassing.

But does this observation undermine the dichotomic logic of this poem? Not really. In all cases, the dichotomy remains stable, in perfect accordance with Schlee's reasoning about conflict.[12] The boundary between 'us', the resisters, and 'them', the invading 'others', is flexible. In any kind of local definition of existing conflict, the local 'we' remains positively charged and stable, just the 'other' against whom 'we' resist (e.g. by joining the Italians in order to resist the rule of Shewa) can be replaced. The borders of resistance change. This poem refers to one of these constructed boundaries. The dichotomic definition of conflict is stable. Only the 'other' can be and will be replaced according to circumstances.

Concluding Remark

The analysis has shown that, even if very short, the poem discussed here offers many layers of interpretation. Its strong performative aspects, its dichotomic view of conflict and its linguistic double layers make it a highly interesting and rich piece of oral literature. Even if the poem seems, at first sight, to be very simple, the analysis reveals the development of a narrative climax with several layers of meaning and with cultural implications of a local tradition of proud militant heroism that strengthens the identity of local people as invincible resisters. In addition, the poem is an interesting local historical document. There are numerous narratives of the anti-Italian resistance of the years 1936 to 1941, but very few of these stem from the rural population. This poem bears witness to how resistance was narrated locally, in poetic performances in a traditional rural setting, creatively integrating the foreign language into local patterns of narration. In retrospect, after the end of Italian occupation, the poem also contributes to a self-definition of local Tigrayans as patriotic participants in the resistance against foreign occupants – which, during the actual occupation took the form of a complicated mixture of fierce opposition to and hesitant or even willing cooperation with the Italians, along with resistance against Amhara rule. But in any case, the local owner of the land resists against the 'other'. Even if he kills, he is the Servant of Life.

Wolbert G.C. Smidt is an ethno-historian at the Seminar of Middle Eastern Studies at the Friedrich Schiller University Jena, carrying out research on historical traditions and cultural practices in Tigray, Ethiopia (Yeha project), in cooperation with the German Archaeological Institute (DAI). He is also an adjunct professor at the Department of Anthropology at Mekelle University and supervises doctoral students in the two Anthropology / History & Cultural Studies PhD programmes. From 1999 to 2010 he was an assistant editor of the *Encyclopaedia Aethiopica* at the Hiob Ludolf Center for Ethiopian Studies at Hamburg University and later worked on historical maps, local concepts of territoriality and borders at the Gotha Research Center of Erfurt University (Ethiomap project).

Notes

1. I warmly thank Häylä Śəllase Gäbräkidan for his communication on this small piece of unusual oral literature and our discussions about it. He came across it during his work on his BA thesis at the Department of History and Cultural Studies on the history of his home town, Färäs May, and kindly made it available to me. See Häylä Śəllase Gäbräkidan (2011), with no reference to this poem. I am also very grateful to Mäᶜarəg Abbay, Wuqro Museum, for further fruitful and lively discussions on linguistic questions. I thank Gianmarco Salvati, Mekelle / Rome, for a first exchange of ideas on this, and I am grateful to Pavia University for having given me the time to work when I was a CICOPS fellow, Dipartimento di studi politiche e sociali, Università degli Studi di Pavia, Italy. It should be noted that this chapter was written before the outbreak of the war in Tigray, which started in November 2020; however, the observations in this chapter on basic patterns of conflict narratives also fit the current situation.

2. See for example Abdullahi A. Shongolo and Schlee (2007).

3. This is the usual Italian spelling of this Ethiopian Christian Ge'ez name in Latin letters, still used today in this form by some people when writing their names in Latin letters. Its meaning is 'Servant of Life' (= of Jesus/God).

4. According to the interviewed elder, this is a reference to the concept of *šəfta*, i.e. 'bandit', a socio-cultural form of resistance and lawlessness.

5. A helpful overview on the Italian influence on languages in the region is Tosco (2008); these influences resulted from the interaction with Italian administration and occupying forces, of which this poem is also an expression. However, the early pidginization of Italian in the region is almost not discussed. The best discussion of Italian pidgin is found in the section 'Simplified Italian of Ethiopia' in Voigt (2007). Some Italian pidgin was observed by Habtä Maryam Marqos in the 1970s. See Habte-Mariam Marcos (1976). Our findings further support these observations with some new material.

6. This phenomena has been mentioned by Voigt (2007: 223): 'The simplification in grammar is very strong . . . The verbal system is reduced to the infinitive (used as present form) and to the past participle (used as past form): *yo läwrare sämbre*, "I work [< inf. *Lavorare*] always [< *siempre*]", *rägasi mänğato*, "the children ate" (instead of the standard *I ragazzi/le ragazze hanno mangiato*). The infinitive is also used as imperative and conditional: *bänire domani* "come tomorrow!"'.

7. Voigt (2007: 223) summarizes this in the following way: 'Simplified Italian shows the typical restructurings as encountered in numerous pidgins. On the phonetic level, some sounds absent from Amharic or Təgrəñña, e.g., [p], [v], [ts], [dz], and the diphthonges [uo], [ie] were changed to [b], [b] (in postvocalic position [ß]) or [w], [s], [z] and [o], [e] respectively, e.g., *vicino* > *baćino* "near", *parlare* >

bärlare "speak".... Unstressed *a* and *i* are changed to ä and ə respectively: *mattina* > *mätina* "morning", *finito* > *fənito* "finished". Under the influence of so many Təgrəñña words ending in *-i* a final Italian *-e* is often changed to *-i*: *pesce* > *bäši* "fish", *miele* > *meli* "honey", *pane* > *bani* "(European-style) bread'".

8. On this see especially Voigt (2007) and Yaqob Beyene (2011). See also Pagliarulo (2004). On another language in Eritrea (Saho), see Banti and Vergari (2008). There were similar developments in Somali: see Mioni (1988); Banti (1990).

9. See the excellent overview of oral literature in the region by Banti (2010).

10. On a war song about Yohannis IV existing in several versions, see Smidt (2007).

11. As mentioned above, as Semitic languages are root-centred, i.e. the main meaning of a word is vested into the consonants, the audience would easily hear the consonantic identity of the 'Italian' and Tigrinya words; the vowels are of secondary importance and usually serve to fine-tune the basic meaning.

12. See especially Schlee's *How Enemies are Made* (2008).

References

Abdullahi A. Shongolo, and Günther Schlee. 2007. *Borana Proverbs in their Cultural Context*. Cologne: Köppe.

Banti, Giorgio. 1990. 'Sviluppo del sistema verbale nell'italiano parlato da somali a Mogadiscio', in Giuliano Bernini and Anna Giacalone Ramat (eds), *La temporalità nell'acquisizione di lingue seconde*. Milan: Franco Angeli, pp. 147–62.

———. 2010. 'Oral Literature', in Siegbert Uhlig and Allessandro Bausi (eds), *Encyclopaedia Aethiopica*, Volume 4. Wiesbaden: Harrassowitz, pp. 38–42.

Banti, Giorgio and Moreno Vergari. 2008. 'Italianismi lessicali in saho', *Ethnorêma* 4: 67–69.

Häylä Səllase Gäbräkidan. 2011. 'The History of Färäs May', BA thesis. Mäqälä: Mekelle University.

Habte-Mariam Marcos. 1976. 'Italian', in Marvin Lionel Bender, J. Donald Boowen, Robert L. Cooper and Charles A. Ferguson (eds), *Language in Ethiopia*. London: Oxford University Press, pp. 170–80.

Mioni, Alberto M. 1988. 'Italian and English Loanwords in Somali', in Annarita Puglielli (ed.), *Proceedings of the Third International Congress of Somali Studies*. Rome: Il Pensiero Scientifico Editore, pp. 36–42.

Pagliarulo, A. 2004. 'La diffusione della lingua italiana in Eritrea: situazione attuale e prospettive future', *Itals, Didattica e linguistica dell'italiano come lingua straniera* II-6: pp. 51–84.

Schlee, Günther. 2008. *How Enemies Are Made: Towards a Theory of Ethnic and Religious Conflicts*. Integration and Conflict Studies 1. New York and Oxford: Berghahn.

Smidt, Wolbert. 2007. 'A War-Song on Yohannəs IV Against the Egyptians, Recited by *Ləğ* Täfäri in Aksum, 1906', *Studies of the Department of African Languages and Cultures* [Warsaw University] 41: 107–31.

Tosco, Mauro. 2008. 'A Case of Weak Romancisation: Italian in East Africa', in Thomas Stolz, Dik Bakker and Rosa Salas Palomo (eds), *Aspects of Language Contact: New Theoretical, Methodological and Empirical Findings with Special Focus on Romancisation Processes*. Berlin: de Gruyter (Empirical Approaches to Language Typology, 35), pp. 377–98.

Voigt, Rainer. 2007. 'Italian Language in Ethiopia and Eritrea', in Siegbert Uhlig (ed.), *Encyclopaedia Aethiopica*, Volume 3. Wiesbaden: Harrassowitz, pp. 222–24.

Yaqob Beyene. 2011. 'I prestiti italiani in amarico e tigrino', *Rassegna di Studi Etiopici (Nuova Serie)* 3: 97–140.

CHAPTER 10

INTEGRATION THROUGH CONFLICT
The Proliferation of Mutually Constituted Sacred Narratives in the Process of State (Re-)Formation in Ethiopia

Dereje Feyissa

Introduction

The centrality of the concepts of integration and conflict to Günther Schlee is evident in the very name of the department he headed at the Max Planck Institute for Social Anthropology and of course in his pivotal works (such as Schlee 2001, 2002, 2008). From the outset Schlee contends that integration and conflict are not mere opposites:

> In the conceptual pair 'integration and conflict', 'conflict' may be understood as the counterpart and opposite of 'integration'; where integration fails, conflicts arise. From certain perspectives, however, this contrast vanishes. If one sees how even in open warfare, opponents become similar in terms of their rhetoric and symbolism down to the details of their attire and threatening gestures, how they traverse the same degrees of escalation in reacting to one another and how they end in the same generalized barbarisms, then one recognizes that conflicts, too, are systems of communication into which one can be integrated ... Through their warlike engagement with each other, the enemies have become integrated into the same system of symbols; they have become culturally similar to each other. (Schlee 2001: 43f)

In a later work, Schlee further expounded on the idea of integration through conflict:

> If we understand our enemies to the extent that we can engage in meaningful hostile relationships with them, we are part of the same social system. Enemies even

tend to borrow from each other culturally or to develop similar cultural forms in response to each other. They develop predictable strategies in dealing with each other 'tit for tat': they engage in arms races and mutual bullying by manoeuvres and parades. Enemies become alike. So, sameness combines with hostility and difference with peaceful interaction. (2008: 11)

Inspired by Schlee's ideas I explored the same theme in my doctoral thesis in the context of inter-ethnic relations, drawing on the example of how the encounter between two radically different modes of ethnic identity formation – the primordial ethnic identity formation of the Anywaa and the constructivist ethnic identity formation of the Nuer – has led to a certain degree of sameness, evident in the modification of the Nuer constructivist identity discourse into an incipient form of primordialization (Dereje 2011). In this chapter I provide additional ethnographic evidence to further substantiate the link between integration and conflict. Specifically, I refer to the politics of entitlement among Ethiopia's religious communities, particularly how the hegemonic discourse of the country's dominant religious community – the Ethiopian Orthodox Church (EOC) – and the historical ownership claim it has advanced over the Ethiopian nation has provoked religious minorities – particularly Muslims and Protestants – to produce their own counter-hegemonic narratives to establish local roots by replicating the nativist discourse of the EOC. Although there are counter-discourses among these religious minorities, the dominant mode of resisting the EOC's hegemonic position affirms the rules of the game set by the latter, i.e. the nativist discourse. Like similar contestations elsewhere, the counter-hegemonic projects of Muslims and Protestants also harbour hegemonic aspiration. The counter-narratives of the Muslims and Protestants are constructed not only in reference to and at the expense of the EOC; they also seek to redefine Ethiopia in their own image, while still referring to the Orthodox hegemon. This has set in motion a new process of contestation, with the EOC assuming a defensive posture. The production of similarity among the entitlement discourses of the religious groups has resulted in the proliferation of 'Great religious traditions' for Ethiopia as 'the chosen nation' (cf. the biblical Solomonic narrative), 'the land of the First Hijra' and 'the land of the Reformation', all essentially variations on the same theme.

The chapter focuses on the mutually constituted Great religious traditions of the EOC and the Muslims in competitive and occasionally violent settings. It is divided into five sections. Section one briefly introduces the major religious groups in contemporary Ethiopia. Section two presents the nativist discourse of the EOC vis-à-vis the Ethiopian state and its national identity. Section three presents the historical and socio-political marginality of Ethiopian Muslims and their narrative strategies of empowerment in contemporary Ethiopia. Section four analyses the hegemonic undercurrents in the Muslim counter-hegemonic narrative and the EOC's reactions. The last section provides a concluding argument.

Religious Groups in Ethiopia

There are five major religious communities in Ethiopia. These are, chronologically, followers of traditional beliefs (derogatorily labelled 'animists' in the 2007 national census and in Table 10.1 herein), Orthodox Christians, Muslims, Catholics and Protestants (evangelical Christians). Each religious community is internally heterogeneous with cleavages ranging from deep theological differences to minor differences in modes of religiosity. They all stand, however, as a group in relation to the 'real' religious other. Table 10.1 shows the membership of the different religions by percentage according to Ethiopia's 1994 and 2007 national censuses.

According to these censuses, the three major religious groups in contemporary Ethiopia are Orthodox Christians, Muslims and Protestants. The introduction and expansion of Orthodox Christianity as the largest and dominant religious community was not the result of organized evangelical activity from outside the country, as was the case elsewhere in Africa, but rather because of the religion's political intimacy with the Ethiopian kings, a historical process that goes back to the fourth century AD when King Ezana of the Axumite kingdom was converted to Christianity (Sergew 1972). Orthodox Christianity remained the official state religion in Ethiopia until the 1974 revolution.

Ethiopian Orthodox Christianity (Hereafter EOC) does not constitute a purely religious phenomenon in the country, but plays an integral role in all aspects of national life. It had maintained its doctrinal and organizational links with the Egyptian Coptic Church, the source of every Patriarch until the mid-twentieth century when Emperor Haile Selassie negotiated the EOC's independence (Kassu 2006). Except during the Era of the Princes (1769–1855) when the church splintered into many factions, the EOC has, rather exceptionally, maintained itself as a unified church throughout its existence (Abir 1980). The inhabitants of the northern Ethiopian highlands (the Amhara, Tigreans and Agaw) are overwhelmingly Orthodox Christians. The Shewan Oromo in the central highlands and segments of the Guraghe are also predominantly Orthodox Christians. Although the EOC had its political leverage over the Ethiopian state, as well as its economic privileges, severely curtailed after the 1974 revolution, it nevertheless has remained the dominant religious group in Ethiopia, constituting 43 per cent of

Table 10.1. Ethiopia's religious demography. Source: 1994 and 2007 national censuses of Ethiopia, Central Statistics Authority.

Year	Christians	Orthodox	Protestants	Catholics	Muslims	Animists	Other
1994	61.6%	50.6%	10.1%	0.9%	32.8%	4.6%	1.0%
2007	62.%	43.5%	18.6%	0.7%	33.9%	2.6%	0.7%
Growth	1.2%	−7.1%	8.5%	−0.2%	1.1%	−1.2%	−0.3%

the country's population (i.e. as of the 2007 census). This dominant status, however, is currently being contested by both Muslims and evangelical Christians. Responding to these challenges the EOC has recently experienced a 'reformist' movement known as *tehadiso*, also known by its detractors as 'ortho-pente' to indicate the Protestant influences. Labelling *tehadiso* a 'sell-out' to Protestantism, a neo-conservative movement has sprung up within the EOC, particularly among the educated youth known as the Mahibere Qudusan, 'Association in the Name of Saints'. The EOC is very apprehensive of the rapid growth of both Islam and evangelical Christianity in contemporary Ethiopia.

Despite the strong identification of Ethiopia with (Orthodox) Christianity, Islam in Ethiopia is as old as Islam itself. The history of Islam in Ethiopia dates back to 615 AD when the companions of the prophet Muhammad (the *sahaba*) came to Axum, fleeing religious persecution by the Quraysh ruling elite in Mecca (see Trimingham 1952; Erlich 1994). Amidst this persecution the Prophet advised the *sahaba* to migrate to Axum where they would be protected by a righteous Christian king, widely known in the Arab world as Najashi. According to the 2007 census Muslims constitute approximately 34 per cent of Ethiopia's more than 80 million people. This makes Muslims the second largest religious group in Ethiopia.

Islam in Ethiopia had an auspicious beginning thanks to the hospitality granted by the benevolent Christian king to the companions of the prophet Muhammad. From early on, however, it had to deal with a politically entrenched (Orthodox) Christianity that flourished under, and in turn helped to flourish, the Ethiopian state, a political intimacy that lasted over millennia. Although Ethiopia's secular turn during the popular revolution of 1974 ushered in a new era of Islamic revivalism, it was not until the 1991 regime change and the modest liberal leanings, the expansion of education and the IT revolution that new fields of possibility were created for Islam in Ethiopia and its global articulation. Islam is the religion of the overwhelming majority of the Somali, Afar, eastern Oromo, Argobba, Harari and Silte. Parts of Guraghe are also Muslim. Ethiopian Muslims belong to the wider Sunni Muslims, predominantly following the Sha'afi school of thought. Mystical Islam, Sufism, is also popular. In the last three decades, a wide variety of Islamic reform movements have also been active in Ethiopia, particularly the Saudi-inspired Salaffiya (also called Wahabiyya) that calls for a literal interpretation and observance of Islamic scriptures.

Protestantism was brought to Ethiopia through the missionary societies in the nineteenth century. As of 2007 Protestants constitute about 18.6 per cent of the total population. They are by far the fastest-growing religious group in Ethiopia, particularly in the urban areas. From close to 400,000 in the early 1960s, Protestants grew to 6 million in 1994 and 13.7 million in 2007. Many of the new converts to Protestantism have an Orthodox background. Persecuted during the military dictatorship of the Derg (1974–1991) and then allowed more freedom due to religious liberalization since 1991, evangelical Christianity's promise of immediate salvation and its modernist profile has particularly attracted educated urban youth (Tibebe 2009). Presently, over 250 religious denominations, churches and ministries are registered with the Ministry of Justice, most of which belong to the Pentecostal and Charismatic spectrum.

The revival of Islam and the exponential growth of the Protestants have generated a siege mentality among followers of the Ethiopian Orthodox Church. It is within this new socio-political context that sacred narratives are situated, signified and contested.

Ethiopia as 'the Chosen Nation' – EOC's Hegemonic 'Great' Religious Tradition

The Ethiopian Orthodox Church is one of the oldest Christian communities in Africa. Although there is some historical evidence that Christian communities had existed in the early Christian era, Christianity became the official state religion of the Axumite kingdom in the fourth century AD (Tadesse 1972: 28). The EOC's self-understanding and the Ethiopian polity assert sacred narratives as the basis for political legitimacy, i.e. the primacy of Ethiopia in the Judeo-Christian tradition as attested by scriptures underscores its present-day claims. Foremost in these sacred narratives is that the name Ethiopia is mentioned more than forty times in the Old Testament (Ullendorff 1967). This special status is further reinforced by the fourteenth-century manuscript known as the Kebre Negest (Glory of Kings). The Kebre Negest provides textual evidence for the Solomonic legend as the foundational myth of the Ethiopian state. It is an account written in Ge'ez of the origins of the Solomonic line of the emperors of Ethiopia. The following summarizes the Solomonic legend that underpins Ethiopia's claim to be the 'chosen nation':

> The Queen of Sheba is a seeker of truth and wisdom and she has heard that King Solomon of Israel is a very wise man. She travels on camel to Jerusalem to meet him and test his knowledge with questions and riddles. The Queen of Sheba tests Solomon's wisdom, asking him many questions and giving him riddles to solve. He answers to her satisfaction and then he teaches her about his god Yahweh and she becomes a follower. The Queen agrees to stay with King Solomon as a guest. An unmarried woman, she warns the King not to touch her. He replies that in exchange she should not take anything of his. He has tricked her, however. In the middle of her first night, she is thirsty and she takes a glass of water. He confronts her and tells her that by breaking her agreement she has released him from his. They spend the night together and when she returns home from his kingdom, she is pregnant with a son. She raises her son Menelik on her own. When he grows up, Menelik decides that he wants to meet his father and travels to Israel to meet King Solomon. When he had reached the age of twenty, Menelik himself travelled from Ethiopia to Israel

and arrived at his father's court. There he was instantly recognized and accorded great honour. After a year had passed, however, the elders of the land became jealous of him. They complained that Solomon showed him too much favor and they insisted that he must go back to Ethiopia. This the king accepted on the condition that the first-born sons of all the elders should also be sent to accompany him. Amongst these latter was Azarius, son of Zadok the High Priest of Israel, and it was Azarius, not Menelik, who stole the Ark of the Covenant from its place in the Holy of Holies in the Temple. Indeed, the group of young men did not reveal the theft to Menelik until they were far away from Jerusalem. When at last they told him what they had done he understood that they could not have succeeded in so bold a venture unless God had willed it. Therefore, he agreed that the Ark should remain with them. And it was thus that it was brought to Ethiopia, to this sacred city of Axum . . . and here it has remained ever since. (Hancock 1993: 85–86)

The text, in its existing form, is at least 700 years old, and is considered by many Ethiopian Orthodox Christians to be an inspired and reliable account (Budge 1932). The Kebre Negest contains the two central stories mentioned in the summary above. Firstly, there is the account of how the Ethiopian Queen of Sheba met King Solomon of Israel in Jerusalem in the tenth century BC, and conceived and gave birth to a son, Menelik, who is later said to have established the Solomonic monarchy in Ethiopia. Secondly, it recounts the transfer of the Ark of the Covenant from Jerusalem to Axum (Ethiopia) after King Menelik's trip to Jerusalem to visit his father King Solomon. This narrative sacralizes the Ethiopian monarchy and the Ethiopian polity at large in more than one way. While the connection to King Solomon provides a scriptural base for political legitimacy for the kings (cf. God's covenant with king David, father of king Solomon),[1] the Ark of the Covenant, which is believed to have been deposited at the Axum Tsion Church, signifies the geographical transfer of divine favour from Israel to Ethiopia. As Edward Ullendorff (1967: 8) noted, 'the Kebra Nagast is not merely a literary work, but it is the repository of Ethiopian national and religious feelings'. As a national epic it has served as the mythological charter for Ethiopia as 'the chosen nation' (Budge 1932; Hancock 1993).

Central to the EOC's self-understanding is the intimacy between church and state in Ethiopian history that continued until the 1974 secular rupture, and by extension the ownership claim it advances over the Ethiopian nation. The Ethiopian state has been ruled by Christian elites who proclaimed Orthodox Christianity as the official state religion of the country, and since 1974 has been ruled by power elites with a Christian background. In effect, the EOC views other religious groups as *mete haymanotoch* (imported religions). Besides, the EOC claims a high moral ground because of how it has accommodated Islam and other Christian denominations. The EOC recognizes the coming of the companions of the prophet Muhammad (the *sahaba*) to Ethiopia in 615 AD (Aba Samuel 2009: 14–15). What it rejects, vehemently, is the Muslim claim that the Christian king Armha who hosted the *sahaba* was converted to Islam. The EOC's major attraction in the narrative of the First Hijra relates to the description of *habesha* (highland Ethiopia) by the prophet Muhammad as the land of righteousness and the hospitality received by the *sahaba* from a Christian king, a gratitude which the Prophet is said to have reciprocated by forbidding Muslims from attacking Ethiopia unless they are attacked first. The reference to the conversion of King Armha (renamed by Muslims as King Ahmed Najashi; see the section below) by the same sources is rejected as biased, and at worst a fabrication by Muslim fundamentalists to advance a political agenda (Aba Samuel 2009).

The recurrent theme in the EOC's representation of Ethiopian history in general and the country's religious past in particular can be condensed into a single Amharic expression: *bagoresin tenekesin* (aggression in return for hospitality). As viewed by the EOC, its accommodation of religious minorities has never been reciprocated by the Muslims and other Christian denominations. In fact, in its view, they have all employed a usurpatory strategy, seeking to expand at the expense of the EOC. According to the EOC's understanding of the relational situation among the faiths, this usurpatory strategy can be traced to the fact that Islam, Protestantism and Catholicism all have external constituencies and therefore ultimately serve the interests of foreign countries. Specifically, the Muslims who assert their 'rights' are on the 'payrolls' of Saudi Arabia, and Protestants are the latest edition of the conspiracy of the Western missionaries. The EOC claims that it alone truly represents the Ethiopian national interest, and provides the country with its dominant national symbols, while highlighting the 'exceptionally' tolerant track record of the Orthodox Church. This position is maintained at the expense of 'inconvenient' historical facts, as noted by the late Hussein Ahmed (2006), who asserted that the EOC claim is based on partisan scholarship that provides a one-sided account of coexistence and tolerance while neglecting the various confrontations that have occurred between religious communities.

Ethiopia as 'the Land of the First Hijra' – the Muslim Counter-Narrative

As stated above, Islam in Ethiopia is as old as Islam itself, tracing its origin back to the coming of the *sahaba* (followers of the prophet Muhammad) in 615 AD. Historical longevity, however, is contrasted with the profound socio-political marginalization of Muslims within the Ethiopian polity, where they were regarded as second-class citizens at best. Muslims in the northern Ethiopian highlands, for instance, were not allowed by law to own land. Indeed, throughout the imperial period Muslims were not referred to as Ethiopian Muslims but 'Muslims in Ethiopia' (Abir 1980). This despite the fact that Islam in Ethiopia spread primarily through the works of Ethiopian Muslim clerics and, except for a small influx of Arab missionaries and traders, the vast majority of Muslims are local people (Hussein 2006).

Islam was introduced to Ethiopia early on through the international trade routes that linked Ethiopia with the Arabian world, as well as through the proselytization works of local Muslim scholars (Hussein 2006). By the ninth century AD, the Sultanate of Shewa emerged at the periphery of the Axumite Christian kingdom in central Ethiopia and stayed in power until the thirteenth century (Tadesse 1972). A more organized and militant Sultanate of Ifat replaced the Sultanate of Shewa towards the end of the thirteenth century (Bahru 2002). The fourteenth and fifteenth centuries were times of intense political and economic competition between the Solomonic Christian kingdom (Abyssinia) and the Sultanate of Ifat and other Islamic principalities (Tadesse 1972). In these protracted hegemonic struggles, the Christian kingdom held the upper hand except for a brief interlude in the sixteenth century, when the balance of power swayed towards Islam with the emergence of the Sultanate of Adal under its capable leader Ahmed Ibn Ibrahim Al Gahazi, popularly known as Ahmed Gragn, and his successful campaigns against the Christian kingdom. In fact, for a period of fourteen years (1529–1543) most of the present-day central and northern highlands came under what Genene (2008) calls 'the aborted Ethiopian Islamic government'. The Christian kingdom survived and revived thanks to the critical military support it received from the Portuguese, in response to the politico-military links between the Sultanate of Adal and the Turkish Empire.

The second half of the nineteenth century marked a renewed struggle for hegemony between the Christian kingdom and the Islamic states, a political process that culminated in the formation of the modern Ethiopian state within which Muslims were integrated as second-class citizens. This second-class status was reflected in various ways: little to no political representation, constrained access to land, limited freedom of worship and limited construction of mosques. Despite its antiquity and large demographic size Islam in Ethiopia has been marginalized by the Christian elites and political elites that represented the Ethiopian state. Notwithstanding the historical roots and demography of Islam in Ethiopia, as Markakis (2003: 2) noted: '[T]he official myth presented Ethiopia as a purely Christian state . . . This myth was widely accepted abroad, and was propagated by the first generation of foreign scholars who studied this country'.

The socio-political reforms brought about by the 1974 revolution and the end of the Christian monarchy partly redressed the marginalization of Muslims in Ethiopia (Hussein 1994). Church and state parted company, and Ethiopia has been a secular state ever since. For the first time in the history of the country, religious freedom was proclaimed and Islam gained parity with Christianity in political dispensation (Abbink 1998; Dereje 2011). The religious reforms of the Derg, however, did not extend to redefining the parameters of Ethiopia's national identity. Despite its ideological commitment to socialism, the Derg was fervently nationalist (Donham et al. 2002), which entailed, among other things, recycling old national (Christian) symbols. Ethiopian historiography, with its 'unbroken'

3000-year-history paradigm (cf. the Solomonic narrative), was left untouched, and it is a historiography still populated by Christian heroes, whereas the Islamic heritage of the country has remained largely silenced. As Braukämper (2002: 4) noted, the 'so called Gragn syndrome was recalled at occasions when Christian Ethiopia felt threatened by the Muslims of the Horn of Africa ... It was used, for instance, during the Ethiopian-Somali war of 1978 to unify and mobilize the Christian highlanders against the invasion of enemies from the east'.

The regime change in 1991 brought yet another opportunity to redress the issue of religious inequality in Ethiopia. While the EPRDF (Ethiopian People's Revolutionary Democratic Front) came to power as a champion of minority rights, its attitude towards Muslims has changed over time. As part of its project of deconstructing 'imperial' Ethiopia, the EPRDF made connections with various marginalized groups, including Muslims. The 1995 Constitution generously provides for religious rights. These have been translated into the emergence of a confident and assertive Ethiopian Muslim community keen to prosper under the new liberalization of the religious sphere. Taking advantage of the freedom of movement, Muslims are now better connected with the Islamic world through Hajj and Umra as well as other forms of travel to Muslim countries (Carmichael 1996).[2]

Furthermore, freedom of expression has meant the flourishing of Islamic literature, with numerous translations of the works of major global Muslim scholars. Religious equality is expressed in the construction of many mosques, although this has provoked a strong Christian reaction in some areas (Hussein 1994, 2006). Responding to the Muslims' rights movement that centres on religiously inclusive citizenship, the EPRDF has also made some historical concessions in the form of greater recognition of the country's Islamic heritage.[3] Ethiopia has indeed transformed fundamentally in allowing individuals from religious minority groups to assume the highest political offices of the country. Whereas the former prime minister Hailemariam Desalegn (2012–2018) hailed from a Protestant minority sect, the current prime minister Abiy Ahmed and his deputy Demeke Mekonen have Muslim backgrounds.[4]

Notwithstanding the EPRDF's liberalization of the religious sphere, nearly four decades after the 'secular revolution' the semantics of the Ethiopian nation are still contested by the various religious groups through competing narratives of entitlement. For the followers of the Orthodox Church, Ethiopia is still the 'chosen nation' and 'an island of Christianity'. Encouraged by the EPRDF's historical revisionism and taking advantage of the modest liberal leanings, Muslims have advanced claims for greater historical and physical space in contemporary Ethiopia. They have been particularly active in contesting the parameters of Ethiopian national identity and renegotiating their 'foreignness' to the Ethiopian polity as presented by the Christian population and implicit in the thinking of the various Ethiopian governments. Many Muslims in Ethiopia and in the diaspora have thus focused in their writing on deconstructing the image of Ethiopia as a Christian Island. They have reasoned that such representation is not only historically unfounded but also seriously undermines the process of state reconstruction and democratization of the Ethiopian polity. In one of its commentaries, for instance, the Network of Ethiopian Muslims in Europe has contested the EOC's claim of autochthony while asserting Islam's long presence in Ethiopia:

> It is to be noted that the Ethiopian state preceded all the Abrahamic religions. Well before the introduction of Christianity in Ethiopia in the 4th century AD the Axumite had already built a sophisticated non-Christian civilization. Like Christianity, Islam was also introduced to Ethiopia from the Middle East at the same time when it was being established in Saudi Arabia. Any ownership claim of the Ethiopian state and its history is thus not only ahistorical but also poses a danger to the peace and security of the country.[5]

In a book entitled *Ethiopian Muslims, 615–1750: A History of Domination and Resistance*, Ahmedin Jebel (2011), an activist and one of the leading Muslim scholars on Christian-Muslim relations in contemporary Ethiopia, has forcefully argued along the same lines in deconstructing the EOC's nativist claim by highlighting its introduction and expansion by Arab missionaries:

> The Arabs had played an important role not only to the expansion of Islam in Ethiopia but also to Christianity as well. The person who converted the first Ethiopian king to Orthodox Christianity in the 4th century AD was the Syrian Bishop Frimentius; the Coptic Church of Alexandria was the patron of the Orthodox Church until the 1950s, and the nine saints who introduced Christianity to the masses in the 5th century were also Syrians. (Ahmedin 2011: 87)

Ahmedin's statements implicitly refer to the Christians' identification of Ethiopian Muslims with Arabs, thus denying them any potential autochthonous claim. The Muslim foundational myth as Ethiopian citizens refers back to the coming of the companions of the prophet Muhammad to *habesha* (Ethiopia) in 615 AD. Contesting the migration of the prophet Muhammad from Mecca to Medina, which is officially considered as the First Hijra among Muslims worldwide, Ethiopian Muslims claim that it is the *sahaba*'s migration from Mecca to Axum that should be considered as the First Hijra: 'The first migration [Hijra] of the Companions and relatives of the Prophet Muhammad to Ethiopia celebrates the birth of freedom of expression and beliefs, whereas, the Second Migration of the Prophet Muhammad to the Madinah celebrates the end of oppression'.[6] The following summarizes the narrative of the First Hijra that organizes Muslims' historical claims as autochthonous to Ethiopia:

> When the Quraysh intensified their opposition of Islam by torturing the Muslims, Prophet Muhammad told his followers to leave for Ethiopia, where 'a king rules without injustice, a land of truthfulness – until God leads us to a way out of our

difficulty'. Ethiopia was at that time ruled by a Christian king, Aṣḥama ibn Abjar, famous for his mercy and equity. News of their intended departure reached Quraysh, so some men were dispatched in their pursuit, but the Muslims had already left to seek out their secure haven, where they were received warmly and accorded hospitality by the Negus, Aṣḥama ibn Abjar (al- Najashi). Among these emigrants were Uthman and Ruqayyah. The second migration consisted of 83 men and 18 women. Ja'far ibn Abī Tālib headed this group.

The migration of the Muslims to Ethiopia, and their reception at the friendly court of Najashi, alarmed the Quraysh. They entertained the fear that Muslims might grow in strength, or find new allies, and then, someday, might return to Mecca to challenge them. To head off this potential threat, such as they saw it, they decided to send an embassy led by 'Amr ibn al-'As to the court of Najashi to try to persuade him to extradite the Muslims to Mecca. 'Amr had brought rich presents for the king and his courtiers to ingratiate himself with them. When the king gave an audience to the emissary of the Quraysh, he said that the Muslims in Ethiopia were not refugees from persecution but were fugitives from justice and law, and requested him to extradite them to Mecca. The king, however, wanted to hear the other side of the story before passing judgement, and summoned Ja'far ibn Abī Tālib to the court to answer the charges against the Muslims. Ja'far gave a most memorable defence. When Ja'far concluded his speech, the king asked him to read some verses, which were revealed, to Muhammad. Ja'far read a few verses from Sura Maryam (Mary), the 19th chapter of the Qur'an. When the king heard these verses, he said that their fountainhead was the same as that of the verses of the Evangel. He then declared that he was convinced of Ja'far's veracity, and added, to the great chagrin of 'Amr ibn al-'As, that the Muslims were free to live in his kingdom for as long as they wished.

Then addressing the Muslims, he said: 'Go to your homes and live in peace. I shall never give you up to your enemies'. He refused to extradite the Muslims, returned the presents which 'Amr had brought, and dismissed his embassy.

The Muslims finally returned from Ethiopia to Medina in 7 A.H. When Najashi died, the prophet announced to the sahaba the day he died and then prayed Salatul Janazah for him, saying that he was a pious man and he was their brother, then he ordered them to ask Allah to forgive him, and to pray with him the funeral prayer for Najashi. This indicates that Najashi was a Muslim. The prophet came to know of his death in Mecca; Najashi embracing Islam through revelation on the day he died.[7]

There are three sacred stories in the narrative of the First Hijra that are central to Ethiopian Muslims. Firstly, there was a strong Ethiopian component in early Islam. 'Umm Ayman (Baraka) and Bilal bin Rabah, two important companions of the Prophet Mohammed, had an Ethiopian background. 'Umm Ayman was the Prophet's nurse who looked after him from his birth, throughout his boyhood and until his marriage. Bilal bin Rabah (the slave of a prominent Meccan) was the third Muslim after the Prophet's wife and Abu Bakr. In fact, Bilal became the first *mu'adhdhin*, the caller for prayer in Islam.[8]

The second story relates to the coming of the *sahaba* to Axum in two waves. The first delegation of sixteen men and women included prominent people, some of whom were very close to the Prophet, such as Uthman bin 'Affan (his son-in-law and the third caliph) and Ruqayya (his daughter). The second delegation of 101 men and women was led by Ja'far Abutalib (his cousin and the brother of the future caliph Ali). Fifteen of the *sahaba* are said to have died in Axum.

The third story relates to the benevolence of King (Najashi) Asmaha (whom the Orthodox Church recognizes as Armha) towards Islam and the belief in his ultimate conversion. Najashi's benevolence is said to have been reciprocated by the prophet Muhammad in the form of his edict: *utruku al-habasha ma tarakukum* ('Leave the Abyssinians/Ethiopians alone, so long as they do not go on the offensive'). According to Islamic traditions this is the reason why the early jihad was not applied to Ethiopia at a time when all countries in the Red Sea subregion succumbed to the new Islamic political and military power (Trimingham 1952; Erlich 1994). The stories that underline the narrative of the First Hijra sacralize Axum (the Ethiopian polity) in the annals of Islamic history, thus forming Axum's alternative sacred geography that parallels the Orthodox Church's claim to have hosted the Ark of the Covenant in the same town.

The First Hijra narrative has been strategically deployed by Muslim leaders in their search for a secure historical foundation for national belonging. They refer to the First Hijra and related sacred narratives as an authoritative historical base to Ethiopian national belonging as well as a moral critique of the present-day violation of Muslims' human rights, such as the right to establish a mosque in Axum or access to land to observe Muslim public holidays on a par with the Christian community.

The Orthodox Church fiercely contests the Muslims' claim that the Christian king who hosted the *sahaba* was converted to Islam. Its version of the story ends with the protection that King Armha (aka Nejashi) gave to the persecuted Muslims in accordance with the Orthodox ethic of accommodation and tolerance. The EOC has extensively written refuting the Muslim historical claims.[9] In 2008 the Mahibere Qidusan (Association in the Name of the Saints) organized a millennium exhibition in which the Najashi issue was presented as the Muslims' 'scramble over Ethiopian history'. Many followers of the EOC now consider the discourse on the Najashi as the first step towards 'Islamizing Ethiopia', as propagated by the Mahibere Qidusan. As one EOC follower noted, 'Islamizing history is a prelude to Islamizing the country and the people'.

Muslims respond to Orthodox Christians' 'denial' of the conversion of King Nejashi by citing the Christian 'double standard' in reading history, while strongly arguing for the Muslim right to construct a mosque in Axum. In an incisive article, 'When History is Narrated', published in many Muslim media outlets as well as popular newspapers, Ibrahim Mulushewa (2009), for instance, criticized the selective memory and 'collusion' between academic and Christian historiography in vehemently denying Najashi's conversion to Islam. Ibrahim contests the Christian historiography at various levels. For one, the Muslim Arab scholars, in the same works where they mentioned Najashi's conversion into Islam, reported the story of one of the *sahaba* being converted to Christianity. Besides, the Arab scholars had also mentioned the clerical opposition that Najashi faced, despite the Christians' contention that had the king converted to Islam there would have been mass unrest. Muslims also bring a third piece of evidence to substantiate their claim that Salatul Ghaib, the first Islamic funeral prayer in absentia that is mentioned in the narrative of the First Hijra, was first said by the Prophet for King Najashi, honouring the favours he did for his companions and accepting Islam. Ibrahim, along with many other Muslim scholars and activists, characterizes the scholarly 'denial' of Najashi's conversion as part of re-establishing the Christian hegemony in Ethiopia, as if allowing the possibility that Ethiopia was ever ruled by non-Christians is a 'contradiction in terms'. Muslims also fiercely criticize Orthodox Christians' refusal to accept the Muslims' demand to construct a mosque in Axum, which compares the Muslim building of a mosque in Axum to the Christians building a church in Mecca:

> Trying to compare the case of Axum with demanding a Mosque in Vatican or a Church in Makah is naive and outrageous. It has a tendency of portraying Muslims as foreigners, as less Ethiopians with less entitlements and rights in their homeland. The Muslims of Axum are not foreigners; they are native people of the region. It is their land and the land of their forefathers that they [have lived in] for more than thousands of years. But, despite that they are still denied to have [a] mosque in a multi-religious secular Ethiopia, which doesn't recognize Axum as a Christian State (City) with a different form of law and governance. It is totally wrong and distractive to compare the case of Axumite Muslims with issues in other countries with different contexts and histories. Such approach does not help in conceptualizing, understanding and addressing the problem. It rather makes things more complex by [bringing] to light another deep-seated prejudice against Ethiopian Muslims – i.e., the problem of accepting the Ethiopian-ness of Ethiopian Muslims and their equal ownership and entitlement of the country.[10]

In Ethiopia's religious landscape the Najashi narrative and other related sacred narratives serve the purpose of repositioning the Ethiopian Muslims vis-à-vis a national identity in the context of a process of state reformation. Accordingly, Ethiopia is not only a special country for the Christians (cf. the 'chosen nation' of the Solomonic narrative); it is also vital for the Muslims of the world in general and the Ethiopian Muslims in particular. Construed in this way, Islam is indebted to Ethiopia for its very survival. The hospitality and the tolerance the *sahaba* received in Ethiopia is said to have been critical to the survival and expansion of Islam (Hussein 2006). Redefining Ethiopia in this way, Muslims would have less trouble identifying with 'Ethiopia the land of the First Hijra' than the

EOC's 'Ethiopia is an island of Christianity'. Tracing the history of Islam to King Najashi thus provides the Ethiopian Muslims with a new foundation myth in reconstructing a national identity. The double facility of the Najashi narrative – reconstructing both religious and national identities – is succinctly depicted in the document that the 2007 delegation of the Ethiopian Muslim diaspora (Badr Ethiopia) produced, which set an agenda for prominent Muslims' citizenship rights issues in contemporary Ethiopia:

> Although we do not have conclusive evidence to claim that Ethiopia is the first country to grant asylum to the persecuted, we understand that Najashi could have well set precedence for the contemporary human right conventions that include protection of the vulnerable and the persecuted. What makes Ethiopia unique in the annals of Islamic history is that the Muslim refugees had lived peacefully with other Ethiopians and this was the basis for the flourishing of Islam in the country to the level it has reached now. King Armha's acceptance of Islam makes Ethiopia not only a land of justice and enlightenment but also the first country where Islam got recognition by a head of state. (Badr Ethiopia 2007: 9)

World Religions, 'Great' Traditions, Hegemonic Aspirations and the National Referent

The Orthodox 'Great' tradition of Ethiopia as 'the chosen nation' and the Muslims' reactive 'Great' tradition of Ethiopia as the land of the First Hijra have something fundamental in common: both, Christendom and the Umma, harbour hegemonic aspirations and are constructed through a reference to an Ethiopian national identity despite their universal pretension. Constructed during the heyday of the intimacy between church and state in the medieval period, the Orthodox narrative of the chosen nation now features as a sort of 'imperial nostalgia'. For a period of two decades under military dictatorship the Orthodox Church had lost its political leverage over the Ethiopian state and the economic privileges associated with that leverage. Religious liberalization since 1991 has opened up a new field of possibility for revivalism among Ethiopia's diverse religious communities. Facing strong competition from Muslims and Protestants, the EOC has gone through a period of reform championed by a neo-conservative movement, largely represented by educated youth, known as Mahibere Qidusan. An anxiety about the future has taken hold among followers of the EOC. The rapid growth of Muslim and Protestant membership and their global articulation has in fact generated a siege mentality among Orthodox Christians. Many of the new converts to Protestantism are ex-Orthodox. The plight of the Christian minorities in Muslim majority areas where there have been escalations of inter-religious conflict is also a source of concern. For instance, the 2006 religious violence in Kemissie and western Oromia and the 2011 attack on Christian minorities in Jimma have revitalized the EOC's ownership claim over the Ethiopian nation.

The traditional mass celebration of the Epiphany has in recent years become a platform where the soul of the Ethiopian nation is claimed and contested. It is common nowadays to see Orthodox youth wearing T-shirts and carrying banners with the words 'Ethiopia is an island of Christianity'.

At a time when the present is considered precarious and the future is imagined as dangerous, it appears that the EOC is bolstering its rapidly eroding hegemonic position by breathing new life into the country's long-standing sacred narrative of Ethiopia as a chosen nation, as defined of course in Orthodox Christian terms. This appears possible not only in the context of religious liberalization but also in the context of the EPRDF's shift in political discourse. The EPRDF had been busy deconstructing the historical bases of the Ethiopian polity, reducing the 3000-year historiographical paradigm into a mere centenary, but lately has assumed a new reconstructionist political posture, particularly since the 2007 Ethiopian millennium. The Ethiopian state, like any other state, looks different when one is administering it from the centre, while at the same time resisting the periphery where the dominant narrative is often of marginalization and victimization. The EPRDF, as was the case with its predecessor the Derg, has felt the need to recycle old national symbols to facilitate war mobilization (Toggia 2008: 323–24). By 2000 the EPRDF had effectively salvaged the idea of Ethiopia and was ready to defend it against ethno-nationalist liberation movements and opposition voices, particularly in Oromia and Somali regional states. A more dramatic change in perspective by the EPRDF regarding Ethiopian history was seen in the events leading to the Ethiopian millennium in 2007 and subsequently. In a speech delivered for the occasion, Prime Minister Meles Zenawi introduced the Ethiopian public to the concept of *hidasse*, the Ethiopian renaissance. According to Meles, the first millennia of Ethiopian history was glorious, producing the greatness of the Axumite civilization. The second millennium was a lost millennium when Ethiopia regressed, deeply mired in protracted conflicts and ravaged by famine. With the capable leadership of the EPRDF Ethiopia was projected to 'reclaim' the third millennium. The EPRDF's new mode of representing Ethiopian history implicitly refers to the Orthodox Christians' 3000-year history, the same history that it was busy deconstructing throughout the 1990s.

Goaded by the counter-narrative of the Muslims and encouraged by the EPRDF's new nationalist profile, the EOC has once again brought its image of Ethiopia into the country's public space. The leadership of the Mahibere Qidusan is in the forefront of reviving the EOC's historical 'ownership' claim of the Ethiopian nation, as suggested by the following excerpt:

> We wonder why we [EOC] are singled out in the discourse of identification of a nation with a certain faith. Look everywhere and you see the same. Even the largest democracy, the US, is identified with the Protestant Church. Isn't it the case that all American Presidents swear with the bible before they assume office? Isn't it the

case that Saudi Arabia will remain a Muslim country no matter how multicultural it becomes? With us it is even different. We have accommodated religious minorities much more than any other country. It is an Axumite (Orthodox) king who protected Muslims when their own people persecuted them in their own country, though this is not duly acknowledged by radical Muslims in contemporary Ethiopia who claim otherwise; that the king who they call Najashi became a Muslim. Who would deny that the EOC is the major contributor in the making of the Ethiopian nation and a repository of its history and values? (Excerpt from an interview with two members of the editorial board of the Mahibere Qidusan publications, 24 August 2010, Addis Ababa)

Prime Minister Abiy's (2018–) more expansive embrace of Ethiopia as a nation is likely to further activate the EOC's nativist claims, while his inclusive rhetoric simultaneously encourages Muslims to invoke Ethiopia's sacred Islamic narratives. Muslims' emphasis is on establishing a local root by mirroring the 'Great' religious tradition of the EOC, Ethiopia's 'autochthon sin qua non'. The political subtext of the First Hijra narrative is the search for a secure sense of national belonging and a historical framework for citizenship rights, which is threatened by the politicization of Islamic identity within the new geopolitical context. A reference to the First Hijra is often made by Muslims in the sense of 'We too have lived in the neighbourhood for a long time', however marginalized they have been. Historical longevity is invoked to counter the securitization of Islam in Ethiopia that stipulates that revivalist movements can only have external referents. In writings and public demonstrations Muslims strongly condemn the hegemonic currents within the EOC's 'Great' religious tradition.

Despite the contested nature of the narrative of the First Hijra and the existence of alternative empowering narratives, the dominant narrative that organizes the Muslim claim for a secured national identity and citizenship rights claim is advanced through the Nejashi narrative. The Muslim contestation of the EOC's exclusivist claim in Axum and other northern towns, for instance, is framed not in the language of citizenship rights but rather as a counter-historical claim that Axum is also a holy city for Muslims in reference to the First Hijra. The EOC exclusively claims the town of Axum, which hosted the 'original' Ark of the Covenant, as its sacred space and has not allowed any mosque or Protestant church to be built within an 18-kilometre radius of the town in all directions. Attempts by local Muslims to build mosques were violently blocked by the EOC with the implicit acceptance, if not outright consent, of the leadership of the Tigray regional state.[11]

Initially invoked as a counter-hegemonic narrative, the narrative of the First Hijra is now presented by Muslims of contemporary Ethiopia as the 'most authentic Great' religious tradition for Ethiopia. The transit to hegemonic aspiration is expressed in an article featured in *Ye Muslimoch Guday* (Muslim Affairs), a popular monthly magazine published by Muslim activists. From a Muslim perspective the First Hijra and the conversion of King Najashi as the first Muslim ruler outside of Arabia is more plausible than the controversial Solomonic legend. They refer to the original Hebraic version of the Bible in which the word Kush is used instead of Ethiopia, unlike in the Greek version. Accordingly, both the Hebraic term Kush and the Greek term Ethiopia refer to Nubia/the Sudan, not to present-day Ethiopia (*Ye Muslimoch Guday* 2009). As such, Muslims do not contest the autochthonous discourse set by the Orthodox per se but instead question its claim while establishing the authenticity of their own claim.

To the extent that both the EOC's 'Great' religious tradition and the Muslims' counter-hegemonic 'Great' religious tradition have the same national referent and subscribe to autochthony as an empowering discourse, we can observe the production of similarity among parties to a conflict, at least at the discursive level. The temptations of 'Great' traditions – in this case, encouraging the matching and, if possible, the beating of one's enemy at their own game – become more abundantly clear to observers of the dynamic religious transformation of contemporary Ethiopia with the emergence of yet another 'Great' religious tradition. Although not the focus of this chapter, the narrative of the Orthodox Church as 'the chosen nation' and the Muslim narrative of Ethiopia as 'the land of the First Hijra' are countered by a third, competing narrative of authenticity put forth by Ethiopian Protestants, who assert that Ethiopia deserves special consideration as 'the land of the Reformation', since, in their view, Ethiopia 'protested' even before Germany did. Like the EOC's and Muslims' 'Great' traditions, the Protestants, too, harbour a hegemonic aspiration. Thus, failing to respond to God's call (the reformation), the EOC, not Ethiopia, will lose favour with God, with one of two outcomes: the emergence of another evangelical movement within the EOC, or the ultimate triumph of Protestantism in Ethiopia evident in the mass conversion of EOC members to Protestantism.

Conclusion

The proliferation of parallel 'Great' religious traditions in competitive and oppositional settings in Ethiopia provides yet another ethnographic example of Schlee's notion of integration through conflict. The Muslim signification of the narrative of the First Hijra speaks to the Orthodox Christians deeply entrenched 'Great' religious tradition of Ethiopia as the chosen nation. As a counter-hegemonic narrative the First Hijra does not question autochthony per se as a basis for political entitlement and ownership claim over the Ethiopian nation, a discourse that was set by its competitive other, Orthodox Christianity. Rather, what it contests is whether the Orthodox claim is sufficiently authentic, while at the same time renegotiating the 'latecomerness' of Islam to the Ethiopian polity. In fact, what started as an inclusionary rhetoric is developing its own authentic flavour by deconstructing the historical basis of the Orthodox claim, and by implication advancing its own autochthony on the basis of a more 'secure' historical basis.

Although there are alternative historical bases for national belonging, Ethiopian Muslims found the narrative of the First Hijra very compelling in countering the deeply entrenched 'Great' religious tradition of the Orthodox Church – an instance of matching an enemy move for move, if not beating them at their own game. Muslims have also found it very useful to de-securitize Islam in Ethiopia: an enduring constraint they have faced within the Ethiopian polity. Here again Muslims are signifying a historical narrative in the same manner as Orthodox Christians have done, i.e. localizing a world religion. 'We too have been around the Ethiopian block' effectively counters the disempowering label of *mete haymanot* (imported religion) applied by Orthodox Christians to religious minorities such as Muslims, which is also implicit in government thinking across political regimes. Not least, the narrative of the First Hijra has additional affordances. It enables the Ethiopian Muslims to simultaneously construct a secure national identity and a universal Islamic identity (Umma). Accordingly, Ethiopian Muslims are not just one among many 'low-rated black Muslims' but descendants of Bilal and Najashi, central actors in early Islamic history. Having a 'Great' religious tradition seems to have attained a doxic status within Ethiopia's religious landscape. No wonder then that other religious groups have also felt the urge to jump on the 'Great' religious tradition bandwagon. The emerging 'Great' tradition of the Protestants that depicts Ethiopia as the land of the Reformation is yet another example of integration through conflict.

Dereje Feyissa holds a doctorate in social anthropology from Martin-Luther University in Halle, Germany. He was a Postdoctoral Research Fellow at Osaka University in Japan and the Max Planck Institute for Social Anthropology. He is currently Adjunct Associate Professor at Addis Ababa University and Research and Policy Advisor to the Life and Peace Institute. He is the author and co-editor of several books, including *Borders and Borderlands as Resources in the Horn of Africa* (London: James Currey, 2010), *Playing Different Games: The Paradox of the Identification Strategies of the Anywaa and Nuer in the Gambella Region of Ethiopia* (New York and London: Berghahn Books, 2011) and *Ethiopia in the Wake of Political Reforms* (Los Angeles: Tsehai Publishers, 2020).

Notes

1. OT, 2 Samuel 7:4–17.
2. Previously there was a Hajj quota imposed on Ethiopian Muslims by the socialist government, averaging 2000 people per year.
3. The Ministry of Culture, for instance, has proposed the Najashi Mosque to the UNESCO as a world cultural heritage. The ministry has also designed a project to turn Negash village into an Islamic centre of learning, with an Islamic university.

4. Although it should be noted that Abiy Ahmed is now a devout Protestant.
5. Retrieved 4 May 2009 from www.ethiopianmuslims.net, 12 April 2009 (author's translation from Amharic).
6. Najib Mohammed, 'The Haven of the First Hijra (Migration): An African Nation Is the Muslims' First Refuge', https://www.soundvision.com/article/the-haven-of-the-first-hijra-migration.
7. This is my summary of the Najashi narrative that I collected from among many Muslims in various regions of Ethiopia.
8. Associated with Bilal, the Prophet is believed to have said: 'Who brings an Ethiopian man or an Ethiopian woman into his house, brings the blessings of God there'.
9. Two prominent books are *Ye haymanot mechachal be Ethiopia aleni?* [Is There Religious Tolerance in Ethiopia?] (2009), by Aba Samuel, bishop of Addis Ababa; and *Ye Islimina Akirarinet be Ethiopia* [Islamic Radicalism in Ethiopia] (2008), by Ephrem Eshete, who was part of the EOC diaspora and lives in the United States.
10. https://www.facebook.com/notes/bilal-seid/mesfin-negash-and-the-case-of-mosque-in-axum/216460595171823/.
11. According to legend (as discussed earlier), the Ark of Covenant given to Moses by God is said to have been brought to Ethiopia by Menelik, the son of King Solomon and Queen Sheba.

References

Aba Samuel. 2009. *Ye haymanot mechachal be Ethiopia Aleni?* [Is There Religious Tolerance in Ethiopia?]. Addis Ababa: Mega Printing Press.
Abbink, Jon. 1998. 'An Historical-Anthropological Approach to Islam in Ethiopia: Issues of Identity and Politics', *Journal of African Cultural Studies* 11(2): 109–24.
Abir, Mordechai. 1980. *Ethiopia and the Red Sea: The Rise and Decline of the Solomonic Dynasty and Muslim European Rivalry in the Region*. London: Routledge.
Ahmedin Jebel. 2011. *Ya ethioipawuyan muslimoch ye cheqon ena tigel tarikh* [Ethiopian Muslims: A History of Oppression and Struggle]. Addis Ababa: Nejashi.
Badr Ethiopia. 2007. Questions Raised by the Ethiopian Muslims Diaspora to the Prime Minister Meles Zenawi. April 2007. Unpublished paper, Addis Ababa. Retrieved from https://www.badrethiopia.org/index.
Bahru Zewde. 2002. *A History of Modern Ethiopia 1855–1991*. Oxford: James Currey.
Braukämper, Ulrich. 2002. 'Islamic Principalities in South-Eastern Ethiopia between the 13th and the 16th Centuries', *Ethiopianist Notes* 1-2: 1–44.
Budge, Wallis. 1932. *A History of Ethiopia, Nubia and Abyssinia*. London: Anthropological Publications.
Carmichael, Tim. 1996. 'Contemporary Ethiopian Discourse on Islamic History: The Politics of Historical Representation', *Islam et Sociétés au Sud du Sahara* 10: 169–86.
Dereje Feyissa. 2011. 'Setting a Social Reform Agenda: The Peacebuilding Dimension of the Rights Movement of the Ethiopian Muslims Diaspora', *Diaspeace Working Paper* 9. Retrieved from www.diaspeace.org.
Donham, Donald L., Wendy James, Eisei Kurimoto and Alessandro Triulzi. 2002. *Remapping Ethiopia: Socialism and After*. Melton, Woodbridge: James Currey.
Erlich, Haggai. 1994. *Ethiopia and the Middle East*. Boulder, CO: Lynne Rienner Publishers.
Genene, Assefa. 2008. *Casting Gragn: The Aborted Islamic Government of Ethiopia (1529–43)*. Addis Ababa: Mega Publishers.
Hancock, Graham. 1993. *Sign and the Seal: The Quest for the Lost Ark of the Covenant*. Clearwater, FL: Touchstone Books.

Hussein Ahmed. 1994. 'Islam and Islamic Discourse in Ethiopia (1973–1993)'. *Proceedings of the 12th International Conference of Ethiopian Studies*. Trenton, NJ: Red Sea Press.

———. 2006. 'Coexistence and/or Confrontation? Towards a Reappraisal of Christian-Muslim Encounter in Contemporary Ethiopia', *Journal of Religion in Africa* 36(1): 4–22.

Ibrahim Mulushewa. 2009. 'When Our History Is Narrated', *Addis Neger*, 15 February.

Kassu, Wudu Tafete. 2006. 'The Ethiopian Orthodox Church, the Ethiopian State and the Alexandrian See: Indigenizing the Episcopacy and Forging National Identity, 1926–1991', PhD dissertation. Urbana-Champaign: University of Illinois.

Markakis, John. 2003. *Ethnic Conflict in Pre-Federal Ethiopia*. Addis Ababa: GIZ.

Schlee, Günther. 2001. 'Dimensions of Comparison at the Department of Integration and Conflict', *Max Planck Institute for Social Anthropology Annual Report 1999–2001*.

———. 2002. *Imagined Differences: Hatred and the Construction of Identity*. Münster: Lit.

———. 2008. *How Enemies Are Made: Towards a Theory of Ethnic and Religious Conflict*. Integration and Conflict Studies 1. New York and Oxford: Berghahn.

Sergew, Hable S. 1972. *Ancient and Medieval Ethiopian History Up to 1270*. Addis Ababa: United Printers.

Tadesse Tamrat. 1972. *Church and State in Ethiopia*. Oxford: Clarendon Press.

Tibebe Eshete. 2009. *The Evangelical Movement in Ethiopia: Resistance and Resilience*. Waco, TX: Baylor University Press.

Toggia, Pietro. 2008. 'History Writing as a State Ideological Project in Ethiopia', *African Identities* 6(4): 319–43.

Trimingham, J. Spencer. 1952. *Islam in Ethiopia*. Abingdon-on-Thames: Routledge.

Ullendorf, Edward. 1967. *Ethiopia and the Bible*. London: Oxford University Press.

CHAPTER 11

'A DIMPLED SPIDER, FAT AND WHITE'
US Exceptionalism and the Accumulation of Terror

STEPHEN P. REYNA

> I found a dimpled spider, fat and white,
> On a white heal-all
> —Robert Frost, 'Design', 1936

The old Yankee poet Robert Frost spent time walking in the woods. In his poem 'Design' (1936), a world is evoked for the reader to contemplate. Envision it: a white spider on a white heal-all flower. White on white: an attractive picture of purity as the poet tramps along a green forest path. But the spider grasps a moth it has killed. This is a world where an initial vision of purity is recognized to be an actuality of awfulness, which moves the poet to ask: what drove the moth to its calamity? To which he responds, a purpose of 'darkness to appall'. The old Yankee poet knew that, in pretty pictures, there could be 'darkness to appall'.

Readers should be aware that this chapter is part of a larger project to which both Günther Schlee and I have been contributing over the last two decades: explaining the actuality of human conflict. My contribution is to craft an anthropology of geopolitics. Geopolitics has historically been a reactionary field dominated by political scientists legitimating imperial control. Think Henry Kissinger! However, geopolitics is crucial, and has a direct impact on humanity's fate. Do you want humanity's fortune in the hands of Kissingers? My goal is to offer a critical form of geopolitics using anthropological insights. Specifically, I analyse what appears to be a pretty picture of American exceptionalism, seeking to know if, in reality, it exhibits a 'design of darkness to appall'.

What is this chapter's primary theoretical intervention? Intervention into theory occurs in the realm of concept formation. Recall that Gilles Deleuze and

Felix Guattari, in *What Is Philosophy?* (1996), thought the job of philosophy was to forge concepts, because these epistemic tools were essential for scrutinizing actuality. The concepts of cargo cult and terrorism are reworked. In both cases, the notions are broadened. The idea that there can be cargo cults of the oppressor is novel, as is a reimagining of terrorism in phenomenological terms.[1] Notions of resistance terrorism and the accumulation of terror are introduced. Then, these concepts are employed to make empirical discoveries. The first of these is that US exceptionalism can be interpreted as an aspect of a cargo cult. The second is that there is a positive relationship between state and resistance terrorism leading to situations of the accumulation of terror. These discoveries inform judgments concerning the design of American exceptionalism.

The argument begins by reporting characteristics of American exceptionalism, suggesting that this exceptionalism is part of a basic design of the United States. Thereafter, further observed properties of this design are reported, which take the narrative into realities of post–Second World War American military operations. Then, reader, you enter a space of horror; for these operations are conceptualized, and observed, in terms of war and terror. The next section reveals approximate and convenient truths of American exceptionalism and, in so doing, introduces a notion of the accumulation of terror. The conclusion speculates upon the critical value of this chapter's speculation.

American Exceptionalism and Cargo Cults

> You are the light of the world. A city set on a hill cannot be hidden ... In the same way, let your light shine before others, so that they may see your good works and give glory to your Father who is in heaven. (Jesus, 'Sermon on the Mount'; Matt. 5:14, 16)

> For we must consider that we shall be as a city upon a hill, the eyes of all people are upon us. (John Winthrop, aboard the *Arbella*, 1630)

> I've spoken of the shining city all my political life ... And how stands the city on this winter night? ... After 200 years, two centuries, she still stands strong and true to the granite ridge, and her glow has held no matter what storm. (President Reagan, 'Farewell Address to the Nation', 1989)

> I believe in American exceptionalism. (President Obama, 2009, in Bryant 2016)

Jesus told his people they were 'a city set on the hill', the 'light of the world' – with it understood that this 'city' of 'light' was the distributive centre of God's good things. Sixteen centuries later, John Winthrop, a founding colonial father, upon landing the *Arbella* in the New World, announced that his government furthering Jesus's work would be the 'city upon a hill', the distributive centre of God's good things. Governor Winthrop's pronouncement was the founding of American exceptionalism: the nationalist ideology that America was a pretty picture – the 'light of the world'.[2] There followed numerous declarations of American exceptionalism, the more recent being those of Presidents Reagan and Obama. One judgement about this exceptionalism is that it makes the United States a distributive centre of cargo in a cargo cult, which assertion may strain credulity. One way of addressing incredulity is to rethink the notion of cargo cults.

Rethinking Cargo Cults

Cargo cults were found, especially after the Second World War, among Melanesian peoples. Revitalization movements, resembling cargo cults, were also reported among Native Americans, such as in the Handsome Lake Movement among the Iroquois in the eighteenth century (Wallace 1969) and the Ghost Dance among Plains Indians in the nineteenth century (Kehoe 2006). These were found among foraging or tribal peoples. Certain relativist and particularist ethnographers might insist that the characteristics of cargo cults are a Melanesian singularity. Nationalistic Americans might relegate such folks to what Michel-Rolph Trouillot (2003) has called the 'savage slot', and reject as scandalous the lumping of their esteemed ideology with that of 'savages'.

I am uncomfortable with such slotting. Scholars are often distinguished as 'splitters' or 'lumpers' – the former disposed to produce narrower concepts, the latter broader ones. Neither disposition seems necessarily the best. What is important is that concepts are not vague or ambiguous, and that they are observable. A virtue of broader concepts is that they allow knowledge of more reality with less conceptual infrastructure. This chapter advances a broader understanding of cargo cults – one that includes the Melanesian variety and those among Native Americans, as well as US exceptionalism.

The study of cargo cults has developed through three phases. The first occurred largely in the 1950s and early 1960s, and offered the classic descriptions and interpretations of Melanesian cargo cults (Worsley 1957; Lawrence 1964; Burridge 1960). A second phase followed in the 1980s, and featured critiques of the earlier work (McDowell 1988; Lindstrom 1993). These accounts problematized the concept, largely on the grounds that it was pejorative, exhibited Western conceptual preconceptions and, worst, lacked empirical referents. A third phase may be said to have been initiated by Holgar Jebens (2004) and Ton Otto (2009), both of whom propose that the term be retained in 'use' (Otto 2009: 88) but that trepidations about its suitability be addressed. I concur. The work of both the first- and second-phase ethnographers indicates that there is something out there in 'social reality' (Otto 2009: 87) that corresponds to cargo cults, but that questions remain regarding how this something can be usefully conceptualized and how its reconceptualization can address justified criticisms. One way of doing this is to place the concept within the mainstream of global history – which requires, first, an understanding of the mainstream.

The 'mainstream' is grasped as the *telos* of macro-human social forms, i.e. those with the greatest powers. In this regard, since the foundation of the state, the mainstream flows towards more and more powerful states – empires expanding through different strategies of imperialism. Associated with imperial growth are different cultural systems (hegemonic or counter-hegemonic), either legitimating empire or struggling against it. Early on, Peter Worsley (1957) and Marvin Harris (1974) placed cargo cults in this mainstream. Adherents of cargo cults possessed millenarian beliefs; that is, they expected a complete revitalization of their society and culture. Worsley understood the millenarian beliefs in cargo cults as expressions of resistance in populations not yet capable of national liberation movements. Harris drew a parallel with the earliest Christians, who, in a world oppressed by expanding Roman imperialism, promised salvation (the cargo), and with salvation, complete revitalization. Christianity's origins, thus, are traced back to a cargo cult struggling against imperial rule. Harris also cites Norman Cohn (1970), who showed that the rebel Christian cults in late medieval and Reformation Europe used their interpretation of Christianity to promise a Golden Age or Paradise on Earth in which Christ would reign for a thousand years, if they resisted the expanding states of their time. These cults, then, promised followers a cargo, Paradise on Earth, which involved change in their social and cultural lives. Worsley, Cohn and Harris placed these forms of cargo cults in the mainstream of struggle against empire. American exceptionalism joins this mainstream as a form of cargo cult struggling to legitimate empire. This involves broadening the scope of the concept.

'Cargo cults' exhibit four properties: they occur in times of stress; they are based on ideological notions of revitalization; they promise cargo; and, often, they have a charismatic leader. Stress here is understood not psychologically but socially as a force leading to dysfunction. Empirical referents of stress vary – but they all involve threats to people's welfare. Imperial oppression and economic malaise are disagreeable stressors. Revitalization ideologies are idea systems with perceptual and procedural components. The empirical referent of the perceptual component is observation of information in spoken or written form that in some way makes it possible to interpret situations as stressed. The empirical referent of the procedural component is observation of spoken or written information specifying what to do to change the situation and bring on the cargo. Cargo is 'good stuff', i.e. desired things. Lindstrom (1993: 193) thought of cargo cults as part of a Western 'meta-discourse of desire'. I concur with him that cargo is about desire but conceptualize this notion differently. Desire (Reyna 2002) involves intentionality and emotion. 'Cargo', so conceived, is the intention to have something, plus the feeling that this intention is well and good. That which is desired may be material (certain Western products) and/or abstract (harmonious social relations, salvation or freedom). It may be unambiguous. Many in Melanesian cargo cults wanted a Jeep. Or things desired may be ambiguous. Just what is freedom? The empirical referent of cargo is observation through verbal or written accounts that such and such is desired.

The charismatic leaders of cargo cults are those who in some manner direct them, while communicating the cult's revitalization messages. Charismatic persons are commonly said to be magnetic, compelling, charming and so on. Of course, the person whom some perceive to be magnetic, compelling and dynamic may be perceived by others as pompous, off-putting and cringe-worthy. (Think Donald Trump.) The empirical referent of a charismatic individual, in a cargo cult, is the perception on the part of observers that, in some manner, s/he communicates information about the cargo and the revitalization promised by the cult, while also directing activities related to that information. If it is observed that, in a time of stress, a revitalization ideology exists, propagated by charismatic leaders and promising cargo, then it is approximately true that the observations are those of a cargo cult. The preceding reconceptualization refutes the notion that the concept of cargo cults should be discarded due to the absence of empirical referents.

A further distinction firmly places cargo cults within the historical 'mainstream'. This distinction is based upon two strikingly opposed functions of the revitalization ideology. On the one hand, these ideas might operate to help the stressed, overwhelmed by powerful, oppressing states. These revitalization ideas produce the main sort of cargo cult recognized in the literature. Melanesians were stressed by the clash of empires during the Second World War, and their beliefs in the cargo they could receive if they followed their revitalization ideologies functioned to relax that stress. Early Christians oppressed by Roman imperial expansion had an ideology in Christian dogma functioning to relieve the oppression. You went to heaven, where you were supernaturally revitalized. The Iroquois and Plains Native Americans endured oppression due to eighteenth- and nineteenth-century settler colonialism. The ideologies of Handsome Lake and the Ghost Dance were designed to relaunch their cultures in the face of colonial abuse. Consequently, these sorts of revitalization ideologies, in the presence of the other three defining properties of cargo cults, result in 'cargo cults of the oppressed'.

Of course, running empires is a risky business – just ask Ozymandias! They tend to come to nasty ends. So empires have their stresses as they 'go bump in the night', accumulating value through oppression and exploitation, in contradiction with others who want to accumulate the value or who do not want to give it up. This being the case, it is conceptually imaginable that there are revitalization ideologies that function to assist the actors who do the stressing. Where such revitalization ideologies exist, in the presence of the other three defining properties of cargo cults, they result in 'cargo cults of the oppressor'. This is what is argued for American exceptionalism.

Recall that the revitalization ideologies in cargo cults are beliefs that if people do such-and-such they will get the cargo. Usually, it is fairly clear who brings the cargo, it being some supernatural entity. American exceptionalism steps in, and its leaders supply to Others, who are oppressed – a revitalization narrative. Sympathetic US leaders see that the oppressed are experiencing stress – due to exploitative economic relations, lousy rulers, crackpot socialist economics, corruption, or what have you. The message to the oppressed, the procedural component of the narrative's underlying ideology, is, then, the following: 'We are the Godly "city on the hill", the "shining light". You do such-and-such. We bring the cargo. You want it, you got it – democracy, capitalism, freedom, prosperity'. Of course, this exceptionalism is a contested ideology, but many among the oppressed 'get it', and when they do, their perception of what it is that is causing them stress is obscured by the oppressors' message, and their understanding of how to proceed legitimates the oppressors' programme.

So, there is a revitalization ideology in American exceptionalism – the belief that America has a supernaturally sponsored, Christian mission to revitalize by bringing 'good things', cargo, to people of the world – democracy, capitalism and freedom. Political, and sometime religious, leaders tend to be the charismatic leaders of American exceptionalism. The Puritan John Winthrop (1588–1649) became governor of the Massachusetts Bay Colony. Presidents – such as Ronald Reagan and Barack Obama – used the bully pulpit of their presidency to disseminate American exceptionalism.

Does American exceptionalism operate in times of stress? Certainly, when Governor Winthrop first articulated his exceptionalism, it was a time when his few Puritan followers had just landed in a bleak land, with every possibility of destruction in the harsh winter. Reagan preached his exceptionalism at a time of economic malaise and political humiliation, following the loss of Iran as a neo-colony. Obama came by his exceptionalism following the most severe economic downturn since the Great Depression, when most people were experiencing declining standards of living, and when the United States had managed to fail in not one but two major wars in Afghanistan and Iraq. There, thus, appear to be two forms of cargo cults – those of the oppressed and those of the oppressor, and American exceptionalism exhibits properties of a cargo cult of the oppressor.

It will be recalled that two reasons for rejecting the term cargo cult were its purported Western bias and its pejorative connotations. Cargo cults were something that occurred among people in the 'savage slot', not among the civilized. This bias is eliminated when those in the West recognize that their social forms are just as much in this 'slot' as those of the Melanesians. Or, as Lindsrom (1993: 182) put it in a different context, 'We are the cargo-cultists'. The pejorative connotation of the term is removed when it is recognized that cargo, as reconceptualized, is not an insulting term but an abstract one denoting objects of desire. Certain students might emphasize, as did Wallace (1956), that what is important in cargo cults is revitalization, and consequently that they are appropriately termed revitalization movements. I sense that it is helpful to keep the word 'cargo', because it is cargo that makes revitalization possible. Some may find the word 'cult' offensive. The concept of cult is ambiguous, with both deprecatory and inoffensive understandings. On the one hand, cults can be understood as small groups with religious beliefs regarded as sinister and deviant; for example, the Cult of Satan. On the other hand, cults are systems of devotion towards some object or figure; for example, the Cult of St Francis. I eliminate ambiguity by understanding cults in the latter sense, with the object of veneration in cargo cults being the cargo. Cargo cults, so conceptualized, are revitalization movements based upon stories about what people want when things go wrong. After all, they dream of things going right – and what is pejorative about that?

To restate this view of cargo cults: they occur in stressful times, feature ideological narratives of revitalization, promise cargo and, often, are headed by charismatic leaders. The novelty in this approach is the claim that there are cargo cults of the oppressor and the oppressed. The central difference between the two is who operates them. In cargo cults of the oppressed, the ideological narratives are generated by actors among the oppressed, the cargos promised are those imagined by the oppressed, and the leaders are members of the oppressed. In cargo cults of the oppressors, the ideological narratives are constructed by some of the oppressors, the cargo promised is imagined by the oppressors, and its leaders are oppressors. The key difference between the two types is that, in the cargo cult of the oppressor, the oppressors communicate the revitalization messages, with its promises of cargo, to the oppressed – the better to obscure their oppression and legitimate their control. American exceptionalism has been offered as a splendid example of an oppressor cargo cult. President Reagan, as he bowed out of political life, asked, rhetorically, how the 'shining city' was standing; to which he replied that it stood 'strong and true', with a persistent 'glow'. The analysis that follows seeks to reveal other aspects of US exceptionalism's design, leading ultimately to speculation about the nature of President Reagan's 'glow'. It proceeds in Socratic fashion – posing and responding to questions. We start with a big question: what is the macro-structural form in which US exceptionalism, the cargo cult of the oppressor, is embedded?

Imperial Design

Think Empire. Empires are important. They are old, having been around at least since Sargon of Akkad (2334–2279 BC) conquered part of Iraq. Since then, they have metastasized, spreading, with the rise of the Euro-American empires at the beginning of modernity (ca. AD 1500), to encompass the entire world. Contra

Wallerstein (1974), empires were not replaced by world systems during the rise of modernity. They are the anatomy of those systems. Nor, during this time, contra certain political scholars (Wimmer and Feinstein 2010), were empires replaced by nation-states. Rather, so-called nation-states have become components of empires – either as core or client states.

Scholars argue that the United States has exhibited some form of empire since its foundation (see, for example, Van Alstyne 1960; LaFeber 1963; Nugent 2008). First, in the short century from 1786 to the 1870s, this empire was a territorial one. Subsequently, in the years following the 1870s, it experimented with different extraterritorial, formal and informal imperial arrangements. Then, in 1950, the US National Security Council issued a policy document called NSC-68,[3] which sought to establish the postwar 'objectives' (NSC-68 1950: 3) of American foreign policy. NSC-68 was written in the context of competition with the USSR, whose 'fundamental design' was believed to be 'world domination' (NSC-68 1950: 17). Given this struggle, NSC-68 maintained that America's 'fundamental purpose' had to be to seek 'world leadership', which involved bringing 'about order and justice' by 'developing moral and material strength', for which a 'strong military posture' was 'essential' (NSC-68 1950: 9–10, 21). The recommendations of NSC-68 were accepted.

Moscow's 'fundamental design' became Washington's 'fundamental purpose', and the 'order' established, as argued in *Deadly Contradictions* (Reyna 2016a), became the 'New American Empire', an autopoetic, complex system – informal, three-tiered, paying strategic rent to its clients. There may be debate over the particularities of this empire; however, there is a convergence of opinion on the Left (Harvey 2003), Centre (Schlesinger 1986; Lundestad 1986; Gaddis 1997), and Right (Ferguson 2004) that post–Second World War America has been an imperial 'order' with global ambitions. Moreover, its enormous development of economic and military resources gives it the 'strength' to be the most forceful empire in history. So what is America? Its design is imperial: one running an imperial cargo cult to help it get what it wants. The next question becomes: what do empires do?

Imperialism, Capitalism and War

> The severed hand on the metal door, the swamp of blood and mud across the road, the human brains inside a garage, the incinerated, skeletal remains of an Iraqi mother and her three small children in their still-smoldering car ... Two missiles from an American jet killed them all ... torn to pieces. (Fisk 2003 on civilian deaths following the US 2003 invasion of Iraq)

Autopoetic complex systems do it – that is, they reproduce and maintain themselves. US imperial re-creation, among other matters, involves the reproduction of capitalist enterprise. Capitalist reproduction is subject to the constraints of economic and political contradictions that can lead to reproductive vulnerabilities requiring fixes. The provision of reproductive fixes to contradictions is the job of elites. Economic elites address contradictions in purely economic matters, for example, by cutting costs, seeking new technology or acquiring larger markets. Security elites use governmental force resources to deal with contradictions. Many of their actions are peaceful, involving the formulation and implementation of policy to improve conditions of capital accumulation. However, some of their actions involve the exercise of violent force. That is, they make war.

There has been considerable debate over the relationship between imperialism, capitalism and war. Lenin (1999) and Bukharin (1929) argued that capitalist imperialism invariably leads to war. My position is that the important question is not whether capitalist forms of imperialism lead to war, but when they do so. When contradictions coalesce and intensify, and peaceful reproductive fixes turn out to be impotent fixations, then what is a hard-pressed imperial social formation to do? It resorts to war. *Deadly Contradictions* (Reyna 2016a) shows how the New American Empire faced considerable political contradictions between 1945 and 1989, and even graver political and economic contradictions subsequent to 1990: contradictions that have not been fixed by economic means. This suggests that US security elites – those at the highest levels of authority over war and peace – would resort to war frequently after 1945. Have they?

There is no body of research that includes, systematically, direct and indirect as well as overt and covert US military operations, especially because of the secrecy surrounding indirect, covert warring. Consequently, estimates of the extent of US governmental violence are approximate. The evidence, however, indicates frequent warring. John Tures (2003) has used a 'United States Military Operations' (USMO) data set generated by the Federation of American Scientists to estimate the frequency of US military activities since 1945. He finds that the United States has engaged in 263 interstate military operations between 1945 and 2002, on the order of 4.6 operations per year. However, 176 of these operations occurred in the 11 years between 1991 and 2002, i.e. about 16 operations per year. One finding of this research is 'that there has been a sizeable jump in the number of U.S. military actions since the end of the Cold War' (Tures 2003: 8). A conclusion follows from the preceding: faced with continual and increasing contradictions since 1945, the United States has waged perpetual war in the form of global warring (i.e. interventions in areas of the globe outside of the US), leaving on battlefields 'severed' limbs, bodies 'incinerated' and 'torn to pieces', raising the question of whether US warring produces terror. However, because there are complications with the concepts of terror and terrorism, it is helpful to specify how these concepts are understood before proceeding.

Conceptualizing Terror and Terrorism

Commonly, terror and terrorism are concepts whose denotations and connotations make them 'fit for purpose' in the ideological armouries of powerful actors. Such definitions of the terms are normally formulated on official or moral grounds. Official definitions – authorized by government agencies – tend to absolve governments from producing terror and terrorism. For example, in the US Code of Laws, domestic and international terrorism are said to 'involve violent acts or acts dangerous to human life that violate federal or state law' (FBI 2015). US officials adjudicate what is or is not lawful, and they habitually judge their government's violence to be legal. Of course, those whom the United States classifies as terrorists equally judge their terror to be legitimate. Their source of legitimacy may be different from that of the Americans (for example, in Muslim instances it may involve a *qadi* [judge] making a *qala* [Islamic legal ruling]); but it is law. Consequently, this results in a situation where all forceful actors proclaim the legitimacy of their violence, thereby defining away terrorism and making it conceptually impossible to distinguish terrorist from non-terrorist violence.

Some conceptualize terrorism on moral grounds and, in so doing, justify horrific violence as good because it is good. Samantha Power, for example, US ambassador to the United Nations from 2013 to 2017 – according to one source, a 'moral compass' of American diplomacy (Forbes 2016) – asserts that 'there is a moral difference between setting out to destroy as many civilians as possible and killing civilians unintentionally and reluctantly in pursuit of a military objective' (Power 2007). The United States is assumed by Power to kill 'unintentionally and reluctantly', and, thus, is not involved in terrorism. Its opponents destroy 'as many civilians as possible', and, consequently, are terrorists. There are problems with such moralizing. First, there is evidence, provided later in this chapter, that the United States knowingly kills large numbers of civilians, who are then classified as 'collateral damage'. Knowingly killing persons, and then classifying them as accidental 'collateral damage', is not so much ethically good as hypocritically outrageous.

Second, those classified by the United States and its Western clients as terrorists do not invariably kill 'as many civilians as possible'. Actually, they are adept at targeting military and governmental assets of Americans or their proxies. When they do kill civilians, and they do, these are normally in relatively small numbers (the exception being 9/11 – the attack on the World Trade Center and the Pentagon on 11 September 2001).[4]

Third, elites who terrorize do not claim to do so on immoral grounds, announcing to the world, 'We're bad, really bad – and we are going to terrorize you'. Rather, they employ hermeneuts, who interpret for ordinary folks what their elites desire (for example, Ambassador Power). These hermeneuts, then, explain the utilization of 'terror' for 'good' moral reasons, which reasons happen to coincide with what the elites want. Terrorism, so understood, is discourse produced to justify elite desires. Given the preceding, there does not appear to be any 'moral compass' that points to the true north of terrorism.[5] How, then, might terror be defined?

Terms are usefully defined by getting to the 'is' of them. The 'is' of something is its reality. 'Getting to' 'is' involves selecting symbols that report empirical referents of it. So, what is the 'is' of terror? It is things happening to bodies whose empirical referent is experience. Consequently, a phenomenological understanding of the term is in order.[6] 'Terror', defined in terms of its empirical referents, is the conscious experience of fear due to violence – at times volatile panic, so strong that it provokes bodily evacuation; at other times nagging dread, replacing tranquillity with persistent and deep anxiety. 'Terrorism' is any and all events that in some manner produce terror. The 'terrorizers' are events causing terror; the 'terrorized' are people experiencing terror. There are human- and nature-made terrorisms. 'Nature-made' terrorism results from hazardous natural events – earthquakes, tsunami, volcanic eruptions and so on – that activate the sense organs of the terrorized. 'Human-made' terrorism results from hazardous events that humans contrive – most of which are political and involve the exercise of violent force that activates the sense organs of the terrorized.

Two sets of conceptualizations pertaining to the terrorized and the terrorists further our understanding of human-made terrorism. The first considers how the terrorized come to experience terror. The second pertains to what the terrorizers do to create the violence that produces terror. Concerning the acquisition of terror, 'unmediated' terrorism is that attained by a person's sense organs perceiving it. S/he sees, hears, smells, tastes or is touched by violence or its consequences. 'Mediated' terrorism is acquired by a person's sense organs perceiving accounts of the terror. S/he sees it on television, reads it in the newspaper or hears about it through gossip. Mass media are currently able to diffuse the fearful happenings rapidly and over great distances. Photographs and films shot at the end of the Second World War of bodies and starving concentration camp victims mediated the sheer terror of the Nazi 'final solution'.

The terms direct and indirect terrorism signal a distinction between ways in which terrorists create violence. 'Direct' terrorism occurs when the terrorists physically cause terror in the terrorized. 'Indirect' terrorism occurs when the terrorizers take a circuitous route to cause terror in the terrorized. An example of direct terrorism occurred in Palestine in 1948, when the main Israeli military force, the Hagenah, along with extremist, underground paramilitaries, namely, the Irgun and the Stern Gang, overwhelmed Palestinians, provoking the *Nakba* (the 'Catastrophe'), terrorizing the more than 700,000 who were expelled from their homes. 'Indirect' human terrorism occurs when one group of actors provides resources to allies, who then use them directly to inflict horrifying violence upon others. During the invasion of Iraq under President George W. Bush, for example, the American government supplied persons who had been involved in organizing death squads in Central America to the Iraqi government to help it strengthen special police commandos, who – so strengthened – went on to terrorize their victims with grim tortures (Mahmood et al. 2013). Bush II's government was in the business of indirect terrorism by helping the Iraqi police to terrorize directly.

Both governmental and nongovernmental forms of direct and indirect terrorisms exist. 'Governmental', or 'state', terrorism involves the exercise of violent force against peoples by police, quasi-military or military agencies of countries' governments. Israeli operations during the *Nakba* were direct, state terrorism. US government assistance to the special police commandos in Iraq was indirect, state terrorism. 'Nongovernmental' terrorism is the exercise of violent force against peoples by actors who are not part of any level of a governing apparatus – ranging from lone-wolf terrorism, where a single individual terrorizes, to rebel movements of various types that terrorize. The United States, with its easy access to guns, facilitates lone-wolf terrorism. Terrorism by rebel movements, widespread throughout the world, has been especially common in Israel following the *Nakba* and included the Palestine Liberation Organization (PLO), which now avoids violence, and Hamas, which does not.

An implication of terrorism's phenomenological conceptualization needs to be made explicit. The US Civil War general William Sherman, whose *chevauchée* through Georgia in 1864 spread unmediated and mediated terror throughout the American South, remarked, 'War is cruelty, and you cannot refine it' (Sherman 1864). War is cruelty. Cruelty causes terror. To make this point, consider one instance of war in a torpid African capital during a civil war. There a friend – let us call him Musa – was making 'une promenade'. He walked in front of a government building. He saw an old man wave a knife at the building. The soldiers who were guarding it machine-gunned him. They threw hand grenades at the body, blasting it apart into 'mini morceaux, mini morceaux', he kept repeating to me when he returned from his walk. Musa had a penchant for categorizing life's troubles as being 'dans la boue' ('in the mud'). What he had just experienced – big, terrifying trouble – was category busting. Beyond mud! So, reflecting upon what he had just experienced, Musa judged, 'Nous sommes dans un monde de merde' ('We are in a world of shit').

Another form of terrorism can be distinguished in terms of its function. Understanding it can be facilitated by recollecting the ancient biblical wisdom, 'All they that take the sword shall perish with the sword' (Matt. 26:52). This suggests that some violence may operate to resist other violence; further, it implies that some terrorist violence may be resisted by other terrorist violence. The concept of resistance has its ambiguities. In this text, it refers to exercises of force resources to eliminate undesired countervailing exercises of force resources. Resistance, as here conceptualized, is not about struggling against a world of shit to make a better world of shit. This is 'mitigation'. Nor is it about struggling against a world of shit to better live in it. This is 'submission'.⁷ Rather, it is struggling in a world of shit to eliminate it. Cargo cults of the oppressed may be those of mitigation, submission or resistance. Our interest is in those of resistance. Some resistance is violent. Violent collective action that terrorizes those producing worlds of shit by terrorizing will be termed 'resistance terrorism'. Now it is possible to return to the question at hand: are the New American Empire's security elites in the terrorism business?

Concerning Apple Pie

February 12, 2010 . . . Circumstances: In a night raid, U.S. forces attacked a home where 25 people, three of them musicians, had gathered for a naming celebration. A newborn was being named that night. One of the musicians went outside to relieve himself. A flashlight shone in his face. Panicked, he ran inside and announced that the Taliban were outside. A police commander, Dawoud, the father of the newborn, ran outside with his weapon. U.S. forces opened fire, killing Officer Dawoud, a pregnant mother, an eighteen year old, Gulaila, and two others . . .

March 16, 2010 – The UN issued a scathing report, stating that the U.S. had killed the women. Villagers told Jerome Starkey, reporting for the *Independent*, that U.S. troops tried to tamper with evidence by digging bullets out of the women's bodies and out of the walls. (Kelly and Pearson 2010, reporting on atrocities committed by US military personnel in Afghanistan)

Something typically done by US citizens is said to be 'as American as apple pie'. I return to this observation and comment upon the above quotation at the end of this section. Previously, it was established that the United States wars a lot. Statistics regarding war mortality and war-induced migration serve as indicators of the number of people experiencing war's terror and, more generally, the amount of terror produced by American warring. Elsewhere (Reyna 2016b), I have reported that, since the Second World War, nine US wars are estimated to have killed over 9,700,000 people. This is a case of underreporting, because it does not include those killed in covert US wars or in wars in which Washington played a significant but indirect role. In other assessments, it is estimated that the United States has killed from 20 to 30 million people since the end of the Second World War (Lucas 2007). Regardless of which estimate is correct, no other country has killed as many people during this period. Many fatalities were non-combatants. One estimate from public health sources has it that 85–90 per cent of deaths in contemporary warfare are civilian (Wiist et al. 2014).⁸ This appraisal has been challenged (Roberts 2010), but the challengers do not deny that civilian deaths in contemporary war are high. US combat operations targeted civilians in the atomic bombing of Hiroshima and Nagasaki; as did the carpet bombing campaigns in North Korea, Cambodia and Laos during the Korean and Vietnam wars and the drone attacks in Africa, the Middle East, Pakistan and Afghanistan of the Bush, Obama and Trump regimes. Analysis of eight post–Second World War US wars (Reyna 2016b) concluded that they resulted in 73,250,000 people becoming internal or external refugees.

This, then, is the evidence: direct state terror visited upon kin, friends and neighbours of the 9.7 million killed by US forces; and direct state terror inflicted additionally on the 73 million refugees fleeing the US killing fields. What is more, mediated state terror was diffused globally to unknown but enormous numbers through television, radio and other public media. The New American Empire produces terror. It inflicts it on those killed, driven to become refugees, or experiencing US warring through the media. Inflicting terror – including 'digging bullets' out of their victims' bodies – is as American as apple pie. This poses the question: what happens when US security elites produce terror?

The Accumulation of Terror

On 20 September 2001, in a Joint Session of Congress, President George W. Bush declared a 'Global War on Terror' (GWOT) that shaped an enormous increase of US global warring in the Middle East, Central Asia, Africa, the Philippines and, to a lesser extent, in Latin America (documented in Reyna 2016a). As of 2014, roughly $1.6 trillion had been spent on military operations since 9/11 (Belasco 2014). GWOT was massive direct, indirect and mediated state terrorism. What happened?

Robert Pape (2010), a political scientist researching suicide terrorism, reports that there were, globally, 343 suicide attacks between 1980 and 2003, of which, at most, 10 per cent were inspired by anti-American sentiment. Since 2004, there have been more than 2000 such attacks, over 91 per cent of which were directed against US and allied forces in Afghanistan, Iraq and other countries. What happened was a huge increase in resistance terrorism in the form of suicide bombings, following American state terrorism. Evidence from three other sources – quantitative data concerning the timing of terrorist attacks, the testimony of anti-US terrorists and statements by members of the security elite opposing them – is examined to know whether it is consistent with that of Pape.

Quantitative Evidence

Reyna (2016b) presents data on the number of terrorist attacks, annually, in Afghanistan, Iraq and worldwide. It is clear that, subsequent to the declaration of GWOT, terrorist attacks steeply increased, globally, between 2001 and 2010. Moreover, if one inspects the individual graphs, one observes the following. In Iraq, between 2001 and 2002, the number of terrorist attacks remains consistently low; thereafter, it rises steeply, evidently, as a consequence of the US invasion. In Afghanistan, the number of terrorist attacks begin to rise steeply subsequent to the US invasion in 2001. These statistics indicate a temporal sequencing: first massive US state terrorism, followed by a terrorist response in Iraq, Afghanistan and globally.

Testimony of Anti-US Terrorists

Discussion of anti-US terrorists will bring us back to the topic of cargo cults. Al Qaeda and the Islamic State (IS) are the two most powerful anti-US terrorist organizations. Both groups are led, or have been led, by charismatic persons – Osama bin Laden, in the case of al Qaeda, and Abu Bakr al Baghdadi, in the case of IS. Both organizations insist they are resisting two Western colonial ventures: first, the political and economic hegemony imposed on the Middle East by the victors of the First World War following the breakup of the Ottoman Empire; and, second, the current 'Crusade' led by the Americans. Both groups follow Muslim Brotherhood and Salafist interpretations of Islam that have been characterized as revitalization movements (Tyrrell 2014: 68; see also Lindholm and Zúquete 2010). Revitalizing will occur through delivery of the cargo of Islamic utopia, thought of as a re-creation of the Caliphate. Consequently, Al Qaeda and IS exhibit the properties identified as characterizing cargo cults of the oppressed.

Spokespersons for each group make clear that, as a result of the American crusader's oppression, their function is to wage jihad against the United States. Al Qaeda, for example, articulated this in a 1998 *fatwa*, attributed to Osama bin Laden (in Mideastweb 2004), declaring that 'for over seven years the U.S. has been occupying the lands of Islam . . . plundering its riches, dictating to its rulers, humiliating its people, terrorizing its neighbors'. As a consequence, he promised, 'We – with God's help – call on every Muslim to comply with God's order to kill Americans' (Mideastweb 2004). Similarly, the popular Salafi preacher Zakir Naik said, 'If he [Osama bin Laden] is terrorizing America – the terrorist, biggest terrorist – I am with him. Every Muslim should be a terrorist. The thing is that if he is terrorizing the terrorist, he is following Islam' (in Von Drehle and Ghosh 2009). 'Terrorizing the terrorist' puts it in a nutshell. Al Qaeda and IS practise resistance terrorism against US state terrorism. Worsley (1957) had suggested that Melanesian cargo cults involved resistance in polities that were incapable of national liberation movements. Al Qaeda and IS might be understood as 'big time' cargo cults contesting the terror of imperial forces with their own terror. Be very clear – cargo cults and resistance terrorism are not conflated, but they can be related. The former may operate to both legitimate and motivate the latter. Al Qaeda and IS promise followers a cargo of the Caliphate if they participate in resistance terrorism and *Jannah* (Paradise) if they die in resistance. In effect, the cargo promised, the Caliphate, is the 'city on the [earthly] hill' or the 'city on the [heavenly] hill'.

Security Elites

At least some Western security elites grasp that state terrorism causes resistance terrorism. The National Intelligence Estimate of 2006, the most authoritative statement of US intelligence, specified that 80 per cent of terrorist attacks against American forces and their allies between 2003 and 2006 in Afghanistan and Iraq were due, in part, to 'fear of Western domination' (NIE 2006: 6), leading the NIE's authors to judge, 'the Iraq war has become the "cause célèbre" for jihadists . . . and is shaping a new generation of terrorist leaders and operatives' (NIE 2006). Lt Gen. Michael Flynn, director of the Defense Intelligence Agency (2012–2014), reported with some asperity, 'We've tended to say, drop another bomb via a drone and put out a headline that "we killed Abu Bag of Doughnuts" and it makes us all feel good for 24 hours . . . And you know what? It doesn't matter. It just made them a martyr, it just created a new reason to fight us even harder' (in Scahill 2015). Sir Sherard Cowper-Coles, Britain's special representative to Afghanistan (2009–2010), stated that Gen. David Petraeus should be 'ashamed of himself'. Sir Sherard was referring to Petraeus's policies during the Afghan war, when 'he . . . increased the violence [and] trebled the number of special forces raids', so that, 'for every dead Pashtun warrior, there will be 10 pledged to revenge' (in Mackenzie 2011). The preceding indicates that at least some of those involved in the GWOT knew of the relationship between state terrorism and resistance terrorism.

The evidence just provided shows that quantitative and qualitative evidence concur: it is apparently true that the relationship between state and resistance terrorism is positive – increases in the former lead to increases in the latter. This is a design whose trajectory is the accumulation of terror.

Conclusion

I smelled the stench of rotting bodies and burning shit. (Wollom Jensen's and James M. Childs' remembrance of soldiering in the Vietnam War, 2016: 88)

Reader, this chapter began with the old poet's report on his jaunt in the woods. You too have been on an outing: a promenade through the geopolitics of the 'city on the hill', the New American Empire. It is time for critical reflection upon the scenic attractions of your amble. These are:

1. The US is an empire.
2. As is the wont of empires, it wars frequently.
3. As it wars frequently, it produces state terrorism.
4. As a state terrorist it causes its opponents to resist, producing resistance terrorists.

Now bring cargo cults into the reflection, which leads to judgements about US exceptionalism. Contemporary geopolitics appears to be occupied by two warring cargo cults – that of the New American Empire's state terrorism opposed by that of Al Qaeda's and IS's resistance terrorism, which interact to grow terrorism. If this is the case, then it implies the following:

1. The US is unexceptional in that it does what empires do – it wars and terrorizes.
2. However, what is exceptional is that, as the most powerful, complex human system ever – generating direct and indirect state terror, resistance terror, unmediated and mediated terror – it is the greatest terror machine in human history.
3. Consequently, the convenient opinion – that the United States is a bringer of a cargo of good things – needs to be replaced by the recognition that it is a cargo cult of the oppressor and that the cargo it delivers is really prodigious amounts of terror, which in turn provokes more terror from the terrorized, resulting in a dynamic of the accumulation of terror.

Recall Musa from the section conceptualizing terror and terrorism. He, like you, had been *en promenade* when he experienced direct, unmediated terrorism – body parts flying all over the place, which shocked him and drove him to cry out, 'We are in a world of shit'. Musa was speaking figuratively. Wollom Jensen and James M. Childs, quoted above, report their battlefield experience of 'rotting bodies and burning shit'. This is because people are often killed in contemporary war due to explosions. These explosions rip bodies apart, mixing their faeces with body parts, which tend to be cooked in the explosion's fire, producing a combined odour of barbecue, shit and eventually rot. If war is terrorism, then terrorism – admitting of no refinements, as General Sherman might say – is literally a world of flame-broiled shit.

As for the 'glow' that President Reagan believed he saw in his final address to the American people, could it not have issued from the burning shit of humans, consumed in order to bring US imperial 'light'? Here is a 'design of darkness to appall', a lot worse than a New Hampshire spider enjoying its breakfast moth.

Stephen P. Reyna is Emeritus Professor, University of New Hampshire, Associated Researcher at Max Planck Institute for Social Anthropology, co-Editor of *Anthropological Theory* and former Senior Research Fellow and Honorary Professor, University of Manchester, UK. He is interested in social theory, political economy, African ethnography and American imperialism. His most recent books are *Starry Nights: Essays in Critical Structural Realism* (Berghahn, 2017) and *Deadly Contradictions: The New American Empire and Its Global Warring* (Berghahn, 2016).

Notes

I am indebted to all who have commented upon this chapter, especially Jonathan Friedman, John Gledhill, Andreas Dafinger, Don Kalb, Keir Martin, Jens Kreinath and John Eidson. Its faults are my own.

1. Gilliam's (2010: 171) approach to 'militarism and accumulation in the United States as a compensatory cargo cult' differs significantly from my conception.
2. For discussions of American exceptionalism, see Lipset (1997); Madsen (1998); Söderlind and Carson (2012).
3. NSC-68 is usefully introduced by Nitze (1980), who directed the project that produced it.
4. With the exception of the year 2001, the fatalities attributable to terrorism in the United States have failed to attain 0.1 per 100,000 (Overton 2015).
5. Asad (2007) has questioned the claims of a moral high ground for Western military violence. Zinn (2007) and Herman (2007) critique Ambassador Power.
6. Phenomenological and biological understandings of terror are offered, respectively, in Morris and Crank (2011) and Yehuda (2001).
7. Scott (1985: 137), for example, famously includes 'rumour, gossip, disguises, linguistic tricks, metaphors, euphemisms, folktales, ritual gestures, anonymity' as expressions of resistance. These, however, might just as well be ways of submitting to nasty situations.
8. Tirman (2011) has written of civilian casualties in US wars. He emphasizes that, through a combined effort, spokespersons for the military, politicians and media hermeneuts hide their true extent.

References

Asad, Talal. 2007. *On Suicide Bombers*. New York: Columbia.
Belasco, Amy. 2014. *The Cost of Iraq, Afghanistan and Other Global War on Terror Operations since 9/11*, Congressional Research Service. Retrieved 16 November 2016 from http://www.biblioteca pleyades.net/archivos_pdf/cost-global-war-terror.pdf.
Bryant, Nick. 2016. 'American Exceptionalism in a Time of American Malaise', *BBC News*, 3 February. Retrieved 16 December 2016 from https://www.bbc.com/news/world-us-canada-35438548.
Bukharin, Nikolai. 1929 [1915]. *Imperialism and the World Economy*. Moscow: International.
Burridge, Kenelm. 1960. *Mambu: A Melanesian Millennium*. London: Methuen.
Cohn, Norman. 1970 [1957]. *The Pursuit of the Millennium: Revolutionary Millenarians and Mystical Anarchists of the Middle Ages*, 3rd edn. London: Granada.
Deleuze, Gilles and Felix Guattari. 1996. *What Is Philosophy?* New York: Columbia University Press.
FBI. 2015. 'Definitions of Terrorism in the U.S. Code', *Federal Bureau of Investigation*. Retrieved 12 October 2015 from https://www.fbi.gov/about-us/investigate/terrorism/terrorism-definition.
Ferguson, Niall. 2004. *Colossus: The Rise and Fall of the American Empire*. New York: Penguin.
Fisk, Robert. 2003. 'It Was an Outrage, an Obscenity', *Information Clearing House*. Retrieved 28 April 2014 from http://www.informationclearinghouse.info/article2426.htm.
Forbes. 2016. '# 41: Samantha Power', *Forbes*. Retrieved 23 June 2016 from http://www.forbes.com/profile/samantha-power/.
Frost, Robert. 1936. 'Design', *Poem Hunter*. Retrieved 26 December 2015 from http://www.poem hunter.com/poem/design/.
Gaddis, John L. 1997. *We Now Know: Rethinking Cold War History*. Oxford: Oxford University Press.
Gilliam, Angelia. 2010. 'Militarism and Accumulation as Cargo Cult', in Faye V. Harrison (ed.), *Decolonizing Anthropology: Moving Further toward an Anthropology for Liberation*. 3rd edn. Arlington, VA: Association of Black Anthropologists, American Anthropological Association, pp. 170–91.

Harris, Marvis. 1974. *Cows, Pigs, Wars and Witches*. New York: Random House.
Harvey, David. 2003. *The New Imperialism*. Oxford: Oxford University Press.
Herman, Edward. 2007. 'Response to Zinn on Samantha Power', *ZNET*. Retrieved 10 December 2018 from https://zcomm.org/znetarticle/responce-to-zinn-on-samantha-power-by-edward-herman/.
Jebens, Holger. 2004. *Cargo, Cult, and Culture Critique*. Honolulu: University of Hawai'i Press.
Jensen, Wollom and James M. Childs Jr. 2016. *Moral Warriors, Moral Wounds: The Ministry of the Christian Ethic*. Eugene, OR: Cascade Books.
Kehoe, Alice B. 2006. *The Ghost Dance: Ethnohistory and Revitalization*. Long Grove, IL: Waveland Press.
Kelly, Kathy and Dan Pearson. 2010. 'Atrocities in Afghanistan: A Troubling Timetable', *Common Dreams*. Retrieved 22 April 2016 from https://www.commondreams.org/view/2010/04/30-10.
LaFeber, Walter. 1963. *The New Empire: An Interpretation of American Expansion 1860–1898*. Ithaca, NY: Cornell University Press.
Lawrence, Peter. 1964. *Road Belong Cargo: A Study of the Cargo Movement in the Southern Madang District New Guinea*. Manchester: Manchester University Press.
Lenin, Vladimir I. 1999 [1917]. *Imperialism: The Highest Stage of Capitalism*. Sydney: Resistance Books.
Lindholm, Charles and José P. Zúquete. 2010. *The Struggle for the World: Liberation Movements for the 21st Century*. Stanford, CA: Stanford University Press.
Lindstrom, Lamont. 1993. *Cargo Cult: Strange Stories of Desire from Melanesia and Beyond*. Honolulu: University of Hawai'i Press.
Lipset, Seymour M. 1997. *American Exceptionalism: A Double-Edged Sword*. New York: W.W. Norton.
Lucas, James A. 2007. 'Study – US Regime Has Killed 20–30 Million People since World War II', Counter-Currents.org. Retrieved 14 December 2015 from http://www.sott.net/article/273517-Study-US-regime-has-killed-20-30-million-people-since-World-War-Two.
Lundestad, Geir. 1986. 'Empire by Invitation? The United States and Western Europe 1945–1952', *Journal of Peace Research* 23(3): 263–77.
Mackenzie, Jean. 2011. 'Afghanistan: Petraeus "Should Be Ashamed of Himself"', *Ground Truth Project*. Retrieved 18 December 2015 from http://thegroundtruthproject.org/afghanistan-petraeus-should-be-ashamed-of-himself/.
Madsen, Deborah L. 1998. *American Exceptionalism*. Jackson, MS: University Press of Mississippi.
Mahmood, Mona, Maggie O'Kane, Chavala Madlena, Teresa Smith, Ben Ferguson, Patrick Farrelly and Guy Grandjean. 2013. 'From El Salvador to Iraq: Washington's Man behind Brutal Police Squads', *The Guardian*. Retrieved 21 June 2016 from https://www.theguardian.com/world/2013/mar/06/el-salvador-iraq-police-squads-washington.
McDowell, Nancy. 1988. 'A Note on Cargo Cults and Cultural Construction of Change', *Pacific Studies* 11(2): 121–34.
Mideastweb. 2004. 'Osama bin Laden's Jihad and Text of Fatwah's and Declaration of War'. Retrieved 24 June 2016 from http://www.mideastweb.org/osamabinladen1.htm.
Morris, Travis and John Crank. 2011. 'Towards a Phenomenology of Terrorism: Implications for Research and Policy', *Crime, Law and Social Change* 56: 219–42.
NIE. 2006. *National Intelligence Estimate 2006-02R, Trends in Global Terrorism: Implications for the United States*, Governmentattic.org. Retrieved 17 December 2015 from http://www.governmentattic.org/5docs/NIE-2006-02R.pdf.
Nitze, Paul H. 1980. 'The Development of NSC-68', *International Security* 4(4): 170–76.
NSC-68. 1950. *A Report to the National Security Council - NSC 68, April 12, 1950*. National Archives, Harry S. Truman Library Museum, Collection: Ideological Foundations of the Cold War, Series: President's Secretary's Files. Retrieved 13 June 2022 from https://www.trumanlibrary.gov/library/research-files/report-national-security-council-nsc-68?documentid=NA&pagenumber=1.
Nugent, Walter. 2008. *Habits of Empire: A History of American Expansion*. New York: Knopf.

Otto, Ton. 2009. 'What Happened to Cargo Cults? Material Religions in Melanesia and the West', *Social Analysis* 53(1): 82–102.
Overton, Jon. 2015. 'Terrorism Is Less Scary Than You Think', *Iowa Peace Network*. Retrieved 11 December 2015 from http://iowapeacenetwork.blogspot.com/2015/01/terrorism-is-less-scary-than-you-think.html.
Pape, Robert A. 2010. 'It's the Occupation, Stupid', *Foreign Policy*. Retrieved 29 December 2016 from http://foreignpolicy.com/2010/10/18/its-the-occupation-stupid/.
Power, Samantha. 2007. 'Our War on Terror', *The New York Times*. Retrieved 10 December 2015 from http://www.nytimes.com/2007/07/29/books/review/Power-t.html?ref=review.
Reagan, Ronald. 1989. 'Farewell Address to the Nation'. Retrieved 13 June 2022 from https://www.reaganlibrary.gov/archives/speech/farewell-address-nation.
Reyna, Stephen P. 2002. *Connections: Brain, Mind, and Culture in a Social Anthropology*. London: Routledge.
———. 2016a. *Deadly Contradictions*. New York and Oxford: Berghahn.
———. 2016b. 'Design of Darkness to Appall'. Retrieved 13 June 2022 from https://www.academia.edu/29070300/DESIGN_OF_DARKNESS_TO_APPALL.
Roberts, Adam. 2010. 'Lives and Statistic: Are 90% of War Victims Civilians?', *Survival* 52(3): 115–35.
Scahill, Jeremy. 2015. 'The Drone Papers', *The Intercept*. Retrieved 17 December 2015 from https://theintercept.com/drone-papers/find-fix-finish/.
Schlesinger, Arthur M. Jr. 1986. *The Cycles of American History*. Boston: Houghton Mifflin.
Scott, James C. 1985. *Weapons of the Weak*. New Haven, CT: Yale University Press.
Sherman, William T. 1864. 'Letter of William T. Sherman to James M. Calhoun, E.E. Rawson, and S.C. Wells, September 12, 1864', *Civil War Era NC*. Retrieved 14 December 2015 from http://cwnc.omeka.chass.ncsu.edu/items/show/23.
Söderlind, Sylvia and J. Taylor Carson (eds). 2012. *American Exceptionalisms: From Winthrop to Winfrey*. New York: State University of New York Press.
Tirman, John. 2011. *The Deaths of Others: The Fate of Civilians in America's Wars*. Oxford: Oxford University Press.
Trouillot, Michel-Rolph. 2003. *Global Transformations: Anthropology and the Modern World*. New York: Palgrave MacMillan.
Tures, J.A. 2003. 'United States Military Operations in the New World Order: An Examination of the Evidence', *American Diplomacy*. Retrieved 4 May 2014 from http://www.unc.edu/depts/diplomat/archives_roll/2003_01-03/tures_military.html.
Tyrrell, Marc W.D. 2014. 'The Use of Evolutionary Theory in Modelling Culture and Cultural Conflict', in Thomas H. Johnson and Barry Zellen (eds), *Culture, Conflict, and Counterinsurgency*. Stanford, CA: Stanford University Press.
Van Alstyne, Richard W. 1960. *The American Empire: Its Historical Pattern and Evolution*. London: Routledge and Kegan Paul.
Von Drehle, David and Bobby Ghosh. 2009. 'An Enemy Within: The Making of Najibullah Zazi', *Time*. Retrieved 30 March 2016 from http://content.time.com/time/magazine/article/0,9171,1927280,00.html.
Wallace, Anthony F. 1956. 'Revitalization Movements', *American Anthropologist* 58(2): 264–81.
———. 1969. *The Death and Rebirth of the Seneca*. New York: Vintage.
Wallerstein, Immanuel. 1974. *The Modern World-System I*. New York: Academic Press.
Wiist, William H., Kathy Barker, Neil Arya, Jon Rohde, Martin Donohoe, Shelley White, Pauline Lubens, Geraldine Gorman and Amy Hagopian. 2014. 'The Role of Public Health in the Prevention of War: Rationale and Competencies', *American Journal of Public Health* 104(6): e34–e47.
Wimmer, Andreas and Yuval Feinstein. 2010. 'The Rise of the Nation-State across the World: 1816–2001', *American Sociological Review* 75(5): 764–90.

Winthrop, John. 1630. 'A Model of Christian Charity', *Collections of the Massachusetts Historical Society*. Retrieved 11 October 2016 from http://history.hanover.edu/texts/winthmod.html.

Worsley, Peter. 1957. *The Trumpet Shall Sound: A Study of 'Cargo Cults' in Melanesia*. London: MacGibbon & Kee.

Yehuda, R. 2001. 'Biology of Posttraumatic Stress Disorder', *Journal of Clinical Psychiatry* 62(S17): 41–46.

Zinn, Howard. 2007. 'Letter: On Terror', *The New York Times*. Retrieved 10 December 2018 from https://www.nytimes.com/2007/08/19/books/review/Letters-t-1.html.

PART III

MIGRATION AND EXCLUSION, DISPLACEMENT AND EMPLACEMENT

CHAPTER 12

FROM BASES OF IDENTIFICATIONS TO ACTS OF EXCLUSION?

Günther Schlee's Contributions to
the Max Planck Research Initiative on Migration

MARIE-CLAIRE FOBLETS AND ZEYNEP YANASMAYAN

Introduction

Germany came to the fore during the so-called summer of migration in 2015 and the research community quickly moved on to an investigation of the participation and inclusion of recently arrived refugees. While the literature covering this field of research is continuously growing, in this chapter we aim to introduce the Max Planck Initiative 'The Challenges of Migration, Integration and Exclusion' which serves as an example of the development of an innovative research programme focusing on societal challenges in Europe, particularly Germany, in the wake of this so called 'summer of migration'. We concentrate in particular on the conceptual angle advanced by the initiative and shed light on a relatively less known aspect of the work of Günther Schlee, renowned for his work on pastoralism, (armed) conflict and identity theory, and its contribution to the study of contemporary societies characterized by migration-related diversity.

Our chapter is divided into two distinct but complementary parts. We first give some background to the initiative, and then focus on the lens of 'exclusion' developed by the initiative and situate the concrete and very generous input this conceptualization received from Günther Schlee and his works.

Genesis and Research Design of the Max Planck Initiative 'The Challenges of Migration, Integration and Exclusion' (2017–2020)

The genesis of the Max Planck Initiative 'The Challenges of Migration, Integration and Exclusion' goes back to the memorable summer of 2015, when European shores saw an impressive peak in the arrival of asylum seekers coming mainly from the Middle East and Africa. It had profound and far-reaching consequences at both the societal and political levels.

At the societal level, new solidarity networks emerged and existing ones were reactivated in the guise of various forms of civic engagement and volunteerism. At the same time, nativist and/or anti-immigrant social movements gained more visibility and support throughout the continent. Politically, European states and, particularly, the European Union (hereafter EU) proved how unprepared decision makers in Brussels and in the individual Member States were to receive so many arrivals at one time. The solidary-sharing frameworks that the EU put forward, such as relocation schemes that aimed to redistribute asylum seekers from Greece and Italy throughout the territory of the various Member States, failed due to lack of political will on the part of some Member States. In a moment when the European institutions as well as individual Member States proved to be ill equipped to deal with the events, Germany stepped up and took the lead with its welcoming attitude, most memorably encapsulated in Chancellor Angela Merkel's famous *Wir schaffen das!* ('We can do it!') pronouncement. The sentence instantaneously became breaking news worldwide.

As Germany took on such a prominent role in the reception and management of migration flows after 2015, scholarly work on migration in Germany also flourished. The Max Planck Society, in line with its mission to promote fundamental research in Germany, called for a cross-institutional, interdisciplinary initiative that would bring together the wide-ranging expertise that was housed in several Max Planck institutes in order to advance new knowledge in the field of migration studies. The joint research programme 'The Challenges of Migration and Integration' (hereafter WiMi) was the result of that effort.

WiMi was a three-year collaborative research programme (March 2017 to February 2020) that was financed by the Max Planck Society and involved researchers from six Max Planck Institutes: the Max Planck Institute for Comparative Public Law and International Law (Heidelberg), the Max Planck Institute for Demographic Research (Rostock), the Max Planck Institute for Social Law and Social Policy (Munich), the Max Planck Institute for Human Development (Berlin), the Max Planck Institute for Social Anthropology (Halle) and the Max Planck Institute for the Study of Religious and Ethnic Diversity (Göttingen).[1]

The task with which the Max Planck Society entrusted WiMi was challenging in several ways. First, it was clear from the outset that there was no shortage of scholarship in the broad field of migration and its numerous societal consequences, and that the literature was growing exponentially. Second, the constellation of disciplines and the various fields of expertise of the different teams that had agreed to join and actively contribute to the WiMi research programme presented a new situation to everyone involved. It was an unprecedented experience for them to be involved in such a multi-disciplinary setting and to be invited to develop a common research programme. In fact, most of the researchers did not know one another, let alone each other's respective scholarly work. Therefore, a great openness to interdisciplinary collaboration would be needed on the part of everyone involved, at the risk of slowing down the whole process, if we hoped to reach mutual understanding and gain new insights. Günther Schlee, from the very start, expressed confidence that we would be able to handle these challenges. He participated with great enthusiasm in every meeting that the teams set up, starting in February 2016, and his input undoubtedly facilitated to a great extent the exchanges among the teams, so much so that on regular occasions his suggestions and interventions provided a decisive orientation to our discussions. His imprint on the dynamic within which the six WiMi teams were able to work together is undeniable.

As noted earlier, the first challenge was to avoid duplicating ongoing research projects and/or already available findings and analyses. With this concern in mind, prior to setting up a concrete agenda for WiMi, we conducted an in-depth review of existing research initiatives and projects throughout Europe, with a particular concern to cover the literature related to Germany as thoroughly as possible.[2] We identified nearly 400 projects and discovered that, strikingly, research on migration to Europe, and to Germany in particular, placed a great deal of emphasis on pathways to successful integration of immigrants and asylum seekers into the host societies. At the same time, we noticed that the processes and mechanisms of exclusion, which by necessity accompany selective migration policies and therefore continue to shape the lives of refugees and newcomers, were still understudied. This preliminary finding provided the focus for the WiMi initiative: the six teams agreed that the core of the several research projects to be undertaken in the three years of the research programme would be the study of mechanisms of exclusion. This would entail having each team use the means and methods of the respective disciplines to document, in the most accurate way possible, the existence of these mechanisms, to understand how they were organized and to assess their societal consequences.

In terms of aims, the partners agreed on giving the WiMi research initiative the following three overarching objectives: first, to provide in-depth studies of the various mechanisms that effectively exclude refugees and newcomers at the different stages of the migration process, with a focus on four main areas or spheres, namely, legal status, socio-economic conditions, health status, and identification with 'emotional communities'; second, to identify some of the major consequences of those exclusion mechanisms, not only for refugees and newcomers, but also for members of the majority societies; and third, to elaborate alternative pathways that might help to prevent the marginalizing effects of exclusion, especially those that raise concerns about respect for human rights.

Despite the rather unusual genesis of the WiMi initiative, all six teams recognized that they had been entrusted with an important mandate by the Max Planck Society. It was determined that the best way to go about addressing this challenge methodologically would be to adopt a three-pronged stance. WiMi would, in its own way, be a multi-disciplinary project: the initiative was bringing together migration researchers from a broad variety of disciplines: law, demography, public health, economics, social anthropology, political science, sociology and history. It would also make use of a variety of methods, including quantitative surveys, register data, qualitative interviews with experts and migrants, archival research and participant observation. Moreover, WiMi would adopt a multi-perspectival position: the aim was to investigate exclusion from the perspectives of a number of different actors. These actors were not limited to state agencies at different levels such as the European Union, the countries of reception and the countries of origin, but also non-governmental actors, members of the 'majority societies', as well as the refugees and newcomers themselves. Last but not least, WiMi took a multi-dimensional approach: instead of viewing inclusion and exclusion merely as opposite and mutually exclusive pathways, it suggested studying inclusion and exclusion as a continuum. Refugees and newcomers find themselves in different positions depending on the sphere of life at stake as well as on the point in time (both in terms of where the migrants are in the migration process and in terms of where a country's migration policies and public opinion are at any given time). The same situation will be experienced differently by different persons. Moreover, exclusion is intrinsically part of social reality; it is often unavoidable and should not be seen as inherently problematic. In other words, exclusion is not monolithic; it is not simply the opposite of inclusion or integration but an inevitable, if highly variable, aspect of it. By adopting this threefold stance, the six WiMi teams took it upon themselves to collect as many relevant data points as possible that would attest to the complexity of (mechanisms of) exclusion.

Of these three aspects, the multi-dimensional approach was undoubtedly the most challenging and, at the same time, the most promising: in order to move beyond the binary thinking of inclusion/exclusion, the WiMi partners agreed to adopt a research framework that rests on analytically distributing mechanisms of exclusion over six constitutive elements: the several actors of exclusion, the acts that lead to exclusion, the various moments when exclusion takes place, the areas in which exclusion can occur, the multiple representations of exclusion, and reactions against exclusion.

The research was to look not only at state actors (i.e. public authorities), but also at non-state actors engaging in exclusionary acts. Moreover, as noted above, exclusion can take place at various moments in one's lifetime; therefore, to get an accurate picture of what exclusion does to a person requires that these moments be carefully taken into account and, if necessary, identified as producing different consequences. Regarding specific areas, the focus would be on the four main areas or spheres identified earlier, namely legal status, socio-economic conditions, health status, and identification with 'emotional communities'. A further element to be considered was the observation that mechanisms of exclusion are also an issue of representations: what exclusion means to one person or community at a certain point in time is not necessarily identical to what it means to another person or community. The reasons for these differences in representation are generally difficult to identify. Finally, mechanisms of exclusion often provoke reactions, particularly on the part of migrants. These reactions also need to be assessed, as they are an integral part of what exclusion produces.

This multi-dimensional approach was geared to capture as closely and directly as possible how the various constitutive elements of exclusion not only play out, but also interact with one another. Exclusion results from a multiplicity of acts of diverse nature that take place in various contexts, at times long before as well as long after effective migration has taken place. It must be approached as a process that does not rest on a clear-cut distinction, but rather evolves along a complex continuum, and it must be studied alongside the effects of acts of exclusion and the reactions they may provoke. This represented a novel approach, and one that was becoming increasingly necessary, particularly in the aftermath of the summer of migration in 2015.[3]

In addition to the abovementioned decisions taken collectively by the six WiMi teams, namely, the focus on mechanisms of exclusion, the three overarching objectives and the three methodological positions, the WiMi teams developed two specific research instruments. With a view to helping researchers overcome the difficulty of familiarizing themselves with the several other disciplines involved in the project, it was agreed to set up a joint glossary and establish a collective bibliography. The function of a glossary may at first sight speak for itself and its compilation appear to be unproblematic; in this case, however, it was more easily said than done. The idea was to establish a list of key concepts that the several teams would use within the framework of their own disciplines and that might require some clarification, either because they were part of the jargon of a specific discipline or because the concepts conveyed different meanings depending on the disciplinary context within which they were used. In other words, the glossary was meant to help avoid conceptual misunderstandings among the teams. The other instrument was a collective bibliography. One of the difficulties when venturing into interdisciplinary work was the lack of familiarity with what counts as fundamental sources and/or common knowledge in disciplines that are not one's own. With this in mind, the teams were asked to suggest two or three works that are considered seminal publications in their own disciplines and which could prove relevant for the other teams and for the overarching aims of the WiMi research initiative. The two main criteria for the selection of publications were that they related to migration and were written in a language that was accessible for outsiders to a discipline.

To date, publications resulting from the research carried out by the teams associated with the WiMi project concentrated on completing this multidimensional puzzle from several perspectives: Hruschka and Rohmann (2021) show how the sheer amount of legislative acts on the domain of migration generated exclusionary effects in Germany during and after the 2015 'crisis'. Dismantling the category of monolithic state, Schader (2020) demonstrates how the same crisis discourse was utilized as a catalyst for change by some municipalities that to a certain extent countered exclusionary policies. Further emphasizing the local variance of accommodation policies in Germany, Seethaler-Wari and Yanasmayan (forthcoming) analyse socio-spatial features of reception centres in Germany and argue that although some offer better opportunities for interaction, exclusion is intrinsic to the ambivalent role of these centres. Focusing more decidedly on the reactions to exclusion by migrants, Hoehne and Scharrer (2021) showed how Somalis in Germany negotiate multiple sociabilities and how delicate it is to navigate them, while Suerbaum (2021) revealed how the trajectory of a person's migration is central to the legal status determination in Germany. WiMi researchers have also paid particular attention to the role of migrants' resources and capital in overcoming exclusion and achieving social mobility in different geographies, including Germany (e.g. Hunkler, Edele and Schipolowski 2021; Scharrer 2020; Hunkler et al., forthcoming). Last but not least, some overarching conclusions and policy recommendations can also be found in Hruschka and Schader (2020) and Yanasmayan (forthcoming). On the whole, all of these contributions strengthened our programme's initial proposition that exclusion and inclusion form a complex continuum. In the remaining pages of this chapter, we underscore what the programme owes to Günther Schlee, both in the sense of his scholarly work as well as in the way he put his shoulder to the wheel and helped to push the programme along.

Günther Schlee's Scholarly Contribution to the WiMi Project

Günther Schlee's contribution to the WiMi research initiative was considerable in at least two ways. On the one hand, as an established scholar on identity formation and the construction of difference, Schlee contributed considerably to the conceptualization of exclusion that we developed for the WiMi research initiative. On the other hand, he gave generously of his time and his longstanding expertise on Africa, where over the course of his entire academic career he has conducted and supervised empirical research in a region that today is one of the major points of origin of refugees to Europe. In what follows, we briefly elaborate on both contributions, beginning with Schlee's conceptual approach to exclusion.

Exclusion of refugees and newcomers is intrinsically linked to the ways in which membership in social or political groups is regulated. Such membership criteria often draw on the idea of perceived 'sameness' within the group doing the including or excluding. As Schlee (2018a: 6) has shown, while anti-immigrant discourses stress 'real or imagined religious or cultural differences' between the 'receiving' society and immigrants, pro-immigrant discourses equally take for granted assumptions of the 'sameness' of the 'receiving society' and do not seek to challenge them. Instead, advocates in support of cross-border migration often underline in a positive way the difference between themselves and migrants, 'sometimes even valuing it as a potential enrichment of the society in question'. Bridging the perceived differences between newcomers and the 'receiving society' has been at the core of integration policies in Europe, so much so that it has become increasingly influential in the regulation of access to citizenship. The emergence and quick proliferation of civic integration measures as conditions for citizenship in Europe (Joppke 2007; Goodman 2010) in response to the so-called 'retreat of multiculturalism' (Joppke 2004) in the early 2000s have also greatly contributed to the idea of a homogeneous receiving society, the contours of which can be clearly drawn and taught to would-be members.

Yet Schlee's work reminds us not only that such homogeneity is always putative, but, more decisively, that 'integration through difference' may well lead to an internally peaceful and stable life in ethnically heterogeneous societies and political units (Schlee 2018a: 3; also see Horstmann and Schlee 2001). In so doing, Schlee (2018a: 14) has argued that processes of integration are much more complex than one would probably wish them to be, and that they cannot simply be reduced to minimizing differences and enhancing sameness. One particularly significant insight that became a cornerstone of the WiMi initiative's approach was precisely the need to question the taken-for-granted relationship between sameness and inclusion. As Schlee (2018a: 13) puts it, 'rejection is more strongly, and with more serious consequence, articulated against the close other than against the distant other'.

Among the several research projects that the WiMi initiative supported, two in particular looked at the experiences of refugees who fell within the category of 'sameness', to draw on Schlee's terminology. They were considered to belong to the 'receiving society' and, therefore, were granted stay permits or expedited access to citizenship. The perception of sameness may have been related to the presumption of a shared history or to certain phenotypic and/or cultural characteristics. Sona Mikulova's project focused on the German Reich citizens or ethnic Germans who had been living in central, eastern, and southeastern Europe and were forced to leave their countries of residence after the Second World War.[4]

Without being subjected to further scrutiny, the expellees were immediately put on an equal footing with the local German population and were granted equivalent legal status. They spoke German as their mother tongue, and they certainly shared cultural similarities with the local populations. Yet, as Mikulova (2018) observes, these similarities were not sufficient to secure their inclusion, and these populations did indeed face various forms of discrimination. For example, the fact that they could claim to adhere to the same religion as the local population did not automatically mean that they were welcomed into the local church communities (Mikulova 2018). Deepra Dandekar's project scrutinized the partition of India and Pakistan in 1947, which led to a shifting of cultural and religious boundaries on both sides of the new border.[5] Dandekar (2018) discusses how people who had previously never been marked out as different suddenly found themselves minoritized in their home settings. This was particularly the case for the Muslim populations who stayed behind in India as well as for Hindus who stayed behind in Pakistan. The prior sameness of these communities was turned into difference by the simple act of underlining identity features other than those that had been emphasized before partition.

WiMi's conceptualization of exclusion drew on insights that had already been developed by Günther Schlee and his team in previous publications and were highly relevant when it came to analysing the present situation in Europe. The contention was that exclusion 'is a function of multiple forms of cross-cutting identities, expressed in acts of identification' (Foblets et al. 2018: 29) that designate 'the ways in which actors engage with the categories on which collective identities are based' (Eidson et al. 2017: 341). The *Current Anthropology* article 'From Identification to Framing and Alignment' by Eidson et al. (of which Schlee is a co-author) represents one of the clearest statements of the theoretical underpinnings of Schlee's research programme. In it, the authors identify two bases of identification, namely framing and alignment, which were particularly applicable in the situations assessed within the framework of the WiMi research initiative, where acts of exclusion were at stake and called out for analysis. Schlee's scholarly work was most valuable in this regard, as it shows that exclusion can occur in contexts where the different framings used to define social categories involved in a concrete situation are incompatible with one another, as well as in contexts where there is a lack of alignment between different components within one and the same social category. It may be helpful at this point to refer to two concrete illustrations that have been analysed by Schlee and his team. The first example refers to 'Germanness' and Islam: there is a very high probability that when one views them in two different frames – citizenship and religion, respectively – they can be compatible social categories. However, when one puts Germanness and Islam together in a single frame – whether 'culture' or 'civilization' – then they can easily become incompatible categories (Eidson et al. 2017: 346). This reveals an underlying mechanism that explains contrasting approaches between people who tend to exclude Muslims from Germany because, in their view, 'Islam does not belong to Germany' and, on the other side, those for whom Germanness and Islam remain in separate categories and can, therefore, be compatible. The same underlying mechanism can also be noticed in Dandekar's project. The reframing of national and religious identity that came about through partition rendered those who adhered to the minority religion incompatible with the national identity.

A second illustration, also drawing on Eidson et al. (2017), shows how the lack of alignment between different components of one and the same social category can lead to exclusion. It concerns the Volga Germans, ethnic Germans who were expelled from the Volga River region in southern Russia during the Second World War, many of whom eventually migrated to Germany. As Eidson et al. remind us, despite their ethnic German backgrounds, many of their new neighbours in Germany aligned them with the category 'Russian' rather than 'German'. Mikulova's project within the WiMi initiative confirmed the observations of Eidson et al. by showing how this lack of alignment for Sudeten Germans was initially a source of exclusion. Eidson et al. (2017) contend that these acts of exclusion are not always based on clear-cut dichotomies; rather, in most cases they are formulated in comparative terms of 'more or less', as if Muslims or Volga Germans are less 'German'. In the specific case of the WiMi research initiative, dealing with the situations of refugees and newcomers, Schlee's approach has proven extremely useful as the empirical data corroborate what has been observed in his previous research, namely, that recognition of 'the framing and alignment of categories of identification' goes a long way towards understanding and explaining why, in concrete situations, some individuals or at times entire populations are 'subject to categorizations that are both unwanted and unavoidable' (Eidson et al. 2017: 347).

Günther Schlee's work helped participants in the project to dissect some of the basic dynamics at play in the background of various forms of exclusion under scrutiny within the framework of the WiMi research initiative. Empirical research conducted under his aegis offers interesting illustrations of what triggers exclusionary choices and how they work out under different historical circumstances and other conditions. His work is also particularly relevant for studying the dynamics of exclusion that emanate from state actors. States are not to be conceived as monolithic players; rather, state-driven processes of exclusion proceed through 'multilayered and multilevel assemblages of bureaucracies and agencies with diverse sets of interests that act within or outside the legal sphere' (Foblets et al. 2018: 29). By the same token, Schlee warns against holding a strict separation between society and state. He emphasizes that governments' courses of action in particular situations are very much dependent on what the actors who effectively hold the power perceive as their interests (Schlee 2018b: 84). Therefore, when it comes to apprehending how various actors enable or, on the contrary, counter mechanisms of exclusion, one should not seek to draw a clear line between private and public actors. To do so would be misguided from an analytical point of view and unrealistic from an empirical point of view. Similarly, relationships between states and ethnic groups should be seen and studied as relationships of interdependency rather than mono-causality. It goes both ways; if it is indeed true that states 'categorize people and can have an influence on "ethnic" identification', one can equally observe how in some cases 'ethnic groups may use the state as a power resource or an instrument for the exclusion of others from resources' (Schlee 2018b: 88). There is no doubt that WiMi team members have gained from rereading some of Schlee's earlier work and from reflecting his way of showing, throughout his empirical observations in various settings, how complex interactions and interdependencies play out. In order to understand how exclusion works and from where (and whom) it emanates, one would be well advised to look not exclusively at state-linked actors, but to extend the gaze to other, non-state actors as well.

As mentioned earlier, in addition to his conceptualization of exclusion, Schlee also offered to the WiMi project his extensive expertise on Africa, particularly on one of the regions that is today still producing large numbers of refugees. Recent scholarly literature reveals that refugees and newcomers who 'make it' to Europe are often middle-class people and do not, as is often presumed, belong to that segment of the population that is, economically speaking, in the most precarious situation (see, e.g. Van Hear 2004; Nieswand 2011, but also see Hunkler et al., forthcoming, on the role of social class in forced migration). Schlee (2017) likewise argues that the root causes of migration should be sought in the limited opportunities for social mobility already *in situ*, that is, in the home country. Migration often entails accepting a lower class status abroad in exchange for elevated social status in the country of origin, a phenomenon dubbed the 'transnational status paradox' by Boris Nieswand (2011), a former doctoral student of Günther Schlee. Many refugees and newcomers find themselves in jobs for which they are clearly overqualified, but the pay is enough to help family members who remain in the home country and sometimes even to build a house there.

Schlee (2017) furthermore pointed out that not all migrants are originally from the major urban areas that tend to be the points of departure for international migrants. Researchers must therefore also take into consideration people's overall migration trajectories, including their initial internal migration from a rural to an urban area. This is a crucial insight that should not be overlooked in (international) migration research. Regrettably, the available scholarly expertise is still 'split into internal and international migration, characterized by different literatures, concepts, methods and policy agendas' (King and Skeldon 2010: 1619). Few studies enquire into the relationship between urbanization and emigration (notable exceptions include Hamilton and Villareal 2011, and King and Skeldon 2010). In one of Schlee's recent case studies (2017), the main reason for internal migration within Sudan from the rural areas along the Nile river to the cities is loss of access to land, in many cases due to the unscrupulous land-grabbing activities of politically and economically more powerful actors. Small-scale farmers are pushed off the land by state or military officials, who appropriate the land and lease it to wealthy (often foreign) investors at rates the local farmers simply cannot afford. Local farmers' access to land has also been negatively affected by irrigation projects and the creation of the new border with South Sudan. Over the years these various factors have rendered access to – not to mention the possibility of actual ownership of – an adequate parcel land for small-scale farming virtually impossible. Deplorable, potentially life-threatening conditions compel many peasants to abandon the places where they lived and to resettle in a city, in surroundings that are unfamiliar to them but where they hope at least to find a job and to make a living, however precarious it may be. Schlee (2017) has collected a significant number of accounts of these former farmers who are occupied in low-paying jobs and in many cases have to wait until they have reached their fifties and accumulated sufficient savings to be able to start a family. Schlee (2017) furthermore observes that this cruel lack of access to basic resources also unequivocally reflects a dramatic political dimension that is grounded in the region's ethnic divides and tensions. Based on decades of ethnographic research in the field, Schlee's data constitute an urgent invitation to have a closer look into the root causes of migration. In the case of his own empirical research, the root causes lie with the reduced chances of social mobility and a decent livelihood in Africa, in combination with life-threatening perils such as famine, often leading to complete dependence on external aid.

A more recent, equally significant insight that emerges from Schlee's empirical work (2017) focuses on the unintended consequences of new technologies, such as biometric passports, that are introduced with a view to controlling migration and population flows more efficiently. Migrants who previously accumulated sufficient earnings to support their families in Africa by travelling back and forth between Europe and their home countries, needing just a single travel document (which they could sometimes even share with others), now feel compelled to stay once they enter the European territory so as not to risk being refused re-entry. Reading Schlee's findings, one notices a startling similarity to labour migration policies that were established in Europe in the 1970s. The moment European states decided to put a stop to the labour migration schemes that had been in place since the end of the Second World War, the 'guestworkers' could no longer travel back and forth freely and had to decide either to become permanent residents of the European country in which they were working or to return permanently to their home countries.

Within the framework of the WiMi research initiative, Schlee enabled three researchers to actively contribute to the project and enrich our understanding of the mechanisms of exclusion that the WiMi research initiative strives to detect and analyse. Tabea Scharrer and Markus Hoehne both focused on Somali migrants in Germany and Africa, including those who, after some time in Europe, decided to return.[6] Their data convincingly demonstrate that refugees and newcomers should not necessarily be seen as the victims of exclusion by state (public) authorities or members of the 'majority societies', which is often the taken-for-granted perception, but that they are also excluded by their fellow immigrants, even those who share the same national, ethnic, linguistic and cultural backgrounds (in Hoehne and Scharrer's case, 'Somaliness' and all that it entails). The decision to return to the country of origin is based on a complex, multi-causal, rational and emotional balancing of pros and cons that goes far beyond an immigrant's sense that they have been denied ('excluded') the right to fully participate in German society. Hoehne and Scharrer's data are proof of the contention noted above, namely, that 'sameness' does not automatically lead to acceptance or inclusion. 'Newcomers' who are joining more established members of 'their' community (i.e. those who arrived in Germany at an earlier point in time) need to adapt to and abide by the expectations that pertain among the members of their community if they want to be accepted. Members of other migrant communities may also not be very welcoming. The testimonies collected by Hoehne and Scharrer (2021) show that such reticence on the part of the established immigrant community can produce several types of reactions from newcomers. A person may, for example, do everything possible to align him- or herself with the expectations of the group. However, as the data also show, whether or not a person decides to abide by the expectations of the community requires a careful balancing of the potential risks and gains of doing so (or not doing so). According to Hoehne and Scharrer, one of the factors to be taken into account in this weighing exercise is that excessive and effusive efforts to demonstrate 'Somaliness' in order to be accepted by the Somali community in Germany may in fact lead to 'self-exclusion' from the German society.

The testimonies gleaned by Hoehne and Scharrer show that Somali migrants in Germany often have to juggle several social identities, some of which are perceived as incompatible. The outcome is a variety of configurations of exclusion and inclusion that more often than not are intertwined (Hoehne and Scharrer 2021). In her most recent project, Scharrer focuses on Somali returnees to Kenya, specifically on parents who remove their children from Europe in order to avoid the possibility that they will become too 'Europeanized'. Are they therefore to be seen as actors of exclusion? Is return migration in this case – voluntary from the point of view of the parents, involuntary for their children – to be apprehended as an act of exclusion? In most cases, the children are not familiar with the people or the ways of living of the Somali communities in Kenya; they therefore face tremendous difficulties in being accepted. In a sense, the parents' decision to send them back to the 'country of origin' puts the children in a new situation of exclusion, making of their parents actors of exclusion, albeit with well-intended social and pedagogical motives.

The third researcher from Schlee's department involved in the WiMi initiative was Zahir Musa Abdal-Kareem.[7] Drawing on Schlee's work on identification and its links to exclusionary practices, he looked at the social interactions between Muslim immigrants and local residents in the German city of Halle-Neustadt. The research focused more particularly on representations of exclusion through standardized emblems and symbols that were used by members of different groups living in Halle-Neustadt to distinguish themselves from one another. One important observation that Abdal-Kareem made was that the marginal social and economic situation of Halle-Neustadt was of pivotal importance in shaping the experiences of inclusion and exclusion that he observed in his fieldwork. Situated at the margins of a former socialist city that remains economically and socially disadvantaged within the unified Germany, Halle-Neustadt itself can be considered 'excluded' or 'disempowered', to use Çağlar and Glick Schiller's terminology (2018). As is also underlined by Çağlar and Glick Schiller (2018: 15), the fact that 'disempowered' cities have fewer economic, political and cultural resources due to their marginal position in national and global networks does not necessarily mean that migrants will be or feel more excluded. Abdal-Kareem's project demonstrated that living in Halle-Neustadt may create an attendant component of spatial exclusion that, perhaps somewhat surprisingly, opens up space for new social relations to develop through 'city-making' in the sense advanced by Çağlar and Glick Schiller.

Conclusion

In February 2018, the Halle–Zürich Centre for the Anthropological Study of Central Asia (CASCA) convened a workshop in Istanbul under the evocative title *Routes of Hope: Transitions and Destinations in Global Migration Flows*. In a paper entitled 'Hope meets Exclusion', Günther Schlee presented some of the preliminary findings of the WiMi research initiative. The paper accomplished precisely what anthropological research invites us to do, that is, to decentre the thinking about the topics we address. To apprehend the complexity of the numerous mechanisms of exclusion that accompany migration, one needs to understand and examine as intimately as possible how people experience their migratory trajectories at all points along the way, from their situation in the country of origin before migrating, through all stages of the migration process, to settling in new surroundings, and even upon returning to the home country if, indeed, return migration is part of the trajectory. It will always be much more complex than one would imagine. The very title of Schlee's paper – 'Hope meets Exclusion' – captured so succinctly, in no more than three words, the way in which members of the WiMi initiative have tried to apprehend exclusion in the German context in the aftermath of the events of 2015.

As we well know, scholarly endeavours can serve more than one purpose. To a certain extent, it is up to the scholars themselves to determine which of these various purposes they will prioritize. For some, conceptualization and theoretical refinement are the major, if not the only, goal; for others, practical application is at least as important. Applied knowledge can come with more or less commitment, more or less engagement, more or less public outreach. Günther Schlee, in his capacity as partner to the WiMi initiative, showed how one person can fulfil all of these purposes at the same time without putting any of them at risk of being overshadowed by another. His personal commitment to the project was no less than remarkable, and his scholarly work has proven to be extremely valuable in terms of inspiration and orientation. As a scholar and a colleague, he was a wonderful team member to have on board when it came to addressing highly sensitive and deeply human issues that required profound mastery of all that anthropology has to offer.

Marie-Claire Foblets is Director at the Max Planck Institute for Social Anthropology, a professor of law at the University of Louvain, and an honorary professor at Martin-Luther-University Halle-Wittenberg and the University of Leipzig. She has published widely on issues of migration law, including the elaboration of European migration law after the Treaty of Amsterdam, citizenship/nationality laws, compulsory integration, anti-racism and non-discrimination, etc. In the field of anthropology of law, her research focuses on cultural diversity and legal practice, with a particular interest in the application of Islamic family law in Europe, and more recently in the accommodation of cultural and religious diversity under State law.

Zeynep Yanasmayan is the head of Migration Department at the German Centre for Integration and Migration Research (DeZIM). She is an interdisciplinary scholar working at the intersection of political science, sociology and socio-legal studies with research interests in citizenship, migration and mobility studies, governance of religious diversity, transnationalism and diaspora politics. She is the author of *The Migration of Highly Educated Turkish Citizens to Europe: From Guestworkers to Global Talent* (Routledge, 2019) and co-editor of *The Failure of Popular Constitution Making in Turkey* (Cambridge University Press, 2020). Her work has previously been published in *Citizenship Studies*, *Political Geography*, *Ethnic and Racial Studies*, and *Law and Social Inquiry*.

Notes

We wish to express our sincere gratitude to Dr Brian Donahoe for his careful editing of this chapter.

1. The initiative is led by Marie-Claire Foblets (Max Planck Institute for Social Anthropology, Halle/Saale) and Steven Vertovec (Max Planck Institute for the Study of Religious and Ethnic Di-

versity, Göttingen) and coordinated by Zeynep Yanasmayan (Max Planck Institute for Social Anthropology, Halle/Saale). The initiative was launched in collaboration with Ayelet Shachar (Max Planck Institute for the Study of Religious and Ethnic Diversity, Göttingen).

2. This gives us the opportunity here to thank Anne Menzel, Alexander Hassler and Luc Leboeuf, who took responsibility for this preliminary mapping exercise. It was intensive and at the same time indispensable work. For details, see Foblets, Leboeuf and Yanasmayan 2018.

3. We have explained in greater detail the conceptual framework adopted by the six WiMi teams in a co-authored working paper titled 'Exclusion and Migration: By Whom, Where, When, and How?' (Foblets, Leboeuf and Yanasmayan 2018).

4. See https://www.eth.mpg.de/4406351/members. Retrieved 24 April 2019.

5. Ibid.

6. See https://www.eth.mpg.de/4472467/project2. Retrieved 24 April 2019.

7. See https://www.eth.mpg.de/4971054/project. Retrieved 24 April 2019.

References

Çağlar, Ayşe and Nina Glick Schiller. 2018. *Migrants and City-Making: Dispossession, Displacement, and Urban Regeneration*. Durham, NC and London: Duke University Press.

Dandekar, Deepra. 2018. 'Refugees in India After 1947', in Aimie Bouju and Andreas Edel (eds), *Similar but Different: Inclusion and Exclusion of Immigrant Communities Sharing Similar Cultural Backgrounds with their Host Societies*. Population Europe Discussion Paper Series Number 8. Berlin: Population Europe, pp. 61–66.

Eidson, John R., Dereje Feyissa, Veronika Fuest, Markus Virgil Hoehne, Boris Nieswand, Günther Schlee and Olaf Zenker. 2017. 'From Identification to Framing and Alignment: A New Approach to the Comparative Analysis of Collective Identities', *Current Anthropology* 58(3): 340–51.

Foblets, Marie-Claire, Luc Leboeuf and Zeynep Yanasmayan. 2018. 'Exclusion and Migration: By Whom, Where, When, and How?', *Max Planck Institute for Social Anthropology Working Papers* No. 190. Retrieved from https://www.eth.mpg.de/pubs/wps/pdf/mpi-eth-working-paper-0190.

Goodman, Sara W. 2010. 'Integration Requirements for Integration's Sake? Identifying, Categorising and Comparing Civic Integration Policies', *Journal of Ethnic and Migration Studies* 36(5): 753–72.

Hamilton, Erin R. and Andreas Villarreal. 2011. 'Development and the Urban and Rural Geography of Mexican Emigration to the United States', *Social Forces* 90(2): 661–83.

Hoehne, Markus Virgil and Tabea Scharrer. 2021. 'Balancing Inclusion and Exclusion Among Somali Migrants in Germany', *International Migration*. Retrieved from https://doi.org/10.1111/imig.12856.

Horstmann, Alexander and Günther Schlee (eds). 2001. *Integration durch Verschiedenheit: Lokale und globale Formen interkultureller Kommunikation*. Bielefeld: transcript.

Hruschka, Constantin and Miriam Schader. 2020. *We Managed – And We Changed in the Process: Selected Conclusions of the Study of the Max Planck Research Initiative 'Challenges of Migration, Integration, and Exclusion' on the Effects of the 'Long Summer of Migration'*. Munich: Max Planck Society. Retrieved from https://www.mpg.de/16180086/MPG-Forschungsbericht-Migration-EN.pdf.

Hruschka, Constantin and Tim Rohmann. 2021. 'Excluded by Crisis Management? Legislative Hyperactivity in Post-2015 Germany', *International Migration*.

Hunkler, Christian, Aileen Edele and Stefan Schipolowski. 2021. 'The Role of Educational Resources in the Labor Market Integration of Refugees: The Case of Syrian Asylum Seekers in Germany', *Journal for Educational Research Online* 13(1): 98–122.

Hunkler, Christian, Tabea Scharrer, Magdelana Suerbaum and Zeynep Yanasmayan. Forthcoming. 'Spatial and Social Im/Mobility in Forced Migration: Revisiting Class', *Journal for Ethnic and Migration Studies*.

Joppke, Christian. 2004. 'The Retreat of Multiculturalism in the Liberal State: Theory and Policy', *British Journal of Sociology* 55(2): 237–57.

———. 2007. 'Beyond National Models: Civic Integration Policies for Immigrants in Western Europe', *West European Politics* 30(1): 1–22.

King, Russell and Ronald Skeldon. 2010. '"Mind the Gap!" Integrating Approaches to Internal and International Migration', *Journal of Ethnic and Migration Studies* 36(10): 1619–46.

Mikulová, Soňa. 2018. 'German Expellees in West Germany After 1945 and Their Integration into Church Communities', in Aimie Bouju and Andreas Edel (eds), *Similar but Different: Inclusion and Exclusion of Immigrant Communities Sharing Similar Cultural Backgrounds with their Host Societies. Population Europe Discussion Paper Series* Number 8. Berlin: Population Europe, pp. 35–41.

Nieswand, Boris. 2011. *Theorising Transnational Migration: The Status Paradox of Migration.* New York: Routledge.

Schader, Miriam. 2020. 'Externalization or Imitation: The 2015–16 Asylum-Seeker Immigration as a Catalyst for Local Structural Change', *Ethnic and Racial Studies* 43(11): 2022–40.

Scharrer, Tabea. 2020. '"It Is Better to Do Business in Africa than in Europe" – Socio-Economic Positionings among Business-Minded European Somalis Moving to Kenya', *Journal of Immigrant and Refugee Studies* 18(3): 270–85.

Schlee, Günther. 2017. 'Wirtschaftliche und Politische Ursachen der Migration aus Afrika', Unpublished introductory remarks delivered at the *Max Planck Forum Wohin? Was passiert, wenn Menschen ihre Lebensgrundlage verlieren, 17 November 2017.* Halle/Saale: Max Planck Institute for Social Anthropology.

———. 2018a. 'Introduction: Difference and Sameness as Modes of Integration', in Günther Schlee and Alexander Horstmann (eds), *Difference and Sameness as Modes of Integration: Anthropological Perspectives on Ethnicity and Religion.* Oxford: Berghahn, pp. 1–33.

———. 2018b. 'Identification with the State and Identifications by the State', in Günther Schlee and Alexander Horstmann (eds), *Difference and Sameness as Modes of Integration: Anthropological Perspectives on Ethnicity and Religion.* Oxford: Berghahn, pp. 78–92.

Seethaler-Wari, Shahd and Zeynep Yanasmayan. Forthcoming. 'Unfolding Socio-Spatial Exclusion: Accommodation Centres at The Height of the "Refugee Reception Crisis" in Germany', *International Migration.*

Suerbaum, Magdalena. 2021. 'Embodying Legal Precarity: Living with Ongoing Short-Term Protection in Germany', *International Migration.*

Van Hear, Nicholas. 2004. '"I Went as Far as My Money Would Take Me": Conflict, Forced Migration and Class', *Centre on Migration, Policy and Society Working Paper* No. 6. Oxford: Compas.

Yanasmayan, Zeynep. Forthcoming. 'Post-2015 Refugees in Germany: "Culture of Welcome", Solidarity, Exclusion?: Introduction', *International Migration.*

CHAPTER 13

DILEMMAS OF IDENTIFICATION
The Trader's Dilemma among Khorezmians in Tashkent

RANO TURAEVA

In this chapter, I reflect on identification as a complex process, focusing on contradictions that arise when actors seeking to procure resources for themselves and their dependents can only do so by incurring obligations to others who make demands on those same resources. The chapter is based on data collected during thirteen months of ethnographic fieldwork in Uzbekistan. From September 2005 to October 2006, I was based in the capital city of Tashkent, where internal migrants from all over the country come in search of economic opportunities but where, for many, regional differences among Uzbeks, which correspond to ethnic differences, make this search especially difficult.

In particular, I focus on people from the region of Khorezm, who serve as an example of internal migrants who are linguistically distinct from Tashkentis. Elsewhere (Turaeva 2016), I have commented extensively on the significance of differences between Khorezmians and Tashkentis, especially as they are made evident in speech. In this chapter, however, I focus not on this first aspect of collective identification, 'we' versus 'they', but on a second, namely, 'we' versus 'I'. The first refers, in the example under consideration, to the solidarity – or the potential for solidarity – among Khorezmians confronting the difficulties of life in Tashkent; and the second refers to the need of individual Khorezmians to provide for themselves and for members of their own household in ways that may conflict with relations of solidarity with fellow Khorezmians who are not household members. As shall be seen, both dimensions of 'we' relationships are more complex than might be supposed. Relations of regional cum ethnic solidarity are often characterized by power imbalances; and the 'self-interest' of the individual

Khorezmian is actually another form of solidarity with a more narrowly defined circle of beneficiaries.

I analyse actual and potential contradictions within the 'we' domain with reference to the model of the 'trader's dilemma', as it has been developed by Hans-Dieter Evers, Heiko Schrader and others (Evers 1994; Evers and Schrader 1994; see also Schlee 2018; van der Grijp 2003). In the analysis of Evers and his co-authors, the dilemma arises when the trader within a peasant society has 'to buy commodities from fellow peasants who are members of their own village community, but sell to others outside their village'; or, alternately, when 'peasant traders' sell products 'to fellow villagers' (Evers 1994: 7–8). In either case, the trader is subject, on one hand, to expectations based on village solidarity and, on the other hand, to market prices that fluctuate independently of village solidarity. The risk is that the trader either alienates fellow villagers by being too much the business person or goes bankrupt by being too much the fellow villager. A common solution to the trader's dilemma, according to Evers (1994: 8–10), is that traders do business only outside of their own group, often by forming their own autonomous group, usually a distinct ethnic or religious minority within the larger society.

The trader's dilemma model can, of course, be extended beyond peasant villages to any situation in which an actor has to reconcile obligations to a larger community, on one hand, and to himself or herself and also to his or her dependents, on the other. In many such situations, however, the 'solution' that Evers and Schrader propose for the trader's dilemma – the ethnic or religious distinction of the trading class – will not be available. Khorezmians in Tashkent are ethnically distinct from Tashkentis, but they are not ethnically distinct from each other, however great the socio-economic differences among them. There is, then, no easy solution to their version of the trader's dilemma. Rather, in each particular case, the contradictions between regional or ethnic solidarity, on one hand, and the narrower economic interest of the individual and his or her dependents, on the other, must be confronted, sidestepped or hidden to the best of one's ability. This is the case for many Khorezmians in Tashkent.

Below, I present selected case studies that illustrate the dilemmas of identification that I have just sketched. First, however, I provide some background information on Uzbekistan and its subdivision in administrative as well as regional/ethnic categories; and then I show how my introductory comments apply to these divisions.

Varieties of Uzbek Identity

'Uzbek' is often taken for granted as a national category, as if citizenship, political belonging and cultural traits would completely overlap. Yet, a closer look at the dynamics of identification in Uzbekistan and, particularly, in the capital,

Tashkent, where people from all over the country meet in pursuit of a better life – especially, a better education and better jobs – shows that when Uzbeks compete for scarce resources and limited economic opportunities, subnational differences become relevant and identity politics are the order of the day. These subnational differences are related to cultural and linguistic traits that are mobilized to create in-group solidarity and to exclude members of other groups in the struggle for resources and opportunities.

It is widely accepted that the modern Uzbek nation is a Soviet creation formed through complex historical and demographic processes, involving several groups. Peter Finke summarizes these processes as follows:

> the Turkic-speaking population, or those elements of it that would later become the nucleus of the Uzbek nationality, comprised three segments: non-tribally organised populations, in their majority former Iranian-speakers . . . ; descendants of the earlier tribes who had settled in the region prior to the Uzbek conquest; and, third, the tribal groups who had arrived after the Shaybanid took possession of the land – primarily speakers of Qipchaq dialects. (Finke 2014: 45; see also Karmysheva 1976; Shanijazov 1978; Zhdanko 1978; Baldauf 1991, 1993; and Ilkhamov 2004)

Uzbekistan is divided administratively into twelve districts, which are called, using the Russian term, *oblasts*: the Tashkent district, the Andijan district, Bukhara, Ferghana, Jizzakh, Kashkadarya, Khorezm, Namangan, Navoi, Samarkand, Surkhandarya and Syrdarya. However, the administrative divisions of Uzbekistan do not correspond to informal distinctions, made most commonly in oral discourse, among five regional categories (Carlisle 1986). The first category is *Tajik*, which includes both *Bukharalik* (or *Bukharskiy* in Russian) and *Samarkandlik* (or *Samarkandskiy*). Many people who are not from one of these two regions categorize their residents together as Tajiks; but Bukharans tend to distinguish themselves from Samarqandis. The second category, *Khorazmlik* (or *Khorezmskiy*) refers to people from the Khorezm region in the far northwest of Uzbekistan. The third category, *Tashkentskiye*, refers to the 'original' inhabitants of the capital city. The fourth category, *Vodiylik* (or *Vodiy*), based on the Uzbek word for 'valley', refers to those from the Fergana Valley. Very often, Vodiylik are considered to be more of a religious subnational group than the others. Finally, the fifth category, *Surqash*, refers to people from the Surhondarya and Qashqadarya regions. Surqash is a derogatory nickname consisting of the first syllables of the two region's names 'sur' and 'qash'. In sum, there are five informal categories of Uzbeks recognized at the discursive level in Tashkent, twelve official administrative districts and one officially promoted Uzbek nation. These categories have great relevance when Uzbeks from various regions come together and interact in big cities, especially in Tashkent.

After the breakup of the Soviet Union, beginning in 1990, the Uzbek state promoted an ideology of nationalism. Yet, beneath this national identity are the regionally-based subnationalities or ethnicities, the members of which engage in identity politics. Following Mary Bernstein (2005: 48), I understand 'identity politics' to be an etic term referring to conflict among those who promote 'competing . . . ways to understand the relationship between experience, culture, identity, politics, and power'. In practice, identity politics may be compared to a game in which people act strategically, using their cultural and economic capital to gain access to limited resources (Bourdieu 1977, 1986). Elsewhere, I have dealt with identity politics involving representatives of various regionally-based ethnic groups in Tashkent (Turaeva 2016). In this chapter, I focus on the identity politics within the community of Khorezmians in Tashkent. Khorezmians are, notably, the regional or ethnic group that is most distinct from the national standard represented by Tashkentis, and, among themselves, they display a high degree of solidarity when compared with other regionally-based ethnic groups. But what happens to this strong sense of 'we' among Khorezmians when they compete not only with others but also among themselves for resources and opportunities in Tashkent? This chapter offers an extended answer to that question.

Identification and Belonging: Questioning the 'We'

The emphasis, in the secondary literature on collective identities and corresponding processes of identification, has been on the constitution or maintenance of the 'we' domain through interaction between 'us' and 'them' (e.g. Barth 1969, 1994; Jenkins 1996, 1997; Elwert 2002). In the process, the inner complexity of the 'we' domain may be neglected. It is true that the literature on the potential contradictions between 'identity', on one hand, and 'interests', on the other, indicates, if somewhat obliquely, that actors may question their commitment to particular 'we'-groups; and that some authors have shown how these contradictions may lead actors to abandon the groups with which they formerly identified (e.g. Barth 1969: 132; Elwert 2002). But what of those situations in which actors have no escape, or only very limited means of escape, once contradictions between group solidarity and their own interests arise? Such situations remain undertheorized and warrant a renewed focus on the complexities of the 'we' within the 'we'-group.

In the following, I delve more deeply into the 'we'-domain, analysing it as a space that is constituted through a series of relations between 'we' and 'I'. The process of 'we'-formation is continuous, as relations within a group – in this case, the Khorezmians – are constantly renegotiated. These relations are themselves full of contradictions that lead to divisions within the Khorezmian community – divisions with which actors must come to terms one way or another.

Economic and political processes generate structural preconditions for individual action – preconditions that are both constraining and enabling (Giddens

1976: 121; Schlee 2008: 58–59). Depending on the social position of various actors, however, these preconditions are constraining and enabling to varying degrees, putting some at an advantage and others at a disadvantage. In some cases, ethnic belonging or collective identification may provide the key for taking advantage of opportunities or overcoming difficulties. Group membership may benefit the individual. However, identification with one's own group can offer both opportunities and traps, as can be shown with reference to the trader's dilemma. Khorezmians in Tashkent are not necessarily 'traders', but they have needs and they have various 'bargaining chips' that they can offer to others in order to gain their help in meeting those needs. When they enter into such transactions with fellow Khorezmians, to whom they are obligated because of shared regional origins and shared ethnicity, they experience the contradictory demands of ethnic altruism and what looks, to members of the ethnic community, like egoism.

In Tashkent, as mentioned above, members of various subnational groups – for example, Tashkentis and Khorezmians, among others – compete for power and resources. Relations among them are, however, hierarchical, with Tashkentis 'naturally' at the top. In Tashkent, Tashkentis have the appropriate *propiska*, the internal passport and residence permit. The *propiska*, which is a legacy of the Russian Empire and the Soviet Union, of which Uzbekistan was once a part, regulates place of origin, residence and belonging for all citizens (Turaeva 2014). In Tashkent, Tashkentis possess the *propiska*; but all others have to apply for it, in order to have the right to stay in the city for longer than three consecutive days. This means that if people from other places wish to work or study in Tashkent, they need to get the *propiska*, which is not easily granted. Because they want to stay or need to stay in Tashkent, but cannot get the *propiska*, at least not on a timely basis, many non-Tashkentis stay illegally in Tashkent, at least for some time. In that situation they are vulnerable to police control and are excluded from many opportunities. It is especially in this situation that Khorezmians need help from their regional compatriots.

Belonging to a group such as the Khorezmians may become a way of achieving inclusion for those who are otherwise excluded. Within the community of Khorezmians in Tashkent, some individuals (such as Halmurad, Dilmurad and Sayora in the case studies below) have the *propiska*, are established in influential positions, and have access to networks of influence extending beyond the Khorezmian community. As Bourdieu (1986: 81) might say, they possess a certain amount of social, cultural and economic capital which gives them privileged access to opportunities and also the ability to make these opportunities accessible for others. But many other Khorezmians who come to Tashkent lack such capital – the *propiska*, the position, and the connections that are necessary to 'make it' there. For them, the best option may seem to be turning to those fellow Khorezmians who have it – but at the cost of falling under their power.

For many Khorezmians in Tashkent, as for many other internal migrants, opportunities are often ethnicity-based. Through fellow Khorezmians, they have at least a chance of living, working, obtaining the necessary documents and taking advantage of other economic opportunities. But they have to decide if they want to become clients of established co-ethnics or risk trying to succeed without such support. Conversely, established and influential Khorezmians have to decide if they are willing to fulfil the role of the patron. Each of these roles offers benefits, and each comes with costs. This is the dilemma faced by Khorezmians in Tashkent: is cooperation with fellow Khorezmians beneficial, or is it a trap? As is evident in the case studies below, often it is both.

Sayora and Dilmurad

Sayora is a Khorezmian who is well-established in Tashkent and so in a position both to help and to benefit from her fellow Khorezmians. She is an entrepreneur in real estate and construction who buys old houses in and around Tashkent from Russians who are emigrating or from elderly Russian couples who want to move from their large, run-down homes into comfortable one-room flats. Then she has these houses renovated or rebuilt and resells them. At the time of my fieldwork, she owned several houses and was able to calculate the substantial profit that she would make after reselling them.

The size of Sayora's team of construction workers, which consists of several young men between the age of 17 and 35, varies according to the season and the ebb and flow of business. All members of the team are, however, dependable but low-cost recruits from Khorezm. In bringing these young men to Tashkent, Sayora can rely on help from her husband – a high-ranking official in the municipal police force who is able to arrange *propiska* for internal migrants. She pays transport costs for her Khorezmian workers and provides housing for them when they arrive in Tashkent. Sayora's construction workers are registered in one of her houses near to her home, but they usually live on the construction site or in adjacent accommodations. On one of the larger construction sites, I saw that many construction workers were sleeping in a big hall on site that was filled with *raskladushkas*, that is, half-meter high aluminium portable travel beds. Outside of Tashkent, workers often live in one of Sayora's un-renovated houses.

Sayora's construction workers have no contracts, only verbal agreements with her. At times, there is no indication of an exact salary at all, since young, unemployed men are usually happy just to be able to start working in Tashkent. When, on top of that, someone provides transport, accommodation and food, they regard themselves as very fortunate indeed: '*Shungaam shukur atamiz boshda!*' 'We praise God at least for that at the beginning!'

Sayora is more than just an employer; she also takes charge of her young workers' lives, for example, by finding wives for the unmarried members of her construction team. During my fieldwork, she said that she had found good girls for two of the 'boys' (*bollara*) and was planning to set the date of the marriages, once she had talked to their parents in their village in Khorezm.

Sometime before my arrival, Sayora had chosen Dilmurad, one of the young men on her construction team, to be its foreman. Sayora got to know him when he was one of the workers helping to build her own new family home.

The title of 'foreman' gives Dilmurad authority over his team members and the reputation of being *katta*, or big, among his friends and relatives back in Khorezm (Turaeva 2022). It also lends to his family and his wife's family back home a kind of social capital that accrues to people who have good contacts in Tashkent. If Dilmurad needs more people for his team, he calls his brother in Khorezm, who then recruits more workers from his network on Dilmurad's behalf. Of the fourteen members of his construction team during my fieldwork, five were kinsmen, one was someone whom he had met in Tashkent, three were related to each other, and the rest were from the same Khorezmian village.

Dilmurad is the boss, and he dictates the 'in house' rules. He even advises his workers on when and where they may go when they are off work and what clothes they should wear. Whoever attempts to deviate from his rules risks his current position and may have to return home, unless he has other options in Tashkent. But the relation of 'boss-employee' becomes complicated when kinship is involved, as is often the case. When he exercises his authority, and if his underlings complain to their families back home, Dilmurad may be accused by their senior relatives of violating the norms of kinship. It is difficult (*qiyin*), Dilmurad told me, when his workers are relatives, because, in such situations, he is 'in between two fires (*ikki otni orasindaman*)'. 'On one side', he continued, 'there are the relatives (*qarindash*), and, on the other, there is the work and responsibilities. But I try to be equal with my workers, and if my relative tries to complain to his family, I will talk to his family myself (*lichna*)'.

One of the workers, named Utkir, was 'very problematic', Dilmurad said, because, often, he did not obey orders and did not learn well. But Dilmurad could not send him home, because he was kin. So they had lengthy discussions, during which Dilmurad threatened to send him back home if things did not improve. Utkir was 19 years old, and he did not like the way Dilmurad treated him. He resented Dilmurad's commanding tone and his injunctions against going downtown in the evening. Utkir hoped to become a headman himself and to stay in Tashkent under better conditions. He said that he had not seen very much of Tashkent yet, although he had already been there for six months.

Dilmurad's relations with workers who are relatives is reminiscent of the trader's dilemma insofar as he has to do well at his job – a job from which he profits –

while managing the obligations of kinship. There is no real solution to Dilmurad's dilemma of 'being between two fires'; rather, it must be continually re-negotiated.

Sayora's relation to Dilmurad displays similar complexity, though she is subject to few, if any, sanctions from his kin. Both are Khorezmians, but he cannot call on the support of the Khorezmian community in order to curb her power over him. Vis-à-vis his construction team, Dilmurad is the boss. But Sayora is his boss. He has the power to recruit as well as fire construction workers, but he still needs the prior consent of Sayora. On more than one occasion, I saw that Dilmurad had discussions with Sayora about new members joining the team. Dilmurad would give references and describe the candidate. Sayora asked about Dilmurad's connection to the candidate, his family background, his skills and the arrangements for wages. If she had reservations about a given candidate, she would politely refuse by saying that he should wait a little – that maybe there would be a job opening in the future.

When I asked Dilmurad about his job, he answered: 'I work under Sayora's arm (*Man Sayorani kolinda ishliman*)'. Dilmurad did his best (*kolimnan galganini atdim*) and 'served well' (*yahshi hizmat atdim*) to gain her confidence. He has shown himself to be hardworking, skilful, loyal, and willing to do extra work for Sayora whenever necessary. His only other option is to leave her service, but he has chosen not to do that.

Sayora is very closely involved in Dilmurad's private life, planning his free time and family matters. Dilmurad discusses his future plans with Sayora – for example, about when, where and how to build his house, and about his children's education. When he or his wife want to travel to Khorezem to visit their parents or attend a special event, they have to get Sayora's permission before going. What is more, Sayora takes part in planning and organizing any life-cycle event for Dilmirad's family, for example, the circumcision of a son. In order not to offend his parents by allowing them to see that Sayora has usurped their authority over him, Dilmurad shares with them the plans that he and Sayora have concocted as if they were his own idea.

The services that Dilmurad fulfils for Sayora go far beyond his responsibilities as the foreman of her construction team. They include shopping for her domestic needs and serving dinner or tea to male guests in her home. Dilmurad and his wife, Rahima, are often in Sayora's home, where they participate in all family events, even in very small gatherings, but often in a servile role, as when they help in the kitchen or Dilmurad serves visiting men. Dilmurad is, however, accepted as a good friend, as 'one of us' (*svoy/ozlarimizniki*) by Sayora's family members and her kin.

Sayora depends on Dilmurad, but is still in a position to end the relationship should it prove necessary. Rationally, however, it was not likely that she would replace him, as she has invested effort and resources in training and financing him. The relationship is exploitative but is still based on trust, which is crucial and not easily established. Because Dilmurad is a reliable foreman who does a good job of managing his team, Sayora has to compromise sometimes in order not to lose a loyal worker.

Dilmurad and Rahima consider themselves to be luckier than most Khorezmians who come to Tashkent. Like many other internal migrants, Dilmurad established contacts in Tashkent who could help him to obtain the *propiska* and find a job and a place to stay before coming. This was necessary, because it is difficult to establish oneself, and it is expensive to live in Tashkent. If Dilmurad had not chosen to work for Sayora on a long-term basis, he would have had to search for another job or join another construction team. Or he could have tried to be independent, recruiting his own team from Khorezm, much as other foremen do.

Dilmurad's current earnings include rather modest monthly wages, accommodations and food provided by Sayora. But if a foreman is 'independent', i.e. self-employed, then he must be able to rely on the earnings from the projects that he completes. It is true that the self-employed benefit from the relatively cheap labour brought in from Khorezm; but it still costs them money to provide accommodations, travel and food for their workers. Unlike his self-employed colleagues, Dilmurad does not have to risk spending money on his team members or concern himself with their trouble with the police. With Sayora, he is financially, legally and existentially secure, whereas the independent construction bosses, especially those lacking contacts, must always run the risk of bankruptcy or of difficulties with state authorities.

Halmurad and His Clients

Halmurad, a Khorezmian, is the head of the Visa Department in the Regional Department of the Ministry of Internal Affairs, i.e. in a police station responsible for a district within the city of Tashkent. I first met Halmurad in 2002, when I arrived in Tashkent to work as a lecturer in a local university and, so, was in need of a *propiska*. He helped me to get a short-term *propiska* and to renew it every six months during the two years that I spent in Tashkent before leaving for Germany. That is what Halmurad does. He helps people to obtain the *propiska* that they need, as he sits in his black leather chair at a long polished table with several different telephones, which seem to ring nearly continuously, creating a cacophony of different ringtones. Halmurad usually lets the landlines ring, while answering the calls on his mobile phone.

Halmurad arranges for the *propiska* and also serves as a good contact if somebody is in trouble with the police. He is well-connected, and he is able to solve any legal problems or problems with papers. He provides these services for a wide range of people, his actual or potential clients, who can be divided into the following three categories. First, there are the 'complete strangers' (*begonalar*), as Halmurad puts it, who turn to him in his official capacity when they need passports or other papers. These clients usually reside officially in the district for which the police station where Halmurad works is responsible.[1] Indirectly, his duties also include supervision of the local registration of residents of the district, although, technically, this is the responsibility of the *passport stol* (Russian for 'passport table', meaning an office responsible for issuing passports and registration stamps for passports). Often, however, clients who have complaints about the *passport stol* come to him with requests, e.g. that fines for failure to renew a passport before its expiration date be waived.[2]

The second type of client includes applicants for exit visas. Usually, these are businessmen who are not necessarily residents of the municipal district where Halmurad's office is located but who make frequent business trips. These are *pullila*, clients who 'have money' and who are, therefore, highly desirable from the viewpoint of the official, especially when they need their exit visas urgently. In such cases, Halmurad's job is to make sure that the application documents reach the right department on time without gathering dust along the way, which is often the fate of the documents of applicants who have not paid the 'special fees' for speeding up the process. What is more, Halmurad also makes sure he has a contact person within the 'right' department who ensures for him that the process is expedited.

The third type of client includes internal migrants from various Uzbek regions, including Khorezm, who have various requests related to their passport or to their quest to obtain or renew a short-term *propiska* in Tashkent. Halmurad complains that 'his own people', i.e. Khorezmians, employ all kinds of tricks to make his services as cheap as possible. One way to get his services for 'free', for example, is mentioning the name of a person to whom Halmurad himself is indebted. Requests backed up with this kind of reference are nearly impossible to refuse. Once Halmurad grants the request, however, the person whose name is used as a reference owes something to him in return. Thus, in Halmurad's office, as elsewhere, people get caught in a continuous state of owing something to somebody, creating a network of various dependencies. If the favour is not repaid, as may be the case, this creates resentment and ill-will, as I could see in Halmurad's dealings with some of the people corresponding to this third type.

Zemlyachestvo and Its Transformations

What is the young Khorezmian, newly arrived in Tashkent to do? He or she needs lodging, work, income, social support and a *propiska*. But going through official channels to get these things, and expecting markets and government agencies to function according to the normative models outlined in the constitution or in supplementary legislation, is a recipe for failure. Everybody knows that. The prospect of fulfilling one's basic needs without the help of family or friends or friends of friends is believed to be impossible, due to economic constraints, state dysfunction, and the largely unspoken conventions governing the social and economic exclusion of various categories of people.

How, then, to proceed? In the first instance, Khorezmian migrants to Tashkent seek social and economic support within their direct families. If no support is available there, they turn to their extended families, to friends from their home village, or to acquaintances of relatives or friends back home.

In the Russian academic literature, the well-known phenomenon of solidarity among Central Asians from the same region, the same city, or the same village is called *mestnichestvo*, which means, literally, 'place politics'. The corresponding Uzbek term is *zemlyachestvo*, which is derived from *zemlyak*, meaning 'countryman', i.e. a person who may enjoy the advantages of regional solidarity. Among internal migrants to Tashkent, the choice of a particular contact and affiliate, the provision of help, or the development of friendship can usually be reduced to this general principle of regional or ethnic solidarity: one shows or should show solidarity in favour of a new associate who is *zemlyak*. In the life stories that I collected during fieldwork, individuals and groups were cited as *zemlyak* or *zemlyaki* (plural) when the basis of the relationship was common regional affiliation or ethnic group membership.

Solidarity based on common regional origins or shared ethnicity, however, is not guaranteed. As one of my Tashkenti informants said: '*Hayot bu bozor*' – Life is a market! And this applies to relations of regional or ethnic solidarity as well. Ultimately, *zemlyachestvo* depends on transactions within a 'market' of solidarity, where supply and demand are negotiated, and transactions take on various forms. As is the case with all real markets, this market is not 'perfect'. Rather, participants may draw on widely varying funds of economic, social and cultural capital in negotiating and wrapping up transactions. Halmurad, for example, can supply at will the coveted *propiska* for those to whom, for one reason or another, he is favourably disposed. Dilmurad can provide a job. And Sayora can provide jobs, housing, even a wife, and, through her husband, the *propiska*. These, then, are the people who exercise command over the resources that migrants require. They possess the knowledge and the capacity to shape their own markets of solidarity by determining the rules of exchange and redistribution. Most migrants, in contrast, have only a little money to offer – or, lacking that, their labour and their loyalty.

When I spoke with Khorezmians in Tashkent about their relationships with their *zemlyaki*, they described some as *boshqacha*, i.e. 'of another kind' or 'something special', and therefore *muhim* or 'important'. Other relationships they described as *bardi-galdi*, or 'come-go'; these were also said to be *yuzaki* (superficial) and *vaqtincha* (temporary). To simplify the exposition, I will refer to these two types of transactional relationships among Khorezmians in Tashkent as type A and type B.

Type A designates an intensive, long-term relationship, often between people of unequal status, one of whom – e.g. a Khorezmian who is well-established in Tashkent – is the patron, and the other of whom – say, a young Khorezmian who has just arrived in the capital – is the client. The personal character of such a relationship is compounded, insofar as the link between patron and client is based on shared regional origins or shared ethnicity and often also on kinship. In this situation, the young internal migrant, who is offered benefits within a limited but secure system of socialization and income generation, has to make choices. The choices are limited because of structural constraints – specifically, the migrant's limited access to resources and opportunities, especially in comparison with the would-be patron. Because he or she is largely excluded from such access, he or she is left with the limited possibilities that are available within his or her own group. Especially in times of uncertainty, and in the absence of social security, interests change accordingly. What one lacks becomes especially valuable. Social security is then more valuable than attempting to obtain more income, which also involves a certain degree of risk. In short, type A relations involve a trade-off. The person in the superior position offers security in the form of employment, lodging, personal involvement, assistance with all kinds of difficulties, but, usually, only modest wages. If this offer is accepted by the person in the inferior position, he or she repays the debt with loyalty, sacrificing financial gain for security. Examples of the type A relationships, given above, include those between Sayora and Dilmurad and between Dilmurad and some of the members of his construction team.

In contrast, type B relationships are superficial and short-term, insofar as at least one party in the transaction attempts to maximize his or her own gain, to the disadvantage of the other. Of course, it is also possible that both parties follow this course. The party in the superior position, say, an official who is able to grant a *propiska*, may opt for profit – e.g. a bribe in the form of a cash payment, an expensive whiskey or new clothes – at the expense of ethnic altruism and solidarity. Conversely, the party in the inferior position may accept a favour that is granted on the basis of ethnic solidarity, and then withhold reciprocation in the form of loyalty or future service, acting instead as a 'free rider', in the sense of game theory. One might say that in type B relationships, at least one party is acting not out of ethnic solidarity but out of self-interest; or both are acting in that way. But, as Schlee has shown (Schlee 2013: 11–15; Eidson et al. 2017: 348, 356), this conclusion must be qualified. When, from the perspective of the offended party, the offending party seems to be acting in 'self-interest', he or she is still acting in the interest of a human community beyond the self. The community in question is, however, not Khorezmians in Tashkent, taken as whole, but the other members of the household to which the offending party belongs. What appears to be 'self-interest' is, in actuality, an alternative form of identification with others. In type B relations, the interests of a more narrowly defined circle of beneficiaries –

usually, oneself and the other members of one's own household – outweigh solidarity with the larger community of *zemlyaki*.

The qualities of the transactions within type A and type B relationships seem to correspond to the 'spectrum of reciprocities' – generalized, balanced and negative – proposed some time ago by Marshall Sahlins (1972: 193), provided, however, that these are understood not as distinct types but as aspects of complex relations that usually cannot be reduced to one type or the other. Type A relations display properties of generalized reciprocity, insofar as the supply of material goods goes in one direction, from the superior to the inferior partner. Such provision is *ot dushi*, 'from the soul', i.e. they involve emotional attachment, resembling *savab* or *sadaqa*, the almsgiving that is an obligation of every Muslim. Simultaneously, type A relations are also balanced, insofar as material provisioning 'must be returned' (*qaytarish garak*), if not in like kind, then in the form of loyalty, dependability and readiness to help in other ways.

In contrast, type B relations are balanced, insofar as they involve simple payment for a service; but they are negative, insofar as at least one of the two parties simply 'makes use of' the other (*paydalanish*), without reciprocating adequately or without being willing to enter into a more intensive, long-term relationship.

In real life, of course, social relations are often ambiguous, because the viewpoints of the parties involved in the relation vary, or because, for each party, his or her viewpoint changes over time or from one situation to another. Such ambiguities are especially evident in the kinds of transactions in which Halmurad, the visa official, partakes. When he is approached by someone who wants an exit visa or a *propiska*, a residence permit, stamped in his or her passport, Halmurad may demand the going rate, so that the petitioner gets the *propiska* and he makes a profit. This is clearly a type B relation, to which neither party is bound, once the transaction is completed. When, however, the petitioner is a Khorezmian who 'plays the ethnic card', appealing to shared connections or to Halmurad's feeling of solidarity for his *zemlyak*, the further development of the relationship depends on a number of variables. It may be that Halmurad grants the petitioner's request, not for a simple cash payment but for future favours. In this case, the petitioner becomes a client who is bound to Halmurad, sometimes at a cost that is not necessarily equitable. If, for example, the petitioner is a doctor, Halmurad may first provide the *propiska*, and then, in the future, make an unspecified number of requests for services, such as a full medical examination for his mother or another of his relatives. In such a case, a relationship has been established that tends in the direction of type A, while being, simultaneously, somewhat exploitative, i.e. negatively tinged.

Of course, there are also cases when the perspectives of the provider and the petitioner do not match – when they entertain contradictory expectations regarding the transaction. For example, in an instance where Halmurad shows magnanimity in anticipation of future favours, the petitioner, or potential client, may or may not feel bound to do him those favours. From Halmurad's point of view, this might be an example of *paydalanish* or negative reciprocity, in Sahlins's sense; but from the petitioner's viewpoint, it might seem like balanced or generalized reciprocity, since he or she 'will give back to Halmurad – and, if not, then God will do so', as one person told me.

From the Trader's Dilemma to the Ethnic Trap

For Khorezmians, the Uzbek capital of Tashkent offers more opportunities for employment and education than they have back home; but it is almost a foreign environment and often a hostile one. From the Tashkenti perspective, Khorezmians deviate more strongly from what they take to be the national norm than any other subnational group. Because Khorezmians are a national minority, and because they have little chance of gaining access to resources and pursuing opportunities through official channels, they depend on each other. Khorezmians who have established themselves in Tashkent can offer contacts, access to employment, political favours, jobs, lodging and security to their *zemlyak*, their fellow Khorezmians. Those who arrive in Tashkent with little in their pockets may have kin, friends or friends of friends among those who are able to help them; but, otherwise, they have little more than their labour and their loyalty to offer.

For all Khorezmians in Tashkent, including both those who need help and those who – because of their wealth, office or connections – are able to help, this creates difficulties that are reminiscent of the trader's dilemma, as described by Evers and Schrader (1994). While they are not all 'traders' in a narrowly understood sense of the word, all Khorezmians in Tashkent, whether potential patrons or potential clients, have something that they want and something that they can offer in exchange in order to get it. And each is motivated to buy cheap and sell dear, in order to maximize gains for themselves and their dependents. At the same time, thrown together in a more or less hostile environment, they are dependent on each other and feel obligated to help each other, either 'from the soul' or to avoid the opprobrium of other members of the Khorezmian community, including their close kin.

Under conditions that resemble Evers's and Schrader's 'trader's dilemma', many Khorezmians in Tashkent fall into an 'ethnic trap' (Turaeva 2016: 198–200). Existential problems that they need to solve are solved by depending on the help of fellow Khorezmians who are in a position to help but who also demand something in return. Thus, accepting such help often brings with it confinement to a world of dependence from which there is little chance of escape. This, in turn, strengthens divisions within a supposed Uzbek 'nation' along lines that are simultaneously regional and ethnic.

Rano Turaeva is affiliated at the Ludwig Maximillian University in Munich and is an associate researcher at the Max Planck Institute for Social Anthropology in Halle (Saale). She has conducted ethnographic research in Central Asia and Russia on topics of migration, entrepreneurship, informal economies, Islam, gender, border studies, identity and inter-ethnic relations. Her texts have appeared in journals such as *Inner Asia*, *Communist and Post-Communist Studies*, *Sociology of Islam*, *Central Asian Affairs*, *Central Asian Survey* and *Anthropology of the Middle East*, among others. She is the author of the book *Migration and Identity: the Uzbek Experience* (Routledge, 2016) and co-editor of *Labour, Mobility and Informal Practices in Russia: Power, Institutions and Mobile Actors in Transnational Space* (Routledge, 2021).

Notes

1. Uzbek citizens are obliged to obtain official permission to leave Uzbekistan, whether they are travelling for business or as tourists. An exit visa is valid for only two years and is subject to renewal. One goes through the same procedure again to obtain another exit visa. Without an interview, the minimum duration of the application process for an exit visa is one month. Interviews are not necessarily required but may be demanded by National Security Service officials (*Slujba Narodnoy Bezopasnosti* or SNB, which is the Uzbek equivalent of the US FBI). The application form for an exit visa consists of fifteen questions, e.g. about the purpose of the trip, the country of destination, and biographical information about the applicant, including his or her employment history and current place of work. The page documenting the applicant's employment history requires a stamp from the current employer. If the applicant is unemployed, the stamp of the neighborhood chair (*mahalla rais*) in the applicant's place of resident suffices. But, without a stamp, the application is invalid. Details and contact information for family members, including the applicant's parents, must also be provided. For children under 16 who are travelling with their parents, a photograph must be submitted as well. Children aged 16 and above must submit a separate application. After the application forms and other documents are submitted to Halmurad's department and processed there, they are forwarded to the central office of the SNB, where they are carefully screened. SNB officials then decide whether or not to issue an exit visa. Usually, no reason is given for the rejection of an application. Two years before I began doing fieldwork, the government established the internal policy (without announcing it publicly) of refusing exit visas to young applicants of working age. This was an attempt to lower the rate of emigration, which had increased dramatically after Uzbek independence. Ironically, however, this official position had the practical effect of making the issuing of exit visas very lucrative because of the money that was then paid 'under the table'.

2. Passports are issued when one reaches the age of 16. On 25 May, which is the last day of school in all primary and secondary schools, teachers, schoolchildren and parents gather on the grounds of the school to celebrate *ohirgi kongiroq* (the last ringing of the school bell). Sometimes, the speeches and musical programmes are supplemented by presentations of passports to school graduates by police officials. Otherwise, one has to pay for the documents, photos and fees that are required for issuing passports. Passports are subject to renewal every ten years. Well-travelled passport holders whose passports are so full of visas and stamps that they have no room for further stamps are required to apply for a new passport, and for new visas, even if the ten-year period is not yet over. The only stamps that are transferred to the new passport are the *propiska*, the registration stamp, though, even in this case,

one must provide additional proof of continued residence. Each of these steps requires the payment of official fees and unofficial contributions in order to facilitate a smooth procedure.

References

Baldauf, Ingeborg. 1991. 'Some Thoughts on the Making of the Uzbek Nation', *Cahiers du Monde Russe et Soviétique* 32(1): 79–96.

———. 1993. *Schriftreform und Schriftwechsel bei den muslimischen Russland- und Sowjettürken (1850–1937)*. Budapest: Akadémiai Kiadó.

Barth, Fredrik. 1969. *Ethnic Groups and Boundaries: The Social Organization of Culture Difference*. Bergen: Universitetsforlaget.

———. 1994. 'Enduring and Emerging Issues in the Analysis of Ethnicity', in Han Vermeulen and Cora Govers (eds), *The Anthropology of Ethnicity: Beyond Ethnic Groups and Boundaries*. Amsterdam: Het Spinhuis.

Bernstein, Mary. 2005. 'Identity Politics', *Annual Review of Sociology* 31(1): 47–74.

Bourdieu, Pierre. 1977 [1972]. *Outline of a Theory of Practice*. Cambridge: Cambridge University Press.

———. 1986. 'The Forms of Capital', in John G. Richardson (ed.), *Handbook of Theory and Research for the Sociology of Education*. New York: Greenwood, pp. 241–58.

Carlisle, Donald S. 1986. 'The Uzbek Power Elite: Politburo and Secretariat (1938–83)', *Central Asian Survey* 5(3/4): 91–132.

Eidson, John R., Dereje Feyissa, Veronika Fuest, Markus Virgil Hoehne, Boris Nieswand, Günther Schlee and Olaf Zenker. 2017. 'From Identification to Framing and Alignment: A New Approach to the Comparative Analysis of Collective Identities', *Current Anthropology* 58(3): 340–59.

Elwert, Georg. 2002. 'Switching Identity Discourses: Primordial Emotions and the Social Construction of We-Groups', in G. Schlee (ed.), *Imagined Differences: Hatred and the Construction of Identity*. Münster, Germany: LIT, pp. 33–54.

Evers, Hans-Dieter. 1994. 'The Traders' Dilemma: A Theory of the Social Transformation of Markets and Society', in Hans-Dieter Evers and Heiko Schrader (eds), *The Moral Economy of Trade: Ethnicity and Developing Markets*. London and New York: Routledge, pp. 7–14.

Evers, Hans-Dieter and Heiko Schrader (eds). 1994. *The Moral Economy of Trade: Ethnicity and Developing Markets*. London and New York: Routledge.

Finke, Peter. 2014. *Variations on Uzbek Identity: Strategic Choices, Cognitive Schemas and Political Constraints in Identification Processes*. New York and Oxford: Berghahn.

Giddens, Anthony. 1976. *New Rules of Sociological Method: A Positive Critique of Interpretive Sociologies*. New York: Basic Books.

Ilkhamov, Alisher. 2004. 'Archaeology of Uzbek identity', *Central Asian Survey* 23 (3-4): 289–326.

Jenkins, Richard. 1996. *Social Identity*. London: Routledge.

———. 1997. *Rethinking Ethnicity: Arguments and Explorations*. London, Thousand Oaks and New Delhi: Sage.

Karmysheva, Balkyz K. 1976. *Ocherki etnicheskoi istorii iuzhnykh raionov Tadzhikistana i Uzbekistana* [Outline of the Ethnic History of Southern Regions of Tadjikistan and Uzbekistan]. Moscow: Nauka.

Sahlins, Marshall. 1972. 'On the Sociology of Primitive Exchange', in Marshall Sahlins, *Stone Age Economics*. Chicago: Aldine Atherton, pp. 185–275.

Schlee, Günther. 2008. *How Enemies Are Made: Towards a Theory of Ethnic and Religious Conflicts*. Integration and Conflict Studies 1. New York and Oxford: Berghahn.

———. 2013. 'Why States Still Destroy Pastoralism and How They Can Learn That in Their Own Interest They Should Not', *Nomadic Peoples* 17(2): 6–19.

———. 2018. 'Introduction: Difference and Sameness as Modes of Integration', in Günther Schlee and Alexander Horstmann (eds), *Difference and Sameness as Modes of Integration: Anthropological Perspectives on Ethnicity and Religion*. New York and Oxford: Berghahn, pp. 1–32.

Shanijazov, K. 1978. 'Early Elements in the Ethnogenesis of the Uzbeks', in Wolfgang Weissleder (ed.), *The Nomadic Alternative: Modes and Models of Interaction in the African-Asian Deserts and Steppes*. The Hague: De Gruyter Mouton, pp. 147–56.

Turaeva, Rano. 2014. 'Linguistic Ambiguities of Uzbek and Classification of Uzbek Dialects', *Anthropos* 110(2): 463–75.

———. 2016. *Migration and Identity in Central Asia: The Uzbek Experience*. London and New York: Routledge.

———. 2022. 'Economy of Favours in Central Asia: Tanish-bilish, kattalar and kichkina'. *Economic Sociology: Perspectives and Conversations* 23(3): 10–16.

Van der Grijp, Paul. 2003. 'Between Gifts and Commodities: Commercial Enterprise and the Trader's Dilemma on Wallis ("Uvea")', *The Contemporary Pacific* 15(2): 277–307.

Zhdanko, T.A. 1978. 'Ethnic Communities with Survivals of Clan and Tribal Structure in Central Asia and Kazakhstan in the Nineteenth and Early Twentieth Centuries', in W. Weissleder (ed.), *The Nomadic Alternative: Modes and Models of Interaction in the African–Asian Deserts and Steppes*. The Hague: De Gruyter Mouton, pp. 137–46.

CHAPTER 14

Is Migrating a Rational Decision?
Motives and Procedures of Qazaq Repatriation

PETER FINKE

Migration has become one of the most thrilling topics in the contemporary social sciences, and research on it is thriving. There is no lack of academic attempts to explain why people are on the move and why migration has increased so dramatically in recent years, just as there is no scarcity in warnings against its massive and uncontrolled character. Obviously, migration has been a constant feature of human existence since its beginning; indeed, in some eras, it has occurred on a grander scale than it does today, proportionally speaking (Bellwood 2013; Castels et al. 2014). But, in recent years, it has started to dominate public discourse and policy-making that is intended to manage the outcome of the seemingly unlimited movement of people across the surface of the globe. The obvious truth that most people tend to stay put – a fact that is equally worthy of explanation, given the often poor conditions under which many live – is often forgotten (Arango 2000).

Classic economic theories suggest that migrating is a rational decision, as people calculate the relative merits of staying or leaving, taking into account the respective advantages and disadvantages of their place of residence and potential destinations, or assessing the scale of the threat that one decision or another poses to their existence. While such theories may also include speculation about the positive and negative effects that migration has for the sending and receiving states and communities, they are largely individualistic in orientation, focusing rather one-sidedly on the economic factors influencing decision-making. Social relationships and the hierarchical structures in which they are embedded are treated merely as variables in calculative games. Consequently, push-and-pull theories – as they are commonly known – have been criticized for neglecting the importance of political and socio-cultural factors in migratory decisions (Arango 2000; Castels et al. 2014).

Alternative approaches have not only added new thoughts and concerns but also shifted the focus of the explanandum. In these models, emphasis falls less on why people leave in the first place than on the factors that explain where they go. For example, they may go where there is already a sizeable community of compatriots, where access to residence permits is relatively easy, or where they may be part of social networks that facilitate finding jobs (Massey et al. 1998; Brettell 2008). Thus, migration happens in chains and this, to a certain degree, prohibits a simplistic economic explanation. A second shift in focus concerns the conditions in and consequences for the countries of both origin and destination. Migration then becomes an expression of highly unequal and exploitative relationships between a capitalist core and a dependent periphery (Portes and Walton 1981; Sassen 1988).

Other researchers, who take yet another approach, deal with the question of integration once migrants have settled, claiming that, in most cases, people maintain close relationships both in their new site and with those in the social environments they left behind – that is to say, they develop transnational ties (Glick Schiller et al. 1992; Portes et al. 1999; Levitt 2001). In all their diversity, these alternative models have all been proposed by those who agree in their critique of push-and-pull theories, which, they insist, are too narrowly economic and neglect the social embeddedness of actors and the systematic power asymmetries to which they are exposed (Smith and King 2012; Brettell 2013; de Haas 2014).

There is, of course, no doubt that migrating is a complex and often painful decision-making process, in the course of which multiple factors must be considered. In most cases, it also affects numerous people, migrants and others, who take part – or try to take part – in its realization. Apart from rational calculation, however one defines it, there are many social constraints and emotional challenges that affect migration. Leaving one's home – even if one is free to choose whether to do so or not – is for most humans not an easy step at all, especially because the benefits of doing so are often only a vague promise (Chibnik 2011). Lack of information is a fundamental component of any act of migration, depending on the media to which one has access and the number of acquaintances already residing in one's prospective destination. Even when readily available, information flows are often highly distorted, while, at the same time, personal attitudes and expectations may override more careful consideration (Williams and Baláž 2012).

Standard rational-choice theory, on which push-and-pull models are ultimately based, does not predict that the outcomes of one's decisions are necessarily satisfactory. It merely says that – given the respective personal goals, the available resources and the subjective expectations regarding potential outcomes – these estimations make sense at the moment they are made. But more recent developments in economics and psychology have made clear that this is a rather crude approach to the reality to which social actors are exposed. Theories of bounded rationality, stressing the fundamental risk aversion that characterizes human decision-making and behaviour, should prompt us to see migration as a rather exceptional case, due to the high degree of uncertainty it entails. Deciding to migrate may typically be based on more or less careful calculation, rather than on 'thinking fast' (Kahnemann 2011); but, even when this is so, it is still based on limited and often distorted information. Conversely, imitation effects and the hope for a better future for oneself or one's children may result in migration without much calculation in the first place.

Cognitive theorists such as Peter Todd and Gerd Gigerenzer (2003) have alluded to the fact that, in a restatement of his idea of bounded rationality, Herbert Simon (1990) stressed its scissors-like character. On the one hand, there is 'the structure of task environments' (Simon 1990: 7), an external factor, which typically places strict limits on the availability of information. And, on the other hand, there are the limited computational skills of human beings, an internal factor. Taken together, however, these blades of the scissors lead to a highly adaptive way of making decisions. Too much information, according to Todd and Gigerenzer (2003), would not be digestible for our calculating brains; and, in a worst-case scenario, it would be paralysing. Therefore, a heuristic approach may, in fact, lead to better results. This implies that, contrary to common assumptions, when people make decisions, it is better to gather less information and engage in less information processing, while focusing on relatively few indicators, drawing analogies between their experience – and the experiences of others – and orienting themselves toward one or a few desirable aims.

When one is analysing migration, either blade of the scissors may come to the foreground, depending on the situation, although of course both of them are constantly at work. On the one hand, there are cases of decisions under conditions of very limited information that often lead to sub-optimal if not disastrous outcomes, as in the case of the people who end up in refugee camps in Libya. On the other hand, there are those who hesitate to make a move, in spite of the more than precarious situation they face in their place of residence – which is why there is in fact far less migration than could be expected on the basis of rational choice theory. In either case, decision-making takes place under conditions of insufficient information and limited cognitive capacities to process it; therefore, one important factor is for people to economize on the variables they take into account before deciding whether and how to migrate.

In this chapter, I take up the case of the repatriation of Qazaqs from Mongolia, demonstrating the complexity and, to some degree, the inconsistency of migratory motives over time. I argue that their case is particularly illustrative, due to the largely free, unrestricted character of their migration, which allows us to examine decision-making processes in a kind of laboratory state. Officially invited by the state bearing their name, the newly independent Republic of Qazaqstan, Qazaq families started, in the early 1990s, to leave Mongolia to find a future in their alleged homeland. Neither state impeded such a move nor did much to prevent the same people from returning to Mongolia or commuting between both countries (Finke 2013). Therefore, a look at successive waves of migration and at individual case studies allows us to study the various factors that induced some families – roughly half of the Qazaq community in Mongolia – to leave the country, and others to stay where they were. It will be shown that economic booms and crises on either side of the border certainly played a huge role in this but that other equally important factors come into play as well.

The basic argument here is that people usually evaluate carefully the pros and cons of moving; thus, they fulfil the prerequisites for being labelled rational actors. But they do this under conditions of severely restricted information and in terms of socially and culturally charged understandings of the world. In this case, the first wave of migration from Mongolia to Qazaqstan was accelerated by the fact that people believed they were going to a place that was similar to their home in Mongolia. Information was not only limited but also deemed to be unnecessary. This proved to be wrong, and cognizance of this mistake caused a sudden end to migration.

In the years following this first wave, only a few Qazaq families left Mongolia, even during times when conditions were promising on the other side of the border. Hesitation was the dominant trait of that time, fuelled by one's own bad experiences or that of others, and augmented further by the insecurity that such a move inevitably entails. In the course of time, however, intensive relationships and frequent visits between communities in both countries significantly reduced the feeling of uncertainty for later generations and opened the way for a new wave of migration. There were still many aspects to be considered, such as job opportunities, school education and political stress in both states, which did not allow for an easy decision and necessarily kept the rationality bounded to some degree. But people had found a way to deal with those aspects of the decision-making process heuristically by focusing on those few issues that were most relevant for them. That is to say, they economized on information-seeking to make information-processing manageable and fruitful.

Qazaqs in Different Parts of the World

Until 1991, Qazaqstan – then the Kazakh Soviet Socialist Republic – was a largely unknown subunit of the Soviet Union, enjoying the highest degree of formal autonomy that the regime granted to its components. Across borders in

Central Asia, this was a period of social and political stability, at least during the latter decades of the socialist era, when people had little reason to leave home. But migration is nothing new in this region. Located in the centre of the Eurasian landmass, the steppes of Qazaqstan had at various times been an important transit zone for the movement of people, goods and ideas, as well as a source for military supply for a series of empires, such as that of the Mongols. Later, in the course of the twentieth century, the region had gradually turned into a backyard for socialist experiments, nuclear testing and large-scale population reshufflings initiated by the government in Moscow.

All this changed abruptly when the Soviet Union fell apart and Qazaqstan became one of the fifteen republics that gained independence. The new state saw itself confronted with a particularly difficult situation. Apart from the challenges of economic and social transformation on a daunting scale, a fate shared by all the former members of the Soviet Union, Qazaqstan was confronted, in its efforts at nation-building, with a particular difficulty, one related to demographic factors, namely being the only republic where the titular group did not form the majority of the population. One reason for that was the massive loss of lives during forced collectivization in the 1920s and 1930s, when an estimated 1.5 million Qazaqs died in famines. The other reason was the large-scale influx, in the early to mid-twentieth century, of European settlers and of deported peoples such as Germans, Koreans and Chechens, who had been deemed to be collaborators with the enemy during the Second World War. In 1989, when the final Soviet census was taken, Qazaqs numbered approximately 8 million, or 40 per cent of the republic's population, with an almost equal number of Russians and smaller numbers of other minorities (Olcott 1981).

Because Qazaqstan shares a common boundary with Russia over several thousand kilometres, this demographic imbalance seemed to the new government to be potentially volatile. The official invitation by president Nursultan Nazarbayev to all Qazaqs abroad, the so-called diasporas, to 'return home and participate in building up the fatherland' (Diener 2009; Kuscu 2012) may be understood as a way to address this perceived problem. Combined with a moderate policy of Qazaqization, this was supposed to provide the state with a distinct face, allowing it to confront nationalist desires in neighbouring Russia. The origin of the Qazaq diasporas goes back to the eighteenth century, when the first groups of Qazaqs left the territory of the contemporary state due to growing pressure by European settlers. In several waves, extending well into the twentieth century, Qazaqs migrated to China, Mongolia, Uzbekistan and further on to Iran, Afghanistan and Turkey. By the time Qazaqstan gained independence, an estimated 4 to 5 million Qazaqs lived outside of the new state, with the largest communities in China, Russia and Uzbekistan. Most of them had little interaction and no traceable kin relations with their compatriots in Qazaqstan (Benson and Svanberg 1998).

The diaspora in Mongolia occupies a special place in this scenario. It is the only country where Qazaqs form the largest minority, consisting of 130,000 individuals, or 6 per cent of the country's population. In much of western Mongolia, Qazaqs even form a local majority, in some districts accounting for up to 90 per cent of the population. A direct connection to Qazaqstan is prohibited, however, by a small strip of land where Russia and the People's Republic of China share a border. In political and economic terms, Qazaqs, in their majority, do not report having experienced any systematic discrimination in Mongolia. Until today, they praise that country as a model of peace and freedom where there are television and radio channels, newspapers and, to a limited degree, school instruction in the Qazaq language (Finke 2004).

Hovd-*sum*, the district of Hovd, where most of the research on which this chapter is based was conducted, exhibits all the characteristics just described. As most of western Mongolia, Hovd is a place well suited for extensive pastoralism, with a landscape featuring high mountain pastures and lower-level desert steppes. It has a cold and arid climate with an annual average temperature of around zero degrees Celsius and with the omnipresent threat of various types of severe winter conditions, known collectively as *dzüd* in Mongolia, that sometimes take a heavy toll on livestock numbers. The history of the district is shaped by frequent and partly overlapping population movements, with Qazaqs as relative newcomers who became the majority only in the 1960s and who retain that status, in spite of the reduction in their numbers caused by migration to Qazaqstan. In Hovd-*sum*, rearing livestock has traditionally been the basis of livelihood, although irrigated agriculture and trade also play a role. Today, steady incomes are limited to the few working in the local administration, in schools or in medical services.

The First Wave of Migration – And a Subsequent Return

This was all very different during socialist times, when regular salaries and a reliable provision with needed goods and services were taken for granted. The sudden end of the planned economy in the early 1990s came as a shock for many and robbed people of a feeling of security and prosperity. The result was a deep crisis, caused partially by the end of subsidies from the Soviet Union and by the breakdown of trade channels within the country and with its neighbours. Poverty struck particularly the urban population and those in small settlements, while pastoralists were able to make a living from the newly acquired private herds, if only by means of subsistence (Finke 2004). It would take a decade for a moderate recovery of the Mongolian national economy to set in, fuelled by the discovery and extraction of natural resources and by a growing urban market for agricultural products.

Such was the situation when the first wave of migration to Qazaqstan set in. This was a period of great turmoil all over the socialist world, culminating in the Soviet Union ceasing to exist in the autumn of 1991. As one of its component republics, Qazaqstan, quasi by default, became an independent state and a potential destination for Qazaqs from other parts of the world. As noted above, the new government in Almaty invited all Qazaqs to come and help build up the new state bearing their name. It promised them houses, jobs and some financial support. A quota system was soon introduced, intended to regulate annual numbers of migrants per country of origin. Once the quota of migrants had been reached, others would still be permitted to come, upon proving their Qazaq ethnicity, but they would be outside the official support programme.

Mongolia was, indeed, the first country affected by this call on a larger scale. When I first went to Hovd in the autumn of 1991, basically everyone – Qazaqs and Mongols alike – would hotly debate the move to Qazaqstan and its consequences. Within two years, an estimated 57,000 Qazaqs had followed the invitation to resettle, close to 40 per cent of the total population at that time. Most affected were minority areas, including the capital of Ulaanbaatar, industrial sites such as Nalaih or Erdenet, and urban and semi-urban settlements such as the provincial centre of Ölgiy. These regional imbalances reflected the unequal effects that the privatization of socialist enterprises had had on different parts of Mongolian society.

Migration numbers were similar for Hovd-*sum*. While overall approximately 35 per cent of the local community left at that time, the majority of these were agriculturalists and inhabitants of the district centre – in the table, the *bag* (sub-district) four and five, respectively. The number of migrants was much lower among pastoralists who resided in the other three sub-districts (Finke 1995).

Although discussions among people were intense, most had only rather vague ideas about Qazaqstan and about what to expect from such a move. Political motives, e.g. the reference to a nation-state bearing their name, were certainly not irrelevant; but, except for a small group of intellectuals from Ulaanbaatar

Table 14.1. Demographic changes in Hovd-*sum*. Source: Statistical Office of Hovd-*sum*.

Bag	1991	1992	1993	1994	1995	1991–1995	2005	2014	2015	2016	2017	1995–2017	1991–2017
1	945	617	562	662	843	–10,8%	982	697	722	721	754	–10,6%	–20,2%
2	1011	885	801	738	778	–23,0%	956	692	719	718	738	–5,1%	–27,0%
3	879	782	779	817	958	9,0%	1064	691	723	719	733	–23,5%	–16,6%
4	945	547	551	676	636	–32,7%	791	609	625	620	632	–0,6%	–33,1%
5	1935	1144	957	1021	957	–50,5%	851	654	688	691	697	–27,2%	–64,0%
Total	5715	3975	3650	3814	4172	–27,0%	4644	3343	3477	3469	3554	–14,8%	–37,8%

and Ölgiy, most migrants were driven by economic factors. What is more, people rarely talked about the potential benefits of life in Qazaqstan; rather, their reasons were grounded overwhelmingly in the precarious situation in Mongolia at that time. In terms of standard migration theory, it was thus the 'push' rather than the 'pull' factors that initiated this first movement. Many perceived the current conditions in Mongolia to be so desperate that no additional information regarding their destination seemed necessary. A rush set in and spread so rapidly that it threatened to deplete the whole Qazaq community in Mongolia within a few years. Apparently, those families who chose to migrate did not care much about accumulating a financial basis to start their new life. The livestock that they had received when the socialist enterprises for animal husbandry were privatized was sold off at very low prices – one sheep, reportedly, for one dollar or a bottle of vodka – or consumed on the spot. Horses and camels were slaughtered in the middle of summer, with lots of the meat being wasted or distributed to kin and neighbours (Finke 2004).

Transport to Qazaqstan was in most cases organized or at least financially supported by the government in Almaty. In the heyday of the first wave of migration, there were several flights a week taking families and their belongings from Ölgiy to the city of Öskemen, and from there, by truck, to other places in the north of Qazaqstan to which they were assigned by the government. Others made the trip by land, which allowed them to take along more of their property. This included, for example, their private yurts, the tents of nomadic Qazaqs; but livestock could not be taken, because it was not permitted to cross the strip of Russian territory located in-between. Once they arrived, migrants received ID cards that qualified them as Qazaqs while they were waiting for formal citizenship to be granted. Since, officially, the first migrants came on work contracts, it would, in most cases, take some years for them to get a Qazaqstani passport.

According to their own accounts, Qazaq migrants – called *oralman* or returnees by their compatriots – were treated less well than they had expected after arriving in Qazaqstan. It is true that most of them were allotted houses that had been vacated by ethnic Russian or German occupants who left Qazaqstan after the collapse of the Soviet Union; and many were able to find work in one of the then still existing cooperatives or state farms. This implies that most were settled in the northern provinces of the country where ethnic Russians and other Europeans had formed the overwhelming majority, often making up 80 per cent or more of the local population. What is more, the few Qazaqs living in the northern regions were highly Russified, at least linguistically – which did not facilitate contact with the new arrivals from Mongolia. Other points of disappointment and frustration included the climate, cold and humid with vast empty steppes and flat territories, and the tense relationships with local residents. 'Society there is broken', *buzilip ketti*, as many remarked, referring in particular to the behaviour of local Qazaqs who they had hoped would be supportive. But, as some admitted, the economic situation in Qazaqstan was not at all favourable when the first wave of migrants arrived, so that local people had little reason to welcome additional competitors for the scarce resources at hand (Finke 2004).

The difficulties and frustrations experienced by these first migrants soon prompted many of them to regret their decision. Beginning in 1994, a return migration set in and within the next two years some 10,000 Qazaqs had moved back to Mongolia, with Hovd-*sum* receiving a proportional share of returnees. Older people had found it to be particularly difficult to adapt to the new conditions in Qazaqstan; but there were also younger families that did not see the future that they had hoped for there. Some of the families who returned had entrusted part of their livestock to friends or relatives before leaving and so had a basis for starting up again after returning. Most, however, had sold everything prior to emigrating and so, in their efforts to build up a new herd or the basis for a new existence, had to rely on the support of kin and friends when they came back. In other cases, returnees became clients of wealthier kin, at least for some time, moving with them throughout the year and helping out with work in exchange for milk and meat. Some were able to use this as an opportunity to build up a herd for themselves again; others were less successful and eventually moved to town when conditions started to improve there.

A number of things are striking in regard to the return migration. One is that the government of Mongolia did nothing to prevent people from leaving and coming back. The attitude among ordinary people was different to a degree. Some would have preferred the migrants to remain in Qazaqstan and be joined there by those Qazaqs who were still in Mongolia. But this position was more typical of urban residents, and even in the cities it did not represent the view of the majority. In rural areas such as Hovd-*sum*, the Mongols I talked with were rather indifferent in that respect. What is also noteworthy is that returning was not really perceived as a failure. There had been good reasons to leave, at least in the eyes of Qazaqs; but there were equally understandable motives for coming back. Those who did come back often faced economic difficulties for a while, but there were no instances of social discrimination, not even by local Mongols, who sometimes even donated livestock to returnees.

Looking at the first wave of migration to Qazaqstan – and, to a certain degree, the return movement to Mongolia that set in as well – it is not only the fundamental lack of information, attributable to 'the structure of the environment', that is striking; even more it is that this deficit seemed irrelevant to most. People had neither notable information about conditions in their destination, nor had they any reasonable estimation regarding possible developments after the demise of the socialist regime, with all its safety and security. But their situation in Mongolia at that time had been so desperate, compared with their standard of living only a few months earlier, that no doubts seemed justified and no careful calculation necessary. As described above, a rush set in that threatened to make the whole Qazaq community in Mongolia disappear within a year or two. It was only the deep disappointment that soon set in – and an equally rushed decision to return to Mongolia – that prevented this. In both cases, information was greatly limited, partly because it was believed to be unnecessary to gather it; and partly because the processing of what little information was available was equally cursory and dominated by a few (and, as it turned out, deceptive) variables.

The Second Wave – Gradually Settling Down

Between the mid-1990s and the early 2000s, hardly any Qazaqs moved in either direction, as people seemed to be waiting for the dust to settle. There were individual cases of migration during this period, mainly for reasons of family reunification; but by and large people stayed put. Careful re-thinking was the dominant strategy of the moment. One reason was clearly the reported difficulties that migrants faced in their new homes in Qazaqstan. No matter how often these were downplayed, the fact that one in five had returned to Mongolia was proof enough that expectations had been overly positive. But a second reason for the stemming of migration was the gradual yet noticeable recovery of the Mongolian national economy, which also affected rural livelihoods in the western parts of the country. Increases in salaries for state employees, financed partially by the growing revenues of resource extraction, were one part of the story; another was the rising prices for agricultural products and the steady improvement in commercial opportunities. Gone were the days of extremely unfavourable terms of trade and exposure to often fraudulent itinerary merchants. By now, market structures had begun to develop, allowing people to make a profit from their surpluses.

Meanwhile, the economic situation had improved also in Qazaqstan. Being endowed with enormous reserves of oil and gas, the country experienced impressive rates of economic growth, which, to a certain degree, manifested themselves in trickle-down effects across the country. Of course, not everyone benefitted and, as is typical in resource-rich countries, the profits were concentrated in the hands of members of a small elite. The distribution of the benefits was also highly unequal both for different regions and for different strata of society, with the northern provinces and, in particular, its migrant population lagging behind. Comparatively speaking, however, a decent proportion was redistributed through salaries and public investments, initiating an amazing upturn for the national economy, so that, by and large, average incomes and living standards were significantly higher than they had been during most of the 1990s. The peak of this boom was sometime between 2000 and 2010, when new crises arose.

With the economic recovery, Qazaqstan became once again a more attractive destination. Therefore, a new wave of migration set in during the early 2000s.

This time, however, it was a rather slow movement of individuals and small groups of related families; and it usually took place after a period of thoughtful consideration. Many of the people I met and spoke with during these days had calculated the pros and cons of moving for years; and, in contrast to the earlier period, they typically refrained from making a decision until the arguments seemed clear enough. Obviously, people now had the advantage not only of superior information beforehand but also of a clear destination, where kin or friends could make preparations for their arrival in Qazaqstan. Another difference was that this time some of the well-off herders were among those who decided to leave Mongolia, selling their livestock for a decent price so that they could start their new lives with some seed capital and survive the first year or two without work. Total numbers are difficult to estimate for this period, but over the years several hundred families left Hovd-*sum* again (cf. Table 14.1).

At this point, the experiences of the first generation of migrants were very much present and had convinced people of the disadvantages of a rushed move. Of course, information was much more readily available as well, because of the high number of kin already abroad and also due to the rise of new communication technologies. People now preferred to play it safe and to stay where they were, if the risk of resettlement seemed too difficult to assess. Such inclinations were presumably reinforced during visits to Qazaqstan, which showed people that even those who did not return to Mongolia often regretted their move in the first place. In fact, until today a strong sense of nostalgia for Mongolia is very widespread among those who have made the move to and stayed in Qazaqstan (Finke 2013).

Still, for those who remained in Mongolia, a move to Qazaqstan was an option, even if they hesitated to disclose this in public. While migration was a dominant theme in conversations, and while people often inquired about the plans of their interlocutors, answers tended to be elusive. At the same time, the attitude towards Mongolia remained ambiguous. On the one hand, the recovery of the national and local economy had made life easier. Most households were far better off than they had been ten years earlier. By now it was possible, with an average income, to feed a family throughout the year – something that had been unthinkable during most of the 1990s. Equally, prices for agricultural and pastoral products had developed positively, allowing families to earn a decent living. Other factors that weighed in favourably for staying in Mongolia were the country's political freedom, its social stability and the lack of any serious ethnic discrimination. Mongolia, as people often said, allows everyone to lead his or her own life, without much disturbance and interference. Opportunities to make a living are plentiful, and political life is more or less democratic.

During this same period, those who had moved to Qazaqstan often changed their location within the country. For more than ten years, families had been moving from one place to another, primarily within the northern provinces, to reunite with kin and former neighbours and friends. In the case of immigrants from Hovd-*sum*, this created two centres of habitation, one in or near the industrial town of Temirtaw in central Qazaqstan and one in Aqsu district of Pavlodar province in the north. By the mid-2010s, migrants from Hovd-*sum* made up the majority of the local population in some villages (Finke 2013). Criteria for choosing a settlement were usually the affordability of housing – rather than job availability – and the existence of kin networks. This prevented most Qazaq from Mongolia from moving to the new capital of Astana or further south towards the booming centres of Almaty or Shymkent.

Obviously, the existence of such networks made movement across borders much easier. Potential migrants now had access to information and to people who could support them before and after a move. Following migration, this did not necessarily make integration any easier and, in fact, added new problems. For example, the incentive to learn Russian – still the essential language in most of northern Qazaqstan – was even lower for the new arrival who had everything prepared and a community of kindred in situ. What is more, increasing numbers did not increase the bargaining power of migrants vis-à-vis local employers or the few owners of large farms who hired seasonal agricultural workers. Many complained that the very term *oralman* had in the meantime turned into a quasi-ethnic category that was applied even to children of migrants who were born in Qazaqstan. One counter-strategy that migrants developed was the strengthening of transnational ties with kin remaining in Mongolia (Finke 2013).

Compared to the first wave of migration, the second was one of careful planning, of lots of postponement, but equally of building on earlier experiences. Statistical data are lacking, but overall the number of migrants in the 2000s was significantly lower than it had been in the early 1990s, despite the impressive economic boom in Qazaqstan. As if following advice from a handbook on bounded rationality, people followed a dominant safety-first strategy. Even those who left Mongolia did so, in most cases, after long periods of reflection; and then they went to places where others from their community of origin, including close relatives, had already settled, thus decreasing uncertainty and transaction costs in starting their new life. However, many more decided to stay in Mongolia, not because they had decided positively in favour of that country but because of uncertainty about the benefits of leaving. In other words, the limiting factor during this period was not information, which was now more easily available and less distorted than it had been during the first wave, but the lengthy and sometimes convoluted calculations that prevented people from making a decision. Retrospectively, this indecision was not always a good strategy either, because, for many, it would have been easier to build up a new existence during Qazaqstan's boom years of the 2000s and early 2010s than it was subsequently. To a certain degree, there was too much information, which was difficult to assess – a situation which tended to make people leave things as they were.

The Third Wave – New Hopes, Concerns and Opportunities

The on-going difficulties that migrants faced upon arrival in Qazaqstan again led to a cessation of movement in the 2010s. Two other factors contributed to this rather sudden halt. One was the end of the fulminant economic boom in Qazaqstan in the wake of the global financial crisis and the subsequent burst of a construction bubble, particularly in the major cities of Almaty and Astana. A second factor was the suspension of the quota payments that the Qazaq government had made to arriving Qazaqs. Informants explained this measure with reference to the frequent abuse of the government's largesse: when people moved back and forth between Mongolia and Qazaqstan several times, they consequently received the money repeatedly. Another reason for stopping payments might have been the Qazaq government's caution vis-à-vis Russia, which it did not want to offend. Right after Russia's annexation of the Crimean Peninsula, which had belonged to Ukraine, another former Soviet republic, any Qazaq policies favouring ethnic Qazaqs over the local Russian minority might have led to disturbances between Moscow and Astana (Finke 2013).

As a result, from around 2013 onward, very little movement happened in either direction. By then, many Qazaq families in Mongolia had reached a decision for themselves to stay and had begun to reinvest in their life there. In Hovd-*sum*, for the first time in decades, new houses were being built and old ones renovated, both in the central settlement and in the pastoral winter camps, while parents now preferred to see their children studying in Hovd or Ulaanbaatar, rather than Almaty or Astana. This time, or so it seemed, people stopped migrating not out of reluctance or caution but because they had made a firm decision to stay. In other words, this time it was the weakening of push factors, rather than pull factors, that led people to settle for staying. The old arguments for each site were still there, but, for most people, the calculation now appeared to be rather straightforward.

By that time, however, the overall number of Qazaqs who had left Mongolia exceeded that of those who had stayed. No exact figures are available, but for Hovd-*sum*, it may be estimated that around 60 per cent of the families residing there in 1991 had resettled to Qazaqstan by the mid-2010s, and the same is probably true for the whole of Mongolia. During the second wave, people were less likely to migrate in large groups of closely related families. Thus, migration tended to result in the dispersion of kin on both sides of the border. As a matter of fact, there is today not a single family that is not divided between both states. This put enormous burdens on people, both socially and economically. All migrants left either siblings or children behind, and, as a consequence, members of separated families are obliged to visit one another fairly frequently. Separation from one's kin was also highly gendered. Brothers tended to move together or follow one another, whenever possible, while their married sisters were usually dependent on the decisions of their in-laws and, consequently, separated from members of their parental family on one side of the border or the other.

Ultimately, this standstill in migration was only temporary, even if combined with serious investments for life in Mongolia. The possibility of migrating was still on everyone's mind, even if arguments for staying were clearly dominant for a while. At the same time, the very process of decision-making had become easier, as it was now supported by modern technology, first-hand experience, and the information provided by kin across the border. For many, the question was no longer whether to go but when and where. People had learned that moving while children are still in school is not a good idea. It will be too late for them to learn Russian properly, and the result might be a mediocre diploma, inferior to the one they could earn in Mongolia. Thus, many decided to wait for their children to grow up. On the other hand, waiting too long could be detrimental as well, because others would take the few jobs available in Qazaqstan beforehand. The question of destination within Qazaqstan was equally challenging, because those places in Pavlodar and Temirtau where the majority of people from Hovd-*sum* had settled did not offer many opportunities. Finally, people had become increasingly aware that migrating or staying were not unrelated decisions. While those who remained in Mongolia now reaped some benefits, mainly by having access to more land, they were well aware of the fact that a further decline of the Qazaq population might jeopardize their status as a favoured minority and cause the district to be dissolved, thus destroying jobs in school and administration.

Things changed yet again in 2018. While the building of new houses in Mongolia was still underway, the orientation towards staying had declined anew, as can be shown with reference to trends in choices regarding education. As mentioned, Ulaanbaatar and Hovd had become attractive places to study again, but this was not to last. Fuelled by a new initiative of the government in Qazaqstan to sponsor students from abroad, people's attitudes changed within a year's time. In 2018, 40 out of 42 graduates from the local school in Hovd-*sum* went to study for a preparatory year in Qazaqstan. This preparatory year was free for all, and if students completed the entrance exams successfully, they could receive a full grant to continue at a local university. To a certain degree, this new programme replaced the quota system, simultaneously increasing the chances of potential migrants to be integrated in the local labour market. And it was clear to everyone I talked with that once their children had completed a university education in Qazaqstan, they would never come back. '*Bala biledi*', 'the children know'. 'When two or three of our sons and daughters study and stay there, we will go as well', as Jaylawkhan put it.

The decision to study in Qazaqstan may initiate a new and potentially final wave of migration, in spite of the fact that life there has not become any easier for the *oralman*. People are now much better prepared, however, for the challenges ahead. Apart from the economic difficulties, which have accelerated again due to the on-going crisis in Qazaqstan, these challenges also include the feeling of not being welcomed by the local population. The fact that many of the later arrivals from Mongolia had moved to settings already dominated by *oralman* where they did not have to bother to adapt to local conditions or to learn Russian only exacerbated the situation. On the other hand, the complaints of the *oralman* about Qazaqstan have also softened. More and more of the families who came during the 1990s and early 2000s have by now been able to have their children admitted to a university, which, in most cases, is the prerequisite for better-paid employment. For many, then, the future seems brighter than the present, if not for themselves then for the next generation.

At the same time, the situation in Mongolia is, in some ways, deteriorating. Difficulties there include an economic slowdown and even a reversal of the previous recovery. But, more importantly, Qazaqs in Mongolia express growing discomfort with their existence as a minority. Many complain that employment policies are increasingly discriminatory, and, because of that, they question their decision to stay. Open calls by Mongols for Qazaqs to go are clearly on the rise, nationally, though they are still rare in the local context. To some degree, such sentiments have been encouraged by political leaders who openly express their dislike of Qazaqs. Thus, while obstacles grow, opportunities seem to shrink, and the future in Mongolia appears to be increasingly jeopardized.

As these lines are being written, the factors just described have not yet resulted in any further decline of the Qazaq population in Mongolia. Individual families have been on the move, but the resulting losses have been compensated by continuing demographic growth. For Qazaqs, it seems, remaining flexible is still a central value – one that has a strong influence on decisions to migrate. What has changed, as has been demonstrated, is that, today, such decisions are well-informed and carefully planned. Gone are both the euphoria and the excessive caution of earlier periods, giving way to a more pragmatic approach. Economic considerations are still important, obviously, but the most decisive variables now seem to be social. When most family members have already moved, and children envision their future abroad, the chances are high that the remaining members will also follow. Even more than before, migration has thus become a joint decision within social networks defined by kinship and related factors.

The situation today thus most closely resembles the scissor model of decision-making, based on heuristic procedures, as proposed by Simon. Information is now readily available and is usually considered sufficient to make reasonable estimations of the pros and cons. In the case at hand, the experiences of former generations constitute guidelines and allow people to concentrate on a few major variables. Crucial considerations are the education of members of the younger generation, along with the age of retirement, which became increasingly relevant as people learned how difficult it was to enter the job market in Qazaqstan in one's forties or fifties. Today, it is easier for people to make decisions, detect correlations or analogies, and to share them with others. People know what to expect and how to prepare adequately, and they do so with a reasonable amount of calculation and hesitation, even if there always remains a moment of risk and uncertainty.

Conclusion

This chapter began with a mildly affirmative statement on the rationality of decisions to migrate. But it has also shown that these are based on a wide range of motives and processes that involve multiple social, political and emotional aspects. For example, such decisions are patterned to varying degrees by age, gender and socio-economic and political standing within the community. In all cases, however, deciding to leave one's place of origin is difficult and often painful, even in cases such as that of the Qazaqs, who were invited to come. And it involves numerous risks that are difficult to evaluate. Indeed, the case of the Qazaq *oralman* displays, over time, a puzzling array of scenarios that do not add up clearly in a simple push-and-pull calculation.

Clearly, human decision-making is calculative. Nevertheless, the case of the Qazaq *oralman* illustrates the fruitfulness of insights from the literature on bounded rationality, as outlined at the beginning of this chapter. The first lesson to take away is that people always make decisions under conditions of risk and uncertainty in one way or the other. Migration is a particularly striking example, as information is by definition limited, while expectations may be grossly inflated. Of course, migration is usually not a case of 'thinking fast' in the sense of Daniel Kahneman (2011); but, especially in its early stages, it is hard to assess its outcomes properly. Therefore, gut decisions or the imitation of others can be expected to be highly relevant. This is very much what happened in the first stage when people left in a rush without much consideration for potential results. In later stages this rather precipitous behaviour gave way to a more hesitant approach, which one would expect in situations of high risk and which was further influenced by news of the negative experiences of the early migrants. As long as conditions are not overtly bad, it is safer to stay at home. It was only at a moment when the various parameters influencing the possible outcomes of one's decision became easier to detect that people started to evaluate the pros and cons of migrating, as well as their individual chances, in a more realistic way.

Considering the case of the Qazaq *oralman* in terms of alternative models of migration, such as those proposed in the introduction to this chapter, may also be instructive. Obviously, migration is always part of a bigger picture of local, national and global politics, and of economic ups and downs. Whether one may classify the *oralman* in Qazaqstan as a new underclass, prone to being exploited and marginalized, is debateable. I doubt that this is a plausible scenario in the long run, as members of the next generation have clearly achieved greater integration, despite being stigmatized as returnee migrants. The *oralman* may also serve as an example of chain migration, as they have tended to congregate in particular settlements in Qazaqstan. Most importantly, however, the patterns of mobility described demonstrate that decisions to migrate were, to a high degree, mutually dependent. Each family leaving Mongolia changed the cost-benefit ratio of the ones staying, albeit in often quite complex and sometimes unforeseeable ways. It also affected the situation of the relatives whom they joined in Qazaqstan as well as the transnational ties across the border.

In any case, the future is as hard to predict for those Qazaqs who, at this writing, still remain in Mongolia as it is for anyone else on the planet. So far, periods of migration based on very little information have taken turns with those of excessive information processing and doubts. The precipitous rush with little consideration for the outcome that shaped behaviour in the early phase of migration was followed by a second phase of hesitation and has now given way to a careful exploration and weighing of arguments for and against such a move. Even when decisions are made, their execution is now characterized by a good amount of advanced planning, with careful attention to timing the move favourably. Crucially, the experiences compiled over the years have provided people with analogies to their own situation, thus allowing them to simplify the complexity of the situation and to find short-cuts to the decision that is right for them. Still, there are risks involved, and everyone is aware of these. Therefore, people try to keep both options open for as long as they can. The past decades have shown all too well that hopes and disappointments can be very close to each other, and that one may turn into the other very quickly.

Who then left and who stayed put? There is no clear answer to this question. Migrants have come from all parts of the Qazaq community in Mongolia, from all age-groups, lineages and professions. In earlier periods, poor families were overrepresented, in later ones less so. This has to do with the relative or, rather, perceived risk involved. Right after Qazaqstanian independence, risk seemed to be practically non-existent for those willing to migrate. This proved to be wrong, and the perception of this error influenced later decisions. Today, for those who have not (yet) left the comfort of a place with which they are familiar, where they know the institutional setting and the rules of the game, staying is, evidently, preferable. This seems to confirm one of the original assumptions of Simon's idea of bounded rationality – that decision-making among human beings is characterized by risk aversion. Time will tell how things will develop.

Peter Finke is Professor of Social Anthropology at the University of Zurich and Co-director of the Centre for Anthropological Studies on Central Asia (CASCA). He has been a Research Fellow at the Max Planck Institute for Social

Anthropology, Halle, as well as a Visiting Professor at the University of New Hampshire and the Middle Eastern Technical University, Ankara. Since the early 1990s he has conducted field research in Mongolia, Qazaqstan and Uzbekistan on issues of economic transformation, institutional change, social cognition, migration and processes of identity formation. His recent publications include *Variations on Uzbek Identity: Strategic Choices, Cognitive Schemas and Political Constraints in Identification Processes* (Berghahn, 2014) and *Qazaq Pastoralists in Western Mongolia: Institutional Change, Economic Diversification and Social Stratification* (Routledge, forthcoming in 2023).

References

Arango, Joaquín. 2000. 'Explaining Migration: A Critical View', *International Social Science Journal* 52(165): 283–96.

Bellwood, Peter. 2013. *First Migrants: Ancient Migration in Global Perspective*. Malden: Wiley-Blackwell.

Benson, Linda and Ingvar Svanberg. 1998. *China's Last Nomads: The History and Culture of China's Kazaks*. New York: M.E. Sharpe.

Brettell, Caroline B. 2008. 'Theorizing Migration in Anthropology: The Social Construction of Networks, Identities, Communities, and Globalscapes', in Caroline B. Brettell and James F. Hollifield (eds), *Migration Theory: Talking Across Disciplines*, 2nd edn. New York: Routledge, pp. 113–59.

———. 2013. 'Anthropology of Migration', in Immanuel Ness (ed.), *The Encyclopedia of Global Human Migration*. Oxford: Blackwell Publishing Ltd. Retrieved from https://doi.org/10.1002/9781444351071.wbeghm031.

Castells, Stephen, Hein de Haas and Mark J. Miller. 2014. *The Age of Migration: International Population Movements in the Modern World*. Basingstoke: Palgrave Macmillan.

Chibnik, Michael. 2011. 'Introduction', in Michael Chibnik, *Anthropology, Economics, and Choice*. Austin: University of Texas Press, pp. 1–19.

De Haas, Hein. 2014. 'What Drives Human Migration?', in Bridget Anderson and Michael Keith (eds), *Migration: The COMPAS Anthology*. Oxford: COMPAS, pp. 184–86.

Diener, Alexander C. 2009. *One Homeland or Two? The Nationalization and Transnationalization of Mongolia's Kazakhs*. Stanford, CA: Stanford University Press.

Finke, Peter. 1995. 'Kazak Pastoralists in Western Mongolia: Economic and Social Change in the Course of Privatization', *Nomadic Peoples* 36/37: 195–216.

———. 2004. *Nomaden im Transformationsprozess: Kasachen in der post-sozialistischen Mongolei*. Münster: Lit Verlag.

———. 2013. 'Historical Homelands and Transnational Ties: The Case of the Mongolian Kazaks', *Zeitschrift für Ethnologie (Special Issue: Mobility and Identity in Central Asia)* 138(2): 175–94.

Glick Schiller, Nina, Linda Basch and Cristina Blanc-Szanton. 1992. *Towards a Transnational Perspective on Migration: Race, Class, Ethnicity, and Nationalism Reconsidered*. New York: New York Academy of Sciences.

Kahneman, Daniel. 2011. *Thinking, Fast and Slow*. New York: Farrar, Straus and Giroux.

Kuscu Bonnenfant, Isik. 2012. 'Constructing the Homeland: Kazakhstan's Discourse and Policies Surrounding Its Ethnic Return-Migration Policy', *Central Asian Survey* 31(1): 31–44. Retrieved from https://doi.org/10.1080/02634937.2012.650004.

Levitt, Peggy. 2001. *The Transnational Villagers*. Berkeley and Los Angeles: University of California Press.

Massey, Douglas, Joaquín Arango, Graeme Hugo, Ali Kouaouchi, Adela Pellegrino and J. Edward Taylor. 1998. *Worlds in Motion: Understanding International Migration at the End of the Millennium*. Oxford: Clarendon Press.

Olcott, Martha B. 1981. 'The Collectivization Drive in Kazakhstan', *Russian Review* 40(2): 122–42.

Portes, Alejandro and John Walton. 1981. *Labor, Class, and the International System*. New York: Academic Press.

Portes, Alejandro, Luis Eduardo Guarnizo and Patricia Landolt. 1999. 'The Study of Transnationalism: Pitfalls and Promise of an Emergent Research Field', *Ethnic and Racial Studies* 22(2): 217–37.

Sassen, Saskia. 1988. *The Mobility of Labor and Capital: A Study in the International Investment and Labor Flow*. Cambridge: Cambridge University Press.

Simon, Herbert A. 1990. 'Invariants of Human Behavior', *Annual Review of Psychology* 41: 1–19. Retrieved from https://doi.org/10.1146/annurev.ps.41.020190.000245.

Smith, Darren P. and Russell King. 2012. 'Editorial Introduction: Re-Making Migration Theory', *Population, Space and Place* 18: 127–33. Retrieved from https://doi.org/10.1002/psp.686.

Todd, Peter M. and Gerd Gigerenzer. 2003. 'Bounding Rationality to the World', *Journal of Economic Psychology* 24: 143–65. Retrieved from https://doi.org/10.1016/S0167-4870(02)00200-3.

Williams, Allan M. and Vladimir Baláž. 2012. 'Migration, Risk, and Uncertainty: Theoretical Perspectives', *Population, Space and Place* 18: 167–80.

CHAPTER 15

Transnational Communities and Shifting Moral Values
Migrants between the Netherlands and the Moluccas

Keebet von Benda-Beckmann

Introduction

The literature on transnational social fields and transnational citizenship has been a welcome addition to migration studies (Glick Schiller 2005). Instead of focusing on the predicaments and exclusionary practices and problems of integration that are the subject of many migration studies, a focus on transnational communities has shown how relationships are maintained and created across borders, highlighting the creative and transformative processes connected with migration. Family relations change in the places of migration, as migrants typically absorb many of the norms of the recipient society. This affects the relationships between migrants and those who stay behind. Within transnational migrant networks, as in networks in general, 'constraints and opportunities varied in accordance with network position' (Crossley 2011: 153). Studies have also demonstrated that migrants take norms with them and that these norms tend to become more conservative in the diaspora. In the process, certain norms come to serve as identity markers, and often nostalgic interpretations of life 'back home' emerge. As Schlee points out, however, these new interpretations should not be regarded as mere 'inventions', but rather as creative constructions that serve specific goals. Schlee (2004: 148) also insists that such constructions are not arbitrary, but they 'consist of elements which support each other, and they make use of local materials. Sometimes old foundations are used, or old building materials are reused. Even very recent social constructs may be generated out of the same processes, thus achieving familiarity, plausibility, and often a degree of pseudo-naturalness'. Ideologies thus created, however artificial and romanticized they may be, still have 'very real consequences in terms of behaviour'. This chapter contributes to this line of enquiry by exploring the real consequences to which Schlee refers – that is, how moral convictions and legal notions change under conditions of migration, how constructed images are used to render a broad range of behaviours both plausible and credible, and how these norms and images are drawn upon in changing modes of social interaction. I will argue that these images and norms throw light on how members communicate within the transnational network, and on the misunderstandings that occur within their relationships, resulting from the different positions of persons within these transnational networks.

The empirical examples for discussing this creative process of changing moral and legal norms and imageries concern relations within the transnational community of Moluccans living in the Netherlands and on the Central Moluccan islands in the eastern part of Indonesia. As a transnational community, they are somewhat exceptional for three reasons. First, the Dutch Moluccan community is still heavily influenced by the experiences of Moluccan veterans in the Dutch colonial army, who share a common military background, educational level and language, speaking exclusively Malay. Fridus Steijlen (2018: 3) calls these veterans 'ethnic soldiers', despite the fact that, ethnically, this group is actually rather diverse.

Second, given the history of their migration, the Dutch Moluccans have formed an unusually close-knit community. Many of the veterans spent most of their adult life in the military bases of the colonial army, and some were even born there. They fought on the Dutch side during the war that ended in Indonesia's independence. Afterwards, in 1951, these soldiers and their families were transported to the Netherlands. There, they were first settled in camps and from 1960 onwards in Moluccan wards, where they lived in relative isolation from the Dutch population at large. This group formed the core of what came to be known in the Netherlands as the Moluccan community.

The third factor that has made the Dutch Moluccans somewhat exceptional for migrant communities was the impossibility of travelling to the Moluccas in the decades following emigration. Initially, they could not travel to the Moluccas because the War for Independence had only recently ended; and, later, because the Indonesian government, fearing separatist sentiments, refused to grant them visas to enter the country. During that time, no face-to-face communication was possible between Moluccans in Indonesia and the Netherlands, although there was an active exchange of letters. It was only from the late 1970s onwards that visas were extended to Moluccans who had opted for Dutch citizenship, and it was not until the 1980s that travelling became affordable for the Moluccan population at large. Since then, many Dutch Moluccans have visited the Moluccas, and quite a number of Indonesian Moluccans have paid visits to the Netherlands.

A small number of Moluccans of the first generation of migration have permanently resettled in the Moluccas.

Their violent military background, their settlement in relative isolation from the rest of the Dutch population, and the long period without face-to-face communication with Moluccans in Indonesia became important elements in the construction of images of Dutch Moluccan identity. These were combined with other elements that drew upon constructed images of a shared culture on the Moluccas. Thus, an image of a Moluccan transnational community emerged that contained elements of care and support, as well as of violence and authority.

History of Moluccan Migration

During the early years of European expansion, the search for spices such as cloves and nutmeg formed an important incentive to find a way to the 'spice islands'. Cloves were indigenous in Maluku proper, in what are now the North Moluccan islands of Halmahera, Ternate and Tidore, while nutmeg was indigenous to the Banda islands south of the Central Moluccas of Seram and Ambon, Haruku, Saparua and Nusalaut. European explorers from Spain, Portugal and the Low Countries competed with the sultans of Ternate and Tidore for control of the spice trade. Spices did not originally grow in the Central Moluccas, but for strategic reasons the Dutch, who came to dominate the market, chose the island of Ambon as their base in the early seventeenth century. There they began successfully to cultivate cloves secretly brought from Ternate in an effort to establish a clove monopoly.

Although the centre of the Dutch colonial empire soon shifted to Batavia on Java, Ambon remained an important stronghold throughout the colonial era. About half the population was converted to Protestantism while the other half was Muslim. Protestants had better access to Dutch education, and many found work in the colonial civil service, with the police, or in the colonial army. Beginning quite early during the Dutch colonization of island Southeast Asia, the Vereenigde Oostindische Compagnie (United East India Company, VOC) and the colonial government recruited men from the Moluccas for the Koninklijk Nederlandsch-Indische Leger (Royal Netherlands East Indies Army, or KNIL) (Steijlen 2015). Although the KNIL included members from throughout the archipelago, Moluccans from Ambon and the surrounding islands dominated. They lived a military life away from the Moluccas in army bases (Ind. *tangsi*, Dutch *kampen*), where their children received some education, generally from Malay-speaking teachers. During the Indonesia War of Independence, 1945–1950, the KNIL soldiers fought on the side of the Dutch.

When the Dutch government finally conferred sovereignty to Indonesia in 1950, it decided to bring indigenous members of the colonial army temporarily to the Netherlands. The government hoped that Moluccan veterans of the colonial army and their families would be able to return to an independent South Moluccan Republic, once that had been founded within an Indonesian federal state.[1] While in the Netherlands, government officials reasoned, the Moluccans could be protected from acts of reprisal to which they would predictably be subject had they stayed in Indonesia. Until a free South Moluccan Republic was established, they would remain safely in the Netherlands. Thus, a group of 3,500 military men and their families, altogether 12,500 persons, arrived in the Netherlands in 1951. To their surprise and immense disappointment they were not to be incorporated into the Dutch army but were discharged, instead entering the Netherlands as civilians.

The veterans and their families formed the core of what would be known, initially, as the 'Ambonese' and only later as the 'Moluccans' – although in fact not all actually had a Moluccan background. Even those who did have a Moluccan background were born or had lived most of their lives on army bases, far away from the Moluccas. In addition, a number of teachers, officials, sailors and navy men, who did not share the same military experience, became part of the Moluccan community.

When Dutch New Guinea, now the Province of Papua, was incorporated into Indonesia in 1962, Moluccans who had continued to serve the Dutch administration there migrated to the Netherlands as well. Although they were seen by the Dutch as part of the Moluccan community, they lived outside of the Moluccan communities and achieved a somewhat higher educational level, including a better command of the Dutch language (Bartels 1989: 40). Finally, there was a very small group of Moluccans who were educated professionals and who immigrated to the Netherlands individually and merged with the Dutch population (Bartels 1989: 29). In the Dutch East Indies, life for the indigenous population at large had been subject to hierarchical colonial conditions; however, the Dutch Moluccans who had served in the colonial army had lived under a strict military regime and had actively participated in an extremely violent and ugly war (Limpach 2014).

The first group of ex-KNIL soldiers to arrive in the Netherlands were placed, with their families, in camps where they awaited the establishment of a South Moluccan Republic within the Indonesian Federation – a dream that never materialized because, against the wishes of the Dutch, Indonesia became a centralized state. Among the Dutch Moluccans, the experience of being discharged and the unfulfilled promise of a South Moluccan Republic gave rise to a deep and long-lasting frustration, even anger, and an intense feeling of being disappointed with and humiliated by the Dutch government, which they had served loyally and which now had let them down. For many years, they lived as stateless people, refusing both Dutch and Indonesian citizenship, waiting in vain for the South Moluccan Republic to be established.

Life in the camps was cramped, frugal, strictly organized and virtually without privacy. Washrooms and bathrooms were shared and food was prepared in communal kitchens. The Moluccan veterans arrived at a time when the Dutch economy was recovering from the Second World War and the labour unions feared that the Moluccans would vie for scarce jobs. The government stipulated that Moluccans were not allowed to enter the precarious workforce, a rule that was an affront to the Moluccan men who had not accepted their discharge and still regarded themselves as soldiers. The government paid for living expenses, but beyond that, individuals received no more than pocket money. Many women earned additional income by working on farms.

Child-rearing was extremely authoritarian, with little room for discussion and severe punishments for misbehaviour. To be sure, in the 1950s, child-rearing among the Dutch was also authoritarian, but punishment of Moluccan children – such as having to stand unmoving outside for hours in wintertime, as told to me in an interview in the early 1990s, or whipping daughters with a belt because they had come home late, as Bartels reports (1989: 90) – was extreme even by Dutch standards of the day. Moluccans' experiences during the years of warfare, the humiliation that the men felt when they were discharged, and the sense of being wary outsiders in the Netherlands must have intensified the harshness of punishment. Additionally, showing respect and deference to one's seniors was a core value taken from the Moluccas.

Dutch Moluccan youth were not under the continuous control of adults, however. As in the Moluccas, younger children were relatively free to do what they wished, but if they transgressed upon the (largely tacit) rules, punishment followed without discussion. As Bartels (1989: 87–90) observes, children learned the rules through observation and punishment rather than by verbal explanation. Those who spent their childhood in the camps would later remember both the freedom they enjoyed in spending their time with their contemporaries and the harsh corporal and psychological punishment that they suffered when caught doing mischief. As the children grew up, their freedom became more restricted, especially in the case of young unmarried women who were kept under close supervision. Camp life was also largely isolated from Dutch society, with the exception of contact with doctors, nurses, social workers and, most important for the children, school teachers. The common language was Moluccan Malay. Since most, if not all, expected to return to a free South Moluccan Republic, there was little incentive to learn Dutch properly. Under these conditions solidarity was strong, but so were the tensions, not least due to the forced absence of meaningful work for the men.

When it became clear that Indonesia would never accept an independent South Moluccan Republic, the Dutch government changed its policies. From 1954 onwards, men were obliged to enter the workforce, which most did with zeal. However, with poor proficiency in Dutch and lacking the necessary skills to compete in the labour market, most found low-paid work solely as unskilled labourers (Bartels 1989: 129). In 1960 a new phase began, when the Moluccans were resettled in wards, built on the fringes of small towns throughout the country. Most welcomed the privacy and comfort of space, warm water and central heating, although some regretted that the solidarity among them was not quite as pronounced as it had been in the camps (Benda-Beckmann and Leatemia-Tomatala 1992: 31). Children went to Dutch schools where they mingled with Dutch children. As a result, their language skills were much better than those of their parents, and they also came into direct contact with Dutch values. A generation of better-educated Moluccans grew up and entered the labour market. But their authoritarian upbringing turned out to be an impediment when they tried to find jobs in a Dutch society that was shedding the hierarchies of the 1950s. Dutch employers and colleagues tended to interpret the Moluccans' ways of showing respect and deference as masking a kind of underhandedness. Unemployment among young Moluccan men of this Dutch-educated generation was high, and this hampered integration in the long run (Veenman 1990, 2001).

Moluccans maintained close relationships with family members in Moluccan wards located in other towns. In addition, organizations of persons from the same village of origin (*kumpulan*) were vital for the preparations that preceded important rites of passage such as baptisms, confirmations, weddings and funerals, upon which much time and resources were expended. Such events were part of an emerging Moluccan diasporic identity, an identity that suffered from the fact that 'normal channels for transmission' with the Moluccas 'were interrupted' (Bartels 1989: 109). The first generation of immigrants had lived away from the Moluccas for most of their lives, and its members had only a vague memory of Moluccan culture. What they taught their children was a highly idealized version in which Moluccan norms were reinterpreted in accordance with this image. This image served to keep alive the longing for a return to a free South Moluccan Republic. It also served to set Moluccan migrants apart from the Dutch environment. In addition, an image of proud and daring but also obedient and loyal soldiers, who had survived a violent war in the service of the Netherlands, rendered plausible their claims to receive support and recognition from the Dutch government and Dutch society at large. Both caring and violent, authoritarian images accompany the Moluccan community to the present day as resources upon which to draw with respect to a wide variety of actual behaviours.

Redefining Kinship Relations

In the Netherlands, Moluccan kinship relations became more broadly defined. Not only were members of the village of origin of one's father considered to be family; rather, the definition of family was extended to the village of origin of one's mother. In addition, the concept of *pela* became a core feature of Moluccan identity. Originally *pela* relations were established between members of distant villages, who promised mutual support in the highly volatile, dangerous times of the sixteenth and early seventeenth centuries, when Ternate, Tidore, the Dutch and the Portuguese fought for dominance over the spice trade in the region. These *pela* relations were seen as ritual kinship upon which Moluccans could rely in order to travel in relative safety from island to island. Marriage among members of villages that were *pela* partners was prohibited, but this had little more than symbolic relevance because of the distance separating the villages.

In the Netherlands, the old institution of *pela* came to serve as an important element of identification, and the interpretation of *pela* was expanded. Within the Moluccas, *pela* relations were traced through the village of the husband, which usually was the domicile of a married couple and their offspring. In the Netherlands, *pela* relations extended to the villages of origin of both husband and wife, or father and mother. This multiplied the number of persons who were considered to be one's *pela*. While, as mentioned above, the prohibition of marriage among *pela* in the Moluccas was virtually irrelevant due to the distance between islands, in this new context it was of real significance. Chances for young people to meet *pela* partners and fall in love with them were high, because *pela* might live together in the same neighbourhood or meet at the many ceremonies and feasts they attended together. Besides, the strict rule that one could not refuse a request for support from a *pela*, and that one should only approach a *pela* if absolutely necessary, attained a greater significance in the Netherlands than it presumably had in the Moluccas (Bartels 1989; Strijbosch 1988; Benda-Beckmann 2007: 267).

In the course of the 1980s and early 1990s, relationships between parents and children changed (Bartels 1989: 44). The aggression and violence in upbringing that was characteristic of life in the camps gave way to a softer form of upbringing that began to resemble child-rearing among the Dutch. Bartels (1989: 403–406) speaks of 'the gentle touch'. A growing sense that young adults should be granted more freedom became evident in their changing relations with their parents. Among the first and second generations, i.e. among those who had been born in Indonesia or in the Netherlands shortly after their parents had immigrated, it had been standard practice for unmarried adult children to live with their parents and hand over their wages to their mother in return for pocket money. In the third generation, this was no longer taken for granted. Unmarried adults continued to live with their parents, but now they merely made a contribution to the household budget, or none at all. Even when contributions were quite substantial, they were offered in a way that made clear that they should not be taken for granted (Benda-Beckmann and Leatemia-Tomatala 1992: 231–33; Benda-Beckmann 2015).

Caring Relations

In the 1980s and early 1990s, among the Dutch Moluccans, a change also occurred in caring relations for children and the aged.[2] The first generation of immigrants was growing old, and was less and less capable of caring for their grandchildren when the parents were at work. Instead, they began to need substantial care themselves. Care for the aged became an important identity marker for Moluccans. From early on, they had grown up with the myth that, on the Moluccas, 'the whole community' cares for the elderly. And that, they felt, was what they had to do in the Netherlands, too. There was a widespread belief among Moluccan immigrants that the Dutch placed their aged parents in homes for the elderly, where they lived a lonely life away from their relatives. That most Dutch elderly were and still are cared for by relatives did not dispel that belief. The Moluccans, in contrast to the behaviour they imputed to the Dutch, took great pride in caring for their ageing parents.

As long as the care of children implied primarily feeding and clothing them, and as long as there were relatively few aged Moluccans who needed extensive care, much time and energy could be spent on such needy parents. However, by the 1990s Moluccans with children had adopted from their Dutch environment a new and more encompassing idea of what constituted appropriate childcare – that is, devoting more time to one's children – and thus there was less time to spend with the aged. Many women felt caught between their duty towards their children and towards their parents. They continued to care for the latter, but not always to the degree that they desired or that was expected by their parents, based on their understanding of Moluccan norms of care. It was not something they talked about, and instead remained a source of silent suffering and tension. Yet putting aged parents in homes for the elderly was out of the question (Benda-Beckmann and Leatemia-Tomatala 1992; Benda-Beckmann 2015). Even today, most elderly Dutch Moluccans are cared for by relatives, although there are now retirement homes with branches for people with a background in the Dutch Indies, featuring special food and personnel (personal communication, Jeanny Vreeswijk-Manusiwa, 9 February 2018).

Extending support and care to relatives back in the Moluccas was also an important expression of Moluccan identification. Connections with the Central Moluccas intensified when travelling to Indonesia became possible from the 1970s onwards. Members of the first generation went to see their close relatives – siblings and cousins, aunts and uncles and even parents. They brought money and gifts for their own relatives, and they also carried money to the relatives of friends or relatives who were unable to make the trip. *Kumpulan* also collected money for the restoration of churches, mosques or dilapidated village halls (Strijbosch 1988). Members of the following generations, who had never been to the Moluccas, also felt obliged to support their relatives there and their parents' or grandparents' communities of origin. Those who could afford the trip travelled to the Moluccas to meet their relatives, but they also wanted to find out about their *adat* – that is, their customs or ways of life – and sought ritual, even transcendental, experiences in the Moluccas.

However, they found a very different society from the one they had created in their imagination after listening to the tales told by the first generation of immigrants, one in which 'the community as a whole' cared for everyone. In the Moluccas care was primarily a matter for close relatives and sometimes extended to neighbours, but there existed little sense that the entire community was responsible for all of its members (Benda-Beckmann 2007: 271–75). When visiting Moluccan communities, they realized that not all elderly were cared for according to the standards of their communities back in the Netherlands, and what care was extended often seemed cold. This came as a shock, and resulted in a sense of shame so deep that few dared talk about it upon their return to the Netherlands (Benda-Beckmann and Leatemia-Tomatala 1992: 242). For a number of older Dutch Moluccans these experiences contributed to their decision not to seek the permanent return to the Moluccas that they had previously envisioned, although it should be added that the overriding reason to remain in the Netherlands was to stay close to their grandchildren.

The second shock was that their Indonesian Moluccan relatives showed little inhibition in asking for money, clothes and various other things, requests that the Dutch Moluccans found inappropriate but difficult to resist. Indonesian Moluccans, in turn, were convinced that their Dutch relatives were very rich. Who else could afford to travel all the way to Indonesia? They did not understand, or did not believe, that the visitors were far from wealthy and had saved for years to make this one trip possible. They approached relatives from the Netherlands in the same manner as they would approach wealthy relatives elsewhere in Indonesia, feeling no qualms about asking for all the support they thought they could get. In contrast to the Dutch Moluccans, wealthy relatives in Indonesia had long learned techniques for evading requests they considered inappropriate.

Over time, educated Dutch Moluccans felt that more was needed than the support of relatives and the restoration of buildings. They began to set up structural development projects, although this came to a temporary halt with the upheavals around the time of the fall of the Suharto regime in 1998. Being Moluccan, they presented themselves to funding agencies as uniquely positioned for such projects, under the assumption that they shared common approaches to work with the Moluccan recipients of the projects. But here, too, Dutch Moluccans met with unexpected differences. Dutch Moluccans, having adopted a Dutch way of organizing, had to deal with differing notions among their counterparts in the Moluccas, whose modes of organization were more clientelist and less interested in accountability.

The Dutch Moluccans, in short, had developed new notions with respect to transnational kin relations, appropriate care and support and related rights and obligations, and they organized projects and acted according to these notions in the Moluccas. Such notions, along with their preconceived images of Indonesian Molucca society, did not match those of the persons at the other end of the intensifying transnational relations.

Authority and Violence

Thus far we have discussed the developing norms for caring relations. There is another strand that deserves attention, one that has to do with authority and violence. Arguably, the harsh child-rearing practices that characterized this immigrant community in its first decades reflected the imagery of violent experiences during the Indonesian War of Independence and the Dutch policies in its aftermath. This imagery of authority and the potential for violence – an important element in Moluccan identity – has been kept alive and, at various times, has been drawn upon in notably different ways. Violence is kept under wraps for the most part, but it may surface in response to developments and occurrences that do not appear to have any particular connection to the past.

In the Dutch Moluccan community, the first outbursts of violence occurred in the 1970s with the occupation of the Indonesian Embassy, the hijacking of a train and the occupation of two schools. These actions were inspired, in part, by the violent kidnappings and killings of the Rote Armee Fraktion (RAF) in Germany and the Brigate Rosse (BR) in Italy, but motivations for the actions of the Dutch Moluccans were entirely different. While the RAF and BR targeted the bourgeois elites, the desperate acts of the Moluccans were intended to force the Dutch government to recognize their special status as loyal allies and to help establish a free South Moluccan Republic. Once again, the Dutch government disappointed the Moluccan community. Instead of entering into serious discussions and negotiations, the government called on the armed forces and brought the occupation and hijackings to a bloody end, believing that only a violent response would quell the call for a free South Moluccan Republic. Although most Moluccans did not support the hijackings, they were furious about the show of force and the lack of sensitivity on the side of the government. Old scars were reopened and the Moluccan community closed ranks against an unresponsive Dutch government – and against society at large. It took half a century, and a court claim for compensation by relatives of one of the victims of the shootings, for the government to open an official enquiry into the question of whether the government had deliberately shot an unarmed hijacker. Heated debate in the media showed how sensitive this violent episode remained. This also occurred in a wider political environment in which the government has been forced to re-evaluate its role in what is now sometimes referred to as the Indonesian War instead of the more common euphemism – *politionele acties*, or police actions.

In a very different way and under different circumstances, and once again induced by external developments, the memory of violence re-emerged in the transnational Moluccan community during the disruptive period surrounding the demise of the Suharto regime at the turn of the twenty-first century. Throughout Indonesia, the armed forces stirred unrest with the help of vigilante groups and thugs. As Schlee (2008: 213) has argued with respect to the similar use of violence among Somali warlords, such strategies served to demonstrate the indispensability of the armed forces in re-establishing and maintaining control, and to secure for them a powerful position within the Indonesian government. The growing tensions between Muslims and Christians in the Moluccas, and the assertions by army officers that Moluccans were still seeking to establish a South Moluccan Republic, provided convenient justifications for allowing them to react in a heavy-handed manner.

On the Central Moluccas, relationships between Muslims and Christians had traditionally been peaceful. Bartels (1978) argues that this is because they believed they had once shared a common pre-Christian and pre-Muslim religion. Although most Moluccan villages were either exclusively Muslim or Christian, several had a religiously mixed population. The provincial capital, Ambon town, was both ethnically and religiously mixed, even though ethnic and religious groups tended to live in separate neighbourhoods. In 1999, the relaxed relationship between adherents of the two religions came to a sudden end when a simple disagreement between a *becak* (bike taxi) driver and a taxi driver evolved into what came close to a civil war in which Christian and Muslim communities were pitted against each other (Klinken 2001). The speed at which violence escalated and the extent of the violence took many Dutch Moluccan observers by surprise. Although the escalation was a direct effect of external meddling by the Indonesian army and allied vigilante groups, the Moluccan code of behaviour that an act of violence called for retaliation was also a contributing factor. However, traditionally the rules of retaliation stipulated that the counterattack should be directed at certain groups of persons only and take place immediately, lest the violence be deemed inappropriate. Moreover, acts of violence should be followed by negotiations among the elderly relatives of the perpetrators. With the demise of the Suharto regime and with threats of secession in various parts of Indonesia, these rules of retaliation were not followed, and the constraining mechanisms, which usually served to prevent the escalation of violence, were ineffective.[3] Often, young men, upon hearing that a church or a mosque elsewhere was ablaze, would immediately set off to avenge this presumed act of violence and fight indiscriminately with persons of the other faith, without knowing the identity of the perpetrators or even the identity of those with whom they were fighting. Elderly relatives, even if they so desired, lacked sufficient authority to restrain them; furthermore, because violence was committed against unknown persons, conducting customary negotiations was difficult to organize. Customary mechanisms were also ineffective because of the involvement of external actors, such as the various branches of the armed forces and vigilante groups. As a result of this violence in the Moluccas, the long-standing good relationships between Christians and Muslim were destroyed, and the population became more segregated than it had been previously.

Dutch Moluccans followed the events with growing anxiety. For some it revived the idea of a longed-for South Moluccan Republic for which their fathers and grandfathers had fought. And a small minority even supported the use of violence, arguing that they could not leave their relatives undefended. But most felt caught between the wish and obligation to help and protect their relatives and the knowledge that any financial support might be converted into weapons, thus contributing to an escalation of the violence, which they strongly rejected.

It was only in 2003, when the political situation in Indonesia stabilized, and the armed forces were confident that they would retain their central position, that the violence ended and negotiations began (Bräuchler 2010). However, the new level of segregation was not undone. This was not only a result of mistrust among Christians and Muslims; it was also an unintended outcome of government policy. For example, the Christian enclave in the predominantly Muslim villages of Hila and Kaitetu had been evacuated when people from a neighbouring village threatened to kill them. As they were warned in time by their Muslim neighbours, there were no casualties, but their houses were set on fire. They fled across the mountain and settled in a related Christian village, where the provincial government financed the building of new houses for them. After peace had returned, leading Muslims in Hila-Kaitetu signalled to their Christian co-villagers that they would welcome their return. However, the provincial government was not prepared to provide additional funding to rebuild their houses in their home village, since, in the eyes of the government, they already had adequate housing. Nor did the evicted persons have the means to rebuild their houses in Hila-Kaitetu. Therefore, they remained in their new Christian village, and Hila-Kaitetu no longer had the mixed population of which its residents had once been so proud.

A third example in which Moluccan men draw on the imagery of violence as a constitutive element of Moluccan identity in order to explain their behaviour concerns the motorcycle club Satudarah (One Blood). Founded in 1990 in Moordrecht by Dutch Moluccans, it is no longer exclusively Moluccan and has many non-Moluccan members; yet it is still regarded as a Moluccan motorcycle club. Since then, it has expanded across the border. It now has seventy-six chapters in eighteen countries and has entered into fierce competition with other motorcycle groups such as the Hell's Angels and Bandolino. Each of these motorcycle clubs is known for violence and involvement in drugs and other crimes for which members frequently have to serve time in prison. But in Satudarah a connection is explicitly made between violence and its specific Moluccan history in that the club's founders saw themselves as the heirs to Moluccan – or, going further back in history, to Alifuru (the indigenous inhabitants of the Central Moluccas) – warriors.[4]

In 2015, when a new generation of leaders came to power in Satudarah, they commissioned a documentary film. The film deserves closer study because of what it reveals not only about the role of violence in the motorcycle club, but also about how the club operates in transnational networks extending to the Moluccas, and about the misunderstandings that occurred when its leaders visited the

Moluccas (Valk and Gavan 2015). For example, in the film, one of the new leaders tells of the extremely violent upbringing that he and his male companions experienced in the camps. The film also shows that Satudarah imposes an absolute ban on disclosing information about the inner workings of the club to outsiders, violation of which is punished by serious bodily violence and eviction from the club. The documentary further shows that members feel an unconditional obligation to obey orders, even if it involves the use of violence when required. The motorcycle club also seems to serve as a safety net for some young, troubled delinquents. As mentioned above, many members, including club leaders, have served time in prison for crimes related to drugs. This is not a reason for exclusion; on the contrary, the documentary shows that a leader is warmly welcomed back after having served his time in prison. The Dutch government is concerned about the high level of violence and the increasing sophistication of drug crimes committed by members of motorcycle clubs and has attempted to convince the courts to ban the clubs outright. On 18 June 2018, the court of first instance of the Hague convicted four leaders of Satudarah for violence against other motorcycle clubs, production of drugs and drug trafficking, illegal possession of arms, and extortion. The court also placed a ban on Satudarah as an organization that encouraged its members to commit criminal offences.

The documentary film also follows four new leaders of Satudarah on their visit to the Moluccas. The purpose of the visit is to allow the new leaders to be confirmed, ritually, and to establish a chapter of the motorcycle club in the Moluccas. The film shows the group being received by the governor of the Province of Maluku, who clearly does not know anything about the motorcycle club – had he realized it was involved in criminal practices, he would not have received them, for drugs are regarded as a serious threat to the public order in Indonesia.

The documentary also shows the performance of the ritual in which motorcycle club leaders seek confirmation of their authority. To that end, they travel to the village of Huku-Anakotta on the island of Seram, the large island north of Ambon, where the 'real' Alifuru lived and where the pre-Christian and pre-Islamic common religion originated. It is there that they find specialists in making connections with the ancestors, who are willing to perform a ritual for them. However, the ritual that is shown in the film has little to do with traditional rituals that are meaningful to the local population. While the Dutch Moluccan participants seem to be nervous and overwhelmed by the transcendental experience of the ritual, the hosts who perform the ritual appear relaxed and even amused. They clearly have never heard of Satudarah, and, during the ritual, they even have to ask the name of the organization for which the ritual is performed. Some of the Satudarah participants speak Malay during the performance, but others speak only Dutch, which their hosts do not understand. This leads to some interesting misinterpretations. The Satudarah leaders say that they have come because they regard the people from Huku-Anakotta as their ancestors (*orang tua tua*), although 'ancestors', in the Moluccan meaning of the equivalent word, only refers to those who are deceased. The hosts from Huku-Anakotta graciously overlook the mistake, invoke God and the ancestors (*nenek moyang*),[5] and tell the Satudarah men, who have travelled all the way to the Moluccas, that they regard them as their brothers.

The documentary film thus shows how the same ritual is interpreted as a mystical and transcendent experience by the Dutch Moluccans and as a slightly peculiar and perhaps playful event by the hosts. This becomes particularly clear when the hosts encourage the Dutch Moluccans to chew the betel nut. If it stays white, they are told jokingly, it means they are bad people, but if it becomes red (which is inevitable when chewed in combination with chalk), they are good people. The documentary gives no evidence that the Dutch Moluccans understand this joke; rather, they seem to take their hosts' statement at face value. On the other hand, there are also no signs that the people who perform the ritual have the slightest knowledge of the violent character of Satudarah. The ritual, in other words, is hardly meaningful for the ritual specialists who perform it, but for the Dutch Moluccans, it has a serious metaphysical significance, obtaining its true meaning in the Dutch context. The imagery of their connection with a long-ago Moluccan history as confirmed by a constructed ritual serves to establish their authority in their motorcycle club in the Netherlands, as well as within their family, as the film seems to suggest.

Conclusions

The common background in colonial military service, the settlement in the Netherlands after Indonesia's independence in 1945, the memories of violent warfare, the humiliation at having been discharged from the colonial army, the disappointment in a Dutch government that could not fulfil its promise of a South Moluccan Republic – together these served to bring about in Dutch Moluccans the construction of an imagery in which specific norms and practices of care and of authority and violence became deeply engrained. In turn, these affected relations of Dutch Moluccans within Moluccan transnational networks and served to strengthen their identity within a Dutch environment that many experienced as hostile, causing them to insist on claims for special treatment and support from the government. The imagery of kinship, of child-rearing in the early days of settlement in the Netherlands, and of typical Moluccan forms of care and support served as a way to navigate between the changing norms of Dutch society at large and their specific Moluccan identity. While care for relatives, especially the elderly, retained a high moral value, the kind of care and the mode of extension changed over time in the Netherlands, where they gradually adapted to Dutch moral notions of care and support. But the change did not occur simultaneously or to the same degree in all generations, which sometimes led to frictions and tensions. During their long and forced physical separation from relatives in the Moluccas, migrants to the Netherlands developed a thoroughly idealized image of community life, which they projected onto their communities of origin. However, once contact was re-established, the moral duties that Dutch Moluccans had developed for the care for relatives and communities on the Moluccas appeared to be ill adjusted to local notions of care, support and organization, putting the relationships between them under pressure.

The violent history in the colonial army and the unmet promises for a South Moluccan Republic also added elements of authority and violence to Moluccan identity that came to serve quite diverse purposes. For the younger generations, for whom child-rearing had become milder, less authoritarian and more discursive in response to the Dutch environment, the image was based on the stories about the extremely authoritarian and harsh child-rearing in the migrant camps. The hijackings in the 1970s drew on an imagery of the violent past and the dream of a South Moluccan Republic, affording their acts of violence a degree of plausibility, even though most Dutch Moluccans no longer believed that the dream of a republic would ever be realized and did not support the hijackings. The hijackings also served to force the Dutch government to take responsibility for the Dutch Moluccans who had served as loyal allies in the colonial army.

The upheavals in Indonesia around the end of the Suharto regime rekindled dreams of a South Moluccan Republic and forced Dutch Moluccans to take a stand. For a small minority, the strong moral obligation to support relatives in need 'back home' required taking the risk of contributing to the violence. Finally, the way that the leaders of the motorcycle club Satudarah presented themselves in their documentary film suggests that the imagery of authority and violence also fed into moral obligations within the motorcycle club and the specific ways of identifying as Moluccans and as a Moluccan motorcycle club. Yet this did not preclude Satudarah from being inclusive of people of different ethnic backgrounds. The leaders sought confirmation on the Moluccas in a created ritual, in which the various participants had diverging interpretations of what the ritual meant, and which served to boost their authority within an exclusively Dutch context.

Finally, the various forms of care and support extended within the Netherlands and to relatives and communities in the Moluccas, and the examples from the documentary film of Satudarah, show that the interpretations of these relationships and the moral ideas and norms related to them have undergone considerable change within the Netherlands. Within the transnational Moluccan networks, they vary according to the position of the participants within these networks.

Keebet von Benda-Beckmann is professor emeritus at Martin Luther University Halle/Wittenberg and Associate at the Max Planck Institute for Social Anthropology in Halle; guest researcher of the Van Vollenhoven Institute for Law and Development at Leiden University; Associated Principal Investigator at BIGSAS at Bayreuth University; and member of the executive body of the Commission on Legal Pluralism. She has published on temporal and spatial dimensions of legal pluralism; anthropological roots of global legal pluralism; dispute management; social (in)security; property; and decentralization. She is co-author of *Political and Legal Transformations of an Indonesian Polity* (Cambridge, 2013) and associate editor of the *Journal of Legal Pluralism*.

Notes

I thank John Eidson for his thoughtful and constructive comments.

1. The South Moluccan Republic was to include what is today the Central Moluccas and the Southeast Moluccas. Dutch Moluccans continued to use the term South Moluccan Republic (Ind. *Republik Maluku Selatan* [RMS]).
2. This section is based on research on local forms of social security that I carried out with my late husband, Franz von Benda-Beckmann, in 1984 and 1985 (Benda-Beckmann and Benda-Beckmann 2007), and on research on the emancipation of Moluccan women in the Netherlands, which I carried out with Francy Leatemia-Tomatala in 1990–1991 (Benda-Beckmann and Leatemia-Tomatala 1992).
3. See Turner (this volume) and Turner (2017) for more on retaliation as a constraining mechanism.
4. Curiously, the emblems on their motorcycle jackets resemble American First Nation motifs. I do not know the reasons for this.
5. In the film, *orang tua tua* and *nenek moyang* are both translated as 'ancestors'.

References

Bartels, Dieter. 1978. 'Guarding the Invisible Mountain: Intervillage Alliances, Religious Syncretism and Ethnic Identity among Ambonese Christians and Moslems in the Moluccas', PhD dissertation. Ithaca, NY: Cornell University.

———. 1989. *Moluccans in Exile: A Struggle for Ethnic Survival – Socialization, Identity Formation, and Emancipation among an East-Indonesian Minority in the Netherlands*. Leiden: Centrum voor Onderzoek naar Maatschappelijke Tegenstellingen.

Benda-Beckmann, Franz von and Keebet von Benda-Beckmann. 2007. *Social Security between Past and Future: Ambonese Networks of Care and Support*. Münster: Lit.

Benda-Beckmann, Keebet von. 2007 [1991]. 'Developing Families: Moluccan Women and Changing Patterns of Social Security in the Netherlands', in Franz von Benda-Beckmann and Keebet von Benda-Beckmann (eds), *Social Security Between Past and Future: Ambonese Networks of Care and Support*. Münster: Lit, pp. 257–79.

———. 2015. 'Social Security in Transnational Legal Space: Limitations and Opportunities', in S. Köngeter and W. Smith (eds), *Transnational Agency and Migration: Actors, Movements and Social Support*. London: Routledge, pp. 245–61.

Benda-Beckmann, Keebet von and Francy Leatemia-Tomatala. 1992. *De emancipatie van Molukse vrouwen in Nederland*. Utrecht: Jan van Arkel.
Bräuchler, Birgit. 2010. 'The Revival Dilemma: Reflections on Human Rights, Self-Determination and Legal Pluralism in Eastern Indonesia', *Journal of Legal Pluralism and Unofficial Law* 62: 1–42.
Crossley, Nick. 2011. *Towards Relational Sociology*. London: Routledge.
Glick Schiller, Nina. 2005. 'Transborder Citizenship: An Outcome of Legal Pluralism within Transnational Social Fields', in Franz von Benda-Beckmann, Keebet von Benda-Beckmann and Anne Griffiths (eds), *Mobile People, Mobile Law: Expanding Legal Relations in a Contracting World*. Aldershot and Burlington: Ashgate, pp. 27–50.
Klinken, Gerry van. 2001. 'The Maluku Wars of 1999: Bringing Society Back', *Indonesia* 71: 1–26.
Limpach, Rémy. 2014. 'Business as Usual: Dutch Mass Violence in the Indonesian War of Independence 1945–1949', in Bart Luttikhuis and A. Dirk Moses (eds), *Colonial Counterinsurgency and Mass Violence: The Dutch Empire in Indonesia*. New York: Routledge, pp. 64–90.
Schlee, Günther. 2004. 'Taking Sides and Constructing Identities: Reflections on Conflict Theory', *Journal of the Royal Anthropological Institute* 10(1): 135–56.
———. 2008. 'Ethnologie und Politikberatung: Erfahrungen mit dem Somalia-Friedensprozess', in John R. Eidson (ed.), *Das Anthropologische Projekt: Perspektiven aus der Forschungslandschaft Halle/Leipzig*. Leipzig: Leipziger Universitätsverlag, pp. 198–216.
Steijlen, Fridus. 2015. 'In and Out of Uniform: Moluccan Soldiers in the Dutch Colonial Army', in Eric Storm and Ali Al Tuma (eds), *Colonial Soldiers in Europe, 1914–1945: Aliens in Uniform in Wartime Societies*. Abingdon: Taylor and Francis, pp. 229–48.
———. 2018. *Tjakalele bij Volle Maan*. Amsterdam: Vrije Universiteit Amsterdam.
Strijbosch, Fons. 1988. 'Informal Social Security among Moluccan Immigrants in the Netherlands', in Franz von Benda-Beckmann, Keebet von Benda-Beckmann, Eric S. Casiño, Frank Hirtz, Gordon R. Woodman and Hans F. Zacher (eds), *Between Kinship and the State: Social Security and Law in Developing Countries*. Dordrecht: Foris, pp. 169–85.
Turner, Bertram. 2017. 'On Retaliation: Conceptual Plurality, Transdisciplinary Research, Rifts, Blurrings and Translations', in Bertram Turner and Günther Schlee (eds), *On Retaliation: Towards an Interdisciplinary Understanding of a Basic Human Condition*. New York and Oxford: Berghahn, pp. 1–25.
Valk, Joost van der and Mags Gavan (dirs.). 2015. *Satudarah One Blood*. Documentary. Amsterdam: Teledoc supported by COBO, Dutch Film Fund, NPO, De Familie Film & TV and NTR.
Veenman, Justus. 1990. *De arbeidsmarkt van allochtonen in Nederland, in het bijzonder van Molukkers*. Groningen: Wolters-Noordhoff.
———. 2001. *Molukse jongeren in Nederland: Integratie met de rem erop*. Assen: Van Gorkum.

CHAPTER 16

MULTISCALAR SOCIAL RELATIONS OF DISPOSSESSION AND EMPLACEMENT

NINA GLICK SCHILLER

In so many places in the world today, impoverished workers and an increasingly precarious middle class seem to be voting or demonstrating their way into fascist movements against those defined as outside the nation. In this fractured political landscape, what can those of us who aspire to social and economic justice do? Joe Hill, a Swedish-American anarchist union organizer of the early twentieth century, who was murdered in Utah by a government firing squad for his activism, advised us to not 'waste any time in mourning. Organize' (Taylor 1990). However, the question of organizing with whom to do what remains unanswered in this response to repressive violence. Answering this question, which falls within the purview of anthropological research and theory building, has become ever more pressing in our current fractious times in which the forces of reaction seem to be doing the most successful organizing. In order to organize effectively for social and economic justice, we need to understand and confront the social dynamics that move people into political life, and then we need to identify ways to respond to those dynamics.

Various lineages of anthropologists have highlighted the need for ethnographers to understand the interconnections between actors on the ground and broader social forces in order to bring about change. Günther Schlee, celebrated in this volume, can be counted among these ranks. Insisting that tracing the interconnections between actors on the ground and institutions of power is an aspect of anthropological research, he has argued that 'any theory about societal processes (the emergence of coherence, integration, conflict or social change) demands that we link the actor's perspective with the system perspective' (Schlee

2018a: 8). Moreover, 'anthropology does have a role in setting political aims and making moral judgments' (Schlee 2018a: 32, n15).

Building on this mandate, this chapter enters into current debates about migration, one of the flashpoints of past and present right-wing politics. I do so in dialogue with Günther Schlee's (2008, 2018a, 2018b) insistence on the significance of the broader interconnections that emerge from various forms of individual interaction. Tracing interconnections, constituted as constructions of the social within networks of differential power, takes us out of the classic and almost ubiquitous Western binary of self and other, native and stranger, local and global.

Deploying a multiscalar approach to the accumulation of capital by dispossession (Çağlar and Glick Schiller 2018), this chapter provides a way to explore the dynamics of power within which people – migrants and non-migrants – constitute their social relations. This exploration entails going beyond ethnographic descriptions of relationships and researching instead the social relations that entangle people in processes that dispossess and displace them. Processes of dispossession can lead displaced people to a politics of difference and exclusion or to a commitment to forging social relations based on shared domains of commonality and aspirations for social justice. The analysis is illustrated with observations drawn from ethnographic fieldwork that Ayşe Çağlar and I have presented in numerous publications, culminating in a co-authored book that situates migrants among the 'makers' of cities (Çağlar and Glick Schiller 2018).[1] We conducted our research in three disempowered but regenerating cities: Halle/Saale, Saxony-Anhalt, in eastern Germany; Manchester, New Hampshire, in the northeast of the United States; and Mardin, Turkey, on the Syrian and Iraqi border. However, in this chapter I focus on Halle and Manchester, where I was personally engaged in the fieldwork.[2]

Theorizing Social Relations without Methodological Nationalism

Critics of methodological nationalism, which underlies so much of migration studies, have argued that many researchers, including those who oppose and support migration, have approached migrants through a homogenizing framework (Wimmer and Glick Schiller 2003; Amelina et al. 2012; De Genova 2013a). A methodological nationalist orientation takes the nation-state as the unit of study and analysis and posits a uniform national culture, which precludes addressing the implications of multiple diversities within the nation-state and within migrant populations. Yet populations living within national borders and those coming from elsewhere vary, in class and wealth, regional culture, rural-urban differentiation, gender, age, sexual orientation, politics and dialect. In contrast, migrants are pictured as uniformly culturally different, frozen, analytically, in a communal, timeless, premodern space (Çağlar 2018; Glick Schiller 2012, 2018).

Even if they are personally supportive of migration and advocate a politics of tolerance of difference and hospitality to migrants, many scholars define migrants as 'strangers' (Alexander 2003; Candea and Da Col 2012). Consequently, they categorize social relations between migrants and non-migrants as 'bridging difference' (Putnam 2007: 138; Wise and Velayutham 2009; Alba and Foner 2015). Migration policy-makers have tended to see migrants as foreign elements who must be integrated because of their supposed difference from some imagined national normality. Urban developers have often celebrated migrants for their 'difference', which they see as contributing to the project of branding cities as diverse, cosmopolitan and open to the world (Binnie et al. 2006).[3] It is becoming increasingly obvious that any approach to migration that uses national history and boundaries to imagine and categorize difference, or that approaches migrants as somehow different from the relationalities that make us human, can readily become a system of exclusion. It is, therefore, politically urgent that scholars, policy-makers and activists move beyond the binaries of difference generated by national imaginaries and theories of otherness. Scholars, especially, must investigate social relations forged as people search for lives that speak to their broader aspirations and desires.

Past Social Theories of Difference and Relationality

In Western social theory, the naturalization of binaries of difference between self/other and native/stranger emerged within a political project of conceptualizing and maintaining social order and cohesion (see, for example, Coser 1998 [1956]).[4] As Schlee (2018a) notes, those holding disproportionate amounts of wealth and power have been concerned to maintain their control and, simultaneously, legitimate the social order and its system of ascribed unequal differences. It is important to revisit several moments in the history of classic Western social and political theory that contributed to the exclusionary nationalist politics of the contemporary moment. This historical retrospective, which provides the foundation for a multiscalar analysis of networked connections of dispossession, displacement and struggles for emplacement on the part of migrants and non-migrants, illuminates a path towards a more liberatory politics.

Theories about the nature of society and its boundaries developed as part of the growth and global expansion of European capitalism over several centuries. When the social sciences emerged, stimulated by Auguste Comte's discussion of the need to develop a scientific approach to social statics and dynamics, its subject of study was human society (Lenzer 1975). For Comte, society was organic in the sense that interdependent social institutions functioned as organs in the social body. The boundaries of the social organism were not the territorial borders of a specific state or nation, but instead included 'the whole of the human species and chiefly the whole of the white race' (Lenzer 1975: 263). In this lineage of social thought – the one to which much of academic social science lays claim – binaries of difference were initially about racialized otherness.

By the late nineteenth century, within renewed imperialist competition, social theorists began to territorialize the concept of society, which they defined within the boundaries of states defined as nations. In this way, concepts of race and nation were brought together. Nationalists imagined each nation-state as a society sharing a patrimony of a common culture, language and biological heritage. Writing in the 1890s, Herbert Spencer defined 'society as a plurality of people occupying a specific territory and between whom various common features obtain' (Martindale 1960: 71). Theorists as well as researchers began to project the notion of enclosed, bounded, racialized and territorialized populations backward into human history before the rise of states or even settled populations (e.g. Tönnies 1957 [1887]).

However, at various times in the development of social theory, unbounded understandings of the social have emerged. Many of these theorists were propelled by their recognition of the global dispossessive nature of capitalist accumulation and by the anti-colonial humanism that this recognition produced. These include, especially, proponents of various forms of Marxist theory, starting with Karl Marx (1887 [1867]), and continuing with the anti-imperialism of V.I. Lenin (1984 [1917]) and Rosa Luxemburg (1951 [1913]). Marx (1887 [1867]: 543) established the groundwork by clarifying that 'capital is not a thing, but a social relation between persons'. This social relations perspective was foundational to the anthropology of Max Gluckman (1940) and others in the Manchester school as well as to Eric Williams' (1944) explorations linking the development of European capitalism, alterations in African political systems, and the Atlantic slave trade.

In a different intellectual lineage, Georg Simmel, writing at the beginning of the twentieth century, also offered an alternative to binary views of the social. Simmel (2002) is usually cited for his discussion of 'the stranger', in which social relations are shaped by a primordial distinction between self and stranger.[5] However, Simmel also developed an understanding of sociability (1949 [1903]) that can lead theorists to highlight the human experiences of commonality of affect rather than difference.[6] This led him to establish social relations as the basis of society. According to Simmel, 'society is the supra-singular structure which is nonetheless not abstract ... Society is the generality that has, simultaneously, concrete vitality' (Simmel 1971: 69, quoted in Emirbayer 1997: 88).

Despite the ongoing theorization of relationalities, in the conjuncture that followed the First World War, the conflation of the nation-state with society became hegemonic. Global interconnections were obscured, and societies conceived as nation-states served as the units of study and analysis in the social sciences for most of the twentieth century. However, the history of methodological nationalist perspectives within the theorizing of social relations is not lineal. For a short conjunctural moment in the last decades of the twentieth century, as the implementation of neoliberal agendas ended tariff barriers and allowed the free flow of finance capital, the global economy, which had been visible during the height of colonial empires in the nineteenth century, was once again readily observable. Scholars around the world transcended the methodological nationalist perspectives of their disciplines and developed a scholarship of globalization and transnationalism.[7] As social relations became mediated by the Internet and as international tourism became a mainstay of economies globally, scholars spoke of the end of borders and boundaries (Mittleman 1994). But migration scholarship never abandoned its homogenized categories of cultural difference. By the first decades of the twenty-first century, racialized culturally homogeneous nation-states were once again being equated with the boundaries of society. Most researchers returned to equating the unit of social cohesion and public welfare with a bounded political unit (e.g. Kymlicka 2015). In this way, while pursuing the question of how to keep society together, they support the continuation of the current social order and its systems of inequality and domination.

Definitions for a Relational Multiscalar Analysis

A relational approach, also identified as a 'transactional approach' in some disciplines (Emirbayer 1997: 287), resonates with those social theorists who emphasize that humans live in networks which, by the nature of their constitution, must be understood as unbounded. In this perspective, the social world is constituted as networks of networks, a transnational social field that extends across political borders. Broadening the initial argument that migrants live in transnational social fields (Basch et al. 1994; Glick Schiller et al. 1992) and building on the work of critical geographers such as Neil Brenner (1999; 2011), Ayşe Çağlar and I have argued that multiscalar perspectives on capital accumulation by dispossession, displacement and emplacement provide an unbounded but power-laden approach to social theory and methodology (Glick Schiller 2015, 2018; Çağlar and Glick Schiller 2018).

The term 'multiscalar' can serve as a 'shorthand to speak of sociospatial spheres of practice that are constituted in relationship to each other and within various hierarchies of networks of power' (Çağlar and Glick Schiller 2018: 8). Multiscalar processes are constituted by global, national, local, economic, political, religious, cultural, organizational, familial and individual actors who develop multiple contending and intersecting networks. In the current conjuncture, scalar trajectories of power are constituted within processes of capital accumulation, including accumulation by dispossession. Through their interactions and contradictions over time, networked actors with differing kinds and degrees of power transform and are transformed by the social and physical world in which they live. These networked actors link together territorially-based but unbounded political and economic units, including households, villages, towns and cities, nation-states and regions.

> The concept of multiscalar social fields enables us to address and capture aspects of social relations through which broader social forces enable, shape, constrain, and are acted upon by individuals . . . Migrants and non-migrants react to dispossessive forces by becoming part of social relations where they contribute to the remaking of the institutional nexus of city-level, regional, national, supranational, and globe-spanning actors. (Çağlar and Glick Schiller 2018: 9)

Among the merits of multiscalar analysis is that by placing migrants and non-migrants within the same networked transformative processes, it eliminates the native-stranger divide produced by thinking in terms of borders. At the same time, as compared to concepts of assemblage, multiscalar analysis specifies the social processes of capital accumulation that actuate contemporary society. These processes constitute the dynamics of social relations as they become connected within networks of unequal power (Brenner, Madden and Wachsmuth 2011). As deployed by most anthropologists, geographers or migration scholars, assemblage theory, which is also a relational approach, remains on the level of descriptions of randomly connected collections, a form of Victorian cabinet of curiosities. In its Deleuzian origins, the assemblage is generated not by a theory of the social but by the psychodynamics of desire.

As a processual and relational analysis, a multiscalar approach discards the notion of levels of analysis which disassemble individual, social, economic and political processes. A multiscalar approach also abandons the concept of embedded territorial scales, which geographers have deployed in the past to denote a fixed hierarchy of bounded units such as household, neighbourhood, city, province and nation-state.[8] In the multiscalar analysis that Ayşe Çağlar and I have developed, hierarchy does not connote fixed relations of territorially-based power but highlights situated, networked relations of unequal power that are produced within processes of dispossession and emplacement (see also Sassen 2014).

Dispossession as a Relational Social Process

Marx (1887 [1867]: 507) used the term 'primitive accumulation' in his analysis of the processes through which populations are dispossessed of their 'social means of subsistence and of production', which are then transformed into capital. Initial forms of dispossession included the violent seizure of land and resources during the expansion of Europe, i.e. the conquest and colonization of another people's land. But they also included what Marx (1887 [1867]: 513) aptly called 'the parliamentary form of . . . robbery' such as the enclosure of the commons in England.

Drawing on Marx's (1887 [1867] and Luxemburg's (1951 [1913]) analysis of the accumulative processes of capitalism, researchers in contemporary critical development studies (Glassman 2006), geography (Harvey 2004) and anthropology (Collins 2012) have investigated the processes of accruing capital by appropriating the social means of subsistence. These processes are now widely referred to as accumulation by dispossession. David Harvey (2004) has argued that dispossessions, especially in the form of urban regeneration and its resulting displacements, have become indispensable to capital accumulation in the current conjuncture. Certainly, in the past several decades, accumulation by dispossession has come to play a prominent role in many economic sectors around the world. Capital is accrued through multiple forms of appropriation rather than at the point of production by workers' direct input of labour.

Forms of accumulation by dispossession include the seizure of precious resources such as minerals or water, public spaces, and individually held or communal land. However, variations on the theme of dispossession also include fines, fees, penalties, usage charges added to rent, debt, confiscation and property forfeiture, some of which Marx began to examine in *Capital* II and III. The expropriation by corporate interests of the wealth accumulated from individual worker's pensions and programmes providing social benefits can also be considered as a form of dispossession. Some forms of appropriation are centuries old but have new monikers such as 'privatization' and 'public/private development'. In public/private development, public money is used to obtain land and buildings – often public and obtained at below market rates – that are then developed for private profit.

It is important to note that the dispossessive legally-enforced processes of expropriation, which are now called financialization, have been defined as an industry – the so-called financial 'services' industry. The growth of financial services since the 1990s has been augmented by the transfer of funds between social actors, especially in the form of debt transactions. Debt is accrued, compiled and sold following loans for housing, transportation, education, household commodities and electronics and also through collection mechanisms that profit from unpaid fines and fees extracted by local authorities or loan agents. Embedded in multiscalar networks that extract capital from the daily lives of people struggling to secure a livelihood, processes of accumulation by dispossession produce not only impoverishment of increasing numbers of people, but rage against government, which increasingly appears as an exploiter of the populace.

Physical and Social Displacements

Dispossession leads to both social and physical mobility, which we can term displacement. People who have become migrants are in point of fact displaced by processes of accumulation by dispossession in multiple forms around the world: the seizure of rural and urban land through legal and illegal means, wars for oil, diamonds and scarce metals such as coltan and cobalt (for electronics and batteries), and the continuing massive debt repayment to global financial institutions from impoverished postcolonial countries, which requires these countries to intensify privatization or elimination of public services and public sector employment. These processes of dispossession and displacement underlie mass migration, whether those who move are categorized by official agencies as refugees or economic migrants. After being physically displaced to a new location, people who have migrated often also experience downward social mobility combined with multiple forms of precarity.

Both migrants and non-migrants experience forms of displacement caused by social relations of dispossession, which produce multiple forms of precarity. Precarity is 'distinct from poverty' (Fassin 2015: 265). It is a 'state of insecurity and unpredictability brought about by neoliberal restructuring of both the terms and conditions of working and living' (Çağlar and Glick Schiller 2018: 19). These alterations include changed working conditions such as: temporary employment, the loss of a liveable wage or social benefits including pensions, the new necessity to pay for privatized basic services such as water, health care, education and transport, the loss of housing through mortgage foreclosure or rent increases because of urban regeneration, property speculation, increased taxes and the necessity of sustaining life and a culturally defined adequate standard of living through debt, accompanied by fees, fines and penalties. That is to say, the displaced may include those who have 'stayed in place' and claim to be 'natives', as well as people of migrant background who have resettled and worked to build new lives. By analysing accumulation by dispossession as social relations that link the disempowered to the powerful here, there and elsewhere within connected social fields, scholars can make visible the relationalities and the dynamics that underlie both increased geographic and downward social mobility.

People moving within states and across state borders experience a despair and dislocation related to the rage experienced by those who face downward social mobility. Those staying within their city, country or region feel increasingly like refugees in their own country. Precarity creates affects: a sense of loneliness in a changing city and world, a desire for companionship, fears about well-being, and a need to search for sources of security and reassurance. These dynamics became intensified globally in the COVID pandemic of the 2020s.

Both migrants and non-migrants respond to their displacements and precarious lives by struggling for emplacement through forming new sociabilities that make life meaningful again. Emplacement can be defined as 'the relationship between, on the one hand, the continuing restructuring of place within multiscalar networks of power and, on the other, a person's efforts, within the barriers and opportunities that contingencies of local place-making offer, to build a life within networks of local, national, supranational, and global interconnections' (Çağlar and Glick Schiller 2018: 20–21).

Theorizers of dispossession and emplacement highlight the processes that can lead dispossessed people – both migrants and non-migrants – into social relations based on 'domains of commonality' (Glick Schiller 2015; Glick Schiller and Çağlar 2016; Çağlar and Glick Schiller 2018). To identify domains of commonality is to acknowledge that dispossessed people may forge social relations that express their shared aspirations for social justice and recognition of their shared humanity. Theorizing the social forces that produce domains of commonality does not erase or deny multiple differences of individual and collective history, experience or social situation. But this theorizing does make possible an understanding of the social relations necessary to build movements against oppression and exploitation.

I am not saying that those who experience displacement and precarity necessarily express solidarity with those others who share the same or similar experiences. People classified as either migrants or natives may face the same underlying political-economic processes, while being subject to differentiating cultural framing of these processes, including narratives of nation, race, religion and gender. 'Precariousness is not something individual and [it is] nothing that exists "in itself" in a philosophical sense; it is always relational and therefore a socio-ontological "being- with"' (Lorey 2011: 1). That means that those who are displaced may express disparate affective states and various kinds of solidarities. The experience of dispossession can be a two-way street in terms of the kinds of social movements that dispossessed people support. In the next section, I provide examples of how analyses of urban restructuring can highlight the processes within which dispossessive and emplacing multiscalar relations of both migrants and non-migrants emerge.

Migrants' Social Relations

Despite their very different geographic and cultural histories, each of the cities that we studied had lost political, economic and cultural power but retained – in the public and religious architecture, abandoned buildings and districts, and public narratives – a historical memory of the city's greater significance in the past. Spurred by images of past urban glory, the leaders of these cities began to look for ways to reinvent their cities, drawing from globally circulating urban regeneration narratives of 'new economy' cities that reinvented themselves based on investments in cutting-edge technologies, culture industries and tourism (Smith 2002). City officials developed elaborate urban redevelopment plans, along with glossy brochures and marketing campaigns. These cities initiated various public-private projects fuelled by state funding and by diverse forms of public borrowing from financial institutions. They also offered publicly funded incentives to corporations and businesses, encouraging them to begin or expand economic activities in the city, with much of the redevelopment focused on city centre renewal. As part of rebranding itself as a global player, rather than a provincial backwater, each city found its own way of indicating that it was open to cultural and religious diversity and that it welcomed migrants.

As a result, the multiscalar actors – urban planners, architectural firms, banks, development corporations, and city, state and national officials – who were central to each city's regeneration projects unleashed a welter of dispossessive processes and engendered new processes of emplacement. In each city, public debt rose, which affected funds available for public services from education to transport; and the cost of living rose, as cities charged more for services and collected more fees to help pay off the debt. Housing costs rose to the point that poor people, generally, could no longer live in the city centre and found themselves displaced to peripheral neighbourhoods, often sharing insufficient infrastructure with newly arrived migrants. The employment opportunities promised in the city redevelopment projections did not match expectations. Most of the new jobs were low-wage and temporary.

Nonetheless, migrants, together with non-migrants, participated in multiscalar processes of emplacement built on shared domains of commonality, as they responded to the dispossessions they were forced to confront. Next, I trace the social connectivities of urban regeneration for both Halle/Saale, Germany, and Manchester, New Hampshire, USA. I identify intersecting territorial scales in which multiple actors reconstituted the physical and social life of the city, and I give some indication of how migrants and non-migrants built social relationships within these restructuring processes.

Multiscalar Example 1:
Entanglement of the Religious, Political and Economic Networks of Emplacement in Halle/Saale, Saxony-Anhalt, Germany

Halle/Saale had been known as a site of science, industry and far-reaching trade networks that began hundreds of years ago and ended with the collapse of the German Democratic Republic in 1989. After German unification, factory, commercial and government workers as well as many professionals lost their jobs. They found themselves displaced by those who had been educated in western Germany and who came to Halle, touting 'proper' credentials, to fulfil short-term work contracts with financial, real estate and commercial corporations. Tens of thousands of people from Halle and other parts of eastern Germany sought work in the west, where they faced stigmatization because of their eastern German accent, origins and training.

Faced with their city's disempowerment, population loss and high unemployment, city leaders sought to regenerated and rebrand Halle. Capital for the redevelopment of the city centre's shopfronts, historic buildings, streets and housing came from a combination of European Union (EU) and German federal, state and municipal government loans and grants. Sites were redeveloped through multiscalar networks of construction companies that extended into western Germany, the EU and Turkey. These companies altered the housing market by reducing the stock of social housing through demolition, rehabilitating other social housing to obtain higher rentals, and building market-rate housing. Redevelopment displaced the poorer population from the city centre; meanwhile, redeveloped shopfronts, initially standing empty, were filled in part by migrant businesses and, increasingly, by multinational corporations.

By the turn of the twenty-first century, leaders in Halle began to rebrand the city, influenced in part by urban developers' global call to cities to rebrand themselves and compete for positions in the new hi-tech economy. In order to portray their city as open to the world and to recruit 'global talent' for its regeneration, Halle city leaders officially welcomed migrants, communicating their message in pronouncements, websites and city policies. In 2001, when national political leaders were still debating whether Germany should be considered a country open to immigration, the lord mayor of Halle emphasized that 'there have always been foreigners in Halle who contribute to the development of the city' and that migrants were part of the city's future (interview FH, 21 November 2001). Her successor developed a 'door opener' section of the city's website that welcomed all 'new residents of Halle', including asylum seekers. She invited all newcomers 'to use the possibilities that Halle/Saale has to offer', saying 'Halle is a cosmopolitan, family-friendly city. It has a rich history with many traditions . . . I sincerely invite you to enrich our city's social, cultural and community life with new ideas and thoughts' (City of Halle nd). In 2013, a mayor with a more business-oriented, neoliberal background took office, but he continued the theme of welcome, saying, 'Every foreigner is part of Halle. Halle has always had foreigners' (interview BW, 21 May 2013).

Within this setting of welcoming narratives and an unwelcoming local economy, some migrants and non-migrants in Halle, although living in a population where most people are atheists, looked to religious congregations as means and sites of emplacement. The world over, in historical and contemporary contexts, migrants have looked to religious organizations to help them to settle in new locations, while maintaining ties with old ones (Warner 1998; Ebaugh and Chafetz 2002). Similarly, non-migrants have built community and identity in the face of dislocating forces within religious networks that stretch across space and time (Hoveland 2021). Generally, migration researchers have viewed religious congregations as ethno-religious institutions, but this is not the whole story. In Halle and Manchester, we found that migrants had founded fundamentalist churches that directly spoke to the changing challenges of displacement and emplacement and encouraged the participation of all believers, both migrants and natives. Whatever their origins, congregants participated in multiscalar religious networks that connected them to more powerful actors. Two such congregations in Halle claimed the city, Germany and the world for those who stood with Jesus (Karagiannis and Glick Schiller 2006; Glick Schiller 2009). Pastor Joshua, from Nigeria, led one of these congregations; Pastor Mpenza, from the Congo, led the other.[9]

At first, speaking to the needs of migrants, Pastor Joshua led congregants in prayers for legal papers, asserting that 'the power of the blood' and 'the everliving presence of Jesus' was more powerful than any government. By 2015, when Pastor Joshua's congregation had become nearly half German through both intermarriage and recruitment, prayers increasingly addressed the precarity of all the members of the congregation. Members prayed for employment, promotion, health and increased wealth and prosperity. Dispossessed by neoliberal restructuring, congregants found ways to belong again by being 'born again' into a social field that stretched far beyond Halle and linked them to powerful people elsewhere.

Both congregations were connected to powerful Christian networks in other parts of Europe, in Africa and in the United States. Pastor Joshua preached in India and New Zealand, as well as in other cities in Germany, and visiting preachers from these networks preached to his congregation in Halle. Both pastors maintained ties to the influential American Pentecostal evangelist, Morris Cerullo, whose World Evangelism organization had offices in the United States, the Netherlands, the United Kingdom and Canada. The organization convened massive prayer meetings in Africa and Asia. Cerullo's network included his personal relations with national leaders in various countries around the world.

Over the years, the Christian networks in which these congregations were embedded took positions against Islam and in support of warring in the Middle East by Israel and the USA. That is to say, while dispossessed members of the two congregations, both migrants and non-migrants, came together for Sunday prayer, weekday prayer meetings and special healing conferences that expressed their aspirations for a better and more righteousness world, they contributed to right-wing global social movements in support of US imperial and neo-liberal capitalist interests.

For example, Evelyn, a long-time member of Pastor Joshua's congregation and a woman strongly opposed to racism, sexism and inequality, was responsible for sending contributions in support of the mission of Morris Cerullo World Evangelism in Israel, in addition to facilitating the congregation's participation in a range of right-wing Christian networks in Germany, in the United States and around the world (Glick Schiller 2005).

Some members of these congregations, including Evelyn, were also participants in Halle's regeneration politics and urban rebranding, which intertwined them in the trajectories of other multiscalar networks. Together with Georg, her

German husband, who had been forced into early retirement as a consequence of the restructuring following German unification, Evelyn was one of several congregation members who engaged in small businesses and international trading. These small entrepreneurs felt that Halle's regeneration offered them opportunities to become part of the city. In 2001, opening a small gift shop in one of the city's many empty shopfronts on the outskirts of the regenerated city centre, Evelyn and Georg obtained merchandise from multiscalar networks that connected Halle to Nigeria, Europe and China. Their shop displayed items that Evelyn thought would be attractive to Halle's emerging upper middle class. However, the city's regeneration did not produce the economic expansion and middle-class consumers that Evelyn and many others anticipated. Instead, the gift shop failed in the face of an economic downturn in the city, compounded by the inflation that accompanied the conversion from the Deutsche Mark to the Euro. After first the gift shop and then her marriage failed, and with her future increasingly precarious, Evelyn looked to Pastor Joshua's congregation and its networks to maintain her emplacement project, as she refashioned herself as an importer and business consultant.

Pastor Mpenza and members of his congregation were also connected to the city's rebranding through their ties with Karamba Diaby, a man of Senegalese origin. After serving as a representative of 'foreigners' in Halle and as an official in the Green Party foundation, Diaby, who had become a member of the Social Democratic Party, was one of the first two black Germans to be elected to the Bundestag, the German parliament. With Diaby's assistance, Mpenza's congregation prayed in a publicly funded centre for migrant integration, constructed within an urban regeneration area of demolished factories, rebuilt with federal, state and local funding. Moreover, Pastor Mpenza and his congregation joined with city and university officials, including the vice-mayor, in public ceremonies in honour of Anton Wilhelm Amo, an eighteenth-century philosopher who was the first African student and lecturer at the University of Halle. The ceremonies contributed to the efforts to project a global, welcoming image of Halle.

In the years between 2000 and 2015, while these fundamentalist Christian church organizations allowed dispossessed people, both migrants and non-migrants, to gain social emplacement by leading them into right-wing politics, other multiscalar organizing in the city brought migrants and non-migrants together in anti-racist movements that welcomed refugees to Halle. Our research documented civil courage movements, ranging from a network of voluntary organizations and churches whose meetings I attended in 2001 to anti-racist and refugee support movements that joined together to welcome Syrian refugees displaced by civil war beginning in 2011. Although religious leaders of Protestant and Catholic mainstream congregations showed scant interest in migrants when we interviewed them in 2001, over the following decades they turned to activism and refugee support. Local Catholic institutions forged links within the sanctuary movement offering protection to migrants without legal papers. The local university served as a base for such organizing over the years. There were also networks of NGOs in the city, linked to broader social movements in Germany and Europe. Embracing the slogan 'no human being is illegal', they organized demonstrations against deportations and held marches and rallies in the name of a common humanity and against all borders. Local networks of organizations, religious and secular, sought ways to welcome the large numbers of refugees, who had entered Europe following an eastern route into Germany in 2015. The Halle city government obtained funding to support local volunteers in their refugee support work.

Meanwhile older women in Halle became part of the transnational network of Omas Gegen Rechts (Grannies Against the Right), which had local organizations in one hundred German cities by 2021. Its members spoke out against 'contempt for human beings, fascism, racism', taking to the streets not 'for our interests or our pensions but for future generations' (Stennett 2019b). In 2020 the Omas, with the support of other local organizations and churches, initiated an anti-fascist demonstration against right-wing demonstrators who had been attempting to take over the public space of Halle's central marketplace.

However, it is important to note that, unlike the activists of the two fundamentalist congregations, anti-racists students and some of their local allies brought binaries of difference into their organizing efforts and social interactions, seeing migrants as exotic others. Therefore, while some migrants were involved in these organizations and some friendships were built between migrants and non-migrants, often non-migrant activists did not build their organizations around a shared 'affective state of precarity as it is psychically sensed, ordinarily experienced, and socially embodied' (Allison 2012: 350). In comparison, the church organizations spoke to the affective dispossession of their members and their sense of 'disaffiliation, unrootedness, [and] social (if not literal) homelessness' (Allison 2012: 354) by offering them a social and moral rebirth, affiliation, and a new sense of belonging.

Meanwhile, some ordinary residents amplified the city's welcoming narrative by strengthening their social relations with new arrivals. For example, after 2015 a school teacher, who had initially formed a discussion group of migrants and non-migrants in her home as a way of teaching German, continued the group's weekly meetings over several years. The meetings had become a form of mutually enjoyed sociability, as participants recognized shared domains of commonality.

Over the years, while city leaders maintained their welcoming narrative, the intensifying contradictions of accumulation by dispossession in Halle, Germany, Europe and the world had produced ever more polarized politics. The growth of the right in Halle built on a long local history of Nazi and neo-Nazi politics, including a local forced-labour concentration camp during the Second World War. In the years after German unification, racist youth vented their rage at their unemployment and new poverty by attacking migrants and students of colour. By 2015, there was increased support for anti-immigrant nationalism among the dispossessed, especially those white Germans who felt abandoned in peripheralized areas of the city. There were attacks on migrant shelters and individuals, and the new right-wing party, the Alternative for Germany (AfD), grew as part of multiscalar networks of racist politics. With € 330,000 and promotional support from a Bavarian foundation, a residence and organizational centre affiliated with the AfD was founded near the university in 2017. Its purpose was to win the alt-right's 'battle for the heads' by providing local young people with a sense of sociability and belonging (Stennett 2019a). In 2019, an anti-Semitic terrorist tried to enter Halle's only synagogue and murdered two people nearby. In 2020 the window of Karamba Diaby's office in Halle was riddled by bullets. People of migrant background, who had been building personal and organizational connections to natives of the city, began to feel increasingly threatened on the streets by openly fascist gestures, graffiti and attacks. At the same time, in response to these violent acts, there was increased public discussion – in the media and in the city's official network of organizations engaged in supporting migrants and 'democracy' – about the fascist multiscalar network organizing in Halle and about the failure of public prosecutors to prosecute those who initiated racist attacks (see Deutsche Welle 2020). In 2021, in this tense setting, Karamba Diaby won his third election to represent Halle in the German parliament.

The international press tends to highlight the aggressive politics of European Christian whiteness, often equating it with eastern Germany, disregarding the dispossessive processes that are shattering aspirations in Germany, as elsewhere, of an equitable democratic society. Meanwhile, local networks of sociability persist, while migrants and non-migrants continue to take to the streets to denounce the threats of fascism.

Multiscalar Example 2:
The Entanglement of Religious, Political and Economic Networks of Emplacement in Manchester, New Hampshire, USA

Manchester, New Hampshire, also claimed a proud history of industry and trade. In the nineteenth and early twentieth century, the city had been the site of massive textile mills and of factories for the production of machine tools and shoes. Its industries were part of production and distribution networks that extended globally. However, beginning in the 1930s, industry left for locations where labour was unorganized and cheaper, so that by the 1960s Manchester was a deindustrialized, disempowered city with an increasingly abandoned city centre.

In the decades that followed, Manchester leaders sought to rebrand and regenerate their city, turning to a broad array of institutions and actors with multiscalar financial networks (City of Manchester 2004, 2006). An architecture firm based in Princeton, New Jersey, with a global set of clients, provided some of the city's redevelopment planning. Little direct private investment was secured for the various city centre regeneration projects. However, city, state and federal urban development programmes offered grants and loans, and multinational financial corporations provided loan capital. Through these connections, developers acquired land for entertainment facilities, upscale condominiums, and office buildings. The central shopping street was rebuilt, with new lighting, pavements and shopfronts, and a meat-packing plant employing hundreds of migrants and locals was replaced by a health-care facility, which also relied in part on migrant labour.

City branders and political leaders saw migrants as valued components in local urban regeneration projects; and, as in Halle, politicians with various political affiliations crafted welcoming narratives. Emphasizing that 'they are us', the Democratic mayor of Manchester in 2002 stressed that migrants were among those who built the city in the past and were also vital to its future (Baines 2002). While, in the years to follow, some city leaders expressed reservations about the city's capacity to welcome large numbers of refugees, a section of the leadership continued to support a welcoming narrative. For example, the Manchester City Council became a member of the 'Welcoming America' network of city governments and non-governmental organizations (NGOs), formed in 2009. This network adopted the 'innovative idea' that 'welcoming leads to prosperity' (Welcoming America 2018). Meanwhile, independent of these development efforts, regenerated and empty city centre shopfronts in Manchester, as in Halle, were tenanted by migrant small businesses, which attracted local consumers and tourists to the city (Cousineau 2019).

As urban regeneration projects within far-reaching networks of financial and political institutions reconfigured the lives of migrants and non-migrants in Manchester, new sociabilities and new political polarizations emerged. Urban regeneration, together with accessible sub-prime mortgages, fuelled a real estate boom that initially provided new emplacement opportunities but that led, over the years, to further dispossession and displacement. Struggling to re-establish themselves, migrants joined their non-migrant neighbours by seizing the opportunity offered by sub-prime mortgage brokers to become home-owners and even landlords. They joined the multiscalar processes of real estate development through which international financial corporations bought up and resold packages of sub-prime mortgages as financial investment opportunities.

Working-class residents, both migrant and non-migrant, bought inflated real estate because of the lack of affordable rentals. Investing in the city's aging housing stock allowed migrants to house large, sometimes multigenerational or extended families and to avoid the discrimination they faced as renters in the housing market. Moreover, the expanded housing industry that accompanied urban regeneration provided an expanded opportunity structure for migrants. Many saw becoming a landlord in a multi-family house as a strategy for economic and social mobility. They also participated in the housing industry as real estate agents, mortgage brokers and employees of banks or local community-based, federally funded organizations that provided support and loans to first-time home buyers.

In urban regeneration, real estate transactions were intimately linked to local political parties and power brokers. From 2000 to 2011, Republican party activists were key players in property development and construction and saw openness to migrants as an aspect of Manchester's regeneration narratives and rebranding. Even after 2011, when the Republican mayor of Manchester argued that the federal government was settling 'too many refugees' in his city, many local Republicans remained less anti-immigrant than their fellow party members in Washington (Siefer 2014).

People interested in property development and financing, including migrants and their family members, often found it beneficial to become activists in the local Republican party. Ties with Republican politicians connected people of migrant background with various corporate, institutional, and governmental actors and opportunities. These social relations were visible at various events, such as the annual Republican party barbecues in Saghir Tahir's backyard. Tahir, an immigrant from Pakistan and a member of the local mosque, became a Republican party activist. He participated in Manchester's regeneration through his construction consulting business, having obtained his initial capital as a small businessman and as someone who acquired devalued property.

Guests at Tahir's annual barbecues included Roy Wieczorek, the former mayor of Manchester, Craig Benson, the multimillionaire 'hi tech' industrialist and Republican party member who had become governor of New Hampshire in 2003, the county sheriff, and multiple other personages involved in local redevelopment, real estate and party politics. Tahir served as member of the New Hampshire legislature, elected initially in the 1990s. Re-elected after the attack on the World Trade Center and Pentagon on September 11, 2001, he served until 2011. Active at the city, state and national political scale, he worked with colleagues in the New Hampshire legislature and with a Republican deputy majority leader of the US House of Representatives to promote a peaceful resolution to the conflict in Kashmir. After his death, one of his sons, Adeel Tahir, became a real estate investor in Manchester and abroad.

Carlos Gonzales, who also attended Tahir's barbecues, was another Manchester Republican party activist in the real estate industry. Like Tahir, an elected member of the New Hampshire state legislature, Gonzalez was also a transnational political actor, having begun his political career in the Dominican Republic while working for the Dominican president (Ballotpedia 2017). After settling in Manchester, Gonzalez established connections with several local and regional Hispanic organizations, but he also built a personal network based on diverse local ties that were not ethnically based. He began by visiting the Manchester offices of both the Democratic and Republican political parties but met with greater interest among the Republicans. Wieczorek, Manchester's Republican mayor in the 1990s, encouraged Gonzalez's political ambitions, saying 'Carlos, I'm of Polish descent. And this city is a city of immigrants. And you might very well be tomorrow the next mayor of the city' (Fabian 2012).

Gonzalez also launched a career in real estate, just as the sub-prime mortgage industry fuelled the expanding local housing bubble. During his tenure as a member of the New Hampshire House of Representatives, he was trained as a mortgage broker through a Fannie Mae fellowship at Harvard.[10] His multiscalar Manchester-based networks linked him to local real estate interests, powerful actors in the Republican party, non-migrants of various class backgrounds in the district he represented, and migrants from around the world who had settled in Manchester, including a close friend from Nigeria and, through him, a fundamentalist pastor named Godsword, also a Nigerian, who cultivated ties in a global religious network.[11]

In the first decade of the twenty-first century, several migrants' political ties of multiscalar emplacement were intertwined within religious networks. Our field notes reveal a range of political actors at events such as Christian prayer breakfasts and potluck dinners at the local mosque. The breakfasts were organized by members of a Christian prayer network of more than twenty predominantly white, non-migrant churches in the Manchester area, led by Godsword, the pastor from Nigeria, and a committee composed of both migrant and non-migrant members. Robert A. Baines, the Democratic mayor of Manchester from 2000 to 2006, Governor Benson, and other political activists attended these breakfasts.

As had been the case in both of the congregations that I came to know in Halle, Godsword's network of congregations, the Resurrection Crusade, maintained ties with transnational fundamentalist Christian organizations, including Morris Cerullo's World Evangelism with its right-wing, imperialist agenda and its campaign for fundamentalist Christians to take control of local, state and national politics. At the time of the presidential elections, congregants were given 'Key Prayer Points', including 'We need great men and women after His heart to occupy every position from the least to the greatest' (Resurrection Crusade 2004). Leaders and the ordinary members of the local mosque, some involved in the city's developing computer industry, also had ties to Governor Benson, who had made his fortune through computer related industries. Through a local private university, which attracted international students from South Asia and the Middle East, the mosque also had ties to various financial institutions and agencies involved in the local and national real estate market, to New Hampshire state agencies, and to federal Congressional committees. In 2003, Governor Benson sent his attorney general and several assistants to a post-prayer potluck dinner at the mosque. The attorney general thanked 'the mosque and its wonderful members for helping introduce me to the diversity of New Hampshire' and went on to say, 'believe me, if you ever have any problem, you have a friend in me. Contact me and I will help you as much as I possibly can' (PB fieldnotes #127, 17 April 2003).

In short, neoliberal restructuring in Manchester provided an initial emplacement of migrants and non-migrants. At a Martin Luther King celebration held at a Greek Orthodox Church in 2003, which was supported by Democrats, Republicans and multiple local organizations, the keynote speaker, Reverend Canon Edward Rodman, a black Episcopalian pastor, stated that 'we all understand each other's suffering, which will give a basis for common compassion and allow us to live in harmony' (field notes, 20 January 2003).

Of course, all was not harmony, and some activists organized initiatives to demand immigrants' rights, improved working conditions and higher wages. For example, the Immigrant Rights Task Force, founded in Manchester in 2002, brought together peace advocates, union organizers, lawyers, health-care activists and representatives of faith communities, some with a migrant background and some without. The Task Force was part of a coalition in New Hampshire that successfully opposed state-level anti-immigrant measures, such as limiting access to drivers' licences and imposing racial profiling to identify non-citizens. However, these organizations, like those formed in Halle, often failed to connect to the daily social relations of commonality that some migrants and non-migrants were building as part of their daily lives.

In 2007, the real estate bubble burst and with it the hopes and aspirations of many working- and middle-class families in Manchester, migrant and non-migrant. In the wake of foreclosures, higher rates of poverty and downward social mobility, political anger flared, and politics polarized (City of Manchester 2014). Republicans in Manchester, as in many other disempowered cities, increasingly organized white working- and middle-class residents to adopt a militant white Americanism and anti-immigrant stance. As a Hispanic member of the New Hampshire Republican party admitted in a local newspaper report in 2016, 'the GOP's once welcoming embrace has grown awkward as anti-immigrant rhetoric grows' (Garcia 2016). Donald Trump lost in Manchester by a small margin in 2016 and a somewhat larger margin in 2020 (New York Times 2016; WMUR 2020). Nonetheless, his initial campaign, presidency and second unsuccessful campaign, all sustained by funding from right-wing billionaires, had an impact on the dynamics of social life. Rage at dispossessions were directed against migrants, people of colour and gay people, and political polarization intensified (McKibben 2016; Robidoux 2016). In Manchester, as in Halle, people of migrant background said that they increasingly experienced overt racism and felt less at home in their daily lives.

Nevertheless, as in Halle, movements of solidarity against all forms of injustice also grew and became more visible, and refugees continued to be welcome (Feely 2015). In 2017, Manchester elected its first female mayor, a member of the Democratic party, who supported refugee settlement as well as neo-liberal regeneration. In 2020, the Black Lives Matter movement, led by youth of colour, including migrant youth, brought together almost a thousand people, including a large number of non-migrant white residents (Gibson 2020).

Challenging the Politics of Otherness: Towards a Multiscalar Anthropology of Social Relations

The goal of this chapter has been to understand the dynamics of social life, which, in so many countries, are moving some people towards violent nationalist movements and others towards participation in movements for social justice and in support of migrants' rights. I began by critiquing social theories that naturalize concepts of natives and strangers. Instead, I explored a form of relational theory, one that analyses the dispossessive processes and networks of displacement and emplacement that move people in particular times and locations to engage in political action.

The relational theory offered here posits that all people, as they seek their livelihoods and strive to build lives with a meaning, constitute themselves within interlinking multiscalar networks of unequal power. As I have demonstrated in this chapter, multiscalar analyses trace networked social relations that stretch across space, named groups, political units, territorial division and multiple forms of institutionalized power. In this volume honouring Günther Schlee, I note that he is among those scholars who offer a non-bounded concept of the social. Departing not from urban studies, as I do in this chapter, but from his (and his many students') work on nomadic peoples, Schlee (1989) has explored how pastoralists' networks have extended across state boundaries and connected them to settled people. In tracing networked social relations not bounded by political units, Schlee has used the term integration. However, his perspective, which extends into the study of institutions of power, speaks to a multiscalar analysis.

Documenting, analysing and explaining the processes through which those who are dispossessed and displaced enter into political action is imperative (Rich 2016). In this vital endeavour, political activists often ignore the insights offered by scholars who have theorized the interconnectedness of social relations through which society is constituted. The research and analysis in this chapter, drawing as it does on a theorization of society as networks of social relations that extend across time and space, can challenge the current politics of difference. It provides a social theory that critiques the legitimization of border walls, agencies and legal mechanisms that leave refugees to drown in the Mediterranean or that delegates 'others' to imprisonment in the bleak industrial complex of detention centres (De Genova 2013b; Santer 2021).

The first step in organizing a politics of aspiration and planetary humanism (Gilroy 2004) is to recognize that migrants and non-migrants can and do join together within the daily relations of urban life. Only by recognizing domains of commonality and deciding to oppose all systems of dispossession and displacement can dispossessed people build movements that claim a common humanity and planetary identity (Gilroy 2004; see also Harvey 2012; Susser 2014; Narotzky 2016; Hansen 2019). Organized, concerted action to alter fundamentally the unequal distribution of wealth and power and to halt environmental catastrophe is urgently needed. However, the path dispossessed people choose as they desperately seek to find a place for themselves in the world is shaped by the political organizing they encounter.

Scholars of migration, dispossession, urban regeneration, populism and social movements must ask how, where, why and with whom people build domains of mutual respect and shared aspirations. If we are to contribute to movements that unite migrants and non-migrants in struggles to win political power and social and economic justice, then our anthropological theory and political practice must come hand in hand.

Nina Glick Schiller is Emeritus Professor, University of Manchester, UK, and University of New Hampshire, USA, and Researcher Partner at the Max Planck Institute for Social Anthropology. Co-Editor of *Anthropological Theory* and Founding Editor of *Identities: Global Studies in Culture and Power*, her books and articles address the relationships between migrants and city making, dispossession and displacement, transnationality of cities and migrants, cosmopolitan sociability, methodological nationalism, long-distance nationalism, comparative urbanism, urban restructuring, categories of epidemic risk, migrant Pentecostalism, care-giving, the ethnic lens and neoliberal multiculturalism. Glick Schiller's ethnographic research spans Haiti, the United States, Germany and the United Kingdom.

Notes

1. Ayşe Çağlar and I were assisted by numerous co-researchers and research assistants over the years. They included, in Halle: Evangelos Karagiannis, Julia Wenzel, Martin Sieber, Marcus Rau, Julia Wenger and Ronn Müller; in Manchester: Thaddeus Guldbrandsen, Peter Buchanan, Molly Messinger, Geraldine Boggs, Hubert Weterwami, Helene Simerwayi and Faten al Hassun; and, in Mardin: Dr Ayşe Seda Yüksel. Students in Halle and Manchester also provided interviews. Thanks to Susan Brown for editing this chapter.

2. Using data from all three cities, we specified the steps entailed in developing a comparative relational multiscalar analysis (Çağlar and Glick Schiller 2021; see also Çağlar and Glick Schiller 2011; Glick Schiller et al. 2006; Glick Schiller and Çağlar 2009, 2011a, 2011b, 2013, 2016; Glick Schiller 2011).

3. Of course, openness to cultural and religious difference has had a long history within the politics of empire. Imperial pluralism has been a mode of governance of ancient and more recent empires (Furnival 1948; Braude and Lewis 1982; Schlee 2018b).

4. Ontologies developed outside the West often posit social relations – human and spiritual – that are multiple, fluid, or mutually constituting, rather than binary (Hunter 2015).

5. João de Pina-Cabral (2018: 435) argues that Simmel saw the individual existing prior to social experience. However, in certain places, Simmel offered a more relational view of society. See Emirbayer (1997) and Donati (2011).

6. Similarly, when Schlee et al. (2018: 230) postulated that humans need an outside force (such as a Martian enemy) to act in terms of a shared human commonality, he is theorizing the relational dynamics of social connectivity. He emphasizes that individuals interact within specific places and times but as part of interconnecting networks of differential power.

7. See for example, the decolonizing social science perspective of Magubane (1971), Mafeje (1976), Harrison (2010 [1991]), Cardoso and Faletto's dependency theory (1979), Wallerstein's world system theory (2011), Eric Wolf's global perspective (1982), and the initial analyses of transnational migration (Kearney and Nagengast 1989; Basch et al. 1994).

8. Our approach builds on the work of those geographers who provide a globe-spanning perspective on territorial scales by viewing them – locally, regionally, nationally and globally – as mutually constituted, relational and interpenetrating territorially referenced entry points (Jessop, Brenner and Jones 2008; Sassen 2014).

9. All names, except for local political officials and global religious leaders, are pseudonyms in order to protect confidentiality agreements.

10. Fannie Mae, officially the Federal National Mortgage Association (FNMA). 'was established in 1938, . . . to create a secondary market for the purchase and sale of mortgages' (Investing Answers 2018).

11. The pastor was among the many who sought security through using a sub-prime mortgage to buy an old, over-valued house. After the economic crisis of 2008, with its housing market crash, in which he and many members of his network faced foreclosure, he moved back to Nigeria.

References

Alba, Richard and Nancy Foner. 2015. *Strangers No More: Immigration and the Challenges of Integration in North America and Western Europe*. Princeton, NJ: Princeton University Press.

Alexander, Michael. 2003. 'Local Policies Toward Migrants as an Expression of Host-Stranger Relations: A Proposed Typology', *Journal of Ethnic and Migration Studies* 29(3): 411–30, DOI: 10.1080/13691830305610.

Allison, Anne. 2012. 'Ordinary Refugees: Social Precarity and Soul in 21st Century Japan', *Anthropological Quarterly* 85(2): 345–70.

Amelina, Anna, Thomas Faist, Nina Glick Schiller and Devrimsel D. Nergiz. 2012. 'Methodological Predicaments of Cross-Border Studies', in Anna Amelina, Devrimsel Nergiz, Thomas Faist and Nina Glick Schiller (eds), *Beyond Methodological Nationalism: Research Methodologies for Cross-Border Studies*. New York: Routledge, pp. 1–22.

Baines, Robert A. 2002. 'Inaugural Address', Manchester, NH: City Clerk's Office, Board of Mayor and Alderman Inaugural Ceremonies. Retrieved 23 April 2013 from http://www.manchesternh.gov/portals/2/departments/city_clerk/agendas_and_ minutes/BMA/2002-01-01-Inauguration.pdf.

Ballotpedia 2017. *Carlos Gonzalez (New Hampshire)*. Retrieved 5 January 2015 from https://ballotpedia.org/Carlos_Gonzalez_(New_Hampshire).

Basch, Linda, Nina Glick Schiller and Cristina Szanton Blanc. 1994. *Nations Unbound: Transnational Projects, Postcolonial Predicaments, and the Deterritorialized Nation-State*. Basel: Gordon and Breach, reprinted in New York: Routledge.

Binnie, Jon, Julian Holloway, Steve Millington and Craig Young. 2006. 'Grounding Cosmopolitan Urbanism: Approaches, Practices, Policies', in Jon Binnie, Julian Holloway, Steve Millington and Craig Young (eds), *Cosmopolitan Urbanism*. New York: Routledge, pp. 1–34.

Braude, Benjamin and Bernard Lewis (eds). 1982. *Christians and Jews in the Ottoman Empire: The Functioning of a Plural Society*. Two volumes: I. *The Central Lands*; II. *The Arabic-speaking Lands*. New York: Holmes and Meier.

Brenner, Neil. 1999. 'Beyond State-Centrism? Space, Territoriality and Geographical Scale in Globalization Studies', *Theory and Society* 28(1): 39–78.

———. 2011. 'The Urban Question and the Scale Question: Some Conceptual Clarifications', in Ayşe Çağlar and Nina Glick Schiller (eds), *Locating Migration: Rescaling Cities and Migrants*. Ithaca, NY: Cornell University Press, pp. 23–41.

Brenner, Neil, David J. Madden and David Wachsmuth. 2011. 'Assemblage Urbanism and the Challenges of Critical Urban Theory', *City* 15(2): 225–40.

Çağlar, Ayşe. 2018. 'Chronotopes of Migration Scholarship: Challenges of Contemporaneity and Historical Conjuncture', in Pauline Gardiner Barber and Winnie Lem (eds), *Migration, Temporality, and Capitalism*. Cham: Palgrave Macmillan, pp. 21–41.

Çağlar, Ayşe and Nina Glick Schiller. 2018. *Migrants and City Making: Dispossession, Displacement, and Urban Regeneration*. Durham, NC: Duke University Press.

———. 2021. 'Relational Multiscalar Analysis: A Comparative Approach to Migrants within City-Making Processes', *Geographical Review* 111(2): 206–32.

Candea, Matei and Giovanni Da Col. 2012. 'The Return to Hospitality', *Journal of the Royal Anthropological Institute* 18: S1–S19.

Cardoso, Fernando H. and Enzo Faletto. 1979. *Dependency and Development in Latin America*. Berkeley: University of California Press.

City of Halle. 'Door Opener'. Retrieved 7 July 2015 from http://tueroeffner-halle.de/ Englisch/information.htm.

City of Manchester. 2004. 'Relocating in Manchester'. Retrieved 8 January 2007 from https://www.yourmanchesternh.com/Business/Relocation.

———. 2006. *Downtown Strategic Plan, Section 2: Exiting Conditions*. Retrieved 5 March 2010 from https://www.manchesternh.gov/pcd/cip/DowntownStrategicPlanSection2.pdf.

———. 2014. *Planning and Community Development Department. Annual Action Plan*. http://www.manchesternh.gov/pcd/cip/ActionPlan2014Draft.pdf.

Collins, Jane. 2012. 'Theorizing Wisconsin's 2011 Protests: Community-Based Unionism Confronts Accumulation by Dispossession', *American Ethnologist* 39(1): 1–15.

Coser, Lewis A. 1998 [1956]. *The Functions of Social Conflict*. New York: Routledge.

Cousineau, Michael. 2019. 'Manchester's South Willow Street: a Magnet for Customers and New Businesses', *New Hampshire Union Leader*, 3 March. https://www.unionleader.com/news/business/manchester-s-south-willow-street-a-magnet-for-customers-and/article_3a9b18c1-9991-5aef-adfe-2f50151dd7d9.html.

De Genova, Nicholas. 2013a. '"We Are of the Connections": Migration, Methodological Nationalism, and "Militant Research"', *Postcolonial Studies* 16(3): 250–58.

———. 2013b. 'Spectacles of Migrant "Illegality": The Scene of Exclusion, the Obscene of Inclusion', *Ethnic and Racial Studies* 36(7): 1180–98.

Deutsche Welle. 2020. *A Year After Synagogue Attack, Halle Residents Struggle Against Racism*. 20 December. Retrieved from https://www.dw.com/en/a-year-after-synagogue-attack-halle-residents-struggle-against-racism/a-55980697.

Donati, Pierpaolo. 2011. *Relational Sociology: A New Paradigm for the Social Sciences*. London: Routledge.

Ebaugh, Helen R. and Janet Chafetz. 2002. *Religion Across Borders: Transnational Religious Networks*. Walnut Creek, CA: Altamira.

Emirbayer, Mustafa. 1997. 'Manifesto for a Relational Sociology', *American Journal of Sociology* 103(2): 281–317.
Fabian, Jordan. 2012. *Q&A with N.H. State Rep. Carlos Gonzalez*. 8 January. Retrieved 14 August 2015 from http://thisisfusion.tumblr.com/post/15510334333/ qa-with-nh-state-rep-carlos-gonzalez.
Fassin, Didier. 2015. 'Introduction: Governing Precariousness', in Didier Fassin and Patrick Brown (eds), *At the Heart of the State: The Moral World of Institutions*. Chicago: University of Chicago Press, pp. 1–12.
Feely, Paul. 2015. 'Manchester Chief: Granite State May Host 500 Refugees, some Syrian', *New Hampshire Union Leader*, 17 November. Retrieved 23 April 2016 from http://www.unionleader.com/Chief-Granite-State-may-host-500-Syrian-refugees.
Furnival, John S. 1948. *Colonial Policy and Practice*. London: Cambridge University Press.
Garcia, M. 2016. *The Risks of Leaving New Hampshire's Latinos Behind*. Boston Globe. https://www.bostonglobe.com/ideas/2016/02/06/garcia/Ks7pHGFGvcW6otyWdoBxoJ/story.html.
Gibson, Sarah. 2020. 'One Month in, N.H. Black Lives Matter Activists Say "We Are Not Going Anywhere"', *New Hampshire Public Radio*. New Hampshire: NHPR.
Gilroy, Paul. 2004. *After Empire: Melancholia or Convivial Culture?* London: Routledge.
Glassman, Jim. 2006. 'Primitive Accumulation, Accumulation by Dispossession, Accumulation by "Extra-Economic" Means', *Progress in Human Geography* 30(5): 608–25, DOI:10.1177/030 9132506070172.G.
Glick Schiller, Nina. 2005. 'Transnational Social Fields and Imperialism: Bringing A Theory of Power to Transnational Studies', *Anthropological Theory* 5(4): 439–61.
———. 2009. '"There is No Power Except for God": Locality, Global Christianity, and Immigrant Transnational Incorporation', in Bertram Turner and Thomas Kirsch (eds), *Permutations of Order*. Farnham, UK: Ashgate Press, pp. 125–47.
———. 2011. 'Localized Neo-liberalism, Multiculturalism, and Global Religion: Exploring the Agency of Migrants and City Boosters', *Economy and Society* 40(2): 184–210.
———. 2012. 'Situating Identities: Towards an Identities Studies Without Binaries of Difference', *Identities: Global Studies in Culture and Power* 19(4): 520–32.
———. 2015. 'Explanatory Frameworks in Transnational Migration Studies: The Missing Multi-Scalar Global Perspective', *Ethnic and Racial Studies* 8(13): 2275–82.
———. 2018. 'Theorising Transnational Migration In Our Times: A Multiscalar Temporal Perspective', *Nordic Journal of Migration Research* 8(4): 201–12.
Glick Schiller, Nina, Linda Basch and Cristina Szanton Blanc. 1992. 'Transnationalism: A New Analytic Framework for Understanding Migration', in Nina Glick Schiller, Linda Basch and Cristina Szanton Blanc (eds), *Towards a Transnational Perspective on Migration: Race, Class, Ethnicity, and Nationalism Reconsidered*. New York: Academy of Sciences, pp. 1–24.
Glick Schiller, Nina and Ayşe Çağlar. 2009. 'Towards a Comparative Theory of Locality in Migration Studies: Migrant Incorporation and City Scale', *Journal of Ethnic and Migration Studies* 35(2): 177–202.
———. 2011a. 'Locality and Globality: Building a Comparative Analytical Framework in Migration and Urban Studies', in Nina Glick Schiller and Ayşe Çağlar (eds), *Locating Migration: Rescaling Cities and Migrants*. Ithaca, NY: Cornell University Press, pp. 60–81.
———. 2011b. 'Downscaled Cities and Migrant Pathways: Locality and Agency without an Ethnic Lens', in Nina Glick Schiller and Ayşe Çağlar (eds), *Locating Migration: Rescaling Cities and Migrants*. Ithaca, NY: Cornell University Press, pp. 190–212.
———. 2013. 'Locating Migrant Pathways of Economic Emplacement: Thinking beyond the Ethnic Lens', *Ethnicities* 13(4): 494–514.
———. 2016. 'Displacement, Emplacement and Migrant Newcomers: Rethinking Urban Sociabilities Within Multiscalar Power', *Identities: Global Studies in Culture and Power, Seeing Place and Power* 23(1): 17–34.

Glick Schiller, Nina, Ayşe Çağlar and Thaddeus Guldbrandsen. 2006. 'Beyond the Ethnic Lens: Locality, Globality, and Born-Again Incorporation', *American Ethnologist* 33(4): 612–33.

Gluckman, Max. 1940. 'Analysis of a Social Situation in Modern Zululand', *Bantu Studies* 14(1): 1–30.

Hansen, Christina. 2019. *Solidarity in Activism*. PhD Dissertation, Faculty of Society and Culture, Malmö University.

Harrison, Faye (ed.). 2010 [1991]. *Decolonizing Anthropology: Moving Further Toward an Anthropology for Liberation*. 3rd edition. Arlington, VA: American Anthropological Association.

Harvey, David. 2004. 'The "New" Imperialism: Accumulation through Dispossession', *Socialist Register* 40: 63–87.

———. 2012. *Rebel Cities: From the Right to the City to the Urban Revolution*. New York: Verso.

Hoveland, Ingie. 2021. 'Value Moves in Multiple Ways: Ethical Values, the Anthropology of Christianity, and an Example of Women and Movement', *Anthropological Theory*, https://journals.sagepub.com/doi/abs/10.1177/14634996211029729.

Hunter, Jack. 2015. '"Spirits Are the Problem": Anthropology and Conceptualizing Spiritual Beings', *Journal for the Study of Religious Experience* 1(1): 76–86.

Investing Answers. 2018. 'Financial Dictionary'. Retrieved 1 December 2018 from https://investinganswers.com/financial-dictionary/real-estate/fannie-mae-fnma-2140.

Jessop, Bob, Neil Brenner and Martin Jones. 2008. 'Theorizing Sociospatial Relations', *Environment and Planning D: Society and Space* 26(3): 389–401, DOI:10.1068/d9107.

Karagiannis, Evangelos and Nina Glick Schiller. 2006. 'Contesting Claims to the Land: Pentecostalism as a Challenge to Migration Theory and Policy', *Sociologus* 56(2): 137–71.

Kearney, Michael and Carole Nagengast. 1989. 'Anthropological Perspectives on Transnational Communities in Rural California', *Working Paper 3, Working Group on Farm Labor and Rural Poverty*. Davis, CA: California Institute for Rural Studies.

Kymlicka, Will. 2015. 'Solidarity in Diverse Societies: Beyond Neoliberal Multiculturalism and Welfare Chauvinism', *Comparative Migration Studies* 3(1): 17.

Lenin, Vladimir I. 1984 [1917]. *Imperialism: The Highest Stage of Capitalism*. New York: International Publishers.

Lenzer, Gertrud. 1975. *Auguste Comte and Positivism: The Essential Writings*. New York: Harper and Row.

Lorey, Isabell. 2011. *Governmental Precarization*, trans. Aileen Derieg. Retrieved 28 April 2021 from https://transversal.at/transversal/0811/lorey/en.

Luxemburg, Rosa. 1951 [1913]. *The Accumulation of Capital: A Contribution to an Economic Explanation of Imperialism*, trans. Agnes Schwarzschild. London: Routledge & Kegan Paul.

McKibben, Bill. 2016. '"The Koch Brothers" New Brand. Review of Dark Money: The Hidden History of the Billionaires Behind the Rise of the Radical Right by Jane Mayer', *New York Review of Books* 63(4).

Mafeje, Archie. 1976. 'The Problem of Anthropology in Historical Perspective: An Inquiry into the Growth of the Social Sciences', *Canadian Journal of African Studies* 10(2): 307–33.

Magubane, Bernard. 1971. 'A Critical Look at Indices Used in the Study of Social Change in Colonial Africa', *Current Anthropology* 12(4/5): 419–45.

Martindale, Don. 1960. *The Nature and Types of Sociological Theory*. Boston: Houghton Mifflin Company.

Marx, Karl. 1887 [1867]. *Capital: A Critique of Political Economy*, trans. from the third German edition by Samuel Moore and Edward Aveling, edited by Friedrich Engels. Moscow: Progress Publishers. Retrieved 1 January 2022 from https://www.marxists.org/archive/marx/works/download/pdf/Capital-Volume-I.pdf.

Mittleman, James. 1994. 'The Global Restructuring and Production of Migration', in Yoshikazu Sakamoto (ed.), *Global Transformation: Challenges to the State System*. Tokyo: United Nations University Press, pp. 276–97.

Narotzky, Susana. 2016. 'Between Inequality and Injustice: Dignity as a Motive for Mobilization During the Crisis', *History and Anthropology* 27(1): 74–92.

New York Times. 2016. 'New Hampshire Election Results'. Retrieved from https://www.nytimes.com/elections/2016/results/new-hampshire.

Omas Gegen Rechts Deutschland-Bündnis. 2020. Retrieved 26 December 2021 from https://omasgegenrechts-deutschland.de/2020/08/12/solidaritaet-ist-unsere-staerke-hetzer-haben-auf-dem-marktplatz-in-halle-nichts-zu-suchen/.

Pina-Cabral, João de. 2018. 'Modes of Participation', *Anthropological Theory* 18(4): 435–55.

Putnam, Robert D. 2007. 'E Pluribus Unum: Diversity and Community in the Twenty-First Century', *Scandinavian Political Studies* 30(2): 137–74.

Resurrection Crusade. 2004. *Calling America to Pray for America's 2004 Elections*. November, flyer in files of Nina Glick Schiller.

Rich, Nathaniel. 2016. 'Inside the Sacrifice Zone. Review of Strangers in Their Own Land: Anger and Mourning on the American Right by Arlie Russell Hochschild', *New York Review of Books* 63(17).

Robidoux, Carol. 2016. 'Trump Dumps on Clintons Over Trade at Former Osram Sylvania in Manchester', Manchester Ink Link, 30 June. Retrieved from https://manchesterinklink.com/trump-dumps-clintons-trade-former-osram-sylvania-manchester/.

Santer, Kiri. 2021. *Bordering Responsibility: The Unaccountable Politics of Migration Control in the Central Mediterranean*. PhD dissertation, Social Anthropology, University of Bern.

Sassen, Saskia. 2014. *Expulsions: Brutality and Complexity in the Global Economy*. Cambridge, MA: Harvard University Press.

Schlee, Günther. 1989. *Identities on the Move: Clanship and Pastoralism in Northern Kenya*. Manchester: Manchester University Press.

———. 2008. *How Enemies Are Made: Towards a Theory of Ethnic and Religious Conflicts*. Integration and Conflict Studies 1. New York and Oxford: Berghahn.

———. 2018a. 'Introduction: Difference and Sameness as Modes of Integration', in Günther Schlee and Alexander Horstmann (eds), *Difference and Sameness as Modes of Integration: Anthropological Perspectives on Ethnicity and Religion*. New York and Oxford: Berghahn, pp. 1–32.

———. 2018b. 'Ruling over Ethnic and Religious Differences: A Comparative Essay on Empires', in Günther Schlee and Alexander Horstmann (eds), *Difference and Sameness as Modes of Integration: Anthropological Perspectives on Ethnicity and Religion*. New York and Oxford: Berghahn, pp. 191–224.

Schlee, Günther, Alexander Horstmann and John R. Eidson. 2018. 'Epilogue', in Günther Schlee and Alexander Horstmann (eds), *Difference and Sameness as Modes of Integration: Anthropological Perspectives on Ethnicity and Religion*. Oxford: Berghahn, pp. 225–30.

Siefer, Ted. 2014. 'Manchester Mayor Gatsas Protests to Refugee Resettlement Group: What about Our Own Kids?', *New Hampshire Union Leader*, 5 August. Retrieved 4 July 2015 from http://www.unionleader.com/apps/pbcs.dll/article?AID=/20140806/NEWS0606/140809428/1006.

Simmel, Georg. 1949 [1903]. 'Sociology of Sociability', *American Journal of Sociology* 54(3): 254–61.

———. 1971. *On Individuality and Social Forms: Selected Writings*. Donald N. Levine (ed.). Chicago: University of Chicago Press.

———. 2002. 'The Metropolis and Mental Life', in Gay Bridge and Sophie Watson (eds), *The Blackwell City Reader*. Oxford: Blackwell, pp. 11–19.

Smith, Neil. 2002. 'New Globalism, New Urbanism: Gentrification as Global Urban Strategy', *Antipode* 34: 427–50.

Stennett, Craig. 2019a. Far Right Spread its Tentacles into University, Eastern Germany. 1 February. Retrieved from http://www.craigstennett.com/blog/far-right-spread-its-tentacles.

———. 2019b. Gertrud Graf, Omas Gegen Rechts, Berlin. 2 February. Retrieved from https://visura.co/craigstennett/projects/gertrud-graf-omas-gegen-rechts?status=Log+in+to+hire+craig.

Susser, Ida. 2014. 'Re-Envisioning Social Movements in the Global City', *Focaal Blog*, 12 November. Retrieved from https://www.focaalblog.com/2014/11/12/ida-susser-re-envisioning-social-movements-in-the-global-city/.

Taylor, Lori. 1990. *Don't Mourn – Organize! Songs of Labor Songwriter Joe Hill*. Retrieved 5 January 2022 from https://drloritaylor.com/articles/dont-mourn-organize/.

Tönnies, Ferdinand. 1957 [1887]. *Community and Society*. Mineola, NY: Dover.

Wallerstein, Immanuel. 2011 [1974]. *The Modern World System 1: Capitalist Agriculture and the Origins of the European World-Economy in the Sixteenth Century*. Berkeley: University of California Press.

Warner, R. Stephen. 1998. 'Immigration and Religious Communities in the United States', in R. Stephen Warner and Judith Wittner (eds), *Gatherings in Diaspora: Religious Communities and the New Immigration*. Philadelphia: Temple University Press, pp. 3–34.

Welcoming America. 2018. 'About us'. Retrieved 9 December 2018 from https://www.welcomingamerica.org/about/who-we-are about us.

Williams, Eric. 1944. *Capitalism and Slavery*. Chapel Hill, NC: University of North Carolina Press.

Wimmer, Andreas and Nina Glick Schiller. 2003. 'Methodological Nationalism, the Social Sciences, and the Study of Migration: An Essay in Historical Epistemology', *The International Migration Review* 37(3): 576–610.

Wise, Amanda and Selvaraj Velayutham. 2009. 'Introduction: Multiculturalism and Everyday Life', in Amanda Wise and Selvaraj Velayutham (eds), Everyday Multiculturalism. Basingstoke: Palgrave McMillan, pp. 21–45.

WMUR. 2020. 'Election Results 2020: How New Hampshire Voted in the Presidential Election'. Retrieved 3 January 2022 from https://www.wmur.com/article/new-hampshire-election-results-2020-town-map/34935446.

Wolf, Eric R. 1982. *Europe and the People without History*. Berkeley: University of California Press.

Epilogue
Emancipatory Cosmopolitanism or Global Neighbourhood?

John R. Eidson, Echi Christina Gabbert
and Markus Virgil Hoehne

Pastoralist communities in the borderlands between Kenya and Ethiopia, under duress from 'development'; Tajiks who travel to Syria to take part in jihad; Serbians who valorize generals whom many others regard as war criminals; Tigrayans who recite poems about resistance to Italian – or Amhara – colonizers; Ethiopian Muslims who challenge the hegemonic nationalist narratives of Orthodox Christians; migrants and 'natives' in Halle, Germany, and in Manchester, New Hampshire, who have been displaced from their homes – what do these and the other case studies featured in this volume have in common?

All of these people lead lives, face difficulties and take actions that the contributors to this volume analyse in terms of conflict, identification, integration, exclusion or emplacement. But does analysis in comparable terms make these cases and their dramatis personae comparable to one another? Or does a focus on identification have the effect of fragmenting people into multiple incommensurabilities, depicting them as prisoners of particular identities? Such is the claim of Nigel Rapport, who, in his commentary on an article in which Günther Schlee and his co-authors present a framework for the comparative analysis of identification processes (Eidson et al. 2017a), urges them not to dwell on how human beings become entrapped in what he calls, citing R.D. Laing, 'phantasies of groupness' but to go 'beyond category-thinking' and to show instead how actors experience the world 'in more open-ended, personal, complex, and even inchoate ways' (Rapport 2017: 353).

Rapport's critique of Schlee and his colleagues raises important questions. Does analysis employing the concept of identity and focusing on processes of identification necessarily entail the reification of groups? Or can it provide a basis for comprehending not only how groups are formed but also how group boundaries may be bridged through taking recourse to alternative bases of likeness, distinction and solidarity? Clearly, the latter is the case – this was our point of departure with the vignette about the herder at the watering hole in northern Kenya on the first page of the introduction to this volume. Rapport misses this point because of his commitment to a widespread but inadequate understanding of the concept of identity and, more generally, because of a misunderstanding of the role of categories in human cognition and communication. In fact, Schlee and his co-authors share Rapport's aversion to collectivist 'phantasies of groupness', but they reject the idea that escaping from such phantasies is the same thing as going beyond 'culture, custom and community'. In any adequate understanding of the concept of 'culture', the cultural means available to actors are always equally capable of facilitating closure and opening, or separation and connection, since human relations are always susceptible to transformation.

Like many critics of the concept of identity, Rapport is convinced that using it with reference to collectivities implies an essentialist theory of motivation: people are thought to behave in a certain way because of their identity, i.e. because of certain essential characteristics that they share with other members of their group. These assumptions underlie the oft-cited critique of how the concept of 'identity' is used in the humanities and social sciences by Rogers Brubaker and Frederick Cooper (2000), which has been reiterated, recently, by Michael Jackson (2019: 95).

By now it should be abundantly clear that this case of mistaking 'identity' bears no resemblance to the way in which Schlee or any of the contributors to this volume employ the term or any of its derivatives, most notably, 'identification'. Schlee sees no simple correspondence between a group, an identity and a certain way of behaving. Rather, in particular social and historical settings, and in various places around the world, actors may avail themselves of a significant, if limited, range of possibilities for understanding their likeness and solidarity with some people and their distinction from others. Actors draw on these possibilities in articulating their relations with others in different ways. Precisely how they do this depends on a whole range of variables, which include the logical possibilities inherent in the available categories of identification, the broader social, political and economic circumstances, the particular situation, and, of course, the actor's motivation. Schlee's achievement is to have outlined these variables systematically (e.g. Schlee 2004, 2008; Eidson et al. 2017a).

Once one takes cognizance of the mutability of identities within limits, the categories of identification that are available to a particular set of actors can be seen as a kind of language for articulating and re-articulating their relations to one another in varying situations and under changing circumstances. In this way, categories of identification – which are one part of what Rapport refers to with the very general term 'culture' – offer to actors the means for expressing their individuality and the particularity of their relations with others. This is actually quite close to what Rapport has written:

> '*Culture*' *is rhetorical practice* ... Experience is expressed through it, the world is explored through it, action is sanctioned through it but culture remains a fund of symbolic or rhetorical forms. It is human usage, individual intentionality, which animates the cultural form and brings it to life in particular instances and in a diversity of contradictory contents. (Rapport 2012b: 103, italics in original)

Precisely. But the logical implication, which Rapport does not draw, is that turning away from 'phantasies of groupness' leads not to freedom from categories but to the possibility of moving among categories and even of manipulating them to a certain degree.

Rapport's misunderstanding of Schlee's project also accounts for weaknesses of his own project, which he calls 'emancipatory cosmopolitanism'. While one can only applaud the ideals implied by such terms as 'cosmopolitanism' and 'emancipation', how one conceives of these ideals and of the path to their realization makes all the difference in the world. For Rapport, the goal of emancipatory cosmopolitanism is nothing less than the 'freeing' of the individual from the 'cultural traditions, ... symbolic classifications and identifications, [and] the structuration of belonging and exclusion of particular communities' (Rapport 2012b: 103) in which he imagines him or her to be entrapped. In his discussion of this entrapment, however, it is not always clear who has entrapped whom. If people are trapped in cultural traditions, have they trapped themselves, or have others trapped them? And, if the latter, is it the powerful who have entrapped the powerless? Or is it the anthropologists and the other exegetes who describe the people they study as if they were trapped? Apparently, it is all of the above, though, in Rapport's reflections, not all of these causes of 'communitarian enclosure' (Rapport 2012b: 102) receive the same degree of emphasis.

According to Rapport, the goal of the individual is, or should be, to become 'Anyone', while the goal of the anthropologist should be to recognize that the human world is made up of individuals who are, or can become, 'Anyone' (Rapport 2012a, 2012b). 'Anyone' is Rapport's updated version of the main character from the fifteenth-century English morality play, *The Summoning of Everyman*. Rapport glosses 'Anyone' as 'the global individual', and he describes him or her as someone who has 'the space to live according to the fulfilment of his or her capacities to author an individual life and the right and encouragement to do so' (Rapport 2012b: 105). The right and the opportunity to become 'Anyone' should not depend, he insists, on 'the "accident of birth"', that is, on 'when and where a human life originates'; rather, 'so far as possible, the life is to be vouchsafed from local contingency' (Rapport 2012b: 106). For the individual actor, pursuit of the goal of becoming 'Anyone' requires going 'beyond category thinking', and the same is required of anthropologists, if they are to be able to recognize and analyse the life of 'Anyone' when they see it (Rapport 2017: 353).

Of course, it is important to note that Rapport's 'emancipatory cosmopolitanism' is one of many versions of a concept that is fraught with contradictions and subject to rather acrimonious debate. In critical reviews of the extensive literature on cosmopolitanism, there have been several attempts to formulate an adequate understanding of this concept and also to reject those versions of it that are deemed to be inadequate, misleading or even compromised ideologically (e.g. Glick Schiller and Irving 2014b; Ribeiro 2014; Werbner 2008). This has resulted in a proliferation of distinctions among various types of cosmopolitanism, each of which allows this or that author to profile his or her views in contradistinction to those of others. For our purposes, it is sufficient to draw a gross distinction between liberal and critical versions of cosmopolitanism. Proponents of liberal cosmopolitanism both advocate and register an extension of ideals such as individual freedom and civil rights from the nation to the world. In this liberal vision, individuals are, under the current conditions of globalization, freed from nationalistic bonds and limitations of movement, which results in the merger of various cultural aspects at local levels (e.g. creolization, hybridization) and, simultaneously, allows people to engage in global flow and transnational lives. At the end of the twentieth and the beginning of the twenty-first century, lives are becoming, or should become, more fluid, flexible and so on (e.g. Appadurai 1996; Appiah 2006). With his emphasis on 'Anyone', the individual who transcends the 'accident of birth' and achieves a cosmopolitan orientation beyond 'culture, custom and community', Rapport may be placed squarely in the liberal camp.

Advocates of critical versions of cosmopolitanism share the emancipatory ethos of the liberal theorists but qualify or object to the liberal vision in a number of ways. Globalization and the corresponding forms of transnational mobility that some people experience are not unique to the turn of the millennium but are an expression of an ongoing process that began several centuries ago with the rise of the modern world system (Friedman 2002). Within this world system, some may find the experience of mobility to be emancipatory; but, for those who are driven from their homes by slavery, land-grabbing or warfare, or who feel that their survival depends on seeking a new home elsewhere, it results from compelling necessity. In short, over and above the ways in which actors identify with others, or adjust their relationships of identification, it is necessary to discover the changing circumstances that make it necessary to do so (Eidson et al. 2017a: 347–49). More particularly, it is necessary to 'expose the power dimensions within any iteration of a cosmopolitan vision, project or programme' (Glick Schiller and Irving 2014a: 6).

In human societies everywhere, the reigning circumstances are determined not only by 'culture, custom and community' but also by the enforcement of people's differential, often widely diverging possibilities of gaining access to land, to the means of production, to financial instruments and to the means of political coercion. Because one always enters into the world under particular circumstances, which are characterized by what is often extreme inequality, Rapport's tendency to de-emphasize the significance of the 'accident of birth' or, more accurately, the actor's position in space, time and social context for his or her life-chances is highly problematic.

To demonstrate the significance of relations of political and economic power for the actor's life-chances, we contrast, briefly, Rapport's example of someone who made the transition to the status of 'Anyone' with an example chosen at random from this volume. Rapport's example is Montaigne, a French aristocrat who, after a life in politics in Bordeaux, was able to retreat to the tower of his chateau, where, on the basis of his wealth and cultivation, he could achieve a semblance of the cosmopolitan ideal by reflecting on his experience in light of the humanist tradition from which Rapport draws inspiration as well (Rapport 2012b). How does Montaigne's situation and how do his life-chances compare with those of members of the Rufaᶜa al-Hoi whom we met in the chapter that Elhadi Ibrahim Osman and Al-Amin Abu-Manga contributed to this volume?

The Rufaᶜa al-Hoi, it will be remembered, are or were pastoral nomads who tended their herds in the pastures of the Blue Nile region in southeastern Sudan, until, beginning in the 1970s, their patterns of transhumance were blocked, increasingly, by the expansion in the region of agro-industry, by civil war, and then by the creation of the new international border between Sudan and South Sudan. Finally, they were forced to settle in unfavourable locations in Sennar State of Sudan, where pasture and water were insufficient for their animals, where their mobility was restricted (making it impossible for them to search for sufficient pasture and water), and where they faced the hostility of local farmers and a lack of government services.

Given the situation of the Rufaᶜa al-Hoi in Sennar State, it is difficult to envision a path that their members could take in a quest to achieve the status of 'Anyone' – except, perhaps, becoming migrants in a global context of growing anti-immigrant sentiment. This was the path taken by the Khorezmians who sought work in Tashkent (Turaeva), the Qazaks who left Mongolia for Qazakstan (Finke), the Moluccans who felt compelled to relocate to the Netherlands (Benda-Beckmann), and the Ghanaians, Nigerians and Congolese who migrated to the city of Halle in Germany or to Manchester, New Hampshire (Glick Schiller); but the chapters devoted to these case studies show that migration does not necessarily bring the people in question any closer than they were before to the preconditions for becoming 'Anyone', in the sense sketched by Rapport. Obviously, not everyone has the same chance of becoming 'Anyone' as did Montaigne – an exceptionally privileged individual, who, in addition, has all the earmarks of the kind of person whom Schlee would call a virtuoso of identificatory flexibility (Eidson et al. 2017b: 355). Despite the emphasis that Rapport places on the individual and on the ideal of individuality, which he has enshrined in his 'Anyone', everyone must necessarily live together with others. But the question is: with which others, how and under what conditions?

Contributors to a volume on critical cosmopolitanism, cited above (Glick Schiller and Irving 2014b), pose the question 'whose cosmopolitanism?' One might amend this question slightly in terms of Schlee by asking whose cosmopolitanism with whom and under which circumstances? If the possibility of enjoying 'emancipatory cosmopolitanism' is confined to global elites, or if people in need can only participate in cosmopolitanism by joining ethnonationalist movements (Glick Schiller, in this volume), i.e. by indulging in what Rapport calls 'phantasies of groupness', then, arguably, it is not worthy of the name. Rather, to qualify as cosmopolitanism in the frankly normative sense of this word, social action must be directed toward creating 'a domain of commonality – however partial, fleeting or contradictory – across categorical identities such as ethnicity, class, sexuality, status, gender and religion' (Glick Schiller and Irving 2014a: 5). It would be illusory, however, to imagine that this domain of commonality might be located 'beyond category-thinking'; such a claim would signal, rather, the imposition of allegedly 'self-evident' categorical distinctions that are favourable to some participants over others. Instead, entering a domain of commonality in which the various participants are sufficiently different to make communication necessary would require a re-selection or a re-adjustment of categories of identification and of perceived category membership in order to make communication possible.

In any given attempt to create such a domain of commonality, what might be the relevant categories allowing such cross-cutting ties? And how might they be set in relation to one another? In beginning to formulate answers to these questions, we turn to a model that takes as its starting point situations in today's world that are characterized by the often unrecognized interconnectedness among people whose positions in the global political economy and whose points of view differ from one another to an extreme degree: the model of global neighbourhood.

The concept of 'cultural neighbourhood' was developed by Ivo Strecker and his students and colleagues in the context of long-term ethnographic research among diverse communities in southern Ethiopia, and it was further elaborated in the edited volume, *To Live with Others: Essays on Cultural Neighborhood in Southern Ethiopia* (Gabbert and Thubauville 2010). In the introduction to the present volume, we have described southern Ethiopia, along with the territories on the other side of the border to Kenya, as a peripheral area populated by members of a large number of relatively small, culturally heterogeneous agro-pastoral communities whose relations vary between alliance and enmity, ritual exchange and raiding. While, in the early twentieth century, members of the British colonial administration in Kenya were appalled by what they understood (in their exoticizing view) to be the 'incessant conflicts' in this region, it is clear that there was no Hobbesian state of *Warre*. Instead, intercommunity relations in this politically decentralized social and cultural world are better characterized as an example of what Alexander Horstmann and Schlee (2001) have called 'integration through difference' and what Gabbert calls 'cultural neighbourhood', which she defines as follows:

> a community across ethnic boundaries that ... embraces enmity and amity, supports cultural diversity, heightens knowledge and facilitates resilience. Cultural neighborhood is place, sentiment and narration, flexible and yet full of rules. Cultural neighbors are aware of and interested in each other, they face each other, get used to each other and develop intimate acquaintance of each other's differences and similarities through time, effort and creativity. (Gabbert 2010: 24)

Importantly, cultural neighbours do not have to be friends, but whether they are friends or foes they are familiar with each other, and this familiarity is the basis for predictability both in peaceful and hostile relations (see also Schlee 2002).

In her continued research in southern Ethiopia, Gabbert has taken the idea of 'cultural neighbourhood' as a point of departure in conceiving of a broader 'global neighbourhood' (Abbink et al. 2014; Gabbert 2014; Gabbert 2018; Gabbert et al. 2021). This concept is useful in the analysis of conflict situations involving diverse actors whose life-projects intersect but who are so distant from one another, culturally, politically, institutionally and spatially, that communication among them seems to be, under normal circumstances, out of the question. The purpose of analysis in terms of global neighbourhood is to expose the interconnection and the divergence among those who qualify as global neighbours as a first step in imagining the possibility of their subsequent convergence.

Examples of the interconnectedness of seemingly disconnected groups and interests may be found in the national and global investment scenarios in East Africa. Here, the global neighbours include local communities, policy makers, investors, NGOs, human rights organizations and scientists, among others. From this list, one can infer that global neighbours include those who have or will meet face-to-face, along with those who most probably never will meet. However, despite the distance that may separate global neighbours, the decisions taken by some, e.g. by investment brokers at a stock exchange, have direct and often devastating effects on the lives of others, e.g. the agro-pastoralists who for centuries have inhabited territories that are now being 'developed'.

Our formulations in the preceding paragraph are enough to indicate that 'global neighbourhood' is not a magical solution to problems caused by international investment and government projects. Rather, it is a way of conceptualizing the problem that draws attention to the full range of actors who should be taken into consideration, to the divergence of their various points of view, to the power differential among them and to the possible bases of conceiving of a 'domain of commonality' with which each could identify, in their own way. Such a conceptualization is urgently needed, as is made clear by the tragic consequences of misrecognition and exploitation to date. With reference to the 'development' of southern Ethiopia, Gabbert describes the regularity with which the actors involved have fallen short in fulfilling the obligations of global neighbourhood in the following terms:

> Administrative efforts to communicate with local populations came too late in the procedures and initially left out people who were drastically affected by changes to their livelihoods. Indeed, villagization schemes to make way for commercial farms have led to hardship for many agro-pastoralists who not only lost their basis for subsistence economy but their aspirations for a future of their own choice, while promises of a brighter future and trickle-down benefits have not manifested for most people . . . This results not only in economic insecurity and hitherto unknown dependencies, it also creates a feeling of loss of a very existence within an environment that was inextricably connected to people's livelihoods, identities and their being in the world . . . The personal suffering of people experiencing the decline of their livelihoods is hardly describable. (Gabbert 2018: 292–93, 294)

Gabbert's colleague, Jon Abbink, sets the situation in southern Ethiopia in broader perspective by noting that '[t]he encroachment on their rangeland follows a familiar path seen many times over: closure, livelihood subversion, impoverishment, and decline' (Abbink 2011: 517). In a time of widely available internet communication (also from the bottom-up) and heightened global power politics (mainly from the top-down), what began as a conflict over who controls which resources can also spiral out of very local settings and become tied to the dynamics of 'terrorism' and 'counterterrorism' on a 'global' scale (Roche and Reyna, in this volume; Hoehne 2014; Reyna 2016).

The key question is, of course: what would it take to get those whom Gabbert identifies as 'global neighbours' to acknowledge one another, to learn from one another and to take action together, despite the dissonance between them? How could different people, who might never meet in person but who are willingly or unwillingly connected through the global economy, rather than through human encounters, be induced to develop mutual respect while making future-oriented choices with global ramifications? For example, would it be possible to base action for planetary survival on the mutual exchange of expertise among global neighbours, so that in times of ecological and climatic crises the local people affected by development are recognized as experts on their ground and 'the most important stakeholders, fellow planners and world makers' (Gabbert 2018: 308)? In attempting to find answers to these questions, one would have to go beyond what Gabbert dismisses as 'so-called stakeholder discussions' in which the people affected by development are called 'partners' but merely 'serve as another element in the planners' tool box' (Gabbert 2018: 289, 308).

Divergence among global neighbours frequently involves the encoding of relations in categorical distinctions that serve to augment it. Thus, the global neighbours of those who wage war on 'terror' include the 'terrorists'; while the global neighbours of advocates of 'development' include those 'backward' people who stand in its way. Insofar as they consider local inhabitants to be 'backward', to belong to a past that they are determined to overcome, many of the 'progressive' people who advocate 'development' think and act in ways that make them highly resistant to the principles underlying global neighbourhood – principles such as the recognition of the value of the experience and the validity of the perspective of other people (Schlee 2021: 67). Development is pursued instead through a politics of exclusion that will continue to displace people in agricultural investment zones. Policy makers, investors and contractors have proceeded with their plans, despite the many works on ecology and food production that warn about the detrimental results of such projects.

> [T]here is a tendency to politicize and discredit scientific reports and local knowledge when they do not fit into the presently dominant ideology. Findings are used selectively to support policies rather than for critical engagement and improvement of the challenges at hand. High modernism is legitimized not only by constructing its opposite: the underdeveloped, vulnerable and/or backward peasant or pastoralist living on so-called wastelands, . . . but also by silencing its critics through words and deeds. (Gabbert 2018: 290)

The problem of achieving convergence among global neighbours, once the divergence of social classes, life-worlds and interests has occurred, is as old as the origins of inequality. Speaking schematically, rather than historically, one might pinpoint the difficulty with reference to the gulf that has opened up between two obligations: first, securing a livelihood for oneself and one's dependents; and, second, contributing to the common good. But what is the 'common good', and who defines it? When a gulf opens up between what are often called 'private' and 'public' obligations, there is a tendency for political and economic elites to acquire the power to define public obligations – contributions to the 'common good' – for others, i.e. for the majority of people. Of course, democratic systems with representative forms of government are designed to address precisely this problem. But democratic systems often function rather imperfectly, sometimes very much so; and often they are absent entirely. As a result, people may be forced to make contributions to the 'common good' such as those that take the form of vacating land on which the government plans to realize its various projects.

Schlee's reflections on the role of group size in processes of identification pertain precisely to the nearly pan-human contradiction dogging the definition of the 'common good'. His latest works on unequal citizenship further those reflections (Schlee 2021). Demanding that people make contributions to the 'common good' without allowing those same people to participate in its definition is just one more expression of a general tendency that Schlee has identified: the tendency of those in positions of power to invoke inclusive identification when broad participation is required to cover the costs of collective action, and then to shift to exclusive identification when they want to narrow the circle of those who enjoy the benefits of that action. This is the logic underlying widely varying forms of betrayal, corruption and exploitation: in each case, someone draws on the contributions of one group, often a relatively large one, in order to accrue benefits for the member of another group, usually a much smaller one. Among the goals of the 'global neighbourhood' project is the clear articulation of the demand that the 'common good' be defined jointly and that those who bear the costs of collective action must also receive a corresponding share of the benefits. Conveying this message to those who see their interests best served by ignoring it is a formidably challenging task; yet it might be the central task of the twenty-first century both retrospectively, when addressing historical injustices, and prospectively, when working together to build a liveable future. As Schlee has noted, '[o]ur common humanity is the collective identity most difficult to mobilize'. 'Yet', he adds, 'the interdependence of the world and the fragility of our environment demand it' (Schlee et al. 2018: 230).

John R. Eidson is a social anthropologist with a PhD from Cornell University and with interests in modern Germany, social theory, historical semantics and the history of anthropology. He has taught at the University of Maryland, the University of New Hampshire, the University of Leipzig and the Martin Luther University of Halle-Wittenberg. He is editor of *Das anthropologische Projekt* (Leipziger Universitätsverlag, 2008) and editorial board member of the *Integration and Conflict Studies* series published by Berghahn Books. After eighteen years as a senior research fellow at the Max Planck Institute for Social Anthropology, he retired in 2020 and continues now with his research as an independent scholar.

Echi Christina Gabbert is an anthropologist and a lecturer at the Institute for Social and Cultural Anthropology at Göttingen University, Germany. Her research foci are agro-pastoralism, music and oral history, political ecology, and peace and conflict studies. Her long-term fieldwork in Ethiopia resulted in the award-winning PhD thesis 'Deciding Peace'. She has extended the 'Cultural Neighbourhood Approach' to 'Global Neighbourhood' scenarios, where global investment schemes meet smallholders' livelihoods, and she is coordinating the Lands of the Future Initiative, an interdisciplinary project about pastoral livelihoods in the twenty-first century. She is also co-editor of the volume *Lands of the Future: Anthropological Perspectives on Pastoralism, Land Use and Tropes of Modernity in Eastern Africa* (Berghahn, 2021).

Markus Virgil Hoehne is lecturer at the Institute of Social Anthropology at the University of Leipzig. He received his PhD from the Martin-Luther University Halle-Wittenberg and worked for ten years at the Max Planck Institute for Social Anthropology in Halle (Saale). His long-term research interests are Somali affairs and the anthropology of conflict; his most recent project deals with forensic anthropology in cultural context, based on research in Somaliland and Peru. He authored *Between Somaliland and Puntland: Marginalization, Militarization and Conflicting Political Visions* (Rift Valley Institute, 2015) and is co-editor of *Borders and Borderlands as Resources in the Horn of Africa* (James Currey, 2010) and *The State and the Paradox of Customary Law in Africa* (Routledge, 2018).

References

Abbink, Jon. 2011. '"Land to Foreigners": Economic, Legal, and Socio-cultural Aspects of New Land Acquisition Schemes in Ethiopia', *Journal of Contemporary African Studies* 29(4): 513–35.

Abbink, Jon, Kelly Askew, Dereje Feyissa Dori, Elliot Fratkin, Echi Christina Gabbert, John G. Galaty, Shauna LaTosky, Jean Lydall, Hussein. A. Mahmoud, John Markakis, Günther Schlee, Ivo Strecker and David Turton. 2014. 'Lands of the Future: Transforming Pastoral Lands and Livelihoods in Eastern Africa', *Max Planck Institute for Social Anthropology Working Papers* No. 154. Retrieved from https://www.eth.mpg.de/pubs/wps/pdf/mpi-eth-working-paper-0154.

Appadurai, Arjun. 1996. *Modernity at Large: Cultural Dimensions of Globalization*. Minneapolis: University of Minnesota Press.

Appiah, Kwame Anthony. 2006. *Cosmopolitanism: Ethics in a World of Strangers*. New York: W. W. Norton.

Brubaker, Rogers and Frederick Cooper. 2000. 'Beyond "Identity"', *Theory and Society* 29(1): 1–47.

Eidson, John R., Dereje Feyissa, Veronika Fuest, Markus V. Hoehne, Boris Nieswand, Günther Schlee and Olaf Zenker. 2017a. 'From Identification to Framing and Alignment: A New Approach to the Comparative Analysis of Collective Identities', *Current Anthropology* 58(3): 340–59.

———. 2017b. 'Reply to Comments on "From Identification to Framing and Alignment: A New Approach to the Comparative Analysis of Collective Identities"', *Current Anthropology* 58(3): 355–57.

Friedman, Jonathan. 2002. 'From Roots to Routes: Tropes for Trippers', *Anthropological Theory* 2(1): 21–36.

Gabbert, Echi Christina. 2010. 'Introduction', in Echi Christina Gabbert and Sophia Thubauville (eds), *To Live with Others: Essays on Cultural Neighborhood in Southern Ethiopia*. Cologne: Rüdiger Köppe Verlag, pp. 13–28.

———. 2014. 'The Global Neighbourhood Concept: A Chance for Cooperative Development or Festina Lente', in Mulugeta Gebrehiwot Berhe (ed.), *A Delicate Balance: Land Use, Minority Rights and Social Stability in the Horn of Africa*. Addis Ababa: Institute for Peace and Security Studies, Addis Ababa University, pp. 14–37.

———. 2018. 'Future in Culture: Globalizing Environments in the Lowlands of Southern Ethiopia', in Jon Abbink (ed.), *The Environment Crunch in Africa*. Cham, Switzerland: Palgrave Macmillan, pp. 287–317.

Gabbert, Echi Christina, Fana Gebresenbet, John G. Galaty and Günther Schlee (eds). 2021. *Lands of the Future: Anthropological Perspectives on Pastoralism, Land Deals and Tropes of Modernity in Eastern Africa*. New York and Oxford: Berghahn.

Gabbert, Echi Christina and Sophia Thubauville (eds). 2010. *To Live with Others: Essays on Cultural Neighborhood in Southern Ethiopia*. Cologne: Rüdiger Köppe Verlag.

Glick Schiller, Nina and Andrew Irving. 2014a. 'Introduction: What's in a Word? What's in a Question?', in Nina Glick Schiller and Andrew Irving (eds), *Whose Cosmopolitanism? Critical Perspectives, Relationalities and Discontents*. New York and Oxford: Berghahn, pp. 1–22.

Glick Schiller, Nina and Andrew Irving (eds). 2014b. *Whose Cosmopolitanism? Critical Perspectives, Relationalities and Discontents*. New York and Oxford: Berghahn.

Hoehne, Markus V. 2014. 'Resource Conflict and Militant Islamism in the Golis Mountains in Northern Somalia (2006–2013)', *Review of African Political Economy* 41(141): 358–73.

Horstmann, Alexander and Günther Schlee (eds). 2001. *Integration durch Verschiedenheit: Lokale und globale Formen interkultureller Kommunikation*. Bielefeld: transcript.

Jackson, Michael. 2019. *Critique of Identity Thinking*. New York and Oxford: Berghahn.

Rapport, Nigel. 2012a. *Anyone, the Cosmopolitan Subject of Anthropology*. New York and Oxford: Berghahn.

———. 2012b. 'Emancipatory Cosmopolitanism: A Vision of the Individual Free from Culture, Custom and Community', in Gerard Delanty (ed.), *Handbook of Cosmopolitan Studies*. London: Routledge, pp. 101–14.

———. 2017. '"Beyond Category-Thinking" – Comment on "From Identification to Framing and Alignment: A New Approach to the Comparative Analysis of Collective Identities" by John R. Eidson, Dereje Feyissa, Veronika Fuest, Markus V. Hoehne, Boris Nieswand, Günther Schlee, and Olaf Zenker', *Current Anthropology* 58(3): 352–53.

Reyna, Stephen P. 2016. *Deadly Contradictions: The New American Empire and Global Warring*. New York and Oxford: Berghahn.

Ribeiro, Gustavo Lins. 2014. 'World Anthropologies: Anthropological Cosmopolitanisms and Cosmopolities', *Annual Review of Anthropology* 43: 483–98.

Schlee, Günther. 2002. 'Introduction', in Günther Schlee (ed.), *Imagined Differences: Hatred and the Construction of Identity*. Münster: LIT Verlag, pp. 3–32.

———. 2004. 'Taking Sides and Constructing Identities: Reflections on Conflict Theory', *Journal of the Royal Anthropological Institute* 10(1): 135–56.

———. 2008. *How Enemies Are Made: Towards a Theory of Ethnic and Religious Conflicts*. Integration and Conflict Studies 1. New York and Oxford: Berghahn.

———. 2021. 'Unequal Citizenship and One-Sided Communication: Anthropological Perspectives on Collective Identification in the Context of Large-Scale Transfers in Ethiopia', in Echi Christina Gabbert, Fana Gebresenbet, John Galaty and Günther Schlee (eds), *Lands of the Future: Anthropological Perspectives on Pastoralism, Land Deals and Tropes of Modernity in Eastern Africa*. New York and Oxford: Berghahn, pp. 59–77.

Schlee, Günther, Alexander Horstmann and John Eidson. 2018. 'Epilogue', in Günther Schlee and Alexander Horstmann (eds), *Difference and Sameness as Modes of Integration*. New York and Oxford: Berghahn, pp. 225–30.

Werbner, Pnina (ed.). 2008. *Anthropology and the New Cosmopolitanism: Rooted, Feminist and Vernacular Perspectives*. London: Routledge.

Afterword

Charisma: Ethnographers and Their Host Societies

Ivo Strecker

'How do I best celebrate my younger mate, neighbour, and academic colleague?', I ask myself as I glance from my farm in Redecke towards Borgholzhausen where Günther Schlee has his abode. This sunny afternoon of 24 March 2019 is so pleasant, and the birds chirp so cheerfully that I decide to begin on a playful note paraphrasing an old Irish joke: 'I don't like to think before I write. I like to be just as surprised as everyone else about what I write.'

The first thought that pops up in my mind is, 'We are celebrating here a truly charismatic personality'. Yes, no doubt, Günther has great charisma, but as soon as I write this, I wonder what I – or anyone else – might mean by it precisely. We know that the ancient Greeks meant by *charis* a superior person's attitude of benevolence and kindness towards subordinates. We know that the Christian apostles, prophets and leaders of the church who bent people's beliefs to their will were said to possess charisma. We know that the heroes, hunters, shamans etc. who tended to act as leaders of their groups had charisma. We know that Max Weber identified charisma as one of the three major types of political rule, i.e. traditional, legal and charismatic; and that he saw charismatic leadership grounded in and deriving from magical or otherwise 'supernatural qualities of a personality', adding that it did not matter whether such qualities were objectively true. And finally, we know that in modern and postmodern discourse charisma is often used more loosely to praise the radiant and captivating character of a person. But in spite of all this knowledge (or perhaps because of it?) we still do not really know what we mean by charisma. Like metaphor and other tropes, it has echo chambers that may cause all sorts of evocations.

The innate qualities of persons undoubtedly play a role, but only when we also take other factors such as hearsay, storytelling, weaving of legends etc. into account can we understand the dynamics of charismatic leadership and meaningfully ask how Günther's charisma may have come about. Night has fallen and I pause now, but I can see already how tomorrow morning I will continue and tell you the tale of how Günther's name became imbued with fame, received an aura and bespoke a certain charisma long before I met him in person.

*

Now it is the morning of 25 March 2019 with strong winds blowing from the northwest and rain splashing against my window. Just the right weather to leave and move – at least in one's mind – to the drier and warmer regions where Jean Lydall and I, as well as Günther Schlee, did ethnographic research during the early and mid-1970s: Günther among the Rendille of northern Kenya and Jean and I among the Hamar of southern Ethiopia. Others also did fieldwork here during this 'blessed' period: David Turton among the Mursi; Uri Almagor and Claudia Carr among the Dassanech; Serge Tornay among the Nyangatom; Don Donham among the Maale; Christopher Hallpike among the Konso; Paul Baxter and Asmarom Legesse among the Boran (later followed by Marco Bassi) . . . and others.

I call this period 'blessed' because it still allowed researchers to closely study local life before the advent of bulldozers (leading to roads, sugar and cotton plantations, towns, churches, loudspeakers!) that from the 1980s onwards were to mercilessly destroy most wildlife and generally the ecological as well as the sociocultural balance of the area. Another metonym of destruction was – of course – the weaponry infiltrating northern Kenya and southern Ethiopia from the war-torn regions in the West (Sudan) and East (Somalia), which has put heavy constraints on ethnographic research ever since.

During the 'blessed' period I observed how in southern Ethiopia and northern Kenya a curious identification of ethnographers and their respective host societies began to emerge. Most of this was hearsay, gossip and even mockery, such as when Asen Balikci – better known for his research and films about the Netslik Eskimo – addressed me at a party (given in Addis Ababa in honour of Judith Ohlmsted) saying: 'Why don't you go and do research among the Hamar, the deadly enemies of the Mursi whom your friend David Turton has chosen to study?' Overtly, this was meant to be play. But later I began to understand the undertone of the joke and realized that it entailed an awareness of the inescapable bonding which over time is bound to develop between researchers and their hosts, as well as the effect of dissonances that may exist between the groups, which 'their' respective ethnographers study.

As Jean and I were to learn once we had come to Hamar, it was in fact Berinas, father of Aike Berinas (Baldambe), 'our' host, mentor and teacher in Hamar, who initiated the animosities between the Mursi and the Hamar to which Asen Balikci referred:

> The country of the Mursu is far and lies across a river, so our ancestors did not know them. It was my father Berinas who started the war with the Mursu. Dedjasmatch Biru who was governor at Bako called Berinas: 'Berinas!' 'Woi!' 'The Mursu are Menelik's enemies, fight them! When the police come to them they kill them. When the Hamar come to them they kill them. When the Amhara come they kill them. Fight them!' Then Berinas showed Biru the way to Mursu. In olden times the Hamar would only look at the fires on the mountains of Mursu. It was Berinas who started the fighting and it was Dedjasmatch Biru who ordered him to do so. (Lydall and Strecker 1979b: 25–26)

Once the fighting had begun, the antagonism between the two groups became so deeply entrenched that the Hamar ritual leader (*bitta*) would routinely curse the Mursi in his annual ritual of protection.

David Turton and I had met in the 1960s when both of us studied at the London School of Economics. We were friends then, but during our years of fieldwork some kind of dissonance developed. I do not want to dwell here at length on what happened. Let it suffice to say that I was deeply hurt when David did not invite me to contribute to 'Warfare among East African Herders', which he edited together with Katsuyoshi Fuki and published in 1979. He knew very well that by then I had closely studied and documented the dynamics of war and peace in South Omo (see the Hamar trilogy, also published in 1979). So it seemed to me that only for some mysterious reason – in revenge of the Hamar *bitta*'s spell? – he excluded me. Later, once the animosities between Mursi and Hamar had ceased, the relationship between 'their' ethnographers – David, Pat, Jean and I – became again one of mutual understanding and friendship.

Things were quite different between myself and Serge Tornay who came to study the Nyangatom (called Bume by the Hamar). Our relationship was not affected by a curse but by a blessing. A generation ago, the Hamar and Bume had conducted elaborate peace-making rituals described in *The Hamar of Southern Ethiopia. Vol. II: Baldambe Explains*, which for the purpose of the present chapter acts as an 'echo chamber' of local memories:

> Then my father slaughtered an ox. The elders gathered together and ate it. Then they called for the end of all fighting: 'May the sickness of the cattle get lost, may the sickness of the goats get lost, may our spear that killed get lost.' ... Then the Bume *bitta* got up and answered: '... Bume, in your belly there is war. Do you see this spear? Do you see this big spear?' 'We see it.' 'Its blade is big, isn't it?' 'It is big.' 'If you should make war, if you should kill the women and children of Berinas, if you should steal his cattle, then this spear will turn back upon you and kill you. Like Berinas' stomach, my stomach has become one and is like the white ox. Now you and Berinas and his children shall become in-laws, friends, one family.'
> Then the ox was slaughtered and the other spear was brought up to *bitta* Elto who buried it in the earth. Isn't then the spear dead? Since the spear was buried the talk of Bume and Hamar has become one. If people start fighting: '*Ai-ai-ai-ai*! Stop it,

stop it, stop it! *Bitta* Elto and spokesman Berinas have put magic into the spear. . . .'. (Lydall and Strecker 1979b: 33–34)

According to the central thesis of the present chapter, the emphatic and well-remembered peace-making between the two host societies – Nyangatom (Bume) and Hamar – will also have influenced the relationship between 'their' ethnographers. In fact, the peace-making leads one to predict that friendship and harmony would develop and prevail between them. So it comes as no surprise that Serge and I entered into a close and cooperative relationship as soon as we were able to meet in the field.

**

Today, 26 March 2019, began with gentle rays of the sun filtering through the trees. Later mighty black clouds rose over the forest, and gradually rain began to fall that now, towards the evening, has given way to a lighter sky that promises the return of the sun, if not this evening then surely tomorrow. In light of my present writing this augurs some brightening up, some kind of arrival followed by a new departure. And so it is! I have now found my central theme with even a title for it: 'Charisma: Ethnographers and Their Host Societies'.

With this chapter I want to pay homage to Günther's achievements as head of the department of 'Integration and Conflict' at the Max Planck Institute for Social Anthropology, Halle/Saale, Germany, and contribute to his research agenda by asking, 'How do interethnic processes of conflict and integration affect the relationships between ethnographers?'

So, what does our 'echo chamber' (i.e. 'Baldambe Explains') tell us about the relationship between the Hamar and the people Günther came to study in 1974 (i.e. the Rendille, Samburu, Gabra, Somali and others whom most Hamar don't distinguish and simply call 'Korre')? Here is what we find:

> In the time of the ancestors, . . . the Korre used to come here, jingle, jingle, their leg bells going: jingle, jingle. One Korre would have four spears, another would have three, another would have two, and they all had shields. The Hamar had no shields and each Hamar had only one spear and one bow, which makes two. Thus they would fight. Early in the morning the leg bells of the Korre would sound *borororo-rorokorrororolololololol* and the Hamar would call: '*Wah! wah! wah!* The Korre have come, have come. Get up, get up, get up.'
>
> Then they would come together to fight, come together, come together. . . They fought all over the country. Then the Korre with their four spears, three spears, two spears and the Hamar with just one spear and a bow, would confront each other. The Hamar would shout: 'Shoot cross-wise with your arrows, shoot cross-wise, shoot cross-wise! . . .'. The Korre had raided our cattle, hadn't they? Then the owner of the cattle called out. Next the bowstring sounded *king, king, king* and the Korre were wiped out. Getting the cattle back from the Korre they came dancing. Thus, the ancestors of the Hamar. (Lydall and Strecker 1979b: 26)

According to the thesis that I try to advance here, the well-remembered battles between the Korre and the Hamar will have influenced the relationship between 'their' ethnographers in one way or other. In particular, the prowess of the Korre must have added to Günther's charisma. In support of this view let us recall that ethnographic fieldwork has often been likened to a 'vision quest', a search for the 'meaning of life', a 'rite of passage'. A successful 'vision quest' enhances a person's social standing. And so it is with ethnographers who embark on fieldwork. The more difficult, demanding and dangerous life in their host societies is the more fame they will eventually gain, and their name will attain a special aura.

There were in fact several aspects under which Günther's fieldwork can been seen as extreme and therefore prone to enhance his charisma: the war-like disposition of his hosts; their desert-like habitat; their magnificent camels; their nomadic life; and – perhaps surprisingly – his youth and physical appearance. Let me briefly detail these aspects one by one.

We know the legendary prowess of the Korre already from 'Baldambe Explains'. But what about the habitat in which Günther lived and moved for several years together with his hosts? During our fieldwork, Jean and I could clearly see how in the transitional zone of southern Ethiopia the mountains east and west of the Rift Valley give way to semi-desert lowlands that extend southward and look like a vast, grey-blue sea. To the north there are the clearly distinct mountains of Ari, to the east the mountains of Borana, and to the west the mountains of Bume and Mursi, but to the south there is only the semi-desert with a hazy blue sky above it. Surely, only brave and hardy people could survive here.

Part of the desert-like environment where Günther did his research are the animals tended by his hosts: splendid herds of camels supplemented by cattle and small stock. From the perspective of the Hamar, nothing is more demanding – and almost impossible to master – than the herding of camels. The Korre are therefore held in high esteem, as is the ethnographer who lives with them in order to study the arduous and joyous sides of camel herding in the semi-desert of northern Kenya.

The fact that the Korre dismantle their homesteads, load them on the backs of their camels and then move to other localities adds in the eyes of the Hamar (for whom most of this is anyway hearsay) to the Korre's and 'their' ethnographer's exotic character. For me a further element added to my perception of Günther, the never-seen-but-often-heard-of ethnographer: he travelled the Kenyan deserts on the backs of camels like Roede Orm – immortalized by Frans Bengtsson – crossed the seas. This image was nourished further by bits of information that reached me about his youth, his tall and strong stature, his long blond hair, and generally – as I thought – Viking like appearance.

**

2 April 2019: Jean and I were away – first at Roland Hardenberg's conference on 'millets' in Groningen and then on a visit to *Ida*, our boat in Varel at the Jadebu-

sen. Upon our return we find the cherry trees blossoming and the leaves bursting out in the bushes and trees around us: time for me to write the final paragraphs of this chapter in which I want to once again strengthen my argument that the relationships pertaining between host societies influence the relationships between 'their' ethnographers.

Our 'echo chamber' tells us not of friendship or alliance between Korre and Hamar, only of fighting. Let's have a look again at the following lines: 'Early in the morning the leg bells of the Korre would sound *borororororokorrorololololololol* and the Hamar would call: "*Wah! wah! wah!* The Korre have come, have come. Get up, get up, get up." And: "Then the Korre with their four spears, three spears, two spears and the Hamar with just one spear and a bow, would confront each other." The Hamar would shout: "Shoot cross-wise with your arrows, shoot cross-wise, shoot cross-wise! . . ."'.

This vivid description of battles between our two host societies, their '*korrororololololol*', '*wah! wah! wah!*' and 'shoot cross-wise, shoot cross-wise!', serves as a perfect analogy of the battles fought between Günther and me on the field of anthropological theory. For seemingly inexplicable reasons (inexplicable as long as one does not take the theory of mutual influence between host societies and 'their' ethnographers into account), we never formed an alliance to strengthen the theoretical paradigms that each of us spent much effort to develop: Rational Choice Theory and Rhetoric Culture Theory. As time went by, I would simply speak of RCT 1 (Rational Choice Theory) and RCT 2 (Rhetoric Culture Theory). Let us have a look at these two ventures.

RCT 1 – Rational Choice Theory

In 1999, when Günther had become one of the founding directors of the Max Planck Institute for Social Anthropology in Halle/Saale, he developed a programme that focused empirically on processes of integration and conflict and theoretically on matters of rational choice in human interaction. A review article entitled 'Understanding Ethnic Conflicts by Rational Choice' by Aleksandar Bošković and Suzana Ignjatovic (2012) has dealt with RCT 1 so well that I quote it here at some length to summarize Günther's venture. Particularly useful is the following passage where the authors compare Schlee with Boudon:

> Let us compare the basic principles of the RCT (as defined by Boudon) with Schlee's theory and research. According to Boudon, RCT is based on six premises: (1) focus on the individual actor; (2) agency can be understood (comprehension is explanation); (3) rationality (there are reasons for actions, conscious or not); (4) consequentialism and instrumentalism (RCT shares this with functionalism, reasons are followed by consequences); (5) egoism; (6) maximization (cost–benefit mechanism is one of the available options to actors). In Schlee's conceptualization of the RCT-

based conflict theory, most of these principles have been applied. First, epistemologically, an individual actor is in focus, even though collective actors are named as particular ethnicities (Nuer, Mbororo, Garra are aggregates of individual choices). Second, understanding the reasons for actors' choices of alliances, identifications, grouping and regrouping, is equal to the explanation (Schlee stays close to the Weberian position, and does not look for 'substantive factors' like culture, religion, etc.). Third, consequentialism and instrumentalism are always present in the explicit link between choice and action. Fourth, actors are rational in the sense that they have 'good reasons' for their agency (not necessarily leading to 'good consequences'). Fifth, egoism is implied in actors' orientation and other 'good causes' are only rhetoric 'rationalizations' in ethnic conflicts. Sixth, the maximization principle is crucially important in Schlee's theory. Maximization is the underlying premise (the cost–benefit calculation of actors) that represents the mechanism for the construction of identities. For example, there is no given collective identity, e.g., the Boran identity is a result of identity preferences, and not its cause. Conflict situations are similar to quasi-markets that offer many options. There is an ongoing process of mapping out of the identity preferences. Not only actors' alliances and enemies, but also the corresponding cognitive products are the result of the maximization principle. This is an important innovation in Schlee's modification of the RCT. He is aware of possible criticisms for putting aside emotional and 'irrational forces'. His reasons are corresponding to 'classical' RCT: actors act 'as if' they were rational, on average, although some irrationalities are present. (Bošković and Ignjatović 2012: 292–93)

As time went by a number of distinguished scholars joined this exploration of the pros and cons of RCT 1, and in 2011 – on the occasion of Günther's sixtieth birthday – they organized a workshop at the Max Planck Institute in Halle/Saale that opened with a roundtable entitled 'Rational Choice and Challenges'. Present were Pierre Bonte, Donald Donham, Dereje Feyissa, Peter Finke, John Galaty, Jürg Helbling, Anatoly Khazanov, Richard Rottenburg, Serge Tornay, Christoph Winter, Olaf Zenker and others. Although the 2011 workshop endorsed and underpinned RCT 1, it also called at times implicitly for an opening towards RCT 2, such as when John Galaty entitled his contribution '(Non) Rational Choice', arguing in the abstract of his paper as follows:

Reasoning is best seen as an illocutionary act, since most choices are 'made' via words and are thus bound up with discourse and the constraints of language. Affects have been demonstrated to underpin the capacity to make decisions, with rationality working in tandem with the emotions. Furthermore, rationality is most often exercised in rhetoric, not as a means to a logical end but as a form of argumentation, aiming at convincing and refuting rather than rigorously arriving at a preferable choice. Without dismissing the exercise of reason, let us be cautious about assuming the evocations of reason exemplify its virtues, and let us examine just how choices are really made, especially – as in the case of East African pastoralists – when words are their most potent enemies. (Galaty 2011)

RCT 2 – Rhetoric Culture Theory

At about the same time Günther began to develop RCT 1 at the Max Planck Institute for Social Anthropology, I embarked on the 'Rhetoric Culture Project' at the Institute of Anthropology and African Studies at the University Mainz. The scholars who first worked most closely with me were Stephen Tyler, Christian Meyer, Felix Girke and Anna-Maria Brandstetter, but as time went by and the Volkswagen Foundation began to fund our conferences, many more joined of whom I can mention here only the few who became editors or co-editors of the first seven volumes in the Berghahn Books series 'Studies in Rhetoric and Culture': Michael Carrithers, Stephen Gudeman, Robert Hariman, Ralph Cintron, Markus Verne, Boris Wiseman and Anthony Paul. At the back of these volumes, the RCT 2 agenda is summarized as follows:

> Our minds are filled with images and ideas, but these remain unstable and incomplete as long as we do not manage to persuade both ourselves and others of their meanings. It is this inward and outward rhetoric which allows us to give some kind of shape and structure to our understanding of the world and which becomes central to the formation of individual and collective consciousness. This series is dedicated to the study of the interaction of rhetoric and culture and focuses on the concrete practices of discourse in which and through which the diverse and often also fantastic patterns of culture – including our own – are created, maintained and contested.

To add further spice to this, here are a few punch lines that Stephen and I wrote for the introduction to *Culture and Rhetoric*, the first volume in our series:

> Like the mythical trickster, rhetoric allows us to turn fact into fiction and fiction into fact. It tempts us to persuade ourselves – and others – to see and feel what we wish, and it leads us to limitless flights of fancy. By means of rhetoric we create phantasms, by means of rhetoric we act like daemons, and by means of rhetoric we conjure up those ideas, values, moral rules and laws that constitute the basis of culture. An awareness of this rhetorical, tropical, fantastic nature of culture helps us to understand the mad, horrific, unspeakable, even unthinkable excesses that characterize the course of human history. And then again, it is the use of tropes that leads us to intimations of transcendence ... and guides our understanding of ephemeral forms of experience. (Strecker and Tyler 2009: 5)

Now, to return to the finding with which I aim to surprise Günther as well as myself in this piece of 'Festschrift' writing: I discovered that the relationships pertaining between host societies are prone to influence the relationships that pertain between 'their' ethnographers. So to end this chapter I would like to repeat the question: why did Günther and I never make an effort to join forces in the field of theory? Why did we never arrange a symposium on 'Rational Choice

Theory versus Rhetoric Culture Theory', 'The Synergy of RCT 1 and RCT 2' or something similar?

My answer is that here the stances of our respective host societies asserted themselves. Günther and I acted on our battlefield of theory just like the Korre and Hamar acted on their battlefield of raiding. We remained apart and conducted our argumentation from a distance. Günther was under the spell of the Korre who throw their spears straight and directly. So – as befits RCT 1 – he argued for the relevance of straight discourse: rational thought and action. I was under the spell of the Hamar who shoot their arrows crosswise, and so – as befits RCT 2 – I argued for the relevance of crooked discourse: rhetorical thought and action.

****

In the afternoon of 3 April 2019, the sun has begun to shine while rain is still falling, creating a curtain in front of the forest across the fields. There is something teasingly unreal in this picture, which goes well with the nature of my gift to Günther. For can any of the mutual influences between ethnographers and host societies of which I have spoken be more than a thought – an intimation, a gesture towards the power of analogy, the sensing of a vast resonance chamber that extends over space and time? Thus, the reality of mutual influence between observers and the observed vanishes like the forest behind a curtain of rain.

*** Finis ***

Ivo Strecker studied ethnology (PhD, 1969, Göttingen University) and later anthropology at LSE, London. He did his 'Habilitation' in Germany (1983). He is Professor Emeritus at the Institute for Anthropology and African Studies, Johannes Gutenberg-University Mainz, Germany, and co-founder of the Rhetoric Culture Project (http://www.rhetoricculture.org/) since 1998. He has over four decades of fieldwork experience in Southern Ethiopia, mainly among the Hamar people, and published widely on it. This work stimulated him to develop the study of rhetoric and culture. He was a visiting professor at the universities of Addis Ababa (1989–1993), Meqelle and Arba Minch (Ethiopia), and was founder of the South Omo Research Centre in Jinka, Southern Ethiopia. He published numerous articles and the book series *The Hamar of Southern Ethiopia* (with Jean Lydall), *The Social Practice of Symbolization* (1988), *Ethnographic Chiasmus* (2010), *Berimba's Resistance* (2013), and co-edited various other books, e.g. *The Perils of Face* (with J. Lydall, 2006), *Writing in the Field: Festschrift for Stephen Tyler* (with S. LaTosky, 2013) and two volumes in the Rhetoric Culture Series (2009 and 2013). He also made ethnographic films and produced a collection of music of the Hamar.

References

Bošković, Aleksandar and Suzana Ignjatović. 2012. 'Understanding Ethnic Conflicts through Rational Choice: A Review Article', *Ethnos* 77(2): 290–96.

Galaty, John G. 2011. '(Non) Rational Choice', Roundtable "Rational Choice and Challenges", *Workshop on the Occasion of the 60th birthday of Günther Schlee, 10–12 July 2011*. Halle (Saale): Max Planck Institute for Social Anthropology.

Lydall, Jean and Ivo Strecker. 1979a. *The Hamar of Southern Ethiopia, Volume I: Work Journal*. Hohenschäftlarn: Klaus Renner Verlag.

———. 1979b. *The Hamar of Southern Ethiopia, Volume II: Baldambe Explains*. Hohenschäftlarn: Klaus Renner Verlag.

Strecker, Ivo. 1979. *The Hamar of Southern Ethiopia, Volume III: Conversations in Dambaiti*. Hohenschäftlarn: Klaus Renner Verlag.

Strecker, Ivo and Stephen Tylor. 2009. 'Introduction', in Ivo Strecker and Stephen Tylor (eds), *Culture and Rhetoric*. New York: Berghahn, pp. 1–20.

Interview with Günther Schlee, Halle (Saale), 10 December 2018

Markus Virgil Hoehne

> Surely, the desire which once made them [i.e. anthropologists] take up the study of anthropology was to explain how people tick and how they interact with each other, rather than denying the possibility of any such explanation. (Schlee 2010: 217)

Markus: Where did you ultimately get the idea to study social anthropology [*Ethnologie*]?

Günther: Due to my family background, I inclined to do something with languages and cultures. I come from a family where everyone was alternately a teacher or a pastor. So languages always played a big role. My father was a secondary-school teacher [*Studienrat*] and a philologist of modern languages. If I had any question, it had to be looked up, and we had three etymological dictionaries on our shelf right by the dining table. *Living German, Living French, Living English [Lebendiges Deutsch . . .]*. Whenever someone used a word and someone else questioned this use, its origins were looked up right away if my father didn't know off the top of his head. And my first contact with anthropology was actually the Museum of Ethnology in Hamburg. I had a great aunt that lived near the museum who I'd visit now and again. I grew up in Heide in Holstein – that's around 120 kilometres from Hamburg. So the trip is manageable for a schoolboy, and affordable. And more or less every time I was in Hamburg I'd go to the Museum of Ethnology. So a certain fascination was always there, also from the stories my father told. He was a teacher of Romanic languages and literature, who had written a study on Spain and had made his way around North Africa on a bike around 1930, writing reports for the local paper. And then my father's stories about America, where he was a migrant worker: North America, that is, in the US – he worked there from

1924 to 1928 to save up for his studies; because in Germany, of course, due to the war and inflation, the family savings kept getting reduced to nothing. We actually come from a family with a longer tradition of learning; like I said, teachers and pastors, in the main. But my father had to re-gain that status, because there were no savings which would have enabled him to study.

Markus: And on your mother's side, what's the story there?

Günther: My mother was a farm girl. My grandfather, whom I never met, was commercially minded – a modern farmer, so to speak. He had the biggest farm in the village. He was the only one to understand the pig cycle, and the first to have a car. Not a traditional, but a modern, commercially minded farmer. And the fact that my mother was a farmer's daughter, this was a boon after the war when one supply bottleneck or another came around, you see. Whereas the father of my father was a pastor, at the end of the day a 'poor church-mouse', my mother came from food production, which can be quite handy in times like those.

Markus: Would you say that your current inclination towards animal and plant breeding and such is influenced by this background?

Günther: I'm a person who's been shaped by the countryside. These two traditions are unambiguously inside me, middle-class and rural. If I have certain left-leaning tendencies and identify with the proletariat, then that is a political decision and not based on my own origins. The nobility, in any case, is something foreign to me. In short, I'm a middle-class, rural individual; and I am distinct from other middle-class people, particularly urbanites, in that I know much more about agriculture. In development-political contexts it has also become clear to me that I'm much better at dealing with languages, that I have a different relationship to languages from most colleagues. That may come from this educated middle-class tradition. I've become conscious of this in the course of my life, that I have these two formative elements within me.

Markus: In other words, the fact that you studied social anthropology didn't worry your parents all too much.

Günther: On the contrary. When I made the decision as to what I would study, my father was already dead. My mother was quite worried whether one could also earn money with that. And then she consulted, as she did quite frequently, the brother of my father, my uncle Ernst – Ernst Schlee, Director of Schloss Gottorf State Museum in Schleswig. Who had studied art history, financed by a monthly dollar-bill that his uncle sent him from America, and who subsisted mainly on oatmeal while studying art history and then became Director of the State Museum in Schleswig-Holstein. That is, practically the only and best position, non-university position, for an art historian in Schleswig-Holstein. And this he was able to get – that was his life experience. And so he said to her, 'let Günther study what he wants; he'll excel at whatever interests him the most, and in the end he'll find a job, too'.

Markus: And what made you choose Hamburg as place of study? Was it simply the most obvious option?

Günther: It was not, no. My sister, Elisabeth, who is two years older – she was studying in Tübingen and in Vienna and then in Kiel in order to become a teacher. The tradition was that you didn't study at one location, but rather changed universities repeatedly. This means, if you'd only studied at one place, you hadn't really studied. Rather, you were supposed to travel to the professors that interested you the most. It was proper to have studied at multiple places.

Markus: Right. But then how to explain Hamburg, as your choice I mean.

Günther: The situation was a toss-up for me. I wanted to do something with languages and cultures, but I didn't know exactly which languages and cultures. And Hamburg had a tremendously broad offering, from Indonesian to Arabic and the African languages and so on; and American Studies, everything. In Hamburg one could study all around the world.

Markus: The professor of anthropology was Hans Fischer?

Günther: Yes, Hans Fischer, whose own research was on the Wampar along the Markham River in the lowlands of New Guinea. And the assistant professor was Jürgen Jensen, who had done research in Uganda. And particular interests were also covered by bringing in second advisors from elsewhere. In my case this came seven years later, when I earned my PhD; there the second advisor was the Africanist Wilhelm Möhlig from Cologne. Because Fischer himself didn't have regional expertise on Africa. But that was no problem. At that time there were many one-man [one professor] institutes, which could nonetheless represent anthropology in its full breadth. And the regional fragmentation of the discipline, as we see today – where people often cease to take notice of each other at all – that didn't exist then.

In the first semester I took Middle Eastern studies [*Orientalistik*], general linguistics, Romanic languages, and social anthropology as main subjects. Then in the second semester I decided that anthropology should be my major, with Romanic languages and general linguistics as minor subjects.

Markus: And Middle Eastern studies?

Günther: There I only took an Arabic course. However, I only gained some speaking skills years after I got my doctorate, when I travelled by land from Hamburg to Bombay to do a reportage for GEO together with a photographer, Heinz

Teufel. On the way we stopped for several weeks in Syria and in Iraq. That was the first time I really communicated in Arabic and could overcome my inhibitions.

Markus: But in the meantime, Arabic has become an important language in your work and day-to-day life.

Günther: Meanwhile I can speak colloquial Sudanese Arabic quite well, because I've been in Sudan on a regular basis since 1996.

Markus: What shaped you during your time in Hamburg? Was Fischer a central influence?

Günther: That he was. He taught the history of anthropology and truly solid fundamentals – one learned a great deal about functionalism and evolutionism, among other things. He gave an overview of the history of the discipline. And above all he taught us the craft of anthropology. He wrote a little book about the genealogical method, which grew out of the course he gave us way back then and over and over to later students. That's all to say, with him, the anthropology of kinship stood on very solid footing, in particular the terminology and techniques; that's one of the specialties of the discipline, and Fischer imparted it with all its technicalities. One simply had to learn a lot of new terms. And the courses consisted to a large degree of reading monographs, which were then discussed as well as compared with each another.

Markus: And this across the entire spectrum, I mean all the continents?

Günther: Yes indeed. Furthermore, Jensen was there. We also had Reinhild Freise for a while as assistant professor. We had Peter Tschohl as a substitute chair once, while Fischer was on leave for a semester. So we did have several instructors there.

Markus: Okay. So Fischer was indeed a formative influence. This Jürgen Jensen – Uganda? What became of him?

Günther: In the end he became a full professor. He was very helpful. He facilitated my first publication in *Sociologus*. The paper on linguistics – on the recognition of arbitrarily named signs; it was a psycho-linguistic study. It was published in *Sociologus* , on the Sapir-Humboldt-Whorf Hypothesis (Schlee 1973). I designed an experiment to find out to what extent naming things influences non-verbal types of performance. I did a psychological experiment for this. Still a beginner studying a different discipline, I simply went to the office hours of a psychology professor and then he authorized an allotment of test subjects, psychology students – just like that, without even asking me if I myself was a psychology student and writing a term paper or something. I remained silent about studying a different subject and being just a beginner. A professor at the army academy in

Hamburg gave me access of his class of lieutenants. So I could conduct a psychological study with a whole array of test subjects. This resulted in my first academic publication.

Markus: When was the first time you actually went to a non-European country?

Günther: Apart from Morocco, which I had reached on one of my hitch-hiking trips, mostly criss-crossing western Europe – that was in fact the trip to Kenya in 1974.

Markus: So the travel with Teufel to Bombay came later?

Günther: That came later, right. That was 1978. That was after my studies. The trip to Bombay also served the purpose of shipping the Landrover which I then had got from the DFG [*Deutsche Forschungsgemeinschaft*, German Research Foundation] from Bombay to Mombasa to use it for my postdoctoral research in Kenya.

Markus: In 1974 you went to Kenya. What brought you to Kenya? How did you arrive at the idea?

Günther: Yeah, so I took Romanic languages and did a lot of Spanish as well. I had taken all the advanced translation courses, Spanish-German, German-Spanish – basically I had studied as much Spanish as a Spanish teacher would have needed. In anthropology and other disciplines open to me, I had taken in everything related to South America. Back then, like many others, I considered this the continent of the future. Che Guevara and so on. There was an interest underpinned by revolutionary sentiments. And then I decided to do a doctoral thesis based on field research rather than work in the library, which [the empirical work] at the time was not completely necessary or generally even that common [in Germany]. And I already had a scholarship from the German Academic Scholarship Foundation [*Studienstiftung des Deutsches Volkes*], but had to write a proposal in order to convert it to a foreign study scholarship and then later to a PhD scholarship. A master's degree was not necessary. It was still possible then to do a combined undergraduate-doctorate [*grundständig promovieren*]. But in order to write this proposal I wanted to have a little experience in the country of study first; I also wanted to select an appropriate field site and to be able to justify this choice. I thought I had to travel there first for a visit. That's why I wanted to go to South America. My plan was to travel through South America on the cheap. And then I discovered that a return ticket to any airport in South America cost 3500 Deutschmark (DM) at the time, while one could fly to Africa and back for 1000 DM. Whereupon I put away my Spanish books, bought a Penguin book titled 'Teach Yourself Swahili', did the basics in the university vacations and then took an advanced Swahili course for one semester, and then I went to Kenya.

Markus: But in Hamburg itself there was hardly anyone who knew their way around Africa, who could tell you concretely, 'that's the place to go', right?

Günther: One of the people who helped me and whom I then visited in Uganda was Jürgen Jensen. That was one of numerous contacts. And those who knew something about Africa I asked for further contacts. They knew some missionaries or university lecturers. Wilhem Möhlig, for instance, was among them. Someone knew that he was a DAAD lecturer in Nairobi at that time.

Markus: An Africanist, a linguist.

Günther: He's a linguist, yes. Then I stuck around Kenya awhile. The north I liked the best.

Markus: Did you go around in the region, Eastern Africa?

Günther: Only a bit. I went as far as Maasailand in Tanzania, as far as the island Buvuma in Uganda, where Jürgen Jensen did his research, and I saw Kampala and then went halfway up Mount Elgon. I travelled around Kenya, Central Kenya that is, and the Samburu District, and I visited the Rendille as well. And that's ultimately the place I liked the best.

Markus: But that was still a time when people seldom made it there, a time when few Whites came to that territory, or was this already somewhat familiar?

Günther: Sure, people would gaze at you. At least in rural areas, that is. With Africans here in Germany, it happens that people want to touch their hair. In Kenya, people also touched my hair and marvelled at me. At what a red mouth I had. And that I was sunburnt. And there were people who mocked me or something. Other people pointed out, 'look, he's also got five fingers'. There I would have liked to say, 'yes, as do frogs and other amphibians; it's pretty widespread, the five-finger thing' [laughs]. As they saw it, you were on the border of humanity, you know? First you had to be classified. If you were also a human or what you actually were. I mean, you yourself were very foreign.

Markus: But with regard to the Kenyan government that was no problem, or did you not ask for permission at all?

Günther: Well, at that time vehicles going to the 'Northern Frontier District' would be checked. I was also frequently inspected later on. You had to write down your name and the car registration number etc. in a book. So in theory the Kenyan government had control over who moved about in the territory. On the other hand, though, they didn't track you down if you didn't return. That is, I don't think it really had any practical function. And for the most part one could roam freely. For staying there and doing research, you needed a research permit. And in order to obtain this, I lived the next year, 1975, for many weeks in Nairobi, as a guest in the household of Wilhelm Möhlig. And getting the official papers was not an easy task. In the end I received a research permit from the Office of the President.

Markus: Did you start at that point with initial linguistic research on the Rendille?

Günther: I had started, the year before, together with schoolboys who knew English or Swahili, to compile word-lists for the Rendille language.

Markus: At that time there was no grammar book for Rendille at all, right?

Günther: No, there wasn't, no. That is, the first sketches that came about, the ones penned by Bernd Heine and so on, were parallel to my own work. For the field research I stayed about eighteen months in the field.

Markus: How did your family take it, that you had suddenly vanished in Africa?

Günther: I think my mother was quite worried. But it was also clear, on the other hand, that if I was in northern Kenya, far away from any communication network, she really couldn't expect letters from me on a regular basis. Letters took several weeks, and apart from that, the next post office was hundreds of kilometres away. So one didn't even try to communicate too often. There were no telephones in northern Kenya. To that extent it was just accepted that if someone was doing field research, one wouldn't hear from them for quite a while.

The whole north of Kenya had no electricity. That came around 1980; it arrived first in the towns and then there were TVs, which ran with VHS tapes and so on. The area was still beyond the reach of the Kenyan TV. Yet, when I started there, the whole area didn't have electricity. In the best case, locals had paraffin lamps.

Markus: How did you get set up there? Did you have enough money from the German Academic Scholarship Foundation for a car and for eighteen months of field research, or did you raise funds externally, or how did you get fixed up? I mean, you had a Jeep there, right?

Günther: I had a Land Rover there. It was a beautiful Land Rover; a station wagon with two rows of seats and auxiliary seats in the back and an opening on top where you could look out. This I bought used from an English farmer there. With money from my mother – that is to say, family savings went into it. Later I sold it again. So I had a car, I had the foreign study scholarship from the *Studienstiftung* and later the PhD scholarship. And, well, I just didn't spend much money. The most expensive item was of course the car. Otherwise, when I was with the Rendille and there was enough milk, I subsisted on milk and blood and meat and such. Now and then, of course, I would also buy a goat and share the meat. Otherwise I consumed the things people gave me; non-perishables like noodles and potatoes and onions I had with me and would cook a bit myself. That was a very spartan lifestyle.

Markus: Were you living in a hut?

Günther: I did at first; it was made out of bent poles, a primitive version of a Rendille house. Nice mats – these of course I didn't have. But covered over with sacks, a dome covered with burlap sacks. Where the sun shone through pretty intensely. And then some months later I'd made local friends, and then lived with a Rendille woman in a Rendille house, as the brother of the mostly absent husband; as an accepted lover.

Markus: And he accepted the fact that you were living together with his wife?

Günther: Yeah, more or less. In that situation one didn't show jealousy. He had also other relationships.

Markus: Was that a part of hospitality?

Günther: It was hospitality; it was also brotherhood. At that point in time I was already taken into the local clan. The woman's husband was my clan-brother, and jealousy among clan brothers is considered to be very bad. One time, years later, when I was back as a post-doc., the woman and I had a quarrel and I moved out. Subsequently the elders fetched me back. This basically shows that it was a relationship that the community accepted and even actively wanted to maintain.

Markus: At that time you were already working on an introduction to the Rendille language, which later appeared in *Buske Verlag* (Schlee 1978), right?

Günther: Yeah, exactly. As I thought of it, I wanted to do an ethnographic work with a high philological standard. And I wanted this work to provide access to Rendille culture by way of the language, to describe it in the words of the Rendille. For that reason I include many texts in the original language. And in order for one to be able to read the original texts, I turned in my dissertation with a guide to the grammar in the form of an appendix. The book with *Buske* essentially belongs to my dissertation as well, in the form it was submitted. Only the later publishers, they thought – that is to say the Marburg series, where the rest of the dissertation on the social and belief system of the Rendille was published (Schlee 1979) – they didn't want a grammatical appendix. They thought that would exceed the frame of an ethnographic publication. And for that reason and through the constraints of publication, the very separation of disciplines that I was trying to avoid was re-established.

Markus: Okay, so you actually wanted to bring together anthropology and linguistics.

Günther: I wanted to bring them together; for me it was one unit. I have a basic philological imprint from my childhood.

Markus: What shaped your theoretical orientation? Was it heavily shaped by the structural functionalism of British social anthropology? The title of your dissertation, *The Social and Belief System of the Rendille*, sounds a bit like a structural functionalist work.

Günther: Yeah, definitely. It's my view that Fischer was somehow a British social anthropologist. If you ignore the fact that he was a German and not a Brit. But what we considered contemporary anthropology was essentially the more recent works coming out of British social anthropology back then, while the German cultural-historical and other studies, they showed up in his course on the history of anthropology. That is, also imparted, but for him that was already history. What was current for him at that time was a functionalist, also in a sense Marxist (without admitting it), materialist, utilitarian, pragmatically informed British social anthropology.

Markus: Had you already read Fredrik Barth at the time or did that come much later?

Günther: During my studies I presented a seminar paper on *Nomads of South Persia* (Barth 1961). That was the contact I had with Barth. *Ethnic Groups and Boundaries* (Barth 1969) was completely off my radar. So I'd been inoculated with Barthian categories, but I'd never read the oft-cited collected volume from 1969. And then, during my time in Bielefeld, in the late 1980s – practically twenty years after the publication of *Ethnic Groups and Boundaries* – it happened to me that I was telling someone about identities and ethnic boundaries with great enthusiasm and my counterpart said, 'yeah yeah, *Ethnic Groups and Boundaries*'. And I thought, 'oh boy, what did you miss?'. Whereupon I read *Ethnic Groups and Boundaries*.

Markus: Not until the Bielefeld era?

Günther: Twenty years too late. I missed out on a great deal of reading material and on what people were discussing, because of these longer periods of time spent in-between in Kenya. And I was reconstructing a lot of things in my head, which other people had already read and could back up with quotes. To some extent, the origins of my insights weren't always known to me, and I probably considered myself more original than I really was. But then I went on to read *Ethnic Groups and Boundaries* – every chapter, not just the introduction – and my reaction was yeah, alright, that's what I actually wanted to say.

Markus: Okay. Maybe we'll come back to that point later. In 1977 you finished your PhD. When did you go to Bayreuth?

Günther: In 1980, after the first post-doc research project. After the research which led to the book *Identities on the Move: Inter-ethnic Clan Relationships in Northern Kenya* (Schlee 1989).

Markus: Did you also do that while in Hamburg?

Günther: After my studies in anthropology, after the degree, I had an unpaid teaching assignment in Hamburg. Parallel to this, I studied two semesters of biology – in case that there'd be no path forward with anthropology. I thought it would be a good idea to have a second qualification in the natural sciences, possibly even to be better versed in practical and technical things if I wanted to go into development aid. And at the same time, I wrote a research application to the German Research Foundation [*Deutsche Forschungsgemeinschaft*] on the topic of inter-ethnic clan relationships in northern Kenya. This was then approved and what resulted, after researching from 1978 to 1980, became the data basis for *Identities on the Move*. This I turned in under a different title as my habilitation dissertation [second book].

Markus: Ah, right. So from 1978 to 1980 you were in Kenya again, more or less to do your habilitation research. And only afterwards did you go to Bayreuth.

Günther: Correct. From winter semester 1980 until summer of 1986 I was in Bayreuth. There I was assistant professor under Christoph Winter. Winter was a specialist on the Chagga in Tanzania. But he was also one of the people who, when I was preparing to do research for my PhD thesis in 1974, was one of my many contacts. I visited him at Kilimanjaro. Winter was appointed to Bayreuth in 1980 and then got me to join him as his assistant. We then started building up the social anthropology programme there. The university was newly founded. Together with representatives of other disciplines we established the first collaborative research centre for cultural identity in Africa [*Sonderforschungsbereich 'Kulturelle Identität in Afrika'*]. And everyone who later came there (Bargatzki, Spittler, Beck, Klute, Alber, etc.), they more or less owe the existence of their chairs to the foundations Winter laid and to the course that he set.

Markus: Okay. And what was Winter's theoretical persuasion, if you can call it that?

Günther: Just as I was of a linguistic and a social-scientific persuasion, Winter was of a legal and social-scientific one. But he also worked on Chagga dialects. He – and Möhlig too, by the way – held law degrees. In Wilhelm Möhlig's case, that is, a lawyer and linguist, and in the case of Christoph Winter – incidentally the brother-in-law of Möhlig – a lawyer and anthropologist. So, Winter had a doctorate in law; from Cologne. He got his graduate degree in anthropology with Evans-Pritchard and Lienhardt at Oxford. Thus I've been shaped by the British twice over. Through Fischer and through Winter. And when, many years later, we had our first external evaluation of the Max Planck Institute (MPI) in Halle, our Dutch reviewer – Frans Hüsken! – he wrote, in order to put something positive in his report, that Schlee represented the positive elements and the strengths of the German tradition and that Chris Hann, the other MPI director in Halle, represented British social anthropology. At which point I told him, it's precisely the opposite. That is, I'm the one who's been moulded by British social anthropology, while Chris Hann is always going on about ancient Eurasian high culture or something, which reminds me more of some romantic German traditions.

Markus: Would you say the structural functionalist influence was as strong in your habilitation? Or did you move on to new theoretical ground and consciously break loose from certain teachers?

Günther: My habilitation was quite unconventional in many regards. There I investigated inter-ethnic clan relationships between groups with highly different languages and across religious boundaries. My field research really opened up a pluri-ethnic space because I investigated clan identities and relationships that cut across ethnic classifications. That breaks with the monographic tradition. That is, everything that we had read was always monographies on specific ethnic groups – one for each group. There was simply nothing else. And in classical British social anthropology, in any case, ethnic groups are represented in isolation and as systems in a state of internal equilibrium.

Markus: Did you deliberately break with that; I mean, was that your objective? Or did you more stumble into your own new perspective?

Günther: Well, the key experience had already come through the Rendille. That is, I was asked by the Rendille if the nine clans of the Rendille were also present among the Germans, and if the Germans also had Gaaldeylan or other Rendille clans. And to that, of course, my answer was no. But through this question I realized, hmm, the question must be based on something. For example, that many Rendille clans also exist among neighbouring ethnic groups; and then I decided to look into that systematically. But from the very beginning, I was of course aware that this monographic tradition, which takes ethnic groups as the natural unit of investigation, was being subverted by my research.

Markus: So did you find theoretical orientations elsewhere?

Günther: Well, I found inspiration, for example, in Paul Spencer's *Nomads in Alliance* (Spencer 1973), which analyses relationships between two neighbouring ethnicities. Spencer doesn't really show a relational network that cuts across a broad region and many ethnic groups. But ethnic double-affiliation and such, that was in Spencer's work. Of course, there are also examples from West Africa and other places, where people had described inter-ethnic clan relationships. But then again, these other authors had remained on a descriptive level, without saying, 'here is something new that has eluded the analytical perspective so far'. The perspective, that clans are not always sub-units of ethnicities, but rather one can flip it around and find ethnicities in clans, did not yet exist. This has then been ascribed to me on some occasions because, even if I wasn't the first to discover this, I did really formulate it fully and make it a subject of discussion – in *Identities on the Move*.

Markus: Back then, during the habilitation phase, did you already have experience in development cooperation?

Günther: We engaged with praxis-relevant topics as students in Hamburg. There we had the working group 'applied anthropology'. That was a student reading circle without a lecturer present. As a group we even co-authored an essay in *Sociologus* with the title '*Wo ist vorne? Sinn und Unsinn von entwicklungspolitischem Eingreifen bei Nomaden in Ostafrika*' ['Which Way Ahead? On Sense and Nonsense of Developmental Intervention with Nomads in East Africa'] (Bundt et al. 1979). This started before my own field research and as a group we picked it up again later, to finish the publication in *Sociologus* in 1979. I then took it up again in the book with Anatoly Khazanov, *Who Owns the Stock?* (Khazanov and Schlee 2012). In that I harked back to the same text. As students we wanted to say something about development interventions, marketization and so on. What function does it have for the nomads to have so much livestock; why do they have this livestock; what do they do with the cattle; what is the sense in maximizing, etc.? But that was already a critical engagement with approaches to development politics. So I always had a certain proximity to this – development research including applied research; even before I went to Bielefeld.

Markus: So that was your second publication ever, right? The first being the psycho-linguistic one in *Sociologus* and the second one with this group of authors.

Günther: Exactly, yes. The second was with Christian Bundt and others, also in *Sociologus*.

Markus: And then came the publications on the Rendille.

Günther: The first book. That was the one on grammar. And then came the second book, and that was the rest of the dissertation, on their social and belief system.

Markus: But what really doesn't show up in your work – as far as I can tell, at least – are any sort of questions about structural power differences, class, exploitation. Considering that you were academically socialized in the 1970s, you allowed astonishingly little Marxism into your work.

Günther: You think so? I mean, Marxism isn't at all foreign to me. Of course, I'd like to distance myself from unilineal models of devolution, etc. But I think, in my work as a whole, there is a healthy dose of materialism. That is to say, I don't believe religious discourse without further ado, but rather relativize it and attempt to link it to material interests. That's the main topic of *How Enemies Are Made* (Schlee 2008). There are people, also in the Max Planck Society, who regard me as a 'crude materialist'. I don't operate in a deterministic fashion, but I do attempt to bring to light how actors' material interests and their ideologies and convictions are related. As a rule, people don't believe in things that harm them. They tend rather to see the world in such a way that they benefit from this way of seeing. And that determines social identification as well. Indeed, the whole theory of identification is based on the idea that people have a conscious or unconscious calculus as to group size, power and access to resources.

Markus: Sure, but to some degree one would actually consider that – subsequent to Fredrik Barth and the critique of his interactionist model – rather as a kind of liberal political orientation. That is, Fredrik Barth was in fact accused of having found or having wanted to find a kind of liberal market-based orientation among the Swat-Pathans (Barth 1959).

Günther: Well, here we have a rationality which in its motivations is heavily shaped by material interests. And that is at odds with bourgeois ideologies that take religious and ideological discourse literally.

Markus: But at the same time it is at odds with Marxist ideology, which takes class-based societies as its starting point and then looks at class formation and class struggle as the motivation behind social, political and economic dynamics. Talal Asad (1972) undertook a class analysis of politics among the Swat. He accused Barth of having ignored structural power differences and the recent historical evolution of exploitative relationships in the Swat valley.

Günther: I have to say, a basic materialist orientation is definitely something I have in common with Marxist approaches. And I also think that through my studies on the marginalization of pastoral groups, for example, I've made a critical contribution. That's all very concrete, based on intensive ethnographic work. As I mentioned, I do have this rural strain; I don't start with the system, I rather start with the meat or the milk or something similarly concrete. But by way of this I do arrive at the global interconnections and at the centre-periphery relationships and at marginalization and disadvantage or exploitation. I mean, one of my book titles is *Pastoralism and Politics in Northern Kenya* (Schlee and Shongolo 2012). That's a book on marginalization and distorted perceptions on pastoral-nomadic people. My wish would be to rehabilitate the pastoral mode of production.

Markus: How was it in Bielefeld? There you were with Elwert, Bierschenk, and other colleagues who worked on larger economic questions.

Günther: Yes! Yeah, I felt comfortable there. Those were the colleagues with whom I communicated most closely. With Elwert – that was a very close bond! Occasionally we were at the same place. In Bayreuth he was once a substitute professor and then in Bielefeld I was his successor. Then he also invited me to Berlin. I knew his family; I knew him very well. And his early death was quite a rupture for me. Yeah, and in Bielefeld I was his successor – not in the same position, because at that time I had an endowed professorship from the Volkswagen Foundation [then the *Stiftung Volkswagenwerk*] and he'd had an assistant professorship or something – but thematically speaking, I was his successor. I inherited some of his students. And, in Bielefeld, I also saw continuity in my becoming the junior partner of Hans-Dieter Evers – H.D. [Ha-De] Evers as he is known – as a member of this group, which shaped the Bielefeld approach to subsistence production. This approach entails the revalorization of local production and a critique of market relationships. That also had an influence on me. It perhaps wasn't the main topic for me, because in my research I wanted to peek into the head of the individual, to look closely at what people were saying and how people made their arguments. For me, the grid was more finely meshed. But I didn't sense a contradiction between my approach and a Marxist approach, or the approaches by Evers or Elwert. If someone had asked me if I was a Marxist, I would have had to give a nuanced answer. Politically speaking, I came to the same conclusions as Marxists on many points; but I did not believe in the classical unilineal evolutionism of the nineteenth century, and not at all in undemocratic forms of government, as sometimes established in the name of Marxist or Socialist revolution.

Markus: The Bielefeld entanglement approach [*Bielefelder Verflechtungsansatz*] was interested in the connection between a subsistence economy and a capitalistic market economy.

Günther: Yes, and indeed I've never studied uncontacted peoples. I never succumbed to this illusion. Although in reality, with the Rendille in the 1970s, one could to a large extent forget about the government and the world economy. But of course I was aware that that's a post-colonial society and such. And I also never romanticized the Rendille as pristine or anything like that. And besides, in later studies, issues of globalization did interest me. I also think that comes out in *How Enemies Are Made*. That is, how – from the Serbs and Bosnians up to pan-Slavism or to the Islamic Umma, etc. – a global identification is instrumentalized and how alliances are sought after and sometimes forged 'worldwide'. So this connection between the various levels of global society has been important to me for a long time. But my starting point was to talk to African farmers or herders in their own language about the things that troubled them.

Markus: In which way are critical perspectives on 'development' still important for you, in your current work?

Günther: At the moment we have the project 'Lands of the Future' and 'Guardians of Productive Landscapes', where we critically take up the discourse on development, criticize land-grabbing in Africa, and consider which benchmarks of productivity we should apply: really only the effectiveness per work-hour, or also the question 'how many people does the land sustain?' And we then arrive at very critical positions on large-scale market production. It takes up themes from the Bielefeld entanglement discourse. The workforce is sucked away, goes to the cities, and they're missing in rural areas. At least this entanglement approach is a critical one, which revalorizes the subsistence economy. And today, under the fashionable catch-phrase 'sustainability', one can return to this even more adamantly, also with regard to concepts like local knowledge and biodiversity.

Markus: Would you ascribe yourself at this point to any kind of theoretical line?

Günther: Well, I've never concerned myself with contemporary trends – never consciously, that is. Naturally I was also exposed in various degrees to trends. But I was always resolute in doing what it was I considered right and never concerned myself with intellectual fashions. I practically skipped the postmodern school of thought with its radical critique of knowledge. In terms of this critique, of reflecting on biases/prejudices and such, I've practically stood still. That is, I never accepted the radical rejection of possibilities for knowledge and the denunciation of knowledge itself as an imposition and pursuit of dominance and so on. Rather, I always wanted to explain; I never gave up the aspiration to explain and was probably old-fashioned in this regard, when others were saying that anthropology has nothing to do with explanation, that it has something to do with writing – it's another way to write. I never went along with that [laughs]. I always held anthropology of kinship in high esteem. And likewise, at times when diffusionism was totally out of fashion, I always appealed to Graebner (1911) and the cultural-historical school in order to clarify, at a smaller scale but with similar categories, the history of northern Kenya and southern Ethiopia. But because no one knew it anymore, it sounded novel again to some [laughs]. I always did my own thing. It would be naive, of course, to say that I wasn't influenced. Naturally I was exposed to every possible influence. But I never wanted to be up-to-date, to adapt to trends, consciously. This has proven to be a good course, because the fashions or trends have somehow always come back to me.

Markus: Would you say there's some kind of continuity: Bayreuth, Bielefeld, Halle. Would you say there's something there, something you've clearly pursued along the way?

Günther: Fredrik Barth once said that when he reads his own book on the nomads of South Persia, when he sees the young man skipping about Badiyya [Arabic for land of the nomads, the Bedouins], about Persia, he doesn't recognize this person as himself; rather, he's changed three times over and today he's a different person. I never felt that way! There are books or manuscripts of mine lying around from thirty, forty years ago that I can pick up and continue writing – revise, I mean. I don't agree with everything anymore, there are later realizations, but it's always the same person speaking there and the same basic interests. In the Rendille book (Schlee 1979), for instance, there's a graphic model with three coordinates in which I say all Rendille can be classified according to age and gender, to clan-membership, or to ritual role. That is, one knows if someone is a man or a woman and how old – age and gender-categories – that is, uncircumcized young boys, warriors, or a married man or woman. There are five values on the dimension of 'age and gender', and then the nine clans and whether someone has a special ritual role. In this way their function is essentially determined. Or one knows what determines the core essentials. And so forth – I don't think I said anything more than that. And in *How Enemies Are Made*, it's the case that nationality/ethnicity, language and religion represent the major dimensions of that space. That is, to break down the identities and make clear the conceptual dimensions. This I have – without using the word identity – in my dissertation of 1977 and published two years later, and until today my thoughts on that remain similar. That is to say, my thought-patterns haven't changed one bit. I was lucky to have had a really good approach, and in the whole course of my working life the questions I've posed have diversified, have been expanded upon, supplemented, empirically enriched and so forth. And naturally in Bayreuth and in Bielefeld and in Halle I also picked up intellectual stimuli. But as to what I did with them – I've always had the same digestive system, so to speak, into which these stimuli entered. In terms of the style of thinking, I've remained the same person. And there are people who say that's a disadvantage. Who say, 'at the most recent AAA [American Anthropological Association] Meeting there were nine panels on religion, therefore we need to do something on religion; now we need to do this, now that, in order to stay up-to-date', and so on – this I never embraced. I always wanted to figure out how I could make sense of people's lives. I had my approach and always kept going and diversified it. This was so from childhood on. I had a linguistic interest and a curiosity about culture. I was interested in recognizing and classifying the world. This goes back to the Old Testament, to Adam: God created the things of this world and Adam was meant to name them. That is, 'bring things into an ordering scheme and classify them'. And that was always my approach.

Markus: Surely a form of taxonomy, too.

Günther: Of course! Yes, for sure. The basic outlines have always been the same. I'm a critic of originality. A doctoral candidate who came to us from the USA, she once told me about a very well-known and very often-cited American colleague who told her, 'Don't bother about learning all these local languages. No one can check anyhow. It's much more important that you coin a concept to your name'. That is, just create something with the goal of appearing original and distinguishing yourself. From a comparative studies standpoint that's counterproductive, that's fatal! And it disrupts any advancement in knowledge. I always wanted to see which of the older insights I can utilize and what I can build upon. Of course I'm critical towards biases and attempt in the interest of advancing knowledge to correct and dismantle prejudices and premature assumptions, but I don't see the primary function of anthropology in critique, as some do. I want to explain the world, the social world. It is highly complex and we don't understand it. Yet we need an understanding of it in order to have a politically meaningful discussion and above all, to overcome a number of crises that approach us and that threaten our survival. For this reason, we have to understand and explain the world. And in this light, we can't throw potentially serviceable approaches overboard in a gesture of originality and innovation. Rather, as to the history of science as a whole, we have to ask ourselves what could be crucial in there – in the existing, older stuff. We need a positive stance towards it. Anthropology has time and again started from scratch; because it is more fashionable to debunk the whole thing as a colonial construct or something and then to start again from scratch. But this, as I've stated in my contribution on paradigm shifts in the book by Olaf Zenker and Karsten Kumoll (Schlee 2010), prevents cumulative insights.

Markus: The one is a cumulative, the other a comparative insight. Where and when did you start working in a culturally comparative vein?

Günther: Right from the beginning, in Hamburg, with Fischer. When the course consists in reading monographs from different parts of the world, what should one discuss? One can only compare them! Fischer himself, by the way, always talked about inter-ethnic relationships. For him there existed these two dimensions: cultural comparison and relationships between cultures. Cultural comparison happens between separate units; inter-ethnic relationships dissolve these boundaries. The scientific question is variation and co-variation! That is, you always need neighbouring cases or similar cases that you can compare with each other.

Markus: Looking back at your career, how would you characterize it?

Günther: I've been a lucky fellow from the start. I was born into a – even if materially, due to the post-war situation, we were obligated to be somewhat frugal –

into an intact middle-class framework; born into a family which offered security and support and which took you seriously as a kid and recognized and seized upon and fostered your talents. No support in a musical direction, sadly, because I was never allowed to learn an instrument – my sister Elisabeth was musically quite talented and I could draw, so I got a few pencils. That is, each child was supported according to his or her talents, but also constricted as a result. But all in all, compared to some childhoods, I had a decidedly lucky situation. Again and again I was supported and encouraged in my studies. Later on I was also lucky: I experienced practically no unemployment. After my PhD I started by writing an application and studied biology in parallel for two semesters. And because I was enrolled as a student, I probably wouldn't have been eligible for unemployment benefits, but it never would have occurred to me that I was unemployed. I also did journalistic work at that time and other things. And on the day of my habilitation lecture I learned that I was being nominated for a position as professor at Bielefeld, so the transition from my time as assistant professor to my first professorship was seamless as well. All in all, it's a piece of good fortune for which one can only be grateful. Which one cannot credit to merit; where one can only say: I've been terrifically lucky! And to be director at the Max Planck Institute for Social Anthropology, even if there have been relationships that weren't so great, or rivalries and such, or enviers – in comparison to all the other possibilities, it is of course the optimal position. It is the best position that a German social anthropologist can have. For the two whole decades [1999–2019] that I held this position, no other German anthropologist had a better basis in terms of funding. Whenever I get a strange idea – which comes to me in a dream, or in the bathtub in the morning – on the same day I have twenty of the most talented young people whom I can share this idea with. Other people my age have no one that will listen to them. That is an unearned piece of luck, where one can only give thanks to one's Maker.

Markus: What was the most important project or the most important accomplishment of your time as Max Planck director?

Günther: Well naturally the Berghahn series is our flagship. It's not thematically open, of course, and in essence reflects our work in Halle – these are works by staff members, students and so on. And that it all comes together relatively well in contexts which complement and round each other off – that's the result of work, no? I can remember a discussion with you, where you came up to me and said you'd made a discovery, something fantastic, that Dereje Feyissa, with whom you shared an office, was working on very similar topics and you wanted to do something together on borders and borderlands (Dereje and Hoehne 2010). And then I said to you, 'yeah, that's why the two of you are here, together, in my department – that was the plan' [laughs]. That is to say, there's a lot of design in the background in order to make the synergy possible in the first place, that the people have something to say to one another. And of course, there's a connection there with my own research interests. The typical ethnographic or anthropological research work is individual. And of course, if one has an institute to run and a huge collective research programme to manage, there is less time for individual field research. Naturally one suffers certain losses. To compensate these losses, the work of colleagues in a wider framework of collaboration has to contribute something to one's own research interests, has to become one's own indirect research. If this collaboration yields a synthesis which is more than the sum of its parts, then this is what we are aiming for! This was the case for the most recent volume on *Difference and Sameness* (Schlee and Horstmann 2018), to which MPI staff members as well as colleagues from outside the MPI contributed. I see that as the propulsion of my academic interests and tie a sense of achievement to that. Yeah, so creating synergies is a success story. There is also the theory related to ethnic relationships, which is a theme that can be traced to my studies in Hamburg. In my own research and together with colleagues, we found out more on the manner in which differences and common ground or sameness can be instrumentalized and how these two relate to each other, also regarding wider dynamics of inclusion and exclusion; we found out some things which are by no means trivial. The other success, of course, is that we've established standards through the documentation of our research – this being the function of the other series at MPI, the *Field Notes and Research Projects*. We set a number of linguistic and methodological standards. I'd say there are few Arabic texts that so faithfully render what the people say, free from nonsensical misspellings and errors of transcription and anglicisms in transcriptions in Latin characters – that is, meet the philological standard of our text editing. So in that series we grapple with, depict, annotate and pre-analyse what people have told us. This follows the very highest standard in our discipline and I am very satisfied with that.

Note

The interview was originally conducted in German; a shortened version was translated by Charlie Zaharoff.

References

Asad, Talal. 1972. 'Market Model, Class Structure and Consent: A Reconsideration of Swat Political Organisation', *Man, New Series* 7(1): 74–94.
Barth, Fredrik. 1959. *Political Leadership among Swat Pathans*. London: The Athlone Press.
———. 1961. *Nomads of South Persia: The Basseri Tribe of the Khamseh Confederacy*. Oslo: Oslo University Press.

―― (ed.). 1969. *Ethnic Groups and Boundaries: The Social Organization of Culture Difference*. Oslo: Universitetsforlaget.

Bundt, Christian, Gertrud Heiland, Hartmut Lang, Rudolf Mathias, Sabine Poppe, Günther Schlee and Ula Stemmler. 1979. 'Wo ist "vorn"? Sinn und Unsinn entwicklungspolitischen Eingreifens bei ostafrikanischen Hirtennomaden', *Sociologus* 29(1): 21–59

Dereje Feyissa and Markus V. Hoehne (eds). 2010. *Borders and borderlands as Resources in the Horn of Africa*. London: James Currey.

Graebner, Fritz. 1911. *Methode der Ethnologie*. Heidelberg: Carl Winter Verlag.

Khazanov, Anatoly M. and Günther Schlee (eds). 2012. *Who Owns the Stock? Collective and Multiple Forms of Property in Animals*. Integration and Conflict Studies 5. New York and Oxford: Berghahn.

Schlee, Günther. 1973. 'Sprachlich gesteuertes Verhalten: die grafische Reproduktion abstrakter Zeichen in Abhängigkeit von deren Benennungen', *Sociologus* 23(2): 127–64.

――. 1978. *Sprachliche Studien zum Rendille: Grammatik, Texte, Glossar; with English Summary of Rendille Grammar*. Hamburger philologische Studien 46. Hamburg: Buske.

――. 1979. *Das Glaubens- und Sozialsystem der Rendille: Kamelnomaden Nord-Kenias*. Marburger Studien zur Afrika- und Asienkunde/A 16. Berlin: Reimer.

――. 1989. *Identities on the Move: Clanship and Pastoralism in Northern Kenya*. Manchester: Manchester University Press.

――. 2008. *How Enemies Are Made: Towards A Theory of Ethnic and Religious Conflicts*. Integration and Conflict Studies 1. New York and Oxford: Berghahn.

――. 2010. 'Epilogue: How Do Paradigm Shifts Work in Anthropology? On the Relationship of Theory and Experience', in Olaf Zenker and Karsten Kumoll (eds), *Beyond Writing Culture: Current Intersections of Epistemologies and Representational Practices*. New York and Oxford: Berghahn, pp. 211–27.

Schlee, Günther and Abdullahi A. Shongolo. 2012. *Pastoralism & Politics in Northern Kenya & Southern Ethiopia*. Eastern Africa Series. Woodbridge, UK, and Rochester, NY: Currey.

Schlee, Günther and Alexander Horstmann (eds). 2018. *Difference and Sameness as Modes of Integration: Anthropological Perspectives on Ethnicity and Religion*. Integration and Conflict Studies 16. New York and Oxford: Berghahn.

Spencer, Paul. 1973. *Nomads in Alliance: Symbiosis and Growth among the Rendille and Samburu of Kenya*. Oxford: Oxford University Press.

TO GÜNTHER SCHLEE, WITH THANKS...

ABDULLAHI A. SHONGOLO

I am honoured to have this opportunity to express my gratitude and my warmest personal regards to Professor Günther Schlee, who has recently retired as Director of the Max Planck Institute for Social Anthropology. It is with great pleasure that I bear witness to my career as a research scientist at that institution, which began in 1999, more than twenty years ago.

I first met Günther Schlee in 1984, when, as a professor at the University of Bielefeld, he was on a research visit to Marsabit, Kenya. I was introduced to him by my former secondary school principal, Mr Tony Troughear, from Australia, who knew me as a prospective researcher. At the time, I was working as a research assistant for Professor Asmarom Legesse of Swarthmore College near Philadelphia, Pennsylvania. The first thing that Günther asked me to do was to collect Borana proverbs that we later analysed for publication. This assignment was, perhaps, a test to determine my competence in conducting field research, for, at that time, I had no academic training, nor had I yet done much research. I would like to quote Günther's evaluation of my work directly:

> When I asked Abdullahi Shongolo in 1984 to collect Boran proverbs, which we would then analyse, illustrate and contextualize in a way which puts also those not fortunate enough to have Oromo as their mother tongue in a position to understand them and to enjoy their wit, we agreed on 1000 as a target for collection. He met this target in no time. (Shongolo and Schlee: 2007: 7)

This first impression of my commitment to research marks the beginning of a long journey that we have taken together until today. Günther began as my employer, but he became a mentor, a colleague, a co-author and a friend.

Over the years, we have done fieldwork together, traversing various parts of northern Kenya and southern Ethiopia. On several occasions, we travelled on foot to many different villages. Sometimes we rode camels. We spent time in remote villages, sleeping on cow hides and drinking raw milk from cows and camels. Günther was at home even under such difficult conditions, unlike many European researchers who dare not submit themselves to such an unfamiliar way of life. He was comfortable living the way that members of the local communities lived and participating in everyday nomadic activities. What is more, people in the field accepted Günther as one of their own. I soon realized that he had no need for an interpreter, since he was fluent in many local languages: Rendille, Boran, Somali and Swahili, the languages of the catchment areas of his field research.

Professor Schlee has always had a profound interest in the history and culture of the communities in northeastern Africa. Among intellectuals, his commitment to the advancement of social anthropology in Africa, and elsewhere, is widely recognized and appreciated. But his connection with the people of these regions has not been limited to academics; rather, everywhere he has gone, he has established social ties. In those places where he has done fieldwork, he has become an elder to whom people have turned for advice and decision-making in community affairs. In short, the people of northern Kenya and southern Ethiopia have good reasons to appreciate his fascination with their way of life, which is based not only on his commitment to scholarship but also on his qualities as a human being.

Where I come from, Günther Schlee's name will always be closely linked with the development of the discipline of social anthropology. He has established cooperative relations that are strong and cordial with many universities and other institutions of higher learning in East Africa, the Horn of Africa, the Sudan and several West African states. All those Kenyans, Ethiopians, Somalis and Sudanese, and also those from West Africa, who have had the privilege of working, interacting and conversing with him will always remember him as someone who dealt with them openly, sincerely and personably, listening carefully with respect and patience.

However, my tribute to Professor Schlee would be incomplete if it stopped with this assessment of his exemplary service to scholarship and to the community. All of us who know him feel that we have personally benefitted in some tangible way from our acquaintance with him. In the last two decades, he has invited many students from the Horn of Africa and elsewhere in Africa to come to the Max Planck Institute for Social Anthropology in Halle, Germany, and to take courses at its sister institution, the Institute for Social Anthropology at the Martin Luther University of Halle-Wittenberg, where he was an honorary professor. Under his supervision, each of them has successfully attained his or her doctoral degree. We all need to express our sincerest gratitude to Günther Schlee for all of his contributions to international, regional, and particularly to pastoral studies in Africa.

I am among those who owe a great personal debt to Günther Schlee. For more than thirty-five years, he has imparted to me the skills and knowledge that have made me who I am today. We have co-authored several books and articles, published in prestigious international scientific journals, which have been read and acknowledged widely all over the world. Beyond our work together on these common projects, I have come to know him as someone who is generous, honest, knowledgeable, courageous and responsible. He has helped and supported me through some difficult times and shared the joyous times. He has encouraged me and inspired me as a mentor, colleague and brother.

I would now like address my words to Günther Schlee directly:

Thank you for helping me to build a strong foundation in a profession that I never thought was within my reach. You opened my eyes to new opportunities and helped me to discover strength that I did not know I possessed, praising my efforts when I performed beyond your expectations. You showed me how to stand my ground and to have a career that I can be proud of. With your help, I have grown into someone who is a recognized scholar in Oromo studies in the Horn of Africa and also in the field of social anthropology internationally.

One of the things I appreciate most about you is your willingness to help me and others in so many different aspects of life. I am lucky to have had a brother like you who has dedicated himself so thoroughly to helping people. It has always been evident that you love what you do with a passion and that you truly want others to succeed as well.

In those early days, when we first met, your advice, support, encouragement and motivation meant everything to me as I struggled with uncertainty and inexperience. You were always there with a kind word that helped me get through some of my darkest times. Thank you for believing in me when I did not believe in myself. Thanks for having been honest with me, for showing me the way to success in the field of research. You showed me not only how to be a better researcher but also how to work hard and effectively. After my retirement, I changed jobs, but what has not changed are the valuable lessons that you taught me. In my life, I hope to affect others positively, as you have affected me.

As you join the seniors of this great nation, I pray for your good health and prosperous future. And may you find life after retirement a happy time with lots of good memories. I also pray that the knowledge and skills that we have gained from you are used well in building a greater nation and a healthy place for all to live. May the Almighty God continue to bless your life and that of your family.

I also take this opportunity to thank those colleagues and friends who, along with Professor Schlee, made my time at the Max Planck Institute so pleasant and so rewarding. Some are already retired, and others may have left the Institute. But I would like to thank everyone who supported and befriended me since my arrival at the Institute as a research consultant in 1999. I will always remember the friendly atmosphere and the good times that we had together. You are my friends, and I will remember each one of you and always hold you in my heart.

The list of people at the Max Planck Institute to whom I owe thanks is long, so I can just mention a few: Viktoria Giehler-Zeng, Viola Stanisch, Bettina Mann, Oliver Weihmann, Ingrid Schüler, Manuela Pusch, Katja Harnish, Armin Pippel, Yossouf Diallo, Janka Diallo, Tabea Scharrer, Markus Hoehne, Kati Broecker, Ronald and Anett Kirchhof, Kathrin Niehuus and many others in the Department of Conflict and Integration, the Department of Law and Anthropology, the Department of Resilience and Transformation in Eurasia and also in the administration and other services. May the Almighty God bless you all!

Reference

Shongolo, Abdullahi A. and Günther Schlee 2007. *Boran Proverbs in their Cultural Context*. Cologne: Rüdiger Köppe Verlag.

Published Works by Günther Schlee (Selection)

Compiled by Viktoria Giehler-Zeng

Monographs and Co-Authored Books

Markakis, John, Günther Schlee and John Young. 2021. *The Nation State: A Wrong Model for the Horn of Africa.* Open Access Edition 14. Berlin: MaxPlanck-Gesellschaft zur Förderung der Wissenschaften. DOI: 10.34663/9783945561577-00.

Schlee, Günther. 2016. 何故为敌: 族群与宗教冲突论纲 [He gu wei di: zu qun yu zong jiao chong tu lun gang; *How Enemies Are Made: Towards A Theory of Ethnic and Religious Conflicts*]. Beijing: She hui ke xue wen xian chu ban she.

Schlee, Günther with Abdullahi A. Shongolo. 2012. *Islam & Ethnicity in Northern Kenya & Southern Ethiopia.* Eastern Africa Series. Woodbridge, UK and Rochester, NY: James Currey.

Schlee, Günther and Abdullahi A. Shongolo. 2012. *Pastoralism & Politics in Northern Kenya & Southern Ethiopia.* Eastern Africa Series. Woodbridge, UK and Rochester, NY: James Currey.

Schlee, Günther. 2008. *How Enemies Are Made: Towards A Theory of Ethnic and Religious Conflicts.* Integration and Conflict Studies 1. New York and Oxford: Berghahn.

Shongolo, Abdullahi A. and Günther Schlee. 2007. *Boran Proverbs in Their Cultural Context.* Wortkunst und Dokumentartexte in afrikanischen Sprachen 24. Cologne: Köppe.

Schlee, Günther. 2004. *Upravlenie Konfliktami: Teorija i Praktika.* Moscow: Deutsch-Russischer Austausch.

Schlee, Günther and Karaba Sahado. 2002. *Rendille Proverbs in Their Social and Legal Context.* Wortkunst und Dokumentartexte in afrikanischen Sprachen 15. Cologne: Köppe.

Schlee, Günther. 1989. *Identities on the Move: Clanship and Pastoralism in Northern Kenya.* International African Library 5. Manchester and New York: Manchester University Press for the International African Institute, London.

Schlee, Günther. 1979. *Das Glaubens- und Sozialsystem der Rendille: Kamelnomaden Nord-Kenias.* Marburger Studien zur Afrika- und Asienkunde/A 16. Berlin: Reimer.

Schlee, Günther. 1978. *Sprachliche Studien zum Rendille: Grammatik, Texte, Glossar; with English Summary of Rendille Grammar.* Hamburger philologische Studien 46. Hamburg: Buske.

Edited Volumes and Special Issues

Bošković, Aleksandar and Günther Schlee (eds). 2022. *African Political System Revisited: Changing Perspectives on Statehood and Power*. Integration and Conflict Studies 26. New York and Oxford: Berghahn.

Gabbert, Echi Christina, Fana Gebresenbet, John G. Galaty and Günther Schlee (eds). 2021. *Lands of the Future: Anthropological Perspectives on Pastoralism, Land Deals and Tropes of Modernity in Eastern Africa*. Integration and Conflict Studies 23. New York and Oxford: Berghahn.

Schlee, Günther and Alexander Horstmann (eds). 2020. 再造异同: 人类学视域下的整合模式 *[Zai zao yi tong: ren lei xue shi yu xia de zheng he mo shi; Difference and Sameness as Modes of Integration]*, translated by Xiujie Wu. Beijing: She hui ke xue wen xian chu ban she; Social Sciences Academic Press.

Härter, Karl, Carolin Hillemanns and Günther Schlee (eds). 2020. *On Mediation: Historical, legal, Anthropological and International Perspectives*. Integration and Conflict Studies 22. New York and Oxford: Berghahn.

Schlee, Günther and Alexander Horstmann (eds). 2018. *Difference and Sameness as Modes of Integration: Anthropological Perspectives on Ethnicity and Religion*. Integration and Conflict Studies 16. New York and Oxford: Berghahn.

Turner, Bertram and Günther Schlee (eds). 2017. *On Retaliation: Towards an Interdisciplinary Understanding of a Basic Human Condition*. Integration and Conflict Studies 15. New York and Oxford: Berghahn.

Finke, Peter and Günther Schlee (eds). 2014. 'Strategii identifikacii v Srednej/Central'noj Azii', *Etnograficeskoe Obozrenie* (4).

Khazanov, Anatoly M. and Günther Schlee (eds). 2012. *Who Owns the Stock? Collective and Multiple Forms of Property in Animals*. Integration and Conflict Studies 5. New York and Oxford: Berghahn.

Schlee, Günther and Elizabeth E. Watson (eds). 2009. *Changing Identifications and Alliances in North-East Africa, Volume 1: Ethiopia and Kenya*. Integration and Conflict Studies 2. New York and Oxford: Berghahn.

Schlee, Günther and Elizabeth E. Watson (eds). 2009. *Changing Identifications and Alliances in North-East Africa, Volume 2: Sudan, Uganda, and the Ethiopia-Sudan Borderlands*. Integration and Conflict Studies 3. New York and Oxford: Berghahn.

Schlee, Günther and Bertram Turner (eds). 2008. *Vergeltung: eine interdisziplinäre Betrachtung der Rechtfertigung und Regulation von Gewalt*. New York and Frankfurt/Main: Campus.

Schlee, Günther (ed.). 2004 (2002). *Imagined Differences: Hatred and the Construction of Identity*. Market, Culture and Society 5. Hamburg, Münster: LIT.

Schlee, Günther (ed.). 2004. *Ethnizität und Markt: zur ethnischen Struktur von Viehmärkten in Westafrika*. Topics in African Studies 4. Cologne: Köppe.

Schlee, Günther (ed.). 2003. 'Identification in North-East Africa', *Africa* 73(3).

Horstmann, Alexander and Günther Schlee (eds). 2001. *Integration durch Verschiedenheit: lokale und globale Formen interkultureller Kommunikation*. Bielefeld: transcript.

Diallo, Youssouf and Günther Schlee (eds). 2000. *L'ethnicité peule dans des contextes nouveaux: la dynamique des frontières*. Paris: Karthala.

Schlee, Günther and Karin Werner (eds). 1996. *Inklusion und Exklusion: die Dynamik von Grenzziehungen im Spannungsfeld von Markt, Staat und Ethnizität*. Cologne: Köppe.

Journal Articles

Schlee, Günther. 2021. 'Animal Production for a More Sustainable Economy', *Nomadic Peoples* 25(1): 107–109. DOI: 10.3197/np.2021.250107.

Staro, Francesco and Günther Schlee. 2020. 'Identity Politics in Contemporary Ethiopia and Sudan; Gouvernement et politiques identitaires en Éthiopie et au Soudan contemporains', *Cahiers d'études africaines* 240(2020): 1005–13. DOI: 10.4000/etudesafricaines.32812.

Schlee, Günther, Verena Böll, Ogato Ambaye and Robert Dobslaw. 2019. 'His Burial and the Rastafarians in Shashamane, Ethiopia', *Visual Ethnography* 8(2): 169.

Schlee, Günther. 2017. '"Civilizations", Eurasia and the Hochkulturgürtel: An Essay About How to Subdivide the World in Terms of Cultural History and What to Explain With the Units Thereby Created', *Zeitschrift für Ethnologie* 142(2): 205–24.

Schlee, Günther. 2017. 'Gewalt und Vertreibung: theoretische, methodische und forschungsethische Probleme der Ethnographie in Konfliktlagen', *Journal für Religionsphilosophie* 6: 128–33.

Schlee, Günther. 2017. 'Omaha Terminologies: Global Distribution Patterns and How They May Have Come About', *Cross-Cultural Research* 51(2): 117–41. DOI: 10.1177/1069397117691011.

Eidson, John R., Dereje Feyissa, Veronika Fuest, Markus Virgil Hoehne, Boris Nieswand, Günther Schlee and Olaf Zenker. 2017. 'From Identification to Framing and Alignment: A New Approach to the Comparative Analysis of Collective Identities', *Current Anthropology* 58(3): 340–51. DOI: 10.1086/691970.

Schlee, Günther. 2016. 'Comment on Chris Hann "A Concept of Eurasia"', *Current Anthropology* 57(1): 18–19. DOI: 10.1086/684625.

Finke, Peter and Günther Schlee. 2014. 'Strategii identifikacii v Srednej/Central'noj Azii: vvedenie', *Etnograficeskoe Obozrenie* (4): 3–10.

Schlee, Günther. 2013. 'Customary Law and the Joys of Statelessness: Idealised Traditions Versus Somali Realities', *Journal of Eastern African Studies* 7(2): 258–71. DOI: 10.1080/17531055.2013.776276.

Schlee, Günther. 2013. 'Territorializing Ethnicity: The Imposition of a Model of Statehood on Pastoralists in Northern Kenya and Southern Ethiopia', *Ethnic and Racial Studies* 36(5): 857–74. DOI: 10.1080/01419870.2011.626058.

Schlee, Günther. 2013. 'Why States Still Destroy Pastoralism and How They Can Learn That in Their Own Interest They Should Not', *Nomadic Peoples* 17(2): 6–19. DOI: 10.3167/np.2013.170203.

Schlee, Günther and Isir Schlee. 2012. 'Ghanaische und Somali-Migranten in Europa: ein Vergleich zweier Diasporen', *Zeitschrift für Ethnologie* 137(1): 1–22.

Schlee, Günther. 2010. 'A Comment on the "Policy Framework for Pastoralism in Africa" adopted by the African Union in January 2011', *Nomadic Peoples* 14(2): 158–63. DOI: 10.3167/np.2010.140211.

Schlee, Günther. 2009. 'Tackling Ethnicity From Different Sides: Marc Howard Ross' Work on Culture and Conflict', *Anthropos* 104(2): 571–78. DOI: 10.5771/0257-9774-2009-2-571.

Schlee, Günther. 2008. 'Comment on Susan A. Crate "Gone the bull of winter? Grappling With the Cultural Implications of and Anthropology's Role(s) in Global Climate Change"', *Current Anthropology* 49(4): 589. DOI: 10.1086/529543.

Schlee, Günther. 2008. 'The "Five Drums", Proto-Redille-Somali, and Oromo Nationalism: a Response to Aneesa Kassam', *Ethnohistory* 55(2): 321–30. DOI: 10.1215/00141801-2007-065.

Schlee, Günther. 2007. 'Brothers of the Boran Once Again: On the Fading Popularity of Certain Somali Identities in Northern Kenya', *Journal of Eastern African Studies* 1(3): 417–35. DOI: 10.1080/17531050701625524.

Schlee, Günther and Krisztina Kehl-Bodrogi. 2007. 'Pilgerfahrten als Feier von Communitas und als Arena', *Zeitschrift für Religionswissenschaft* 15: 155–78. DOI: 10.1515/zfr.2007.15.2.155.

Schlee, Günther. 2006. 'Comment on Nathalie Peutz "Embarking on an Anthropology of Removal"', *Current Anthropology* 47(2): 236–37. DOI: 10.1086/498949.

Schlee, Günther. 2005. 'Language and Kinship: Introductory Remarks on a Debate', *Zeitschrift für Ethnologie* 130(1): 317–22.

Glick Schiller, Nina, Boris Nieswand, Günther Schlee, Tsypylma Darieva, Lale Yalçın-Heckmann and László Fosztó. 2005. 'Pathways of Migrant Incorporation in Germany', *Transit* 1(1): https://transit.berkeley.edu/2005/schiller/.

Schlee, Günther. 2004. 'Comment on Jon Holtzman "The Local in The Local: Models of Time and Space in Samburu District, Northern Kenya"', *Current Anthropology* 45(1): 79–80. DOI: 10.1086/379635.

Schlee, Günther. 2004. 'Taking Sides and Constructing Identities: Reflections on Conflict Theory', *Journal of the Royal Anthropological Institute* 10(1): 135–56. DOI: 10.1111/j.1467-9655.2004.00183.x.

Schlee, Günther. 2003. 'Comment on Sandra Gray et al.: Cattle Raiding, Cultural Survival, and Adaptability of East African Pastoralists', *Current Anthropology* 44(S5): S23–S24. DOI: 10.1086/377669.

Schlee, Günther. 2003. 'Integration und Konflikt', *Entwicklungsethnologie* 12(1/2): 74–95.

Schlee, Günther. 2003. 'Introduction: Identification in Violent Settings and Situations of Rapid Change', *Africa* 73(3): 333–42. DOI: 10.2307/3556907.

Schlee, Günther. 2003. 'Redrawing the Map of the Horn: The Politics of Difference', *Africa* 73(3): 343–68. 10.2307/3556908.

Schuster, Peter, Rudolf Stichweh, Johannes Schmidt, Fritz Trillmich, Martine Guichard and Günther Schlee. 2003. 'Freundschaft und Verwandtschaft als Gegenstand interdisziplinärerer Forschung', *Sozialer Sinn* 1: 3–20. http://www.digizeitschriften.de/dms/resolveppn/?PID=PPN598191607_0004|log7.

Schlee, Günther. 2002. 'Régularités dans le chaos: traits récurrents dans l'organisation politico-religieuse et militaire des Somali', *L'Homme* 161(1): 17–49. DOI: 10.4000/lhomme.138.

Schlee, Günther. 2000. 'Identitätskonstruktionen und Parteinahme: Überlegungen zur Konflikttheorie', *Sociologus* 50(1): 64–89.

Schlee, Günther. 1999. 'Comment on Martin Sökefeld "Debating Self, Identity and Culture in Anthropology"', *Current Anthropology* 40(4): 439–40. DOI: 10.1086/200042.

Schlee, G. 1999. 'Pronizaemost' graniz w teorii konflikta', *Zurnal Sociologii i Social'Noj Antropologii* 2(1): 36–47.

Schlee, Günther. 1998. 'Identidades múltiples y cross-cutting ties (nexos transversales) en la teoría de los conflictos: aspectos somalí y oromo', *Revista Mexicana de Sociologia* 60(3): 197–244.

Schlee, Günther. 1997. 'Neue Literatur zur Ethnizität in Ost- und Nordost-Afrika', *Zeitschrift für Ethnologie* 122(2): 229–42.

Schlee, Günther. 1995. 'Ethnizität und interethnische Beziehungen in Kenia: Vorbemerkungen zu den Fallstudien von Falkenstein und Odak', *Zeitschrift für Ethnologie* 120(2): 191–200.

Schlee, Günther. 1995. 'Regelmäßigkeiten im Chaos: Elemente einer Erklärung von Allianzen und Frontverläufen in Somalia', *Africa-Spectrum* 30(3): 274–92.

Schlee, Günther and Kurt Salentin. 1995. 'Ernährungssicherung in Nomadengebieten Nordkenias: Ergebnisse einer Lehrforschung', *Zeitschrift für Ethnologie* 120(1): 89–109.

Schlee, Günther and Abdullahi A. Shongolo. 1995. 'Local War and its Impact on Ethnic and Religious Identification in Southern Ethiopia', *GeoJournal* 36(1): 7–17. DOI: 10.1007/BF00812521.

Schlee, Günther. 1994. 'Die Generationslänge in Darfur und anderswo: ein methodisches Problem am Beispiel der Ethnographie von Ulrich Braukämper', *Zeitschrift für Ethnologie* 119(2): 273–79.

Schlee, Günther. 1994. 'Gumi Gaayo: Some Iintroductory Rremarks', *Zeitschrift für Ethnologie* 119(1): 17–25.

Schlee, Günther. 1994. 'Der Islam und das Gada-System als konfliktprägende Kräfte in Nordost-Afrika', *Sociologus* 44(2): 112–35.

Schlee, Günther. 1993. 'Inter-ethnic Clan Identities, Ethnicity, Centrisms and Biases: A Response to Paul Spencer', *Africa* 63(4): 591–600. DOI: 10.2307/1161008.

Schlee, Günther. 1991. 'Les réseaux de relation intra & inter-ethniques chez les nomades du nord Kenya', *Bulletin des Études Africaines de l'INALCO* 8.1988(16): 73–95.

Schlee, Günther. 1989. 'Nomadische Territorialrechte: das Beispiel des kenianisch-äthiopischen Grenzlandes', *Die Erde* 120: 131–38. http://www.digizeitschriften.de/dms/resolveppn/?PID=GDZPPN002998033.

Schlee, Günther. 1989. 'Zum Ursprung des Gada-Systems', *Paideuma* 35: 231–46.
Schlee, Günther. 1985. 'Interethnic Clan Identities Among Cushitic-Speaking Pastoralists', *Africa* 55(1): 17–38. DOI: 10.2307/1159837.
Schlee, Günther. 1984. 'Intra- und interethnische Beziehungsnetze nordkenianischer Wanderhirten', *Paideuma* 30: 69–80.
Schlee, Günther. 1984. 'Nomaden und Staat: das Beispiel Nordkenia', *Sociologus* 34(2): 140–61.
Schlee, Günther. 1984. 'Une société pastorale pluriethnique: Oromo et Somalis au Nord du Kenya', *Production Pastorale et Société* 15(automne): 21–39.
Bundt, Christian, Gertrud Heiland, Hartmut Lang, Rudolf Mathias, Sabine Poppe, Günther Schlee and Ula Stemmler. 1979. 'Wo ist "vorn"? Sinn und Unsinn entwicklungspolitischen Eingreifens bei ostafrikanischen Hirtennomaden', *Sociologus* 29(1): 21–59.
Schlee, Günther. 1973. 'Sprachlich gesteuertes Verhalten: die grafische Reproduktion abstrakter Zeichen in Abhängigkeit von deren Benennungen', *Sociologus* 23(2): 127–64.

Chapters in Books

Schlee, Günther. 2022. 'Retaliation, Mediation and Punishment in Ankole: Revisiting the Chapter by Oberg', in Aleksandar Bošković and Günther Schlee (eds), *African Political System Revisited: Changing Perspectives on Statehood and Power*. Integration and Conflict Studies 26. New York and Oxford: Berghahn, pp. 122–38.
Schlee, Günther. 2021. 'Unequal Citizenship and One-Sided Communication: Anthropological Perspectives on Collective Identification in the Context of Large-Scale Land Transfers in Ethiopia', in Echi Christina Gabbert, Fana Gebresenbet, John G. Galaty and Günther Schlee (eds), *Lands of the Future: Anthropological Perspectives on Pastoralism, Land Deals and Tropes of Modernity in Eastern Africa*. Integration and Conflict Studies 23. New York and Oxford: Berghahn, pp. 59–77.
Schlee, Günther. 2020. 'Mediation and Truth', in Karl Härter, Carolin Hillemanns and Günther Schlee (eds), *On Mediation: Historical, Legal, Anthropological and International Perspectives*. Integration and Conflict Studies 22. New York and Oxford: Berghahn, pp. 116–31.
Schlee, Günther. 2020. '导言：论差异性与共同性作为社会整合的方式 [Introduction: Difference and Sameness as Modes of Integration]', in Günther Schlee and Alexander Horstmann (eds), 再造异同：人类学视域下的整合模式 *[Difference and Sameness as Modes of Integration]*. Bejing: Social Sciences Academic Press, pp. 1–49.
Schlee, Günther. 2020. '国家认同与国家给予的身份认同 [Identification with the State and Identifications by the State]', in Günther Schlee and Alexander Horstmann (eds), 再造异同：人类学视域下的整合模式 *[Difference and Sameness as Modes of Integration]*. Bejing: Social Sciences Academic Press, pp. 109–27.
Schlee, Günther. 2020. '双族群共存：三种情形的比较研究 [Three Dyads Compared]', in Günther Schlee and Alexander Horstmann (eds), 再造异同：人类学视域下的整合模式 *[Difference and Sameness as Modes of Integration]*. Bejing: Social Sciences Academic Press, pp. 238–63.
Schlee, Günther. 2020. '存异而治：一项关于帝国的比较研究 [Ruling over Ethnic and Religious Differences: A Comparative Essay on Empires]', in Günther Schlee and Alexander Horstmann (eds), 再造异同：人类学视域下的整合模式 *[Difference and Sameness as Modes of Integration]*. Bejing: Social Sciences Academic Press, pp. 264–313.
Härter, Karl, Carolin Hillemanns and Günther Schlee. 2020. 'On Mediation: Historical, Legal, Anthropological and International Perspectives on Alternative Modes of Conflict Regulation', in Karl Härter, Carolin Hillemanns and Günther Schlee (eds), *On Mediation: Historical, Legal, Anthropological and International Perspectives*. Integration and Conflict Studies 22. New York and Oxford: Berghahn, pp. 1–11.

Härter, Karl, Carolin Hillemanns and Günther Schlee. 2020. 'Conclusion', in Karl Härter, Carolin Hillemanns and Günther Schlee (eds), *On Mediation: Historical, Legal, Anthropological and International Perspectives*. Integration and Conflict Studies 22. New York and Oxford: Berghahn, pp. 219–21.

Schlee, Günther, Alexander Horstmann and John R. Eidson. 2020. '结语 [Epilogue]', in Günther Schlee and Alexander Horstmann (eds), 再造异同：人类学视域下的整合模式 *[Difference and Sameness as Modes of Integration]*. Bejing: Social Sciences Academic Press, pp. 314–21.

Schlee, Günther and Keebet von Benda-Beckmann. 2019. 'Introduction', in Timm Sureau and Yelva Auge (eds), *Understanding Retaliation, Mediation and Punishment: Collected Results of the International Max Planck Research School on Retaliation, Mediation and Punishment (IMPRS REMEP)*. Max Planck Institute for Social Anthropology, Department Integration and Conflict Field Notes and Research Projects 25. Halle/Saale: Max Planck Institute for Social Anthropology, pp. 1–18.

Schlee, Günther and Joanna Pfaff-Czarnecka. 2019. 'Die Anfänge der Sozialanthropologie in Bielefeld: Günther Schlee im Gespräch mit Joanna Pfaff-Czarnecka', in André Kieserling and Tobias Werron (eds), *Die Fakultät für Soziologie in Bielefeld: eine Oral History*. Sozialtheorie. Bielefeld: transcript, pp. 101–14.

Schlee, Günther. 2018. 'Identification with the State and Identifications by the State', in Günther Schlee and Alexander Horstmann (eds), *Difference and Sameness as Modes of Integration: Anthropological Perspectives on Ethnicity and Religion*. Integration and Conflict Studies 16. New York and Oxford: Berghahn, pp. 78–91.

Schlee, Günther. 2018. 'Introduction: Difference and Sameness as Modes of Integration', in Günther Schlee and Alexander Horstmann (eds), *Difference and Sameness as Modes of Integration: Anthropological Perspectives on Ethnicity and Religion*. Integration and Conflict Studies 16. New York and Oxford: Berghahn, pp. 1–32.

Schlee, Günther. 2018. 'Ruling Over Ethnic and Religious Differences: A Comparative Essay on Empires', in Günther Schlee and Alexander Horstmann (eds), *Difference and Sameness as Modes of Integration: Anthropological Perspectives on Ethnicity and Religion*. Integration and Conflict Studies 16. New York and Oxford: Berghahn, pp. 191–224.

Schlee, Günther. 2018. 'Three Dyads Compared: Nuer/Anywaa (Ehtiopia), Maasai/Kamba (Kenya) and Evenki/Buryat (Siberia)', in Günther Schlee and Alexander Horstmann (eds), *Difference and Sameness as Modes of Integration: Anthropological Perspectives on Ethnicity and Religion*. Integration and Conflict Studies 16. New York and Oxford: Berghahn, pp. 173–90.

Schlee, Günther, Alexander Horstmann and John R. Eidson. 2018. 'Epilogue', in Günther Schlee and Alexander Horstmann (eds), *Difference and Sameness as Modes of Integration: Anthropological Perspectives on Ethnicity and Religion*. Integration and Conflict Studies 16. New York and Oxford: Berghahn, pp. 225–31.

Schlee, Günther. 2017. 'Customary Law and The Joys of Statelessness: Somali Realities Beyond Libertarian Fantasies', in Bertram Turner and Günther Schlee (eds), *On Retaliation: Towards an Interdisciplinary Understanding of a Basic Human Condition*. Integration and Conflict Studies 15. New York and Oxford: Berghahn, pp. 208–35.

Schlee, Günther. 2017. 'Interethnische Beziehungen', in Bettina Beer, Hans Fischer and Julia Pauli (eds), *Ethnologie: Einführung in die Erforschung kultureller Vielfalt*. 9th edn. Ethnologische Paperbacks. Berlin: Reimer, pp. 213–28.

Schlee, Günther. 2017. 'Prólogo', in Soledad Jiménez Tovar (ed.), *Pertenencias múltiples, identidades cruzadas: nuevas perspectivas sobre Asia Central*. Mexico: El Colegio de México, pp. 9–11.

Schlee, Günther. 2017. 'Preface', in Fazil Moradi, Ralph Buchenhorst and Maria Six-Hohenbalken (eds), *Memory and Genocide: On What Remains and the Possibility of Representation*. Memory Studies: Global Constellations. London and New York: Routledge, pp. XIV–XVI.

Schlee, Günther. 2017. 'Zum Zusammenhang von Förderungsformen und akademischer Kultur', in Stefan Schaede (ed.), *Unvermeidliche Königsdisziplinen? zur forschungspolitischen Relevanz des Selbst-*

verständnisses von Geistes- und Sozialwissenschaften im norddeutschen Raum. Loccumer Protokolle 16. Rehburg-Loccum: Evangelische Akademie Loccum, pp. 105–13.

Ismailbekova, Aksana and Günther Schlee. 2017. 'El parentesco en Asia Central desde una perspectiva comparatista', in Soledad Jiménez Tovar (ed.), *Pertenencias múltiples, identidades cruzadas: nuevas perspectivas sobre Asia Central*. Mexico: El Colegio de México, pp. 49–86.

Schlee, Günther. 2015. 'Competing Forms of Land Use and Incompatible Identifications of Who is to Benefit From Policies in the South of the North: Pastoralists, Agro-Industry and Farmers in the Blue Nile Region', in Sandra Calkins, Enrico Ille and Richard Rottenburg (eds), *Emerging Orders in the Sudans*. Mankon: Langaa Research & Publishing CIG, pp. 121–37.

Schlee, Günther. 2015. 'Wie Terroristen gemacht werden', *Jahresbericht 2014*. Munich: Max-Planck-Gesellschaft zur Förderung der Wissenschaften, pp. 18–22.

Schlee, Günther and Echi Christina Gabbert. 2015. 'Dynamics of Identification: Research on Northeast Africa at the Max Planck Institute for Social Anthropology in Halle/Saale', in Wolbert G.C. Smidt and Sophia Thubauville (eds), *Cultural Research in Northeastern Africa: German Histories and Stories*. Ityopis: Northeast African Journal of Social Sciences and Humanities; Extra Issue 1. Frankfurt/Main: Frobenius-Institut;Addis Ababa: Goethe-Institut; Mekelle: Mekelle University, pp. 229–37.

Schlee, Günther. 2014. 'The Construction of Life Phases and Some Facts of Life', in Sophie Roche, *Domesticating Youth: Youth Bulges and Their Socio-Political Implications in Tajikistan*. Integration and Conflict Studies 8. New York and Oxford: Berghahn, pp. IX–XVII.

Schlee, Günther. 2014. 'How Terrorists Are Made'. *Annual Report 2014*. Munich: Max Planck Society for the Advancement of Science, pp. 23–26.

Schlee, Günther. 2014. 'Regional Political History and the Production of Diasporas', in Liisa Laakso and Petri Hautaniemi (eds), *Diasporas, Development and Peacemaking in the Horn of Africa*. Africa Now. London: ZED, pp. 28–50.

Osman, Elhadi Ibrahim and Günther Schlee. 2014. 'Hausa and Fulbe on the Blue Nile: Land Conflicts Between Farmers and Herders', in Jörg Gertel, Richard Rottenburg and Sandra Calkins (eds), *Disrupting Territories: Land, Commodification & Conflict in Sudan*. Eastern Africa Series. Woodbridge, UK and Rochester, NY: James Currey, pp. 206–25.

Schlee, Günther. 2013. 'Kollektivnaja identićnost' gorožan: razmyšlenija o masštabach goroda i razmere gruppy', in Marina Ju. Martynova (ed.), *X Kongress ètnografov i antropologov Rossii: Moskva, 2-5 ijulja 2013 g.; tezisy dokladov*. Moscow: IÈA RAN, pp. XIII–XXII.

Schlee, Günther. 2013. 'Préface', in Remadji Hoinathy (ed.), *Pétrole et changement social au Tchad: rente pétrolière et monétisation des relations économiques et sociales dans la zone pétrolière de Doba*. Paris: Karthala, pp. 9–10.

Schlee, Günther and Martine Guichard. 2013. 'Fulbe and Uzbeks Compared', in Peter Finke and Günther Schlee (eds), *CASCA: Centre for Anthropological Studies on Central Asia; Framing the Research, Initial Projects*. Field Notes and Research Projects/Max Planck Institute for Social Anthropology, Department Integration and Conflict 6. Halle/Saale: Max Planck Institute for Social Anthropology, pp. 25–62.

Finke, Peter and Günther Schlee. 2013. 'Introduction', in Peter Finke and Günther Schlee (eds), *CASCA: Centre for Anthropological Studies on Central Asia; Framing the Research, Initial Projects*. Field Notes and Research Projects/Max Planck Institute for Social Anthropology, Department Integration and Conflict 6. Halle/Saale: Max Planck Institute for Social Anthropology, pp. VI–IX.

Schlee, Günther. 2012. 'Interethnische Beziehungen', in Bettina Beer and Hans Fischer (eds), *Ethnologie: Einführung und Überblick*. Ethnologische Paperbacks. Berlin: Reimer, pp. 429–44.

Schlee, Günther. 2012. 'Multiple Rights in Animals: An East African Overview', in Anatoly M. Khazanov and Günther Schlee (eds), *Who Owns the Stock? Collective and Multiple Forms of Property in Animals*. Integration and Conflict Studies 5. New York and Oxford: Berghahn, pp. 247–94.

Schlee, Günther. 2012. 'Neue Technologien in der Tundra: High-Tech-Geräte, Raumwahrnehmung und Raumorientierung der nomadischen und sesshaften Bevölkerung in der russischen Arktis', in Sonderforschungsbereich 586 (eds), *Differenz und Integration: Wechselwirkungen zwischen nomadischen und sesshaften Lebensformen in Zivilisationen der Alten Welt; Abschlussbericht 01.07.2008 - 30.06.2012*. Leipzig: Leipzig University, pp. 319–46.

Schlee, Günther. 2012. 'Preface', in Katja Werthmann and Tilo Graetz (eds), *Mining Frontiers in Africa: Anthropological and Historical Perspectives*. Mainzer Beiträge zur Afrikaforschung 32. Cologne: Köppe, p. 7.

Schlee, Günther. 2012. 'Prologue', in Karen Witsenburg and Fred Zaal (eds), *Spaces of Insecurity: Human Agency in Violent Conflicts in Kenya*. African Studies Collection 45. Leiden: African Studies Centre, pp. [v–vi].

Khazanov, Anatoly M. and Günther Schlee. 2012. 'Introduction', in Anatoly M. Khazanov and Günther Schlee (eds), *Who Owns the Stock? Collective and Multiple Forms of Property in Animals*. Integration and Conflict Studies 5. New York and Oxford: Berghahn, pp. 1–26.

Paul, Jürgen and Günther Schlee. 2012. '(Ehemalige) Nomaden und pastorale Landnutzung im Wandel von Macht- und Marktbeziehungen: Ost-Buchara/Süd-Tadschikistan, 1868–2008', in Sonderforschungsbereich 586 (eds), *Differenz und Integration: Wechselwirkungen zwischen nomadischen und sesshaften Lebensformen in Zivilisationen der Alten Welt; Abschlussbericht 01.07.2008 - 30.06.2012*. Leipzig: Leipzig University, pp. 231–46.

Schlee, Günther. 2011. 'Afterword: An Ethnographic View of Size, Scale, and Locality', in Nina Glick Schiller and Ayse Caglar (eds), *Locating Migration: Rescaling Cities and Migrants*. Ithaca, NY: Cornell University Press, pp. 235–42.

Schlee, Günther. 2011. 'Fulbe in wechselnden Nachbarschaften in der Breite des afrikanischen Kontinents', in Nikolaus Schareika, Eva Spies and Pierre-Yves Le Meur (eds), *Auf dem Boden der Tatsachen: Festschrift für Thomas Bierschenk*. Mainzer Beiträge zur Afrikaforschung 28. Cologne: Köppe, pp. 163–84.

Schlee, Günther. 2011. 'Suggestions for a Second Reading: An Alternative Perspective on Contested Resources as an Explanation for Conflict', in Andrea Behrends, Stephen P. Reyna and Günther Schlee (eds), *Crude Domination: An Anthropology of Oil*. Dislocations 9. New York and Oxford: Berghahn, pp. 298–302.

Schlee, Günther. 2010. 'A Comment on the "Policy Framework for Pastoralism in Africa" Adopted by the African Union in January 2011', *Nomadic Peoples* 14(2): 158–63.

Schlee, Günther. 2010. 'Epilogue: How do Paradigm Shifts Work in Anthropology? On the Relationship of Theory and Experience', in Olaf Zenker and Karsten Kumoll (eds), *Beyond Writing Culture: Current Intersections of Epistemologies and Representational Practices*. New York and Oxford: Berghahn, pp. 211–27.

Schlee, Günther. 2010. 'Preface', in Dereje Feyissa and Markus Höhne (eds), *Borders & Borderlands as Resources in the Horn of Africa*. Eastern Africa Series. Woodbridge, UK and Rochester, NY: James Currey, pp. VIII–IX.

Schlee, Günther. 2010. 'Preface', in Echi Christina Gabbert and Sophia Thubauville (eds), *To Live With Others: Essays on Cultural Neighborhood in Southern Ethiopia*. Mainzer Beiträge zur Afrikaforschung 27. Cologne: Köppe, pp. 9–11.

Schlee, Günther. 2010. 'Preface', in Olaf Zenker and Karsten Kumoll (eds), *Beyond Writing Culture: Current Intersections of Epistemologies and Representational Practices*. New York and Oxford: Berghahn, pp. VII–VIII.

Schlee, Günther and Patrick Heady. 2010. 'Terminology and Practice: European Kinship in a World-Wide Perspective', in Patrick Heady and Martin Kohli (eds), *Family, Kinship and State in Contemporary Europe, Volume 3: Perspectives on Theory and Policy 3*. Frankfurt/Main and New York: Campus, pp. 347–74.

Schlee, Günther. 2009. 'Changing Alliances Among the Boran, Garre and Gabra in Northern Kenya and Southern Ethiopia', in Günther Schlee and Elizabeth E. Watson (eds), *Changing Identifications and Alliances in North-East Africa; Volume 1: Ethiopia and Kenya*. Integration and Conflict Studies 2. New York and Oxford: Berghahn, pp. 203–23.

Schlee, Günther. 2009. 'Descent and Descent Ideologies: The Blue Nile Area (Sudan) and Northern Kenya Compared', in Günther Schlee and Elizabeth E. Watson (eds), *Changing Identifications and Alliances in North-East Africa, Volume 2: Sudan, Uganda, and the Ethiopia-Sudan Borderlands*. Integration and Conflict Studies 3. New York and Oxford: Berghahn, pp. 117–35.

Schlee, Günther. 2009. 'Introduction', in Günther Schlee and Elizabeth E. Watson (eds), *Changing Identifications and Alliances in North-East Africa, Volume 1: Ethiopia and Kenya*. Integration and Conflict Studies 2. New York and Oxford: Berghahn, pp. 1–13.

Behrends, Andrea and Günther Schlee. 2009. 'Lokale Konfliktstrukturen in Darfur und dem Osten des Tschad oder: Was ist ethnisch an ethnischen Konflikten?', in Walter Feichtinger and Gerald Hainzl (eds), *Krisenmanagement in Afrika: Erwartungen - Möglichkeiten - Grenzen*. Internationale Sicherheit und Konfliktmanagement 3. Vienna: Böhlau, pp. 159–78.

Dereje Feyissa and Günther Schlee. 2009. 'Mbororo (Fulbe) Migrations From Sudan into Ethiopia', in Günther Schlee and Elizabeth E. Watson (eds), *Changing Identifications and Alliances in North-East Africa, Volume 2: Sudan, Uganda, and the Ethiopia-Sudan Borderlands*. Integration and Conflict Studies 3. New York and Oxford: Berghahn, pp. 157–78.

Schlee, Günther and Elizabeth E. Watson. 2009. 'Space and Time: Introduction to the Geography and Political History', in Günther Schlee and Elizabeth E. Watson (eds), *Changing Identifications and Alliances in North-East Africa, Volume 1: Ethiopia and Kenya*. Integration and Conflict Studies 2. New York and Oxford: Berghahn, pp. 15–31.

Watson, Elizabeth E. and Günther Schlee. 2009. 'Introduction', in Günther Schlee and Elizabeth E. Watson (eds), *Changing Identifications and Alliances in North-East Africa, Volume 2: Sudan, Uganda, and the Ethiopia-Sudan Borderlands*. Integration and Conflict Studies 3. New York and Oxford: Berghahn, pp. 1–27.

Schlee, Günther. 2008. 'Ethnologie und Politikberatung: Erfahrungen mit dem Somalia-Friedensprozess', in John Eidson (ed.), *Das anthropologische Projekt: Perspektiven aus der Forschungslandschaft Halle/Leipzig*. Leipzig: Leipziger Universitätsverlag, pp. 198–216.

Schlee, Günther and Bertram Turner. 2008. 'Rache, Wiedergutmachung und Strafe: ein Überlick', in Günther Schlee and Bertram Turner (eds), *Vergeltung: eine interdisziplinäre Betrachtung der Rechtfertigung und Regulation von Gewalt*. New York and Frankfurt/Main: Campus, pp. 49–67.

Turner, Bertram and Günther Schlee. 2008. 'Einleitung: Wirkungskontexte des Vergeltungsprinzips in der Konfliktregulierung', in Günther Schlee and Bertram Turner (eds), *Vergeltung: eine interdisziplinäre Betrachtung der Rechtfertigung und Regulation von Gewalt*. New York and Frankfurt/Main: Campus, pp. 7–47.

Schlee, Günther. 2007. 'Conflict Resolution and Reconciliation as a Component of the Improvement of Farming System Project (IFSP)', in Wolbert G.C. Smidt and Kinfe Abraham (eds), *Discussing Conflict in Ethiopia: Conflict Management and Resolution; Proceedings of the Conference 'Ethiopian and German Contributions to Conflict Management and Resolution', Addis Ababa 11 to 12 November 2005*. Vienna, Zurich, Berlin and Münster: LIT, pp. 119–44.

Schlee, Günther. 2007. '"Diebe haben keine Kinder": Väter, Gevattern, Erzeuger und die soziale Konstruktion des Biologischen', in Johannes F.K. Schmidt, Martine Guichard, Peter Schuster and Fritz Trillmich (eds), *Freundschaft und Verwandtschaft: zur Unterscheidung und Verflechtung zweier Beziehungssysteme*. Theorie und Methode: Sozialwissenschaften. Konstanz: UVK, pp. 261–90.

Guichard, Martine and Günther Schlee. 2007. 'Einblicke in die Verwandtschaftsethnologie', in Johannes F.K. Schmidt, Martine Guichard, Peter Schuster and Fritz Trillmich (eds), *Freundschaft* und Verwandtschaft: zur Unterscheidung und Verflechtung zweier Beziehungssysteme. Theorie und Methode: Sozialwissenschaften 42. Konstanz: UVK, pp. 249–60.

Schlee, Günther and Fritz Trillmich. 2007. 'Verwandtschaft und Freundschaft im Verhältnis von biologischer, sozialer und handlungstheoretischer Rationalität', in Johannes F.K. Schmidt, Martine Guichard, Peter Schuster and Fritz Trillmich (eds), *Freundschaft und Verwandtschaft: zur Unterscheidung und Verflechtung zweier Beziehungssysteme*. Theorie und Methode: Sozialwissenschaften. Konstanz: UVK, pp. 369–94.

Schlee, Günther. 2006. 'The Somali Peace Process and the Search for a Legal Order', in Hans-Jörg Albrecht, Jan-Michael Simon, Hassan Rezaei, Holger-C. Rohne and Ernesto Kiza (eds), *Conflicts and Conflict Resolution in Middle Eastern Societies: Between Tradition and Modernity*. Schriftenreihe des Max-Planck-Instituts für Ausländisches und Internationales Strafrecht I, Interdisziplinäre Forschungen aus Strafrecht und Kriminologie 13. Berlin: Duncker & Humblot, pp. 117–67.

Schlee, Günther. 2005. 'Forms of Pastoralism', in Stefan Leder and Bernhard Streck (eds), *Shifts and Drifts in Nomad-Sedentary Relations*. Nomaden und Sesshafte 2. Wiesbaden: Reichert, pp. 17–53.

Schlee, Günther. 2004. 'Einleitung', in Günther Schlee (ed.), *Ethnizität und Markt: zur ethnischen Struktur von Viehmärkten in Westafrika*. Topics in African Studies 4. Cologne: Köppe, pp. 1–10.

Schlee, Günther. 2004. 'Somalia und die Somali-Diaspora vor und nach dem 11. September 2001', in Hartmut Lehmann (ed.), *Koexistenz und Konflikt von Religionen im vereinten Europa*. Göttingen: Wallstein, pp. 140–56.

Schlee, Günther. 2003. 'Interethnische Beziehungen', in Hans Fischer and Bettina Beer (eds), *Ethnologie: Einführung und Überblick*. Neufassung. Berlin: Reimer, pp. 375–90.

Schlee, Günther. 2003. 'Komplementarität oder Feindschaft: das Doppelgesicht der Ethnizität', in Rüdiger Fikentscher (ed.), *Islam and Coca Cola: Begegnungen der Kulturen nach dem Irak-Krieg*. Halle/Saale: Mitteldeutscher Verlag, pp. 115–30.

Schlee, Günther. 2003. 'North-East Africa as a Region for the Study of Changing Identifications and Alliances', in Rajko Muršič and Irena Weber (eds), *MESS: Piran/Pirano, Slovenia 2001 and 2002*. MESS: Mediterranean Ethnological Summer School 5. Ljubljana: Filozofska fakulteta, Oddelek za etnologijo in kulturno antropologijo, pp. 137–50.

Schlee, Günther. 2002. 'Introduction', in Günther Schlee (ed.), *Imagined Differences: Hatred and the Construction of Identity*. Market, Culture and Society 5. Münster and New York: LIT; Palgrave, pp. 3–32.

Schlee, Günther. 2002. 'Mobile Forschung bei mehreren Ethnien: Kamelnomaden Nordkenias', in Hans Fischer (ed.), *Feldforschungen: Erfahrungsberichte zur Einführung*. Neufassung Ethnologische Paperbacks. Berlin: Reimer, pp. 133–51.

Schlee, Günther. 2002. 'Regularity in Chaos: The Politics of Difference in the Recent History of Somalia', in Günther Schlee (ed.), *Imagined Differences: Hatred and the Construction of Identity*. Market, Culture and Society 5. Münster and New York: LIT; Palgrave, pp. 251–80.

Schlee, Günther. 2001. 'Einleitung', in Alexander Horstmann and Günther Schlee (eds), *Integration durch Verschiedenheit: lokale und globale Formen interkultureller Kommunikation*. Bielefeld: transcript, pp. 17–46.

Schlee, Günther. 2001. 'Identitätspolitik: zur sozialen Konstruktion von Feindschaft', in Heiko Schrader, Markus Kaiser and Rüdiger Korff (eds), *Markt, Kultur und Gesellschaft: zur Aktualität von 25 Jahren Entwicklungsforschung; Festschrift zum 65. Geburtstag von Hans-Dieter Evers*. Market, Culture and Society 11. Münster, Hamburg and London: LIT, pp. 167–79.

Schlee, Günther. 2000. 'Introduction: une ethnicité dans des contextes nouveaux', in Youssouf Diallo and Günther Schlee (eds), *L'ethnicité peule dans des contextes nouveaux: la dynamique des frontières*. Paris: Karthala, pp. 7–14.

Schlee, Günther. 2000. 'Introduction: Identity Discourses and Practical Politics; Redrawing the Map of the Horn; The Politics of Difference'. *Afrika 2000: 17. Tagung der Vereinigung von Afrikanisten in Deutschland, 2000*. Leipzig: African Studies Association in Germany (VAD).

Schlee, Günther. 2000. 'Les peuls du Nil', in Youssouf Diallo and Günther Schlee (eds), *L'ethnicité peule dans des contextes nouveaux: la dynamique des frontières*. Paris: Karthala, pp. 207–23.

Diallo, Youssouf, Martine Guichard and Günther Schlee. 2000. 'Quelques aspects comparatifs', in Youssouf Diallo and Günther Schlee (eds), *L'ethnicité peule dans des contextes nouveaux: la dynamique des frontières*. Paris: Karthala, pp. 225–55.

Schlee, Günther. 1999. 'Cross-Cutting Ties: Grenzen, Raub und Krieg', in Waltraud Kokot and Dorle Dracklé (eds), *Wozu Ethnologie? Festschrift für Hans Fischer*. Kulturanalysen 1. Berlin: Reimer, pp. 315–31.

Schlee, Günther. 1999. 'Nomades et état au nord du Kenya', in André Bourgeot (ed.), *Horizons nomades en Afrique Sahélienne: sociétés, développement et démocratie*. Hommes et Sociétés. Paris: Karthala, pp. 219–39.

Schlee, Günther. 1998. 'Gada Systems on the Meta-Ethnic Level: Gabbra/Boran/Garre Interactions in the Kenyan/Ethiopian Borderland', in Eisei Kurimoto and Simon Simonse (eds), *Conflict, Age & Power in North East Africa: Age Systems in Transition*. Eastern African Studies. Oxford: James Currey; Nairobi: East African Publishing; Kampala: Fountain; Athens: Ohio University Press, pp. 121–46.

Schlee, Günther. 1998. 'Some Effects on a District Boundary in Kenya', in Mario I. Aguilar (ed.), *The Politics of Age and Gerontocracy in Africa: Ethnographies of the Past & Memories of the Present*. Trenton, NJ and Asmara: Africa World Press, pp. 225–56.

Schlee, Günther. 1997. 'Cross-Cutting Ties and Interethnic Conflict: The Example of Gabbra Oromo and Rendille', in Katsuyoshi Fukui, Eisei Kurimoto and Masayoshi Shigeta (eds), *Ethiopia in Broader Perspective: Papers of the 13th International Conference of Ethiopian Studies; 12.- 17. Dec. 1997 2*. Kyoto: Shokado, pp. 577–96.

Schlee, Günther. 1996. 'Das Nebeneinander der Diskurse: neue Nationalismen und ältere Loyalitäten in Äthiopien', in Helmut Buchholt, Erhard U. Heidt and Georg Stauth (eds), *Modernität zwischen Differenzierung und Globalisierung: kulturelle, wirtschaftliche und politische Transformationsprozesse in der sich globalisierenden Moderne*. Münster: LIT, pp. 119–26.

Schlee, Günther. 1996. 'Regelmäßigkeiten im Chaos: die Suche nach wiederkehrenden Mustern in der jüngeren Geschichte Somalias', in Günther Schlee and Karin Werner (eds), *Inklusion und Exklusion: die Dynamik von Grenzziehungen im Spannungsfeld von Markt, Staat und Ethnizität*. Cologne: Köppe, pp. 133–60.

Schlee, Günther. 1996. 'Traditionelle Töterideale, Islamisierung und der Islam als Feindbild', in Erwin Orywal, Aparna Rao and Michael Bollig (eds), *Krieg und Kampf: die Gewalt in unseren Köpfen*. Berlin: Reimer, pp. 135–46.

Schlee, Günther and Abdullahi A. Shongolo. 1996. 'Oromo Nationalist Poetry: Jarso Waaqo Qooto's Tape Recording About Political Events in Southern Oromia, 1991', in Richard Hayward and Ioan M. Lewis (eds), *Voice and Power: The Culture of Language in North-East Africa; Essays in Honour of B. W. Andrzejewski*. London: SOAS, pp. 229–42.

Schlee, Günther and Karin Werner. 1996. 'Inklusion und Exklusion: die Dynamik von Grenzziehungen im Spannungsfeld von Markt, Staat und Ethnizität', in Günther Schlee and Karin Werner (eds), *Inklusion und Exklusion: die Dynamik von Grenzziehungen im Spannungsfeld von Markt, Staat und Ethnizität*. Cologne: Köppe, pp. 9–36.

Schlee, Günther and Rüdiger Korff. 1995. 'Die Doktorandenausbildung an der Fakultät für Soziologie', in Franz-Xaver Kaufmann and Rüdiger Korff (eds), *Soziologie in Bielefeld: ein Rückblick nach 25 Jahren*. Bielefeld: Verlag für Regionalgeschichte, pp. 208–16.

Schlee, Günther. 1994. 'Ethnicity Emblems, Diacritical Features, Identity Markers: Some East African Examples', in David Bokensha (ed.), *A River of Blessings: Essays in Honor of Paul Baxter*. Syracuse, NY: Maxwell School of Citizenship and Public Affairs, pp. 129–43.

Schlee, Günther. 1994. 'Kuschitische Verwandtschaftssysteme in vergleichenden Perspektiven', in Thomas Geider and Raimund Kastenholz (eds), *Sprachen und Sprachzeugnisse in Afrika: eine*

Sammlung philologischer Beiträge, Wilhelm J. G. Möhlig zum 60. Geburtstag zugeeignet. Cologne: Köppe, pp. 367–88.

Schlee, Günther. 1994. 'Loanwords in Oromo and Rendille as a Mirror of Past Inter-Ethnic Relations', in Richard Fardon and Graham Furniss (eds), *African Languages, Development and the State: [workshop held at the School of Oriental and African Studies, in April 1991]*. London and New York: Routledge, pp. 191–212.

Schlee, Günther. 1993. 'Historische Ethnologie', in Thomas Schweizer, Margarete Schweizer and Waltraut Kokot (eds), *Handbuch der Ethnologie: [Festschrift für Ulla Johansen]*. Ethnologische Paperbacks. Berlin: Reimer, pp. 441–57.

Schlee, Günther. 1992. 'Ritual Topography and Ecological Use: The Gabbra of the Kenyan/Ethiopian Borderlands', in Elisabeth Croll and David Parkin (eds), *Bush Base: Forest Farm: Culture, Environment and Development*. London and New York: Routledge, pp. 110–28.

Schlee, Günther. 1992. 'Traditional Pastoralists: Land Use Strategies', in Salim B. Shaabani, Markus Walsh, Dennis J. Herlocker and Dierk Walther (eds), *Mandera District*. Range Management Handbook of Kenya II,4. Nairobi: Republic of Kenya, Ministry of Livestock Development (MOLD), Range Management Division, pp. 122–35.

Schlee, Günther. 1992. 'Traditional Pastoralists: Land Use Strategies', in Salim B. Shaabani, Markus Walsh, Dennis J. Herlocker and Dierk Walther (eds), *Wajir District*. Range Management Handbook of Kenya II, 3. Nairobi: Republic of Kenya, Ministry of Livestock Development (MOLD), Range Management Division, pp. 140–49.

Schlee, Günther. 1991. 'Erfahrungen nordkenianischer Wanderhirten mit dem kolonialen und postkolonialen Staat', in Fred Scholz (ed.), *Nomaden, mobile Tierhaltung: zur gegenwärtigen Lage von Nomaden und zu den Problemen und Chancen mobiler Tierhaltung*. Berlin: Das Arabische Buch, pp. 131–56.

Schlee, Günther. 1991. 'Traditional Pastoralists: Land Use Strategies', in H.J. Schwartz, Salim Shaabani and Dierk Walther (eds), *Marsabit District*. Range Management Handbook of Kenya II, 1. Nairobi: Republic of Kenya, Ministry of Livestock Development (MOLD), Range Management Division, pp. 130–64.

Schlee, Günther. 1991. 'Zur rechtlichen Verwendung von Sprichwörtern bei den Rendille (Nordkenia)', in Anette Sabban and Jan Wirrer (eds), *Sprichwörter und Redensarten im interkulturellen Vergleich*. Opladen: Westdeutscher Verlag, pp. 162–74.

Schlee, Günther. 1990. 'Altersklassen und Veränderungen der Lebenslauffalter bei den Rendille', in Georg Elwert and Martin Kohli (eds), *Im Lauf der Zeit: ethnographische Studien zur gesellschaftlichen Konstruktion von Lebensaltern*. Spektrum: Berliner Reihe zu Gesellschaft, Wirtschaft u. Politik in Entwicklungsländern 25. Saarbrücken and Fort Lauderdale, FL: Breitenbach, pp. 69–82.

Schlee, Günther. 1990. 'Das Fach Sozialanthropologie/Ethnologie seit dem Zweiten Weltkrieg', in Wolfgang Prinz and Peter Weingart (eds), *Die sog. Geisteswissenschaften: Innenansichten*. Suhrkamp-Taschenbuch Wissenschaft 854. Frankfurt/Main: Suhrkamp, pp. 306–12.

Schlee, Günther. 1990. 'Holy Grounds', in Paul Trevor William Baxter and Richard Hogg (eds), *Property, Poverty and People: Changing Rights in Property and Problems of Pastoral Development*. Manchester: Department of Social Anthropology and International Development Centre, University of Manchester, pp. 45–54.

Schlee, Günther. 1989. 'The Orientation of Progress: Conflicting Aims and Strategies of Pastoral Nomads and Development Agents in East Africa: A Problem Survey', in Elisabeth Linnebuhr (ed.), *Transition and Continuity of Identity in East Africa and Beyond: In Memoriam David Miller*. Bayreuth African Studies Series Special issue. Bayreuth: Breitinger, pp. 397–450.

Schlee, Günther. 1989. 'The Oromo Expansion and Its Impact on Ethnogenesis in Northern Kenya', in Taddese Beyene (ed.), *Proceedings of the Eighth International Conference of Ethiopian Studies: University of Addis Ababa, 1984 2*. Addis Ababa: Institute of Ethiopian Studies, pp. 711–23.

Schlee, Günther. 1988. 'Camel Management Strategies and Attitudes Towards Camels in the Horn', in Jeffrey C. Stone (ed.), *The Exploitation of Animals in Africa: Proceedings of a Colloquium at the*

University of Aberdeen, March 1987. Aberdeen: Aberdeen University African Studies Group, pp. 143–54.

Schlee, Günther. 1988. 'Die Islamisierung der Vergangenheit: von der Rückwirkung der Konversion somalischer und somaloider Gruppen zum Islam auf deren oral tradiertes Geschichtsbild', in W.J.G. Möhlig, H. Jungraithmayr and J.F. Thiel (eds), *Die Oralliteratur in Afrika als Quelle zur Erforschung der traditionellen Kulturen = La littérature orale en Afrique comme source pour la découverte des cultures traditionnelles.* Collectanea Instituti Anthropos 36. Berlin: Reimer, pp. 269–99.

Schlee, Günther. 1988. 'Das Weltmodell der Enzyklika', in Karl Gabriel, Wolfgang Klein and Werner Krämer (eds), *Die gesellschaftliche Verantwortung der Kirche: zur Enzyklika Sollicitudo rei socialis.* Arbeiterbewegung und Kirche 9. Düsseldorf: Patmos, pp. 200–204.

Schlee, Günther. 1987. 'Somaloid History: Oral Tradition, Kulturgeschichte and Historical Linguistics in an Area of Oromo/Somaloid Interaction', in Herrmann Jungraithmayr and Walter W. Müller (eds), *Proceedings of the Fourth International Hamito-Semitic Congress: Marburg, 20–22 September, 1983.* Amsterdam Studies in the Theory and History of Linguistic Science/4 44. Amsterdam and Philadelphia: Benjamins, pp. 265–315.

Schlee, Günther. 1985. 'Mobile Forschung bei mehreren Ethnien: Kamelnomaden Nordkenias', in Hans Fischer (ed.), *Feldforschungen: Berichte zur Einführung in Probleme und Methoden.* Ethnologische Paperbacks. Berlin: Reimer, pp. 203–18.

Schlee, Günther. 1982. 'Annahme und Ablehnung von Christentum und Islam bei den Rendille in Nord-Kenia', in Niels-Peter Moritzen (ed.), *Ostafrikanische Völker zwischen Mission und Regierung.* Erlangen: Lehrstuhl für Missionswissenschaften, pp. 101–30.

Schlee, Günther. 1982. 'Zielkonflikte und Zielvereinheitlichung zwischen Entwicklungsplanung und Wanderhirten in Ostafrika', in Fred Scholz and Jörg Janzer (eds), *Nomadismus - ein Entwicklungsproblem? Beiträge zu einem Nomadismus-Symposium, veranstaltet in der Gesellschaft für Erdkunde zu Berlin vom 11. - 14. Februar 1982.* Abhandlungen des Geographischen Instituts Anthropogeographie 33. Berlin: Reimer, pp. 97–109.

Schlee, Günther. 1978. 'Soziale, kosmologische und mythologische Bezüge der Verben "herauskommen" und "sich drehen" im Rendille', in Herrmann Jungraithmayr (ed.), *Struktur und Wandel afrikanischer Sprachen: Vorträge vom 20. Deutschen Orientalistentag, Erlangen 1977.* Marburger Studien zur Afrika- und Asienkunde/A 17. Berlin: Reimer, pp. 162–70.

Encyclopedia Entries

Elwert, Georg and Günther Schlee. 2015. 'Conflict: anthropological aspects', in James D. Wright (ed.), *International Encyclopedia of the Social and Behavioral Sciences* 13. 2nd edn. Amsterdam: Elsevier, pp. 620–26. DOI: 10.1016/B978-0-08-097086-8.12232-9.

Schlee, Günther. 2015. 'Language and Ethnicity', in James D. Wright (ed.), *International Encyclopedia of the Social and Behavioral Sciences* 13. 2nd edn. Amsterdam: Elsevier, pp. 251–55. DOI: 10.1016/B978-0-08-097086-8.53054-2.

Scholz, Fred and Günther Schlee. 2015. 'Nomads and Nomadism in History', in James D. Wright (ed.), *International Encyclopedia of the Social and Behavioral Sciences* 16. 2nd edn. Amsterdam: Elsevier, pp. 838–43. DOI: 10.1016/B978-0-08-097086-8.62018-4.

Schlee, Günther. 2010. 'Orma', in Siegbert Uhlig (ed.), *Encyclopaedia Aethiopica, Volume 4:O-X.* Wiesbaden: Harrassowitz, pp. 53–54.

Schlee, Günther. 2007. 'Inter-Ethnic Clan Relations', in Siegbert Uhlig (ed.), *Encyclopaedia Aethiopica, Volume 3: He-N.* Wiesbaden: Harrassowitz, pp. 173–75.

Schlee, Günther and Richard Pankhurst. 2007. 'Kenya, Relations With', in Siegbert Uhlig (ed.), *Encyclopaedia Aethiopica, Volume 3: He-N.* Wiesbaden: Harrassowitz, pp. 386–89.

Schlee, Günther. 2001. 'Klan und Lineage', in Jacob E. Mabe (ed.), *Das Afrika-Lexikon: ein Kontinent in 1000 Stichwörtern*. Stuttgart: Metzler; Wuppertal: Hammer, pp. 295–96.
Schlee, G. 2001. 'Language and Ethnicity', in Neil J. Smelser and Paul B. Baltes (eds), *International Encyclopedia of the Social and Behavioral Sciences* 12. Amsterdam, Paris, New York and Oxford: Elsevier, pp. 8285–88.
Schlee, Günther. 2001. 'Nomadismus', in Jacob E. Mabe (ed.), *Das Afrika-Lexikon: ein Kontinent in 1000 Stichwörtern*. Stuttgart: Metzler; Wuppertal: Hammer, pp. 455–57.
Schlee, Günther. 2001. 'Scherzverwandtschaft', in Jacob E. Mabe (ed.), *Das Afrika-Lexikon: ein Kontinent in 1000 Stichwörtern*. Stuttgart: Metzler; Wuppertal: Hammer, pp. 536–37.

Max Planck Institute for Social Anthropology, Department 'Integration and Conflict' Field Notes and Research Projects, Series Editor and Author
(source: https://www.eth.mpg.de/dept-schlee-series-fieldnotes)

Al-Amin Abu-Manga, Elhadi Ibrahim Osman and Günther Schlee. 2021. *Farmers and Herders in the Blue Nile Area. Conflict or Symbiosis? Part II*. Volume 27.
Al-Amin Abu-Manga, Elhadi Ibrahim Osman and Günther Schlee. 2021. *Farmers and Herders in the Blue Nile Area. Conflict or Symbiosis? Part I*. Volume 26.
Günther Schlee and Al-Amin Abu-Manga. 2017. *Fulɓe in the Blue Nile Area of Sudan: Field Notes and Interviews*. Volume 16.
Isir Schlee and Günther Schlee. 2015. *Rendille and Ariaal – a Linguistic and Cultural Affiliation Census II*. Volume 13.
Günther Schlee. 2015. *'Civilisations', Eurasia as a Unit and the Hochkulturgürtel: An Essay about How to Subdivide the World in Terms of Cultural History and What to Explain with the Units Thereby Created*. Volume 11.
Awad Alkarim and Günther Schlee. 2015. *Pastoralism in Interaction with Other Forms of Land Use in the Blue Nile Area of Sudan III: The Methods of Citizen Science in the Study of Agropastoralism*. Volume 10.
Isir Schlee and Günther Schlee. 2014. *Rendille and Ariaal - A Linguistic and Cultural Affiliation Census I*. Volume 9.
Günther Schlee. 2014. *Das Glaubens- und Sozialsystem der Rendille. Kamelnomaden Nordkenias. German Original of Volume VII, Reprint*. Volume 8.
Günther Schlee. 2014. *The Social and Belief System of the Rendille: Camel Nomads of Northern Kenya. English Version: Halle 2014 (German Original: Berlin 1979)* Volume 7.
Peter Finke and Günther Schlee (eds). 2013. *CASCA - Centre for Anthropological Studies on Central Asia*. Volume 6.
Awad Alkarim and Günther Schlee. 2013. *Pastoralism in Interaction with other Forms of Land Use in the Blue Nile Area of the Sudan II: Herbarium and Plant Diversity in the Blue Nile Area, Sudan*. Volume 3.
Isir Schlee and Günther Schlee. 2012. *The Moiety Division and the Problem of Rendille Unity: A Discussion among Elders, Korr, 21st January, 2007. Rendille Text and English Translation. (Belel Ichoow Sagi Ren'dille is Liikeeno. Tooloo Makhaballe, Korr, Tahere 21 Januari, 2007. Af Ren'dilleka Kiiye af Ingereza Lülaabe)*. Volume 2.
Günther Schlee and Elhadi Ibrahim Osman. 2012. *Pastoralism in Interaction with Other Forms of Land Use in the Blue Nile Area of the Sudan: Project Outline and Field Notes 2009–10*. Volume I.

INDEX

Abu-Hujar, 67, 69
accumulation
 by dispossession, 15, 311–15, 322
 primitive accumulation, 313
action, theories of, 10, 15, 353, 355
adat, 298
adornment, 31–32
affairs, 34, 39, 41. *See also* infidelity
Africa
 East Africa, 7, 12–13, 30, 41, 49, 53, 101n2, 154, 189, 341, 349, 353, 362, 368, 378
 Horn of Africa, 2, 7–8, 204, 378–79
 Middle Eastern and North Africa (MENA), 156, 164, 166, 170
 north-eastern Africa, 4–5, 87, 190, 378
 West Africa, 5, 13, 60n2, 69, 72, 78, 85–86, 89–91, 93–94, 96–97, 99–100, 118, 126n13
agency, 1, 10–11, 28–29, 33, 41, 43, 45n3, 156, 159, 352–53
age-set system, 30, 52–54, 58–59, 168–69
Ahmed Gragn, 203–4
Aike Berinas, 348–50. *See also* Baldambe
Akyeampong, Emmanuel Kwaku, 86, 89–90, 96–98, 101n9
aliens, 88–89, 92–94, 97, 99–100, 101n7
 Aliens Compliance Order (Ghana), 89, 94, 97
alliance, 2–3, 6, 53, 80, 116, 155, 161, 163, 165, 167, 169–71, 192, 340, 352–53, 367, 371
allochthone, 87
American exceptionalism, 216–18, 220–22, 232, 233n2
ancestors, 163, 303–4, 305n5, 349–50. *See also* nenek moyang
anthropology, anthropologist, 1, 4, 9–10, 14, 27–28, 40, 49, 106–9, 123–25, 126n4, 136–38, 174–76, 182–3, 183n2, 216, 246, 251–52, 357, 308–9, 311, 313–14, 327–28, 337–38, 352, 357–61, 365–66, 368, 371, 373, 375, 378–79. *See also* Max Planck Institute for Social Anthropology
audio-visual, 106–8, 123–25
British tradition, 365, 367
German tradition, 365, 367, 374

Arab(s), 63, 69, 71–72, 74, 78–80, 82n6, 82n8, 82n16, 83n21, 83n29, 95, 97–98, 126n13, 164, 166, 168, 199, 202–3, 205, 208, 212, 359–60, 372, 375
Arbore (Hor), 2, 6, 45n3
Ark of the Covenant, 201, 207, 211, 214n11
Ari, mountains of, 351
Ariaal, 50, 56–58, 61n3
Armha, seventh century Ethiopian king, 202, 207, 209
Asmarom Legesse, 348, 377
assemblage, 101n1, 117, 155, 157, 162, 247, 313
assimilation, 49–50, 52–53, 55, 57, 163
aura, 348, 351
authority, 5, 7, 40, 52, 64, 70, 74–77, 80, 95–96, 115, 154–55, 160, 165, 169–70, 179, 181, 189, 198, 224, 231, 242, 250, 261–63, 293, 300–1, 303–5, 314
autochthone, 86–100, 101n2
Axum, Axumite, 198–201, 203, 205, 207–8, 210–11, 214n10

Badiyya, 372
Badr-Ethiopia, 219
Baggara, 64, 71, 82n3
bagoresin tenekesin, 202
Baldambe, 348–51
Ballotiral, 107, 111–18, 120–21, 123, 126n10
banditry, 12, 145, 186, 189–90, 194n4
Bantu, 56
Barber, Karin, 109, 124
Barth, Fredrik, 365, 369, 372
Bayreuth, 366, 370, 372
beads, beading, 31–32, 34, 36, 39, 42, 45n1. *See also* adornment
belonging, 1, 31, 34, 36, 44, 63, 72, 74, 78, 85, 91, 101, 111–12, 135, 138, 144, 154–56, 160, 162, 165, 168, 170–71, 178, 207, 211, 213, 258–59, 319, 321–22, 337
Berinas (Balambaras), 348–50
Bielefeld, 365, 368, 370–72, 374, 377
 Bielefeld entanglement approach, 370–71
Bierschenk, Thomas, 370

bilingualism, 50, 56–57
Blue Nile (river), 67, 70
Boran Oromo (Borana), 2, 30, 56, 58, 348, 351, 353, 377
Bosnia and Herzegovina, 176, 179–81
boundaries (ethnic, national), 3, 5–6, 18nn2–3, 49, 55, 58–60, 78–79, 81, 86–87, 136, 276, 310–12, 327, 335, 341, 365
bravery, 33, 39, 43, 179
Brubaker, Rogers, 9, 15, 336
Buut (district), 69, 74

camels, 29, 31, 56, 82n3, 158–59, 200, 279, 351, 377–78
Cameroon grassfields, 112–18, 126n10
capital, 15, 29, 44, 138, 221, 223–24, 227, 244, 258–59, 261, 265, 273, 282, 309, 310–14, 317, 319, 323–24, 370
care, 30, 79, 293, 298–99, 304–5. See also health care
  caring relationships, 147, 298–99, 304–5
cargo cult, 13, 217–23, 230, 232, 233n1
  of the oppressed, 221–22, 228, 230
  of the oppressor, 217, 220–22, 232
cattle, 3, 6, 29–40, 43–45, 56, 58, 70–71, 73–74, 78, 82n3, 90–93, 95, 112, 114, 118–19, 126n13, 349–51, 368
Chagnon, Napoleon, 41
character, 91, 113, 118, 120–21, 123, 266, 337, 347, 351
charisma, 70, 200, 219–22, 230, 347–48, 350–51
children, 37–39, 41, 43–44, 53, 56–57, 89, 96, 118, 126n8, 126n14, 135, 147, 175, 194n6, 223, 250, 262, 269n1–2, 274, 283–86, 293, 295–300, 304–5, 349, 365, 372, 374
choice, 1, 11, 28, 32, 41, 66, 120, 138, 149, 166, 176, 247, 253–54, 274, 285, 342, 353, 359, 361. See also decision-making; rationality: rational choice
Christian-Muslim relationships, 205
Christianity, 12, 45n2, 96–97, 112, 141, 190–91, 194n3, 198–210, 212–13
circumcision, 30, 262, 372
citizenship, 69, 73, 78–79, 85–94, 96–100, 101n3, 139, 202–5, 209, 211, 228, 245–46, 256, 259, 269n1, 279, 291–92, 294, 326, 343
civil rights, 90, 109, 118, 338
civil war, 5, 11, 18n3, 64, 66–67, 69, 71, 75, 78, 80–81, 82n10, 135, 145–47, 227, 301, 320, 339
civilization, 182, 205, 210, 221, 246
clan, 1–3, 6, 10–11, 18n3, 36–37, 44, 49, 53–54, 78, 85–86, 94, 154, 158–59, 162, 164–65, 169, 364, 366–68, 372
  clanship, 53–54
class, social, 6–7, 58, 94, 138–39, 202–3, 248, 256, 287, 308–9, 320, 323, 325–26, 340, 343, 358, 368–69, 374

cohesion, social, 3, 154–56, 159–60, 162–63, 165, 167, 169, 171, 172n1, 310, 312
collectivity, 9–10, 18n4, 55, 59
colonialism, 3, 5, 13, 16, 30, 45n1, 49, 52, 55–58, 61n4, 86, 88, 97, 101n2, 112, 138, 145, 180, 189–90, 193, 217, 220, 230, 292, 294, 304–5, 312–13, 335, 373
  colonial boundaries, 49
  colonial government, 32, 36, 53, 69–70, 87–90, 94, 99, 293, 340
commonality, 59, 309, 311, 316–17, 321, 326, 328, 329n6, 340–41
common property, 59–60
compensation, 74, 80, 115, 154, 156–62, 166–71, 300
Comte, Auguste, 310
conflict, 1–5, 7–8, 10–13, 18n3, 27–29, 44, 50, 52–55, 58, 60, 64, 66, 91, 98, 105–16, 120–21, 123, 125n2, 135–37, 139–40, 142–49, 151n7, 155–57, 159–60, 162–63, 166–70, 176, 180, 183n3, 186, 191–93, 194n1, 196–97, 209–10, 212, 216, 255, 258, 308, 324, 335, 340–42, 350, 352–53
  conflict theory, 8, 10, 308, 353
  narratives of, 12, 191, 193, 194n1, 197, 209, 212
Cooper, Frederick, 9, 15, 336
corruption, 7, 17, 89, 113, 115, 221, 344
cosmopolitanism, 56, 310, 318, 339
  critical vs. liberal cosmopolitanism, 338, 340
  emancipatory cosmopolitanism, 335, 337, 340
cowards, cowardice, 33, 40–43
crime, 180–82, 183n2, 192, 302–3
Croatia, 179–81
cross-cutting ties, 1, 3, 18n2, 165, 246, 340
culture, 16, 18n2, 27–29, 32–34, 43–44, 45nn1–2, 45n4, 46n5, 49–51, 53–55, 57, 60, 61n5, 69, 72, 78, 83n29, 86, 91–93, 95, 97–99, 101nn4–5, 107–13, 116–18, 120–21, 123–24, 126n18, 175–76, 179, 181–82, 186, 190–91, 193, 194n1, 194n4, 196–97, 211, 213n3, 219–20, 245–46, 250–51, 256–59, 265, 273, 275, 293, 296, 309, 311–12, 315–18, 328n3, 336–38, 340–41, 348, 353–54, 357, 359, 364–67, 371–73, 378. See also neighbourhood: cultural neighbourhood; rhetoric culture theory
  cultural heterogeneity, 2, 112, 340
  cultural homogeneity, 14, 16, 168, 245, 312
  cultural rights, 12, 175, 181
  cultural similarities, 196, 246
Cushitic peoples and languages, 49, 78
  Cushitized Nilotes, 55
  Eastern Cushitic speakers, 55, 57
  Eastern Nilotic speakers, 55

Damazin, 65–68, 70–73, 78, 81, 82n2, 82n6, 82n14, 83n28

danger, discourse of, 144, 151n8
Dassanech, 348
decision-making, 28, 160, 240, 272–75, 285–88, 353, 378
Degodia clan, 158–59, 163, 165
Deleuze, Gilles, 216, 313
dependency, 14, 138, 140, 144, 189, 198, 247, 249, 255–56, 264, 268, 273, 284, 288, 329n7, 342–43
Derg (the military council that led the revolutionary government of Ethiopia, 1974–1991), 199, 203, 210
descent, 2–3, 33, 89, 154–55, 161, 163, 165, 169, 172n6, 213, 257, 325
  patrilineal descent, 3, 167
development, 5–8, 33, 60n1, 83n28, 106, 109–12, 116–17, 126n2, 126n7, 175, 299, 314, 317, 335, 342–43, 358, 266, 368, 371
Diaby, Karamba, 320, 322
diaspora, 13–14, 94, 96, 204, 209, 214n9, 276, 277, 291
  diasporic identity, 296
difference, 1, 11, 16, 34, 49, 55, 77–79, 86, 92, 99, 107, 113, 116, 165, 176, 197–98, 222, 225, 243, 244–46, 255–57, 309–12, 316, 321, 327, 328n3, 329n6, 341, 368–69, 375
  binaries of, 310–11, 321
  difference and sameness, 101n7, 245, 375
displacement, 13, 15, 17, 55, 57, 309–10, 312, 314–18, 320, 323, 327–28, 335, 343
dispossession, 2–3, 17, 308–17, 319–323, 326–28
Dutch government, 293–96, 300, 304–5
Dutch people, 292–99, 304–5
Dutch Moluccan identity, 292–95, 297–305, 306n1

echo chamber, 347, 349–50, 352, 355
Elwert, Georg, 370
empire, 97, 203, 219–20, 222–24, 228–32, 259, 276, 293, 312, 328n3
  British Empire, 3
  Ethiopian Empire, 2–3
empiricism, 8, 12, 27, 29, 156, 161, 164, 170, 177, 217, 219–20, 226, 244, 248–49, 292, 352, 361, 372
  critical empiricism, 4
emplacement, 13, 15–17, 308, 310, 312–13, 315–18, 320, 322–23, 325, 327, 335
EPRDF (Ethiopian People's Revolutionary Democratic front, ruling party of Ethiopia 1991–2019), 204, 210
Erikson, Erik, 176–77
Ethiopia, 1–3, 7, 12, 51, 66, 70, 106, 125n1, 140, 158, 186, 188–92, 194n3, 194n5, 196–213, 213n1, 214n5, 214nn7–9, 214n11, 335, 378. See also Badr-Ethiopia; empire: Ethiopian Empire
  Ethiopian Orthodox Church (EOC), 197–202, 204–5, 207, 209–12, 214n9
  oral literature of, 186, 190, 193, 194n2
  southern Ethiopia, 1–3, 6, 29, 78, 340–42, 348–49, 351, 355, 371, 377–78
ethnicity, 2–3, 7, 10, 16, 27, 49–50, 57, 78, 85–86, 90, 101, 105–7, 111–12, 116, 121, 123, 125, 176–77, 258–60, 265–66, 278, 340, 353, 367–68, 372
  ethnic trap, 268
ethnography, 2, 4–7, 27, 86, 107, 109, 123, 125, 145–46, 151n7, 155, 164, 166, 168, 197, 212, 218, 249, 255, 308, 340, 347–52, 354–55, 364, 369, 375
  dialogical ethnography, 4–5, 108, 126n4
ethnonyms, 50–51
Evans-Pritchard, E.E., 367
Evers, Hans-Dieter, 256, 268, 370
exclusion, 13–15, 27, 29, 59, 60n2, 80, 90, 93, 113, 141, 161, 182, 239, 242–48, 250–51, 253n3, 291, 303, 309–10, 335, 337, 343. See also exclusion; inclusion
  acts of exclusion, 113, 239, 242–43, 246–47, 250
  exclusion continuum, 242, 244
  mechanisms of exclusion, 14, 142, 241–43, 247, 249, 251, 310
extremism, 140–42, 145, 179, 226

farmer-grazier conflict, 113–14, 120
farmer-herder relation, 92, 111–13, 115–16, 120, 125
farming, 5–7, 30, 46n5, 56, 64, 66–67, 69, 72, 74–81, 82n9, 87, 90–94, 112–16, 126n13, 145, 249, 279, 283, 295, 339, 342, 347, 358, 363, 371
fascism, 177, 321–22
  fascist imperialism, 325
fatwa, 230
fieldwork, 1–2, 4–5, 16, 63, 86, 105–7, 109, 111, 120, 124, 126n16, 144–46, 172n2, 251, 255, 260–61, 265, 269n1, 309, 344, 348–49, 351, 355, 377–78
fighting, 35, 37, 52, 59, 67, 71, 75, 80, 82n10, 82n15, 82n17, 92, 137, 139–40, 142, 145–48, 150n2, 163, 190–91, 231, 301, 349–50, 352
financialization, 314
Fischer, Hans, 359–60, 365, 367, 373
food production, 8, 31, 37–39, 91, 94, 105, 263, 294, 298, 343, 358
freedom, 11, 27–28, 30–32, 44, 124, 143, 147, 158, 174, 181, 203–5, 220–21, 277, 282, 295, 297, 337–38
friendship, 6, 265, 321, 349–50, 352
frontiers, 58, 94, 362
Fulani, 63–64, 70–71, 73, 78, 81, 82n11, 82n16, 83n27, 86–87, 89–93, 95, 99–100, 113. See also Fulɓe; Mbororo; pulaaku

Fulɓe, Pullo (sing.), 63, 64, 66, 69–74, 78–81, 82n18, 83n21, 91, 111–13, 118–19, 125n1, 126n13. *See also* Fulani; Mbororo; *pulaaku*
future, 17–18, 34, 56, 59–60, 69, 96, 114, 148, 155, 160, 169, 207, 209–10, 262, 266–67, 274–75, 280, 286, 288, 318, 320–21, 323, 342, 344, 361, 371, 379

Gabbert, Echi Christina, 6, 101, 341–42
Gabra, 2, 58, 350
game theory, 266
Garre, 2, 78
generation, 4, 13, 32–36, 39, 55–57, 69, 88, 90–94, 97–100, 114, 124, 156, 163–64, 172n1, 172n6, 175, 203, 231, 275, 282, 286, 288, 293, 296–99, 302, 305, 321, 323, 349
  generational conflict, 28, 44, 167
  generational tensions, 34, 305
genocide, 179–82, 183n2
Germany, 4, 9, 13–14, 17, 105, 107, 123, 126n16, 175, 212, 239–41, 244–47, 250–51, 263, 276, 279, 300, 309, 317–22, 335, 339, 350, 357–58, 361–63, 365–67, 374–75, 378
  German Reich, 245
Ghana (former Gold Coast), 5, 85–100, 101nn3–7, 109–10, 113, 339
Girinti (place in South Sudan), 71–72, 82n16
global neighbourhood, 340–44
Graebner, Fritz, 371
grassfielders (of Cameroon), 112, 115
group ranches (in Kenya), 5, 55, 58–60
group size, 2–3, 9–12, 18n3, 136–40, 142–43, 148–50, 155, 159–60, 163, 165, 343, 369

Halle/Saale, 60, 105, 252n1, 309, 317–18, 350, 352–53, 357
Hamar, 348–52, 355
Hamburg, 357, 359–62, 366, 368, 373, 375
Hausa, 66, 86–87, 89–90, 92–96, 99–100, 101n4, 101n7, 112, 116, 118
Hawiye clan, 158
Heide/Holstein, 357
Helander, Bernhard, 18n3
health care, 315, 323, 326
herders, herding, 1, 5–6, 17, 18n1, 29–31, 34, 37–38, 43–44, 57–59, 66, 69, 74, 76, 78, 80, 82n7, 82n9, 90–93, 107, 111–16, 118, 120, 125, 126n13, 158, 168–69, 277, 280, 282, 336, 339, 349, 351, 371
hidasse (Ethiopian notion of the renaissance), 210
Hijra, first, 82n11, 197, 202, 205–9, 211–13, 214n6
homage, 28, 350
Homo oeconomicus, 11
Homo sociologicus, 11
Horn of Africa, 7–8, 204, 378–78

Hovd-*sum*, 277–78, 280, 282–85
humanity, 12, 60n1, 175, 183n2, 216, 316, 321, 328, 344, 362
hunter-gatherer, 1, 105

identity, identification, 1–2, 4–5, 7–15, 17, 18n4, 27, 30–32, 34, 36, 41, 46n5, 49–50, 53, 55–59, 69, 85–86, 88–93, 95–99, 108, 136–38, 144, 147, 149, 151n8, 154–56, 160–63, 165–66, 168–71, 174, 176, 178, 180–82, 190, 193, 195n11, 197, 203–5, 208–11, 213, 230, 239, 241, 243, 244, 246–48, 250–51, 255–56, 258–59, 266, 291, 293, 296–98, 300–2, 304–5, 318, 326, 328, 335–39, 342–44, 353, 365–70, 372. *See also* diaspora: diasporic identity; religion: religious identification
  alignment of categories of, 152, 246–47
  category-thinking, 335, 337, 340
  collective identity, 9, 12, 18n4, 28, 30, 55, 85, 101n1, 155, 161, 246, 255, 258–59, 336, 344, 353 (*see also* collectivity)
  critique of the concept of, 335–36
  Dutch Moluccan identity, 293, 301–2, 304–5
  framing of categories of, 10, 246, 335
  identity creation, 27, 88, 186, 340
  identity politics, 10, 163, 191, 211, 257–59, 336
  'phantasies of groupness', 335–37, 340
  social-psychological identity, 9, 18n4
  Uzbek identity, 256–57
Iloibonok (laibons), 52
Iloikop, 50–55, 61n4
Iloogolala, 50–53
Iloshon, 50, 52–55, 57, 59–60. *See also* territorial sections
imperialism, 2, 13, 16, 17, 202, 209, 216, 219, 222, 230, 311, 328. *See also* fascism: fascist imperialism
  US imperialism, 223–24, 232, 319
inclusion, 14, 149, 204, 211–12, 140, 242, 245–46, 250, 305, 343
  inclusion and exclusion, 10–11, 27, 29, 136, 142, 149, 155, 165–66, 242, 244, 250–51, 375
India, 89–90, 101n2, 293, 319
  India, partition of, 246
infidelity, 34, 38–39
information processing, 274–75, 281, 288
Ingessana, 64, 69, 77
integration, 4, 8, 12–17, 50, 53–54, 69, 92–93, 96, 99–100, 101n5, 101n8, 123, 125, 157–58, 162–63, 165, 179, 193, 196–97, 203, 212–13, 239–42, 245, 273, 283, 285, 288, 292, 296, 308, 320, 327, 335, 341, 350, 352
International Criminal Tribunal for the Former Yugoslavia (ICTY), 179–80, 183n2

INDEX • 399

Islam, 14, 29, 67, 72, 78, 82n10–11, 94–96, 107, 111, 117–18, 120, 134, 138–42, 144, 148, 154, 158–59, 199–209, 211–13, 213n3, 225, 230, 246–47, 303, 319
  Islamist, 137, 139–40, 145, 147–48, 150, 214n9, 230
Italy, 194n1, 240, 300
  Italian colonialism, 190, 193
  Italian-Ethiopian war (1936–1941), 189, 192–93

Jensen, Jürgen, 359–60, 362
jihad, 12, 17, 93, 135–37, 145–47, 149–50, 207, 230–31, 335

Kapferer, Bruce, 177–78
Kebre Negest, 200–1
Kenya, 2, 5, 7, 18n5, 30–31, 43, 45, 45n1, 50–51, 56, 60, 60n1, 60–61n3, 87, 158, 250, 335, 340, 351, 361–63, 365–66, 377–78
  British in Kenya, 2, 32, 45, 340
  northern Kenya, 1–5, 8, 18n3, 27, 29, 32, 49–51, 54, 61n3, 78, 158, 336, 348, 351, 362–63, 366, 369, 371, 377–78
  postcolonial Kenyan state, 2–3, 5, 30, 49–50
Khazanov, Anatoly, 353, 368
Khorezm region (Uzbekistan), 255–58, 264
  Khorezmians, 14, 255–60, 262–68, 339
kinship, 6, 18, 105, 155, 162–63, 261–62, 266, 286, 296–97, 304, 360, 371. *See also* descent: patrilineal descent; lineage
  affinal ties, 2, 6, 78, 167, 283, 288
  inter-marriage, 55–56, 94, 319
  marriage, 1, 3, 32, 34–42, 44, 56, 89–90, 93, 98, 100, 126n14, 169–70, 200, 206, 260–62, 265, 284, 297, 320, 372
Kisongo, 50–53, 55, 58, 61n3
kitala (status of a woman among Samburu), 38–39
Koninklijk Nederlandsch-Indische Leger (KNIL, Royal Netherlands East Indies Army), 293–94
Korre, 350–53, 355
kumpulan, 296, 268
Kwavi, 50, 52

Laing, R.D., 335
Laikipiak, 39, 50–51, 53, 56–57
Lake Turkana, 1, 55, 57
language, 9, 50, 54–57, 85–86, 91–95, 99, 101n4, 115, 124, 155, 165, 186–91, 193, 195n8, 211, 244, 277, 283, 292, 294–96, 311, 336, 353, 360, 363–64, 371–72. *See also* poetry
  pidgin language, 119, 188–89, 194n5
  social context of, 55–56, 186
Lebanese, 86–87, 89–90, 96–100, 101n3, 101n9
Lienhardt, Godfrey, 367

lineage(s), 10, 39–40, 44, 85, 162–65, 168, 288
linguistics, 4, 10, 49, 51, 55, 57, 78, 112, 123, 193, 194n1, 250, 257, 279, 359–60, 362–63, 365–66, 368, 372, 375. *See also* bilingualism
literature
  anti-colonial literature, 190
lmurran, lmurrani (sing.), 29–44, 45n1, 45n4, 46n5. *See also* war: warrior
Lydall, Jean, 348
Lynn, John, 29

Maa (language), 5, 49–51, 54–56, 60n3
Maasai, 5, 34, 49–60, 60n1, 61n4, 362
Madison, Soyini, 109
Mahibere Qidusan (neo-conservative movement related to EOC), 199, 207, 209–11
Malik Aggar, 70–71, 77
Manchester, New Hampshire, 309, 317–18, 322–26, 328n1, 335, 339
manyatta (*imanyat*), 58
Marsabit, 58, 377
Marx, Karl, 14, 313–14
Marxism, 311, 365, 369–70
Max Planck Initiative Challenges of Migration, Integration and Exclusion (WiMi), 13, 239–40, 242, 252n1
Max Planck Institute for Social Anthropology, 1, 4, 13, 60n1, 63, 105, 124, 125n2, 186, 196, 240, 252n1, 350, 352, 354, 367, 377–78
Max Planck Society, 240, 242, 369
Mazmuum, 67, 74–77
Mbororo, 63–64, 70, 72–73, 107, 111–21, 126n10, 126nn13–14, 353
MBOSCUDA (Mbororo Social and Cultural Development Association), 111, 116, 121, 126n13
media, 28–30, 55, 86, 89, 92, 105, 108, 113, 123–24, 126n12, 126n15, 126n17, 144, 147–48, 151n5, 180–81, 183n2, 207, 226, 229, 233n8, 273, 300, 322
Menelik II, Emperor of Ethiopia, 2, 200–1, 214n11, 349
Merlan, Francesca, 28–29
methods, 5, 86, 105–10, 112–13, 123–25, 145, 149, 151n6, 241–43, 248, 309, 311–12, 360, 375
  methodological nationalism, 309, 311–12
  quasi-experimental methods, 106–7, 123–25
  video-documentation, 5, 106–7, 121, 123
migration, 2, 4, 13–15, 18n3, 33, 54, 56, 60, 69, 75, 82n11, 87, 93–94, 96, 98, 125, 136, 199, 205–6, 214n6, 228, 239–45, 247–51, 253n3, 260, 269n1, 272–88, 291–94, 297, 309–10, 312–13, 315, 318, 328, 329n7, 339
  causes of, 248–49
  'push and pull' theories of, 272–73, 279, 284, 287

migrant groups, 13, 85–87, 89–90, 92, 94–95, 98–100, 139, 250, 321
seasonal migration, 66–67, 71, 79, 82n13, 90–91
south-north migration, 13, 56, 64, 67, 90
summer of migration 2015, 13, 239–40, 243
urban-rural migration, 248, 309, 315
welcoming narratives, 318, 321, 323
Mladić, Ratko, 172, 179–83, 183n2, 184n5
Möhlig, Wilhelm J. G., 359, 362–63, 366
Moluccas, 291–99, 301–5, 306n2
Moluccan wards in the Netherlands, 292, 295–96
Moluccans, 14, 292–305, 306n1–2, 339
Mongolia, 14, 274–86, 288, 339
Montaigne, 339
morality, 337
moral duties, 205
Morocco, 12, 156, 159, 163, 166, 168–69, 172n2, 361
multi-disciplinary research, 45, 241–43
multiscalar, 15–16, 308, 312, 314–15, 317–20, 322–23, 325
multiscalar analysis, 309–10, 312–13, 327, 328n2
multiscalar relations, 15, 17, 308–9, 312, 315–16, 327
Mursi (Mursu), 51, 348–49, 351
museum, 60n1, 194n1, 357–58
Muslims, 12, 78, 91, 94–96, 98, 101n4, 101n7, 111–12, 135, 137, 141, 143, 148, 182, 197–99, 201–13, 213n1, 214n5, 214n7, 225, 230, 246–47, 251, 267, 293, 301–2, 335
myth, mythology, 166, 174, 176–79, 182–83, 200–1, 203, 205, 209, 298, 354

nationalism, 15–16, 57, 98, 176–79, 203, 210, 218, 252, 257, 276, 309–12, 322, 327–28, 335, 338, 340
natives, 15, 80, 82n4, 82n19, 83n31, 87–88, 94, 101n2, 112, 208, 218, 220, 309–10, 313, 315–16, 322, 327, 335
neighbourhood, 1, 3, 30, 45n4, 49–51, 55, 58–59, 72, 78, 87, 89, 91–93, 96, 101n2, 101n9, 116, 119–20, 158, 176, 183, 211, 229, 247, 276–77, 279, 283, 297, 299, 301–2, 313, 317, 323, 335, 340–44, 347, 367, 373
cultural neighbourhood, 18n2, 45n4, 55, 340–41, 373
global neighbourhood, 335, 340–44
Nejashi (Muslim name for the Axumite king), 207, 211
nenek moyang, 304, 306n5
neo-Nazis, 321
Netherlands, the, 14, 291–99, 304–5, 306n2
nomads, 1, 4, 6–7, 64, 66, 69–74, 77–81, 82n7, 82n13, 83n33, 91–93, 118, 120, 126n13, 158, 168, 279, 327, 339, 365, 367–68, 370, 372
nomadic lifestyle, 6, 72, 351, 378
NSC-68, 223, 233n3
Nyangatom (Bume), 41, 348–50

Olosho (sing.). *See* Iloshon, territorial section(s)
Omas Gegen Rechts, 321
Omo, South, 349
orality, 4, 12, 83, 109, 124, 164, 186, 188, 190–91, 193, 194n1, 195n9, 257
oralman, 279, 283, 285–88
Oromo, 2, 158, 190, 198–99, 377, 379
ortho-pente (in Ethiopia), 199
otherness, 310–11, 327

pastor, 319–20, 325–26, 329n11, 357
pastoralism, 2–8, 14, 27–30, 41, 51, 57, 59, 60nn1–2, 63–64, 66–67, 69–70, 73–77, 91–93, 112–13, 117–18, 125n1, 158, 239, 277–78, 327, 335, 341–43, 353, 369
anti-pastoralist bias, 8
pastoral futures, 342
pastoralist-agriculturalist relations, 3, 5–7, 61n4, 64, 77, 158, 277
pasture, 3, 7–8, 44, 45n4, 57–59, 60n2, 63, 66, 69–70, 76, 78–79, 82n12, 90–91, 97, 126n13, 168, 277, 339
patron-client-relations, 260, 266, 268
peace, peace-making, 6, 8, 13, 17, 18n5, 28–29, 34, 44, 66, 69, 71, 77, 110, 112, 116, 126n13, 139, 143–45, 147–48, 167, 175, 197, 205–6, 209, 224, 245, 277, 301–2, 324, 326, 341, 349–50
pela, 296–97
performance, 5, 29, 31, 36, 43–44, 55–56, 105–11, 113, 116–21, 123–25, 126n4, 126n8, 126n14, 143, 157, 166, 169, 186, 188–89, 191–93, 303–4, 360
Philadelphia, Pennsylvania, 377
poetry, oral, 188, 193
political structure, 54, 149–50, 258, 369
politionele acties, 300
Popular Defense Forces (PDF, in Sudan), 67, 69–70
power, 4, 13, 15, 18n3, 27, 38, 40, 50, 80, 86, 109–10, 124, 140, 144, 147, 154–57, 159–66, 167, 169–71, 174, 179–80, 190, 201, 203–4, 219, 247–48, 255, 258–59, 262, 273, 283, 302, 308–10, 312–13, 315–16, 319, 324–25, 327–28, 329n6, 338–39, 341–43, 355, 368–69
control of power, 155
imbalance of power, 109, 163, 255, 313
military power, 13, 180, 207
power relations, 11, 17, 154–55, 157, 162, 169, 248, 255, 258–59, 309, 312–13, 315, 327, 329n6, 339

precarity, 315–16, 319, 321
propiska, 259–60, 263–67, 269n2
  propiska office, 264
proportionality, 161, 163, 167, 272
proverbs, 109, 124, 164, 377
pulaaku, 91, 111, 118. See also Fulani; Fulɓe; Mbororo
Purko, 50, 53, 55, 57–58, 60n3

Qazaqstan (Kazakhstan), 14, 272, 274–88

Rachamimov, Alon, 29
Rapport, Nigel, 335–40
  'Anyone', Rapport's concept of, 337–39
rationality, 11, 15, 177, 182, 250, 271, 273, 275, 287, 352–53, 355, 369
  bounded rationality, 14–15, 274–75, 283, 287–88
  rational choice (theory, RCT 1), 10, 273–74, 352–54
Rasht Valley, Tajikistan, 136, 138–41, 143–44
real-estate, 260, 317, 323–26
reciprocity, 59, 156, 162–63
  balanced reciprocity, 156, 161, 267–68
  generalized reciprocity, 267–68
  negative reciprocity, 267–68
reform, 199, 203, 208–9, 212–13, 219
refugee(s), 51, 53, 61n4, 144, 206, 209, 214n6, 229, 239, 241–42, 245, 247–48, 250, 274, 315, 320–21, 323–24, 326–27
  refugee crisis, 244 (*see* migration: summer of migration 2015)
relationality, 43, 138, 160, 162, 202, 310–13, 315–16, 327, 328n2, 329nn5–6, 329n8, 367
relativism, 174–75, 181, 183
religion, 10, 15, 78, 82n11, 85, 90, 92, 94–95, 99, 101n4, 109, 112, 135, 145, 148, 197–201, 203–5, 208–13, 214n9, 221, 245, 303, 316–18, 320, 340, 353, 369, 372
  Christian fundamentalism, 15, 209, 320–21, 325
  religious boundaries, 246–47, 367
  religious identification, 10, 78, 97–99, 112, 135, 162, 170, 177, 201, 208–9, 246, 257
  religious networks, 137, 141, 205, 197–99, 202, 209, 222, 312, 317–19, 321–22, 325, 328n3, 329n9
  religious segregation, 198, 256, 301
Rendille, 1–2, 4, 10, 18n3, 46n6, 53, 56–58, 78, 348, 350, 362–65, 367–68, 370, 372, 378
reproduction, 38, 40–41, 44, 223–24
Republican Party (US), 324–25
resistance, 12, 17, 58, 75–76, 78, 139, 145, 186, 190–93, 194n4, 197, 205, 217, 219, 227–32, 233n7, 299, 335
resources, 1–3, 5–7, 10, 27, 59, 66, 70, 78, 86, 139–40, 147, 163, 187, 191, 223–24, 226–27, 244, 248–49, 251, 255, 257–59, 262, 265–66, 268, 274, 277, 280–81, 296, 313–14, 342, 369
retaliation, 12, 154–57, 159–68, 170–71, 172n5, 301, 306n3
returnee(s), 14, 16, 63–64, 71, 74–78, 82n13, 206, 249–51, 261, 275–77, 279–81, 288, 299
revenge, 154–55, 158–59, 161, 166, 167, 231, 349
rhetoric culture theory (RCT 2), 337, 352–55
rights, 4–6, 12, 44, 76, 88–91, 94, 96, 99–100, 101n3, 113, 118, 156–57, 159, 163, 168, 174–76, 202, 204, 207–9, 211, 250, 259, 299, 326–27, 337, 341. See also civil rights
  economic rights, 88, 90, 175
  human rights, 12, 17, 109, 126n8, 174–76, 181, 207, 209, 242, 341
  political rights, 90, 96, 175
  socio-economic rights, 59–60, 90, 96, 175
risk, 6, 32, 40, 220, 249–50, 256, 260–61, 263, 266, 274, 282, 287–88, 305
role-playing, 106–23, 126n3, 126nn9–12, 126n15
Rosseiris, 65, 68, 70, 72, 83n23
Rufaᶜa al-Hoi, 63–64, 67, 69–72, 74–75, 77–80, 82n18, 83n30, 339

sahaba, 199, 201–2, 205–8
Sahlins, Marshall, 268
Sakuye, 2, 18n3, 78, 158–59
Salatul Ghaib, 208
Samburu, 5, 10, 16, 28–35, 37–45, 45n1, 45nn4–5, 50–51, 53–54, 56–58, 60n3, 350, 362
sameness, 9, 14, 101n8, 176, 197, 245–46, 250, 375. See also difference
Satudarah (motorcycle club), 302–5
scale, geographic and political, 12–13, 15–17, 28, 33, 40, 136–39, 142–44, 146, 148–49, 313, 317, 324, 329n8, 342
secession, 69, 71, 74–75, 79, 82n17, 192, 301
security, 6, 64, 66, 70, 75, 80–81, 90, 95, 106, 141, 147–48, 151n5, 205–6, 211, 213, 223, 266, 268, 269n1, 277, 280, 315
  security elites, 224, 228–29, 231
  social security, 6, 80, 105, 147, 175, 266, 306n2, 314–15, 343, 374
sedentarization, 5, 8, 63–64, 66, 72, 78, 87, 91–93, 126n13
segmentary societies, segmentarity, 9, 54, 56, 64, 85–86, 96, 154, 156, 159, 162–66, 168–69, 198, 257
sexuality, 27–35, 38, 40–44, 45n3, 181, 309, 319, 340
Schlee, Elisabeth, 359, 374
Schlee, Ernst, 358
Schlee, Günther, 1–4, 6–8, 10–16, 18n3, 27–28, 44, 50, 81n1, 105–6, 124, 136, 138, 139,

142, 149, 154–56, 159–60, 163, 165–66, 170–71, 176, 186, 193, 196–97, 212, 215, 239, 241, 244–49, 251–52, 266, 291, 308, 327, 335–37, 339–40, 343–44, 347–48, 352–53, 367
Serbia, 12, 17, 174, 176–77, 179–83, 183nn3–4, 184n5, 335, 370
Simmel, Georg, 311, 329n5
Simon, Herbert, 286, 288
social complexity, 3–4, 49, 55, 166, 171, 373
social structure, 1, 10–11, 28, 33, 40, 50, 54, 59, 149, 163, 165, 176, 178, 272, 291–2, 311, 315, 317
society, 3, 8, 14–15, 28, 33, 40, 44, 51, 56, 60, 60n1, 64, 86, 96–97, 99, 101n8, 108, 111, 113, 117–18, 120, 126n14, 136, 142–43, 154, 156, 159, 161, 164, 165, 167, 170, 178, 181, 199, 219, 239–42, 245, 247, 250, 256, 278–79, 281, 291, 295–96, 299–300, 304, 308, 310–13, 322, 327, 329n5, 338, 347–48, 350–53, 355, 368–71
solidarity, 6, 10, 12, 14, 59, 78, 154–55, 157–58, 160–64, 166–71, 172nn5–6, 175, 178, 240, 255–58, 265–67, 295–96, 316, 326, 336
Solomonic narrative, 197, 200–1, 204, 208
Somali, Somalia, 2, 8, 11, 13–14, 18n3, 18n5, 35, 139–40, 158, 162, 189, 195n8, 199, 204, 210, 244, 249–50, 301, 348, 350, 378
space, locality, 35–37, 54, 74, 76, 95, 98, 138, 140, 145, 149, 164, 204, 211, 296, 337
Spain, 108, 293, 324, 326, 361
Spencer, Herbert, 311
Spencer, Paul, 367–68
social anthropology. *See* anthropology
South Sudan, 5, 55, 63–67, 69–75, 77–81, 82n2, 82n5, 82n8, 82n10, 82nn16–17, 249, 339
Srebrenica, 179–82, 183n4
state, 5–7, 14, 30, 63–64, 72–80, 82n2, 83n25, 83n33, 87, 90, 92, 95–96, 116, 138–44, 146–50, 151n6, 151n10, 170–71, 177, 180–82, 192, 196–203, 205, 208–10, 217, 219, 225, 227, 229–32, 242, 247–50, 257, 265, 275–76, 278–79, 281, 294, 309–11, 313, 315, 318, 320, 323–27, 339, 358
state actor(s), 106, 113–15, 138, 141, 149–50, 166, 227, 242, 247–48, 263, 317, 324
the monolithic state, 244, 247
welfare state, 175
strangers, 1, 15, 83n29, 90, 92–93, 96, 99, 101nn4–5, 263, 309–11, 313, 327. *See also* aliens
subjects, 16, 28, 38, 69, 87–89, 97, 101n2, 108, 110, 117, 137, 247, 356, 362, 360–61
Sudan, 4–6, 8, 55, 63–65, 68–71, 74, 79–81, 81n1, 82n12, 82n17, 83n25, 106, 125n1, 126n13, 212, 248, 339, 348, 360, 378

Blue Nile State, 5–6, 8, 63–67, 69–73, 77–81, 81n2, 82n4, 82n6, 83n21, 83n23, 83n27, 339
Sennar State, 63–64, 67–68, 70, 72, 74–76, 78–80, 81n2, 339
Upper Nile Province (today South Sudan), 66, 69, 71
White Nile Baggara, 64, 71, 82n3
Swahili, 33, 43, 56–57, 361, 363, 378
Swarthmore College, 378

Tajikistan, 12, 16, 17, 135–48, 150, 150n3, 151n5, 151n7, 151n10, 257, 335
taxonomy, 373
territoriality, 137
territorial politics, 50, 59, 216, 231–32
territorial section(s), 16, 53, 55, 87, 327 (*see also* Iloshon; Olosho)
territory, 2, 52, 57–58, 87, 94, 97, 99, 155, 167, 169, 223, 240, 249, 276, 279, 310–11, 329, 362
terror, 137, 140, 142, 144, 146, 216–17, 224–30, 232, 233n6
accumulation of, 216–17, 229, 231–32
counter-terrorism, 135, 137, 142, 148, 150, 342
terror group, 12, 136–37, 142–43, 146, 149–50, 151n5, 226, 230
terrorism, 13, 17, 135–38, 140–50, 151nn5–6, 217, 224–32, 233n4, 342
terrorist, 12–13, 18n5, 135–40, 143–49, 151nn5–7, 225–26
topography of, 136–38, 146, 148–50, 151n5
war on, 12, 136, 140, 143, 146, 217, 229, 343
Teufel, Heinz, 360–61
Theatre for Development, 109–12, 117, 126n3, 126n7, 126n12, 126n15, 126n17
theory. *See also* action; conflict; game theory; identity; migration; rationality: rational choice theory; rhetoric culture theory
Tigray, 12, 16, 186, 190–93, 194n1, 211, 335
Tigrinya literature, 187–89, 192, 195n11
Tornay, Serge, 348–49, 353
trader's dilemma, 6, 255–56, 259, 268
transnationalism, 13–14, 98, 248, 291, 312, 329, 338. *See also* migration
transnational networks, 156, 292, 302, 304–5, 321
transnational ties, 125, 273, 288, 293, 299–300, 325
trans-border movements, 49, 90, 28
Troughear, Tony, 377
Turkana, 30, 56–57
Turton, David, 348–49

uncertainty, 70, 96, 155, 162, 169, 266, 274–75, 283, 287, 379

universalism, 12, 16, 154, 174–75, 213
urban regeneration, 314–18, 320, 324–25, 328
Uzbekistan, 14, 141, 255–57, 259, 269n1, 276. *See also* identity: Uzbek identity

video-documentation, 5, 106–8, 121, 123, 182
violence, 1, 3, 5, 7, 13, 28, 30–31, 33–34, 38, 40, 43–44, 45n1, 46n5, 52, 55, 66, 77, 88, 91, 95, 112, 115–16, 120, 137, 140, 142–44, 147, 150, 156–60, 163, 166–70, 177–78, 197, 209, 211, 224–28, 231, 233n5, 293–94, 296–97, 300–5, 308, 313, 322, 327
  interethnic, 3, 30, 35, 46n5, 52, 55, 91, 95, 177

war, 7, 13, 27–28, 36, 38, 40, 44, 66, 71–73, 77, 139, 140, 177, 179–81, 191, 194n1, 204, 210, 217–18, 220, 223–24, 226, 228–32, 245, 247, 249, 276, 292, 294–96, 300, 311, 321, 335, 343, 348–49, 351, 358, 373. *See also* civil war; terror: war on terror

US wars, 11–12, 136, 140, 143, 146, 180, 224, 227–29, 231, 343
warfare, 7, 18, 27–30, 32–35, 38, 40–41, 43, 45, 74, 196, 228, 295, 304, 338, 349
warlord, 11, 301
warrior, 30, 33, 41–42, 58, 94, 179, 231, 302, 372 (*see also lmurran*)
war song, 40, 195n10
Warre, Hobbesian state of, 340
we-groups, 16, 88, 191, 256, 258
Winter, Christoph, 353, 366–67
women, 5, 14, 16–17, 27–29, 32–44, 45nn3–4, 107, 110–11, 113–14, 116–21, 126n8, 126n14, 148, 167, 175, 200, 206–7, 214n8, 228, 295, 298, 306n2, 319, 321, 325, 349, 364, 372

Ye Muslimoch Guday newspaper, Facebook page, 211–12
Yugoslavia, 175–76, 179–80, 183n2

Zongo, 92, 94–96, 101n4, 101n7

www.ingramcontent.com/pod-product-compliance
Lightning Source LLC
Chambersburg PA
CBHW051523020426
42333CB00016B/1753